# Approaches to Teaching
## *The Story of the Stone*
## (*Dream of the Red Chamber*)

# Approaches to Teaching
## *The Story of the Stone*
## (*Dream of the Red Chamber*)

Edited by

*Andrew Schonebaum*

and

*Tina Lu*

The Modern Language Association of America
New York    2012

MLA and the MODERN LANGUAGE ASSOCIATION are trademarks
owned by the Modern Language Association of America.
For information about obtaining permission to reprint material from
MLA book publications, send your request by mail (see address below)
or e-mail (permissions@mla.org).

Library of Congress Cataloging-in-Publication Data

Approaches to teaching the story of the stone (Dream of the red chamber) /
edited by Andrew Schonebaum and Tina Lu.
    pages cm. — (Approaches to teaching world literature ; v. 120)
    Includes bibliographical references and index.
    ISBN 978-1-60329-110-1 (hardcover : alk. paper)—
    ISBN 978-1-60329-111-8 (pbk. : alk. paper)
1. Cao, Xueqin, ca. 1717–1763. Hong lou meng—Criticism and interpretation.
2. Cao, Xueqin, ca. 1717–1763—Study and teaching.
I. Schonebaum, Andrew, 1975–  II. Lu, Tina.
    PL2727.S2A85  2012
    895.1'34—dc23  2012038661

Approaches to Teaching World Literature 120
ISSN 1059-1133

Cover illustration for the paperback edition: *Daiyu Burns Her Poems*, by Xiaozhou,
studio of Sun Wen, late Qing. © Lüshun Museum, Dalian, China.

Third printing 2019

Published by The Modern Language Association of America
85 Broad Street, suite 500, New York, New York 10004-2434

www.mla.org

*Dedicated to the memory of*
*David Hawkes (1923–2009)*

My one abiding principle has been to translate *everything*—even puns. For although this is . . . an "unfinished" novel, it was written (and rewritten) by a great artist with his very lifeblood. I have therefore assumed that whatever I find in it is there for a purpose and must be dealt with somehow or other. I cannot pretend always to have done so successfully, but if I can convey to the reader even a fraction of the pleasure this Chinese novel has given me, I shall not have lived in vain.

—David Hawkes, from the
introduction to his translation
of *The Story of the Stone*

# CONTENTS

# ACKNOWLEDGMENTS

We are both grateful to David Rolston for his attentive reading of the entire manuscript and for sharing his own materials, many of which have been adapted and incorporated here. Shuen-fu Lin shared course materials with us as well. James Watt of the Metropolitan Museum of Art, Sophie Volpp, and Chlöe Starr were gracious enough to read parts of the manuscript and offer their thoughts. We would also like to thank David Wang and Bob Hymes for their support of this project, the Chiang Ching-kuo Foundation for funding the Ming-Qing workshop devoted to this volume in November 2008, Joe Gibaldi for his support from the beginning, Sonia Kane and James Hatch of MLA for their efforts in seeing the manuscript through to publication, Michael Kandel for his copyediting work, and Paul Banks for his production work.

The creation of this book has mirrored its purpose: to help students share and appreciate a great work of literature. For Andy, editing this volume has been a wonderful education, not just because of what he learned but also because of the people with whom he learned. He thanks some talented students for their thoughts at an early stage of this project: Katherine Atwill, Robert Compagnon, Lars Dabney, Serena Longley, Emma Malinen, Willem Molesworth, Morgan Kennedy, David Bisson and Jonathan Bisson, Henry Antenen, Laura Peskin, and Josh Breslow. He thanks Marta Hanson for her help and advice during different stages of this project and Maram Epstein for sharing ideas and syllabi and introducing him to Tina; the Columbia Heyman Center for the Humanities and the Committee on Asia and the Middle East for their support during the fellowship year 2006–07; and Barnard College, SUNY New Paltz, and Bard College for collegial and material support. Finally he thanks Chava, Ella, and Maggie for their patience, encouragement, and distraction, not necessarily in that order.

This volume has been a conversation among friends, the circle of whom has expanded over the course of the last decade. Tina would like to thank the two old friends who began this conversation — Matt Sommer and Haun Saussy — and also those who worked steadily and patiently during the many years that this volume has gestated, especially Tobie Meyer-Fong and Maram. The Center for East Asian Studies at the University of Pennsylvania generously funded the conference in 2001 that became the kernel for this volume. And of course all the energy that Tina contributed was generated by the warmth of her home and by Stuart, Tovah, Natalie, Eli, and Adie.

# PREFACE, ON CITATION AND ORTHOGRAPHY

We tie our volume to the David Hawkes and John Minford translation and strongly believe that it is *the* English version of *Honglou meng* to use. Thus we retain its romanization system for names of characters. We generally refer to *Honglou meng* as *The Story of the Stone* (or *Stone*) and use the translation in the Penguin Classics edition except where noted. Citation follows this format: volume, chapter, page, and each number is separated by a period. For example, "(1.5.200)" is "volume 1, chapter 5, page 200." (When only two numbers appear, the chapter is not given—either because a different element of the volume is cited, such as an introduction, or because the chapter was already given in the discussion.) But sometimes we use the title *Dream of the Red Chamber*—for instance, when talking about films available under that title. When quoting the Chinese, we use the Renmin Wenxue 人民文學 two-volume edition (its pages are numbered consecutively).

Characters from Chinese literature are hyphened when they have a multi-syllabic given name. Jia Baoyu in this volume is Jia Bao-yu, as in the Hawkes and Minford translation, and Du Liniang from *The Peony Pavilion* is Du Li-niang. Names of actual people, such as scholars and actors, are not hyphened (e.g., Lin Yutang), except when they themselves hyphen their names (e.g., I-Hsien Wu). This difference should help readers keep the fictional separate from the real. Personal names of real people do not follow any one romanization system but are presented as they would be found in a library, except where noted. Chinese last names, usually one syllable, are most often written first: Lin Yutang is Dr. Lin, Cao Xueqin is Mr. Cao. But Ling Hon Lam is Professor Lam. When in doubt, the reader can consult Works Cited. We use traditional Chinese characters throughout.

When romanizing words and the names of fictional characters, we use the standard pinyin system, adopted by UNESCO (e.g., *qi* instead of *ch'i*), except in a few cases where a word has achieved popular use in English (*Tao* instead of *Dao*, *Zen* instead of *Chan*, etc.). We do not follow Hawkes and Minford with their historical English spelling of place-names: we have Beijing, Nanjing, Suzhou, Hangzhou, Yangzhou, and Guangzhou instead of Peking, Nanking, Soochow, Hangchow, Yangchow, and Canton, in order to facilitate finding these places on a current map. Where places or words could be pronounced in different ways, (e.g., *Changan* could be *Chang'an* or *Chan'gan*), we mark the syllable break with an apostrophe.

Hawkes presents a good explanation of Chinese pronunciation in volume 1 of *Stone*. His brief (and approximate) note on the spelling and pronunciation of pinyin romanization gives these equivalents: c = *ts*, q = *ch*, x = *sh*, z = *dz*, zh = *j* (11).

Chinese characters are included in this volume, to conform to the MLA's recent publication policy of giving in its original form text in a language not using the Latin alphabet as well as to aid those students who are learning Chinese or just beginning serious inquiry into *Stone*. As we discuss in detail in the materials section of this volume, Hawkes and Minford have done a remarkable job of translation, particularly in capturing the tone of the original. But because Hawkes consults and translates from many different early editions, none of which are considered authoritative, it is nearly impossible for us to stitch together a version of the Chinese that would correspond to the translation.[1] We follow what is as close to a standard modern edition as any (Renmin Wenxue 人民文學) in quoting the Chinese, but there are some disconnects between "original" and translation. Authors including the Chinese text when quoting a passage from *Stone* will sometimes amend the translation. Quotations from primary sourses other than *Stone* are often not presented with the Chinese original because of similar textual issues. When an existing English translation is available and suitable, we asked contributing authors to use it. Hawkes and Minford give us a translation that seeks to preserve tone and meaning, but alongside the standard original it may occasionally look overly free. Readers who would like a very literal translation are encouraged to consult Gladys Yang and Yang Xianyi's *A Dream of Red Mansions*.

NOTE

[1] Fan Shengyu is in the process of preparing a bilingual edition of *Stone* to be published by Shanghai Foreign Language Education Press in 2012. In it, he notes when Hawkes departs from the Renmin Wenxue edition but does not specify which text was followed in those instances.

# Part One

# MATERIALS

# Introduction

*Dream of the Red Chamber* . . . is the greatest of all
Chinese novels.
> —C. T. Hsia, *The Classic Chinese Novel*

Of all the world's novels perhaps only *Don Quixote* rivals
*The Story of the Stone* as the embodiment of a nation's
cultural identity in recent times, much as the epic once
embodied cultural identity in the ancient world.
> —Stephen Owen,
> *Norton Anthology of World Literature*

Scholars and readers alike have agreed that *The Story
of the Stone* is the greatest Chinese novel, but about the
nature of its greatness lively differences of opinion have
swirled from its first appearance.
> —Pauline Yu,
> *Longman Anthology of World Literature*

The nostalgia for and idealization of a lost world in *Stone*
capture the modern Chinese reader's feelings about the
entire traditional Chinese culture; at the same time its
ironic, critical self-reflexivity intimates the burden of
modernity.
> —Wai-yee Li, "Full-Length Vernacular Fiction"

*The Story of the Stone* (or *Dream of the Red Chamber*) is critically acclaimed, popular, and long. This story of an extended family centers on its women and on relationships. Among the many plot arcs are the "choice" the hero must make between two talented and beautiful women and the deceit that leads to the death of one, the hero's journey toward enlightenment, and the moral and financial decline of a noble family.

*Stone* continues to influence culture in China. Proof of the continuing passion of its readers is the number of sequels and rewrites of the ending. The first sequel was published in 1796, just four years after *Stone*'s publication; two sequels appeared in 2006, and at least fifty-six were published in between. Works that might be called fan fiction are still popular, such as the 2004 *Murder in the Red Mansions*, which was written and published in Japan (紅楼夢の殺人), mainland and Taiwan translations appearing in 2008 and 2006. An English translation, *Murder in the Red Chamber*, appeared in 2012. Books that plumb or reveal *Stone*'s wisdom on many topics have also been common. For example, the 2009 *Honglou Fortune* (available in English) is a guide to managing wealth based on principles supposedly laid out in *Stone*. A $16 million, fifty-episode TV series of

林黛玉，聪慧敏感，孤高自
许，与宝玉相恋却无法结合，得知
宝玉与宝钗成婚，焚稿呕血而死。

贾宝玉，反……一故，
意。与黛玉思想一致，
黛玉夭亡，出家为僧。

贾政，荣国府主人，
的卫道士，强迫儿子宝玉留意于礼
义之间，委身于经来之道。

王熙凤，贾链……要里不……
两面三刀，说东打……
在贾府中，是一个人物。

Fig. 1. A deck of playing cards that ranks the characters in order of importance. Dai-yu and Bao-yu are the jokers, Jia Zheng is an ace, Xi-feng a king,
and so on.

*Stone* finished production and aired in 2010. It was preceded by the *Red Mansions* Casting Contest, in which millions of viewers voted on whom they wanted
to play the lead roles; 236,000 actors tried out.

   *Stone* has also been featured in the marketplace and department store. Playing cards (fig. 1), teapots, CDs, stamps, comic books, pottery, snuff bottles, lanterns, vases, figurines, coins, and ashtrays, merchandise of every quality, can be
found in many homes and under many display cases. In the 1920s and 1930s,
cigarette packs included collectible pictures of characters from *Stone*. There are
*Stone*-themed hotels, food festivals featuring menus of dishes from the novel,
and *Stone* theme parks where you can dress up as your favorite character or take
a ride through Bao-yu's trip to the land of illusion. This impulse to experience
*Stone* is not new: Shanghai brothels of the 1920s and 1930s featured prostitutes

who took the names of its female characters. *Stone* has infiltrated the Chinese language, spawning books of quotations. Families refer to their spoiled only sons as their "little Jia Bao-yu," and many girls are characterized as either a self-centered Dai-yu or a dutiful Bao-chai.

Readers are interested in *Stone* not just for its vivid portrayal of characters and its incredibly intricate structure but also for its depiction of virtually every facet of eighteenth-century life in China, for its treatises on connoisseurship, for its catalogs of artifacts, and for the quality and variety of its poetry.

In part 1 of this volume we provide readers, students, and teachers with information that will aid them in pursuing their inquiries into *Stone*. Our hope is that the essays in part 2 will serve as an accessible introduction to all the major topics teachers might want to cover in the classroom. Indeed many of the readings we recommend for further study are written by the contributors to this volume. Our aim is also to inspire scholarly interest. While there is enough work on *Stone* in Chinese (and other languages) to fill several lifetimes of study, the available work on *Stone* in English can be managed in one. We offer a guide to some of the confusing aspects of *Stone* and suggest topics, questions, and sources to get readers and teachers started who wish to pursue *Stone* in more detail on their own.

# Materials in the Hawkes and Minford Translation

Our volume uses the David Hawkes and John Minford translation of *Honglou meng*, titled *The Story of the Stone*; it is the translation scholars most often use. In its five volumes Hawkes and Minford present many aids to the reader, some of them very important. We do not wish to duplicate those materials, but since teachers rarely teach all five volumes of *Stone*, we list them here for reference and reminder.

The introduction to volume 1 of *The Story of the Stone* (subtitled by Hawkes "The Golden Days"), which is probably the most-read essay about *Stone*, focuses on its complex textual history, especially its circulation in manuscript before its publication in 1791–92. Hawkes discusses the importance of the Red Inkstone group of commentators, who seemingly worked with the author, Cao Xueqin, to revise the story while it was still in manuscript. He goes on to discuss what we know of Cao (previously romanized as Ts'ao) and the abiding belief by many that the primary male protagonist of *Stone*, Jia Bao-yu, is a representation of the author at an earlier age. Cao's biography and the importance of the early commentators lead to the issue of the authorship of the last forty chapters of the total hundred and twenty. Some believe that a man named Gao E wrote them; others view him simply as an editor. Where these last forty chapters lie on this author-editor spectrum is still a matter of debate.

In the appendix to volume 1, Hawkes explains the meaning of the cryptic dream that Bao-yu has in chapter 5, in which the fate of many of the main female characters is supposedly revealed. Readers new to *Stone* may not pick up on these meanings without the help of the appendix, but it is important for students to understand them as well as to realize that Bao-yu does not. All the Hawkes-Minford volumes include a list of characters in the back and a brief description of who they are. Since keeping all the names straight in *Stone* is a challenge for new readers — there are over four hundred names — these lists are invaluable. But they are not comprehensive, containing only the characters that appear in each volume. Note that the volume breaks were decided by the translators and do not represent natural divisions in the narrative. At the end of the character lists are small but useful family trees for the Jia and Wang families. Students often do not notice these materials unless they are pointed out to them.

The preface to volume 2 discusses other textual issues, in particular how Hawkes dealt with corrupt passages. Appendix 1 of volume 2 explains the basic rules and patterns of regulated verse in Chinese poetry, an important topic considering how significant poetry is to the overall meaning and structure of *Stone*. Students may benefit more from I-Hsien Wu's discussion of poetry in this volume, or even by consulting Hawkes's *A Little Primer of Tu Fu*. Hawkes explains in appendix 2 how Chinese dominoes are played and how the various hands have names and meanings. In appendix 3 he explains the riddles from chapter 51.

In his preface to volume 3 Hawkes expands his explanation of textual matters by discussing the difficulty of reconciling early claims about *Stone* found in the manuscripts. (Examples of inconsistencies in these early editions that he encountered in the translation are examined in appendixes 1–6 of volume 3.) He deals with the question of authorship of the last forty chapters, to which Minford returns in his prefaces to volumes 4 and 5.

In the preface to volume 4, Minford reminisces about his and others' search for the garden of *Stone* and discusses Gao E and Cheng Weiyuan, the men primarily responsible for bringing *Stone* to print. Appendix 1 in volume 4 presents translations of the prefaces written by Gao and Cheng to the novel's first printed edition. Teachers can use these prefaces in a number of ways, one of which is simply to point out how popular *Stone* was even before its publication. Appendix 2 discusses the octopartite essay that was the core of the exams leading to official careers and that Bao-yu must study to master if he is to please his father. The third appendix is devoted to the story about knowing the sound; it explains the valuation of literature on the basis of transmitting emotion, particularly from the author to a particular reader rather than to a general reader or to many anonymous ones, as traditional poetry in English is often valued. Teachers could help students understand different ways of appreciating literature using this piece. Minford's preface to volume 5 briefly discusses his opinion about the authorship of the last forty chapters.

# Editions and Translations

## *Chinese Texts and Editions*

There are three basic categories of *Story of the Stone* texts: early manuscripts, early printed editions, and modern printed editions. The manuscripts have received the most attention from scholars, especially in China and Taiwan. The more important versions are known as the "Reannotated Commentary on the *Story of the Stone*, by Red Inkstone Studio" (*Zhiyan zhai chongping shitou ji* 脂硯齋重評石頭記), which has commentary dated from 1754 to 1784. Hawkes discusses these in the introduction to the first volume of his translation (34–46). Essentially, there are five versions. The Jiaxu manuscript of 1754 (*jiaxu* 甲戌 refers to a year of the reign of the emperor), the most famous, was discovered in Shanghai in 1927 and purchased by Hu Shi. As with all the other Red Inkstone commentary manuscripts, it had eighty chapters, although only chapters 1–8, 13–14, and 25–28 remain of the Jiaxu version. Most of the Red Inkstone manuscripts are referred to by dates in the traditional sixty-year cycle. There is a note that reads, "When Red Inkstone copied and annotated for the second time in the year *jiaxu*, he used the title *Story of the Stone* again" 至脂硯齋甲戌抄閱再評仍用石頭記 (1.1.8b; my trans.). Even though *jiaxu* refers to the lunar year that largely corresponds with 1754, we cannot assume that the Jiaxu manuscript we now have is the original and not a transcription, and the process of transcribing such a lengthy text could introduce many errors in or variants to the text. Nonetheless, this manuscript seems to be the earliest extant.

Many paratextual items and comments appear in other versions of the manuscript and in different forms. Taken together, the versions contain pre- and postchapter comments, single- and double-column interlineal comments, and marginal comments (fig. 2). The oldest manuscripts have been accorded authority by Chinese scholars as well as by Hawkes and Minford. Many of the standard modern editions are based on them. The 1982 Renmin edition 人民文學出版社 in simplified characters, the Taiwan Liren 里仁書局 edition (1984) in traditional characters, and the revised 1996 Renmin edition (with 2,318 notes and 1,033 collation notes) are all based on manuscript versions, particularly on the Gengchen manuscript (also refers to a year of the reign, *gengchen* 庚辰 1761) for the first eighty chapters and the Cheng Jia 程甲 printed edition (see below) for the last forty. Much ink has been spilled in the debate over the identity of the author and the author's relation to the major manuscript commentators, "Red Inkstone" 脂硯齋 (*Zhiyan zhai*) and "Odd Tablet" 畸笏叟 (*Jihu sou*), and many minor ones. The comments on the manuscript shed light on many questions of authorship and interpretation, but it is important to remember that these were not widely available to the reading public until 1941, when the Jiaxu manuscript was first published. Other manuscript versions were made available in photoreprints afterward, but for one hundred

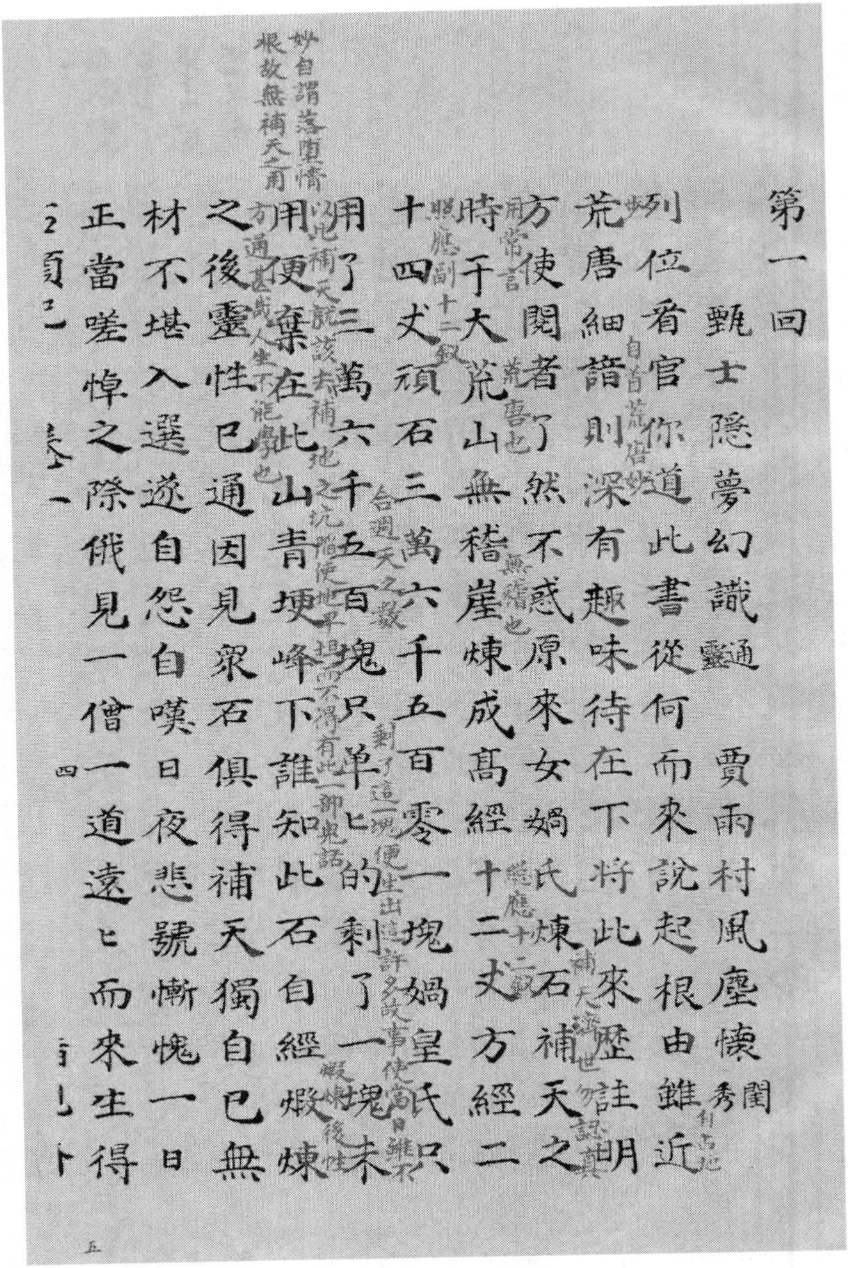
第一回
甄士隱夢幻識通靈
賈雨村風塵懷閨秀
列位看官你道此書從何而來說起根由雖近
荒唐細諳則深有趣味待在下將此來歷註明
方使閱者了然不惑原來女媧氏煉石補天之
時于大荒山無稽崖煉成高經十二丈方經二
十四丈頑石三萬六千五百零一塊媧皇氏只
用了三萬六千五百塊只單ㄟ的剩了一塊未
用便棄在此山青埂峰下誰知此石自經煆煉
之後靈性已通因見眾石俱得補天獨自己無
材不堪入選遂自怨自嘆日夜悲號慚愧一日
正當嗟悼之際俄見一僧一道遠ㄟ而來生得

Fig. 2. A page from the opening of chapter 1 of the *jiaxu* 甲戌 edition of the *Stone* manuscript featuring interlineal and marginal comments from Red Inkstone (1754?) and Hu Shi, among others. The comments were originally made in red ink. Rpt. in *Qianlong jiaxu zhiyan zhai chongpin shitou ji* (Taipei: Hongye shuju youxian gongsi, 1981), 1.1.4a fifty years the only editions that were available to the reading public were 120-chapter versions.

The first printed edition of *Stone* was edited by Cheng Weiyuan (1742?–1818?) and Gao E (1738?–1815?) and is generally dated to 1791, based on the date of Gao's preface. A second edition containing many corrections appeared in 1792. The first of these Cheng-Gao 程高 printed editions is usually referred to as the Cheng Jia, the second as the Cheng Yi 程乙 edition. The Beijing Normal University 北京師範大學 edition (with 3,380 notes) bases all one hundred twenty chapters on the Cheng Jia edition. The influential first Renmin Wenxue 人民文學 edition (1957, 1959, 1964, and 1973 versions), which Hawkes consulted, is based on the Cheng Yi edition. The complete Gao *Story of the Stone* 紅樓夢高 manuscript is referred to as such because it contains a comment signed by Gao E, and some think that he had a part in the preparation of the Cheng-Gao editions (fig. 3). Minford translates the prefaces to these first printed editions, in which the editors detail the difficulty they had in finding and piecing together manuscript fragments of the last forty chapters (4.385–88). There are at least three different printings of the Cheng-Gao editions, all with variants. These editions were printed without commentary and largely superseded by those with commentary, prefatory essays, pictures, character lists, and other paratexts.

The first of these annotated editions was published in 1811 and reprinted with added commentary in 1830 under the title "Illustrated *Story of the Stone* with Newly Added Commentary" (*Xinzeng piping xiuxiang honglou meng* 新增批評繡像紅樓夢). In 1832 an annotated edition was published by Wang Xilian (c. 1800–1876?) entitled "Newly Commentated, Illustrated, Complete Edition of *Story of the Stone*" (*Xinping xiuxiang honglou meng quanzhuan* 新評繡像紅樓夢全傳). In addition to Wang's chapter-end comments, it included the preface by Cheng Weiyuan, a new preface by Wang, and prefatory essays entitled "Evaluations of the Characters of *Story of the Stone*" and "Questions and Answers on *Story of the Stone*," by Tu Ying; "Explanation of the Diagram of Grand Prospect Garden," by Huang Cong; "Prefatory Poems on *Story of the Stone*," by Zhou Qi; and "General Comments," "Phonetic Glosses," and in some editions "List of Errors," by Wang. These comments and prefatory materials were popular and incorporated in whole or part into most subsequent commentary editions, even those from different commentators and publishers. Editions were also produced featuring comments by Yao Xie (1805–64) and Zhang Xinzhi (fl.1828–50) in the late nineteenth century.

An edition called the *The Affinity of Gold and Jade, Fully Illustrated, with Additional Comments and Illustrations* (*Zengping buxiang quantu jinyu yuan* 增評補像全圖金玉緣) appeared in 1884 (fig. 4). It includes interlineal and postchapter notes by Zhang Xinzhi as well as postchapter comments of Wang Xilian and Yao Xie. It also contains a preface by Huayang Xianyi; an essay "How to Read *Story of the Stone*," by Zhang Xinzhi; Wang Xilian's preface and "General Comments"; part of Zhu Lian's "Commentary on *Story of the Stone*" but called in this edition "General Remarks by the Owner of Ming Studio"; "General

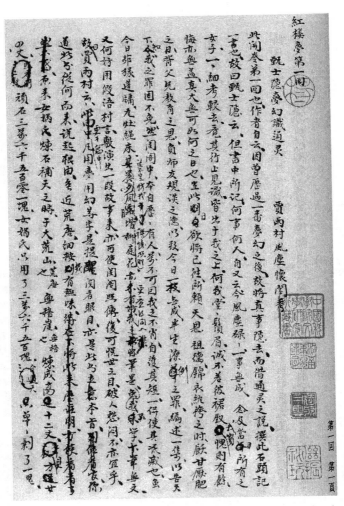

Fig. 3. A page from the opening of chapter 1 of the Qianlong 乾隆 hand-written copy, the earliest complete version (though much is still in debate). It is referred to and reprinted in Chinese as "The Gao [高] *Story of the Stone.*" The stamps are the name seals affixed by previous owners or commentators. Rpt. in *Qianlong chaoben bainian hui Honglou meng gao* (Beijing: Zhonghua shuju, 1963), 1.1.1a

Comments by Yao Xie"; "Someone Asked" (same as "Questions and Answers on *Story of the Stone*"), by Tu Ying; the anonymous "Twelve Poems on Incidents in the Grand Prospect Garden"; prefatory poems by Zhou Qi; Wang's phonetic glosses; and Huang Cong's "Explanation of the Diagram of Grand Prospect Garden." This edition was reprinted and further expanded over the years. That it was widely available is evidenced by the relatively numerous remaining editions, the poor quality of the paper, and the cheap ink.

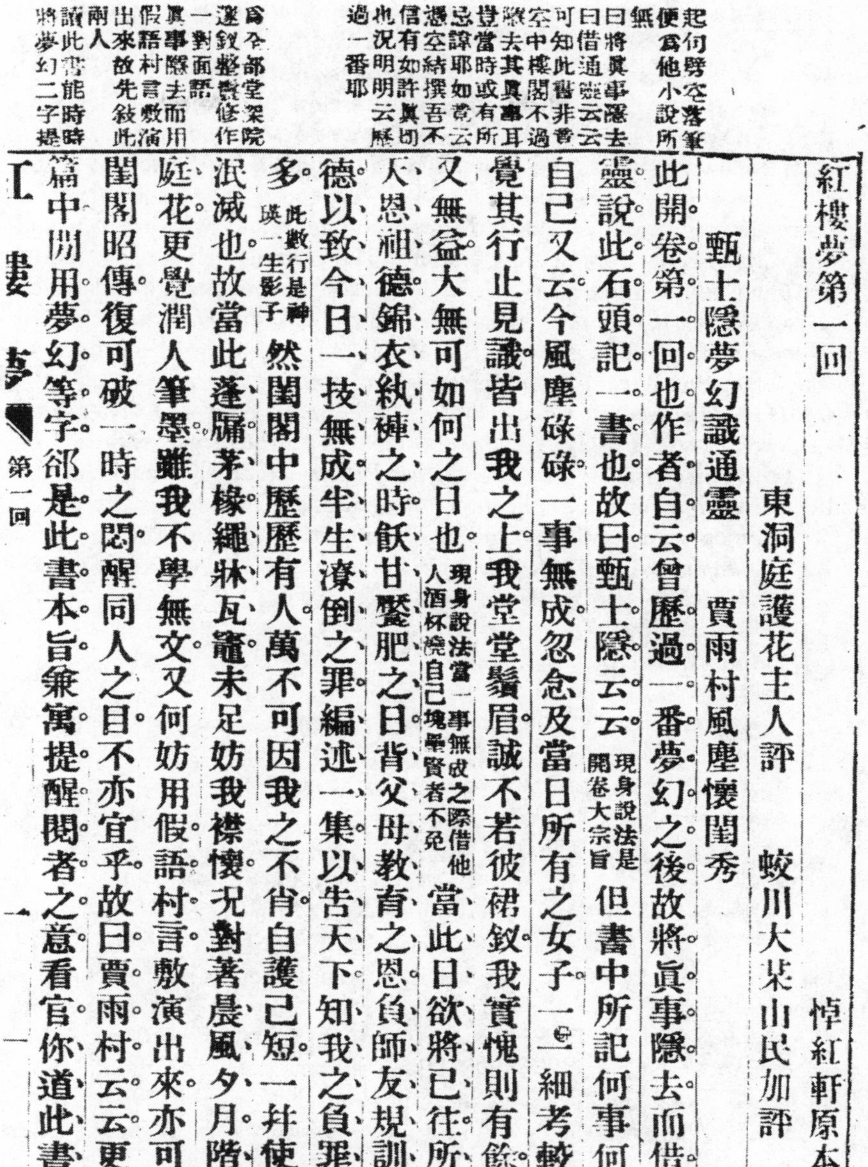

起何劈空落筆
便爲他小說所
無
日將眞事隱去
日借通靈云云
可知此書非著
空中樓閣不過
幾去其眞事耳
豈當時或有所
忌諱耶如意云
憑空結撰吾不
信有如許眞切
也況明明云歷
過一番耶
爲全部堂架院
逐欽整齊修作
一對面語
眞事隱去而用
假語村言敷演
出來故先敍此
兩人
讀此書能時時
將夢幻二字提

紅樓夢第一回　　悼紅軒原本

東洞庭護花主人評　　蛟川大某山民加評

甄士隱夢幻識通靈　　賈雨村風塵懷閨秀

此開卷第一回也作者自云曾歷過一番夢幻之後故將眞事隱去而借通靈說此石頭記一書也故曰甄士隱云云（現身說法是開卷大宗旨）但書中所記何事何人自己又云今風塵碌碌一事無成忽念及當日所有之女子一一細考較去覺其行止見識皆出我之上我堂堂鬚眉誠不若彼裙釵我實愧則有餘悔又無益大無可如何之日也（現身說法當一事無成之際借他人酒杯澆自己塊壘賢者不免）當此日欲將已往所賴天恩祖德錦衣紈袴之時飫甘饜肥之日背父母教育之恩負師友規訓之德以致今日一技無成半生潦倒之罪編述一集以告天下知我之負罪固多（此數行是神瑛一生影子）然閨閣中歷歷有人萬不可因我之不肖自護己短一并使其泯滅也故當此蓬牖茅椽繩牀瓦竈未足妨我襟懷況對著晨風夕月階柳庭花更覺潤人筆墨雖我不學無文又何妨用假語村言敷演出來亦可使閨閣昭傳復可破一時之悶醒同人之目不亦宜乎故曰賈雨村云云更於篇中間用夢幻等字卻是此書本旨兼寓提醒閱者之意看官你道此書從

紅樓夢　第一回　一

Fig. 4. The first page of chapter 1 from a popular 1927 edition of *The Affinity of Gold and Jade*, with marginal and interlineal comments in characters smaller than those of the main text.

Readers wanted commentary editions. Some volumes of *Stone* contained advertisements that solicited new commentary, which would be published in subsequent editions. Some volumes had covers and title pages promising a commentary edition but without comments, a clear ploy to sell undesirable, unmarked texts. Publishers reprinted prefatory essays and comments, editing them or changing titles as they saw fit. Because publishing *Stone* was clearly good business, many, many different editions resulted.

There are many heavily annotated editions of *Stone*, and there are also modern reprints of older commentary editions. The edition used for this volume is that published by Renmin Wenxue Chubanshe, annotated with explanatory notes by the *Story of the Stone* research institute at the China art institute under the supervision of Feng Qiyong (b. 1924). We note when quotations from the Hawkes and Minford translation are drawn from other editions.

The *Three Commentators* Story of the Stone (*Sanjia pingben honglou meng* [SJPB] 三家評本紅樓夢) is a modern edition that reprints commentaries from the 1884 edition of *The Affinity of Gold and Jade* and is widely available. There is also an excellent book that collects commentaries and prefatory material from eight traditional commentators, entitled The Story of the Stone *with Comments by Eight Commentators* (*Zhongjiao bajia pingpi honglou meng* 重較八家評批 紅樓夢).

## English Translations

The Hawkes and Minford translation *The Story of the Stone* is the edition used throughout this volume, unless otherwise noted.[1] There are two other complete translations of *Stone* into English. The first is by Yang Xianyi and Gladys Yang, published under the title *A Dream of Red Mansions*, in Beijing by the Foreign Languages Press, 1978–80. The Yangs' is quite a literal translation, but it includes a few passages that the Hawkes-Minford does not.[2] Older editions of this translation use a strange variant of the Wade-Giles romanization system (without umlauts or apostrophes) that was common in the People's Republic of China until the pinyin system was officially adopted. There is another complete translation, by B. S. Bonsall under the title *Red Chamber Dream*, currently available online from the University of Hong Kong Libraries. H. Bencraft Joly, the vice-consulate of Macao, translated the first fifty-six chapters and published them in two books in 1892 under the title *Hung lou meng; or, Dream of the Red Chamber*. (This translation was reprinted in 2010 as *The Dream of the Red Chamber*.)

There have been a few abridged translations of *Stone*, probably most notably that of Chi-chen Wang in *Dream of the Red Chamber*. Wang published his drastically abridged version in 1929 (the publishers were Doubleday, Routledge) and a much-expanded, retranslated version in 1958 (Doubleday, Twayne). For many years, his was the most common version of *Stone* in English and often the only one known to readers in the West. Its popularity may have been enhanced by the preface written by Mark Van Doren, but this work of adaptation obscures much of the original. (For a discussion of the history and influence of early translations of *Stone*, see Schonebaum, "Dreams.") The first Wang translation focuses almost exclusively on the love relationship between Jia Bao-yu and Lin Dai-yu, while the revised translation really is an outline of the plot, although it preserves the mythical frame of the Stone and Crimson Pearl Flower. In the absence of an abridged Hawkes-Minford translation, one option for classroom use is the Yang and Yang translation abridged by editors at the Commercial Press in Beijing in 1985 and available from Cheng and Tsui in Boston (499 pages). The editors of that volume do not acknowledge which chapters of the original correspond to their table of contents, but the episodes that it contains are usually preserved in their entirety. One drawback of the abridgement of the Yangs' translation is that, like the modern film versions and the television series, it ignores the mythological frame of the novel. It skips the first chapters with the origin of the Stone, of Zhen Shi-yin, the discussion of novels with Vanitas, and so on. The virtue of the book lies mainly in the faithful preservation of some of the more quotidian scenes. (The third edition of the *Norton Anthology of World Literature*, interestingly, focuses almost exclusively on the issues presented in the first few and final chapters of *Stone*.)

H. C. Chang, in his *Chinese Literature: Popular Fiction and Drama*, presents a good translation, with extensive footnotes, of the scene "A Burial Mound for Flowers," taken from chapter 23. It is highly recommended but might be confusing for those accustomed to Hawkes and Minford, since Chang uses the Wade-Giles romanization system and the names of the maids are translated differently (e.g., Aroma is Bombarding Scent).

# Commonly Taught Selections

It is difficult to decide how much and which parts of *The Story of the Stone* to select if teachers are unable to devote an entire course to the novel. Probably the most common solutions are to teach all of volume 1 (chs. 1–26), chapters 1–17, or chapters 1–12. Some teach the first three volumes (chs. 1–80). Some have made their own abridged versions of the complete work. There are other ways of using *Stone* in class, however, depending on the kind of course and amount of time available. In the past few years there has been a flourishing of anthologies of world literature, most of which use the Hawkes-Minford translation when they excerpt *Stone*. These, along with a few good anthologies of Chinese literature, present interesting selections from *Stone* that merit consideration.

Some anthologies, like *The Longman Anthology of World Literature*, focus on the dual pressures put on Jia Bao-yu (Damrosch et al.). Bao-yu's father, who represents traditional Confucian practice and belief, requires Bao-yu to study, put away his frivolous pursuits with his girl cousins, pass the imperial examinations, and become a gainfully employed official and eventually head of the Jia household and a model of Confucian morality. His mother expects him to marry a sensible, healthy, and industrious girl with whom he can produce the offspring that will continue the Jia family line and restore the Jia clan to their former status as one of the wealthiest and most respected families in the empire. This approach includes chapters like 17, where Bao-yu undergoes the rigor of naming places in the garden while receiving the criticism of his father and his father's retinue of literary gentlemen. Such an approach might also present a selection from chapter 33 in which Bao-yu is savagely beaten by his father (though this chapter is not in *Longman*). The pressures put on Bao-yu are well illustrated by the "choice" he faces between his cousins Lin Dai-yu and Xue Bao-chai. Dai-yu is the only member of the family who sympathizes with Bao-yu's aversion to study and to his responsibilities as the sole male heir, while Bao-chai is sturdy, sensible, filial, and in other ways a model Confucian woman. *Longman's* selections from chapters 23, 27, 28, 29, 30, 34, 94, 96, 97, and 98 show how this opposition culminates in Dai-yu's death and Bao-yu's marriage to Bao-chai. Emphasizing the themes of Bao-yu's pressures, romantic attachment, or two ideals of female beauty (an approach that would make *Stone* a good paring with *The Tale of Genji*) is likely the most common way, though certainly not the only or even best way, to adapt *Stone* for the classroom.

Focusing on the romance in the novel between Bao-yu and Dai-yu, in which Bao-chai serves as a rival or foil, is a time-honored reading of *Stone* and the approach taken by *The Norton Anthology of World Literature* (Lawall et al.). The dangers of this approach, aside from reductionism, are to overemphasize adolescent love (as opposed to sentiment) and to neglect what many see as the other main character: Wang Xi-feng. Reducing the novel's complexity in this way does make teaching *Stone* a more manageable endeavor, and some might argue that a focus on adolescent love suggests the novel's universalism, unlike depictions of difference from its Western counterparts. One way to make the lesson a bit more complex is to include the episode of Jia Rui and his Mirror for the Romantic in chapter 12: the episode allows students to see that the love story in *Stone* is itself a mirror for the romantic. They become better readers than Jia Rui, realizing the illusory nature of love. One virtue of the *Norton* selections is that they include scenes in which characters read other texts, even the forbidden *Story of the Western Wing*, which Bao-yu and Dai-yu use as a code to discuss their feelings. Students get a sense of the role poetry plays, of how it is used to communicate emotion.

Another approach is to follow Bao-yu's journey toward enlightenment, as does *The Bedford Anthology of World Literature* (Davis et al.). His brief sojourn in the realm of red dust is bookended by readers encountering the story of and on the Stone. This approach might survey selections from chapters 1, 3, 4, 5, 6, and 8, covering origins, the characters of Dai-yu and Bao-chai, the introduction of Bao-yu to the Land of Illusion, his early experiments in the arts of love, and the matching inscriptions of his jade and Bao-chai's locket. It might cover the development of his relationship with Dai-yu, the awkward encounter of chapter 32, and her vow to waste away in chapter 89 after hearing of Bao-yu's engagement, followed by her death in chapters 97 and 98. *Bedford* includes selections from chapters 119 and 120, in which Bao-yu's journey is brought to completion. This approach embraces the ending of the novel, attributed to Gao E and supposedly based on Cao's original notes or intention. Many, including Hawkes and Minford, believe the ending is equal in quality to the first eighty chapters. The complete tale is the version most often read in the last two centuries in China, so why not teach the ending? We learn that Bao-yu succeeds in the imperial examinations and that he disappears, like Zhen Shi-yin, whom we meet again and who expounds the nature of passion and illusion, while Jia Yu-cun concludes the Dream of Golden Days. Since Bao-yu's journey in the human realm is one of enlightenment through sentiment, it makes sense to teach the end of the novel. (Table 1 compares the selections of *Stone* in the Norton, Longman, and Bedford anthologies.)

An interesting selection is that of Cyril Birch in his *Anthology of Chinese Literature* (Cao and Gao, "Red Chamber Dream"). He excerpts chapters 63–69 (in his own translation), the episodes in which Jia Lian takes You Er-jie as a concubine in secret, they are discovered, and Xi-feng cunningly drives Er-jie to suicide. Birch omits the tragic story of You San-jie, who kills herself after her fiancé unjustly breaks off their engagement. San-jie's story would be instructive to include, since it presents both an ironic twist — it is her association with the Jia family that makes her fiancé suspect her virtue — and an interesting comparison of the bold San-jie and her meek sister, Er-jie. The melodramatic story of the You sisters is one of the few episodes of *Stone* to become part of the regular repertory of Peking opera, and Tong Zhiling (1922–95), a famous opera singer, starred in a 1962 film version of the San-jie story (*You Sanjie* 尤三姐). Although this selection has little to do with major plot arcs of *Stone*, it lends itself to courses on Chinese civilization or women's roles. It could also be

Table 1: Selections from *Stone* in Four Anthologies of World Literature

| Norton (2nd ed.) | Norton (3rd ed.) | Longman | Bedford |
|---|---|---|---|
| from 1: origin of the stone; discussion of novels; Zhen Shi-yin's dream | the same; Jia Yu-cun | the same as Norton (2nd ed.) | the same as Norton (2nd ed.) |
| | from 2: Jia Yu-cun discusses Jia and Zhen families with Leng Zi-xing. | the same | |
| | all of 3 | from 3: Lin Dai-yu arrives in the Jia household and meets Jia Bao-yu. | the same |
| | | | from 4: Xue Bao-chai arrives in the Jia household. |
| short summary of 2–25 | | from 5: Qin-shi's bedroom; Bao-yu's dream visit to the Land of Illusion | 5 |
| | | | from 6: Bao-yu's first experiment in the art of love |
| | | | from 8: Bao-yu and Bao-chai discover corresponding inscriptions. |
| | | | short summary of 8–31 |
| | from 17: the naming of the garden; discussion of poetics | the same | |
| | | from 23: forbidden books; burial mound for flowers | |
| all of 26 | | | |
| all of 27 | | from 27: Dai-yu rebuffs Bao-yu and laments the fate of fallen flowers. Bao-yu overhears her poem. | |
| all of 28 | | the same | |
| all of 29 | | the same | |
| all of 30 | | from 30: Dai-yu cries into handkerchief; she chastises Bao-yu for being so casual with his female cousins. | |
| all of 31 | | | |

| | | | | |
|---|---|---|---|---|
| **all of 32** | | | | **from 32:** Dai-yu is happy about an overheard compliment but concerned about matching inscriptions and kylins. |
| **all of 33** | | | | **short summary of 33–88** |
| **all of 34** | **from 34:** Bao-yu is placed in Aroma's care. Bao-yu sends handkerchiefs to Dai-yu, on which she writes poems. | | | |
| **summary of 35–96** | | | | **from 89:** Dai-yu vows to waste away after hearing of Bao-yu's engagement. |
| | | | | **from 90:** Dai-yu hears good news and begins to recover. Grandmother Jia decides Bao-yu is to marry Bao-chai. |
| | | | | **short summary of 91–95** |
| | **from 94:** a strange omen; Bao-yu's jade lost | the same | | the same |
| **from 96:** Dai-yu learns that Bao-yu will marry Bao-chai. She falls desperately ill. | | the same | | |
| | **from 97:** Dai-yu burns her poems and prepares to die. Bao-chai marries Bao-yu. | **from 97:** Dai-yu burns her poems and prepares to die. | the same | the same as Norton (3rd ed.) |
| **all of 97** | | | | |
| **short summary of 98–120** | **from 98:** Dai-yu dies. Bao-yu has a revelatory dream, convalesces, and warms to Bao-chai. | the same | the same | **from 98:** Dai-yu dies. Bao-yu has a revelatory dream. **summary of 99–118** |
| | **from 119:** Bao-yu says goodbye to his family, passes the exams, is lost. | | | the same |
| | **from 120:** Jia Zheng sees Bao-yu one last time. | | | the same |

Chapter numbers are in boldface. The Longman has footnotes that mention plot points skipped by its selections. No anthology includes the final half of 120.

compared productively with the Jia Rui episode of chapters 11 and 12 and with those listed in the table below that discuss the moral and financial decline of the Jia household to present a fascinating portrait of Wang Xi-feng.

Two other anthologies of Chinese literature, H. C. Chang's *Chinese Literature: Popular Fiction and Drama* (383–404) and Victor Mair's *The Columbia Anthology of Traditional Chinese Literature* (Cao and Gao, "Burial Mound"), take an aesthetic approach in presenting an iconic scene from the novel, the burial mound for flowers in chapter 23. The scene is symbolic in that Dai-yu, herself the incarnation of a flower, here is tending to her "own" grave. The scene also employs forbidden romantic literature: Bao-yu is emboldened by *The Western Chamber* (*Xixiang ji* 西廂記), and Dai-yu, overhearing lines from *The Peony Pavilion* (*Mudan ting* 牡丹亭; Hawkes translates the title as "The Soul's Return"), is able to give shape to her feelings. Teachers might use this passage to discuss aspects of Chinese aesthetics, reading practice, and the traditional suspicion of novels and plays. The passage might also be paired with the scene when Dai-yu returns to the same spot in chapters 27 and 28, presenting examples of fine (and foreboding) poetry. It could also be used to start a discussion of funerary rites, ancestor worship, and other rituals for the beloved dead.

The story of Wang Xi-feng is not anthologized anywhere and rarely appears in syllabi that include *Stone*, though Xi-feng is a perennial favorite with students. This story of ambition, responsibility, mismanagement, illness, and death works particularly well in the classroom. When coupled with the story of Aroma, it gives entrée to discussion of gender roles, hierarchy, and retribution. It also provides an oblique way to treat the otherwise unwieldy story of the decline of the Jia household in general, considering how Xi-feng is visited by Qin-shi's ghost twice—the first time to warn her to economize and plan for the future (ch. 13), the second time to reprimand her for not doing so (ch. 101). The diminishing splendor of the funerals that Xi-feng must oversee, culminating in the shoddy affair that is her own funeral, is another way to consider the fall of both Xi-feng and the Jia family (Qin-shi's funeral in chs. 13–15, Jia Jing's in ch. 64, Er-jie's in ch. 69, Grandmother Jia's in ch. 110, and Xi-feng's in ch. 114).

The story of the Jia house in decline can be presented through other groupings. One might track the building and ruin of the garden as it becomes privatized, desolate, and then perhaps haunted (chs. 16–18, 23, 40, 55–56, 73–74, 78–79, 89, 102, 116). The garden is a symbol of the purity contrasting with the outside world, the wealth of the Jia family, childhood, the land of illusion, and yet it is often overlooked as one of *Stone*'s main characters. Readings might also include Xi-chun's thwarted efforts to paint the garden (chs. 42, 50, 52). The fall of the Jias could also be presented through an examination of Grannie Liu's visits (chs. 6, 39–42, 113, 119). Grannie Liu witnesses the splendor of the Jias and is the butt of their jokes, but she outlives most of the them and saves Xi-feng's daughter from being sold into concubinage.

Ideally *Stone* should be read in its entirety, but teaching some of it is preferable to teaching none of it.

# Naming Practices and Glossary of Names

In China, the surname comes first. Traditionally there were multiple personal names, including the given name (*ming* 名) and the "courtesy name" (*zi* 字 or *biaozi* 表字) usually given to or taken by men when they reached twenty years, marking their coming of age. Women sometimes were given a courtesy name upon marriage. According to the *Book of Rites* (*Liji* 禮記), it is disrespectful for others of the same generation to refer to a man by his given name, which is reserved for his elders and himself. Friends and colleagues use his courtesy name, particularly on formal occasions or in writing. The courtesy name is usually disyllabic (two Chinese characters) and usually bears some relation to the given name. In *The Story of the Stone*, Bao-yu never receives a courtesy name.

There was also the studio, style, or pen name (*hao* 號), often self-selected, composed of three or four Chinese characters, and having no relation to either the given or courtesy name. The pen name was often a personal or whimsical choice, perhaps alluding to something or containing a rare character, as might befit an educated literatus. Another possibility was to use the name of one's residence. For instance, Su Shi (1037–1101), a Song dynasty statesman, artist, and poet, took as his pen name "resident of Eastern slope" *Dongpo Jushi*, because he built a residence while in exile. An author's pen name was also often used in the title of his collected works — in this case, the works of Su Dongpo.[3]

Certain names were taboo. The name of the emperor was taboo to everyone, and he was referred to by his reign name. Parents' names were taboo to children, and they had to refer to their parents obliquely, as Dai-yu does when she uses her mother's given name, Jia Min, in chapter 2 of *Stone*. Jia Yu-cun says, "Of course! I have often wondered why it is that my pupil Dai-yu always pronounces '*min*' as '*mi*' when she is reading and, if she has to write it, always makes the character with one or two strokes missing" (1.2.82) "怪道這女學生讀至凡書中有 '敏' 字, 皆念作 '密' 字, 每每如是, 寫字遇著 '敏' 字, 又減一二筆 ..." (1: 32).

There is structural significance to many of the names in the novel. The overlap in the names Dai-yu, Bao-yu, and Bao-chai suggests the relationship between the three:

Dai-**yu**　黛玉 "Black Jade"
**Bao-yu**　寶玉 "Precious Jade"
**Bao**-chai 寶釵 "Precious Clasp" or "Precious Hairpin"

Note that the surname *Jia* 賈, as in the Jia family, is a homophone for "false" 假 while *Zhen* 甄, as in Zhen Bao-yu, is a homophone for "true" or "real" 真. Thus the protagonist Jia Bao-yu is the "false" or "fake" Bao-yu. Jia Zheng's 賈政 name suits his personality, since it recalls the *zheng* of *zhengfu* 政府, "government," or of *zhengming* 正名, Confucius's concept that good government must start with the "rectification of names." Some readers like to remember that Jia is a homophone with a character meaning "false" and so think of Jia Zheng as "false government" or "falsely upright."

Other major characters have significant names. Adamantina (Miao-yu 妙玉) and Crimson (Lin Hong-yu 林紅玉) both have *yu* 玉, "jade," in their names, though Crimson's name is changed to Xiao-hong 小紅 because of its similarity to Bao-yu and Dai-yu (at the end of ch. 24; the change is not included in *Stone*). The major women characters in *Stone* also have interesting names. Xi-feng's forceful personality and refined pedigree may be suggested by her name, which is that of a man (3.54.29). One way of following the fall of the Jia clan is to mark the fortunes of the four springs, Yuan-chun, Ying-chun, Tan-chun, and Xi-chun. If the four *chun* (*chun* is "spring") are read together in order—that is, Yuan, Ying, Tan, and Xi 元迎探惜—according to the Red Inkstone commentary, it sounds like "actually/indeed should be sighed over and pitied" (*Yuan ying tan xi* 原應嘆息).

The Jia family uses some particular naming conventions that the reader should be aware of, such as common elements to indicate members of the same generation in a family. Instances of this are the use of *chun* 春 in the female cousins' names, *dai* 代 in the oldest living male generation of the Jias, and *yu* 玉 in Bao-yu's generation. Names were listed in descending order by generation and position in that generation. The list of attendees at Qin-shi's funeral is an example of such a hierarchical list (1.13.259). The convention of using respectful names is difficult even to the characters. In chapter 3, Dai-yu does not know how to address Xi-feng until someone whispers in her ear that it is "cousin Lian's wife" (91). Observing ritual formalities was complicated and time-consuming. In the garden, the young people, all within a year or two of each other in age, have a hard time remembering who is senior to whom; thus they abandon trying to observe the formalities of address (2.49.474). The garden inhabitants address one another in a disordered way, but there is no escape from the kinship terms for older and younger brother and sister as applied broadly to mark age. Bao-yu, for instance, always calls Dai-yu "younger sister" and Bao-chai "older sister."

In their translation of *Stone*, Hawkes and Minford treat characters according to class. Although this system can present a rigidity that may not reflect the realities of life in mid–Qing dynasty China (early eighteenth to mid-nineteenth century), it is a great help to readers of the novel. The translation of names separates masters from servants. The master class stays Chinese, their names romanized according to the pinyin system (with hyphens), like Jia Zheng or Lin Dai-yu. The names of maids and servants are translated: Aroma, Skybright. Religious people (Taoists and Buddhists) are given Latin names, like Sapientia. Actresses are given French names, like Parfumée. There are a few exceptions to this rule, however. Not all servants' names are translated. Older male servants tend to be referred to by their surnames, like Zhou Rui. Their wives tend to be referred to (as in Chinese) by reference to their husbands. Married female servants have "Mama" or "Nannie" (if they are nurses) preceding their surnames. This privileging of seniority or age among servants is the same in the original and Hawkes's translation.[4]

Many of the names of minor characters are puns relying on close homophones. While they do not deserve undo attention in the classroom, they do hint at a playfulness and complexity that might be fun to note or significant for advanced students. Here are some examples:

Bu Shi-ren 卜世仁 is a shopkeeper and maternal uncle of Jia Yun. His name sounds like *bu shi ren* (不是人 "not a man" or "inhuman"). Hawkes has this association in mind when he mentions a name that could be translated as Hardleigh Hewmann in his introduction (1.31).

Calamity is a Zhen family servant who loses Ying-lian. His name, Huo Qi 霍启 puns with *huo qi* (祸起 "calamity arises"). Hawkes translates his name as "calamity" (1.1.61–62), which is problematic in that families were careful to give their servants names that were auspicious (e.g., De-gui: ["Get honors"] or Lai-fu: ["Prosperity arrives"]). It is unusual in a Chinese novel for a servant of Huo Qi's status to get a surname, but this is probably done precisely for the pun.

Cheng Ri-xing is one of Jia Zheng's literary gentlemen. His name 程日形 sounds like *chengri xing* (成日興 "having fun every day").

Feng Yuan 馮淵 is Caltrop's first purchaser. He is originally attracted to men but falls in love at first sight with Caltrop and intends to marry her. He is beaten savagely by Xue Pan's servants and dies three days later. Xue Pan is brought up on charges of murder. Feng Yuan's name is a homophone for *feng yuan* (逢冤 "meets injustice").

Jia Yu-cun 賈雨村 is a careerist claiming relationship with the Rong-guo family, benefiting from the patronage of Zhen Shi-yin. When we first meet him, he is eking out a living as a scrivener, one who sells scrolls and inscriptions to make a living. His given name, Jia Hua 賈化, is a homophone for "false words" (*jia hua* 假話). The "face" or literal meaning of *yucun* is "rainy village," but taken with his surname, *"jiayu cun"* 假語存, it sounds like "false words preserved," which parallels the homophone of Zhen Shi-yin's name: "true words concealed." "Jia Yu-cun" can also be interpreted to mean *jiayu cun (yan)* (假語村[言] "false words clothed in rustic language"), another way of saying "fiction in the vernacular." As for Jia Yu-cun's pseudonym, Shi-fei 時飛, it connotes *shifei* 實非 "truth and falsity" or "actually false." A more common meaning of *shifei* is "dissension." Someone who stirs up *shifei* is a troublemaker. Jia's hometown is Hu Zhou 胡州, a homonym for "gibberish" (*huzhou* 胡謅).

Moonbeam, Xia Jin-gui's maid, plots with Xia Jin-gui to seduce Xue Ke. Her name, Bao-chan 寶蟾, sounds like *bao chan* (飽饞 "satisfying one's hunger").

Shan Ping-ren 单聘仁 is another of Jia Zheng's literary gentlemen. His name sounds like *shan pianren* (擅骗人 "good at deceiving people").[5]

Wang Ren 王仁 is Wang Xi-feng's elder brother. He takes advantage of birthdays and funerals at the Jia house to embezzle money. His name is a homophone for *wang ren* (忘仁 "forgetting benevolence" or "blind to all forms of human decency"). Jia Lian says as much in chapter 101 (4.53).

Wang Shan-bao's wife is a meddlesome old woman and trusted servant of Lady Xing (Aunt Xing). She is the one who leads the inspection in the garden of the maids' things. Her name, 王善保, sounds like *wang shangbao* (往上報 "report [tell on someone] to one's superior").

Zhan Guang 詹光 is one of Jia Zheng's literary gentlemen. His name sounds like *zhan guang* (沾光 "taking advantage").

Zhao Quan 趙全, Commissioner of the Embroidered Jackets (leader of the Imperial Guards), has a name that sounds like *chao quan* (抄全 "confiscate everything").

Zhen Shi-yin 甄士隱 is a retired gentleman of Suzhou and father of Caltrop (Ying-lian). After his daughter disappears and his house burns, he goes off with a Taoist monk to faraway places. His story bookends *Stone*. His name sounds like *zhen shi yin* (真事隱 "true facts concealed" or 真士隱 "true scholar in seclusion").

Zhen Ying-lian 甄英蓮 is Zhen Shi-yin's daughter, who is kidnapped and ends up in the Jia mansion as a maid named Caltrop. Her name sounds like *zhen ying lian* (真應憐 "worthy of pity").

# Chronologies and Maps

As in much of Chinese poetry, in *Stone* the name and style of each residence in the garden are a clue to the character of its inhabitant.[6] Dai-yu, whose surname is Lin 林 ("forest" or "grove"), resides in a bamboo grove, and the house of Bao-chai, whose surname is Xue 薛, a homophone for "snow" (*xue* 雪), is compared to a snow cave. Bao-yu, who delights in all things red (see ch. 19), things that themselves are symbols of his attachment to the mundane world (red dust) with all its cares, is housed in Crimson Joys Court (*Yihong yuan* 怡红院), which Hawkes translates as the "House of Green Delights" from the imperial concubine's line "Crimson Joys and Green Delights" (1.18.364). Syntactically, a better rendering might be "House of Delighting in Red." Of the seven different dwellings, the more distinctive are described twice. The first description is made during Jia Zheng's tour of the garden in chapter 17 (supplemented by information given during Yuan-chuan's tour in chapter 18); in the second, we see the Garden through the wide eyes of Grannie Liu in chapters 40 and 41.

Dai-yu lives in the Naiad's House and has a parrot that recites verses (2.35.175). Her residence in Chinese is the Xiao-xiang Hermitage 瀟湘館. The Xiao and the Xiang, two rivers in Hunan Province, are the subject of numerous misty landscape paintings. The bamboo grown along the Xiang belongs to a speckled variety known as the Xiang Queens bamboo; the speckles are supposedly the stains of tears shed by the two queens of Xiang who later became goddesses. Thus, Dai-yu is called "River-Queen" (2.37.217). Her place has three small, neatly furnished rooms with a veranda shaded by bamboo. A winding pebble path leads to the door. A stream runs through the back courtyard into the bamboo grove in front (1.17.330–2). The bamboo grove suggests seclusion, otherworldliness, and tears; the narrow, winding path reflects an introverted stance; and the running stream is a sign of a lively mind.[7]

Bao-yu's residence, Green Delights, is entered through a moon-shaped rose trellis leading into a courtyard with some small palms, a small rock garden, and a large crab apple tree, supposedly from the Kingdom of Women (1.17.345). The courtyard is enclosed on three sides by covered walks, with Bao-yu's apartments forming the remaining side. There are five rooms created by a maze of exquisitely carved wooden partitions, the shelves of which are filled with antiques and curios. A mirror door, "an imported contraption," which opens between Bao-yu's bedroom and the back courtyard, compounds the sense of a labyrinth (3.54.24). It confuses Jia Zheng as well as Grannie Liu. Green Delights also has false windows and doors inserted into the partitions and trompe-l'oeil paintings on the walls. A cloistered part of the residence is filled with exotic birds in cages of various colors (described in 1.26.511), which adds to the maze and trap symbolism. Bao-yu's residence, named for the crab apple blossoms, is suggestive of the title *Dream of Red Mansions*. Red Rue Studio (*Jiangyi xuan* 絳芸軒) is used as an alternative name for Green Delights in the titles of chapters 36 and 59 and in chapter 8 of the sixteen-chapter manuscript version, but it seems to be Bao-yu's study, since it exists before the garden is built. Bao-yu's residence suggests that Bao-yu is indeed trapped in a world of things, ornamentation, and feelings; the mirror on the door suggests illusion leading, perhaps, to enlightenment.

Bao-chai lives in All Spice Court 蘅蕪苑 (1.17.340–42). Her suite of five rooms with awnings and a veranda is hidden behind a tall rock garden overgrown with creeping herbs that give off a fragrance that is reminiscent of chapter 8, before the building of the garden, when Bao-yu detected a delightful fragrance about Bao-chai caused by her "cold fragrance pills" (191). Her rooms are excessively bare, with only a vase of the coarser Tingware holding a few chrysanthemums for decoration. There is an explicit lack of trees, marking the place as anti- or non-Dai-yu, because Dai-yu is associated with trees and bamboo. The fragrance denotes purity of character; the unadorned interior denotes thrift and the simpler female virtues. But the overall plainness and whiteness, which Grandmother Jia thinks inauspicious, are an omen of a sad ending. Note that the rocks and cave-like apartments suggest a tomb.

Other residences have significance. One bearing mention is Pear Tree Court, where the twelve young actresses are housed (1.17.350). The name is appropriate, because Emperor Xuanzong of the Tang dynasty trained his three hundred musicians in a pear orchard. There are also puns in place-names. Readers should pay attention to the layered meanings in almost all the names in chapter 1, both of people and of places. Green Meadow Peak (*Qing Geng Feng* 青埂峰), where the Stone is originally abandoned, is a near homonym for *qing gen* 情根 ("root-origin of feeling-desire"). The character Cao Xueqin is mentioned as working on *Stone* in his Nostalgia Studio for ten years. In Chinese the studio name is *Dao Hong Xuan* 悼紅軒, which might also be rendered "Mourning over the World of Red Dust."

Time is imprecise in *Stone*. It flows quickly at the very beginning and end of the novel but spans only two or three years for the middle eighty chapters or so. In chapter 103, Jia Yu-cun says it has been nineteen years since he last saw Zhen Shi-yin, an event from chapter 1 (5.94). But the end of the novel slows down too, since in chapter 120 we are told that Bao-yu is nineteen (361). References to ages and the precise passage of time are particularly unreliable in the last forty chapters. An example is the age Yuan-chun is said to be at her death: 43 (4.95.311). Since Bao-yu was old enough to be taught by her before she entered the palace, she would have had to enter the palace in her late twenties or early thirties, remaining unmarried until then.

Time is marked in the novel mainly by seasons, festivals, and birthdays. It is often difficult to determine how much time has passed and how old everyone is. In Chinese tradition, you are one at birth, then become a year older, with everyone else, on the New Year. That Hawkes and Minford translate in terms of years the Chinese way of reckoning age tends to reduce the ages given in the original by one. Using the Western count introduces another ambiguity.

Similarly, years of documents and events in *Stone* are given, in the original, as one in a sixty-year cycle, a practice that Hawkes and Minford date to the eighteenth century. For example, the date of Jia Jing's advanced degree is given as "17__" (1.13.263). The cyclical date in the Chinese text cannot be automatically matched to any century, and the translators' practice in this instance is contrary to the explicit statements in chapter 1 that the events in the novel do not belong to any dynastic period.

Ages in *Stone* are almost plastic. Caltrop, Skybright, Aroma, and Bao-chai are all the same age (3.63.229). We are told that Ying-chun, Tan-chun, Xi-chun, Bao-chai, Dai-yu, Xiang-yun, Li Wen, Li Qi, Bao-qin, Xing Xiu-yan, and Bao-yu are all fifteen, sixteen, or seventeen in chapter 49 and that they all get so confused trying to remember who is senior to whom that they give up trying (2.473). In other words, a primary way in Chinese to determine age—terms of address that indicate seniority—and thus mark the passage of time is confused in the novel.

When we meet Bao-yu, he is on his way to be incarnated, but in chapter 2, he is already seven or eight years old. Dai-yu is six when we first meet her, and she says in chapter 3 that she is a year younger than Bao-yu. In chapter 5 we are told that Bao-chai is just a bit older than Dai-yu (1.124), which suggests that Bao-yu is older than both girls. But in chapter 22 Bao-chai has her fifteenth birthday and in chapter 23 Bao-yu's age is mentioned as thirteen, two years less than Bao-chai's. In chapter 25 the monk and Taoist say that it has been thirteen years since they saw Bao-yu. If Bao-yu is a year or two younger than Bao-chai, Dai-yu is only twelve. But in chapter 45, she is fifteen, and we know that exactly one year passes from chapter 18 to chapter 53, which should make her thirteen. In chapter 62, Bao-yu celebrates a birthday that would put him at sixteen or seventeen, on the basis of Bao-chai's and Dai-yu's stated ages, but he is much younger by the reckoning of the monk and Taoist. Between chapter 63, when Jia Jing dies, and chapter 76, two years pass. This makes Bao-yu eighteen or nineteen, but in chapter 78 we are told that Skybright was sixteen when she died and she is the same age as Caltrop, Bao-chai, and Aroma (3.63.229), which suggests that Bao-yu is still sixteen. The next point at which we know Bao-yu's age is chapter 103, when Jia Yu-cun says to Zhen Shi-yin that it has been nineteen years since he last saw him, and Bao-yu is nineteen when last seen in chapter 120.

The passage of time in the novel might be reversed in the classroom. Some teachers spend an entire class on chapter 1, an hour on chapters 2 and 3, and so on, speeding up until they reach the last few chapters, then slowing down again, spending an hour on chapter 120.

In the table of appendix 2 of Andrew Plaks's *Archetype and Allegory in* The Dream of the Red Chamber we can see that the fortunes of the Jia family are followed through the turning of six years, and *Stone* seems to cover Bao-yu's life from about age twelve to nineteen. The structure of the novel is intricate. Readers and traditional commentators have noticed an elaborate patterning of events in *Stone*, an alternation of fortunes and tones in and between chapters. Since chronological time is so imprecise, the transition of one emotion into another or between scenes of action and scenes of dialogue or description provides the only reliable measure. Just as *Stone* makes use of, in its form and content, the conquest cycles of yin and yang and the five phases (discussed in this volume by Schonebaum; Epstein; and Lu), so it also moves between the emotions and tones of elegance, baseness, joy, sorrow, union, separation, harmony, conflict, prosperity, and decline.

Space, like time, is imprecise in *Stone*. One of the most prominent spatial ambiguities is the conflation of north and south in China. The Jia family originally hails from Nanjing, on the Yangzi River, about 550 miles south of where they now live, Beijing. As Hawkes points out in the introduction to volume 1 of *Stone*, the girls are the "twelve beauties of Jinling" (Nanjing), though many of them have never been there. In most other regards—street names, proximity to the palace, the proliferation of kangs (heated platforms to sit or sleep on) throughout the house, and so on—the action of the novel takes place in Beijing. There is a good deal of travel in the vast Qing Empire, most of it between Beijing and Nanjing, for funerals, business, and official matters, travel usually done via the Grand Canal (fig. 5). Spatial confusion of the Jia world might be explained by the author's using his background in his creation of fictional characters. Interference from historical-familial models produces inconsistency in the text. That Yuan-chun visits her family only once after becoming an imperial concubine seems strange but might be because the historical model was married to a prince who lived far away and not, as it is in the novel, in the nearby palace.

Traditional scholarly interest in *Stone* as a roman à clef has led many readers to assume that the world of the novel is the world of its author. The argument can be made that *Stone*'s lack of clarity in time and space is a direct result of the author's disguising of real events and people in the eighteenth century. The Red Inkstone commentary suggests that the description of the Jia household and garden is intended to frustrate any attempt to map everything out, but numerous scholars have devoted themselves to doing just that. Despite the success that some have had in charting the passage of time in *Stone*, others feel that it is best to live with the imprecision.[8]

Students may benefit from seeing the variety of ways of imagining the spatial world of *Stone*, particularly the garden. The exercise may help them sympathize with Xi-chun's frustrated project of painting the garden. Ambiguity in *Stone* is more important than its resolution. The garden seems so vast at times that characters lose their way in it, but at other times it is quite small, enabling secrets to be discovered, conversations to be overheard, and unintended meetings to take place. With the leitmotif of dream, the interplay between truth and fiction, and the suggestion that the garden is the Land of Illusion, the authors may simply be more comfortable with nebulous time and space than scholars are.

Many scenes in *Stone* have led to iconic, sometimes reductive, pictorial representations of characters. Scholars such as Wu Hung have pointed out how

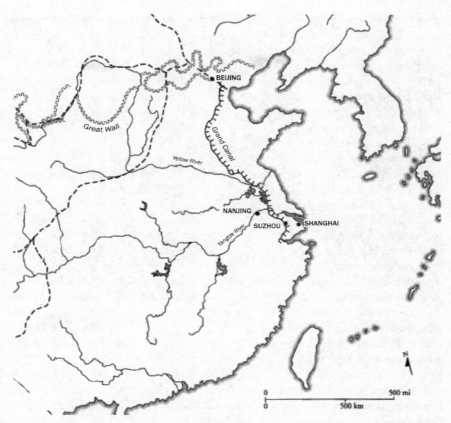

Fig. 5. Map of the eastern Qing Empire showing Beijing (Peking), Nanjing (Nanking), Suzhou (Soochow), the Great Wall, and the Grand Canal (map by Andrew Schonebaum)

visual depictions in *Stone* often parallel poses in painting albums of beautiful women that became popular in the seventeenth and eighteenth centuries. Often, printed editions of *Stone* included prints of characters as they are portrayed in famous scenes: Xiang-yun drunkenly sleeping outside while flower petals fall on her, Dai-yu burying flower petals, and Bao-chai chasing butterflies. Paired butterflies often signified the courtship of young lovers, and to have Bao-chai chasing them with childlike exuberance instead of ruminating on the meaning implied by their flitting about contrasts her innocence with those interested in love, sex, and marriage. Looking at three versions of this last scene, from chapter 27, we see that the image of Bao-chai does not change much, but the garden in the background does (fig. 6). On the left, the rocks and plants in the foreground suggest the naturalness, openness, and wildness of the garden. The bridge in the background with the stream underneath points to spaces beyond.

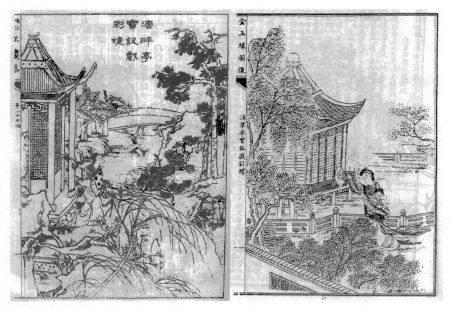

Fig. 6.  Bao-chai chasing a butterfly, from chapter 27. *Left*, from 1927? *Jing jiao*; *right*, from 1884 *Zeng ping*

Fig. 7.  This image of Bao-chai presents a complicated and ambivalent stance toward space in the garden. From Wang Zhao's 1888 *Honglou meng xie zhen* 紅樓夢寫真 ("Portrait of *Dream of the Red Chamber*")

Fig. 8. This image shows the scale of the garden but little of its expansiveness. 大觀園圖 Anonymous. Collection of the Palace Museum, Beijing

On the right, walls in the foreground and background enclose the area, and the plants suggest a more orderly, constructed space. Other images present the garden as highly structured in landscape and architecture (enclosed buildings, bridges, and walls) but including a great expanse through a circular doorway in a garden wall that has no top, to clouds of smoke trailing into the distance (fig. 7).

An intriguing variety of attempts have been made to represent the garden and its position in the Jia family mansion. For other images, see the essays in this volume by Dore Levy and by Shang Wei. Some of the garden images published in late-nineteenth- and early-twentieth-century editions of *Stone* are impressionistic and seem to be at ease with the ambiguous representation of space in *Stone.* Figure 8 is indebted to the school of "scholars enjoying themselves in a landscape," as Grandmother Jia suggests Xi-chun should do with her painting of the garden (2.42.336).

The image in figure 8 is more interested in portraying the spirit of the place than the actual layout, given that there are no walls around the garden or even an end to it. Buildings and pavilions here are emphasized, as is the garden's capacity to hold many of the novel's characters.

Other artists provide blueprints of the garden. In a book on the architecture of *Stone* published in 2006, Huang Yunhao presents two precise visions of the garden. In the first, the garden is situated in the Jia family compound (fig. 9). The Rong-guo side of the family is on the left, the Ning-guo side on the right. The garden is in the upper left quadrant. This blueprint suggests that the entire compound is approximately a thousand by two thousand feet or forty-five acres. In the second, the garden is about 590 feet on a side, giving about 350,000 square feet or eight acres—taking up approximately a fifth of the Jia mansion or about seven American football fields (fig. 10).

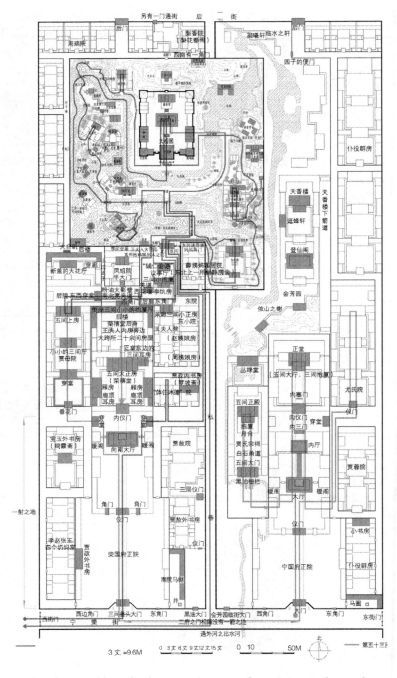

Fig. 9. A diagram of the Jia family mansion (Huang Yunhao 41). © 2006 China Architecture and Building Press

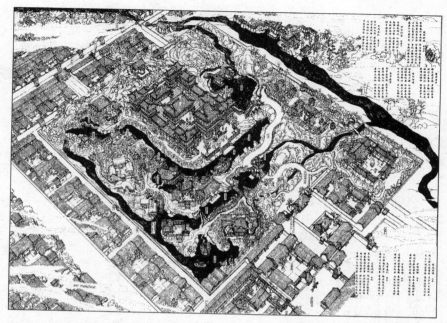

Fig. 10. An isometric image of the garden and surrounding Jia compound (Huang Yunhao 93).
© 2006 China Architecture and Building Press

This isometric view of the garden is interesting not just because of the detail but also because of the degree to which the relatively open and asymmetrical space of the garden contrasts with the highly patterned layout of the rest of the mansion. Green Delights is in the corner of the garden that is furthest to the right in this image.

# Study Questions

These groups of questions are designed to encourage close reading and help students grapple with complex topics and characters.

*Narrators*   How is the story in the novel told to us? Who is the narrator? Is the narrator omniscient? trustworthy? What is the narrator's relationship to the Stone, Jia Bao-yu, the author, and the reader? From whose point of view do we witness the events in the Jia family? Can we believe a story that tells us what it is about (1.1.51)? Is this an odd or Chinese way for a novel to begin?

*Zhen Shi-yin and Jia Yu-cun*   What is the significance of the characters Zhen Shi-yin and Jia Yu-cun? Consider the meanings of their names. Late in the story, why does Shi-yin refuse to recognize Jia Yu-cun? What is the meaning of their conversation (5.103.92–95)?

*Mysterious Figures*   What is the significance of the Taoist priest and the Buddhist monk? of Vanitas (1.1.47–48, 52–56, 63–64)? Consider Dai-yu's "scabby-headed old monk" (3.90), Jia Rui's Taoist claiming to be able to cure retributory illnesses (12.251), and the monk who finds Bao-yu's missing jade (5.117.299). Are these all the same monk? The Won-Done Song and its commentary are famous. What do they mean in the novel (1.1.63–65)?

*Land of Illusion*   Is Bao-yu's dream in chapter 5 *the* dream of the Red Chamber? What is the significance of the fantastic, impossible objects in Qin-shi's room? How would you describe the fairy Disenchantment's attitude toward love and lust? What is the Ford of Error (1.5.147–48)? In chapter 116, Bao-yu dreams, for only the second time, of the Land of Illusion. What has changed and why? Does he understand the registers more than he did the first time? On awakening, he seems changed. How so? Is the second visit to the Land of Illusion crucial? Is Bao-yu replicating Zhen Bao-yu's experience (4.93.268–71)?

*Qin-shi*   Who is Qin-shi, and what is her role in the novel? (See, in volume 1, 5.125–30, 148; 6.149; 7.183; 10.224–28; 11.234–36; 13.255–66; 533–34 [appendix]. In volume 5, see 101.48–49 and 111.209–10.)

*Jia Rui*   Is Jia Rui a victim? What do his illness and its cure mean? Some believe that the Jia Rui episode was dropped into *Stone*, originally written for another novel. What do you think? What is the significance of the "Mirror for the Romantic" (1.1.51, 12.251)?

*The Garden*   Some feel that Prospect Garden is one of the most important characters in the novel. How is it described in chapters 17 and 18? What are its origins? Some believe that the residences in the garden reflect their inhabitants' character traits. Do you agree or not? Consider the description and comments on the new residences of Dai-yu (1.17.330–31), Li Wan (334–35), Bao-chai (339–40), and Bao-yu (344–47). How does the initial tour of the garden go with Jia Zheng, his entourage, and Bao-yu? What happens to Bao-yu when he arrives at the main hall (342–43)? What do we learn from Stone's note (1.18.357–58)? Why does Yuan-chun name the garden Prospect Garden (364–65)? Why paint the garden? What kinds of problems are involved in its painting (2.42.334–43)? Is privatization of the garden a good idea? What are the reforms, and what is behind them (3.55.56–57, 55.62, 56.66–77, 57.122)? Are the economy and politics of the garden enclosed? Note attempts to close off the garden, increased surveillance (59.135), and Bao-chai on locking gates (62.192–93). Why is Xi-feng admonished to keep a closer eye on the garden? What are the results of this supervision (4.90.219)? What does it mean that by chapter 99 only Li Wan, Tan-chun, and Xi-chun remain living in the garden? Is the garden really haunted (5.102.66–76)?

*Worlds and Levels*    One popular reading is that of the two worlds of *Stone*: the utopian or Pure Land aspects of Prospect Garden versus the reality of the rest of the home or outside world. How many different worlds or levels of existence appear in the novel? How do they interact?

*Arguments and Misunderstandings*    The arguments between Bao-yu and Dai-yu are some of traditional readers' favorite scenes. How do these arguments arise? Why do the two fight so much? Are their differences resolvable? What do Bao-yu and Dai-yu fight about? Why do readers love these fights so much? Consider in depth one of the most carefully depicted fights in the novel (2.29.84–90).

*The Jade*    Bao-yu's jade is (at least in part) a talisman. It claims to ward off evil influences (1.8.189). Why does the jade lose its power (1.25.505)? How is it restored? What does the jade's glow mean (4.85.120)? Why does Bao-yu become insensate when he loses his jade in chapters 94–95? What does it mean that so many false jades and replicas turn up (4.95.309–11)? Is the loss of the jade a supernatural event or a mundane one? What solution does the family come up with to cure Bao-yu (4.96.326)? What is the relation of Bao-yu to his jade? How can he give his jade back (5.117.302–03)?

*Jealousy*    Xi-feng and Bao-yu are attacked by black magic in chapter 25. Why? Mother Ma is put in prison on charges of practicing black magic for a fee (an offense punishable by death). Who is the culprit (4.81.39–43)? Aunt Zhao is possessed by a spirit and dies (5.112.237–113.242). Is this misfortune the working of karma, retribution, black magic, or something else? Is Aunt Zhao's story a part of the jealousy and envy motif in *Stone*? How does her status as a concubine compare with that of the maids? Is she a sympathetic character?

*Bao-chai and Dai-yu*    Compare Bao-chai and Dai-yu. How are they introduced? Why are they both sick, and what do their illnesses mean? Is the narrator more sympathetic to one of the pair or not? Are Dai-yu's problems internally
or externally caused (is Dai-yu responsible for her fate)? Is Bao-chai scheming
and devious? Are the women an antagonistic or a complementary pair? How
does each see the other? How does Bao-yu see them?

*Yuan-chun*    What is Yuan-chun's role in *Stone*? Consider in detail her visit
home in chapter 18. How does what Yuan-chun says about the Jia family later
in the novel (4.83.88–89) resonate with what others have said about it (e.g.,
Bao-yu, Grannie Liu)? What does it mean for the Jias when she dies (95.310)?

*Past and Future*    How should we interpret references in *Stone* to characters'
pasts (the debt of tears) or to their futures (the ledgers in the Land of Illusion)?
What purposes do these references serve? What functions do the many omens
in *Stone* serve (1.22.450, 4.94.286, 5.101.62, 120.360)?

*Bao-yu*    Jia Bao-yu is both one of the most beloved and one of most detested
of all fictional characters in China. Why? Is he particularly strange or modern?
What do you think about him? How is he characterized by the fairy Disenchantment? What does "lust of the mind" mean (1.5.146)? Bao-yu is distraught over
the fact that so many of the young women in his life have died or married and
moved away. Yet he marries and generally does little to prevent the misfortunes
of these women. How can we be reconciled to this passivity? How does Zhen
Bao-yu help us understand Jia Bao-yu?

*Gender and Sex*    How does masculinity work in *Stone*? How is it defined?
What is Bao-yu's relationship to Qin Zhong? to Jiang Yu-han? to the prince
of Bei-jing? How does *Stone* depict homosexual relationships? What does
Bao-yu mean when he says "girls are made of water and boys are made of mud"
(1.2.76)? What do we learn from the schoolyard ruckus (9.208–13)? Why is it
that the tomboy Xiang-yun speaks about all difference in the universe in terms
of yin and yang (2.31.122–25)? Does Jia Zheng beat Bao-yu in chapter 32 because of rumors about his sexuality? What do we learn about gender and sexuality during the banquet with Liu Xiang-lian (2.47.436–45)? What do you make
of the cross-dressing and gender confusion in *Stone* (e.g., 2.49.479–80, 20.505,
3.63.222)?

*The You Sisters*    Even though it is a beloved part of the novel, some think
that the story of You San-jie and You Er-jie (chs. 63–70) was written separately
from the rest of the novel and then stitched in. Others think that only the San-
jie and Liu Xiang-lian plot was stitched in (3.620–23). Does this subplot have a
different feel from the rest of the novel? Does it lend the novel special mean-

ing? Does it matter that much of this plot takes place outside the Jia manor? What do you think of You Er-jie? of San-jie?

*Beginnings*    Some scholars see the first six chapters as a series of introductions, each opening the novel in a different way (Grannie Liu's visit in chapter 6 would be the last). Film and television versions of *Stone* often begin with Big Jiao's rant of chapter 7 (183). How many distinct introductions do you see? What different purposes do they serve? Which do you think is best?

*Authority Figures*    How are parent-child relationships portrayed in *Stone*? In some ways, Bao-yu is torn between two sets of influences, those of Grandmother Jia and those of Jia Zheng. What is Jia Zheng like as a father? Does his attitude toward Bao-yu change (4.84.98–103)? What kind of influence is Grandmother Jia? She loves Bao-yu but at times seems unwise. Is her shortcoming a criticism of Chinese households? Has something good and wonderful been perverted here? Or is there just something corrupt about this old woman's authority?

*History of the Quotidian*    To the best of your knowledge, does *Stone* give an accurate or illuminating portrait of China in the eighteenth century? How does the information on Chinese life contained in it relate to what you know about China from sources other than the novel? Consider, for instance, Grannie Liu's stories that Lady Wang and Grandmother Jia like best (2.39.271–72). Is the poetry society a version of society at large? is the family? Do you feel that Cao Xueqin is critical of this particular society?

*Poetry*    Formally and socially, how does poetry work in *Stone*? How many kinds of poetry appear, and how are they used in the novel? What function do the poetry clubs play in the novel? What are the criteria for choosing a topic (2.37.236)? What are the formal requirements for linked verse? How does the author use the writing of it to characterize the members of the poetry club (50.488–95)?

*Purity and Transgression*    In chapter 40, after visiting a number of the young women's rooms, Grannie Liu finds her way to Bao-yu's. What do we learn about gender norms in terms of interior decorating? It is clear that her napping in Bao-yu's room is a violation, perhaps supporting Adamantina's feelings about Grannie Liu's visit. Where are the circles of purity? Do they overlap with the garden's borders? What do you make of this sense of violation? Is it right? artificial?

*Maids*    Do the maids in *Stone* function as foils that complement the more complex and interesting members of the Jia family, or do they have personalities of their own? Do they have the power to influence members of the family? What would be the implications of that power? Do the maids help sustain the status quo of hierarchical human relationships in the Jia household, or do they subvert and threaten it? How eroticized is the place of the maid? What kind of relationships do you see between the masters (or mistresses) and the maids? For example, what is going on between Sunset and Jia Huan (chs. 61–62)? between Golden and Bao-yu? between Nightingale and Dai-yu? between Aroma and Dai-yu? between Patience and Xi-feng? between Patience and Jia Lian? What about the character Crimson? What do you make of her flirtation with Jia Yun (ch. 26)?

*Religion and Cosmology*    How does *Stone* present religion? How are ghosts, demons, sorcery, and the supernatural depicted? Are there differences between the first eighty chapters and the last forty chapters in this regard? What omens and talismans appear in *Stone*? How are they interpreted? What do the discussions of these suggest about how the cosmos is conceived? How do the natural, human, and supernatural interact?

*Xi-feng*    Consider the conversation about Wang Xi-feng (1.6.156–57) and the description of her typical day in chapter 6. What do you think about her acting as go-between in chapter 15? of the way she handled the situation with Bao Er's wife (ch. 44) or the situation with You Er-jie? Consider the business with Zhang Hua, You Er-jie's erstwhile fiancé (3.68.340–42, 349–50, 69.356–59). What is her relationship to Bao-yu? to Jia Lian? to Patience? What about the fact that Xi-feng is only marginally literate? What features of storytelling does she parody?[9] How does she compare with Lao Lai-zi (3.54.29, 31–32)? Is there significance to her miscarriage and illness (3.55.45–46)? How is she vulnerable (64)? Are Xi-feng's and Qin-shi's illnesses similar (72.420, 72.425–26, 72.428)? Xi-feng is visited by Qin-shi in chapters 13 and 101. What transpires at these meetings (1.13.256–57, 5.101.48–49)? What does Xi-feng worry about (51)? What does her fortune suggest (62–63)? Consider her death. She is visited by images of the dead and by a lively Grannie Liu. What arrangements do they make? What are Xi-feng's last words? (5.113.242–50, 114.256). What is her funeral like? Who pays for it (114.256, 259–61)? Is there a moral to her story?

*Finances*    How rich are the Jias, and what is their financial situation really? Consider when money is collected for Xi-feng's birthday party (2.43.345–51), when Li Wan is working on funding for the poetry club (3.45.385–89), when Dai-yu explains her financial status to Bao-chai (2.45.398), or when it is time to collect from the harvest (53.562–65). From whom did Xi-feng learn her management strategies (2.46.407)? There is a clear distinction between private money and public money among the Jias. To what extent are they financially individual and to what extent does the family operate as a collective? What does it mean to have one's own money in this context?

*Dreams*   What is the function of dreams and dream-like spaces in *Stone*? Are dreams a window onto other planes of existence, or are characters merely mistaking dream for reality?

*Decline*   Who is responsible for the moral and financial decline of the Jia household? Consider how authority figures in the Jia family (Grandmother Jia, Jia Zheng, Lady Wang, and Wang Xi-feng) manage the household. What does the miserable turnout at Grandmother Jia's party (3.76.501, 76.507) suggest in general? What do Dai-yu, Xiang-yun, and Adamantina do at the party, and what does it mean (513–25)? What are other signs of decline?

*Status*   A great deal of attention in this novel is directed toward status—or, more precisely, precedence. Who ranks above whom in the complicated social world of the Jia residence? How does Dai-yu regard her own status? How does Bao-chai? Why would their status in the family be different? How about Jia Huan or Tan-chun? How are children of concubines and main wives treated differently (3.55.62)? How does Bao-yu feel about status? What happens to status in the garden (2.49.474)? What happens when the dowager consort dies (ch. 58) and virtually all the members of the older generations leave? How does this change upset other hierarchies? Consider how different hierarchies collide (Tan-chun and her mother, Swallow and her aunt) and how jockeying for status pervades all interactions. Recall the rosters of the important funerals, the attendees at the New Year's celebration, or Grandmother Jia's eightieth birthday (1.13.259). Do we learn anything new about how the family is organized (3.71.395–98, 407)?

*Grannie Liu*   Grannie Liu turns out to be quite an important and complex character. Does she act the clown, or is she instead making clowns of the Jias (2.40.279–81, 286–91, 302; 41.304–09)? Is her relationship with the Jias affectionate, or is there a trace in it of the adversarial? It seems clear that some sort of exchange is taking place between the Jias and Grannie Liu. What is being traded for what? Is Grannie Liu a version of Grandmother Jia? Why is she so important—even necessary? Is there a Marxist message to her story?

*Search of the Garden*   The idea of things leaking out of the garden (money and information) and things leaking into it (pornography and bad behavior) is important (3.77.536–37). The two are connected. Xi-feng tells Bao-yu that a search is taking place because something is missing, but in fact it's because something has appeared (3.74.467). How is the permeability of the garden's borders significant (3.73.443, 73.445, 74.456)? How have they been preserved? Why are they breaking down now?

*Ritual Mourning*   How to deal with the beloved dead through ritual sacrifice is a central motif in *Stone*. Consider Bao-yu's sacrifice for Golden (2.43.355–62),

Dai-yu's comments on how to sacrifice (prompted by watching a scene from *The Wooden Hairpin* [2.44.364]), Bao-yu's discovery of the sacrifice one actress makes for another and his advice about how to sacrifice (3.58.124–26, 58.132–33), and how Dai-yu's comments on Bao-yu's elegy for Skybright turn it into one for her (79.582–83; 4.89.201–03). Bao-yu desires to dream of Dai-yu after her death but cannot. We might view this as an inability to sacrifice for her, to revere the dead. How does he deal with this problem (5.109.172, 109.176–82)? What do we learn about ritual from *Stone*? Do you think the novel as a whole can be spoken of as one sacrificial lament for Dai-yu?

*Twelve Beauties of Jinling*    What are the fates of the twelve beauties of Jinling (the fifteen women Bao-yu reads about in the registers of the ill-fated fair are: Dai-yu, Bao-chai, Yuan-chun, Tan-chun, Shi Xiang-yun, Adamantina, Ying-chun, Xi-chun, Wang Xi-feng, Qiao Jie, Li Wan, and Qin-shi from the first register; Caltrop [Zhen Ying-lian] from the second register; and Skybright and Aroma from the third register)? Do you think that *Stone* really is an account of their lives, as the author claims? A passage that Hawkes puts in the introduction of volume 1 usually opens the Chinese versions (1.20–21). How would this knowledge change your reading?

*Significant Minor Characters*    Some characters, like Grannie Liu, Caltrop, the monk, the Taoist, Jia Yu-cun, and Shi Xiang-yun, serve as a window onto the Jia family. They disappear for long periods, then reappear at significant moments. What kinds of characters are these? Through whose eyes do we see the most? Do they give us some objectivity, or are they just additional unreliable narrators?

*Causality*    To some, it seems obvious that Bao-yu and Bao-chai's marriage is foreordained. Yet the wedding takes place only when a number of plots converge: Xue Pan's trial, the loss of Bao-yu's jade, Dai-yu's illness, Yuan-chun's death, Jia Zheng's rushing away on a new posting. Is there causality between these events and the wedding, or do they all converge in a big rush of misfortune? Whose fault is this tragic wedding?

*Loss of Sympathy*    A number of characters—especially Lady Wang and Grandmother Jia—become noticeably less sympathetic in the second half of the novel. Do they change, or are their preexisting faults somehow magnified? When Dai-yu tells Grandmother Jia, "Your love for me has been in vain!" (4.97.341), what does she mean, and how does Grandmother Jia interpret this comment?

*Bao-yu and Dai-yu*    Bao-yu and Dai-yu seem linked. An example of this linkage is when he refers to her dream of chapter 82 (4.97.344). What is the nature and extent of this connection? How do you interpret their interaction in chapter 96, when Dai-yu hears of the plan to marry Bao-yu to Bao-chai (96.336–39)?

When Bao-yu hears of Dai-yu's death, he collapses and has a dream. What happens in this dream? What does it mean that the man throws a stone at Bao-yu's chest (82.65, 97.344, 98.371–73)? What does it mean when Nightingale reflects, "better by far the destiny of plant or stone, bereft of knowledge and consciousness but blessed at least with purity and peace of mind" (5.113.255)?

*Women's Writing*     What is the status of women's writing in *Stone*? Why does Caltrop wish to learn poetry? What does Dai-yu teach her about it (2.48.450–60)? Compare Caltrop's poems with one another (48.464, 49.467). What is Bao-chai's attitude toward Caltrop and poetry (48.462–64, 49.474)? What do you make of Bao-qin's literary talent? of Adamantina's? of Dai-yu and Bao-chai's? What does it mean that Dai-yu burns the handkerchiefs and the rest of her poems right before she dies? Are we sorry to lose the person or the work (4.97.351–53)? What is the role of female suicide in *Stone*? Is Dai-yu's death suicide?

*Major Events*     In chapters 90 to 100, the primary drama is Bao-yu and Bao-chai's marriage (and Dai-yu's simultaneous death). In chapters 101 to 110, the drama—also one of the climaxes of the novel—is the fall of the Jias. Some readers see the first as the climax of the novel, some readers the second. Do you think the novel is more about the love affair between cousins or more about the fall of the Jias? What do you think the relation is between these two plots?

*The Real Bao-yu*     Is Zhen Bao-yu the real Bao-yu? Is this what Jia Bao-yu should become, or does "real become not-real when the unreal's real" (1.1.55; see 5.115.272–78)? As a result of their encounter, Bao-yu goes into a decline. Why?

*Literature in Literature*     What literature is read in *Stone*? Is there a difference between public reading and private reading? What kind of literature does Tealeaf bring Bao-yu to read and why? Why does Bao-yu read the play *Western Chamber* while Dai-yu buries the flowers? Why does Dai-yu have an outburst when Bao-yu recites two lines from the play (1.23.463–64)? How do Bao-yu and Dai-yu speak to each other through shared literature? What does Bao-chai tell Dai-yu during their sisterly talk, and how does Dai-yu take it (2.40.301, 42.332–34)? What does Grandmother Jia say about boudoirs in romances (40.296)? What does *Stone* (or the Stone) say about literature in chapter 1? Who wins the argument over Bao-qin's reference to the *Western Chamber* and *The Return of the Soul* (2.51.513–15)? How do Bao-chai's and Bao-qin's ideas on romantic literature and poetry compare (2.51.513–15, 52.539)? What prompts Bao-yu's sudden appreciation of the *Zhuangzi* (1.22.439)? Is he a good reader? In chapter 113, he returns to the *Zhuangzi*. Why? Has his reading changed? What does it mean that Bao-yu puts away the *Zhuangzi* in chapter 118?

*Hearing and Overhearing*    What sorts of things are overheard in *Stone* and by whom (1.17.348, 22.437, 22.439, 23.465, 26.516, 2.27.27, 28.41, 44.369, 3.66.304, 79.582, 4.89.205, 89.207, 90.215)? Why do Bao-yu and Dai-yu have a conversation about music (4.86.151–55)? What does Adamantina have to say about how to play the *qin*, and how does it compare with what Dai-yu has said (87.171–73)? Why does Bao-yu advise Dai-yu not to play the *qin* so much (89.204)? To what does "knowing the sound" refer (86.153, 93.266, 3.391)? What are its implications for *Stone*?

*Aroma*    In chapters 34 and 36 (2.34.165, 36.199, 36.204), it becomes clear that Aroma's status has changed. What is she now? Do you think Aroma still belongs in the conversation about the relation between maids and mistresses (39.260–61)? How is her return home (51.515–19) comparable to Yuan-chun's visitation in chapter 18? What is going on with Aroma in chapter 82? We get inside her head for one of the first times in the novel. Why does she go to talk with Dai-yu, and what is the outcome of that conversation (4.82.58–61)?

*Golden*    What happened to Golden? We hear competing versions—from Lady Wang (2.32.138) and Jia Huan (33.146)—and of course we witness her death. Do we get a definitive sense of why she killed herself? Why is Bao-yu's sacrifice to Golden treated so mysteriously (43.355–362)? What does Dai-yu say about Bao-yu's making sacrifice to Golden (43.364)? How does this sacrifice remind us of Bao-yu's fascination with Grannie Liu's story of the statue (39.270–74)?

*Echoes and Shadows*    Throughout this enormous novel are echoes of the relationship between Bao-yu and Dai-yu. For example, in chapter 34, Bao-yu sends Dai-yu two old handkerchiefs, and she earlier gave him one of hers. Why is there another handkerchief exchange (between Jia Yun and Crimson) in chapters 24 and 26? Consider Dai-yu's musings on such romantic love tokens after she hears that Bao-yu and Xiang-yun both have gold kylins. In chapter 36, we see the little actress Charmante, who bears a striking resemblance to Dai-yu, fight with Jia Qiang. What influence do these double or shadow relationships have on our interpretation of the relationship between Bao-yu and Dai-yu?

*Caltrop*    What role does Caltrop—formerly Zhen Ying-lian, finally Lily—play in *Stone*?

*Skybright*    How does Skybright get sick, and what are the consequences of her illness (2.51.520–24)? What aggravates it (51.525, 52.534–36, 52.547–56)? Note the association with crab flowers (51.529), being left alone on one's sickbed (52.533), and the performance of "The Meeting in the Sickroom" (53.581–82). What is Skybright's connection to the crab flower (3.77.540–41)? Is Aroma jealous of Skybright (77.538–41, 548–49)? Why does the author insert the incident with Skybright's cousin's wife forcing herself on Bao-yu right after the scene in which he and Skybright exchange tokens (77.544–48)? The idea of borders and permeability is at play in the death (betrayal?) of Skybright. How does information leak out of the House of Green Delights? Bao-yu and Skybright's last conversation is marked by another exchange, this time of undershirts (77.545). What do you make of that, especially in contrast with Bao-yu's exchanges with others? Do his efforts to commemorate her as a person do justice to her (78.570–85)? Are Grandmother Jia and Lady Wang agreed about Skybright (554–56)? What does the maid tell Bao-yu about Skybright's death (78.561–63)? How does his "Ballad of the Winsome Colonel" (567, 570–74) compare with the elegy for the hibiscus spirit (575–81)? How do Dai-yu's revisions affect the elegy (582–84)?

*Dai-yu*   Consider Dai-yu's susceptibility to illness (2.51.531), the smell of medicine (51.529–30, 52.533, 52.538–39), and the statement "the sharp-witted don't live long" (532–33). In chapter 82, Dai-yu seems to have a change of heart and advises Bao-yu to study hard for an official career. How can we explain this change (4.82.52)? Dai-yu has a dream in chapter 82—what is it about, and what does it mean (62–69)? What does the physician say about her illness (83.77–80)? How is her dream like or unlike other dreams in this novel? What is the relation between the dream and her physical symptoms (82.66–67)? Does one cause the other? Is Dai-yu's personality and fate her fault? What do you make of the physician's report? Is it an explanation that accounts for everything? What does Dai-yu's recovery in chapter 90 say about the nature of her illness, about karma? What does it mean to be lovesick (90.216–17)?

*Foreign Objects*   How do the characters in *Stone* talk about foreign locations, objects, and people (2.51.512–13, 52.536, 52.540, 52.544)? Consider examples of the exotic, such as snuff and medicine (536–37) and the Western girl (539–34). What do they tell us?

*Marriage*   What are Bao-yu's feelings on marriage (3.59.138–39)? What is the problem with Ying-chun's marrying Sun Shao-zu (72.421, 72.432, 77.52, 79.584–86, 80.606, 80.611–13)? What is Bao-yu's reaction (79.586)? What is the cumulative effect on him of the betrothals and removal of girls from the garden (589–91)? Why is Bao-yu upset about Ying-chun? What solution does he offer, and what does it tell us about him (4.81.32)?

*Government*   In chapter 78, Jia Zheng makes references to the government (3.78.567). Comments on this topic are rare in *Stone*. Some scholars believe that there are anti–Qing dynasty sentiments in *Stone*. Do you agree? Is it strange that the narrative turns at perhaps the most dramatic moment (Dai-yu's death and Bao-yu's marriage) to Jia Zheng's new government position? Why might this be? Why is Jia Zheng impeached? What are the official reasons, and what are the real reasons (5.102.76–78)? What does the emperor ask him (104.103–04)?

*Xia Jin-gui*    What type of person is Xia Jin-gui (3.79.588, 79.591–92)? How does her marriage to Xue Pan affect Caltrop and Bao-yu (589)? Is Jin-gui a foil for another character? What does she say about the Jia family (4.83.91–92)? What is the purpose and significance of the Jin-gui episode in which Moonbeam and she try to seduce Xue Ke (91.228–35)? Is Jin-gui meant to be purely comical (ch. 103)? Does the subplot bear any relation to the larger story?

*Authorship*    We can reliably attribute the first eighty chapters to Cao Xueqin. The next forty chapters are at best stitched together out of his detailed drafts, at worst written entirely by another person (or people). Consider why what we have by him ends at chapter 80. Are there significant differences between the first eighty chapters and the last forty?

*The Raid*    What does the search of the Jia mansions reveal (5.105.113–17)? What are the repercussions of the search? Who is at fault, and who is punished? Are the imperial search and confiscation justified? How does the search of the garden parallel this raid? Jia Zheng and Grandmother Jia finally discover the financial facts of the Jia family in chapter 107. What does this discovery tell us about the Jias and perhaps about large, official families in general? How do Jia Zheng and Grandmother Jia deal with the news about the Jia finances? How do the stewards and servants respond (144–49)? We know that the imperial search has been a long time in coming, but still there are specific causes. Is there—as in Dai-yu's death—one person most at fault? Who do you think that person is (104.104, 106.128–33, 106.137–38, 107.140–41, 107.152–55)? Just as the imperial search, the robbery of Grandmother Jia's apartments is a sign of internal corruption. Who planned the robbery and why (think back to ch. 89)? What does it mean that the Zhen family is restored to power? Some feel that the search and confiscation do not seem as traumatic as they ought to. What do you think? Is the family's ultimate restoration of good fortune real, or will they just slide again in "chapter 121"?

*Lists*    What function do lists of physical attributes, food, medicine, clothing, and other objects have in *Stone* (1.3.91, 7.168–69, 10.227–28, 13.270, 18.372–73, 23.460, 2.28.46, 42.340–41, 53.561–62; 3.56.79, 71.395–96, 5.105.119–121)?

*Cao Xueqin*    Why did the author, Cao Xueqin, introduce himself in the first chapter of the novel (1.51)? What is his role in the final chapter (120.375)? What do you make of the author's portrayal of his role (or Gao E's portrayal of Cao's role)?

*Endings*    Are you satisfied with the ending of *Stone*? Is it convincing that Bao-yu can be such a good Confucian while also going off with the monk and Taoist? What does his disappearance say about (Confucian) obligation and ritual versus (Buddhist-Taoist) enlightenment? Are they mutually exclusive or complementary? What do you think about the marriages of Qiao-jie to Ban-er and Aroma to Jiang Yu-han? What do you think about the reappearance of Jia Yu-cun and Zhen Shi-yin and their discussion? What do you think about the story of how this novel came to be published? Where is the ending inadequate (there are some obvious points of inconsistency, for example)? Can you think of a more fitting ending? Now that you have read to the end, what do you think this novel was about? Is it really a story of Buddhist enlightenment? A Confucian morality tale? A story about a family? About a romance? None of the above? Which of the titles from chapter 1 is the best at encapsulating the novel?

# The Instructor's and Students' Library

This volume is the first to attempt a comprehensive introduction to major issues when teaching or studying *Stone* in English. For those who seek to move beyond these introductory essays, we provide a selection of articles and books for further reading, with suggestions for useful groupings.

## *Entries in Reference Works*

Because *The Story of the Stone* is unique in the history of Chinese literature, not just as a crowning achievement in long narrative fiction but also in its synthesis of other genres, teachers and students may be interested in entries in important reference works, both because such entries are generally short and because they are situated among summaries of other works and genres that *Stone* references, quotes, appropriates, or influences. The most venerable of these references is the two-volume *Indiana Companion to Traditional Chinese Literature*, edited by William Nienhauser. For it, top scholars wrote essays explaining genres and eras as well as many short entries on individual authors or anonymous works. The entry on *Stone* has long been used as an introduction to the work (Minford and Hegel). Wilt Idema and Lloyd Haft's *Guide to Chinese Literature* gives brief entries about major works and genres. Because it is organized chronologically and by genre, teachers may find it useful in locating *Stone* in the Chinese literary tradition. The hardcover edition's extensive bibliography is much shorter in the paperback edition. The Columbia Project on Asia in the Core Curriculum has published three good books, one of which, *Masterworks of Asian Literature in Comparative Perspective: A Guide for Teaching* (B. Miller), is particularly worthwhile for teaching *Stone* in the context of world or Asian literature. It features essays by top scholars on Chinese, Japanese, and Indian literature, from classical to modern times, and contains essays on *Stone*, *The Journey to the West*, *The Travels of Lao Can*, *The Stories of Lu Xun*, *Camel Xiangzi (Rickshaw)*, *Classical Poetry*, *Records of the Grand Historian* and *Zhuangzi (Chuang Tzu)*. All its essays feature topics for discussion and guides for further reading. The other two books by the Columbia Project are *Asia: Case Studies for the Social Sciences: A Guide for Teaching* (Cohen) and *Asia in Western and World History: A Guide for Teaching* (Embree and Gluck).

   *The Columbia History of Chinese Literature*, edited by Victor Mair, is a volume of forty essays arranged by genre and topic. Critics may complain that the essays do not tie together well and that as a history, read from beginning to end, the volume is disjointed, but each essay is accessible and the right length for, say, an undergraduate survey course. The discussion of *Stone* by Wai-yee Li is authoritative and interesting, putting *Stone* in the context of other Chinese novels (*xiaoshuo* 小說) ("Full-Length Vernacular Fiction"). *The Cambridge History of Chinese Literature*, edited by Stephen Owen and Kang-i Sun Chang, will likely become a valuable reference work, as the *Cambridge History of China* is the standard reference in English for that topic (see Peterson). Shang Wei's "The Literati Era and Its Demise, 1723–1840" in *The Cambridge History* covers *Stone* in depth as well as the literary milieu informing and informed by it. Both these volumes feature entries on topics and periods that situate *Stone* in a long and complex literary tradition.

## Introductions in Anthologies

A few anthologies have been including scholarly translations of Chinese literature and introducing them at the highest levels. For a discussion of those that select portions of *Stone*, see the "Editions and Translations" section of part 1. Many anthologies also have introductions to *Stone*—particularly the world literature anthologies from Norton and Longman with introductions by Stephen Owen and Pauline Yu, respectively. The Norton, Bedford, and Longman anthologies of world literature also suggest texts with which *Stone* might be paired in the classroom. They also have instructor resources, providing additional introductory information as well as online materials that illustrate important points for students and offer study questions, quizzes, and so forth.

## Biographical Resources

Little is known about Cao Xueqin, and answers to the enduring question of how much of *Stone* is autobiographical are probably too complex and inconclusive to attempt in the classroom. That said, Jonathan Spence's *Ts'ao Yin and the K'ang-hsi Emperor, Bondservant and Master*, about Cao's grandfather Cao Yin, is a wonderful book to read alongside *Stone*. Cao Yin formed the center of an illustrious family's rise and fall over five generations. The book is essentially an institutional history of the Kangxi reign (1661–1722), a fascinating period in China's dynastic history, and especially of the Qing dynasty. More than that, *Ts'ao Yin* is about what it meant to be a textile commissioner and salt censor; to host the emperor in your home; to be a member of the upper class, along with the industrial, financial, administrative, and cultural ramifications of that membership. Spence's book illuminates much about the historical context that produced *Stone*. His discussion of the status of bond servants is of particular importance. Some say what eunuchs had been for the Ming (or against the Ming, eventually), bannermen were for the Qing. Spence treats Cao Yin's role in the compilation and printing of the *Complete Tang Poems*, the purchase of copper, and the distribution of rice. He discusses *Stone* explicitly with regard to the emperor's (Yuan-chun's) visits in the sections "Ts'ao [Cao] Yin and the Southern Tours" (138–51) and "Southern Tours in the *Dream of the Red Chamber*" (151–57).

A book that teachers might use to spark conversation is *Between Noble and Humble: Cao Xueqin and the* Dream of the Red Chamber, a translation of the venerable Redology scholar Zhou Ruchang's 1992 *Cao Xueqin xin zhuan* 曹雪芹新傳 ("A New Biography of Cao Xueqin"). While Zhou's early work is famous as foundational research on *Stone*, this book makes controversial claims. He is known to be hostile to Gao E, the editor or author of the last forty chapters of *Stone*. Zhou claims that Gao was a palace scholar embroiled in a literary conspiracy and believes that Heshen, the evil favorite minister of the Qianlong emperor, masterminded a scheme to have Gao compose an uplifting ending for the novel. In the process, Gao destroyed the first eighty chapters of Cao's masterpiece by turning it into a harmless love story. Zhou recently published a new critical edition of the first eighty chapters that purports to excise all Gao's contributions and restore Cao Xueqin's original narrative. In *Between Noble and Humble*, Zhou makes or restates other claims that have been widely challenged. He claims, for instance, that Red Inkstone was a female relative of Cao. Some scholars feel that Zhou adds to what is known about Cao and *Stone* things that are improbable and based on scant evidence. The book has no citations or bibliography but is fascinating, both because it features thoughtful conjectures about Cao Xueqin and his world by an eminent *Stone* scholar and because it models the persistent obsession of so many with the author and provenance of *Stone*.

## Critical Studies: Articles and Book Chapters

Academic articles on *Stone* and its contexts are given here in two groupings.

### Gender, Sexuality, and Desire: One Course on *Stone*

One approach that we have found valuable in semester courses on *Stone* is to follow the theme of sex, sexuality, and gender. Along with readings from *Stone*, teachers could assign an article or two for each class meeting. One might rely largely on a single companion volume, Ellen Widmer and Kang-i Sun Chang's *Writing Women in Late Imperial China*. In the first weeks of class, readings might focus on women's lives in the seventeenth and eighteenth centuries: Dorothy Ko's "The Written Word and the Bound Foot," Martin Huang's "The Self Displaced: Women and Growing Up in *The Dream of the Red Chamber*" (*Literati* 75–108), and Janet Theiss's "Managing Martyrdom: Female Suicide and Statecraft in Mid-Qing China." What is commonly referred to as the cult of *qing*, a literati obsession with love, desire, and passion, could be the thematic grouping of secondary texts for the next few weeks. Students have responded well to chapters 3 ("Beginnings: Enchantment and Irony in *Hung-lou meng*"), 5 ("Self-Reflexivity and the Lyrical Ideal in *Hung-lou meng*"), and 6 ("Disenchantment and Order in *Hung-lou meng*") in Wai-yee Li's *Enchantment and Disenchantment*. Maram Epstein's *Competing Discourses* has a useful chapter on desire (ch. 4, "Reflections of Desire in *Honglou meng*"). This theme may also be paired with stories of women reading, and often dying from reading, romantic literature. See Widmer's "Xiaoqing's Literary Legacy and the Place of the Woman Writer in Late Imperial China" and Judith Zeitlin's "Shared Dreams: The Story of the Three Wives' Commentary on *The Peony Pavilion*."

Teachers could ask students to consider the relation of gender to connoisseurship, with reference to the first few chapters of Zuyan Zhou's *Androgyny in Late Ming and Early Qing Literature*, which discuss androgyny as an aesthetic ideal in Chinese philosophy and culture in the period leading up to the writing of *Stone* (Zhou also has a chapter treating this topic with regard to *Stone* [155–98]). Literature about and guides to appreciating women's beauty and virtue are also pertinent to *Stone*. Katherine Carlitz's "Desire, Danger, and the Body: Stories of Women's Virtue in Late Ming China" pairs well with chapter 3 ("Obsession") in Zeitlin's *Historian of the Strange: Pu Songling and the Chinese Classical Tale*, because some see the late Ming dynasty (16th–17th cents.) obsession with obsession as a precursor to the early Qing dynasty (17th–18th cents.) obsession with desire. In late imperial China, connoisseurship was related to courtesan culture. Three historical articles discuss this particular kind of appreciative discourse; they clearly inform and reflect *Stone*'s descriptions of the girls in the garden: W. Li, "The Late Ming Courtesan: Invention of a Cultural Ideal"; Ko, "The Written Word and the Bound Foot"; and Catherine Vance Yeh, "Reinventing Ritual: Late Qing Handbooks for Proper Customer Behavior in Shanghai Courtesan Houses."

Teachers could move on to talk about same-sex encounters in *Stone*, their precedents, and the implications of homosexual desire in Chinese society. Giovanni Vitiello's "Exemplary Sodomites: Chivalry and Love in late Ming Culture," Sophie Volpp's "The Literary Circulation of Actors in Seventeenth-Century China," and Matthew Sommer's "The Penetrated Male in Late Imperial China: Judicial Constructions and Social Stigma" are all important essays in the field and often paradigm-challenging for students. Teachers might also consider the represented body, by selecting one of Charlotte Furth's many important essays on medicine, perhaps "Blood, Body, and Gender: Medical Images of the Female Condition in China, 1600–1850." The way *Stone* influenced painting and how painting is a way of reading are discussed in Wu Hung's "Beyond Stereotypes: The Twelve Beauties in Qing Court Art and the *Dream of the Red Chamber*." How women wrote and read poetry and fiction and how that mode of representation is represented are examined by Angelina Yee ("Self"), Haun Saussy, and in Widmer (*Beauty*).

## *Stone* in a Variety of Historical and Cultural Contexts

A course that seeks to place *Stone* in its historical and cultural contexts might assign Craig Clunas, *Superfluous Things* (esp. ch. 6, "Anxieties about Things: Consumption and Class in Ming China") as a way of discussing the many lists of things in *Stone*. Susan Naquin's *Peking: Temples and City Life* (esp. ch. 1, "Introducing Peking," gives students some geographic orientation as well as ideas of the issues in city life in eighteenth-century China. Evelyn Rawski's *The Last Emperors* discusses imperial consorts (like *Stone*'s Jia Yuan-chun) and bond servants (131–34, 166–81). Spence gives an important account of the Manchu institution of bond servants (*Ts'ao Yin* 1–41). To provide literary contexts, teachers might assign Colin Mackerras, "The Drama of the Qing Dynasty"; Plaks, "The Chinese Literary Garden" in *Archetype and Allegory* (146–77); or Zeitlin's entry on *xiaoshuo* in Franco Moretti's edited volume *The Novel*.

Women's education and writing as modes of agency and also as objects of connoisseurship are discussed by Susan Mann in "Learned Women in the Eighteenth Century" and "Writing" in *Precious Records* (76–120). For situating the many women in *Stone* in or against standard practice, William Rowe's "Women and the Family" goes well with Tina Lu's chapter "*Hongloumeng* and the Borders of Family" in *Accidental Incest* (201–38). Spence's "Ch'ing," on food, gives students perspective on *Stone*'s representation of elite culture. Furth's "Concepts of Pregnancy, Childbirth, and Infancy in Ch'ing Dynasty China" shows students that the Jias subscribed to many common, even folk, notions about the body. Finally, teachers may want to broach the subject of authorship, authority, and intent or the use of fiction to write history, in the discussion of *Stone*'s textual history. Hawkes's introduction to volume 1 of *Stone* may leave much to be desired but does present most of the textual issues in a way that students can understand (15–46). Students could discuss the translated prefaces in the appendix to volume 4 of *Stone*. The wonderful example of traditional Chinese criticism and the authoritative, descriptive bibliography of *Stone* texts (for advanced undergraduates or graduate students) are in David Rolston's *How to Read the Chinese Novel* (196–243, 456–84).

## Historical and Cultural Contexts: Books

A book by two of our contributors, Susan Naquin and Evelyn Rawski, entitled *Chinese Society in the Eighteenth Century*, has made for good classroom material. The first half of it goes particularly well with *Stone* in a course that seeks to include an examination of daily, if elite, life during the height of one of China's great dynasties.

There are two collections of essays that the reader might make use of as a supplement to this one. The first is Paul Ropp's *Heritage of China*, which presents authoritative essays on early civilization in China; the evolution of the government system; the Confucian tradition; Buddhist and Taoist traditions; science and medicine; women, marriage, and the family; Chinese economic history; Chinese art, poetry, and fiction. Some of these essays, like David Keightley's article on what made China Chinese and Albert Feuerwerker's on one thousand years of economic history in comparative perspective, are audacious in their scope but thought-provoking.

Corinne Dale did a service to the field of Chinese literature when she collected eleven essays on different genres and themes in Chinese literary history: *Chinese Aesthetics and Literature*. Some of these essays (Owen, "Omen"; W. Tu [in Dale, 27–40]) have a great deal of overlap with essays in *Heritage of China*, and the Ropp essay ("Distinctive Art") is reprinted from it, but this book also makes a good supplementary text, although for a course that focuses on *Stone* more as literature than as literary product of its time.

For those teaching a course on Chinese philosophy or looking at *Stone* vis-à-vis religion, politics, and philosophy, the standard anthology has been William Theodore de Bary et al.'s *Sources of Chinese Tradition*, which presents selections (in translation) in two large volumes of the major primary texts of the last 2,500 years. The *Hawai'i Reader in Traditional Chinese Culture* presents many of the same texts (usually in different translation) but defines civilization more broadly, with a wider variety of texts and images but less depth on philosophical issues (Mair et al.).

Teachers who (rightly) want to emphasize the poetry in *Stone* may consider using as a supplement James Liu's *Art of Chinese Poetry*, a classic introduction to Chinese poetry. Liu's little book (164 pp.) has been hailed for its concision and elegance. Part 1, in which Liu discusses the Chinese language, particularly with reference to poetry, is of great use to teachers who would like to disabuse students that reading Chinese is akin to watching images flash by one's eyes (as many American modernists thought). Part 2 is a succinct account of four attitudes that have determined the understanding and evaluation of poetry in China. Part 3 strives for a synthesis of these attitudes, presenting what are essentially Liu's opinions. Scholarly reviewers, including David Hawkes and James Hightower, consider this a valuable book. Much is left out, and there are trifling arguments to be made (Hawkes finds it strange that Liu claims that Chinese poets were never drunk but rather "rapt with wine" [673]), but teachers will find this a text that sparks lively discussion about how poetry works in culture and in *Stone*.

Liu also has published a volume entitled *Chinese Theories of Literature*. The criticisms of this book are that the six categories into which he divides the thousands of years of discourse on the topic of literature in China are artificial, that each category is not treated equally, and that there are omissions, oversimplifications, and only passing reference to important subjects. That said, this introduction to the topic is intelligent and sophisticated. Interested readers should move to Owen's *Readings in Chinese Literary Thought*, but at 674 pages, it might be a bit much for a supplementary text to *Stone*.

## Critical Studies on Stone: Books

Single-volume studies of *Stone* in English naturally are filled with detail that readers new to *Stone* may find overwhelming. But *Stone* was the work of a lifetime, and exploring its problems and complexities is also the work of a lifetime for many. Teachers will find some chapters of these books useful in the class-room and may want to pursue them for more advanced study.

Anthony Yu's *Rereading the Stone: Desire and the Making of Fiction in* Dream of the Red Chamber is organized around two broad issues: the claim of fictionality and the narrative of desire. This book is widely regarded as one of the best on *Stone* in recent decades written in any language. It is both historical and comparative. The first chapter discusses earlier approaches to *Stone* and argues against the common reading of it as an historical document. Yu claims that the primary merit of *Stone* is its insistence that it is a work of fiction (3–52). In chapter 2, Yu discusses desire and presents a genealogy of the concept *qing* 情 ("emotions," "passion," "love") that ranges through thousands of years of history and philosophy and culminates in *Stone*, the primary subject and message of which is *qing* (53–109). These first two chapters provide broad historical, theoretical, and comparative context for later specific interpretations of *Stone*. In chapter 3, Yu addresses what he sees as *Stone*'s central paradox, that the illusion of life can be grasped only through the illusion of art (110–71). Chapter 4 discusses the ability of poetry, drama, and fiction to awaken passion in their readers and drive them to self-dramatize, like Bao-yu and Dai-yu (172–218). Chapter 5 analyzes Lin Dai-yu as a tragic heroine who is both the victim and agent of her misfortune (219–55). Many will find Yu's work challenging, but it is valuable to scholars with an interest in comparative perspective.

Perhaps more appropriate for readers new to *Stone* is Dore Levy's *Ideal and Actual in* The Story of the Stone. Little of the Western-language scholarship deals directly and with such erudition with many of the questions that Hawkes and Minford's first-time English readers are likely to have. Levy provides a brief and accessible overview of recent scholarship on *Stone* but also puts their work to good use in her own sensitive and well-articulated readings. Her chapter headings address important issues: "Ideal and Actual, Real and Not-Real," "Family Togetherness: Patterns of Authority and the Subversion of Family Structure," "Pre-existing Conditions: Retributory Illness and the Limits of Medicine," "A World Apart: Poetry and Society in the Garden of Total Vision," "Poetry and Epiphany: The Chiming of the Void." Some take issue with some claims — for example, that Bao-yu's eccentricities can be explained as symptoms of attention deficit disorder — but such differences of opinion might spur classroom debate.

Plaks's *Archetype and Allegory in* The Dream of the Red Chamber is probably the best-known book-length work devoted to *Stone*. The first three chapters — "Archetype and Mythology in Chinese Literature," "The Marriage of Nu-kua and Fu-hsi," and "Complementary Bipolarity and Multiple Periodicity" — set up a discussion about archetypes in chapter 4, "The Archetypal Structure of *Dream of the Red Chamber*," from which students might benefit. Similarly, chapters 6, "Western Allegorical Gardens," and 7, "The Chinese Literary Garden," set up the discussion of *Stone*'s allegorical stories and spaces in chapter 8, "A Garden of Total Vision: The Allegory of the Ta-kuan Yüan," with wide-ranging comparisons between Western and Chinese aesthetic and literary traditions. Some teachers employ just chapters 4 and 8 in the undergraduate classroom because the others are so complex. Perhaps most important in Plaks's book is the treatment of the intricate structure of *Stone*. His concepts of complementary bipolarity and multiple periodicity have been discussed by other scholars as fundamental structuring units of *Stone* and other Chinese fiction. In the classroom, *Archetype and Allegory* might be paired with a review of it by C. T. Hsia. Hsia accuses Plaks of focusing exclusively on *Stone*'s structure and narrative logic, aspects that are particularly Chinese, rather than on the more universal, human aspects of the novel. If yin and yang are fundamental principles that constantly change into each other, "why take joy or sorrow seriously if one follows the other as surely as night follows day?" (192). Jing Wang also has a sustained critique of Plaks's book in her article "The Poetics of Chinese Narrative." Students in our classes have benefited from the heated discussions generated by the desire to understand differences, to overemphasize them, or to neglect them for the universal.

Although Widmer's *The Beauty and the Book: Women and Fiction in Nineteenth-Century China* is less a critical reading of *Stone* than a history of its influence on women readers, it may be beneficial in the classroom. It explores the social and literary events leading up to the publication of the first female-authored Chinese novel, in 1877, *Honglou meng ying* 紅樓夢影 ("In the Shadow of *Dream of the Red Chamber*") (Gu Taiqing). Widmer's book will help teachers interested in either women's writing or the rise of the novel. While academics trained in European literature are not surprised by the connection between women and the novel, the situation in China was different. Widmer explores that difference throughout her book but with particular reference to *Stone* in her introduction and chapters 5, 6, and 7. Chapter 7, "*Honglou meng* Sequels and their Female Readers," may be paired with Feng-ying Ming's article on science fiction sequels to *Stone* and, in this volume, Keith McMahon's essay to discuss the desire to write sequels and fan fiction as a way of reading (or misreading) a beloved work. Widmer's "Afterword: Women and 'The Rise of the Novel' in China" will be of interest to teachers or scholars of the novel genre in world history.

Louise Edwards's *Men and Women in Qing China: Gender in* The Red Chamber Dream largely applies Western feminist theory to the study of *Stone*. Edwards surveys mainland Chinese criticism of *Stone*, from the novel's first publication in 1791–92 until 1949 (the founding of the People's Republic of China). Teachers may also want to employ the last chapter of this book at this point, "*Hongxue* after 1949 and Gender Equality," which reviews mainland criticism since 1979. It seeks to rescue *Stone* from the ideological criticism of Mao and his followers but makes little attempt to understand the dynamics of gender and power in Chinese society, which might prompt classroom debate about *Stone* criticism on the mainland and some discussion of trends in scholarship. Edwards argues that Bao-yu suffers from the typical male dilemma, for which symbolic castration, retreat or monkhood, is the typical solution (33–49). She acknowledges that Cao subverts dominant paradigms about sexual ideologies, but she challenges the often made claim that *Stone* is a feminist novel (50–67). She expands on the theme of women corrupted by power. The characters Xi-feng and Bao-yu indicate to her that the negative attitude in the Qing dynasty toward transgressing gender boundaries was more severe for women than for men. Edwards makes the point that women warriors in a poem by Bao-yu, but mostly in another novel, *Flowers in the Mirror* 鏡花緣, function to uphold the sexual ideology of patriarchy (87–112). Chapters 7 and 8 might pair well in the classroom—"Jia Family Women: Unrestrained 'Indulgent Mothers'" and "Men of the Jia Clan: Responsible or Degenerate"—since Edwards argues that *Stone's* depictions of the positions of men and women are equally insightful.

Xiao Chi's *The Chinese Garden as Lyric Enclave: A Generic Study of* The Story of the Stone will appeal more to advanced students of Chinese literature. This book concerns itself with lyricism in a variety of novelistic genres. The introduction puts *Stone* in its immediate contexts, along the lines of the Stone's own conversation with Vanitas on pages 48–51 of the novel. Xiao synthesizes a great deal of Chinese and Western scholarship on *Stone* while setting up an examination of the novel as the apogee of lyricism at just the moment when lyricism in novels was beginning to wane and causing authors anxiety about its future. He then considers the garden as the location for beauties and beautiful women as a representation of idle aesthetes and makes the interesting claim of a conceptual third world (based on Yu Ying-shih's famous conception of the two worlds) of *Stone* (135–48). He shows the indebtedness of *Stone* to late Ming dynasty texts such as Li Suiqiu's manual on how to appreciate feminine charms in garden settings, *Hua di shiyi* 花底拾遺 ("Picking Up the Petals Left Behind by the Flowers"). Locating *Stone* in textual traditions in this way, Xiao shows how Bao-yu follows the rules of these prescriptive texts, at least regarding the girls in the garden. The strengths and weaknesses of Xiao's close readings are tied to the influence of traditional commentary. For example, his list of "ugly events" is meant to match the nineteenth-century critic Yao Xie's list of elegant occasions (191–246). But his assumption that the Red Inkstone commentary is absolutely authoritative limits the scope of his criticism.

Liu Zaifu, a prolific writer, scholar, and critic, published *Reflections on* Dream of the Red Chamber, which was translated into English in 2008. Liu consciously avoids scholarly approaches to *Stone* in this work and even remarks, "The more than two hundred random thoughts collected in this book are no more than 'sudden realizations' I jotted down as I read the novel. They are by no means 'serious scholarship'" (xvi). For this reason, teachers might find in this book some entrées into *Stone* that provoke discussion in the classroom or reading group. There is much in *Reflections* to recommend it—the many paragraph-length thoughts on *Stone* and Chinese culture by a Chinese scholar and seasoned reader of *Stone* are most helpful. Longer meditations on specific topics relate to the spiritual value or Zen logic of *Stone*. Liu's consideration of Wang Guowei's essay (discussed by Wang Xiaojue in this volume) might be of interest to advanced students. Liu's book makes connections to many works of world literature and also to other works in the Chinese tradition. The clarity of its prose is further enhanced by the translator (Shu Yunzhong), who benevolently follows Hawkes and Minford's names for characters (e.g., translating "Qingwen" as "Skybright").

## Selected Web Sites

There are not many Web sites in English devoted to the serious study of *Stone*, although sites that contain reliable information related to its teaching are too numerous to discuss here. Two other translations of *Stone* are available on-line: by B. S. Bonsall (http://lib.hku.hk/bonsall/hongloumeng/index1.html) and H. Bencraft Joly (www.gutenberg.org/etext/9603). A good survey of editions of *Stone*, by David Steelman (http://etext.virginia.edu/chinese/HLM/hlmitre2.htm) contrasts a bit with Rolston in *How to Read the Chinese Novel*. Example courses on or related to *Stone* are available at the Columbia University Expanding East Asian Studies site: www.exeas.org. A plot synopsis by Michael McKenny is available online (http://alsandor.net/solarguard/china/hong/index.html). It is recommended for teachers but not for students. Speaking generally, avoid the CliffsNotes that pertain to *Dream of the Red Chamber*. Written by a Chinese mainland scholar in the 1980s, it is littered with ideological (Marxist) readings about feudalism and exploiting the peasants, and so on. It is not based on the Hawkes-Minford translation (names appear differently), and what is subtle or complex in the novel is lost in oversimplification. Many of the most useful sites are in Chinese or Japanese. The site 紅楼夢年表 *Honglou meng nianbiao* ("A *Stone* Chronology"; http://pingshan.parfait.ne.jp/honglou/nenpyo.html) presents a detailed description of the ages of Bao-yu, Dai-yu, and Bao-chai throughout the novel. *A Dream of Red Mansions: Anasoft A and Anasoft B* (www.speedy7.com/cn/stguru/english/redmansions.htm) makes available plain-text versions of early Chinese editions of *Stone*.

## Film and Television Resources

The following films and television versions of *Stone*, with English subtitles, are currently available: *Dream of the Red Chamber* 紅樓夢 (1944), directed by Bu Wancang; *The Dream of the Red Chamber* 紅 樓夢 (1962), directed by Yuan Qiufeng (a musical); *The Dream of the Red Chamber* 金玉良緣紅樓夢 (1977), directed by Li Hanxiang (a musical); *Dreams of the Red Mansion* 紅樓夢 (1987), directed by Wang Fulin (36 episodes). For more on these resources, see Ling Hon Lam's and Xueping Zhong's contributions to this volume.

NOTES

1 For a detailed description of commentary editions of *Stone*, see Rolston, *How to Read* 456–84. On the commentary about the novel, see Martin Huang's essay in this volume.

2 The Yangs base their translation on two manuscript editions (the first eighty chapters are based on the Youzheng large-type edition with a preface by Qi Liaosheng; the last forty are based on the revised second Cheng version), but they amend and supplement it with selections from other editions, perhaps unavoidably but also unmistakably creating a new version of *Stone*, as Hawkes and Minford do.

3 For more examples, see the index of names below for the pen names that commentators on *Stone* chose for themselves.

4 Being married or unmarried does not seem to be the dividing line, since Brightie is married and fairly senior but still referred to by his personal name (surely given by his employers for its auspicious ring) both in the original and in the translation by Hawkes.

5 Cao Xueqin and the commentators see phonetic puns in places where standard users of Mandarin might not. For them *qin* rhymes with *qing*, and *ping* rhymes (or is close enough for the purposes of the pun) with *pian*.

6 This section is indebted to H. Chang 383–403.

7 See Confucius, *Analects* 6.21: "The wise find pleasure in water; the virtuous find pleasure in hills."

8 For two examples of such time charting, see Plaks, *Archetype* 242–44. Imprecision with regard to time and other contradictions in the last forty chapters of *Stone* are evidence to some, like Hawkes, that those chapters are the result of work done by Gao E as a conscientious editor of disparate and fragmentary texts rather than his creation out of whole cloth. Had Gao E created out of whole cloth, there would be few or no contradictions, loose ends, and mistakes.

9 Contemporary readers will associate the title *Feng qiu huang* 鳳求凰 ("The Phoenix Seeks a Mate") with the story of Sima Xiangru 司馬相如 and Zhuo Wenjun 卓文君, which takes place in the second century BCE, rather than with the one in *Stone*, which takes place in the Five Dynasties period (907–60 CE).

*Part Two*

# APPROACHES

# Introduction

*Andrew Schonebaum*

## *Ways of Reading* The Story of the Stone

In a long work like *Story of the Stone*, there is much to interest students: kidnapping, corruption, sex, brawls, loan sharking, black magic and exorcisms, mournful longing, fulfilled and unfulfilled desire, multiple wives vying for power, officials rigging court cases, seductresses luring men to their deaths, and all manner of daily joys and traumas. But perhaps the best way to approach *The Story of the Stone* is to consider how it understands itself or, rather, how it suggests it should be understood to the reader. In chapter 1, the narrator tells us that different readers have named this story with five different titles: *The Story of the Stone* (*Shitou ji* 石頭記; the origin of this title is not explained), *The Tale of Brother Amor*, *A Mirror for the Romantic*, *Dream of the Red Chamber* (which Hawkes translates as *A Dream of Golden Days*), and *The Twelve Beauties of Jinling*. Additionally, a popular printed edition of the novel features the title *The Affinity of Gold and Jade* (given to the novel in the late nineteenth century, in part to avoid censorship of the novel known as *Story of the Stone* or *Dream of the Red Chamber*). These various titles, some adopted for later printed editions but none more enduring than *Dream of the Red Chamber* (*Honglou meng* 紅樓夢), hint at the novel's rich textual history and are keys to understanding its complex narrative.

The title *Story of the Stone* points to the protagonist Jia Bao-yu, an eccentric boy who grows up in a wealthy household among many girl cousins and maids during the moral and financial decline of his powerful family. The jade in his mouth when he was born points to his previous incarnation as the magical Stone rejected by the goddess Nü-wa as unfit for repairing the sky.[1] This jade always hangs around Bao-yu's neck—or is conspicuously missing—yet its existence is hardly questioned by the novel's characters. Teachers commonly focus on Bao-yu's gradual, often unwitting, and unique journey toward enlightenment through love and loss, passion and detachment.

The stone-like qualities of Bao-yu resonate throughout the novel. He is the "precious jade of spiritual understanding" (*tongling baoyu* 通靈寶玉; Hawkes translates this as "Magic Jade" [1.8.189]), which is one of the engravings on the jade in his mouth at birth; he is also a dumb rock, which the Buddhist monk and the Taoist often call an "absurd" or "stupid" stone 蠢物 (*chunwu*) (1.1.54). These qualities of mind are reflected in the appearance of jade, which may be cloudy or spotted or have an inner luminosity. We know that Bao-yu eventually returns to his stony form, since the entire story of his human incarnation is carved on him when Vanitas discovers the Stone at the base of Greensickness Peak in chapter 1. Ultimately, the question is if Bao-yu, whom we assume to be the Stone, has benefited from his trials. Has he attained understanding, or is he still a stubborn (unknowing and unteachable) rock? This major theme of knowledge and enlightenment is hinted at by two alternative titles, *The Tale of Brother Amor* and *A Mirror for the Romantic.*

The paradox of attaining enlightenment through passionate attachment to anything is reflected in the oxymoronic name "Brother Amor" that Vanitas takes for himself. Monks are supposed to renounce ties to the world, but Bao-yu is driven to seek enlightenment through the very experience of attachment and desire.[2] The process by which he attains enlightenment, through attachment to his girl cousins, the experience of their loss, and ultimately his detachment from worldly things, is called into question by the novel's existence, since it supposedly was written as a record of these young women so they would not be lost to memory. The irony of enlightenment through attachment as a theme is applied to the experience of reading fiction as well. Just as Vanitas did when he read this story engraved on the Stone, the reader of *Stone* must work through a contemplation of Form or Appearance, and the feelings they engender, to reach some kind of truth, which is knowledge of the Void—that everything in the phenomenal, human world is empty and transient (1.1.51). In this regard, the novel is either jesting at or lamenting the inescapable realization that Buddhist detachment and fictional aesthetics constantly undermine each other.

The title *A Mirror for the Romantic* more clearly addresses the relation between fiction and knowledge. Mirrors play a large role in *Stone*, hinting at the illusory nature of all things but particularly of self-knowledge. The narrator claims that he has faithfully presented a record of true happenings, but that claim is immediately and consistently called into question by the fantastic nature of the story and by the story's own insistence on its constructedness (50–51). The mirror is a Zen Buddhist image for a clear mind and a life that is not focused on the self. It also calls up the image of flowers in a mirror and of the moon in water, images from Buddhism popular in Chinese poetry that express the ephemerality and insubstantiality of things. The mirror also points to the episode of Jia Rui's magic mirror (ch. 12), which is ultimately also about reading fiction, and the episode of Bao-yu's dream of his real doppelgänger, Zhen Bao-yu (ch. 56). The play of rhetoric throughout the novel on real (*zhen* 真) and unreal (*jia* 假) constantly reminds the reader of the novel's obsession with the paradoxes of truth in fiction and fictive truth.

*The Story of the Stone* is only partly the story of Jia Bao-yu and the Stone's journey toward enlightenment. It also preeminently features women and considers the fate of a large family. The title *The Twelve Beauties of Jinling* recalls the mostly sad fates predicted for the major heroines in the registers of the "ill-fated fair" that Bao-yu reads in his dream in chapter 5 (131). Jinling is the old name for Nanjing, the capital of several imperial dynasties in southeastern China, familiar to Cao Xueqin from his youth. The title emphasizes the women in this household as well as things feminine. It also intimates nostalgia for people and places recalled from childhood. The many girl cousins, maids, nuns, and other young women in *Stone* are, according to words attributed to the author in the "preface," the reason he wrote the novel.

The world of the garden is ideal, at least for Bao-yu, because its inhabitants are exclusively young, unmarried women. The focus on women in *Stone* is important for a few reasons. It presents a remarkable challenge to the traditional norms of patriarchal Confucianism.[4] The emphasis on their beauty, taste, literary and artistic talents, political savvy, sensitivity, and morality is unique for and ahead of its time. Their activities and achievements defetishize them and call into question the elite place of males in society. That the novel also dramatizes the politics of literary art by focusing on female poetic talent makes it an engaging classroom text.

The story of Wang Xi-feng, the young woman manager of the Jia family finances and household servants, is arguably as important as that of Bao-yu. She is a perennial favorite with students, who are interested in how she both conforms to and challenges stereotypes about women. The financial and moral decline of the Jia family is her story as much as anyone's, reflected in the gradual loss of the garden and its female inhabitants. The "twelve beauties" title, which draws attention to the many other important characters in *Stone*, contrasts starkly with *The Affinity of Gold and Jade*, a title that picks up on the debate about which is the better match for Bao-yu or, indeed, which is the more ideal woman, Lin Dai-yu or Xue Bao-chai. But although *Stone* can be viewed as a triangle of romantic attachment, the many sad stories and few happy ones of the women of the Jia family deserve more attention in the classroom.

The title by which the novel is known throughout the Chinese-speaking world—*Honglou meng* or *Dream of the Red Chamber* (also *A Dream of Red Mansions*)—likely owes its popularity to its expression of splendor. The towered buildings denoted by *lou* 樓 (more than a "chamber") and the "pervading *redness*" of the novel and the opulence it connotes conjure images of wealth, power, and decadence for most readers (1.45). Gates and pillars of the very wealthy were painted red in traditional China, as were the front steps to royal palaces. Many readers are drawn to the material culture in the novel, the many descriptions of lavish objects in the Jia household. Textiles, paintings, furniture, unusual trinkets—all have complicated modes of signifying, and all involve matters of taste, wealth, culture, connoisseurship.

Many are drawn to *Stone* as a morality tale, because it tells of the near collapse of such a splendid family as a result of its mismanagement. Red points to the red dust by which Buddhism refers to the earthly realm, which contrasts sharply with the luxury brought to mind by the vernacular use of *red*. Also coupled with *Stone*'s world of opulence is the phenomenon of dream, which suggests transience and fantasy. Dreams in *Stone* are windows onto both the real world and the land of illusion. The dream is a figure for *Stone*'s content and overall vision. There are more than twenty dreams in the novel. In its refusal to commit to a linear time or uniform space, the narrative itself is dream-like.

## *Some Characteristics of* Xiaoshuo

It is unnecessary and perhaps not even useful to judge long Chinese fiction by the standards of the European novel. The defining characteristics of the Chinese novel are independent of their evaluation according to Western understandings of what a novel is. Unfortunately much widely read, early scholarship in English on the classic Chinese novels was apologetic, saying that most of them were unrewarding compared with Western fiction and that only *Stone* and a few other works "possess[ed] enough compensating excellences to appeal to the adult intelligence" (Hsia, *Classic Chinese Novel* 1). Many works of long vernacular fiction in China are every bit as complex as European novels; they also predate them. But it is more important to understand why long vernacular fiction became popular in China at the beginning of the seventeenth century and what relation it bore to other developments in the empire and the world. The novel in China was an innovative genre, as it was elsewhere but with important differences.[5]

The novel resists definition. As Terry Eagleton says, "It is less a genre than an anti-genre. It cannibalizes other literary modes and mixes the bits and pieces promiscuously together" (1). Nonetheless, let us make a few broad statements about the modern novel in the West. It is linked to the emergence of the middle class. It has roots in the romance — the world of heroes and villains begins to contend with the world of quotidian desires and the minutiae of daily life. The modern novel presents such themes as sex and marriage, money and property, social mobility, and the nuclear family. Its sphere is secular, empirical rather than mythical or metaphysical, and it concerns itself with culture more than nature. Romance gives way to realism; nobles give way to commoners. The novel has a suspicion of classical authority, and its investigative focus often gives it a subversive or reformist spirit. Novels are also written in a particular style, often that of an individual author.

Early terms for the novel in China did not have a precise definition. The word for novel in China (and Japan and Korea) is, literally, "small talk" or "trivial discourse" *xiaoshuo* 小說. Its earliest uses (Han dynasty, 206 BCE–220 CE) mean something more along the lines of "miscellany." Only as late as the late sixteenth century did *xiaoshuo* come into common use as a term for full-length prose fiction, as it does today. *Xiaoshuo* still can mean anything from a short story to a very long work, like *The Story of the Stone*. To indicate longer works, *xiaoshuo* is usually qualified with words like "full-length" or "chapter-based." But the lack of an exact term for the premodern Chinese novel does not mean that the genre was poorly defined or understood. The generic category into which *The Story of the Stone* best fits has chronological boundaries beginning around the turn of the sixteenth century with two (of the six) classic Chinese novels, Luo Guanzhong's *Three Kingdoms* 三國演義 (*Sanguo yanyi*) and Shi Nai'an and Luo's *Outlaws of the Marsh* (also known as *The Water Margin*; 水

滸傳 [*Shuihu zhuan*]). (Both works are available in a good English translation: *Three Kingdoms*, by Moss Roberts; *Outlaws*, by Sidney Shapiro.) The point at which the traditional novel in China gives way to the modern novel is usually identified as 1919 but might be traced back to the last decades of the nineteenth century. This was the period of experimentation with new forms leading up to a self-conscious rejection of the classic novel by cultural reformers in favor of the new, Western narrative model.

In China, the novel grew out of the historical tradition. It developed from accounts of the strange and along with other such stories was considered less important than dynastic accounts, essays on the Confucian classics, or poetry. In fact, works of vernacular fiction were often called unofficial histories. Folk origins and a long tradition of storytelling might also explain why the early Chinese novels, such as *The Three Kingdoms*, *Outlaws of the Marsh*, and Wu Cheng-en's *Journey to the West* (also known as *Monkey*; 西遊記 [*Xiyou ji*]) are often repetitive, attempting to incorporate all the various extant stories into one cohesive narrative. Yet this repetition is often significant: characters serving as shadows of other characters and situations echoing other situations bring out nuances of meaning through comparison. Andrew Plaks calls this patterning "figural recurrence" (*Four Masterworks* 87). Scholars generally consider *Plum in the Golden Vase* (also known as *The Golden Lotus*; 金瓶梅 [*Jin ping mei*]), originally published in 1618, as the first Chinese novel that was wholly the creation of one author and had no antecedent in the oral tradition.[6] *Plum in the Golden Vase* influenced *Stone* perhaps because it was less indebted to history. That *Stone* is the most complex example of the traditional Chinese novel might be attributed to the fact that it (along with *The Scholars* in the mid–eighteenth century) was the last of these so-called classic novels and thus could borrow from its predecessors while developing the genre.

Premodern Chinese novels, unlike most works of fiction that preceded them and that were written in the terse, classical language of scholarship and official documents, tended to be written in an early vernacular, which in turn came to be viewed as fusty and elite by moderns.[7] That these novels contain a great amount of poetry in the classical language, which coexists with the surrounding vernacular narrative,[8] shows the influence of traditional Chinese dramatic art, which also fuses vernacular narrative and classical lyric. In fact, the novel and serious drama in China influenced each other, sharing the same narrative structures and motifs as well as readers, publishers, and often the same authors. The poetry in Chinese novels creates an interaction and tension between high and low diction, between literati and popular culture.[9] It marks the novel even more than drama as a hybrid genre. The great works of vernacular fiction self-consciously exploit this hybridity by playing with generic and linguistic differences to achieve ironic disjunctions or harmonious visions based on complementary opposites.

Some argue that the novel in China grew out of particular historical conditions in the sixteenth and seventeenth centuries, as it did in Europe in the seventeenth and eighteenth. Increased urbanization and a population shift to urban centers of the Yangzi River delta region, increased printing and literacy, the move to an economy based on silver money, overseas colonization and trade, and incipient industrialization seem connected to the appearance of the novel in China and are represented in it. Both Chinese and European novels document a shift from the old elite and the pretensions of classical literature toward a broader, more generously encompassing literature. The new literary form is inventive and has subject matter that appeals to a wider audience — namely, depictions of the quotidian, of mundane settings and middlebrow characters. It resists or subverts those political and cultural forces that previously kept this stratum of society from being represented. Domestic works reflect a literary fascination with material culture in the poetry of useful things but also show the reader a familiar world of sights, smells, and sounds. Eighteenth-century novels in particular serve historians of China with a repository of meticulously documented artifacts of daily life.

The premodern Chinese novel, like its European counterpart, is notable for its treatment of sex and gender. In this respect, the full-length Chinese fictional narrative diverges from most of the literature that precedes it. It is particularly feminist, and if *Stone* is not feminist, the feminine is given a central place in it. In many Chinese novels, women still appear in popular generic stereotypes — the abandoned lover, the shrew, the whore, the devoted mother — but there are indisputably a greater sensitivity to and more carefully drawn representations of women than we find in most of the traditional literature.

Perhaps most important for the comparative study of Chinese and European novels is the "paradigmatic use of irony as its primary rhetorical mode for exploring the labyrinth of autonomous identity and defining the intrinsic limitations of self-realization" (Plaks, "Novel" 211). Irony goes with other characteristic rhetorical devices of novelistic discourse, such as reliable and unreliable narrators, changing points of view, and layers of voice and registers of dialogue. It creates a sense of slippage between subjectivity and objectivity.[10]

In discussions of the evolution of the traditional Chinese novel, *Stone* is often placed at the modern end of the spectrum. It is one of the first if not the first piece of Chinese vernacular fiction in which feelings are of primary importance. Yet the characterization of Bao-yu is not just about his persona (first-person narratives were not the favored form for vernacular literature in China until well after *The Story of the Stone*); it also involves the contesting forces in the self, the family, society, and even the cosmos.

It is this protracted, concentrated, and multifaceted exploration of feelings in a long narrative that has led readers, almost from the moment of its publication, to associate *Stone* more with the venerable genre of classical poetry than with *xiaoshuo*. Given the already entrenched hierarchy of literary genres by late-eighteenth-century China, such association automatically elevated the stature of the text. Small wonder that many modern critics label *Stone* a lyric novel. This focus on the novel's emotive features and language is understandable and often illuminating, but it has a liability: it reinforces the still prevalent tendency to read the novel as autobiography. Poetry has been the premier mode of composition for millennia, and its ability to reveal the innermost thoughts and feelings of its creator is enshrined in the familiar slogan "poetry articulates one's aspirations" (*shi yan zhi* 詩言志) (Owen, *Readings* 40). Thus the narrative episodes in the novel, the linguistic inventions, the characters, the varieties of emotions, the twists and surprises of plot, and the multiple points of view are all read as expressions of the author. Students in class should be warned about this critical bias in the novel's reception history. It is helpful to remember that traditional Chinese readers of, say, *The Three Kingdoms* seldom bothered to consider whether it was Cao Cao or Zhuge Liang who expressed the author or final redactor's feelings, and few worried whether it was Guanyin, Tripitaka, or Monkey who mouthed the views of the *Journey to the West*'s putative author. That context should indicate the special character and burden of *Stone*.

The Chinese novels in the premodern period were primarily written by literati for literati.[11] The educated elite wrote novels to entertain their friends, relatives, and in some cases their wives. Most novels were not written with publication in mind. Although novels were profitable, the writing of fiction was not a respected endeavor. Reading novels was something to be done in private, and writing them was a game by which the author might showcase his education and cleverness to his peers, for fun. It was quite a while after *Stone* before printed novels were attributed to particular authors—or before authors felt it acceptable to claim their novels.[12]

Because they were written by and for the most educated members of Chinese society, the novels considered to be masterworks are incredibly intertextual. In referencing, borrowing, and incorporating varieties of sources, particularly poetry, the Chinese novel is unparalleled in complexity. The degree to which this display of knowledge is incorporated into a story varies from novel to novel, but most agree that *Stone* is beyond compare with regard to how its poetry and other intertexts inform the characters and narrative. A detailed account of how *Stone* interacts with the Chinese literary tradition and derives its meanings from other texts is best left to an annotated edition, which does not yet exist in English.

## *The English* Story of the Stone

From 1973 to 1986, Penguin published the complete English edition of *The Story of the Stone*, translated by David Hawkes and John Minford. Gladys Yang, who cotranslated the same work, *Honglou meng*, under the title *A Dream of Red Mansions*, remarked that her competitors' version was "one of the great translations of this century" (G. Yang 621). At over 2,500 pages, *Stone* requires a semester to itself if we are to teach it in its entirety. Making selections can be difficult. Students will want to know what happens next or what happened in skipped sections, when their teachers give them only a few excerpts in survey courses. This difficulty often caused *Stone* to be left off a syllabus. It is a sad contradiction that the book that tells us the most about Chinese culture is not taught at all because it teaches too much. But with the increasing popularity of world literature in academic circles, and the increasing presence of China on the world stage, it is time to publish a book to help teachers deal with such an important work.

The Hawkes and Minford translation is a remarkable work of literature. One of the aims of our volume is to draw attention to this classic, which is available and accessible. The translators did a wonderful job of conveying the literary allusions, the parallel structures, the symbolism, and the poetry.[13] By interpreting as well as translating, they allow the readers of *Stone* to gain some ownership of the text. But their work could benefit greatly from an annotated—and abridged—edition. Our volume serves the teacher who wishes to offer selections of *Stone* as well as the teacher or reader who intends to take on the entire novel. Many of the essays in this volume serve as extended commentary, providing historical background, context, and literary approaches for those who have no time to do extensive outside reading on the novel.

The textual history of *Stone* is complex: there are at least eleven extant manuscript versions, four different early printed editions, and ten or eleven different printed commentary editions. The number of different editions is fifty-four or more. The Hawkes and Minford translation does not follow any one text exclusively; it is a mélange of them, edited by translators who, seeking coherence of a good story, neglected passages or terms that introduced contradiction. Needless to say, this editing required them to make choices that changed the wording and meaning of sentences and passages.[14]

Teachers of *Stone* should know what some feel is missing from this translation. One example is the "pervading redness" and the love, feelings, and femininity it connotes throughout (1.45). Bao-yu suffers from love of (all things) red sickness 愛紅的毛病兒 (263; left out of the Hawkes translation on 1.19.392). The novel in general is also a bit more racy and vulgar than the subtle, slightly fusty British style conveys ("baggages" would be "bitches" to American readers, and "sod" would be "fuck"). Many of the novel's passages have strong sexual overtones and include homosexual and homosocial relationships; they become even more veiled in the translation.

Hawkes and Minford at times needed to choose between different recensions of a text. In a few instances they made clear what to many premodern readers was not. In some editions of *Dream of the Red Chamber*, for instance, the Stone in chapter 1 decides to be incarnated in the world of men, and the crimson pearl flower decides to go also, in order to pay him a debt of tears. Some editions have Qin Zhong revive before he dies at the end of chapter 16, to give Bao-yu encouragement to study hard for the examinations in a scene reminiscent of and resonant with that of chapter 13, when Qin-shi (the ghost?) appears to Xi-feng and advises her to economize and plan for the future. The narrator in chapter 18 of some editions thanks the monk and Taoist for bringing him to the garden, which is so enchanting and beautiful. These passages were left out of the translation, but providing students with them (some are available in the Yangs' translation) may stimulate interesting conversations. One of the more conspicuous changes made by Hawkes is moving what in most Chinese editions are the first lines of chapter 1, words attributed to the narrator, to his introduction (20–21). The reason is that they were originally commentary, then later made part of the novel, but to just about everyone who has bought a copy of *Dream* in the last century, they are the first words of the novel.[15]

A few aspects of the Hawkes-Minford translation need restating here. Names of characters are either transliterated or given a translation on the basis of the character's class. If the name is transliterated, such as Leng Zi-xing or Xue Bao-chai, the character belongs to the educated or moneyed class; if the name is translated—Skybright or Parfumée for example—the character is a servant, performer, or religious practitioner. The translation also has paratexts, including character lists, diagrams, and notes in the appendixes, which students rarely notice on their own. They range from the essential, such as Hawkes's discussion of the registers of the ill-fated fair in chapter 5, to discussions of minor characters and textual inconsistencies. Hawkes focuses on the poetry in his translation. He generally translated the poetry first, then the narrative. Students should be encouraged to engage the poetry as well as the narrative and to discuss how one informs the other.

## Structure and Content of This Volume

Our volume offers scholarly interpretations of major issues and provides background that we hope will allow teachers to come up with their own approaches. Contributors were asked to present topics of contention so that professors new to *Stone* might more easily make selections that fit their course. Each essay in this volume deals with a major issue, the many sides of which students may productively argue. Our contributors have taught *Stone* in courses dedicated solely to it; in surveys of Chinese, East Asian, and world literature; in courses on the novel genre, Chinese and East Asian civilization, gender, and Chinese history.

The essay topics are interconnected. By assigning groups of them to students, teachers can use *Stone* in a variety of classes. Examples of such groupings are Chinese literature, music, and aesthetics (Scott; Wu; and Levy); reading and education (Lam; Millward; Huang; and Saussy); bodies and identity (Sommer; Lupke; Schonebaum; Epstein; and Lu); the "stuff" of *Stone* (Meyer-Fong; Ni; and Shang); text and beyond (Lu; McMahon; Shang; and Zhong); *Stone* studies and intellectual history (Saussy; Minford; Wang; and Friends); and *Stone*'s relation to the challenge of history (Furth; Rawski; and Shahar).

This volume parallels the paratexts found in most printed editions of Chinese novels before 1949. Early modern editions of *Stone* had many prefatory essays and much commentary to help understanding (and at times to suggest particular readings). There would be prefaces advocating traditional or new approaches, a guide to reading, a list of common questions and answers given to them, a long list of characters with descriptions and commentary, and a list and discussion of the places in which the main characters live in the garden. A popular 1927 edition contains 152 pages of introductory material. As yet there are no editions that translate the front matter, back matter, and marginal and interlineal commentary that so many readers experienced as part of any good *Stone* text. But our volume takes a step toward providing the reader of *The Story of the Stone* in English with an experience similar to those that Chinese readers had for two hundred years. One of the things that made commentary editions so popular is that they turned first-time readers into second-time readers without the necessity of rereading the book. A novel as complex as *Stone* otherwise requires rereading if one is to achieve the clearly desired effects of the narrative. We hope that our volume will provide that service as well.

## NOTES

[1] The relation that Bao-yu has with his jade, the stone of spiritual understanding, is a good topic for debate. Similarly, it is not clear what relation the Stone had with Crimson Pearl Flower, whether it was love or merely a fancy for it.

[2] On enlightenment through attachment, see the seventeenth-century novel *Xiyou bu* 西遊補 ("A Supplement to *Journey to the West*"), by Dong Yue, translated as *A Tower of Myriad Mirrors*. Its appendix contains a translation of the author's commentary on the dialectic of attachment through desire and enlightenment.

[3] These two images are explicitly given in the second song of the "Dream of the Red Chamber" suite: "All, insubstantial, doomed to pass. / As moonlight mirrored in the water / Or flowers reflected in a glass" (1.5.140) 一個空勞牽掛. 一個是水中月, 一個是鏡中花 (1: 82).

[4] *Stone* is not the first Chinese novel to foreground women. In general, the foregrounding of women is often viewed as characteristic of the genre in the nineteenth century.

[5] For an introduction to the Chinese novel and why the term *novel* applies, see Plaks, "Novel."

[6] The best translation of *Jin Ping Mei* is that of David Tod Roy, under the title *Plum in the Golden Vase or Chin P'ing Mei*. As of 2012, the first four of a planned five volumes (eighty of a hundred chapters) have been published. A complete translation, though based on an inferior recension and lacking much of the important poetry, is that of Clemont Egerton, published as *The Golden Lotus*.

[7] Many reformers of the republican period in China (1911–49) felt that *Stone* was part of the classical tradition of literature and needed to be overthrown in favor of a modern, vernacular one, but it was still considered a work of vernacular literature in comparison with the language used to write much of the literature before the late sixteenth century. In fact, when Wang Li, a towering figure in modern Chinese linguistics, wrote his famous and influential *Modern Chinese Grammar* (1943), his examples were taken almost exclusively from *Story of the Stone*. See Norman 152–53.

[8] Classical Chinese is at least as different from modern Chinese as Latin is from Italian or French.

[9] But some of the poetry in traditional Chinese novels is doggerel.

[10] Readers of *Stone* often lose sight of the ironic vision at its core, because of its evocation of the splendors and pleasures of traditional Chinese civilization. For a fuller discussion of irony in the premodern Chinese novel, see Plaks, *Four Masterworks*.

[11] There are many kinds of Chinese novel, including what Wilt Idema and Lloyd Haft call chapbooks, which, because of their simple language, must have been written for the only moderately literate. The literary value of the chapbooks and how to distinguish between chapbook and novel are matters of scholarly debate. The popularity of these early, nonliterary novels, as judged by the number published, is not in question. It is also certain (it is to any teacher of *Stone*) that many readers read *Stone* at different levels, with some, for instance, blithely skipping over the poetry.

[12] There were exceptions to this rule. For instance, a great number of novels were attributed to Luo Guanzhong, the putative author of *The Three Kingdoms*.

[13] In the literature on this translation, as on any translation, more attention is paid to what is lost than to what was added. It is important to note that Hawkes and Minford add quite a bit of cultural context to their translation in order to avoid using footnotes.

[14] Hawkes writes in his introduction, "In translating this novel I have felt unable to stick faithfully to any single text. I have mainly followed Gao E's version of the first chapter as being more consistent, though less interesting, than the other ones; but I have frequently followed a manuscript reading in subsequent chapters, and in a few, rare instances I have made small emendations of my own" (1.45–46). In other words, he followed the basic text established by Gao E (specifically, the "Cheng yi" text 程乙本, as reproduced by Renmin Wenxue Press), but every now and then he allowed himself to deviate from it. (Minford seems to have followed the Renmin Wenxue edition for the last forty chapters.) Some of the most noticeable editorial decisions are the occasional notes to the reader from *Stone* (e.g., 2.53.578), which are not found in most editions. When they do occur, they are not as clearly differentiated from the rest of the narrative as they are in the translation.

[15] Haun Saussy translates these words in his first essay in this volume.

# GETTING STARTED

# Authorship and *The Story of the Stone*:
## Open Questions

*Haun Saussy*

Interpreting a work of literature begins with questions. But the questions readers ask about the *Story of the Stone* change from time to time. Some questions become possible only with a broad change in assumptions about literature, authorship, and reading. One question that may seem obvious to the present-day reader was hardly pursued by readers and commentators of this novel in the first hundred and fifty years of its circulation: Who wrote *Dream of the Red Chamber* or *Story of the Stone*?

The short answer is Cao Xueqin (c. 1715–c. 1763). But, as often happens, the long answer is more informative. Editions of *Story of the Stone* today, Chinese and English alike, state on their title pages that the novel is the work of Cao Xueqin, supplemented by Gao E (c. 1738–c. 1815). But how do we know this? The name Cao Xueqin occurs in the work's first chapter, but only as one of a series of names, some patently fantastic and others merely unknown, of people who are said to have rewritten or edited earlier versions of the book. Why should posterity have settled on Cao Xueqin as the author? How did this name manage to move from the inside of the novel to its front cover?

Early manuscript copies of the novel do not include an author's name, and the first edition to reach a wider public, Gao E and Cheng Weiyuan's movable type printing of 1792, notes in its preface, "No one knows for sure who wrote this book" (Cheng). A typical late-nineteenth-century edition bears on its title page *Zengping huitu Daguan suolu* 增評繪圖大觀瑣錄 ("A Trifling Record of Events in the Grand Prospect Garden, Newly Annotated and Adorned with

Illustrations") and, on a separate slip pasted onto its cover, *Zengping buxiang quantu Shitou ji* 增評補像全圖石頭記 (*"The Story of the Stone*, Illustrated Throughout, Supplemented with Portraits, and Newly Annotated") (a copy of this edition is in the East Asia Library of the Standford Univ. Libs.). The difference of titles is accounted for by a Shanghai law forbidding the sale of *Honglou meng* or *Shitou ji* in the city, but the impression given by the added verbiage is that publishers and readers made much of extras such as illustrations and appreciative commentary.[1] For more than a hundred and thirty years after the novel's first publication, its title sheet and first page remained innocent of any author's name.

When the novel itself gives guidance on the question of its authorship, it is in a suspiciously playful tone. The Cheng-Wei edition of 1792 opens with a paragraph in which someone claims to cite the author on his original intent:

This is the first and opening chapter. The author himself states: "Having lived through an unreal dream, I have concealed the original facts [*jiang zhen shi yin qu* 將真事隱去, homophonous with the name of the fictional character Zhen Shi-yin] and, adopting the fiction of 'spiritual enlightenment,' I have written the present *Story of the Stone*." So it speaks of "Zhen Shi-yin," and so on. But what are the events and who are the people recorded in this book? He himself goes on to say: "Having made an utter failure of my life, I found myself one day, in the midst of my poverty and wretchedness, thinking about the female companions of my youth. As I went over them one by one, examining and comparing them in my mind's eye, it suddenly came over me that those slips of girls—which is all they were then—were in every way, both morally and intellectually, superior to the 'grave and mustachioed signior' I am now supposed to have become. The realization brought with it an overpowering sense of shame and remorse, and for a while I was plunged in the deepest despair. There and then I resolved to make a record of all the recollections of those days I could muster—those golden days when I dressed in silk and ate delicately, when we still nestled in the protecting shadow of the Ancestors and Heaven still smiled upon us. I resolved to tell the world how, in defiance of all my family's attempts to bring me up properly and all the warnings and advice of my friends, I had brought myself to this present wretched state, in which, having frittered away half a lifetime, I find myself without a single skill with which I could earn a decent living. I resolved that, however unsightly my own shortcomings might be, I must not, for the sake of keeping them hid, allow those wonderful girls to pass into oblivion without a memorial. . . . I might lack learning and literary aptitude, but what was to prevent me from using invented speeches and rustic language [*jia yu cun yan* 假語村言, homophonous with the name of the fictional character Jia Yu-cun] to enliven the telling of a story? In this way the memorial to my beloved girls could at one and the same time serve as a source of harmless entertainment and as a warning to those who were in the same predicament as myself but who were still in need of awakening." So he says "Jia Yu-cun" and so forth. Wherever this chapter speaks of "dream" and "unreality" and the like, this is meant to reawaken the reader's awareness of the author's purposive design (1:1).[2]

此開卷第一回也. 作者自雲: 因曾歷過一番夢幻之後, 故將真事隱去, 而借 "通靈" 之說, 撰此 "石頭記" 一書也. 故曰 "甄士隱" 云云. 但書中所記何事何人? 自又云: "今風塵碌碌, 一事無成, 忽念及當日所有之女子, 一一細考較去, 覺其行止見識, 皆出於我之上. 何我堂堂鬚眉, 誠不若彼裙釵哉? 實愧則有餘, 悔又無益之大無可如何之日也! 當此, 則自欲將已往所賴天恩祖德, 錦衣紈褲之時, 飫甘饜肥之日, 背父兄教育之恩, 負師友規談之德, 以至今日一技無成, 半生潦倒之罪, 編述一集, 以告天下人: 我之罪固不免, 然閨閣中本自歷歷有人, 萬不可因我之不肖, 自護己短, 一併使其泯滅也. ... 雖我未學, 下筆無文, 又何妨用假語村言, 敷演出一段故事來, 亦可使閨閣昭傳, 復可悅世之目, 破人愁悶, 不亦宜乎?" 故曰 "賈雨村" 云云. 此回中凡用 "夢" 用 "幻" 等字, 是提醒閱者眼目, 亦是此書立意本旨.

When the passages purportedly spoken by the "author" are removed, the editor's framing utterance is limited to five points:

1. This is the first and opening chapter.
2. So it speaks of "Zhen Shi-yin," and so on.
3. But what are the events and who are the people recorded in this book?
4. So he says "Jia Yu-cun," and so forth.
5. Wherever this chapter speaks of "dream" and "unreality" and the like . . .

Apart from the identification of the opening chapter, the remaining points of this paragraph all bear on the dual nature of the novel's content: a background of real people and events, we read, is here masked by a literary technique that the editor names "'dream' and 'unreality' and the like." Both the assertion that real events underlie the fiction and the assertion that the fiction is fictive are credited to the author, who is otherwise unknown to the reader. But what authority lies behind this attribution of authorial intent? The Red Inkstone family of commentaries suggests that the paragraph was added to the novel by a younger brother of Cao Xueqin, named Cao Tangcun, but there is no independent evidence for this claim. Some readers hold that the paragraph is a piece of commentary by an early reader that has crept into the novel through successive copyings; others see it as a piece of mock commentary deceptively inserted by the novel's main author. Is the paragraph part of the novel or not, and does the difference affect the novel's credibility? In any event, since (or although) this prefatory passage tells us that the whole story is a dream and not to be taken at face value, we may be unable to take it at face value even if its account of the meaning of the book corresponds to the "author's." Nothing is to be taken literally except—this is the condition for playing the game—the statement that says that the novel is not to be taken literally (see K. Yau). The opening passage puts us on notice that *The Story of the Stone* is a far from straightforward novel and requires a similar agility from its reader.

Gao and Cheng admitted with admirable honesty that "No one knows for sure who wrote this book," but from the very start of our experience as readers we are faced with other readers' need to know the author's history and motives, if only to settle the question of what such important thematic threads as dream and unreality really represent. In its tone and concerns this paragraph resembles the many commentaries composed by devotees of the novel and added to its nineteenth-century editions. For these readers, the novel is full of insights and truths, all the more profound for wearing the appearance of a slight, self-indulgent fiction about spoiled, idle young aristocrats. Any attempt to draw from these readings of the work a profile of the author suggests a complex personality: a moralist intent on diagnosing the ills of the age and the illusions that lead people to destruction, a skilled exponent of the classics and parts of the Buddhist canon, and a writer passionately involved in the fates of his fictional characters.

For most readers of the novel until the early twentieth century, the question "Who wrote *Story of the Stone*?" amounted to asking what sort of person the author was, not which individual. A smaller group of readers took the motto "original facts concealed" as an invitation to probe for historical information that would unveil the meaning of the novel as well as its author's name: to read the novel, in short, as a roman à clef. The extensive 1916 commentary by Wang Mengruan and Shen Ping'an took the novel to be a disguised account of the love of the Shunzhi emperor (who reigned 1644–61) for the former courtesan Dong Xiaowan, a passion that allegedly led the emperor to abdicate and seek refuge in a monastery. Wang hypothesizes that only a court insider with access to extraordinarily sensitive documents could have written the book, and he supposes that the emperor himself, after abdicating, signed a draft of his reminiscences with the sobriquet the Passionate Monk. This draft would have been rewritten by a series of insiders, the last of whom must have been named Cao Xueqin. Historians assure us that these facts are imaginary, however, and Wang's efforts to correlate every event in the novel with some aspect of the intimate life of the early Qing court soon appear tedious and disorderly.

Cai Yuanpei's 1917 reading draws up a different suspect profile for the author of the novel. Published not long after the revolution that saw the end of the Manchu imperial dynasty's two and a half centuries of occupation rule, Cai's decoding of the novel makes it a lament for lost Chinese nationhood. His allegory has Jia Bao-yu stand for the seals of state, now fallen into the hands of an illegitimate dynasty (hence his name, which punningly translates as "false precious jade"; what jade indeed could be more precious than the emperor's authenticating seal?). Zhen Bao-yu, who is much talked about though a rare presence in the story and whose name sounds like "true precious jade," stands for the missing line of Ming sovereigns. The women in the story stand for Chinese—now subordinate in their own country—and the men, correspondingly, for Manchus. For Cai, the author must have been "a passionate nationalist" and a sharp critic of those Chinese who eventually went over to serve the "illegitimate" rulers. A similar reading was recently defended by Pan Zhonggui, whose interpretation of the novel points to an author who would have lived through the disasters of the fall of the Ming, witnessed the sacrifices of loyal subjects, and observed the powerful Manchu repression that made these sacrifices useless. Once more, the meaning found in the novel directs the reconstruction of its author's psychology.

Hu Shi (1891–1962), the Columbia University–educated philosopher of pragmatism and advocate of literary reform who was China's preeminent intellectual of the 1920s and 1930s, had no patience for the generalizing moral interpretations of one group or the highly specific topical allegories of the other. For him, neither amounted to anything more than speculation, and the only interpretation of the novel that he could accept would be based on historical fact. It was jumping the gun to talk about what the book meant: "What we need to do," said Hu Shi,

> is base ourselves on reliable editions and reliable information, determine who exactly the author of this book was, uncover the history of this author and his circle together with the time in which the book was composed, and investigate the various editions and publishers of the work. This is the proper sphere of *Honglou meng* studies.
>
> 其實 . . . 我們只須根據可靠的版本與可靠的材料, 考定這書的作者究竟是誰, 作者的事迹家世, 著書的時代, 這書曾有何種不同的本子, 這些本子的來歷如何. 這些問題乃是 "紅樓夢" 考證正當的範圍.
>
> ("*Honglou meng*" 585–86)

Literal, historical information was needed, not timeless teaching or topical allegory. The passage in which the Stone's story is said to have passed from the Passionate Monk (formerly Vanitas) to Kong Mei-xi to "Cao Xueqin [who] in his Nostalgia Studio worked on it for ten years" (1.1.51) contained one genuine historical name among the various fantastic personas, one figure who appeared in other documents of the period: Cao Xueqin. Not much was known about him, though a persistent legend associated his family's former dwelling in Nanjing with the Sui Garden of the famous poet Yuan Mei (1716–98). Xueqin's grandfather Cao Yin (1658–1712) was a conspicuous figure in the China of his time, for he managed the Nanjing textile manufactures and collected the salt duties

of the region on behalf of the imperial household, two extremely lucrative and
strategic positions; he was even something of a confidant of the Kangxi emperor.
When the emperor visited the southland, Cao Yin organized his progress and
on four occasions hosted the imperial party. But Cao Yin died, leaving massive
debts and the accounts of the salt and textile enterprises in bad shape. His son,
Cao Fu, was allowed to continue in the father's place, but after the accession of
the suspicious and vengeful Yongzheng emperor in 1721, the Cao family were
deprived of their rank, stripped of most of their wealth, and forced to leave
their residence in Nanjing. Xueqin would have been a teenager at the time of
his family's fall.[3]

Applying these details to the blanks of the novel, Hu Shi declares that "we
can be sure that the *Honglou meng* is Cao Xueqin's autobiography. . . . We must
keep in mind that at its very beginning, the *Honglou meng* unambiguously states
that 'The author himself says. . . .' . . . How clearly this is stated! . . . So, Cao
Xueqin is also the miserable and remorseful 'I' of this opening passage!" 可以
明白 "紅樓夢" 這部書是曹雪芹的自叙傳了 我們總該記得 "紅樓夢" 開端時,
明明地說着: "作者自云" 這話說得何等明白! 那麼, 曹雪芹即是 "紅樓夢" 開
端時那個深自忏悔的 "我"! (598–99). Hu Shi's historicism killed two birds with
one stone, for he claimed to have found not only an author for the novel but also
an adequate interpretive framework (the book as autobiographical fiction).

Hu Shi's detective work founded one of the main approaches to *Story of the
Stone* in the modern period: the tireless pursuit of historical materials concerning the Cao family, research into social and economic conditions at the time of
its writing, and efforts to fill out the biography of Cao Xueqin, the presumed
original of the fictionalized version presented to us in the novel. The goal is,
it sometimes seems, to dissolve the creative work of the author back into the
conditions from which it arose and to turn the novel into a high-grade historical
document.

In the decades after Hu Shi's essay revolutionized *Stone* scholarship, manuscripts of the work predating its first appearance in print began to be published.
Several contained comments (at beginnings and ends of chapters, between the
lines, and in the upper blank area of the pages) by a person whose pen name was
Zhiyan zhai ("Red Inkstone," as Hawkes translates it) and by his or her close
associates. These comments bore out Hu Shi's theory, for Red Inkstone was
clearly an intimate friend of Cao Xueqin's, perhaps even a member of the family, and never missed an opportunity to insert personal reminiscences into the
flow of the story: "Exactly as I remember her." "My heart breaks to relive this
scene today." "I was there too." Other figures in this group of commentators
also seem to have been part of the Cao circle. While the Red Inkstone family of
comments often point out subtleties of fictional technique and guess at hidden
meanings, their importance has been greatest for the historicist wing of *Stone*
studies.

The Red Inkstone annotations go up only as far as chapter 80. No manuscript in this family contains the last forty chapters of the presently accepted

version; in fact, many presages in the first two-thirds of the novel are contra-
dicted by developments of the last third; Red Inkstone's comments, too, speak
of outcomes different from those narrated by the 120-chapter text. Gao E's
preface to the 1792 printing acknowledges that for years he too was frustrated
by the incompleteness of every manuscript copy he could find of this wonderful
novel. But one day, he tells the reader, his friend Cheng Weiyuan unexpectedly
bought a fuller manuscript version, which he, Gao E, then set about editing
and polishing and now presents to the public (1: 31–32).[4] Readers have always
suspected that this story covers a more prosaic reality: that Cheng and Gao saw
the opportunity for profit in publishing a work already famous in manuscript,
that they recognized that rounding out the story would make it even more desirable. But what did Gao E have to go on when he composed the last forty chapters? What was contained in the chapters that Cheng Weiyuan unexpectedly
acquired? Cheng's preface to the first woodblock printing refers to an original
table of contents that had 120 chapters. Were there surviving members of Cao
Xueqin's circle who could have passed on the design of the unrealized whole?
Did Gao rely, though inconsistently, on a Red Inkstone commentary with its
frequent allusions to future events? What, in a word, is the degree of Gao E's
contribution — in what measure is he too the author of *Story of the Stone*? Between his editing a preexisting manuscript and his inventing the last third out
of whole cloth, various positions have been sketched out, based usually on interpretive conclusions. Most readers sense a boundary at chapter 80 and feel
that the continuation is written in a different voice, one less imaginatively vivid
in capturing details of character and action, readier to assimilate story patterns
from legend or other vernacular collections, more conformist in morality, more
predictable in imagery and rhetoric (Wu Shih-Chang). Others feel that the so-
bering of fantasy and the greater conventionality of the last third reflect not a
change of authorial hand but the gradual maturing of the book's hero, Bao-yu,
and the transition from the sheltered garden life to a harsher everyday world (A.
Yu; Xiao Chi). Does the novel exhibit artistic unity, or does its conclusion serve
mostly to evoke the mirage of what a complete *Story of the Stone* by the real
Cao Xueqin would have been like? Both attitudes toward the integrity of the
novel find justification in the many points of contrast between the text of the
Red Inkstone manuscripts and the two Cheng Weiyuan–Gao E printings (contrasts that give us a sense of Gao's fictional technique). Both attitudes bear interpretive fruit; both are likely to appeal to the same reader by turns, as the reader
is solicited by the different voices of the *Stone* and its chameleon narrator. Perhaps questions of authorship and historical context are always, in this case, fated
to reduce to the pull of rival interpretations.

The manuscript versions of the novel present a special problem, for they do
not all derive from a single archetype. Comparison of variant texts suggests, as
do some comments by Red Inkstone, that the author circulated draft chapters
among a group of intimates who responded with suggestions, protests, praise,
and attempts at interpretation. Occasionally a batch of chapters might be lent

out to unrelated people who failed to return them. Different versions of the same chapter might circulate simultaneously, and revisions in one version were not always taken into account in other copies. It thus appears that Cao Xueqin's circle of first readers contributed substantively to the novel (Odd Tablet, for example, records having ordered him to give Qin Ke-qing a better fate than was originally planned for her [1.42]). If taken as a work of collective imagination, the novel seems less deceptive in its claims to have no author (except a self-inscribing Stone) and to have emerged from a sequential process of editing and rewriting in which "Cao Xueqin in his Nostalgia Studio" is only one of many relays (51). Perhaps it was interpretive wisdom, not only a lack of information, that led the nineteenth-century commentators to seek the intentions of the book rather than of its maker. "Who wrote the *Story of the Stone*? — I did. — How can you say that? — Every sentence of it clawed its way out from my own heart" 或問: "'石頭記' 伊誰之作?" 曰: "我之作." "何以言之?" 曰: "語語自我心中爬剔而出" (Tu Ying).

## NOTES

[1] For a publisher's advertisement seeking new commentary to novel texts, see Rolston, *How to Read* 2.

[2] For a photoreproduction of this Chinese text, see the frontispiece in Yisu, *Honglou meng juan* (vol. 1). The sentences from "Having made" to "aptitude" and from "In this way" to "awakening" are quoted from Hawkes's translation, (1.20–21). Hawkes omits part of this section for clarity.

[3] On the Cao family's fortunes, see Spence, *Ts'ao Yin*.

[4] Somewhat different retellings of the story of the restored chapters are given in Cheng and in *Honglou meng* [2002] 1: 32 (in the introduction by Cheng Weiyuan and Gao E).

# Five Questions for
# a New Reader of *The Story of the Stone*:
# A Historian's Primer for Volume 1

*Charlotte Furth*

Like many contributors to this collection of essays, I honed my knowledge of *The Story of the Stone* by teaching a college class on it. Given ten to fifteen weeks together with a captive audience, I learned to coax, prod, and cajole my general education students, most with little or no background on Chinese culture or history, into an engagement with the novel that was lively and often rich in insights for all concerned. The college classroom is indeed a place for Cao Xueqin's masterpiece to become recognized as part of today's more global literary canon. But there is another, perhaps larger audience out there that we are missing.

Not long ago, I read Jane Smiley's *Thirteen Ways of Looking at the Novel*, built around her project of reading one hundred novels. For Smiley this project was both an overview of the history of the genre, informed by her own virtuosity as a master of the craft, and a meditation on the novel's importance in the modern age for developing our human sense of self and of possible worlds. Her list roams over European literature, from Boccaccio, Cervantes, and Madame de Lafayette to contemporary favorites like John Updike, Vladimir Nabokov, and Milan Kundera. It includes one work in Arabic (Mahfouz's *The Harafish*) and three in Japanese (Murasaki, Tanizaki, Mishima) but not a single Chinese novel. Of course one must grant that such lists are always shaped by an individual's tastes and preferences, yet *Stone* resonates with Smiley's own identified novelistic themes of family conflict, relationships between the sexes, and frontiers of human intimacy—all domains of experience that she argues have been profoundly shaped through the cultivation of sensibilities that novels especially foster. Translation is not the problem: even the most literate anglophone readers access most of their classics through English-language translations, and her list embraces Icelandic sagas as well as Russian, German, Italian, Spanish, and Japanese favorites. With the excellent David Hawkes and John Minford English-language version available now for more than twenty years, clearly *Stone* could become another modern classic as well as a work that opens the door on unexplored aspects of the history of fiction as a genre. Surely it could find more general readers than have come forward so far—consider not only students but also book club groupies, retirees, speed readers, Jane Austen addicts, and people embarked on those travels and sojourns in the woods, on islands, or around the world that provide a period of refuge from everyday life. From the Harry Potter books to *Lord of the Rings* to TV serials like *The West Wing* and *The Sopranos*, the extended narrative with large casts of characters still has the power to generate dedicated readers who steep themselves in the minutiae of their preferred characters, spawning fanzines, costume reenactments, and sequels both mock and serious. Inside the People's Republic of China, *Stone* (usually called *Dream of the Red Chamber*) has this sort of place in the popular culture today. You can find versions of it in comic book abridgements, in traditional opera, in television miniseries, and on the Internet, and you can visit two theme parks, one in Shanghai and one in Beijing, where fans stroll the garden pavilions, dress up in costumes as their favorite personages, and dine from menus based on the novel's sumptuous banquets.

English-language readers (not only students) have often told me that the book is difficult to get into. Too much is unfamiliar, and there is just too much of it. Here I think a historian's perspective can make a contribution that may elude the more sophisticated literature specialists whose job it is to understand and teach Chinese fiction. Basic questions of text and context can seem a little old-fashioned to today's academic humanists. Between the linguistic challenges of sinological interpretation and the temptations of postmodern hermeneutics, there is a great deal for specialists on Chinese literature to talk about, while the task of fitting the history of fiction into a larger framework of historical cultural studies of China remains in its infancy. The historian can do two things: one is to recognize and deal with some of the basic questions about the nature of the very unfamiliar society that formed the authors and readers of this book; the other is to use techniques of primary source analysis to help students tease out of the story itself some plausible answers to their questions about the social world *The Story of the Stone* takes for granted.

*The Story of the Stone* is haunted by questions about the truth of fiction and the illusoriness of everyday mundane experience—ontological questions that are posed by its creator as well as by our modernist literary interpreters. But a historian's guide to the novel should not take this issue as a point of departure. The readers I am thinking about need a primer. Primers explain much that is obvious to experts, though hopefully in a way that will not be dismissed as simplistic. Primers also need to guard against explaining too much. You hope to give your reader an assist over obstacles as they appear along a complex path, without depriving literary travelers of the pleasures of pulling ahead to make discoveries on their own. In this spirit I offer an outline, around five basic questions, of how to get started reading *Story of the Stone*. There could be a good many more, but these five are relevant to engaging with volume 1.

## What Did Eighteenth-Century Authors and Audiences Expect a Novel to Look Like?

First of all, imagine an upper-class society whose members have both education and a great deal of leisure time. Reading and writing in the classical language are highly valued, but the poems, diaries, recollections, essays formal and informal, and occasional pieces that a cultured man or woman is likely to produce in it are not destined for wide circulation. A commercial print book market for classical and vernacular writings flourishes, but only a fraction of the literary flood finds an outlet there. There are no newspapers or magazines. Now imagine a down-at-the-heels literary gentleman who, having declined to pursue or failed to achieve an official career, whiles away his time weaving a long narrative of a rich family's rise and fall based loosely on his own past. Manuscript chapters accumulate slowly, are read to friends and kinsmen over wine, are passed around, copied by hand, discussed and altered over a couple of decades.

When the author, Cao Xueqin, died in 1763, the novel was unfinished. Commentaries written between the lines and on the margins of several of the manuscript copies bear witness to the personal interventions in the text by readers who were close to the author, and sometimes changes were made by the author himself. Although a complete 120-chapter version of *The Story of the Stone* was commercially published in 1791–92, under the title *Dream of the Red Chamber*, printing for profit had never been the author's goal, and until the beginning of the twentieth century the novel was treated as anonymous. Nonetheless, at least thirteen separate editions were reprinted over the course of the nineteenth century, as *Stone* joined other popular novels, stories, and plays in the vernacular language that were laying claim to a place in the literary sun that still shone most brightly on the classics.

Eighteenth-century readers understood that producing a novel was a leisurely process designed for an intimate audience, and they welcomed the very personal communication with the writer that reading invited. They had the habit of adding handwritten notes in the margins of novels, using comments to enter into dialogue with the author and to share their responses with others. The characters seemed just as real as the readers' friends and family, and the novel's illusion of historicity was entered into enthusiastically. Readers of the manuscript versions of Cao Xueqin's book included some of his family intimates; the real-life models for certain characters dominated many readings of the novel; and a respected tradition of Chinese commentary on the work assumed it was a roman à clef, to be unlocked through literary detective work, into the history of the Cao family.

But eighteenth-century writers and readers were not simply producing and consuming naive stories or purely personal anecdotes and memoirs. The novel, as an extended prose narrative of linked episodes and imaginary characters, had been an established Chinese literary form for over three hundred years. Early Western critics, who assumed that Chinese novels were the product of a simple narrative art form drawing on oral traditions, complained about the lengthy, episodic structure; about the primacy of dialogue over interior monologue; about the intrusion of poems or learned disquisitions; and about the hundreds of characters. Chinese novels indeed carried these markers of the genre's roots in public performance—whether the tales of storytellers, the songs of balladeers, puppet theater, or traditional opera—but novelists had learned to shape their many-chapter narratives around yin-yang alternations of mood, often imagined in ten-chapter units, and around long arcs of development that typically reached a high point midway before descending from yang to yin.[1] They liked to create character types based on standard roles in stage performances and to group characters into complementary personality pairs. The inclusion of poems highlighted lyricism and subjectivity. Learned passages evoked culture as play and encouraged the connoisseur to appreciate apt literary and historical allusions. Further, just as theatrical performances featured prologue and envoi, a well-crafted novel could draw on framing devices to enlarge the canvas and foreshadow destiny.

Finally, the habit of commentary, so evident in the manuscript versions of *Stone*, functioned as literary criticism, establishing authorial intention, reader response, and the interplay between them that made the production and consumption of novels in Ming-Qing China uniquely embedded in group sociability. Important novels were published not as the products of a single author's vision but in editions where commentators also had their say, encouraging reading between the lines and inspiring spin-offs, and where implicitly the genre itself was subjected to scrutiny. These are some of the expectations that eighteenth-century fiction fans would bring to the table as they opened a novel and began to read—perhaps with their own commentator's brush in hand.

## Why Should I Pay Special Attention to the Opening Chapter?

A student's first response to the opening chapter is likely to be disorientation. Where are we? What time is it? And who is telling this story anyway? Within a few pages, the reader is transported from cosmic realms where the repair of heaven is presided over by the goddess Nü-wa to a shadowy void where immortals wander and have conversations with a magic Stone, and then down to earth to the very concrete and historic city of Suzhou, where finally ordinary human characters make their appearance. Eons pass in a flash, and the reader is informed that the complete story of the Stone is already finished and carved on the Stone, which awaits being taken to the mortal world, where various authors, including someone named Cao Xueqin, will edit and transmit it. Readers reasonably suspect that they are being played with, and also that these fantastical riffs are meant to hint at serious messages. Both are true.

Chapter 1 is doing at least three important things: it is introducing the multilayered voices through which the story will be told, it is providing a pretale that foreshadows the arc of the story as a whole, and it is suggesting that there is an allegorical level at which the novel's deeper themes will be explored.

First, the narrator addresses the reader and, like a balladeer in a teahouse or a commentator writing in a book's margins, engages his audience directly, offering remarks on the action. But then the Stone, a bit of otherworldly cosmic rock brought to earth, is set up to be author, narrator, and hero of the story. The protagonist is a young man named Bao-yu ("Precious Jade" in Chinese) and is said to have been born with a jade stone in his mouth. The claim of fusion or nondifferentiation of author and subject is conveyed though the further conceit that the Stone's story is inscribed on its body's surface. The Stone speaks straightforwardly as an author in prefatory words, swearing that what it writes is entirely "a true record of real events" (1.1.51). But this otherworldly introduction undercuts the claim that we have a straightforward historical narrative or memoir. Protagonist, Stone, storyteller, and author are engaged in a game of hide-and-seek. In entering into a conversation with the text, the reader is invited to think about how the literary imagination works and about the act of reading itself.

Second, chapter 1 establishes a framing pretale that serves as prologue for the action to come. As the story moves to the historical city of Suzhou, the reader is introduced to the retired scholar Zhen Shi-yin and his friend, the poor student Jia Yu-cun. In the space of about ten pages, they meet, part, and undergo stunning reversals of fortune. Jia rises to official rank and position, while Zhen loses everything: his child is kidnapped, his house burns down, and when he is reduced to being a dependent on his wife's miserly parents, he abandons the world for the life of a mendicant holy man. Since the characters Zhen and Jia disappear almost entirely for the next 115 chapters, this brief story anticipates the larger narrative's trajectory of decline and fall of a wealthy family.

The third theme at work is karma and the nature of illusion. Today's reader is probably vaguely familiar with karma as the Buddhist belief that living beings undergo a cycle of many lives connected by an invisible bond of karmic consequences. This belief fostered a rich Chinese Buddhist folk cosmology of an underworld where the dead are judged and reassigned to new lives and identities and where the records of past lives and future fates are kept and known. Though in Buddhism no one has access to individual memories of former existences, in the popular religious imagination traces of such knowledge can surface, and since they foreshadow the future, they have a prophetic resonance. Karma provided ordinary Chinese with some explanation for the vicissitudes of fate. It also provided the author of *Story of the Stone* a culturally resonant vehicle for literary foreshadowing, allowing readers to anticipate the destinies of the characters in the novel.

The story of Zhen Shi-yin and Jia yu-cun works against readers' expectation or hope that karma rewards good and punishes evil. The message religious teachers offer is hardly a comforting one. The selfish, careerist Jia (whose surname name is a pun on the word for "false" or "inauthentic") rises in the world and forgets his erstwhile benefactor, Zhen (whose surname puns on "true" or "genuine"), in the latter's time of troubles. Moreover, the holy men who warn

Zhen scold him for loving his child too much and advise him to abandon her. Religious wisdom appears harsh and inhuman, and its messengers are uncouth madmen.

Chapter 1 also prepares the reader for the important themes picked up and developed further in chapter 5, through the metanarrative device of the Land of Illusion, a dream world. Dream is often a vehicle for human communication with a domain beyond ordinary experience. The Land of Illusion appears in dreams in which the characters are given hints about the karma in their lives. Zhen dreams of two immortals who are taking souls awaiting reincarnation through its portals to assume human form and experience their destinies. He awakes from his dream without having gone through this entryway himself, prefiguring his renunciation of the world to follow the teachings of the two immortals. In chapter 5, a dream takes Bao-yu and the reader through the gateway into the Land of Illusion itself, guided by its presiding spirit, the fairy Disenchantment. Both reader and hero are disoriented. Students quickly see that this is a dream of beautiful women and love, but is Bao-yu being encouraged to love or warned against it? Enchanting goddesses entertain him with song and poetry. The translator tells the reader that the poems in the two song suites performed for Bao-yu contain riddles identifying major young female characters and hinting of sorrow that awaits them. An anglophone student who is unfamiliar with the work may feel something that a Chinese reader cannot, a sense that these song riddles are opaque, about characters not yet encountered in the story. Such a reader is more open to the aura of erotic invitation that suffuses the narrative and to being puzzled by the fairy's contradictory discourse. On the one hand, she brings the dreaming adolescent hero messages from dead ancestors about the responsibilities of manhood and warns against the folly of believing that love can be distinguished from lust. On the other hand, she is mistress of the joys of the bedchamber who presides over Bao-yu's sexual awakening. Modern readers are all familiar with the illusion of love as celebrated in the Lorenz Hart lyric "Falling in love with love is falling for make-believe." But as Bao-yu is horror-struck at the verge of the Ford of Error and wakes to the everyday reality that he has just had a wet dream, it is difficult for the Land of Illusion to stay contained in the purely psychological domain of human sleep or the beatitudes of romantic sentiment.

Wait a minute, someone will say. Does this story really mean to tell us that all love is an illusion? Surely the point isn't that love is merely sex. Maybe there is some deeper Buddhist truth here that life itself is a dream and illusory. But if life is illusory, why are we reading on and on about the Jia family? If everything is foreordained, where is human free will? Don't we need these questions answered before we can believe in the reality of these characters and their experiences?

Readers who can get this far at the end of chapter 5 are on the way to being able to appreciate Anthony Yu's important insight that the *Story of the Stone*'s metanarratives interweave a Buddhist ontology about illusion and reality together with an artist's reflection on the illusionism of fictional worlds (267).

> Truth becomes fiction when the fiction's true;
> Real becomes not-real when the unreal's real.    (1.1.55, 1.5.130)

> 假作真時真亦假,
> 無為有處有還無.    (1: 10, 74)

This enigmatic couplet, adorning the gateway to the Land of Illusion, invites discerning readers to wrestle with the metanarrative.

## Who Are All These People?

A primer should not linger too long on these vast metaphysical themes. Millions of readers, including Mao Zedong and many modern-minded Chinese, enjoy *Story of the Stone* as a social novel or as thinly disguised autobiography and are convinced that it conveys much of the historical reality of upper-class Chinese life in the eighteenth century. Beginning with the teahouse gossip between Jia Yu-cun and an acquaintance in chapter 2, followed up in chapter 3 with the description of the orphan heroine Lin Dai-yu's arrival at the Jia mansion to take up residence with her maternal grandmother, readers are introduced to a family embedded in a social world as densely realized as any from the pen of Charles Dickens, Honoré de Balzac, or Jane Austen.

With their two mansions, multigenerational hierarchy, profusion of marriage connections, and flock of vaguely related hangers-on, the Jias and their establishment exceed anything most readers today would define as a family. Readers quickly sense that this family is outsized and also dysfunctional, to use today's pop psychology language, but they are not prepared for the intricate rules of kinship that govern such things as meals, visiting, birthday celebrations, and holidays. Nor can they easily see how daily incidents involving these practices also help readers trace character development and personal relationships, as well as reveal conflicts that supply narrative drive and tension. Leo Tolstoy knew that "each unhappy family is unhappy in its own way" (1). But to gain insight into the Jia family's particular conflicts in the social world of kinship, a world that eighteenth-century readers would have taken for granted, we turn to the insights of anthropologists. Today anthropologists of China look back on a full century of ethnographic field work and are more interested in modern change and regional diversity than in any presumably normative, traditional Chinese family system. But some of the basics of the anthropology of kinship do help us understand the relationships in this fictional household.

To start off, the family is patrilocal, patrilineal, and joint; all its male members are presumed descended from a common apical ancestor. Ethnographers distinguish between the larger group, which is defined ritually by common ancestors, the lineage, and the coresident group, which is the family. Although the family ideal was for several generations to live together and maintain a common purse under the guidance of its senior male, the Ning and Rong are branch lineages that have divided into separate residential units some time before the beginning of the story. However, their mansions are adjoining and the unity of the kin group is made visible in a single ancestral temple, which is dedicated to the memory of their forebears in the fifth ascending generation: two brothers, the duke of Ning-guo and the duke of Rong-guo. Four generations of Jia kin live side by side in the Rong compound, close to the Confucian ideal of five generations under one roof. In ethnographic perspective, relationships in such families are shaped by lineage ritual ties, age and gender hierarchy, and marriage politics.

In such Chinese big families, ritual unity finds expression in the ceremonies performed in the ancestral temple, and it is elaborated by the rules of precedence that order all males by age and generation. The Jia ancestral temple is attached to the Ning-guo mansion, and when Lin Dai-yu arrives at her new home, she must first pay a ceremonial visit to the Ning-guo residence, which is senior, even though she will be sheltered by her grandmother, who belongs to the Rong-guo branch, which is junior. This precedence is based on the instructions of the great neo-Confucian scholar Zhu Xi (1130–1200), mentioned in *Stone* as Zhuxius (3.56.68), which allocated family ritual responsibility according to the principle of primogeniture, vesting it in eldest sons of eldest sons, even though the economics of a joint family were egalitarian, dividing inheritances equally between elder and younger brothers and between male cousins (agnates). Therefore, as often happens in large kin groups, the Ning males tend to be older than their generational peers in the Rong mansion, and the lineage head in ritual matters is Cousin Zhen, who belongs to the same fourth descending generation as Bao-yu and his girl cousins, who are all adolescents. Attuned to such norms, an eighteenth-century reader would quickly sense that the Ning-guo senior males are poor custodians of the family's ritual responsibilities. They would notice that Cousin Zhen is in charge because his father—in fact the eldest Ning-guo male—has abdicated his leadership role by retiring to a Taoist monastery. They would be prepared for the scene in chapter 7 where Cousin Zhen is cursed by the drunken family retainer, Old Jiao, for the sexual scandal that underlies Cousin Zhen's extravagant grief and inappropriately grandiose funeral on the death of his beautiful young daughter-in-law, Qin-shi.

At the Rong-guo mansion there are similar contradictions between ritual role and personal behavior of the two senior men in residence, both middle-aged sons of the matriarch Grandmother Jia. Sir Zheng, father of Bao-yu, is the second son and therefore the ritual junior to his feckless brother Jia She. Sir Zheng's lower position is out of alignment with his prestige as the only successful public official in the family. But neither man pays any attention to the actual management of his complex household and many servants. Nor is the Ning-guo mansion better served by the leadership of Cousin Zhen. If the anthropological stereotype of the patrilineal, patrilocal, joint family system imagines a senior male in charge of the economy and administration of household and lineage, the Jia men all fall short. When the ghost of Qin-shi in chapter 13 warns that a prudent family provides for hard times by setting up a trust for the education of the young and the sacrifices to the dead, she is alluding to the tradition of lineage-based charitable estates long esteemed by Confucian moralists and granted tax advantages by the imperial state. But the Jia men show no interest, and domestic management is left to the women.

The women in a family were assigned ritual rank on the basis of their husbands' rank, in a firmly patriarchial, sex-segregated order, but the reality was more complex. Anthropological analysis of women in a traditional kinship system seems to veer between two poles. One presents women as liminal creatures, who unlike their brothers are only temporary members of their natal families. A woman brought into the family as a bride in an arranged marriage is a stranger, and she threatens the solidarity of brothers and the loyalty of a son to his parents. The strict submission of a young wife to her mother-in-law controls this threat conjugal intimacy poses to a family system based on the hierarchy of age and the privileging of males. The other pole presents a uterine family of mothers and children and a multigenerational matrifocal network that gives older women great authority, albeit informal, in domestic matters, authority in both marriage arrangements and household management.

It is relatively easy to see the liminality of women in the adolescent female cousins of the novel, as their lives move toward the inevitable moment of departure from their natal homes, their fate hostage to the families into which their elders will marry them. Given that arranged marriage remained normative in China down to the middle of the twentieth century, the novel's representation of it as a tragedy for girls (and for sensitive young men like Bao-yu) has been a wellspring of the novel's popularity as well as evidence that the domestication of desire was a familiar and tension-laden issue for eighteenth-century upper-class families. Demographers and anthropologists alike have shown that for young women of good family in this period there were no alternatives to marriage. Spinsterhood was virtually unknown. In *Stone* a Buddhist nun's vocation is portrayed—realistically—as eccentric, bordering on disgraceful, whereas the spinster's respected role as family caretaker is reserved for the life path of a chaste widow, someone like Li Wan, who brings honor to the family by remaining to serve her dead husband's parents. Historically, chaste widowhood was seen by many widows as preferable to a remarriage arranged by the in-laws that would lower the woman's social status and might involve separation from her children. Acknowledging this reality, *Story of the Stone* makes Li Wan more contented and untroubled than her sisters-in-law and cousins-in-law facing the uncertainties of betrothal and marriage.

If *Stone* encourages readers to sympathize with young women as victims of the marriage system, its portrayal of the sex-segregated inner quarters is rich in social detail about the domestic power networks woven out of matrilineal and matrilateral relationships. Such a network exists around Grandmother Jia, one of the great matriarchs of Chinese fiction. Her ritual authority is based on the fact that she is the last surviving member of the fourth ascending generation and on the filial obedience owed her by her adult sons, Jia She and Jia Zheng. Because of this seniority, she goes by her husband's lineage name, Jia, rather than by her natal surname of Shi. However, her female network is the product of many generations of intermarriage in a few rich families, shaped by surname exogamy. While young men are forbidden to marry women with the same surname as their own, the family's women supply candidates from their matrilateral connections. The Shi, Wang, and Xue families have in the two previous generations produced women who married into the Jia lineage, and these ties are parodied in a comic poem in chapter 4. Surnames are the key to unraveling the past that brings to Grandmother Jia (who was born a Shi) visiting granddaughters named Shi (Xiang-yun) and Xue (Bao-chai). But it is the affinal Wang family that is the most intricately woven into the Jia inner quarters. Grandmother Jia's daughter-in-law is Lady Wang, wife of Sir Zheng, and somehow Sir Zheng's brother's son (Jia Lian) has married Lady Wang's brother's daughter, her niece (Wang Xi-feng). Moreover, Aunt Xue, visiting the Rong-guo household from Nanjing with her daughter Xue Bao-chai, turns out to be Lady Wang's younger sister.

English-language readers, used to the relatively impoverished bilateral kinship system of the Anglo-Saxon world, tune out these intricacies, and in any case translations simplify the all-important distinctions between male and female lines of descent incorporated into Chinese kinship nomenclature—distinctions that not only illustrate the role of senior women in marriage negotiations but also provided eighteenth-century readers with social clues as to why Lin Dai-yu was at a disadvantage as a candidate for Bao-yu's hand. At issue is the common traditional practice of cross-cousin marriage.

However utopian their deployment in the novel, visiting customs that bring a circle of young cousins to gather in Prospect Garden reflect female-centered eighteenth-century upper-class practices that eased the isolation of sex segregation for women and also had a potential for aligning romance and marriage. Cross-cousin marriage (among cousins with different surnames) could foster both compatibility in a conjugal couple and the integration of a bride into a household ruled by her mother-in-law. While visiting, matrilateral kin could seek partners for their children and cross cousins could meet decorously as potential mates. The genealogical records of cross-cousin marriage show that matrilateral alliances were more common than patrilateral ones: a niece of a young man's mother was more likely to be chosen as his wife than one of his father. Faced with this network of alliances, Lin Dai-yu, who may also be Grandmother Jia's granddaughter but is the daughter of Sir Zheng's dead sister, is indeed the orphan she claims to be. The union of Xue Bao-chai and Jia Bao-yu would carry the matrilineal marriage ties of these families into the third generation. The power of sisterhood emerges in this unfamiliar familial context as a matron's preference to have her sister's daughter become her own daughter-in-law.

## How Can You Follow Tales of Love If You Don't Know the Rules of the Sexual Game?

A long-haired young man who dresses in medallioned Japanese silk damask and wears a gold coronet, who has servants clothe and bathe him, and who likes to play with women's cosmetics and help women with their makeup—can he be a proper hero? For many of today's student readers, especially males and not just American ones, Bao-yu is a hard sell. They reject him as a playboy: he is spoiled, childish, an overemotional Peter Pan fleeing adulthood, and, to sum up, simply too feminine. Or, they ask, could he be gay? Yet the story provides Bao-yu with a whole gallery of female admirers and a robust array of sexual adventures ranging from dalliances with male actors and liaisons with maidservants to intense if unconsummated love affairs with more than one woman. His appearance and behavior raise questions about the norms of gender difference that prevailed in the eighteenth century. His amorous adventures and relationships raise questions about eighteenth-century understandings of desirability and about the boundaries of acceptable male sexual conduct pertinent to our moral judgments of *Stone*'s exploration of romantic themes.

We want to look first at the prevailing cultural signs of sexual difference and second at the way social factors—the hierarchy of masters and servants, the place of polygamy in the marriage system—order expressions of erotic desire. The adventures of the adolescent hero are given a darker counterpart in the narrative of the sexual lives of senior Jia males, but together they raise a key interpretive issue: was this novel about a profoundly female-identified young man intended to challenge eighteenth-century regimes of gender and sexuality, or did it remain largely bound by them?

In philosophical discourse, the masculine and the feminine were folded into the dynamically interacting cosmological forces of yin and yang. They were aspects, not the foundations, of the resonant binary quality of the world at large: light and dark, fire and water, hot and cold, active and passive, high and low, manifest and latent, and so on. In natural philosophy, yin and yang involved not only opposites but also the ceaseless process of change by which they interacted and transformed each other. In chapter 2, gossiping about the Jia family in a teahouse, Jia Yu-cun sketches a portrait of Bao-yu with a bit of pedantic philosophizing: Bao-yu belongs to the class of people who are neither absolutely good nor absolutely evil but endowed at birth with a mixture of benign and malign humors characteristic of lovers, artists, and aesthetes. The translator's English language of Galenic bodily humors only clumsily communicates a Chinese cosmology of yin and yang forms of the primal stuff of the universe, qi, shaping natural and social worlds and including human temperament and gender identity. The assertion of hybrid possibilities here is congruent with a cultural pattern that makes sexuality an aspect of gender, not essentialized in the body or expressed in specific forms or objects of desire. Since yin-yang qualities are never unmixed and always in dynamic interaction, they supply a relativistic language that allows for the play of personality and temperament in imagining desirability in persons of both sexes.

Consider the reservoir of yin-yang images that evoke temperament and relationships among the main characters. Dai-yu's yin qualities are expressed in her affinity for water and wood and are seen in her frequent tears and her nom de plume (River Queen), while her pavilion hints of scholarly reclusion, and its furnishings, built of speckled bamboo, suggest the tears of an ancient heroine. Her rival, Xue Bao-chai, on the other hand, is symbolically associated with the bright, firm qualities of gold and metal, while her plain taste in clothing and decor hints of Confucian rectitude. What then of the explicitly hybrid Bao-yu, whose yang nature is embodied in the qualities of his jade amulet: hardness, luster, and purity? If there is any other character who matches his complexity—his yang nature as Precious Jade and his yin flight to the inner quarters and the company of women—it might be Wang Xi-feng. She is emphatically yang in temperament, given her managerial competence, which is complemented by her brilliant dress as well as her name (Phoenix, the symbol of fire and the south). Here yin and yang, deemphasizing the reproductive roles or the forms of desire preferred by these two characters, return the reader to the theme of gender, pairing the female-identified hero with a heroine whose masculine talent for leadership and command is corrupted by the social rules confining its expression to domestic management.

As aspects of personality, yin and yang accommodate variation, but the strict hierarchy of social roles defined by gender, kinship, and age remains rigidly bounded. In these social confines, or perhaps because of their rigor, there was ample room for what moderns would call gender-bending play. Following a not uncommon social practice of the time, the Jias pride themselves on giving their girls gender-neutral personal names, a mark of their commitment to educating daughters. Whether cross-dressing accompanied actual elite festivities to the extent suggested by the novel is hard to say, but the adventures of a woman disguised as a man sparked the plot of many popular entertainments. Cross-dressing by both sexes was institutionalized in the sex-segregated world of opera actors and performance. In the eighteenth-century, most opera was performed by single-sex troupes, usually male, which made the circuit of temple fairs and were hired by rich families. Some families had their own troupes, as did the imperial aristocracy. The male actor who specialized in female roles could become a celebrity, courted by powerful men. In the novel, Bijou is such a figure, a royal favorite. But only the power of his patron separates him from the ordinary female impersonator, who was more vulnerable, an eroticized and feminized young male whose function was to entertain—and service—the more privileged men who employed him.[2]

In the novel, male homoeroticism is treated casually, portrayed as schoolboy crushes or youthful flirtations on Bao-yu's part, while incidents involving the older married men, Jia Lian and Cousin Zhen, tend toward encounters during a night of drinking on the town. The tone of the narrative is comic rather than scandalized, but it would be a mistake to take this treatment as evidence for societal tolerance of homosexuality as we understand it today.

The history of Chinese law shows that Qing society treated homosexual and heterosexual transgressions in exactly the same way—conceding sexual power to older, higher-ranking men and punishing those whose sexual acts violated normative gender, age, and status hierarchy. The penetrated male occupied a debased position, and this role could be tolerated in adolescents, who would grow out of it, and it was accepted as natural in the lowborn. In the mocking narrative of the Stone, homoerotic episodes add to the carnival of Jia male dissipations, but they do not construct anyone's sexual identity.

More troubling to modern students is the sexual politics of master-servant relationships, where the issues of hierarchy and gender involve maidservants and their masters, and their mistresses as well. Why, students will ask, should we accept the intimacy of Bao-yu and his maid Aroma as freely entered into, when she is clearly a family bondwoman who belongs to him? And what are we to think of the implied relationship between the maid Patience and Jia Lian, her mistress's husband? If it reflects an eighteenth-century acceptance of the power of upper-class men to command the sexual services of their servants, many Americans will be reminded of the contemporaneous practices of plantation slavery in the United States. Qing law did not protect a servant woman from her master's sexual advances, though it might consider them a mitigating factor if the situation provoked her to violence against him. The novel points to an important difference between American and Chinese forms of human bondage here. In China, the institution of polygamy in theory gave a maidservant a path to legitimize her situation, which wives and mothers could see as either an opportunity or a threat. If the position of a first wife was unassailable, based on rituals arranged by parents and conducted before the ancestral altars, the door remained open to a succession of secondary wives and concubines along a continuum of more or less well defined status. For a wife, the power to select the partners who would share her home and her husband's bed was significant and hard-won, but she was not always able to wield it successfully. Resourceful wives often chose their husband's concubines for them, and moralists praised the wives for their lack of jealousy. However she entered a household, a concubine had to surrender social motherhood of her children to the first wife; it was the price of seeing them acknowledged as legitimate. In this social context it is not surprising that the Aroma–Bao-yu relationship, sanctioned by Lady Wang, feels like a marriage. If we wonder what, for a young man in a polygamous society, counts as a legitimate sexual relationship, the answer is: One his mother or wife approves of.[3]

Although Stone keeps to the premise that all love is carnal, the narrative, in describing the romances of the adolescent hero, must work with the conventions of physical separation and emotional reserve expected of chaste lovers. Because *famous romance of chp 23*

Charlotte Furth 91

the action takes place almost entirely in a large household run according to the gregarious communal practices of Chinese family life, unfamiliar readers can easily miss the significant moments that pass between two people in a crowded room. In a domestic space where a large heated platform bed, a kang, served group seating during the day and was where one unrolled sleeping quilts at bedtime, parents, children, siblings, and cousins often slept together. Servants providing personal attentions might occupy a couch close by their masters or mistresses. Where people are seldom alone, privacy may become a matter of a third party's looking the other way.

In such a gregarious environment, little things matter. Readers can miss the significance accorded a touch on a girl's hand or arm by an eligible young man. In the light of the Confucian axiom that "after the age of seven [boys and girls] do not sit on the same mat," such gestures carried a heightened connotation of impropriety (*Li Ki* 10.51). In the absence of physical expression, romantic feelings might be channeled into exchanges—gifts or poems—which were widely used in other forms of social interaction as well. But the reticence surrounding even verbal expressions of passion was such that one of the tropes of eighteenth-century Chinese romances was that lovers intuit each other's thoughts through wordless communication. *Stone* adopts this stance, portraying Dai-yu as instinctively knowing Bao-yu's heart, and at the same time offers incidents in which two people in love fall into misunderstanding.

It is against this background that a reader may begin to realize that the encounter between Bao-yu and Dai-yu in the garden in chapter 23 is an important love scene. A tête-à-tête over a book, teasing repartee over some lines of verse, soon interrupted, ends with the heroine alone listening to snatches of opera. Her accusation that he is taking advantage of her makes sense when one considers the books and verses they are reading—passages from China's most famous romance, Wang Shifu's *Story of the Western Wing* 西廂記—and the aria she overhears from the equally famous opera, Tang Xianzu's *Peony Pavilion* 牡丹亭, in which the dreaming heroine hears the song of a lover seeking her in a deserted garden. For a modern reader, the setting of a late spring garden scattered with the petals of spent flowers, hinting at Robert Herrick's "Gather ye rosebuds while you may," can evoke transcultural resonances in the carpe diem mode. But imagine a reader who does not recognize allusions to the balcony scene in *Romeo and Juliet*! Saturated with lyrical allusion and metaphor, chapter 23 of *Stone* creates its romantic mood from a literary repertory known and loved by readers—one that showed the power of art to transform emotions, both in the story and in the minds of eighteenth-century readers of the story.

## Is Prospect Garden like a Real Chinese Garden? Or Is It a Chinese Eden?

The dramatic high point of volume 1 of *The Story of the Stone* is chapters 16 through 18, which narrate the building of Prospect Garden and the ceremonial visit there of Bao-yu's exalted older sister, the imperial concubine, whom the garden is designed to honor. For eighteenth-century Chinese, Prospect Garden would have been instantly recognizable as a lavish version of the kind of ornamental landscape any cultured scholar would desire to have at his disposal. From the Song dynasty (960–1279) forward and especially after the sixteenth century, elite Chinese designed and built such scholar gardens, wrote about them, lavished fortunes on their embellishment, and enjoyed them as private retreats. Earlier versions of the scholar garden remained close to agrarian life, a productive horticultural space featuring rural landscape, orchards, vegetable crops, and fishponds. But the famous gardens of the late Ming and high Qing periods (sixteenth through eighteenth centuries) were the hobbies of extremely wealthy men. They were urban, not rural, hidden behind walls instead of embracing vistas, and filled with rare plants and craftily sculpted rocks, and their spatial amplitude was the result of carefully designed illusion rather than park-scale acreage. Enjoying them was about fantasies of withdrawal from the demands of official life, about scholarly leisure, artistic connoisseurship, and luxurious display. The Yangzi River delta city of Suzhou, which in the novel is the birthplace of Lin Dai-yu, is still famous for scholar gardens, which are visited by tourists today much as they were in the eighteenth century. Chinese fans of *Stone* still debate whether any known historical gardens were the inspiration for Cao's invention, pointing to the fact that his wealthy grandfather, an imperial textile commissioner, did in fact construct a garden to receive the Qing emperor Kangxi on one of the emperor's famous southern tours of the empire.

In chapter 17, readers can get a taste of the social and aesthetic conventions that surrounded these gardens as they read about a stroll through the newly finished grounds: the artificial mountain at the entryway; the pavilions and winding paths across streams widening out to ponds; the scattered, half-hidden cottages; a teahouse, temple, and other rustic hideaways; the main reception hall, as one circles around, flanked by a white marble memorial arch. Unfolding as the visitor moves, such a garden never reveals the design of the whole at once but encourages the viewer slowly to weave its individual elements into a comprehensive image of the world in microcosm. Designed for philosophical reflection and with a painterly eye, such a garden leads its owner not to pick up a trowel or prune a bush but to adorn the landscape with words. Bao-yu impresses his father and his father's friends with apt poetical names for particular sites and also makes some critical comments that reflect eighteenth-century debates about the artifice that lay behind such cunning exercises to evoke the natural world.

But despite its historical points of reference, something about Prospect Garden soon begins to strike readers as excessive. Its opulence is nothing less than imperial in scale. Physically separated from the masculine spaces of the Jia households as well as from the city beyond, it becomes an idealized feminine sphere. Under normal practices of sex segregation in a family, one would expect the inner quarters, including gardens, to be used by old and young women alike, together with the men. In Prospect Garden, young unmarried women have taken over the life of poetry, art, and philosophy that the culture expected of the male literatus in his scholar's garden. The narrative that provides residences there only for these women and their single male kinsman, Bao-yu, is extremely implausible, requiring the plot device of an imperial command to be accomplished.

Therefore readers will begin to suspect that Prospect Garden is not only a male fantasy of a life of pleasure surrounded by beautiful women but also a novelist's alternative universe. If English readers start thinking of literary gardens as allegories going back to the Garden of Eden, they are on the right track. Images suggesting its purity are plentiful: it is associated with females, who we are told are made of water while males are made of mud. The maidenly innocence of its genteel inhabitants extends to the vows of chastity of the young lay Buddhist nun Adamantina, who is invited to take up residence in the garden's temple. Much is made of the carefully guarded entrances and exits and of the engineering that diverts the main watercourse, which forms the garden's streams and ponds, through weirs in the walls separating it from the city. In chapter 23, when Dai-yu instructs Bao-yu to bury the fallen blossoms in the clean earth of the garden rather than let them be washed away through the downstream weir to the city outside, the allegory of the garden as a site of innocence and purity, sheltered from the grime and corruption of the mundane world, is expressed at its fullest. The garden is a refuge from what Buddhists call the world of red dust.

Prospect Garden does seem Edenic here, but Buddhist and Christian allegories diverge. Where Eden is the paradise a sinful humanity had to leave in order to know mortal life, Prospect Garden is a place its young residents enter in order to taste the joys that mortal life can offer. It is a playground for youth escaping the burdens of adulthood—career, duty, marriage—yet growing into experience as well. As a microcosm of a cosmic order of flux driven by the dynamic forces of yin and yang, the garden cannot possibly remain unsullied by the human nature of its inhabitants or unchanged by the passage of time its seasonality attests to. Bao-yu and Dai-yu read erotic poetry together, and from this beginning the garden is shadowed by carnality, even as an inescapable part of love, and by loss, because death and departure will overtake its residents. The Buddhist garden of earthly delights is also a vale of tears, and its transitory and ultimately illusory nature must be recognized if mortals are to find true enlightenment.[4]

This Buddhist allegory of Prospect Garden is hinted at in a couple of seemingly casual references that few beginning readers are likely to notice. In designing the garden, the Jias start with the existing All Scents Garden attached to the Ning mansion (1.16.319) in chapter 5. All Scents Garden was the site of the picnic that preceded Bao-yu's famous dream that took place in the adjoining chambers occupied by his ritual aunt Qin-shi. In chapter 17, when Bao-yu tours the newly completed garden with his father and his father's friends, he experiences a strange emotion as he passes through the marble arch leading to the imperial consort's pavilion—"a sign that he must have known a building somewhat like this before" (343) 倒像那裡曾見過的一般 (1: 229). A fantastical literary garden that is devoted to pleasure and love and that recalls the hero's dream of love and evokes in him a sense of the uncanny will lead the reader to realize that Prospect Garden is the Land of Illusion. Eden, emptied of humanity, may remain a pristine ideal; Prospect Garden becomes a Buddhist allegory of experience. It blooms and withers with the ebb and flow of human desires and longings, but it is also a fictional world, imagined, the stuff of dreams.

NOTES

[1] For an example of such development; see the "Chronologies and Maps" in part 1 of this volume.

[2] For more on the workings of yin and yang in *Stone*, see both Schonebaum and Epstein in this volume; for more on gender and sexuality, Sommer in this volume.

[3] For more on maids and bond servants, see both Rawski and Lupke in this volume.

[4] For more on gardens in *Stone*, see Levy in this volume.

# Readership and Reading Practices:
## *The Story of the Stone* in Premodern China

### *Martin Huang*

Ever since the mid–seventeenth century, when commentators, such as Jin Shengtan (1608–61), made popular the practice of fiction commentary, editions of vernacular fiction without accompanying commentary became rare. In commentary editions of fiction, comments are often printed on the top margin of a page and sometimes inserted between the lines; lengthier comments appear at the end of and occasionally before each chapter. It was difficult for a reader to ignore the comments printed alongside the text proper when reading a novel. Reading a work of vernacular fiction therefore often meant reading the words of another reader at the same time. There were also collected commentary editions, such as those of *The Story of the Stone* published in the late nineteenth century, in which comments by different people were printed side by side, highlighting the possibility of different interpretations. The publication of commentary editions of fiction began to lose its popularity at the turn of the twentieth century, when publishers started to produce modern typeset and Western-style punctuated editions of traditional fiction, from which all the earlier commentaries had been expurgated. Consequently, the experience of reading a commentary edition of fiction in traditional China was significantly different from that of reading a reprint edition of the work today.[1]

There is ample documentation of the crucial role played by readers in the long writing process of *The Story of the Stone*. For many decades before the novel saw its first printing in 1791–92, it circulated in the form of hand-copied manuscript among a small group of readers composed mainly of the author's relatives and friends—like many fictional works during that time. On some of these manuscript copies still extant today, which are generally known as the Red Inkstone editions of *The Story of the Stone*, we sometimes come across a commentator's complaint that the author, Cao Xueqin, failed to revise a certain part of the novel according to his suggestions. Sometimes a commentator advised the author to delete a passage. For example, the episode of Qin-shi's affair with her father-in-law, Jia Zhen, in chapter 13 was expurgated by the author because a member of the Red Inkstone group believed that it might be too scandalous, given the novel's autobiographical implications.

Obviously these readers enjoyed a special relationship with the author, and they were not shy about telling him how to write. They seemed pleased to have inside information about his intentions, about the real-life models for the novel's characters, and about how the author's life informed his writing. One commentator suspected that he was the model for Bao-yu. The Red Inkstone commentators were assuming several roles simultaneously: they were readers, commentators, editors, and sometimes even coauthors. Some of their comments became part of the text of the novel in the repeated process of copying, and there were many different versions of the novel in circulation at the same time, a result of the textual mutability often associated with manuscript culture. What added to this mutability was that the novelist died before he could complete the work, as one of the Red Inkstone commentators informs us. That the boundary between author and reader was often blurred granted these commentators a special authority in interpreting, editing, and rewriting the novel. They showed particular interest in the theme of the decline of an aristocratic family, and they liked to read the novel as a family saga. Since none of the Red Inkstone editions go beyond chapter 80, the clues to later chapters provided by their comments became an important source of information as to how the novel was to have been concluded.

Another group of early readers of the novel in manuscript were made mostly of the author's friends and acquaintances, such as Yong Zhong (1735–93) and Ming Yi (b. c. 1740), who probably did not personally know the Red Inkstone commentators. Some were members of the aristocracy, and their responses to the novel often took the form of poetry. One of their central concerns was the question of desire and its ramifications. Their writings on the novel, though not large in quantity, became an important source of information about Cao Xueqin. We know much more about his grandfather, Cao Yin (1658–1712), who was a bond servant and adviser of the Kangxi emperor (r. 1662–1722).

The readership changed dramatically after the 120-chapter *Story of the Stone* (without the Red Inkstone commentary) was first published.[2] It was such an instant hit that a second edition, revised, came out the following year. (The Red Inkstone commentaries, gradually forgotten by the reading public, were rediscovered in the early twentieth century.) The readership rapidly expanded. By the beginning of the nineteenth century, according to Hao Yixing (1757–1825), a renowned scholar of Confucian classics, almost every family in the capital had a copy of the novel. There was even a popular saying that reading all the books and poems available would be useless if one could not carry on a conversation about *The Story of the Stone* commentary (Yisu, *Hongloumeng juan* 354–55).

New commentary editions of the novel appeared in the early 1800s. Among them, the most popular and influential was published by the commentator Wang Xilian (c. 1800–c.1876). Wang's family was involved in the business of book printing, and they once published a new edition of the classic novel *The Romance of the Three Kingdoms*. Wang took advantage of the popularity of *Stone*, and his edition proved to be a great success. Conservative in his views, he read the novel as a cautionary tale about the overindulgence of desire. Emphasis on the didactic function of fiction had long been a tradition in fiction commentary, but Wang was the first to offer detailed analyses of the novel's narrative structure. He divided the novel into twenty-one sections, considering the ups and downs of the Jia family fortunes to be the main trajectory of plot development: for example, section 6 (chs. 17–24) is about the rise of the Jia family, section 11 (53–56) is about the peak of its fortunes, section 14 (70–78) is about its decline, and section 19 (104–12) is about ruination.

Zhang Xinzhi (fl. 1828–50), an itinerant scholar who worked as a secretarial clerk on the staffs of local government officials, was another commentator whose readings of the novel influenced its reception in the last few decades of the nineteenth century. Zhang spent more than twenty years writing comments on the novel, but they were not published in his lifetime. His commentary edition of the novel first appeared in 1877. He read the novel as an elaborate allegory of the idea of self-cultivation as expounded in such core Confucian classics as *The Doctrine of Mean* 中庸 and *The Great Leaning* 大學. *The Book of Changes* 易經 was another Confucian classic he liked to refer to in interpreting the novel.[3]

Yao Xie (1805–64), a book collector, scholar, and prolific writer, was an un-usual commentator in his approach to the novel. Given the enormous length and complexity of the novel, he believed that common readers needed help to understand it, so his comments were intended to be a reading aid or reference tool. He was the first to pay so much attention to the chronology of the novel, to the ages of various characters and inconsistencies among their ages. He was known as the statistician of *The Story of the Stone* for the data he collected: the total number of Jia family members, the total number of their maids, their expenditures, their income. Although known for his keen eye for detail, Yao Xie could also be perceptive on large interpretative issues, such as the structure of the novel. He proposed to divide the novel into three parts: the first four chapters as prologue, chapters 5–116 as the main story, chapters 117–20 as the conclusion.

The comments by Wang Xilian, Zhang Xinzhi, and Yao Xie were published in a collected commentary edition in 1884. It soon became the most popular and influential edition of the novel during the late Qing and early republican periods and saw many reprints.[4] As a result, these three commentators on *The Story of the Stone* were the most prominent at the beginning of the twentieth century.

One issue many commentators dwelled on is the characterization strategies used by the novelist. They divided the characters into different interrelated groups by proposing the concept of *yingzi* 影子 ("reflection" or "shadow").[5] For example, in his comments at the end of chapter 8, Zhang Xinzhi contends that Aroma is the reflection of Bao-chai, Skybright the reflection of Dai-yu (Feng Qiyong et al. 210).[6] The first pair tend to be received favorably by others in the novel thanks to their accommodating personalities and social skills, whereas the second pair often get into trouble because of their assertiveness and short temper. The commentator Hong Qiufan (c. 1815–c. 1889) suggested that if one character has a reflection, the reflection in turn can have a reflection, thus form-ing a group of characters who mirror one another. For example, because they resemble each other in appearance and personality, Skybright is the reflection of Dai-yu, and Fivey is the reflection of Skybright; Aroma is the reflection of Bao-chai, and Musk is the reflection of Aroma (459). A network of reflections results. Agreeing with Zhang Xinzhi that Aroma is Bao-chai's reflection, Hong Qiufan adds that Aroma is reflected in Musk, because both maids are cautious and accommodating. In the novel, someone actually says that Musk is another

Aroma. Consequently, two contrasting groups of characters are led by Dai-yu and Bao-chai, who are often contrasted. A related characterization strategy commentators have drawn readers' attention to is the use of one character as a foil for another. Chen Qitai (1800–64) repeatedly notes that Shi Xiang-yun is a foil to Bao-chai (97). In his comments on chapter 32, Chen points out that Shi Xiang-yun, like Bao-chai, is jealous of Dai-yu but, unlike Bao-chai, who often avoids revealing to others what is on her mind, is almost too straightforward (129). Shi Xiang-yun states what Bao-chai would like to but dares not. Chen Qitai alerts us to many places in the novel where Shi Xiang-yun functions as a mouthpiece for Bao-chai, whose reticent personality gives the author few opportunities to allow the readers to enter directly into her mind. All this analysis of the novelist's characterization techniques reveals the frequent use of intercharacterization strategy to emphasize the collective and relational nature of the characters. Skybright, for example, is constantly compared horizontally — with other maids, such as Aroma and Patience, who have similar importance in the development of plot and similar social status. She is also compared vertically — with Dai-yu and with the maid-actress Parfumée, who differ in their importance in the novel and in their social status. The physical and emotional resemblances between Skybright and Dai-yu are set against the constant contrast between Skybright and Aroma. Readers' understanding of Skybright is therefore always conditioned by their knowledge of other characters.

Many of these commentators' reading strategies remind us of that of close reading made popular by the school of New Criticism in the Anglo-American literary tradition. An example is their interpretation of an episode in chapter 36. Sitting beside Bao-yu, who is taking a nap, Aroma embroiders a pinafore. She has at her side a fly whisk, its handle made of the horn of a white rhinoceros. Bao-chai wonders why Aroma has a fly whisk in the bedroom. After being told that Aroma needs it to drive away small flying insects that bite, Bao-chai points out that such insects breed inside flowers and are attracted to anything fragrant and that they fly in because sweet-smelling flowers are growing outside the house. Later Bao-chai is so drawn to the pattern of mandarin ducks Aroma is embroidering on the pinafore that, when Aroma leaves for a break, Bao-chai sits down at the very same spot. Zhang Xinzhi reads the "fly-whisk with a handle of white rhinoceros-horn" (2.36.201) as a phallic reference, since in traditional erotic literature rhinoceros horn is a common euphemism for the male sexual organ. He further reminds the reader that Bao-chai's remark that "this kind of insect breeds inside of flowers" (201) echoes the line "[the honeybee] pushed and squeezed trying to get inside" (28.57) in the erotic song sung by the prostitute, who entertains Bao-yu and his friends in chapter 28. Commenting on the pinafore and its embroidered patterns and colors, Zhang asks, "What kind of bird is the mandarin duck? What kind of game is taking place among the lotuses? Where is the part of the body that is below the abdomen and is supposed to be covered by the pinafore? What kind of thing is white outside and red inside? All these are extremely significant" 鴛鴦是何鳥？戲蓮是何事？兜在肚

下是何處? 外白裡紅是何象? 此乃點題 (Feng Qiyong et al. 866). It is also in this very symbolic as well as compromising situation that Bao-chai overhears the napping Bao-yu's confession in dream that Bao-yu prefers the marriage of wood and stone over that of gold and jade. Zhang Xinzhi's almost Freudian reading of this episode sheds light on one of the few scenes in the novel where Bao-chai's subconscious is depicted. In the words of Hong Qiufan:

> Bao-chai has been a very thoughtful and careful person all her life. She usually leaves a scene whenever there is the possibility of causing gossip or suspicion. Why should she behave so carelessly in such an intimate situation this time? This must be due to her secret wish to be close to Bao-yu. Being alone with him is exactly what she has been waiting for, just as a honeybee is always attracted to fragrant flowers. The author wants to test the reader's attentiveness by taking advantage of Bao-chai's moment of carelessness. Just recall Bao-chai's deliberate attempt to keep her distance from Bao-yu in chapter 30 to see whether she is really being "careless" here.

> 寶釵一生精細, 到處留心, 形影之間, 亦必籌度行走, 以避嫌疑. 而況孤男曠女, 枕度床帷, 反至漫不經心呼! 分明欲親芳澤, 竊喜無人, 如小蟲只聞香即撲. 作者稱其不留心, 特以試讀者之眼力耳. 如謂真不留心, 則請回憶第三十回中 "遠著寶玉" 之言便悟.
> (881)

Another group of commentators read *The Story of the Stone* as a roman à clef, although this approach began to be in fashion only in the early twentieth century. Some interpreted the entire novel as an elaborate account of the love affair between the first emperor of the Qing dynasty and Consort Dong Xiaowan and the palace intrigues during the mid–seventeenth century or as a veiled criticism of the Manchu regime. The rise of the so-called modern study of *Stone*, initiated by scholars such as Hu Shi, resulted from the attempt to refute that approach by shifting the focus to the author of the novel and by emphasizing its autobiographical implications. The roman à clef approach proved to be of little value from the perspective of literary analysis, but it appealed to many readers at that time. New readings that use this approach are still being proposed by some Chinese critics, only now the novel is interpreted as a narrative about the palace intrigues during reign of the Yongzheng emperor (1723–35).

To appreciate fully the reception of *Stone* in the history of the Chinese novel, we should not overlook the new role of the female audience. *Stone* is the first traditional Chinese novel for which we have substantial documented evidence of a large female readership. Its popularity even led a woman author to try her hand as fiction writer. Gu Taiqing's (1799–1877) sequel to *Stone*, titled *In the Shadow of* Dream of the Red Chamber, first published in 1874, was also the first Chinese novel that could be identified with certainty as written by a woman (for sequels to *The Story of the Stone*, see McMahon in this volume). There is little information available on women readers or writers of fiction before *Stone*, although we have ample evidence of women's deep involvement in poetry and drama. Some scholars have speculated that many authors of the so-called scholar-beauty fiction in the late seventeenth and early eighteenth centuries might have had female readers as the targeted audience, but so far there is not much evidence to substantiate that claim. The history of the Chinese novel is quite different from that of the Western novel. The English novel, for example, relied heavily on women's active participation as both authors and readers.

Unlike the earlier classic novels of the Ming dynasty, such as *The Romance of the Three Kingdoms* (Luo Guanzhong), *Outlaws of the Marsh* (*The Water Margin*) (Shi and Luo), *The Journey to the West* (Wu Cheng'en), and *The Plum in the Golden Vase*, something in this eighteenth-century novel's subject matter and style struck a chord among the literate women. While works such as *The Plum in the Golden Vase* are also about domesticity and private passion, *The Story of the Stone* seems to deal with these topics in a manner much less scandalous so that boudoir readers can openly acknowledge their involvement as fiction readers, commentators, and even authors. Hong Qiufan observes, "*The Story of the Stone* demonstrates the deepest respect for the boudoir. Its description is seldom explicit when it comes to sex. The only exceptions are a few cases where those involved are all vulgar characters" "紅樓" 一書最尊重閨閣, 凡曖昧事皆不明寫, 有明寫者, 率皆不等人物 (166). *Stone* seems to have shown more delicacy toward gentlewomen and boudoir women, the main component of its female readership.

An early female reader who left her impressions of the novel in the form of writing is Zhou Qi. Her husband was none other than the commentator Wang Xilian. Her poems on the novel are printed in his commentary edition of the novel. She apparently gained access to *Stone* through her husband and probably contributed to his commentary project with her own readings. In a preface to her poems on the novel, she recounts a dream she had in which she defended herself against criticism by a conservative man who said that women should have nothing to do with writing poems, not to mention writing poems on a novel such as *The Story of the Stone* (see Widmer, *Beauty* 151). So women still faced strong opposition with regard to their roles as readers of fiction, even though some of them were supported by the male members of their families. Zhou Qi's preface suggests that there was a large group of women who read and even commented on fictional works in defiance of their society's disapproval.

Many women in nineteenth-century China were able to read openly *The Story of the Stone* because of the tolerant family environment they lived in. They typically read the novel with family members and were able to exchange views on it with one another. For example, in a collection of a hundred poems on *Stone* published during the Tongzhi period (1862–74), two dozen are by several women who were closely related or friends. Two of these women were the first and second wives of the compiler of the book, the Master of Western Garden; the third was his sister-in-law, the fourth a friend of the first wife, and the fifth the sister-in-law of the second wife. One has the impression there was a family salon devoted to the reading of *Stone*. For these women readers, the preferred medium of commentary was poetry, the most accepted literary form of self-expression for women in late imperial China. Another way to comment on the novel was writing prefaces for publications related to it. Quite a few women authors contributed prefaces to sequels of *Stone*, in the form of a prose essay.

So far we have found no edition of *Stone* or critical monograph on the novel that was compiled or authored by a woman from that period, although we know that some women were involved in commentary projects by men. In his comments on the novel, Hong Qiufan frequently refers to and even quotes a certain Lotus Fairy Female Historian, who was one of his pupils. He considered her to be his friend and fellow reader. Sometimes he quotes her to support or corroborate his own interpretation of the novel, praising her as an insightful reader not only of the novel but also of his readings of it (88); at other times, he recounts how the two debated (1572–73), suggesting the deep involvement of this female reader in his project of commentary.

An anecdote often mentioned as a proof of readers' passions about *Stone* is how some came to blows when they chose sides between Dai-yu and Bao-chai, the two rivals in the love triangle with Bao-yu. Interestingly enough, the division between Dai-yu supporters and Bao-chai supporters was confined to the male readers; there was no such division among women readers. To the best of my knowledge, few women readers from that period were negative toward Dai-yu in their writings on the novel. On the contrary, they were almost unanimous in their admiration of her. Dai-yu, who is far more assertive than Bao-chai and more inclined to jealousy in her love for Bao-yu, no doubt had less appeal to male readers in a society where jealousy of a woman was a problem for a husband with more than one wife. Dai-yu must have won sympathy from female readers trapped in a polygamous household where they were not supposed to complain about unfairness. It has been reported that some female readers were so heartbroken after reading *The Story of the Stone*, empathizing with Dai-yu for her sad fate, that they literally died. A careful examination of women's reception of the novel should help us better appreciate the gendered nature of fiction reading in late imperial China.

The role of *The Story of the Stone* in changing the gender composition of the audience for fiction is a question worth further exploration (Widmer, *Beauty* 181–277). The novel certainly provoked unprecedented enthusiasm from female readers, and the traditional prejudice against women reading fiction seems to have lessened considerably as a result of the popularity of this novel.

## NOTES

[1] For a comprehensive study of Chinese fiction commentary, see Rolston, *Traditional Chinese Fiction*. See also Rolston, *How to Read*. Fiction commentary saw a limited revival in recent decades in China, although it was mainly confined to works of classic fiction from the premodern period. The novelist Wang Meng published his own

commentary edition of *The Story of the Stone* in 1995, and its revision appeared in 2005. More recently (2009), the critic Zhou Ruchang put out a commentary edition, placing his commentary alongside those of the Red Inkstone.

2 The editors explained that they did not reprint the commentaries from the hand-copied manuscripts because they did not want the already long novel to become even longer. See their "Joint Foreword," translated in *Stone* (4.388).

3 For more information on Zhang Xinzhi and an English translation of some of his commentaries on the novel, see Rolston, *How to Read* 316–40.

4 A page from one of these reprints is shown in figure 4 in the "Materials" part of this volume.

5 *Yingzi* may bring to mind the Western concept of double: one character mirrors another. But it does not have the strong psychological implication of the double, in that the reflection does not necessarily imply a split self. Both a character and its reflection usually maintain independent status as a novelistic entity. *Yingzi* is a concept more rhetorical than psychological, although there can be psychological affinity between a character and its reflection.

6 All subsequent references in my discussion of the nineteenth-century commentators' readings of the novel are, unless-otherwise noted, to Feng Qiyong et al.

# The End of *Stone*

## Tina Lu

By the middle of the eighteenth century, the books that most people read were imprints prepared for commercial publication. In contrast, *The Story of the Stone* was neither circulated in a marketplace nor an imprint. The novel was written to be read, of course—but not to be purchased. It appeared only in manuscript during its writer's lifetime and was passed around in hand-copied versions from acquaintance to acquaintance. (My students have been known to complain when we attempt to read the whole novel over the course of a semester; imagine copying out by hand what in English translation would run over 1,700 pages.) Martin Huang writes of how odd a premodern person would find our current texts, stripped of commentary and paratext, a chorus of readers reduced to a solo authority ("Author[ity]"). Cao Xueqin himself no doubt would be shocked to know that all modern readers encounter his work through mass-produced imprints.

Eleven hand-copied versions have emerged that date from before the first printed version of 1791–92. They are all slightly different, and it is certain that others (perhaps many others) circulated but have since been lost. The earliest manuscript bears the date 1754, about a decade before Cao Xueqin's death. David Hawkes's translation of the first eighty chapters does not follow any single edition but rather picks and chooses—in many respects the only reasonable decision under the circumstances—since among these manuscripts there is simply no such thing as a definitive version, and even within manuscripts there are minor, but insuperable, internal contradictions.

Scholars have argued that our notion of an authoritative version might be a product of print culture, in which the author's control of a final text makes economic sense. Manuscripts that reflect an author's process are much more fluid, and *Stone*'s surviving manuscripts are marked not just by different copyists' errors but also by significant differences. For example, in the first chapter of Hawkes's translation (based on the 1791–92 imprint), the Stone is a passive object carried off to the mortal world by the monk, but in the 1754 manuscript the Stone actively appeals to the monk and the Taoist before they agree to take him.

Differences among versions arose in part through how the manuscripts were circulated, among close friends and relations whose opinions and comments might have shaped a new draft. What must have happened is that one copy was returned to Cao Xueqin and then sent to someone else, while another version, shaped by those comments, was being written, soon to be sent out. Since the readers were all people Cao Xueqin knew, these first commentaries all speak not just of intimacy with him but also of familiarity with the events described in the novel—hence such references to shared experience as "I was there" and "I remember it as if it were yesterday." Many scholars guess that the two most important commentators, Red Inkstone and Odd Tablet, were relatives of Cao Xueqin, and episodes like Qin-shi's untimely death in chapter 15 shed light on how complicated the relationship was among the text, the author, and these early commentators. Odd Tablet urged the author to alter Qin-shi's story, presumably because in its original form he found something too scandalous about it. In some ways the authorship of these early chapters, surviving in multiple forms and shaped by input from friends, is a matter of just as much critical interest as that of the concluding chapters.

Some of these early manuscripts are quite short (the 1754 manuscript contains only sixteen chapters) and none of them extend past chapter 80, or the end of Hawkes's volume 3. At this point of the novel, even though the reader has plenty of hints as to what happens later, the two main plotlines — namely, what happens to the household as a whole and how each of the cousins is to marry and become fully adult — remain almost entirely unresolved. We know that the Jias will run afoul of the emperor and meet with financial ruin; we know that Bao-yu and Dai-yu will not marry; we know that the Stone will finally attain enlightenment; through the rebuses in chapter 5, we even know something of the fates of the female cousins.

The first generation of readers had to satisfy itself with that vague sense of how things would turn out. In contrast, the 1791–92 imprint contains 120 chapters and continues to the novel's end. In its preface (translated in its entirety at the end of Minford's volume 4 [385–88]), the bibliophile Cheng Weiyuan explains that he was able to gather together from multiple sources enough fragments to assemble a skeletal conclusion to the novel. He goes on to add that he sought the help of his friend Gao E in "removing what seemed superfluous and making good any gaps" (385) 細加釐剔, 截長補短 (Feng Qiyong et al. 1). Cheng Weiyuan does not know who wrote the novel and insists that he and Gao E served only an editorial function.

The claims of Cheng Weiyuan invite some suspicion. The two main ones here do not even quite square: if all the extant copies end at chapter 80, how was he able to buy chapters piecemeal, searching everywhere "from antiquarian book collectors to piles of old discarded papers" (385) 自藏書家甚至故紙堆中, culminating with the purchase of ten chapters all at once from a peddler? And if he was able to gather thirty-odd chapters, why has no fragment beyond chapter 80 ever surfaced from any other source? We may assume that as popular as the novel was, other early collectors would have sought out copies in the marketplaces of Beijing. But in the two centuries since, no other fragment beyond chapter 80 has ever resurfaced, even as many versions of the first chapters have.

Nonetheless, despite these peculiar claims as to the conclusion's provenance, commentators and readers from the nineteenth century did not approach the last third of the novel any differently than they did the first two-thirds. Nor should their acceptance of the conclusion surprise us, because in many respects these forty chapters do an admirable job of tying up the threads from the first eighty. They contain some of what traditional readers considered the novel's most memorable scenes, as, for example, when Dai-yu staggers from her deathbed to burn the handkerchiefs that were given to her as a gift from Bao-yu and that she inscribed with poems.

The last chapters also contain much of the novel's plot. Bao-yu's jade mysteriously goes missing, and Bao-yu descends into a state of idiocy. After years of putting it off, Grandmother Jia and Lady Wang finally decide on his bride: they arrange a match with Bao-chai, whose mother is in no position to protest since she is heavily relying on the Jias' money and power to rescue her son, Xue Pan, who is in legal trouble yet again. Instead of dealing with the idiotic Bao-yu's displeasure, Xi-feng comes up with the plan of tricking Bao-yu into thinking that his bride is actually his beloved Dai-yu, who tragically dies at the very moment he marries Bao-chai.

The family's fortunes decline when Jia Zheng is dismissed from his office and the imperial concubine Yuan-chun dies. Shortly thereafter, the Ning-guo house is raided. Financial ruin seems to be averted when Grandmother Jia disperses many of her belongings, but then the household is robbed. Gradually, Bao-yu recovers his mind but develops a newfound emotional detachment. After he and Jia Lan take the examinations, he disappears. When the family is forgiven and redeemed after the boys pass, it is in permanently reduced circumstances.

The actual fall of the family is ingeniously and carefully constructed, picking up threads from earlier subplots. During the raid, Officer Zhao finds a chest full of promissory notes, evidence of Xi-feng's usurious loans (issued not solely to enrich herself but also to keep the profligate household afloat). The Embroidered Jackets who search the Jia household carry an imperial edict accusing Jia She of having abused the power of his office against commoners. Much earlier, in chapter 48, after hearing of a phenomenal collection of fans owned by a poor man named Stony, Jia She tries to buy them; when Stony refuses, Jia Yucun cooks up false charges against him and presents the fans to Jia She as a gift after Stony is thrown in jail. In another incident, which spans chapters 65 to 69, Jia Lian takes as a chamber wife You Erjie, but he so fears his wife's jealousy that he keeps the relationship a secret from her. When Xi-feng finds out, she pretends to welcome the girl into the Jia household but secretly seeks out Erjie's childhood fiancé, Zhang San, who has descended into poverty. The match was dissolved with no hard feelings on either side, but Xi-feng forces money on him to bring charges against Jia Lian for wife stealing. As we find out later from a conversation overheard by the servant Bao Yong, these allegations against the Jias were initiated by Jia Yu-cun, afraid that misbehavior on the part of the Jias will implicate him.

Nonetheless, despite the seamless way in which the plot of the last forty chapters picks up threads from the opening, once modern philological techniques were directed toward the novel, the last third was vulnerable to charges that it was not only inferior but forged. Many scholars of the novel, including the leading lights of the New Redology—study of the novel informed by rigorous philological analysis—disapproved of the ending. In the early part of the twentieth century, Hu Shi and Yu Pingbo identified the author of the first eighty chapters as Cao Xueqin and the author of the last forty as Gao E. Scholars of a later generation took it further: to men like Zhou Ruchang, study of the novel involves scraping away all evidence of these false forty chapters and attempting to restore Cao Xueqin's "own" conclusion. On the basis of hints from the first eighty chapters, Zhou Ruchang even wrote a reconstructed twenty-eight-chapter conclusion (*Hongloumeng de zhengushi*).

The anger directed toward Gao E is colored by residual anti-Manchu sentiment. In her essay in this volume, Evelyn Rawski, among others, has written about the ambiguous ethnic status of the real-life Caos and the fictional Jias. We might call them culturally hybrid. In contrast, Gao E was simply a Manchu, and some scholars have attributed the conclusion's political stance to his desire to suppress the novel's seditious tone or at least to shape the novel to hew more closely to safe political sentiments. (But note that the novel was circulated pseudonymously not to avoid political reprisal. It is characteristic of the genre that premodern novels did not carry their authors' names.)

The positions are entrenched. Some sinologists, like Anthony Yu, believe the final chapters to be authentic; others, like Wai-yee Li, believe them to be second-rate and fraudulent (*Enchantment*). Although most of the evidence has been scoured again and again, no incontrovertible argument has been made. However, I believe that the preponderance of the evidence lies on the side of Cheng Weiyuan's preface. I find convincing some version of what he writes there — that the final chapters are largely the work of the author of the first eighty and that Gao E's work was primarily editorial. For one thing, the two halves of the novel are not on equal epistemological footing, since it is far easier to disprove than to prove. For all the new redologists' certainty as to the fraudulent nature of the last forty chapters, attempts to expose them definitively as false have not been successful. One very persuasive computer analysis of stylistic markers points to a single author for all one hundred twenty chapters (B. Chan).[1]

In 1959, a 120-chapter manuscript version of the novel was discovered, dating to the Qianlong reign. To those who believe Cheng Weiyuan's preface, this manuscript is rock-solid proof. But some discredit its independent transmission. Like the imprints, it is titled *Dream of the Red Chamber*, whereas the earlier manuscripts were called *Story of the Stone*. Furthermore, this manuscript's versions of various chapters draw on other manuscripts. Even the explicit reference to Gao E at the end of chapter 78 — "read by Lan Shu" 蘭墅閱過 (Gao E's style) — is to some evidence that supports Cheng Weiyuan's preface, while to others it is damning proof that this manuscript too was contaminated by him.

Though Cheng Weiyuan was probably prevaricating when he described how he acquired them, somehow he did come to possess skeletal versions of the last forty chapters that were authored by Cao Xueqin. His account of how his friend Gao E stitched these together and filled lacunae to construct a coherent narrative rings true. Any quick inspection of the novel's sequels (see Keith McMahon's essay in this volume) reveals how poorly writers just a few generations removed treated the same material.

But parts of the conclusion are clearly the product of another hand. One of the most convincing arguments against the authenticity of the second half is based not on stylistic differences but on a close reading of the conclusion. Huang suggests that we might approach the novel's conclusion as if it were a sequel ("Boundaries"). Clearly the last few pages couldn't have been written by Cao Xueqin. In chapter 120, the monk rereads the inscription on the Stone and observes that what was left incomplete before has been finished:

> But at the time it was unfinished; the cycle within it was incomplete. There was in the earlier version none of the material relating the Stone's return to the source. I wonder when this rather admirable last installment can have been added? (5.120.374)

> 我從前見石兄這段奇文, 原說可以閱世傳奇, 所以曾經抄錄, 但未見返本還原. 不知何時復有此一佳話? (2: 1604)

This certainly sounds like a tongue-in-cheek explanation added by a later editor. Vanitas's plans that follow are even more suggestive: "I had better copy it down again in this complete form and find someone in the world with leisure on his hands to publish it and transmit its message" (374) 你這抄錄的尚無舛錯, 我只指與你一個人, 托他傳去, 便可歸結這一新鮮公案了 (1604). In chapter 1, the Stone with the story inscribed on it is transmitted from one person to another, just as the manuscript was. (Vanitas carries the Stone around; it is passed to a series of redactors.) In chapter 120, Vanitas has turned into an editor whose work represents the penultimate step before publication. The beginning and end allude to very different circumstances of writing and transmission. If the novel's wonderful opening is a meditation on the manuscript, passed from hand to hand and transformed by each contact, then the novel's conclusion concerns the circumstances that led to publication, so the inscribed Stone has turned into something like a carved woodblock.

Some criticisms of the conclusion arise out of misplaced expectations. It is important to recall that standards for the conclusion of late imperial long fiction were quite different from our ideas about how a novel ought to end. Even when a single authorship is not in dispute, Chinese novels often do not tie up threads carefully. Complaints that scholars have leveled against the last few chapters of the late-sixteenth-century novel *The Plum in the Golden Vase* (the single greatest influence on *The Story of the Stone*) include the hastiness of the plot's resolution and the moral simplicity of the conclusion—ceteris paribus, the same criticisms, though somewhat milder, leveled at *Stone*'s ending, even though no one suggests that the last chapters of *Plum* are a forgery. So in and of itself, the failure of *Stone* to follow through on suggestions from earlier in the novel (especially the predictions in chapter 5 for the characters' fates) is not decisive one way or the other.

Taking a step back, we can see that two distinct problems have been unfortunately conflated: that of quality, whether the end measures up to the beginning, and that of authorship, or whether the beginning and end were written by the same hand. On the question of quality, there is some agreement. Even a casual modern reader approaching the text in translation senses that the last forty chapters have a different feel from those preceding, and not just because Hawkes has passed on the task to John Minford: time moves at a different pace, the chapters are linked in such a way as to speed through exposition, the characters are depicted in a more simplistic light, and each of the various subplots moves toward a resolution colored by moral judgment.

Minford's assessment of these last forty chapters, inseparable from his short biographical sketch of Gao E, should be taken with more than a grain of salt. Minford accepts Cheng Weiyuan's explanation but attributes the difference in tone between the two parts of the novel to the differences between Cao Xueqin's and Gao E's lives. Cao Xueqin was an aristocratic dissolute; Gao E came from a well-connected banner family, succeeded in the examinations in middle age, and occupied minor but respectable offices until his retirement in old age. Minford goes on to mesh much of the novel's conclusion with what we know about Gao E: in his view, a series of family losses that struck just as Gao E must have been writing explains why volume 4 speaks in so affecting a way of life's tragedies. He suggests that Gao E was less able to tap into his own experiences for the last few chapters, which explains why they are less satisfactory than those preceding.

Minford makes the same primary assumption as the Chinese scholars of the novel, conflating authorship and literary quality, when in fact we ought to keep them separate, if for no other reason than that we have so little information about either Cao Xueqin or Gao E. Using Gao E's other writings to prove that the second-rate nature of the last forty chapters means they must be the product of his brush leaves us with the logically consistent imperative to examine Cao Xueqin's other writings, but those are almost nonexistent. Instead of conceiving of Gao E as a hack and Cao Xueqin as a genius who could do no wrong and thus attributing the worst parts of the novel to the one and the best to the other, let us consider why the novel abruptly changes at chapter 80. If there is something special about this place in the novel, the last forty chapters must sound different, no matter who wrote them.

The entire middle portion of the novel—loosely speaking, volumes 2 and 3—carefully steers away from treating either of the two major plot arcs, the fates of the young people (especially Bao-yu) and of the household as a whole. Instead, after volume 1, the novel introduces a number of minor characters, many of whom, like Xue Baoqin, a mix of Bao-chai and Dai-yu in temperament, bear a certain morphological resemblance to the original cousins. These characters are brought in gradually until we are told, in chapter 49, that the garden is replete with doubles:

> The Garden's society was now larger and livelier than it had ever been before. With Li Wan as its doyenne it numbered—if you counted Xi-feng

as an honorary member—thirteen people: Li Wan, Ying-chun, Tan-chun, Xi-chun, Bao-chai, Dai-yu, Xiang-yun, Li Wen, Li Qi, Bao-qin, Xing Xiu-yan, Bao-yu, and Xi-feng. Apart from the two young married women, the rest were all fifteen, sixteen or seventeen years old. Most of them were in fact born in the same year, several of them in the same month or even on the same day.    (2.473)

此時大觀園中比先更熱鬧了多少. 李紈為首, 餘者迎春, 探春, 惜春, 寶釵, 黛玉, 湘雲, 李紋, 李綺, 寶琴, 邢岫煙, 再添上鳳姐兒和寶玉, 一共十三個. 敘起年庚, 除李紈年紀最長, 他十二個人皆不過十五六七歲, 或有這三個同年, 或有那五個共歲, 或有這兩個同月同日.    (1: 657)

If, as is clear in chapter 8, when Bao-chai shows Bao-yu her gold pendant, Bao-chai and Dai-yu are Bao-yu's main emotional attachments, over the course of the next volumes, the two young women each gradually accumulate proxy after proxy. The connection of the proxies to the Jias becomes increasingly dilute, and as characters the proxies become less and less distinctive. When we examine the character lists at the end of each volume, each list is longer than the last. By volume 3, Hawkes lists well over two hundred characters.

This growth cannot be sustained. Chinese fiction—and perhaps especially late imperial Chinese fiction—always struggles to balance too few characters (whose interaction cannot propel plot) with too many (whose connection with one another attenuates to nothingness). In volume 3, our ability to keep characters straight is strained. A number of the inconsistencies scholars have found in the first eighty chapters can be explained by the difficulty of juggling several hundred characters. For example, Hawkes's translation cleans up confusion in the original texts among several of the servants, including Bao-yu's page Tealeaf, whose name changed in midstream.

Other patterns established earlier have also reached the breaking point. Volume 3 as a whole depicts what is very much the last season of the characters' childhoods: we are now several years after Bao-yu's sexual awakening, and Bao-chai is two years older than Bao-yu. It becomes more and more improbable that no one has given serious thought to these young adults' marital futures.

Volume 3 concludes with two events that foreshadow the resolution of the two main narrative arcs: the ransacking of the Garden and the death of Skybright. There are hints throughout the novel that Aroma is a stand-in for Bao-chai and Skybright the same for Dai-yu. In selecting a concubine for Bao-yu, Lady Wang chooses between the two maids, just as later she will choose one cousin to be Bao-yu's bride. Like Bao-chai, levelheaded Aroma is well liked by the adult women, while spirited, sharp-tongued Skybright, whose physical resemblance to Dai-yu is remarked on several times, inspires Lady Wang's dislike. In chapter 77, having lost favor with Lady Wang, Skybright is turned out of the household and dies alone and neglected, and her death sends Bao-yu into a tailspin of grief. This death is an emotional proxy for Dai-yu's eventual death.

The decline of the Jia household has become more marked, but nothing definitive happens. In place of the ransacking of the household that will take place in chapter 105, chapter 74 relates how Lady Wang orders a search of the Garden, after Lady Xing sends her a little purse she found with a pornographic picture embroidered on it. Outraged and brokenhearted, Tan-chun compares this ransacking with the one to come:

> The searching will begin soon enough in this household when the day of confiscation arrives. Didn't you hear the news this morning about the Zhens? *They* tempted fate, just as we are now doing, by carrying out a quite unnecessary search of their own servants, and now there is a confiscation order against them and they are being searched themselves. (471)

> 你們別忙, 自然連你們抄的日子有呢! 你們今日早起不曾議論甄家, 自己
> 家里好好的抄家, 果然今日真抄了.                                          (2: 1030)

Culminating in a confrontation between Tan-chun and an older servant, the search of the girls' private quarters seems a violation that can scarcely be topped—and indeed, in literary terms, it is not topped by the imperial search that takes place in volume 4.

Though Skybright's death and the Garden's ransacking prepare us for the denouement, neither does anything to forward the plot. Nonetheless they are depicted with such emotion that Dai-yu's death and the mansion's search seem anticlimactic when they come, and it is impossible to imagine another ten or twenty chapters in the same vein: no new characters can be added, and further disasters cannot compete with those that have already taken place. From the perspective of narrative, chapter 80 seems a critical breaking point. The same pace and tone that have carried the novel thus far must be abandoned.

One of the main criticisms readers have had of the final forty chapters is that so much plot has been deferred that when the text finally does recount what happens, the effect is that of mechanical exposition. No chapter of the last forty fails to contribute to the interlocking narratives of the family's fate and Bao-yu's marriage, whereas one might almost say that none of the previous forty do. More than a hundred chapters recount the family's decline, but the raid on the household, their period of humiliation, and the restoration of their fortunes take place over the course of just fifteen chapters.

The other main criticism of the conclusion has to do with its moralizing tone, so different from the rest of the novel. But that too can be explained by a problem in narrative that comes to a head in chapter 80. Why was this novel so difficult to end? Why—no matter what their authorship—is the tone of the concluding chapters so different from that of the chapters preceding? Traditional commentators of Chinese fiction tended to read texts moralistically, and all writers knew that their characters were being judged by readers. *Stone* occupies a curious position vis-à-vis the values of mainstream eighteenth-century

Chinese society, which were frugality, study, chastity, and obedience. While in general the period represents the high watermark for the straitlaced values of Confucianism, Bao-yu and Dai-yu are both uncomfortable in its confines. The cousins' moment of greatest communion takes place in chapter 34, after Bao-yu has been beaten almost to death by his father for his various moral failings—not just for his possible dalliance with a maid but also for his refusal to study. Dai-yu is anxious for Bao-yu's life but almost equally anxious that he may change. He reassures her by dismissing his father and the orthodox social values he embodies: "I wouldn't change if he killed me" (2.159) 就便為這些人死了, 也是情願的! (1: 452).

Just as much as the two overarching narratives of family decline and Bao-yu's marriage, this conflict must be resolved at the novel's end: the novel must choose whether it subscribes to mainstream values or to what for its time were countercultural ones. Is the Jias' profligate lifestyle to be condemned or enjoyed? Is Bao-yu's refusal to study to be celebrated or corrected? For most of the novel, the novel revels in adopting both positions. Take a scene like this one, in which Bao-yu pontificates cheerfully to Skybright about objects:

> These things are there for our use. What we use them *for* is a matter of individual taste. For example, fans are made for fanning with; but if you prefer to tear them up because it gives you pleasure, there's no reason why you shouldn't. What you *mustn't* do is to use them as objects to vent your anger on.
> (2.31.116)

> 這些東西原不過是借人所用, 你愛這樣, 我愛那樣, 各自性情不同. 比如那扇子原是扇的, 你要撕着玩也可以使得, 只是不可生氣時拿他出氣.
> (1: 422)

She mischievously takes him for his word and asks for his fan to tear. Bao-yu laughs as she rips it apart. Another maid comes in and scolds them both, whereupon Bao-yu seizes *her* fan and hands it to Skybright to tear: "The two of them, Bao-yu and Skybright, then burst into uproarious laughter" (117) 二人都大笑 (422). Bao-yu's playfulness and the smallness of the stakes mean that we can simultaneously recognize Bao-yu's wastefulness and appreciate his joie de vivre.

But other scenes force us to pick one position. Consider the scene in which Bao-yu visits Dai-yu, who is taking a nap. He climbs into bed with her, and the two cousins chat facing each other. After he threatens to tickle her, he tells her a whimsical story about mice. Is this innocent play between children, to be celebrated, or an inappropriate flirtation that can take place only in a household where the adults have entirely abdicated responsibility?

The ambiguity is even more unsustainable when we must appraise a character as a whole. We may sympathize with Bao-yu, whose antipathy to study sets him outside mainstream values, but are we meant to go so far as to admire him? Jia Lan, Li Wan's son and Bao-yu's nephew, is brought up carefully by his widowed mother; he is studious and well-behaved, perfectly comfortable with orthodoxy, everything that Bao-yu is not. Are we as readers to regard Jia Lan as his mother's reward for her sacrifices or to disdain him because of his limitations? For much of the novel, the answer is both, and our censure of him is mitigated by his extreme youth. These ambiguities of character can be maintained for eighty chapters, but eventually the novel must choose sides.

Volume 5 suggests that Jia Lan is praiseworthy: after passing the examinations, he represents the family's redemption and future. But in rejecting the 1791–92 imprint, Zhou Ruchang has an altogether different reading of the character (*Hongloumeng de zhengushi*). In his reconstruction of how the novel was meant to end, Jia Lan is a hypocritical villain, almost as bad as Bao-yu's half-brother Jia Huan; instead of helping his cousin Qiao-jie (the victim of Jia Huan's plotting) in her hour of need, he preaches sanctimoniously to her. There is no evidence in any version of the first eighty chapters of anything so vicious in Jia Lan's character.

Zhou Ruchang's choice of a position diametrically opposed to that of the 1791 edition is illustrative. In general, modern readers find the novel's countercultural figures more sympathetic than the conforming ones. The distance between us and eighteenth-century values is especially great when we try to imagine the entire framework of belief in China then. In the twentieth century, those traditional values had become so withered and impoverished that an ethical and internally rich life based on them was impossible to conceive. In that eighteenth-century state, imperial institutions like the examinations possessed a great vitality, and even someone like the free-spirited Cao Xueqin, who seems never to have seriously attempted an official career, could not entirely escape its pull. For both him and Gao E, it was possible to be an upstanding citizen and morally whole person in the framework of mainstream eighteenth-century values.

We might think of the first eighty chapters as hypotheticals whose full range cannot be treated. Throughout the novel, there are hints of dissatisfaction over many features of the status quo: concubinage, the status of maids and bond servants, even arranged marriage and the status of women more broadly. We get close to an experiential sense of how difficult and cruelly unfair life could be for a young woman in the eighteenth century—for Dai-yu and for women as different from one another as Caltrop, Tan-chun, and Skybright. Still, it is important to distinguish between these imagined life histories and a systematic critique. It seems to have been impossible to imagine a world without an emperor, without families organized around patriarchies, without the imperative to leave male heirs. In the absence of such a critique—impossible to form in 1750, impossible to avoid in 2000—Jia Lan is not a villain but a rather bland young boy, more wholesome but duller than his uncle.

I began work on this volume ten years, two universities, and four children ago. Back then I thought that the project was a simple one of interpretation: to gather together sinologists to serve as native informants who would explain the novel to nonspecialists in American colleges and universities. Things look a little different now. The last decade has seen unparalleled growth in the Chinese economy and vigor in the Chinese cultural sphere, and it has become clearer than ever that no matter how many Anglophones read the novel, non-Chinese will never constitute more than the tiniest portion of the novel's readership.

In 2005, Liu Xinwu, a Chinese fiction writer who first came to prominence in the late 1970s, gave a popular series of lectures on *Stone* on television. Here is the core of *Qinxue*, Liu's study of *Stone* inspired by Qin Ke-qing, Jia Rong's young wife, who dies early in the novel: Liu proposes that Qin-shi was based on the illegitimate daughter of the historical crown prince, who was rejected by the Kangxi emperor. The Caos took her into their home, hoping that the crown prince would be reinstated and they would be rewarded; but later, their eldest daughter (Yuan-chun in the novel) betrayed this hidden princess. If I keep slipping back and forth between speaking of the real-life Caos and the Jias of the novel, and between Jia Yuan-chun and some imaginary daughter of the Caos, it is because Liu Xinwu himself makes little distinction between the two.

Mainstream redologists have no patience for this kind of analysis, criticizing it on factual and historical grounds, but consumers of books, participants in online discussions, and television viewers have an unquenchable thirst for it. Liu Xinwu says Qin-shi is really a princess. But perhaps she is only Qin-shi. Why can't the novel be read as it stands? Quite aside from reasonable concerns about provenance, we can see that the main question about the novel's end—namely, whether it is true to the spirit of the beginning, or as true as it possibly can be, given the constraints of the middle of the eighteenth century—is really the same as the question leveled at the first eighty chapters: Are they in fact about what they say they are about?

The theoretical problem that Liu Xinwu wants to address is the place of traditional China in the modern world. When he insists that Cao Xueqin could not say what he wanted to say because of the Literary Inquisition or because he wanted to protect his family or because there was a massive conspiracy afoot, I think of Freudian displacement or Derridean deferral. In recent years, Zhou Ruchang has become obsessed with the incredible notion that Gao E was not a clumsy redactor but instead an evil henchman of Heshen, the Qianlong emperor's corrupt favorite. According to Zhou, Gao E took possession of the novel's real conclusion and purged it, at Heshen's behest, as part of a conspiracy that involved the innermost court circles. Why go to such lengths to argue that the novel, and especially its end, is not what it says it is?

Instead of accounting for the novel's lack of revolutionary sentiment through the success of a complicated conspiracy, we might look to the wholeness of premodern society, which made it impossible to conceive of something else. There might never have been a culture with a sturdier orthodoxy than Yongzheng's China. Why drag in the Literary Inquisition, Heshen, and palace intrigue?

Our project is one of triangulation, but not what I had thought ten years ago. From our historical distance, one of the trickiest challenges in reading *Stone* is determining how far it stands outside the moral framework of mainstream

Chinese eighteenth-century culture and then determining how far that culture is from our own. In some form or other, most of the essays in this volume address this challenge.

In looking for continuity, Chinese scholars (Liu Xinwu included) fail to see distance. In seeing continuity, they dare to do what we do not: propose and write an alternative ending for the novel. Refusing to acknowledge that our world is far from that of the novel, they decide that the novel is far from itself, that it does not say what it means.

It is no coincidence that Zhou Ruchang lays the conspiracy at Heshen's feet, at the moment that the glories of Qianlong's reign and of the High Qing itself come to an end, soon to be replaced by the diminishment of the Unequal Treaties, the Opium War, and modernity. That was the fork in the road. Before that, some imagined, was the lost whole novel; after that, a patched mess—an emblem of our postlapsarian present. Anxiety about a world that has lost its coherence is displaced onto a text that can no longer say what it means.

NOTE

[1] But another linguistic comparison of how questions are phrased in the two halves of the novel suggests that the two were written in slightly different dialects and that the conclusion has more northern characteristics (H. Yu).

# The Garden and Garden Culture in *The Story of the Stone*

*Dore J. Levy*

Prospect Garden (*Daguan yuan* 大觀園) is the central work of art, and the symbolic center, of *The Story of the Stone*. It is a miniature world that exists simultaneously on several levels: physical, metaphoric, allusive, and allegorical. Each level of the garden is interreferential in the world of the novel and metareferential in encompassing the world of the reader. When the Stone as narrator states the purpose of his novel in chapter 1, he could be describing the idealized function of traditional Chinese gardens as environments for physical and spiritual refreshment:

> My only wish is that men in the world below may sometimes pick up this tale when they are recovering from sleep or drunkenness, or when they wish to escape from business worries or a fit of the dumps, and in doing so find not only mental refreshment but even, perhaps, if they will heed its lesson and abandon their vain and frivolous pursuits, some small arrest in the deterioration of their vital forces. . . . (50)

> 只願他們當那醉淫飽臥之時, 或避世去愁之際, 把此一玩, 豈不省了些壽命筋力? 就比那謀虛逐妄, 卻也省了口舌是非之害, 腿腳奔忙之苦.
> (1: 6)

Reading this text, the Taoist Vanitas immediately reaches enlightenment, as surely as if he had himself lived the years of experience, attachment, disappointment, and ultimate disillusionment of the hero of the narrative, Bao-yu, whose personation of the Stone is represented by the jade he wears on a cord around his neck. In short, the reader who fully enters the world of the novel enters Prospect Garden with the mind of the hero and vicariously shares all the moments that lead to his liberation from that world, of which Prospect Garden is the heart.

Any study of this subject must be indebted to Andrew H. Plaks's ground-breaking study of the garden as literary and allegorical topos in *Archetype and Allegory in* The Dream of the Red Chamber (1976). David Hawkes judiciously translates *Daguan yuan* as "Prospect Garden," suggesting, in addition to its purpose as a symbolic microcosm of the world, that this garden provides an opportunity for an enlarged view of the world from within its precincts. Plaks's rendering of the name as "Garden of Total Vision" extends this notion, tracing the term *daguan* from its first mention in hexagram 20 of the *Book of Changes* to denote the all-encompassing perspective of the ruler, through Zhuangzi's and other Taoist thinkers' use of the term for extraordinary insight, to its Buddhist allegorical significance—namely, the state of insight into the significance of all experience attained with enlightenment, "a vast vision within an enclosed space" (Plaks 181; see 179–81).

Physically, Prospect Garden lies squarely in the tradition of elaborate literati gardens as personal retreats and environments of hospitality. It also alludes to the danger of lèse-majesté in their evocation of the luxury of the precincts of imperial gardens—likewise to their frequent use as refuges when the rich and influential retired from public life in order to avoid charges of misconduct or even sedition. The *locus classicus* of the personal literary garden is the glorious estate known as the Golden Valley Garden of the third-century poet Shi Chong. Though Shi Chong called it his cottage retreat, the Golden Valley became a byword both for extravagance and for the doom of the politically compromised individual, whatever his resources. The tales of the poet's fabulous parties during his exile are balanced by his final tragedy. When his part in an antigovernment plot was uncovered and he was sentenced to death, his favorite concubine, Green Pearl, threw herself off one of the garden's pleasure towers to give her master an example of courage. Gardens are the most fragile and ephemeral of ecosystems, and Shi Chong's garden has endured far longer in literature—nearly two thousand years—than it did in real life. Its reputation and the fate of its owner, however, link the literary Prospect Garden to a fateful image of prosperity and rise, decline and fall, which no Chinese reader would have missed from the first mention of its building. Even in Prospect Garden's exclusive society, Shi Chong's extravagance with human feeling as well as with worldly resources is critiqued by the garden's preeminent poet, Dai-yu:

> *Green Pearl*
> Pebble or pearl—to Shi Chong it was only a rich man's whim:
> Do you really believe your undoubted charms meant so very much to him?

It was fate, from some past life preordained, that made him take his rash
  stand,
And the craving to have a companion in death's dark, silent land.

(3.64.257–58)

綠珠
瓦礫明珠一例拋,
何曾石尉重嬌嬈.
都緣頑福前生造,
更有同歸慰寂寥.　(2: 892)

As a literary topos, Prospect Garden also evokes the long tradition of *fu* 賦
("rhyme-prose" or "rhapsody"), a poetic genre that reached its zenith at the Han
dynasty court with grand visions of imperial gardens and parks as allegorical
representations of the empire at large and of the imaginative mind of the poet.
The original palace gardens are said to have been built by Emperor Wu of the
Han dynasty (r. 140–86 BCE) to attract immortals to visit his capital, since it had
proved impossible for mortal travelers to reach their dwellings. The idea was
that such lovely places would entice immortals to land for a brief respite in their
flights through the air. In the rhapsodies that celebrate imperial gardens, notably the "Shang-lin Park," by Sima Xiangru (179-127 BCE), the allegory of the
garden as empire also leads to a moral climax, when the emperor proclaims that
such gardens for his pleasure alone are wasteful extravagance and opens their
gates for the benefit of all his subjects (Watson, *Chinese Rhyme-Prose* 49).

In *The Chinese Garden*, Maggie Keswick describes the impact that the first
complete description of a Chinese garden had in the West. A Jesuit priest, Père
Attiret, whom the Qianlong emperor had employed as a painter at his court
in Beijing, wrote a letter that was published in Paris in 1749. His descriptions
of the emperor's passion for gardening in his incomparable Yuanming Yuan
圓明園 ("Garden of Perfect Brightness"), where the Jesuits were housed during the summer heat, caused a sensation—not least because Père Attiret mar-
veled that, unlike the rectangles, straight lines, and symmetry that governed
European garden design, Chinese gardens avoided such signs of imposed order,
their elements "plac'd with so much Art that you would take it to be the Work
of Nature" (translation by Sir Harry Beaumont in 1749). Keswick sums up the
revelation of this vision from China for European garden design: "While the
French treat nature as if it were architecture, planting trees and clipping hedges
into walls, the Chinese try to make the many architectural elements of their
garden conform to an ideal of natural irregularity" (123).

The essentials of Chinese garden design could not have been more different
from European ones, from the ideology of the garden's relation to nature to
its metaphoric representation of the dwellings of the immortals. The Chinese
garden's evocation of nature is of a piece with Chinese lyrical poetics; the visitor to a garden hopes to experience integration with the environment, much as

a reader of a Chinese poem aspires to integration with the poet's experience and inspiration. The notion of the garden as a glimpse of the dwellings of the immortals differs fundamentally from the Western notion of the garden as imitation of the earthly paradise from which an omnipotent God drove fallen humanity for disobedience to his will. No such sentient power governs the relation of humanity to nature in China. The Chinese garden refreshes body and spirit by encouraging the contemplation and appreciation of humanity's organic position in nature, not of a fall from grace. As such, the Chinese garden becomes the perfect environment for metaphors of all human experience. Prospect Garden figures Bao-yu's progress from senseless stone to a creature of hope and attachment, from his disappointment and disillusionment to his final return to an enlightened state of senseless stone.

Whatever the size of a Chinese garden, certain elements are regarded as crucial to its aesthetic purpose. According to the seventeenth-century garden engineer Ji Cheng, author of *The Craft of Gardens* (*Yuanye* 園冶, China's first prescriptive manual of garden design—*yuanye* literally means "garden smelting"), selection of a convenient site allows more frequent and more personal participation in the garden's conception and building. The word "building" is significant here, for although in the West one thinks in terms of planting a garden, in China a garden is referred to as an architectural phenomenon (19). Wherever the location, it must be secluded from the commotion of the city, even if that sense of seclusion is achieved by architectural ingenuity rather than geographic removal from an urban setting. The most common separating device is a plastered wall, usually white but sometimes painted gray or some other unobtrusive tone, enclosing the entire garden space. While the girdling of the garden by a wall sets the space apart from any other "natural" landscape, it marks the boundary in which the imagination is free. Peaks, groves, pagodas, and other landmarks glimpsed over the garden wall enlarge both the physical view and the mental vision, as the wall reminds the viewer that this constructed space is a microcosm of the larger world.

Even the smallest garden contains several buildings, designed to enhance the diversity of contemplative experience by evoking as many human environments as possible: from luxurious tea platforms to fishing perches, from secluded libraries in bamboo groves (an essential of literati gardens) to moonlit pavilions hovering over flowing water, from miniature temples to bowers for amorous assignations. Although not usually intended for permanent residence, such buildings could be used year-round, as the cycle of the seasons offered ever-changing views of the garden and encouraged admiration of all its phases. Greenery was essential but never took the form of lawns, so dear to European garden art, which to the Chinese evoked a pastoral style of life associated with the barbarian nomads beyond China's borders. Plantings were designed to reflect the beauties of each season; they included flowering and fruiting trees, fragrant perennials, evergreen bamboos and pines, deciduous shrubs and trees that turned a lovely color when touched by frost and assumed interesting shapes when bare or covered with snow. These living garden elements were set off by rock formations, which also appeared to change with the seasons and over years, as the garden grew around them. Cunningly placed rocks recalled the mountains from which they came. Finally, the presence of water, flowing or still, represented the pulse of the earth. No Chinese garden was complete without water, the element that bound all life together, a reminder of the nature of life in easy reach of eye and ear.

Rocks, combined with streams and pools, formed the basis of the garden's plan. The Chinese word for landscape (*shanshui* 山水) means literally "mountains and waters," while a common phrase for making a garden, again translated literally, is "digging ponds and piling mountains." The garden designer strives, by both contrasting and pairing opposites, to give the illusion that a garden, however small, extends indefinitely. This principle must be built in during the construction of the garden, but as the garden matures, the feeling of it as a microcosm of the world should deepen.

Prospect Garden combines the Chinese imperial heritage of garden design and symbolism with the tradition of elaborate literati gardens. It is first conceived in chapter 16, when the Jias plan to construct a "separate residence for a visitation" from Jia Zheng's eldest daughter, the imperial concubine Yuan-chun. When Jia Zheng is first summoned for an imperial audience, Grandmother Jia is alarmed: an imperial summons may just as well send an individual to be executed as to be promoted. But the news is good, even stupefying: "Your eldest young lady has been appointed Chief Secretary to the Empress and is to become an Imperial Concubine" (1.304) 說咱們家大小姐晉封為鳳藻宮尚書, 加封賢德妃 (1: 203). It is a compliment to Yuan-chun and her family that her sagacity and upbringing have given her the kind of literary ability and personal discretion to be in frequent attendance on the empress and that her personal charms have caught his imperial majesty's eye.

Soon after this announcement, the family receives the decree that allows households to establish a separate residence for their daughters in the emperor's service, so the family may be granted a home visit from them. This explanation is given in the presence of Nannie Zhao, an intimate of Xi-feng and Jia Lian by virtue of her standing as Lian's wet nurse. The scene is full of affectionate and occasionally off-color teasing, but Nannie Zhao has the experience to put this privilege into historical and political perspective. As they reminisce about the lavish entertainments that their extended families provided for a previous emperor, she remarks, "'Twere no more than paying for the Emperor's entertainment with the Emperor's own silver. No family that ever lived had money enough of its own to pay for such spectacles of vanity!" (315) 也不過是拿著皇帝家的銀子往皇帝身上使罷了！ 誰家有那些錢買這個虛熱鬧去? (210). This privilege is a more subtle form of control than the consternation caused by an imperial summons, for in the guise of honoring filial piety by allowing his concubines to see their families, the emperor requires that the families throw money into the economy in the name of their daughters' security. Prospect Garden is built in one year, at the expense of thousands of ounces of silver, as the Jias scramble to prepare a residence fit for their daughter's visit. Even spurred by imperial command, such rapid completion of a garden so large and lavish could be achieved only in a work of fiction. This project is an implicit criticicism of the vanity of an emperor who requires grandiose constructions to make his benevolence a reality.

Prospect Garden is regarded by the senior Jias as a practical work of craft, the best that money can buy. But what they see as a site for a unique formal occasion (the imperial concubine's one holiday from the imperial palace to visit her home), the children of the house will find to be a universe. In literary and symbolic terms, it *is* a universe: the buildings, promenades, waterways and pools, hills and dales, not to mention the plants, embrace every aspect of a wealthy and privileged family. Its various prospects and sites evoke as many different styles and environments as possible: from imperial dignity (Hall of Reunion) to a simple rural farmhouse (Sweet-Rice Village), from luxurious prosperity (House of Green Delights) to a secluded retreat (Naiad's House). In this world, the works of art that Bao-yu and his companions encounter throughout their daily lives vibrate with metaphoric significance, though they are usually unaware of it. Luxury of fabric and furnishings, objects by famous artists, precious works of art and craft, even objects imported from Europe embody a world that the reader knows is destined to collapse.

Critics have proposed many real-life gardens as the models for Cao Xueqin's fictional one: the palace of Qianlong's favorite, Heshen (1750–99, later the property of Prince Gong [1833–98]); the Xitang ("West Court") in Nanjing, which was attached to the residence of the textile commissioner (and may well have been the site prepared for the Kangxi emperor's visit in 1705); the poet Yuan Mei's Suiyuan 隨園 in Nanjing, as the poet himself claimed; and, more obscurely, another garden well known to the Caos, two li to the west of the North Gate of Nanjing, the Shitou yuan 石頭園 ("Stone Garden") (Spence, *Ts'ao Yin* 302–06).[1] The most frequently invoked model was perhaps the greatest imperial garden of all time, Emperor Yongzheng's grand project, the Garden of Perfect Brightness. It is curious that none of these identifications has significantly influenced the illustrations of Prospect Garden. This absence points to a major interpretative division between critics who insist that works of art necessarily imply analogues in real life and artists to whom the biographical fallacy seems an unfair constraint on the powers of individual genius. In figure 1, Prospect Garden is depicted with emphasis on the abundance of rocks and buildings. The layout focuses on the architecture: the garden's principal structures are labeled in the order of Jia Zheng's tour of them in chapter 17. Sun Wen's depiction (fig. 2) is much more open, the boundaries of the garden being less distinct from surrounding nature—a conspicuous feature, since the garden is located in a city. This imagining of Prospect Garden focuses more on "digging ponds and piling mountains" and expresses the desire to create a contained space that seems to extend indefinitely.

Fig. 1. "Daguan yuan tu," from *Zengping butu Shitou ji* 增評補圖石頭記 ("Annotated Illustrated *Story of the Stone*"), Shanghai, 1930

1. Main Gate
2. Path Winds Upwards to Mysterious Places
3. Drenched Blossoms Weir
4. Drenched Blossoms Pavilion
5. Naiad's House (Dai-yu)
6. Green Delights (Bao-yu)
7. All Spice Court (Bao-chai)
8. Sweet-Rice Village (Li Wan)
9. Prospect Hall

Fig. 2. Sun Wen's plan of the garden from *Quanben Honglou meng* 全本紅樓夢 ("The Complete *Dream of the Red Chamber*"), © Lüshun Museum, Dalian

Inspiration may have come from any or all of these gardens, and more—any view, any resting spot that Cao Xueqin encountered in his difficult life could have found its way into his perfect microcosm of the world's experience. But as to the inspiration for Prospect Garden's overall design, we may identify a popular literary source as well. In the first tour of the garden in chapter 17, Cao Xueqin constantly alludes to Ji Cheng's *The Craft of Gardens*, especially in the essential structures of rock, water, and buildings. When considerations of logistics and economy lead the Jia family to insist that they build the garden within the confines of the existing family property instead of breaking new ground outside the city, this decision is perfectly in accord with Ji Cheng's preference. *The Craft of Gardens* emphasizes that the purpose of a garden is separation from the noise and scrabble of daily life, even in a city. As primarily a landscape engineer, Ji Cheng preferred to achieve this end by structural ingenuity rather than by geographic separation: "If you can find seclusion in a noisy place, why there is no need to yearn for places far from where you live" (47).

Keeping the garden in the family's grounds keeps the family's affairs there as well. The Jias combine the existing garden resources of both households—the All Scents Garden of the Ning-guo side and the former Rong-guo Garden, where Jia Zheng's elder brother, Jia She, is housed—and other ground into approximately one acre within the confines of the family property. Cousin Zhen agrees to the incorporation of his All Scents Garden, where his daughter-in-law, Qin-shi, hanged herself in the secluded pavilion they had used for their assignations. This suicide was explicit in Cao Xueqin's original draft, but when pressed by one of his readers, he changed her cause of death to a lingering gynecological problem—albeit one whose diagnosis is replete with the symbolism of improper sexual activity (Levy 70–72). Plowing All Scents Garden to make it part of a seemly whole may be read as a metaphor for what the unwilling author's rewriting did: it covers up Qin-shi's real cause of death but does not eradicate the traces, which affect other characters. Qin-shi's spirit reappears near the end of the novel to show Grandmother Jia's maid, Faithful, how to take her own life and save her honor (ch. 111). The history of Prospect Garden figures the archaeology of the novel.

Whatever the Jia family's reasons for incorporating their old gardens into a new one, Cao Xueqin abides by Ji Cheng's principles. A garden cannot hope to reproduce nature, but it can evoke it by echoing all natural forces in their appropriate balance. Keswick summarizes the ideal: "[J]ust as a great landscape painting acquires, over time, the calligraphy of connoisseurs as colophons around its margins, so the garden acquires history, life, and meaning from poems that record the feelings of those who, maybe a hundred years before, enjoyed the same sight and sounds and scents that are still there" (Ji Cheng 24).

The first tour of Prospect Garden is best known, perhaps, for the literary inquisition of Bao-yu by his father, Jia Zheng, as he puts the boy through his paces in front of the band of literary gentlemen—Jia Zheng's inevitable sycophants. For the Chinese literati, poetry adds a necessary dimension to garden appreciation, and when Jia Zheng orders Bao-yu to provide inscriptions and couplets, he argues:

> These inscriptions are going to be difficult. . . . By rights, of course, Her Grace should have the privilege of doing them herself; but she can scarcely be expected to make them up out of her head without having seen any of the views which they are to describe. On the other hand, if we wait until she has already visited the garden before asking her, half the pleasure of the visit will be lost. All those prospects and pavilions — even the rocks and trees and flowers will seem somehow incomplete without that touch of poetry which only the written word can lend a scene.    (1.17.324–25)

> 這匾額對聯倒是一件難事. 論理該請貴妃賜題才是, 然貴妃若不親睹其景, 大約亦必不肯妄擬, 若直待貴妃游幸過再請題, 偌大景緻, 若干亭榭, 無字標題, 也覺寥落無趣, 任有花柳山水, 也斷不能生色.    (1: 217)

According to Keswick, "[t]hree kinds of writing are commonly found in gardens: names, inscribed couplets, and the appreciative poems of visitors, often written to commemorate particularly enjoyable days or elegant gatherings" (150). These writings would ordinarily accumulate over decades in the life of a garden as part of its social and aesthetic growth, so Bao-yu is right to resent his father for pressing him to cram generations of appreciation and response into an afternoon of forced composition. The literary gentlemen do have some sense of this problem and try to intervene on Bao-yu's behalf when the conflict between father and son becomes too intense. Part of the struggle is a typical intergenerational one: the garden demands "that touch of poetry" to celebrate its creation, but Jia Zheng and Bao-yu have very different ideas of how the Garden should be celebrated.

Bao-yu does best when he combines his romantic approach to appreciating scenery with orthodox references to classical texts. When he names the artificial mountain seen when the gate first opens (a signature Ji Cheng feature) "Pathway to Mysteries," he satisfies his father's desire for a dignified yet original title, while expressing his own anticipation of the possibilities of life before him. It is the boy's first step into the place that will be the heart of his lifetime of experience, and in that light "Pathway to Mysteries" reminds the reader of the novel's allegorical frame and Bao-yu's trajectory toward enlightenment. He continues fair with the many buildings in natural settings and viewing sites over water, but comes to grief at "Sweet-Rice Village," a miniature farm complete with livestock, crops, and thatched cottages. Mulishly ignoring his father's approval of the place's "quietness and natural simplicity," Bao-yu objects to the use of the term "natural" in such a context:

> A farm set down in the middle of a place like this is obviously the product of human artifice. . . . It sticks up out of nowhere, in total isolation from

everything else. It isn't even a particularly remarkable view—not nearly so "natural" in form or spirit as those other places we have seen. The bamboos in those other places may have been planted by human hands and the streams diverted out of their natural courses, but there was no *appearance* of artifice. . . .                                                          (336)

卻又來! 此處置一田莊, 分明見得人力穿鑿扭捏而成. 遠無鄰村, 近不負郭, 背山山無脈, 臨水水 無源, 高無隱寺之塔, 下無通市之橋, 峭然孤出, 似非大觀. 爭似先處有自然之理, 得自然之氣, 雖種竹引泉, 亦不傷於穿鑿.                                                                       (225)

His father's burst of outrage cuts off his peroration. The father-son conflict is rooted in the genuine divergence of worldviews as well as of life experience. Firmly set in his social and political context, Jia Zheng accepts what Plaks notes as conventional in both China and the West: "the entire idea of a garden is by definition one of artificiality—of constructing an artifact using the stuff of nature as materials" (*Archetype* 161). Furthermore, Jia Zheng sees the little farmstead as an image of the country retreat of the poet Tao Qian (365–427), who lived in retirement for twenty-two years rather than compromise his spirit by remaining in official life. Tao Qian was the founder of field-and-garden poetry, which celebrates the connection between the contemplative intellectual and nature. Bao-yu's worldview, quite unknown to Bao-yu on a conscious level but clear to the reader, comes from his origin in the Land of Illusion. He even uses the phrase *daguan* (rendered by Hawkes as "remarkable view") to describe what the little farm lacks. Jia Zheng's and Bao-yu's two perspectives can never be reconciled. By common sense and in terms of garden aesthetics, Bao-yu has a point—what is a farm doing in such a place? But the boy's naïveté about the strength of conventional social and aesthetic modes cannot prevail against a system of philosophy and art that reads simplicity and naturalness into a thoroughly artificial construction of rustic life. But he has been incarnated to learn, through the span of a mortal existence, the essential unity of conscious creation (human artifice) and spontaneous generation (nature) as complementary aspects of the universe of experience, and Prospect Garden is the world in which that experience will take place.

Bao-yu nearly comes to grief again when they reach the main reception hall of the imperial concubine's separate residence. Jia Zheng deprecates the showiness of the building while conceding that his daughter's exalted position now demands it. Bao-yu is simply struck dumb, in the grips of an overpowering sense of déjà vu. This hall reminds him of the palace of the fairy Disenchantment, but his dream from chapter 5 is too deeply buried for him to recall it to conscious memory. Yuan-chun, during her visit, will change the provisional name Precinct of the Celestial Visitant to Hall of Reunion. Both names point, in different ways, to the palace in the Land of Illusion: the first alludes to Disenchantment herself, the second to the reunion of Bao-yu and Dai-yu as Stone and Flower, after their worldly karma is completed.

As the party winds its way through the rest of the garden, Bao-yu recovers sufficiently to show that he is more than a match for his elders when it comes to poetic associations of youth and transcendence for the imperial concubine's pleasure. A slightly malicious jibe is aimed at Jia Zheng when they visit the building that later becomes Bao-yu's residence. Yuan-chun will name it the House of Green Delights (*Yihong yuan* 怡红院, literally, "the house of the pleasures of youth"; *hong* ["red"] denotes youth in Chinese—to get an idiomatic translation, Hawkes substitutes "green," the color of youth in the West, for "red"). To the mature members of the party, it is a confusion of corridors and partitions, with no regular rooms at all. Jia Zheng actually loses himself in the maze, dodging a huge mirror when he sees but does not recognize his own party coming toward him, bumping into trompe-l'oeil doors. Cousin Zhen, who has acted as overseer to the construction, considerately leads him out the back to the entrance of the garden again. These passages and choices, even the mirror, are for Bao-yu, not for Jia Zheng.

How does Yuan-chun, the imperial concubine for whom this paradise has been constructed, feel about it? She sighs and remarks, "Oh dear, this is all so extravagant!" (1.18.357) 默默叹息奢华过费 (1: 237). Her pleasure in the beauty of the garden seems second to her delight in the titles and inscriptions written by her adored little brother, Bao-yu. Before she was called to service in the palace, she was his first teacher, and once she has visited the garden, it is as if she conceives of it as her avatar to guide and protect him in her absence. Appreciating the world that the garden has the potential to be, she includes Bao-yu in her command that the garden be occupied by the children, so that he may have its full benefit—as the name she gives the place, Prospect Garden, implies:

Embracing hills and streams, with skill they wrought:
Their work at last is to perfection brought.
Earth's fairest prospects all are here installed,
So "Prospect Garden" let its name be called!    (365)

衔山抱水建来精,
多少工夫筑始成.
天上人间诸景备,
芳园应锡大观名.    (1: 242)

The roles of Mysterioso and Impervioso (the Taoist and Buddhist who find the lamenting Stone near Greensickness Peak and propel him into the mortal world) as guides and guardians of the incarnated Stone have been much noted, but the role of Yuan-chun as Bao-yu's guardian angel in the Jia household is also remarkable. Whatever her regrets, she strives to turn her position to her family's good, especially by invoking the benevolence of the emperor in all her family interactions. She thanks him for his compassion by naming Prospect Garden's main hall the Hall of Reunion, and she lays this building at her sovereign's feet in the couplet she composes for the entryway:

For all earth to share, his great compassion has been extended,
　that children and humble folk may gratefully rejoice.
For all ages to admire, his noble institutions have been promoted,
　that people of every land and clime may joyfully exult.　(364)

天地啟宏慈,
赤子蒼頭同感戴,
古今垂曠典,
九州萬國被恩榮.　(241)

Aware, perhaps, of the fragility of gardens, certainly of the vanity of aspiration, she decrees that the garden must be the site of experience, even if it cannot be hers and even if its ideal is doomed to flourish only for a short time. Just when Bao-yu and Dai-yu are demonstrating their adolescence by sharing forbidden books of romance and poetry, Yuan-chun's decree arrives: "Bao-chai and the other young ladies of the household are to reside in the Garden. The Garden is not to be kept closed. Bao-yu is to accompany the young ladies into the Garden and to continue his studies there" (1.23.455) 命寶釵等只管在園中居住, 不可禁約封錮, 命寶玉仍隨進去讀書 (1: 309). Removing the younger generation to the garden seems an ideal solution to the inevitable pressures on the family of having a gaggle of adolescents on top of them in the main residence. While on the mundane level, this move seems to undermine parental authority by giving the young people more independence and self-determination, on the cosmic level, Yuan-chun's decree serves the karmic mission Bao-yu received from Mysterioso and Impervioso in the first chapter. The final proof that Yuan-chun is crucial to his spiritual progress is revealed after her death, in Bao-yu's second dream of the Land of Illusion in chapter 116. As he sees the spirits of the young women he has known and loved turning into monsters, Impervioso shines a mirror in his face and shouts, "By the order of Her Grace the Imperial Jia Concubine I have come to save you!" (5.116.293) 我奉元妃娘娘旨意, 特來救你 (2: 1547). When Bao-yu questions his savior, the monk chides him for his slowness in understanding the experience his sister has supported: ". . . predestined attachments of the human heart are all of them mere illusion, they are obstacles blocking our spiritual path" (293) 世上的情緣都是那些魔障 (1548). When Bao-yu awakes, he is ready to leave the mundane world forever.

　As a resident of Prospect Garden, Bao-yu is the only male member of the Crab-Flower Club, a poetry society founded by his sister Tan-chun with the invitation, "Why should the founding of poetry clubs be the sole prerogative of the whiskered male, and female versificators allowed a voice . . . only when some enlightened patriarch sees fit to invite them?" (2.37.214) 孰謂蓮社之雄才, 獨許鬚眉, 直以東山之雅會, 讓余脂粉 (1: 487). This distinctive group and their poetry have been studied in many other contexts.[2] In the context of the garden, the poems celebrate its many seasons, places, and occasions; they idealize a place that is already an ideal. In order to survive their inevitable departure from the garden, the children must discover the potential of poetry as a vehicle for the development of self-awareness, if not awareness of the vanity of existence. The many plays, with their beautiful poetry, that the children view during private entertainments in Prospect Garden have this same potential. The plays inevitably reflect the inhabitants: the lines can be a casual entertainment, an avenue of romantic release, or a glimpse of the possibility of transcendence—it all depends on the state of the listener or, if poetry is being composed, the poet. The vast array of poetry in every genre, for every member of the garden, complements the garden's panoply of views and environments. Both hold the possibility of lyrical and spiritual transcendence for the reader as well as for the characters in *The Story of the Stone.*

Jia Zheng's fatuous remarks about rustic simplicity are ironically recalled when a true rustic, the redoubtable Grannie Liu, appears and is treated to a weekend sojourn among her distant relatives. In chapter 40, she makes a second visit to the Jia mansion, to bring return gifts for the largesse given to her when her family was in dire straits. There is no pretension about her: her family farms for a living, and she brings the first fruits of the year's harvest to her benefactors as a mark of gratitude and respect. Charmed by the prospect of conversing with a lady as old and as much of a survivor as she is, Grandmother Jia invites Grannie Liu to prolong her visit. As a gesture of hospitality and to amuse themselves, the ladies of the Rong-guo house entertain Grannie Liu with a thorough tour of the garden. As the amazed old lady views its wonders, we get a view of the garden as a living environment imbued with the personalities of its inhabitants.

From her first glimpse of the garden, Grannie Liu appreciates it as a work of art:

> You know, we country folk like to get a picture at New Year that we can stick up on the wall. Every year just before New Year the farmers come into town to buy one. Many's the time of an evening when the day's work was done we've sat and looked at the picture on *our* wall and wished we could get inside it and walk around, never imagining that such beautiful places could really be. Yet now I look at this Garden here, and it's ten times better than any picture I ever saw. If only I could get someone to make a painting of it all, just the way it is, that I could take back to show the others, I do believe I should die content!          (2.40.280)

> 我們鄉下人到了年下, 都上城來買畫兒貼. 時常閒了, 大家都說, 怎麼得也到畫兒上去逛逛. 想著那個畫兒也不過是假的, 那裡有這個真地方呢. 誰知我今兒進這園一瞧, 竟比那畫兒還強十倍. 怎麼得有人也照著這個園子畫一張, 我帶了家去, 給他們見見, 死了也得好處.    (1: 532)

Whereupon Grandmother Jia proposes that her great-niece, Xi-chun, paint the garden. When it turns out that the old lady is serious, Xi-chun's dismay is acute:

". . . as I was too scared to refuse, I've got myself into a mess" (2.42.336). Bao-chai, sympathetic, provides a critique of the garden that sums up its scope and the impossibility of reproducing it in a painting:

> . . . the trouble is that the Garden itself was designed rather like a painting, with every rock, every tree, every building in it carefully and precisely placed in order to produce a particular scenic effect; and if you tried to get your impressions of all of these different scenes onto paper exactly as they are, they simply wouldn't make a picture. . . .                    (337–38)

> 這園子卻是象畫兒一般, 山石樹木, 樓閣房屋, 遠近疏密, 也不多, 也不少, 恰恰的是這樣. 你就照樣兒往紙上一畫, 是必不能討好的.                    (571)

Bao-chai, as usual, is right. That Xi-chun is unable to carry out the project should not surprise us. Prospect Garden is captured only in the literary medium of the novel.

The introduction of Grannie Liu shows Prospect Garden as an amusing environment. Unfortunately, the incursions of outsiders into the garden often have a negative effect. One could argue that the growth of awareness of the outside world plants the seeds of the garden's destruction, spoiling its sanctity as a refuge from responsibility, adulthood, and time. In chapter 55, Xi-feng's miscarriage forces her to relinquish many of her household duties, and Lady Wang turns the management of the garden over to Tan-chun. As aware as her older sister, Yuan-chun, was about the dangers of extravagance, Tan-chun proposes an organizational structure that will allow the garden, if not to yield a profit, at least to be self-sufficient:

> Now of course, a family like ours couldn't possibly put its garden under contract and turn it into a business . . . it would look too mercenary. On the other hand, when you know how valuable everything is, it seems a terrible waste of natural resources not to have a few people whose special job it is to look after it. . . .                    (3.56.69)

> 若此時也出脫生發銀子, 自然小器, 不是咱們這樣人家的事. 若派出兩個一定的人來, 既有許多值錢之物, 一味任人作踐, 也似乎暴珍天物.                    (1: 765)

If the people who are responsible for looking after the garden's plantings can use its bounty to supply the household with such necessities as bamboo shoots for the kitchen and flowers for vases, if the surplus fruit can be taken to vendors, and if the valuable pharmaceutical plants of All Spice Court can be properly harvested and sold, the laborers will make a tidy profit on the side, the household will have plenty, and youthful idealism will stand alongside ancient prescriptions for universal prosperity.

Idealist she may be, but of all the inhabitants of the garden, Tan-chun is the one most mindful of what the future holds. The elders of the household have assumed that, because of the imperial concubine's dispensation, the children in Prospect Garden are somehow in a state of timeless and inviolable innocence. This was neither Yuan-chun's intention nor expectation—did she not go to the imperial palace to lose her innocence? The children are far more aware than the adults that their childhood is ending; moreover, they see quite clearly what is happening in the adult world from which they are thought to be sheltered.

Tan-chun, firmly believing that the family's integrity rests on the loyalty of their servants, proposes that the staff share in the profit of the garden. Unfortunately, the basis of mutual respect and trust this system requires is rudely disrupted when a mentally handicapped serving girl discovers in the garden a purse decorated with erotic figures. Ladies Xing and Wang, feckless as ever and each having her own agenda and animosity toward the other, unleash a vice squad of eager toadies to search the garden and weed out elements of sexual corruption. The elder ladies delude themselves that the purpose of this inquisition is to preserve the innocence of the garden's inhabitants. Predictably, the search is a fiasco. Whatever the children's state of innocence, such a disturbance cannot but shake its foundations. Tan-chun attempts to shield her staff from rude treatment, insisting that her effects be searched first and scolding the inquisitors:

> I must say, I cannot understand this eagerness to meet trouble half-way. The searching will begin soon enough in this household when the day of the confiscation arrives. . . . A great household like ours in not destroyed in a day. . . . In order for the destruction to be complete, it has to begin from within. (3.74.471)

> 你們別忙, 自然連你們抄的日子有呢! . . . 自己家裏好好的抄家, 果然今日真抄了. 咱們也漸漸的來了. 可知這樣大族人家, 若從外頭殺來, 一時是殺不死的. . . . 必須先從家裏自殺自滅起來, 才能一敗塗地!
> (2: 1030)

The family's strength is dependent on every member of the household. The draconian measures of search, seizure, and expulsion, which result in the deaths of two of the principal maids, Skybright and Chess, the degradation of many others, and the public humiliation of all the garden society mean that the family will have no internal solidarity on which to depend in a crisis, no reliable trust or loyalty left among the remaining staff. From this moment, signs of decay and ill-omen in the garden begin to drive away its inhabitants.

Prospect Garden remains a powerful environment of poetic inspiration, though of a valedictory kind. These moments center on the young women. In chapter 76, Dai-yu and Shi Xiang-yun celebrate the mid-autumn moon by composing linked couplets in the Concave Pavilion, a little building on the water's edge named by Dai-yu as part of the imperial concubine's naming activities. Xiang-yun points out how unusual this combination of physical and poetic environment is:

> Whoever made this Garden must have been quite an educated person. The place where we are now is obviously called the Convex Pavilion because it is on top of the convex hill, and Concave Pavilion must have been given its name because it is in a hollow. These two words "concave" and "convex" are very seldom encountered in literature. Their use in landscape gardening for the naming of features must be even rarer. To my mind the linking together of these two pavilions by so unusual a pair of names suggests that they must have been specially designed for viewing the moon from: Convex Pavilion for those who like the small, remote moon of the mountains and high places, Concave Pavilion for those who prefer the silky whiteness of the great orb reflected in the surface of the water.                                                                           (3.514)

> 可知當日蓋這園子時就有學問. 這山之高處, 就叫凸碧; 山之低窪近水就叫作凹晶. 這 "凸" "凹" 二字, 歷來用的人最少. 如今直用作軒館之名, 更覺新鮮, 不落窠臼. 可知這兩處一上一下, 一明一暗, 一高一矮, 一山一水, 竟是特因玩月而設此處. 有愛那山高月小的, 便往這裡來; 有愛那皓月清波的, 便往那裡去.                                                                           (2: 1061)

When the girls descend to the pavilion, the garden shows them its poetic best:

> A great white moon in the water reflected the great white moon above, competing with it in brightness. The girls felt like mermaids sitting in a shining crystal palace beneath the sea. A little wind that brushed over the surface of the water making tiny ripples seemed to cleanse their souls and fill them with buoyant lightness.                                                                           (515)

> 只見天上一輪皓月, 池 中一輪水月, 上下爭輝, 如置身於晶宮鮫室之內. 微風一過, 粼粼然池面皺碧鋪紋, 真 令人神清氣淨.                                                                           (1063)

For the final touch, a lone flute begins to play from somewhere over the hill, and Dai-yu and Xiang-yun capture this moment, aided by the unexpected appearance of the unshorn nun Adamantina in a lovely set of linked pentameters.

Adamantina is the garden's most eccentric inhabitant, representing the Jia family's highest moral aspirations and their greatest disappointment. Her name contains the character for "jade" (yu 玉), which links her both to Bao-yu, to whom she is mortifyingly attracted, and to Dai-yu, whose poetic nature she deeply appreciates. Since the garden's designer included "a nun's retreat hidden in a little wood" (1.17.344), the Jias were obliged to find a nun to occupy it. Adamantina, the daughter of a highly educated official family from Suzhou,

is an accomplished scholar and has a most fastidious temperament. There are
many precious objects in her Green Bower Hermitage that she proudly displays to Bao-yu, Dai-yu, and Bao-chai, despite her professed detachment from
worldly concerns. After Grannie Liu's visit, Adamantina insists on discarding the
valuable enameled porcelain cup of Chenghua ware that Grandmother Jia used
to share tea with her guest, because it has been contaminated by the old lady's
peasant touch. Adamantina often appears unexpectedly, especially when Bao-yu
is about, and at his request donates the luscious boughs of red plum blossom for
a winter meeting of the Crab-Flower Poetry Club. Her self-proclaimed purity
is not proof against the disintegration of the Jia household, and she falls prey to
exactly the kind of opportunistic hangers-on Tan-chun would have discouraged.
After the mansion is burgled during Grandmother Jia's funeral procession, one
of the rascals returns, drugs her and her companions, and carries her off to an
unknown fate. Adamantina's debacle, however, is not a symptom of imperfection of the garden but rather the manifestation of the imperfection in herself
that she brought with her and that, even in such seclusion, destroyed her. The
register of the twelve beauties of Jinling foretold her end in its sixth entry:

> For all your would-be spotlessness
> And vaunted otherworldliness,
> You that look down on common flesh and blood,
> Yourself impure, shall end up in the mud.   (1.5.134)

> 欲潔何曾潔,
> 雲空未必空.
> 可憐金玉質,
> 終陷淖泥中.   (1: 77)

Even before Adamantina's ravishment, perceptions of Prospect Garden degenerate into superstition and exploitation. It is as if, once the young ladies begin
to be married off and are sent away from the family to meet their fates outside,
the garden loses its heart. The girls go from the self-contained innocence of
childhood to the self-conscious vulnerability of maturity. Bao-yu is most unhappily affected by these developments and in chapter 94 notices that the crab apple
trees adjoining his House of Green Delights are about to bloom — wildly out of
season. Grandmother Jia insists that this unseasonable blossoming is auspicious,
but the young people know better. Tan-chun secretly thinks, "This must be an
ill-omen. Everything that is in harmony with nature prospers, and things out of
season, out of time, fade and die . . ." (4.94.287) 此花必非好兆. 大凡順者昌,
逆者亡. 草木知運, 不時而發, 必是妖孽 (2: 1301). Sure enough, before the day
is out, Bao-yu's jade disappears, and Bao-yu is well on his way to losing his
wits. Seeing that he is incapable of acting on his own behalf, Grandmother Jia
removes him from the garden and plans a hasty wedding for him with Bao-chai.
When Dai-yu accidentally learns of this wedding, she pitches into a decline,

expiring at the very moment Bao-yu takes Bao-chai as his wife. Months later, when Bao-yu tries to reenter Prospect Garden for refreshment, Aroma intervenes, warning him that the now-empty garden has seemed haunted since Dai-yu's death. The Jia elders even went so far as to conduct a formal exorcism (ch. 102). Convinced that he hears ghostly weeping from Dai-yu's former residence, the Naiad's House, Bao-yu bursts out, "How could I have wounded you so! . . . It was my father and mother who made the choice. In my heart I was always true to you!" (5.108.170) 林妹妹, 林妹妹, 好好兒的是我害了你了! 你別怨我, 只是父母作主, 並不是我負心 (2: 1461–62). This is Bao-yu's last visit to the garden. His life in the imitation of Disenchantment's Paradise of Truth is over: his next destination must be beyond illusion.

NOTES

[1] There is an interesting problem regarding Yuan Mei's alleged reference to the Cao garden as his own in the *Suiyuan shihua* 隨園詩話 (*Poetry Talks of the Casual Garden*). That attributed statement appeared in an 1824 edition of *Poetry Talks*. The 1790 and 1792 editions of *Poetry Talks*, printed by Yuan Mei himself (i.e., financed by the still-living poet), did not have the few sentences identifying the novelistic garden with Yuan's own famous Casual Garden in Nanjing. Scholars have speculated that the 1824 addition of this intriguing detail could have been forged, especially since the author of that statement refers to the work as *Honglou meng*, the title of the published novel, whereas all the manuscripts are titled *Shitou ji*. Note that the publications of *Poetry Talks* practically coincided with those of the first printed editions of the full-length, one hundred twenty-chapter novel.

[2] See I-Hsien Wu's essay in this volume. See also Levy, ch. 4.

# Religion in *The Story of the Stone*

## *Meir Shahar*

The supernatural is present in *The Story of the Stone* from the very beginning. The novel that was hailed by Chairman Mao Zedong as a great achievement of social realism (see Xiaojue Wang's essay in this volume) opens not with the tensions of class struggle but with a goddess smelting the azure heavens. Its religious aspect precedes its economic, social, and even psychological concerns, as the author outlines his characters' divine origins before delving into the earthly making of their identities. Furthermore, at the very outset the reader is informed that the principal hero's human career is no more than a brief interlude in his otherworldly existence. Bao-yu's life on earth is but a dream (*Dream of the Red Chamber*), from which he ultimately awakens into a higher reality.

To the Western reader, the novel's religious aspect is likely baffling. How could a hero be made of stone? Who are the two eccentric saints who bring him into the world? And most intriguing of all: How does the search for liberation coexist with the novel's minute attention to the fabric of worldly existence? *Stone* is remarkable for its detailed realism. The rich texture of social relations and material objects from which its narrative is woven seems to belie otherworldly concerns. The dream of Bao-yu's life has been crafted with such loving attention that one wonders whether its author truly intended to shatter it by a vision of religious awakening.

Two paths open to us as we try to disentangle the novel's religious significance. The first is a historical inquiry into the origins and meaning of specific spiritual motifs. The themes of eccentricity and sainthood, Buddhist enlightenment, and sacred stones merit each a brief genealogical introduction that places them in the Chinese cultural context. The second and more challenging path concerns the roles that these motifs assume in the narrative. For all its concern with spiritual liberation, *The Story of the Stone* is a novel, not scripture. Whichever religious motifs the author borrowed from his cultural environment were given new meanings in the context of his artistic vision. Cao Xueqin's unique genius transformed the shared cultural symbols of his time, weaving them into a remarkable tapestry that illuminates such varied themes as desire and social order, enlightenment and the meaning of fiction. The novel's religious aspect should be explored therefore in connection with the author's other concerns.

In this short essay I combine the two approaches: historical inquiry into the origins and significance of specific religious motifs and commentary on the role of those motifs in Cao Xueqin's masterpiece. My discussion of origins is intended for readers with no background in Chinese religion; my observations on their role in the narrative draw on the insights of contemporary scholars. My intention is not to be exhaustive but merely to provide an outline of some aspects of the novel's rich religious texture.

## *Jade*

Affectionate Chinese mothers often call their child Precious Treasure (*baobei* 寶貝). In Bao-yu's case, however, Precious Jade (Bao-yu 寶玉) is not only an endearing diminutive but also a statement of fact: Bao-yu *is* a precious stone, which following a romantic encounter in heaven has been sent to the human realm to experience the illusion of worldly existence. When the drama of its earthly incarnation is over, it returns to the Great Void, whereupon its life story is miraculously engraved on it. *The Story of the Stone*, then, has been inscribed on the Stone. Luckily for the reader, the absentminded Taoist Vanitas happened upon it and copied its saga.

In his rocky aspect Bao-yu is not unique. Chinese fiction features another unforgettable character who likewise emerged from a stone. This is the heroic monkey protagonist of the sixteenth-century *Journey to the West* 西遊記, Sun Wukong (nicknamed in English Monkey). How could these beloved figures be equated with insentient stones? On the most general level the answer lies in the Chinese concept of nature, which is radically different from the Judeo-Christian one. For the Chinese, there was no dichotomy between spirit and matter. Theirs was a vision of a continuity of being in which all modalities of existence—animate and inanimate alike—come from the same vital force. Called in Chinese *qi* 氣, the vital energy is neither solely spiritual nor exclusively material—it is both. Hence human beings are organically connected to everything in the universe, from rocks and trees to the Great Void. As one intellectual historian has noted, "it is not at all difficult for the Chinese to imagine that an agate or a piece of jade can have enough potential spirituality to transform itself into a living being" (W. Tu 43).

If stones, like human beings, are endowed with religious potential for awakening, then it is not inconceivable to rank them according to their degree of spirituality—in which case jade would rank first. For thousands of years, jade has enjoyed the position of most potent Chinese gem. Its significance in Chinese culture has ranged from the political realm (in which it served as a symbol of royalty) to the aesthetic sphere (in which it was favored as a jewel and objet d'art), to the religious area (in which it signified immortality). Archaeological excavations have revealed to us that as early as the first millennium BCE, jade was believed to safeguard eternal life. In some cases the protective stone was placed under the deceased's tongue (recalling Bao-yu's precious amulet); in others, the deceased's entire body was covered by jade plates, which sealed it from the harmful influence of sinister spirits. Identifying his protagonist as a piece of jade, the author bestows on him an aura of spirituality (even magic power) and an air of artistic refinement that has been associated with the gem (J. Wang, *Story*).

Jade is further employed by Cao Xueqin for purposes dictated by his own creative agenda. Indeed, he displays virtuosity in the range of meanings assigned to his protagonist's magic stone. David Hawkes is likely correct when he suggests that at least in one instance Bao-yu's jade stands for masculinity. When in a fit of adolescent hysteria Bao-yu tries to smash his precious jade, he betrays his sexual confusion: "None of the girls has got one" [Bao-yu sobbed uncontrolla-bly]. "Only I have got one. It always upsets me. And now this new cousin comes here who is as beautiful as an angel and she hasn't got one either, so I *know* it can't be any good" (1.3.104) 家裡姐姐妹妹都沒有, 單我有, 我說沒趣, 如今來了這們一個神仙似的妹妹 也沒有, 可知這不是個好東西 (1: 50). Here the jade functions as a phallic symbol (see Hawkes's comment [1.32]).

Its occasional sexual connotations notwithstanding, the Stone serves its au-thor first and foremost to reflect on the meaning of fiction. As Anthony Yu has demonstrated, the fiction of the Stone enables the author to ponder in his nar-rative the creation, the dissemination, and the reception of the narrative itself (110–71). The following example demonstrates the Stone's role in the creation of reflexive fiction. When he catches his friend Qin Zhong in the act with little Sapientia, Bao-yu promises to settle accounts with him in bed. The reader is left in the dark as to the (presumably sexual) punishment that follows, because of the narrator's declared ignorance: "As for the 'settling of accounts' that Bao-yu had proposed to Qin Zhong, we have been unable to ascertain exactly what form this took; and as we would not for the world be guilty of a fabrication, we must allow the matter to remain a mystery" (1.15.300) 寶玉不知與秦鐘算何帳目, 未見 真切, 未曾記得, 此是疑案, 不敢篡創 (1: 200).

This feigned ignorance is due to the fiction that his informant—the Stone—is not present: on this particular night, it was taken for safekeeping by Xi-feng. Since the Stone was not there to witness Bao-yu and Qin Zhong, the narrator has no way of knowing what transpired between them. The reader recognizes, of course, that the Stone's whereabouts are determined by the author. This de-lightful literary joke reminds us that *Stone* is a consciously crafted fiction. No wonder the Red Inkstone commentary marvels at the brilliance of this passage, which combines a playful sexual innuendo with a zestful insight into the making of literature (*Zhiyan zhai* 15.158).

I have spoken of the spiritual and aesthetic connotations of jade in Chinese culture. It should be remembered, however, that the "precious jade" that is Bao-yu has been found unfit to repair heaven. That is a slightly deformed or deficient stone leads us to another association of stone that is at work in Cao's novel. In some Chinese Buddhist texts, stone stands for stubborn obtuseness. Great preachers are those capable of leading even insentient rocks to enlighten-ment. Cao Xueqin makes use of the Stone's stubbornness no less than its spiri-tuality. His Bao-yu is simultaneously a precious gem and a foolish stone that is bound to experience the consequences of its folly before being awakened to the illusory nature of worldly existence.

## Eccentricity and Sainthood

In Cao Xueqin's narrative—as in Chinese religions generally—the divine sphere and the human realm are not separated by an impassable abyss. The border between the heavenly Great Void and the earthly Land of Illusion is permeable. Two messengers travel back and forth between the mortal and immortal realms. They usher the novel's protagonist into the human world, and they reappear at critical junctures of his earthly existence. After Bao-yu loses interest in human affairs, he seeks their company and returns with them to the paradisiacal Greensickness Peak from which he originally issued. Other characters encounter the heavenly emissaries (either one or both) at pivotal moments. The two forewarn Caltrop's and Dai-yu's parents of the fate awaiting their daughters, and they lend Jia Rui the magic mirror that leads to his grotesque death as he fails to heed their warning—gazing into the looking glass's front side of carnal lust instead of its back side of self-realization. By contrast, Zhen Shi-yin and Liu Xiang-lian are guided by the monk and Taoist to religious awakening, following which they abandon society for reclusive lives.

Cao Xueqin's divine messengers represent two different faiths: Taoism and Buddhism. This variety might appear puzzling to a Western monotheistic perspective, which highlights the competition—even hostility—between religions. (We are not accustomed to have Christian priests, Jewish rabbis, and Muslim muftis walk hand in hand.) However, China's polytheistic faiths tend to be mutually tolerant. Indeed, by the time *Stone* was authored, the slogan of "the three religions unite into one" had been widely accepted. The idea was that by addressing different aspects of human existence, the three great traditions of Confucianism, Taoism, and Buddhism led to the same ultimate truth. Like most of his contemporaries, Cao Xueqin was not concerned with the doctrinal differences between Taoism and Buddhism. Rather, the Taoist and the Buddhist represented for him an identical urge toward spiritual liberation.

The Taoist and the Buddhist are equally eccentric. The two scruffy old men are a far cry from the white-robed angels or rosy-cheeked cherubs of the Western tradition. These hidden saints are odd in behavior as well as in appearance, laughing loudly and gesticulating widely. They are referred to as mad by the narrator and by fellow characters alike. The heavenly emissaries' mental weirdness is reflected by their physical deformity—one limps, and the other's shaven pate is covered by scars. Dirty and lice-infested, they wear tattered clothes. The first stanza describes the Buddhist, the second the Taoist:

> A bottle nose he had and shaggy brows,
> Through which peeped eyes that twinkled like bright stars.
> His robe was patched and torn, his feet straw-shod,
> His unclean pate blotched with unsightly scars.
> . . . . . . . . . . . . . . . . . . . . . . . . . . .
> Up, down he hopped on his unequal legs,
> From mud and puddle not a stitch left dry.
> Yet, if you asked him where his dwelling was,
> "Westward of Paradise" he would reply.        (1.25.504)

鼻如懸膽兩眉長,
目似明星蓄寶光,

破衲芒鞋無住跡,
醃臢更有滿頭瘡.
. . . . . . . . . . .
一足高來一足低,
渾身帶水又拖泥.
相逢若問家何處,
卻在蓬萊弱水西. (1: 345)

The idea of the crazy saint is old in Chinese tradition. As early as the first centuries BCE, Chinese literature celebrated divine madmen who hid their sanctity under a mask of outrageous behavior and shabby dress. The trope implies that social norms hinder the search for truth. Liberation, it suggests, can be sought only outside the political order. The social marginality of the holy fool is often reflected in physical deformity. The pages of such Taoist classics as the *Zhuangzi* 莊子 (c. 250 BCE) are populated with mutilated and crippled sages. Hideous-looking holy men, whose ugliness estranges them from human society, are endowed with magic powers that can move heaven and earth. "Uglyface Tuo was ugly enough to give the whole world a fright . . . nonetheless wild creatures would couple where he stood. . . . This was obviously a man with something different about him" (Graham 79).

Such was the attraction of the crazy saint that it crossed the boundaries between China's diverse religions. Sages who asserted their independence by disregard for conventional behavior figured equally in the classics of Taoism and of Buddhism. In both traditions, lowly menials who worked unnoticed in the temple's kitchen were often discovered to be more enlightened than the pompous abbot. The two religions also celebrated eccentric saints in visual art. Carefree and humorous immortals are a favorite topic of Taoist-related painting, as holy fools and weird ascetics are commonly depicted in Buddhist frescoes. Since Buddhism arrived in China from India, local artists accentuated its saints' eccentricity by exaggerating their foreign features. Indian religious paragons such as the arhats were endowed with a humorous air, as Chinese artists highlighted their bushy eyebrows, bulging eyeballs, and large noses. Occasionally, to enhance the comic effect, a foreign saint was shown sporting a beard (despite the Buddhist custom of tonsure) and wearing earrings.

The idea of the holy fool extended from the human to the divine realm. The Chinese pantheon features numerous clownish gods. As their human counterparts, these eccentric divinities cross the boundaries between different religions. Divine fools figure in the heavenly pantheons of Buddhism, Taoism, and the Chinese popular religion. A group of clownish and carefree drunkards is venerated by the Taoists under the title of Eight Immortals, and the beloved Buddhist god Jigong is nicknamed Crazy Ji. These jovial deities reveal the significance of humor in the Chinese religious tradition. Unlike the Western monotheistic faiths, in which the divine is approached by "fear and trembling" (in Søren Kierkegaard's definition), Chinese religions are often easygoing.

Chinese gods are often fond of a good joke. Indeed, foreign divinities who were incorporated into the Chinese pantheon were often colored in humorous hues. Even though in India he was imagined as a somber ascetic, the messianic Buddha Maitreya became in China a jolly good fellow, whose jovial potbellied image welcomes visitors to Buddhist temples (Shahar 39–40).

Eccentric saints were not only a literary trope but also a social reality. When Cao Xueqin was writing his novel, itinerant miracle workers roamed the Chinese landscape. Most were Buddhist, but some were Taoist. As mirrored in *The Story of the Stone*, they functioned as healers and fortune-tellers. They intoned spells, wrote charms (which, burned and mixed in water, were swallowed by the devotees), and sometimes combined rituals of exorcism with martial arts demonstrations. An itinerant lifestyle distanced these folk healers from the religious establishment. Instead of living in the big monasteries, they stayed in humble village shrines or in the houses of the laity. Many disregarded their faith's monastic codes, especially the Buddhist dietary prohibitions against meat and wine. Thus wandering saints were far removed from and held no ecclesiastic post in the monastic community.

The veneration of itinerant miracle workers probably reflected resentment of organized religions. Eccentric magicians were worshipped precisely because their madness estranged them from the monastic establishment, which was accused of corruption. *Stone* censures hypocritical clerics no less than venal officials. Recall the greedy abbess Euergesia, who abets Wang Xi-feng's crimes (1.15.296–98). The author's fondness for itinerant eccentrics accords with his hostility toward deceitful priests.

The image of the carefree sage extended from the religious to the aesthetic sphere. As early as the first centuries CE, Chinese literature celebrated the lighthearted genius who dashes off poems in the heat of wine. That nonconformity was considered by some artists a precondition for individual expression and creativity leads us to the autobiographical aspect of *Stone*'s cult of eccentricity. Its author was himself a bohemian who, in his own words, "frittered away half a lifetime, [finding himself] without a single skill with which [he] could earn a decent living" (1.20). Instead of fulfilling his family's expectation of a respected public career, Cao wasted his life writing a novel that, even had it been published, would not have earned him the kind of recognition associated with the genre nowadays. "All men call the author fool; / None his secret message hears," he tells us (1.1.51) 都云作者痴，誰解其中味 (7). No wonder he feels affinity with such characters as Zhen Shi-yin and Bao-yu, whose obsessions with art, love, and liberation have turned them into social misfits.

Inherited from the Chinese religious landscape, the eccentric saint fits perfectly into the contrapuntal structure of Cao's masterpiece. It has been pointed out that *Stone*'s episodes and characters illuminate each other by difference or resonance. The author conceived his characters in contrasting pairs, "subtly shaping an implicit system of values wherein the individual characters find their place" (Yee, "Counterpoise" 613). The mad Buddhist, the lame Taoist, and the carefree Zhen Shi-yin (who joins them) serve as foils to career figures such as Jia Yu-cun, who subverts justice for personal gains. Their estrangement from the sociopolitical order illuminates that order's hypocrisy and corruption.

## Liberation and Social Order

*Stone* is a story of religious awakening. Experiencing the turmoil of love and the pain of ensuing loss, the protagonist is led to the realization that earthly existence is meaningless. Bao-yu awakens from the dream of the Red Chamber as a wandering monk. Forsaking his wife and family, he is lastly revealed to his father as an ascetic with "shaven head and bare feet, wrapped in a large cape made of crimson felt" (5.120.359) 光著頭, 赤著腳, 身上披著一領大紅猩猩氈 的斗篷 (2: 1594). His journey to enlightenment is shared by other characters. Harboring spiritual aspirations since her childhood, his third cousin Xi-chun chooses to become a nun rather than marry (5.115.269–71, 118.318–21). Zhen Shi-yin joins the mad monk and the lame Taoist after experiencing the terrible loss of his daughter (1.1.65), and Liu Xiang-lian does the same after the shock of his fiancée's suicide. Slashing his queue, he severs "the . . . strands / That bind [him] to the world and its annoys" (3.66.307) 掣出那股雄劍, 將萬根煩惱絲一 揮而盡 (2: 924).

The idea of liberation from worldly existence was brought to China during the first centuries CE. Buddhism considers the world ontologically false and experientially painful. According to the Indian-born faith, existence is transitory and hence inherently afflictive. In this world we are forever bound to lose that which is dear to us. Therefore, liberation can be found only outside this life. Only by breaking out from the relentless cycle of birth, death, and rebirth are we able to escape suffering. The Buddhist concept of salvation, which has had a tremendous impact on China, entails radical liberation from the world as we know it.

Needless to say, these brief lines do not encompass the complexity and variety of Buddhist thought. In the course of its historical evolution and geographic spread, Buddhism has witnessed the emergence of countless schools of thought. Some Buddhist philosophers came to affirm the very world from which they sought to escape. For them liberation did not entail a transcendental sphere separate from the painful realm of experience; rather, it required a new perspective on the familiar world of suffering. "Form is not distinct from emptiness; emptiness is not distinct from form," the *Heart Sutra* tells us, meaning probably that there is no realm of attainment (emptiness) distinct from the transitory world of loss and bereavement. As if to undermine its own soteriology, the scripture (which in its present form was likely written in China) goes on to discredit the very notion of salvation: "There is no suffering, arising [of suffering], extinction [of suffering], or path; no knowledge and no attainment" (Nattier 155–56).

Its doctrinal variations notwithstanding, the urge for liberation has remained a defining Buddhist trait, finding an institutional expression in monasticism. Monks and nuns have figured throughout the history of the faith, across the entire Buddhist world, regardless of philosophical standpoints. The Buddhist priesthood is made of monks. Unlike Judaism and Islam (which do not recognize celibacy), the Buddhist cleric, like his Catholic counterpart, is a person who has chosen to renounce worldly ties. Following the example of the founder of the faith, the Buddha Śākyamuni, monks and nuns forsake family and society for spiritual liberation. With some exceptions, they do not work, marry, or bring offspring into the illusory world of transmigration, from which they seek to escape.

The Buddhist promise of salvation has been at once attractive and difficult for the Chinese to swallow. Even as the notion of liberation resonated with native spiritual needs, accounting for the faith's great success in China, it clashed with the culture's social and religious norms. Chinese family values, sanctioned by the hegemonic Confucian ideology, placed supreme importance on filial piety. Chinese individuals were expected to care for their progenitors in this life—and in the next. As long as one's parents were alive, one was expected to sustain them. When they passed away, one was supposed to provide for them by sacrificial offerings. The filial burden was particularly heavy for sons, as daughters were commonly lost to their natal families when married off. A male offspring was expected to bring into the world children that would provide for his ancestors' welfare. By the very fact that they failed to procreate, Buddhist celibates disrupted the continuity of ancestral worship, condemning generations of their ancestors to eternal suffering. From a Confucian perspective, monks were traitors to their families.

Buddhist apologists were fully aware of the contradiction between the monastic ideal and the native family values. Over the centuries, they developed various methods for accommodating Buddhist monasticism and Confucian filial piety, arguing that a monk's or nun's religious merit would provide for his or her ancestors better than sacrificial offerings. The famous Chinese legend of the Bodhisattva Avalokiteśvara (Guanyin) illustrates their attempts to negotiate the tension between individual salvation and paternal authority. According to the eleventh-century story, the bodhisattva had been incarnated as Princess Miaoshan. When she came of age, Miaoshan refused her father's order to marry. The enraged king sentenced her to death, but she was miraculously spirited away from the execution ground. Years later, the king was afflicted by a terrible disease. No remedy was found throughout his kingdom, until a mysterious monk arrived on the scene. Gouging out his own eyes and cutting off his arms, he offered them as medicine to the king, who was instantly healed. Recognizing that his savior was his own daughter, the king became her ardent devotee, whereupon he was graced with her divine epiphany as the goddess of a thousand eyes and a thousand arms.

The legend provides an etiological explanation for Avalokiteśvara's multi-headed, multihanded iconography, which was brought to China from India. The typical Tantric image of a thousand eyes and a thousand arms is explained as a reward for the goddess's filial sacrifice. For our purpose here, the myth is significant for its attempt to resolve the contradiction between Buddhist celibacy and Confucian family values. Miaoshan's choice of the nunnery defied her father's command, but it provided her with the power to rescue him. The offspring's Buddhist vocation becomes the means for the parent's salvation. Not surprisingly, the legend has been used by Chinese women as a charter for celibacy. (Dudbridge).

Buddhist apologetics notwithstanding, the conflict between monasticism and family was to characterize the history of the Indian faith in China. In one sense, *Stone* could be read as an extended expression of the discord between Buddhist religiosity and Confucian morality. The novel is, after all, the story of a person's struggle against familial authority. Defying paternal expectations, Bao-yu chooses to desert wife and family for the sake of individual salvation. Admittedly, in the current ending, he goes through the motions of passing the examinations and (presumably) providing his family with an heir. But no attempt to mitigate the rupture between Confucian values and Buddhist celibacy could mask the hero's urge to personal liberation. In the end, Bao-yu chooses Buddhist salvation over the performance of his socially ordained roles.

If *Story of the Stone* tells of the discord between individual salvation and social norms, it is equally an epic of tragic love. Just as Bao-yu's religious quest clashes with his familial obligations, his search of individual love clashes with the prevailing system of arranged marriage. *Stone*, then, is concerned with the conflict between individual expression, whether in the romantic or religious sphere, and social norms. The author appears to side with those eccentric saints whose dedication to their inner feelings has estranged them from family and society.

Equally hampered by social obligations, love and the search for spiritual fulfillment are not unrelated. *Stone* suggests that those capable of feeling (enchantment) are more apt to achieve enlightenment (disenchantment). Those who love intensely enough will mourn intensely enough to realize the emptiness of the illusory world. As the fairy Disenchantment predicts, Bao-yu has been endowed with a "blind, defenseless love" that will result in pain and lead to religious awakening (1.5.146). Here we approach the oxymoron of Brother Amor or the Passionate Monk. The stone that is Bao-yu, like its first reader, Vanitas, has engendered passion followed by regret and awakening. The novel's opening chapter explains:

> As a consequence of all this, Vanitas, starting off in the Void (which is Truth) came to the contemplation of Form (which is Illusion); and from Form engendered Passion; and by communicating Passion, entered again

into Form; and from Form awoke to the Void (which is Truth). He therefore changed his name from Vanitas to Brother Amor, or the Passionate
Monk (because he had approached Truth by way of Passion), and changed
the title of the book from *The Story of the Stone* to *The Tale of Brother
Amor*.                                                                    (51)[1]

從此, 空空道人因空見色, 由色生情, 傳情入色, 自色悟空, 遂改名情僧,
改 "石頭記" 為 "情僧錄."                                                (1: 6–7)

The Buddhist language of illusion is used interchangeably with the *Stone*'s
discourse of its own fictionality. Just as the world is ontologically groundless, so
is the product of the artistic imagination. The Land of Illusion into which the
reader follows Bao-yu is both the experiential world (in the Buddhist sense) and
the novel (which is by definition fiction). The Buddhist musings on the nature
of reality are thus seamlessly intertwined with *Stone*'s pondering of its own artistic fantasy. Buddhist philosophy and literary reflexivity are combined in the
novel's motto, which applies both to the dream of living and to the delusion of
reading:

> Truth becomes fiction when the fiction's true;
> Real becomes not-real where the unreal's real.   (1.1.55)

假作真時真亦假,
無為有處有還無.   (10)

The metaphor goes both ways. Buddhist vocabulary is employed as a tool
of literary theory, just as the experience of reading serves to convey Buddhist
philosophy. On the one hand, "the author has succeeded in turning the concept
of world and life as dream into a subtle but powerful theory of fiction" (A. Yu
141). On the other hand, the experience of reading is likened to the chimera
of worldly existence. Enchanted by the work of art, the reader is gripped by its
fiction, only to wake up and realize its illusion. The vicarious moment of living through fiction could serve therefore as a Buddhist exercise, rehearsing the
dream of earthly existence:

> When grief for fiction's idle words
> More real than human life appears,
> Reflect that life itself's a dream
> And do not mock the reader's tears.   (5.120.376)

說到辛酸處,
荒唐愈可悲.
由來同一夢,
休笑世人痴!   (2: 1605)

The application of Buddhist vocabulary to literary theory brings us back to the fact that *Stone* is a novel, not scripture. Whatever his spiritual aspirations, Cao Xueqin chose to express them in a form that defies orthodox religiosity. From a Buddhist perspective, the writing of thousands of pages of fiction would be a waste of time, for art is ultimately tangential to spiritual liberation. By contrast, Cao's dedication to his literature indicates that he did not seek religious salvation. Rather, he found consolation in artistic creation. Like Vladimir Nabokov, he sought the "refuge of art" (311).[2]

The loving detail with which Cao recorded his life reveals the depth of his attachment to it. The seriousness of his artistic endeavor, and his painstaking efforts to reconstruct his past, belie the Buddhist ideal of detachment. As Li Wai-yee pithily observes, Cao Xueqin "is deeply committed to all that he questions: the aesthetic illusion he creates, his own past, and the lyrical ideal of the tradition" (*Enchantment* 267). If *The Story of the Stone* is directed toward liberation from the world, it is equally torn by longing to that lost world itself.

NOTES

[1] On *Stone*'s paradoxical association of love and enlightenment, see W. Li, *Enchantment*; A. Yu; and Q. Li 122–34.

[2] I am grateful to my student Or Biron for this reference.

# The Banner *Story of the Stone*

## Evelyn S. Rawski

*Story of the Stone* has been studied by many scholars, but relatively little attention has been paid to the work as a depiction of Qing banner society. The neglect is especially surprising given widespread recognition of the banner origins of the novel's two authors, Cao Xueqin and Gao E. To what extent and in what ways can *Stone* be characterized as a novel of a bannerman household? How does the banner background affect readings of the novel? And finally, if the novel is centered on the society of the Qing conquest elite, how does one explain its widespread appeal to Han Chinese literati?

### Banner Society in the Qing

The Qing dynasty (1644–1911) was founded by a northeast Asian people who claimed descent from the Jurchen, who had ruled part of north China during the Jin dynasty (1115–1260). The founder of the Qing ruling house, Nurhaci, was a minor tribal chieftain who emerged as a regional power in the northeast. In 1616 he accepted the title of *han* (Manchu for "khan") and established the Later Jin state. Two years later, citing grievances against the Ming dynasty (1368–1644), Nurhaci began to directly challenge Ming control of the northeast. This struggle was continued by his son, Hongtaiji, who transformed the people of the region into a new group, the Manchus. In 1636, Hongtaiji took on the Chinese title of emperor and proclaimed the establishment of the Qing state. When Hongtaiji died, his half brother, Dorgon, directed the entry of Manchu troops into China proper in 1644, which began the final phase of the Manchu conquest of the Ming.

Banners, originally small hunting groups loyal to Nurhaci, developed from 1601 onward into large civil-military units. Those who joined Nurhaci and Hongtaiji were enrolled into companies, each consisting (in theory) of three hundred warrior households. Companies were subsumed under banners, which before 1644 were led by Nurhaci and Hongtaiji's kinsmen, the banner lords. Banners became administrative units for registration, conscription, taxation, and mobilization of the tribes and peoples who enlisted in the Manchu cause before 1644. By that time eight Mongol and eight Chinese banners had been added to the eight Manchu banners that were organized in 1616.[1] The Manchu conquest of the Ming, completed in 1683, was accomplished with a multiethnic fighting force organized into the banner system.

What we call Manchu society was in reality the society of the Manchu, Mongol, and Chinese martial bannermen. These banner designations did not conform, at least not in the seventeenth century, to ethnicity: some Mongols who had initially belonged to the Manchu banners remained in them even after the

Mongol banners were created, Korean and Russian companies could also be found in the Manchu banners, and Han Chinese bond servant companies who bore the flags and drums of the banner lords and the *han* (the leader of the banner lords) were also part of the Manchu banners.

By providing a mechanism for incorporating the diverse peoples of northeast Asia under one regimen, the banners facilitated the creation of a Manchu nation. Even as Hongtaiji led his followers to the military conquest of the Ming dynasty, he and other leaders were reinforcing a distinctive, separate group identity. The name *Manchu* itself was adopted in 1635 by Hongtaiji, as a restoration of the name by which his ancestors were identified. Like the commissioning of a new writing system, accomplished in several phases from 1599 to the 1630s, Manchu became an identity that superseded the tribal designations of the Jurchen and other northeastern peoples whom Nurhaci and Hongtaiji had united by force. The Manchu people included hunter-gatherers living close to the Russian settlements in Siberia (the new Manchus [*ice Manju*]); Haixi Jurchen, who resided along the northeast coast; and southern Jurchen, the group to which Nurhaci belonged.

The relation of Manchu to banner identity has been a subject of some debate. Except for a brief period in the 1640s, the banners constituted a conquest elite governed by laws separating them from the civilian population, the former Ming subjects, by dress and residence. After 1648, the bannermen in Beijing were assigned to residences surrounding the imperial palace and the central government ministries in the Tartar or Inner City. Only bannermen were initially allowed to live in the Inner City; Han Chinese were moved into the southern Chinese or Outer City and could not enter the Inner City at will. Outside Beijing, bannermen who manned garrisons located at strategic sites throughout the empire also lived in walled settlements segregated from the civilian population.

Despite obvious differences in their cultures and languages during the conquest period, the separation of bannermen from the civilian or subject population tended to cause them to become Manchu over the course of the late seventeenth century. For the most part, bannermen married within the banners. Banner society was marked by gradations of status that cut across the Manchu, Mongol, and Chinese martial banner designations and played a major role in determining the life prospects open to an individual. This highly stratified society had a graded nobility, free commoners, and several groups of hereditary slaves.

The preeminent group, imperial kinsmen, were direct descendants of emperors or the collateral descendants of Nurhaci's brothers. Unlike the Ming, which bore the heavy fiscal burden of an ever expanding number of imperial descendants, the Qing reduced the number of perpetual princedoms; discriminated against collateral descendants; and limited special privileges, high stipends, and access to power to a favored few. Below the imperial lineage, there was a small banner nobility descended from military heroes. The most prestigious nobles were descended from Nurhaci's Five Councilors, who served before 1616. The Niohuru clan of Eidu, the Suwan Gūwalgiya of Fiongdon, and the Donggo clan of Hohori were among the eight great houses of the Manchu nobility, and their descendants enjoyed favored access to high military and civil positions.

Especially in Nurhaci's lifetime, talented warriors could rise to high positions and be awarded titles and imperial kinsmen brides. Eastern Mongol leaders who joined the Manchu cause with their followers were also incorporated into the banner organization, and like other bannermen, they were eligible to sit for special examinations to qualify for office. Khalkha (Qalqa) Mongols to their west, in what is today Mongolia, were reorganized into a separate group of approximately two hundred banners, subsumed under eighteen leagues. These Outer Mongols were under the jurisdiction of the Court of Colonial Affairs, while all other nobles fell under the jurisdiction of the Board of Personnel. The Outer Mongols enjoyed greater autonomy but were under the administrative purview of specially appointed Qing high officials.

The conquest elite also included men who had served the Ming, then switched sides. Wu Sangui, Shang Kexi, and Geng Jimao were three Ming generals who came over to the Manchu cause and were rewarded with princely titles and imperial brides. Although these Han Chinese adherents lost everything in their unsuccessful rebellion (1673–81), many lesser figures founded noble lines that persisted throughout the dynasty.

Most ordinary bannermen were free men. After the conquest, bannermen were either settled in strategic garrisons or on agricultural lands in north China and the northeast homeland. In addition to filling hereditary military posts, they became eligible to compete in the civil service examinations under special quotas and to serve in the bureaucracy. The Qing established schools to educate and train bannermen in Manchu and scheduled special examinations in Manchu (later also in Mongolian), which qualified successful candidates for office.

Bond servants—the Manchu term, *booi*, means "of the household"—were descendants of Mongol, Korean, and Chinese prisoners of war enslaved and registered in separate companies under the banners. Although bond servants were subject to the same laws that applied to all bannermen (as distinct from the subjugated Ming populace), their servile status distinguished them from the freemen who composed the bulk of the banner forces. The status of the *booi* was not very different from that of slaves, who were called *aha* in Manchu or *booi aha*. Both *aha* and *booi* were legally defined servile groups in the Qing. Whereas *aha* worked in the fields, *booi* were in domestic service. Occupying the lower rungs of the banner hierarchy, they were not (at least not by law) permitted to intermarry with other banner groups. After the upper three banners (Bordered Yellow, Plain Yellow, and Plain White) came under the emperor's personal control in the late seventeenth century, *booi* in these banners became the emperor's household servants. With the Manchu conquest, their activities were "elevated from a family level to a state level of operations" (Kessler 28).[2]

## The Novel and Banner Society

According to scholars, the primary author of *Story of the Stone*, Cao Xueqin, belonged to a family that was part of the "banner-bearers and drummers" registered under the Manchu Plain White Banner.[3] His ancestor Cao Xiyuan seems to have become a bond servant during the Manchu capture of Shenyang in 1621; some branches of the family remained in the northeast into the eighteenth century. When Dorgon was purged after his death in 1650, control over his Plain White Banner shifted to the emperor. As one of the "upper three banners" of the emperor, bond servants in the Plain White Banner were eligible for positions in the Imperial Household Department. Gao E, who is credited with the last forty chapters of *Stone*, was registered in the Chinese martial Bordered Yellow Banner and had a minor official career (4.20–22).

*Story of the Stone* focuses on the domestic life of young cousins in a wealthy household in decline. The novel describes attributes and activities typical of a bannerman family. The adult males of this aristocratic household are educated, with at least some of them — Jia Zheng is the exemplar — engaged in literati pursuits, yet the Jia males frequently ride on horseback and practice archery, activities associated with the banner and not the Han Chinese literati lifestyle during the Qing period. The senior men kneel in Manchu style to receive imperial communications. Jia Zheng is sent on a wide variety of imperial assignments: supervising relief measures, serving as an education officer and as Jiangxi grain intendant, and holding a post in the Ministry of Works (3.70.384, 71.394, 5.99.29). Jia Rong's great-grandfather was a general and hereditary noble of the first rank; the title is reduced with each transmission, so Jia Zhen, Rong's father, is only an "Honorary Colonel" and a hereditary third-rank noble (1.13.263). When a family member becomes ill, Grandmother Jia can call on a specialist from the imperial College of Physicians. When Jia Jing dies, the emperor grants the family permission for the coffin to be brought from the Taoist temple into the city, contravening the prohibition.

The Jia diet features dishes that would not be unusual in banner circles. In one chapter, the bailiff arrives with produce from the Jia estates as the household prepares to celebrate the New Year. The meat includes three kinds of deer, wild boar, sheep, goats, and bear paws (2.53.561–62), reminiscent of the seasonal shipments of local meat received for consumption by the imperial household from the northeast. Father Ripa, residing in Peking during the Kangxi reign, observed that "an enormous quantity of game," which included stags, wild boars, pheasants, and partridges, was shipped to the Forbidden City from October to March (Rawski, *Last Emperors* 47). In the novel, when Bao-yu and his sister Tan-chun visit Grandmother Jia in the winter, the first dish served is unborn lamb stewed in milk. Grandmother says this is a health food for old people and suggests that the youngsters try instead the fresh venison. But Bao-yu chooses pickled pheasant with his rice (2.48.483).

The Jia family is enmeshed in social relationships with nobles and princes yet is insecure in its own status. Despite its wealth, it adopts the position of the inferior in encounters with the prince of Bei-jing and other notables. Although they are not blood relations, Grandmother Jia and the other senior ladies must escort the coffin of a dowager consort to the imperial tombs. The family enjoys imperial favor but trembles whenever it receives an imperial summons, because it does not know whether to expect good or bad fortune. Its worst fears are eventually realized when the emperor sends the imperial guards to search the Jia mansions in a criminal investigation that results in punishment for the senior men of the family. The uneasiness over imperial whim that permeates the novel accurately reflects the Cao family's bond servant background.

Despite — or because of — their low status, bondservants in the upper three banners enjoyed special opportunities to rise above their station through imperial appointment. The Manchu rulers used bond servants to control and supervise eunuchs, another low-status group of people who had long served Chinese emperors in the palace. The Imperial Household Department, which performed diplomatic and fiscal duties extending far beyond its primary responsibility for managing the household affairs of the emperor, was staffed by bannermen, bond servants, state slaves, and eunuchs in a complex internal system of checks and balances.

The Imperial Household Department had jurisdiction over customs bureaus that collected taxes on goods in transit at key points in long-distance trade routes from the northwest, the Yangzi delta, and at Canton. It also managed imperial manufactories in Nanjing, Hangzhou, and Suzhou, where silks and other textiles for court use were produced. Cao Xueqin's father, grandfather, and great-grandfather were all superintendents at these manufactories, from the Kangxi reign (1662–1722) to the Yongzheng reign (1723–35). His grandfather, Cao Yin, was appointed in 1690 as superintendent of the Suzhou Imperial Textile Factory, then transferred in 1693 to the Nanjing factory, a post he held for twenty years. From this post and four terms as head of the Liang-Huai salt controllership, he accumulated great wealth. He acquired a reputation "as a connoisseur of special dishes at banquets, as a collector of rare books, and as host to men of letters" (Hummel 741). Less known to his contemporaries were his services as a confidential imperial agent, whose reports on corrupt bureaucrats reached the Kangxi emperor through the secret palace memorial system.

How did bond servants attract imperial favor? One of the ways cited in *Story of the Stone* occurs in a discussion between You-shi and Xi-feng about Big Jiao, an unmanageable manservant. You-shi explains the origins of his privileged status:

> When he was young he went with Grandfather on three or four of his campaigns and once saved his life by pulling him from under a heap of corpses and carrying him to safety on his back. He went hungry himself and stole things for his master to eat; and once when he had managed to get half a cupful of water, he gave it to his master and drank horse's urine

himself. Because of these one or two acts of heroism he was always given special treatment during Grandfather's lifetime.                (1.7.181)

只因他從小兒跟著太爺們出過三四回兵, 從死人堆裡把太爺背了出來, 得了命; 自己挨著餓, 卻偷了東西來給主子吃, 兩日沒得水, 得了半碗水 給主子喝, 他自己喝馬溺. 不過仗著這些功勞情分, 有祖宗時都另眼相待.
                                                                            (1: 113)

The Jias are bond servants whose wealth and social prominence stem from the merit of earlier ancestors: the family's noble titles were due to the achievements of Jia Zheng's grandfather and great-uncle, and the imperial edicts sparing Jia Zhen and Jia She from the heavy punishments stipulated by law ascribe imperial mercy to these ancestors' merit (5.107.141–43). In actuality, Manchu rulers did not ennoble bond servants, but there is no doubt that the affluence and literati pursuits of the Jia senior men reflected the social reality of Cao Yin's life.

*Story of the Stone* makes numerous references to the aristocratic social networks in which the Jia family moved. The Jia men and women go to parties at the mansions of princes and dukes; their funerals and birthday parties are attended by personages. The social whirl is exemplified by a description of the eight days of entertainment with banquets marking Grandmother Jia's eightieth birthday:

> [T]he twenty-eighth would be for imperial kinsmen, princes and princesses of the Blood and their consorts, Royal Highnesses, Serene Highnesses and members of the high nobility; the twenty-ninth would be for Ministers of State and Civil and Military Governors and their wives; the thirtieth for official colleagues and their wives and members of other clans related to the Jia family by marriage; on the first of the eighth month a family party would be given by Jia She, on the second one by Jia Zheng and on the third one by Jia Zhen and Jia Lian; on the fourth a joint entertainment would be given by all members of the Jia clan irrespective of age and seniority; and on the fifth there would be another joint entertainment organized by Lai Da, Lin Zhi-xiao and the other senior domestics.
> (3.71.349–50)

二十八日請皇親附馬王公諸公主郡主王妃國君太君夫人等, 二十九日 便是閣下都府督鎮及誥命等, 三十日便是諸官長及誥命並遠近親友及 堂客. 初一日是賈赦的家宴, 初二日是賈政, 初三日是賈珍賈璉, 初四 日是賈府中合族長幼大小共湊的 家宴. 初五日是賴大林之孝等家下管 事人等共湊一日.
                                                                            (2: 977–78)

Jia sons and daughters also marry into other prominent banner families. Daiyu's father, Lin Ru-hai, and Xiang-yun's family both had ancestors with noble titles; Ying-chun's husband comes from a family of hereditary army officers; and

Tan-chun is married to the son of the commandant of Haimen. The high status of relations by marriage is also tied to the Imperial Household Department. This connection is enjoyed by the Wangs, the natal family of Xi-feng and Lady Wang, and the Xues of Bao-chai's family. According to the novel, the Wangs had the honor of entertaining the emperor on one of his southern visits, when Grandfather was in charge of the tributary missions—an honor distinguishing the historical Cao Yin's career (1.16.314).

Another peculiarity of the Cao family history that is duplicated in *Story of the Stone* concerns the importance of women in a bond servant family's social mobility. When Jia She and Jia Zheng converse with a visitor, Feng Zi-ying, Jia Zheng muses on the decline of great houses, Jia She asserts that nothing can happen to their family, and Feng chimes in, "Of course not . . . with a family that from Lady Jia [the grandmother] down to the younger generation has such an impeccable record" (4.92.260) 果然, 尊府是不怕的 . . . 你家自老太太起至於少爺們, 沒有一個刁鑽刻薄的 (2: 1283). Such references to women (Feng is referring to the imperial concubine in the current generation of Jia women) as major contributors to the fortunes of a great house would make no sense in a Han Chinese social context but were completely accurate and appropriate in the bond servant context. Cao Xueqin's great-grandfather, Cao Xi, married a nurse of the Kangxi emperor's, Ms. Sun, and the emperor's affectionate recollection of her undoubtedly advanced Cao Xi's career.

Only bannermen's daughters and bond servant's daughters were eligible for entry into the imperial harem, according to the Qing regulations. The empress and higher-ranking consorts for imperial princes and the emperor were selected by a triennial draft of beautiful women from the daughters of banner officials, who had to present themselves for inspection at the palace before they could be betrothed to others. Daughters of bond servant officials in the upper three banners who served in the Imperial Household Department were subject to an annual draft for palace maids but could also be promoted into the harem. In *Story of the Stone*, much is made of the entry of the eldest Jia daughter, Yuan-chun, into the palace in this fashion. She is eventually promoted into the ranks of imperial consorts.

The description of the wealth and lifestyle of the Jia family agrees with information available on the actual circumstances enjoyed by a favored bond servant like Cao Xueqin's grandfather, Cao Yin. The family eats red emperor rice, which is specially grown for the imperial table. The family possesses "restricted garments and skirts for palace use" (5.105.115) and other fashionable curiosities, such as a Western clock and a painting using Western perspective, which startles Grannie Liu. On one of her visits, Grannie enters Prospect Garden, where she sees a "young woman smiling at her in welcome," which turns out to be a painting. " 'Strange!' she thought. 'How can they paint a picture so that it sticks out like that?' " (2.41.318).

One of the clearest signs of high status was the ownership of slaves. As Preston Torbert noted, servile groups in the banners could be classified into four categories. At the bottom were the state slaves, who were bannermen enslaved for major economic and political crimes. State slaves registered in the upper three banners were, like the *booi*, eligible for palace service. In 1738, they were granted the same status under criminal law as *booi*, but their social status continued to rank below bond servants. Above them were the indentured servants of the *booi*. Then came ordinary *booi*. At the top of the social scale were the few, like the Caos, who enjoyed imperial favor.

Despite their servile status, *booi* could own slaves, as do the Jias. *Story of the Stone* refers to several different categories of slaves that the Jias own. Perhaps the most symbolically prestigious slaves were foreigners who had been captured in battle and bestowed by the emperor. In a conversation with one of the young actresses purchased by his family, Parfumée, Bao-yu wants to dress her up as a boy, with "a big fur cap" and "tiger-boots." When he doubts that she could successfully pretend to be his page, she replies, "Tell them I'm a *foreign* page. Your family's got several foreign pages" (3.63.237) 咱家現有幾家土番, 你就說我是個小土番兒 (2: 877).

Parfumée was purchased in Suzhou to perform plays during the home visit of Yuan-chun, the imperial concubine (1.16.316). Many of these actresses are eventually sent out to be adopted into families, to be married off. Their status resembles that of Aroma, Bao-yu's maid, who tells Bao-yu that she "is not one of your house-born slaves." She was purchased, and her family plans to buy her out of service "next year" (1.19.386). Jia Lian and Lin Zhi-xiao have a conversation about arranging a marriage between Sunset, one of Lady Wang's maids, and Brightie. Lin Zhi-xiao argues that the boy is "drinking too much and gambling and getting up to all sorts of capers. I know they're only slaves (*nücai*), but marriage is for a lifetime after all" (3.72.432) 旺兒的那小兒子雖然年輕, 在外頭吃酒賭錢, 無所不至. 雖說都是奴才們, 到底是一輩子的事 (2: 1003).

It is not clear in the text whether Brightie was a house-born (i.e., hereditary) slave, as was Lai Da. The Jia house rules do distinguish between hereditary and purchased (indentured) slaves. As explicated by Tan-chun to her natural mother, Aunt Zhao, "home-reared" or hereditary slaves receive lower payments to cover funeral expenses than do servants from "outside" (3.55.51–52). In other words, indentured servants like Aroma enjoy higher status than hereditary slaves.

In Qing times, ordinary Chinese commoners as well as bannermen could own hereditary slaves. The mother of the chief steward of the Rong-guo mansion, Lai Da, chats with Xi-feng, who congratulates her on her grandson's appointment to a government post. She responds:

"Thirty years it is since you were born," I said, "and all that time, in actual fact, you've been a bondservant. Yet through the kindness of our Masters you . . . were taught to read and write like a gentleman's son . . . I doubt you know how the word "bondservant" is written. (2.45.390)

你今年活了三十歲, 雖然是人家的奴才, 一落娘胎胞, 主子恩典 . . . 也是公子哥兒似的讀書認字 . . . 你那裡知道那 "奴才" 兩字是怎麼寫的. (1: 602)

There is no Chinese term that is a precise equivalent for the Manchu *booi*. In the passage cited above, Hawkes translates *nücai* as "bondservant," but in Lai Da's mother's concluding peroration, when she admonishes her grandson to be grateful to the master who "did this for you, that was born a *nücai*," David Hawkes translates the same term as "slave" (390).

The Jias, who are bond servants, own *nücai*. Their *nücai* are themselves able to purchase slaves. Skybright, one of Bao-yu's maids, was originally purchased as a child by Lai Da to serve his wife. When Grandmother Jia took a liking to her, Lai Da's wife gave her to the mistress, and subsequently Grandmother Jia assigned Skybright to serve Bao-yu (3.77.542). The novel takes pains to point out that even lowly slaves like Skybright lived lives of luxury that free peasants could not imagine, just as low-status bond servants could be raised by imperial order to the peaks of wealth and authority. When Grannie Liu first meets Wang Xi-feng's chief maid, Patience, she mistakes her for her mistress, because Patience is dressed in silks and satins and wears gold and silver ornaments in her hair (1.6.158). A household such as the Jias regarded good treatment of their slaves as an important sign of their status. This treatment included educating especially bright boys like Lai Da's grandson, who eventually is appointed a district magistrate (2.45.390).

Many incidents in *Stone* illustrate the enormous gap between the law, which drew a firm line between master and slave, and the actualities of life in a large extended household. The Jia servants take on some of the status of their master and some of his authority. Patience, Wang Xi-feng's maid, acts as a gatekeeper, determining which individuals will have access to the mistress. Faithful, Grandmother Jia's maid, has an equally powerful position, so the other members in the household tread carefully where these individuals are concerned.

Both Patience and Faithful exercise authority through performance of their daily duties. Some servants possessed symbolic capital from their association with the ancestors of the current masters. For this reason Big Jiao cannot be effectively disciplined. When Jia Rong tries to stop his drunken abuse, he bellows:

> Don't you come the Big Master stuff with me, sonny boy! Never mind a little bit of a kid like you, even your daddy and granddaddy don't dare to try any funny stuff with Old Jiao. If it wasn't for Old Jiao, where would you lot all be today, with your rank and your fancy titles and your money and all the other things you enjoy? It was your great-granddad, whose life I saved when he was given up for dead that won all this for you, by the sweat of his brow. And what reward do I get for saving him? Nothing.
>
> (1.7.182)

> 你別在焦大跟前使主子性兒. 別說你這樣兒的, 就是你爹, 你爺爺, 也不敢和焦大挺腰子! 不是焦大一個人, 你們就做官兒享榮華受富貴? 你祖宗九死一生掙下這家業, 到如今了, 不報我的恩.                                      (1: 114)

Because they perform maternal functions, nurses and wet nurses take on part of the prestige of the parental role. Just as the emperor rewarded his former wet nurse, Cao Yin's mother, so Bao-yu must honor his wet nurse. In chapter 19, Nannie Li, who has been pensioned off, comes to visit Bao-yu's quarters. She picks up a bowl of koumiss (fermented mare's milk) that Bao-yu saved for his maid Aroma and drinks it. When the maids warn her that Bao-yu will be angry, Nannie Li retorts that he owes her much more:

> Do you mean to tell me that Aroma counts for more with him than I do? He ought to stop and ask himself how he grew up to be the big boy he is today. It's my milk he sucked, that came from my own heart's blood: that's what he grew up on. And you mean to tell me that now, if I drink one bowlful of *his* milk—cow's milk—he's going to be angry with me?     (384)

> 難道待襲人比我還重? 難道他不想想怎麼長大了? 我的血變的奶, 吃的長這麼大, 如今我吃他一碗牛奶, 他就生氣了?     (258)

Bao-yu may regard Nannie Li as a tiresome old woman, but the larger society's attitudes toward the relationship of child and wet nurse give her a claim on him. His own relationship with Aroma exemplifies the occasionally paradoxical nature of the master-servant bond. Even though Aroma is an indentured servant, she has some authority over him, delegated to her by Bao-yu's mother, Lady Wang, and by Grandmother Jia.

Aroma and the other confidential maidservants of the Jia family are portrayed as intelligent and loyal human beings, on a par with their masters in terms of their sensitivity to human feelings. At the same time, the novel depicts the arbitrary power of the masters and the tragic consequences when a maid incurs the master's displeasure. When Bao-yu's maid Skybright is brought to the attention of his mother by a disgruntled servant, Lady Wang decides that Skybright is a depraved young female who will lead her son into a dissolute life, so she dismisses the ailing woman and sends her home to die. Xi-chun's maid, Picture, and Ying-chun's maid, Chess, are also abruptly dismissed (3.74.464–66, 77.532–35).

*Story of the Stone* uses the plight of the Jia servants to make an important point about the situation of masters. Many of the disasters in the novel occur to both servants and masters. The search for illicit articles to weed out bad influences in the chambers of the young cousins in the Jia mansion parallels the search of the Embroidered Jackets (a kind of imperial secret police) through the Jia mansion (5.105.113–17). As a result of such an investigation, Jia She is sentenced to penal service on the Mongolian frontier, and Jia Zhen is stripped of his hereditary rank and sent to the maritime frontier (7.112–55). Whereas the author openly mourns the sad fates of the Jia women and their maidservants, he puts the blame for the punishments of the Jia men squarely on their inability to maintain discipline in their households.

## Reading the Novel in Qing Context

*Story of the Stone* refers to the Confucian canon and preparation for civil service examinations, but its heart lies elsewhere. Buddhism and Taoism are important cultural presences in the novel; so is the banner society and specifically the bond servant society of the Qing period. The structure of banner society sets the framework for the plot and affects certain authorial choices. The ending leaves the Jias much reduced in circumstances but with two new degree holders and the prospect of a partial restoration of the family fortunes. Here the novel diverges from the actual poverty of the Cao family after its dismissal from office at the hands of the Yongzheng emperor.

The Cao family's impoverishment was closely linked to lavish expenditures incurred by virtue of their close ties with the imperial family. Cao Yin hosted the Kangxi emperor on four of the emperor's six southern tours (1699, 1703, 1705, 1707), which entailed building a miniature palace to house him during his visit, elaborate entertainment and gifts, and the cost of lodgings for the enormous imperial entourage. While enjoying the enormous prestige and public recognition bestowed by these signs of imperial favor, Cao Yin died owing the government over half a million taels of silver. The emperor appointed Li Xu, Yin's colleague and relation by marriage, to a year as Yangzhou salt controller in order to clear this debt, but the additional arrears incurred in his office at the textile manufactory remained unpaid until 1728, when the Yongzheng emperor ordered the confiscation of the property of Yin's adopted son, Cao Fu, to clear the accounts. At this stage, the Cao family is said to have still owned thirteen residences, almost 2,000 mu (330 acres) of land, and their household was 114 persons, including servants. The year 1728 marks the end of the Cao sojourn in Nanjing and their move into modest quarters in Beijing.

Although the Cao family's inability to pay off the arrears in government accounts was the ostensible reason for the purge, Jonathan Spence rightly points to several contributing factors (*Ts'ao Yin* 263–67, 269–72). The Kangxi emperor was indulgent to Cao Yin's family and intervened in their favor because of his fondness for his former nurse, Cao Yin's mother, and for the services rendered to him by his deceased bond servant. Spence cites several such interventions, not only immediately after Cao Yin's death but also in 1715, when the sudden death of Cao Yong left the family without an heir, and in 1716, when audits discovered even more arrears in the accounts.

Yinzhen, the Yongzheng emperor, held quite a different attitude. Perhaps because of questions about the legitimacy of his succession (Silas Wu, *Passage* 179–83, 185–86), he was suspicious of his father's former confidants, as he was of the secret palace memorials (Silas Wu, *Communication* 69–72). The new emperor also feared that bond servants might overstep their legal bounds. In a 1726 edict, he reminded officials that the distinction between master and slave, strictly observed in Manchu society, must not be blurred as Manchu officials took on Chinese customs: "the distinction of master and slave, once determined, cannot be changed throughout one's life and extends beyond oneself to one's wife, children, clothing, food, and livelihood" (Wei, Wu, and Li 19).

Yinzhen viewed *booi* as "petty, dishonest, and disobedient" (Spence, *Ts'ao Yin* 283). Moreover, his personal interest in fiscal issues may have made him particularly intolerant of sloppy handling of government accounts. Shortly after he ascended the throne, Li Xu and other bond servants like Cao Fu were investigated and found wanting. Commenting on Cao Fu's personnel evaluation, the emperor wrote, "This man is really no good" (288).

Writing during the Qianlong reign (1736–96), Cao Xueqin would have found it politically inadvisable to adhere too faithfully to the narrative of his own family's decline: such an account might catch the emperor's attention in an unwanted way. In the novel, it is not the emperor's arbitrariness but rather the decadent and immoral lifestyle of the senior Jia males that is to blame for the destruction of the family.

The novel's treatment of the fate of the Jia daughters and the Jia maids is somewhat different: unable to determine their own fates, they are victims of those in authority. The life of Bao-yu also invokes this theme of helplessness. He empathizes with his female cousins but cannot alter the disposition of their lives; no matter how favored a grandchild he is, he cannot prevent Skybright's dismissal and untimely death. Similarly, the Jia senior men and women, although they determine the fates of the younger generation, are themselves powerless against imperial authority. At most, they can attempt to cultivate relationships that will mitigate the harshness of imperial edicts. Bao-yu's ultimate liberation from this scheme of things is in the mainstream of Buddhist and Taoist teaching but can also be construed as a response to the precariousness of his family's position in the Qing political system.

## Moving beyond Banner Society

Many aspects of *Story of the Stone* indicate that the Jias were not a Han Chinese family but rather belonged to the banners; not only that, they were one of the small group of bond servant families who became powerful and affluent in imperial service. Why, given the anti-Manchu bias of Chinese literati at the close of the Qing dynasty, was this identification not an impediment to the novel's widespread popularity?

Several factors might be cited. The first is that information that confirms the non-Han social background of the Jias is concealed or masked. The main action of the novel deals with the dynamics of a wealthy extended family and the relationships of its younger generation, in a manner that many Han Chinese readers found familiar. Just as one can ignore implicitly contradictory features of a scene that one regards as incidental, readers could bypass the numerous citations of noble titles and descriptions of non-Han Chinese cultural customs to focus on the story of Bao-yu and the young girls with whom he grew up.

Scholars have noted that Cao Xueqin masked the biographical details of his family history when he re-created the world of his childhood in *Story of the Stone*. The power of the Qing rulers, even before the Qianlong inquisition and the Yongzheng emperor's ruination of the Cao family, provided ample reason for the exercise of caution. Cao's strategy of self-censorship included introducing deliberate confusion in specific allusions that might be taken amiss. For example, descriptions of the aristocratic milieu incorporate enough elements of the actual Qing system to seem authentic but are carefully mixed with imaginary and anachronistic elements.

In one instance of obfuscation, the Qing policy of reducing noble titles with each generational transmission is assumed in the novel's description of aristocratic personages, but they all have titles, such as the prince of Bei-jing (1.14.284), that are imaginary (the characters 北靜君王 are not the ones designating the modern capital 北京). In another example, the imperial guards who invade the Jia mansions to search out evidence for criminal prosecution are designated not by the Qing but by the Ming name for this group. The specific title that Yuan-chun first received, *nüshi* 女史 ("female scribe") (1.2.81), was used from the Tang dynasty (618–907) through the Ming but not in the Qing dynasty. Yuan-chun's title when Yuan-chun is installed as an imperial consort did not exist during the Ming or Qing dynasties. The Chinese term that is used to describe her death, *hongshi* 薨逝, is a made-up amalgam of *hong* 薨, the verb used to describe the death of princes and high-ranking consorts, and *keshi* (溘逝), which is the verb for the death of lower-ranking court personages (4.95.310). As a result, the reader is presented with a compendium of Ming-Qing society as a backdrop for the plot.

Similar confusion in the locale of the major action has been noted by *Stone* scholars. The Jia ("false") and Zhen ("real") families exemplify the attempt to create a locale that is not specific to Beijing or Nanjing, the northern and southern cities central in the existence of the Cao family. Nanjing seems to have been where Cao Xueqin was born (perhaps in 1715) and raised before moving to Peking in 1728. References to unmistakably northern customs, several of which were cited earlier, are mixed with references to southern customs—for example, the consumption of betel nuts (4.82.58).

The novel was written in Chinese, and the language also functions to mask several aspects of banner society. The first printed edition appeared in 1791–92, but the existence of a manuscript copy, purchased in Peking in 1769, suggests that annotated manuscript versions circulated soon after Cao Xueqin's death, if not before. The conflation of the many servile statuses in the banners into one term, *nücai*, blurs the banner distinctions and suggests to readers that they were the same as those found in Han Chinese commoner society.

The novel is similarly coy in its depiction of the social status of the Jia family. The title awarded to Jia Dai-hua, Jia Zhen's grandfather, seems to be a take-off on Tang dynasty military designations and the Qing practice of conferring honorary generalships on the deserving. There is no direct identification of the family as bond servant in origin, and the only individuals described as *nücai* are the Jia servants. Yuan-chun's initial palace appointment as a female secretary and her subsequent installation as *Xiande fei* 賢德妃 (second-ranking imperial consort) are both highly unlikely (1.16.304, 203). Whereas daughters of banner officials were selected as brides, the bond servant daughters selected through the palace maids draft tended simply to be classified as maids. Palace maids who were promoted into the harem were given low-ranking titles as imperial consorts and required to produce sons before climbing into the higher ranks.

The novel's complete omission of details on whether Bao-chai and her female cousins had bound feet is worth noting, given its focus on the women in this large, extended family. During Cao Xueqin's lifetime, daughters of well-to-do Chinese families had their feet bound when they were children, but banner daughters were legally banned from following this practice. Since Bao-chai was born into a banner family, she should not have had bound feet. In the official Qing regulations, we have orders from emperors punishing bannermen whose daughters appeared for the beautiful women inspection with bound feet (bannerwomen did not bind their feet, but they may have worn elevated shoes that made their feet look smaller, emulating the Han Chinese ideal of feminine beauty). Was the omission of what might be regarded as an ethnic marker another masking device by the author? Or was it part of a social reticence to bring up the subject, given the erotic connotations of bound feet?[4]

One unintended consequence of Cao Xueqin's strategy of concealment was that the novel transcended its social context and appealed to a wider readership. Hawkes suggests that its first readers were "Manchu noblemen" (1.16), and it would be interesting to learn how they read the novel (despite reports of a Manchu-language version, the overwhelming probability is that even banner readers read the novel in Chinese).[5] The many Han Chinese literati in the nineteenth century who made *Stone* famous, however, seem to have largely favored the love story and the loving depiction of life in a wealthy extended family. The twentieth century's revived interest in drawing out the banner culture of the authors is a reflection of the importance of contemporary circumstances in both the creation and reception of literature. At the same time, as its continuing popularity demonstrates, *Story of the Stone* is a great work of literature that transcends the particular culture of its creators. Awareness of the banner backdrop simply adds another layer to this complex novel.

## NOTES

[1] More background information on the Manchu state and the Qing dynasty can be found in Rawski, *Last Emperors*. On the banner system, see Elliott.

[2] On the servile status of bond servants and the Manchu view of it, see Torbert 56–58.

3 Biographies of Cao Yin and Cao Xueqin are in Hummel 737–39, 740–42.

4 On the historical development of foot fetishes, see Ko, *Every Step*.

5 Yisu lists a Xibo Manchu translation of *Stone* (*Hongloumeng shulu* 82). Gimm reports the sighting of a Manchu transliteration of the novel by Walter Fuchs in a Peking bookshop about 1940 (95), but there is no Manchu-language *Stone* listed in Huang Runhua's union catalog of Manchu-language works held in the People's Republic of China.

# Bao-yu's Education

## *James Millward*

More than anything else, Bao-yu fears interviews with his father, Jia Zheng, who inevitably berates his son for failing to devote himself to serious study. Yet Bao-yu is anything but stupid, and he is certainly well read: in naming the vistas in the family's Prospect Garden, for example, or in numerous discourses with his cousins and maids, he displays a broad knowledge of poetry, history, fiction, and such esoteric subjects as Taoism and Buddhism. He is clearly a reader—the problem from Jia Zheng's point of view is that Bao-yu likes reading the wrong things. What should he be learning, and why?

In eighteenth-century China there were two generally recognized and approved purposes of education. One was moral improvement, viewed as important for society as a whole. Education aimed at this goal was seen as proper not only for elite men but also for women, the poor, and even some non-Chinese minorities.

The other purpose of education in imperial China was to enable a young man to master the curriculum of the state examinations, success at which opened the way to official position, elite status, and wealth for scholars and their families. The idea of selecting government personnel by examination dates from the Han dynasty (206 BC–AD 220), though it was only after several centuries that the process was systematized and opened to candidates from other than the top elites. Although, realistically, the examination system was never open to everyone, there were rational, meritocratic elements about it. The Qing system in the early eighteenth century, at the time Cao Xueqin wrote *Story of the Stone*, largely continued the institution as elaborated during the previous Ming dynasty (1368–1644), with exams at the prefectural, provincial, and palace levels, each higher level open only to those successful at the lower, qualifying exams. Success at the prefectural exam afforded a measure of prestige in local society but no access to official position. Those who passed the exam at the next, provincial level were eligible for low, quasi-official positions. But only those who made it all the way to Beijing and passed the metropolitan exams could become magistrates or fill higher jobs in the hierarchy of civil governance. (There were martial exams for military positions, and Manchus and Mongols could take advantage of special preferences—a kind of affirmative action for the ruling conquest elite.)

Preparing for and taking the successive exams was for most a decades-long process, involving not only knowledge of the prescribed Confucian canon of Four Books and Five Classics, much of which had to be memorized, but also familiarity with a large body of officially sanctioned commentaries. Exam essays had to be written in a fixed format, the eight-legged essay, which itself required much practice to master. Graders of the exams took into account political correctness, writing style and penmanship and sometimes the political, family, and scholarly connections of candidates—though efforts were made to prevent nepotism and factionalism from corrupting the selection process. The exams were held in examination compounds, rows of small cells nearly in the open air. Stories of the torment suffered by exam takers in these conditions abound: one common trick to defeat fatigue, supposedly, was to tie one's queue to a beam in the ceiling to prevent oneself from nodding off during the three-day exam ordeal. It's no wonder Bao-yu could work up little enthusiasm for this career path.

In addition to the examination curriculum, elite men generally also read belles lettres, unofficial history, poetry, drama, non-Confucian philosophy including Taoism and Buddhism, and, to a lesser degree, fiction. Such readings were frowned on by neo-Confucians (albeit hypocritically, since most read the same things themselves).[1] Men, and increasingly elite women, were expected to be able to produce occasional poetry and be familiar with the masterpieces of literature and drama; however, too great an affinity for these aesthetic writings was a sign of moral weakness. Not only did these noncanonical works distract from more serious moral pursuits, they also introduced a whole range of anti-Confucian values, including monastic retreat from the family and the free expression of romantic love. Such non-Confucian values could be tolerated only when contained in a Confucian frame. For example, the Jia family is happy to support various Taoist and Buddhist institutions but horrified when Xi-chun and Bao-yu begin to take their Buddhism seriously and express a desire to take religious vows. The Jias are justly proud of Bao-yu's facility with lyric composition; they worry, however, that the young man indulges himself in self-expressive arts to the detriment of his moral development and prospects for official position.

Bao-yu embraces the notion of study for aesthetic cultivation and even, in his own way, for spiritual development. He greatly enjoys poetry and fiction. What he abhors is the scholastic approach to the Four Books and Five Classics, the Song dynasty neo-Confucian interpretations of this canon, and the rigid formalism of the eight-legged essays (octopartite compositions) that exam candidates had to master. He can abide neither the naked careerism of exam worms nor the hypocrisy of older men who drone on about the Confucian virtues but fail to live up to them in their own affairs. This attitude looks like adolescent rebellion, but in fact Bao-yu's distaste for the orthodox state curriculum was shared and frequently voiced by eighteenth-century literati, many of whom embraced new approaches and tackled new problems in their scholarship, either questioning the authenticity of the canonical texts themselves or seeking to direct intellectual endeavor toward more practical pursuits.

In late imperial China, there were different types of pedagogy for different types of student. Well-off families did not send their children to schools but hired tutors to teach them at home: so Lin Dai-yu was taught as a girl by Jia Yu-cun, and a boy like Bao-yu would under normal circumstances likewise have had a tutor. This practice was also a way in which rich families patronized up-and-coming scholars, forging connections that could be beneficial later on (e.g., Jia Yu-cun using his position to help the Jias).

In mid-Qing times there were also schools aimed at providing literacy and basic knowledge of classics and improving texts such as the *Classic of Filiality* (孝經 *Xiaojing*) to poor students who might or might not hope to take the civil service exams. The state-run school system employed during the Ming dynasty was moribund by Qing times and had been replaced by various types of private and community-funded schools, including both charity or free schools and clan schools (both exclusively for boys). There were also higher learning academies where particular philosophies and schools of scholarship were promoted. Most schools were funded by local elites, whose reasons for doing so were not entirely altruistic. The rich and powerful families in a clan provided endowments or otherwise funded the education of less well-off members and close associates of the clan, often feeding and housing them as well, as a way of maintaining the corporate strength of the lineage. (Jokey Jin is a beneficiary of this system, and the free meals he takes at school greatly help his widowed mother's finances [1.10.271].) Local elites voluntarily maintained charity schools for nonrelatives in the belief that education contributed to social stability.

Clan and charity schools were usually one-room establishments, presided over by a single teacher. Unlike the private tutors of children in rich house-holds, these schoolteachers had low social status, it being assumed that they had come to teaching as a last resort, after failing at other endeavors. Certainly the attitudes of the students in the Jia clan school toward their teacher, Jia Dai-ru, reflect such an attitude. In the classroom, younger students learned to read by first memorizing ten characters a day, written on cards that were then strung to-gether. They practiced writing with a brush and read simple didactic texts such as the *Three-Character Classic* (三字經 *Sanzi jing*), which was written in catchy verse to aid memorization. Once they had mastered a few thousand characters, older boys began memorizing the Four Books (*The Analects of Confucius* [論語 *Lunyu*], *Mencius* [孟子 *Mengzi*], *Great Learning* [大學 *Daxue*], *Doctrine of the Mean* [中庸 *Zhongyong*]), which formed the core of the examination canon; they also studied the Five Classics (*The Book of Changes* [易經 *Yi jing*], *The Book of Odes* [詩經 *Shi jing*], *The Book of Rites* [禮記 *Li ji*], *The Classic of History* [書經 *Shu jing*], and the *Spring and Autumn Annals* [春秋 *Chun qiu*]), as well as key commentaries on both sets of texts. As they approached the day when they would take the first of the three-tiered examinations, they read model eight-legged essays and tried their hand at composing them themselves.

The schoolroom brawl in which Bao-yu, Qin Zhong, and the other boys are embroiled is rightly one of *Stone's* most famous scenes and is also one of the novel's most pointed commentaries. What should be a somber learning envi-ronment, steeped in the wisdom of the sages, descends into chaos. The ideal-ized image of lineage harmony, which a grand family like the Jias would wish to convey and which a clan school was meant to promote, shatters before the reality of class, clan rank, and other differences among the boys: "there are nine kinds of dragon and no two are alike" (1.9.206) 一龍生九種, 種種各別 (133). Cao Xue-qin is also poking fun at the exclusive masculinity of the examination-focused curriculum and schoolhouse atmosphere. This is one of the few scenes in the novel with no girls or women in it; the chapter number, 9, is a yang 陽 or masculine number (as is its multiple, chapter 81, in which Bao-yu returns to school). Yet the school is soon revealed to be a hotbed of boy-boy love, with poor students trading "bum-cake" for the sponsorship of the oafish Xue Pan (1.9.208). (The Chinese word Hawkes translates as "bum-cake" is *shaobing* 燒餅, a layered sesame flatbread. It is often eaten with a long, thin, deep-fried cruller sandwiched between its folds.) This is but another pointed example of the subversions of proper order with which the novel is rife, foreshadowing the fall of the Jia family.

The classroom's loutishness and carnality contrast markedly with the refined and accomplished scholarship of Bao-yu's girl cousins in the garden. Though Bao-chai and even Dai-yu are well acquainted with the classics and both exhort Bao-yu to take his studies of the Four Books more seriously, the cousins' poetry club, painting, zither (*qin* 琴) playing, and similar pursuits represent the type of learning that was treasured by the cultured literati but that had little relevance to the imperial examination track. Indeed, the question of how much and what kind of women's learning was appropriate runs through the novel. It was a frequent subject of debate among Chinese scholars from the late Ming through the eighteenth century, in response to rising female literacy and a raft of social changes that challenged conservative neo-Confucian notions of women's proper roles. The author evokes this debate directly, telling us that Li Wan's father—a director of education, no less—subscribed to the adage "it is precisely the woman without talent who is virtuous" or, as Hawkes translates it more plainly, "a stupid woman is a virtuous one" (1.4.108).

This proverb notwithstanding, not even staunch Confucians thought women were best kept ignorant. Rather, the Confucian ideal of an educated woman (exemplified by Li Wan) was a stern moral exemplar, a maternal figure whose learning was focused on properly raising and educating her children in the ancient ways. Though only modestly educated herself, Li Wan successfully devotes her widowhood to supervising her son Jia Lan's preparation for the examinations. The late Ming scholar Lü Kun and the eighteenth-century thinker Zhang Xuecheng both espoused women's education directed to such a goal, while frowning on women writing poetry.

Lin Dai-yu, on the other hand, embodies the Romantic ideal for women in late imperial China. Her ethereal beauty, deep emotional sensitivity, and natural poetic intelligence inspire her poems with an unsurpassed elegance. That she dies young only heightened her aesthetic appeal for traditional readers. Yuan Mei, a Qing writer, is (in)famous for promoting an aesthetic education for talented young women like Dai-yu and accepting them as his students.

The issue of what constituted a proper education was thus even more complicated for women than for men during the late imperial period. From the moralists' perspective, women were viewed as morally weaker than men and more susceptible to the passions expressed in affective literature. However, there was a growing romanticization of marriage during this period, and many works of contemporary literature portray the ideal wife as intellectual and aesthetic companion to her husband. The characterization of Bao-chai captures this cultural paradox, and for this reason many traditional and modern commentators call her hypocritical. Bao-chai is as well read as Bao-yu and Dai-yu and composes poetry as well as they do. However — though she has eagerly read them herself — she affects pious horror at romances, including the two great romantic dramas *The Western Chamber* (*Story of the Western Wing*) and *The Return of the Soul* (*The Peony Pavilion*) that Bao-yu repeatedly quotes to Dai-yu. And Bao-chai echoes the Confucian ambivalence about an aesthetic education when she lectures Dai-yu to the effect that although the girls practice poetry writing and calligraphy, it is neither their "proper business" nor even that of boys. Boys should be reading the texts that will help them gain office and govern the country, while girls should confine themselves to spinning and sewing. If they must read, let them read only improving books (2.42.333–34).

Bao-chai later adds, "a girl's first concern is to be virtuous, her second is to be industrious. . . . The last thing girls of good family need is a literary reputation" (3.64.236) 總以貞靜為主，女工還是第二件 (2: 891). Of course, Cao Xueqin's book has made Lin Dai-yu and Bao-chai among the most famous literary heroines in Chinese literature. Bao-chai's homilies, Bao-yu's distaste for the exam curriculum, and the characterizations of Li Wan and Lin Dai-yu all reflect the contradictions of the age.

NOTE

[1] Neo-Confucianism is a type of Confucianism dating from the Song dynasty that formed the basis of Confucian orthodoxy in the Qing (1644–1911). It attempted to merge basic elements of Confucianism, Taoism, and Buddhism. See Meir Shahar's essay in this volume for more on Confucianism.

# Medicine in *The Story of the Stone*: Four Cases

## Andrew Schonebaum

We might read some of the main characters of *Story of the Stone* differently with a little knowledge of Chinese medicine.

Medicine and illness are topics that tell us much about how people think about life. Students should begin to reflect that concepts even for something as fundamental as the body are culturally conditioned, that metaphors and literature are powerful in the creation and circulation of knowledge, and that popular culture can influence both what and how regular people know things, even through science.

A problem is that students have strong assumptions as to the inherent truth of modern science and biomedicine, perhaps because they have been little exposed to medical themes in Western cultural history and perhaps also because they have little experience with illness and death in their young lives. But since everyone has a body and everyone gets sick, approaching *Story of the Stone* from the perspective of the cultural history of medicine can prove quite engaging.

The scientific, biomedical understanding of illness arose only recently — even in the West. Opposition to the shocking idea that doctors spread infection by going straight from the mortuary to the surgery table ruined the career of early hand-washing advocates in 1850. Beginning in 1867, Joseph Lister promoted the systematic implementation of antiseptics in the hospital to prevent infection. Sterilization of surgical instruments became widespread in 1881, the use of rubber gloves in 1900. Germ theory, claiming that microorganisms were responsible for many diseases, was confirmed by the isolation of a bacillus by Robert Koch in 1884. Before that, it might be said that metaphor and meanings of illness or symptom sets defined medical knowledge. Now, metaphor usually follows it. We still believe that being out in the cold is why we catch colds and that chicken soup is good for body and soul. We not only have to battle AIDS but we still have to battle the belief that it is a disease of gay men or of people far removed from us geographically or ethnically. There is a long tradition of locating the origins of venereal disease outside national or community borders. Syphilis, the name of which was coined in an Italian poem entitled "the French disease," was called the Venetian malady by the French, the Spanish disease by the Dutch, the Polish disease by the Russians, the Canton sore by the Japanese, and so on. We think that ulcers are caused by stress, that tumors result from keeping emotions bottled, and that depression is not an illness but the predisposition of a morbid personality.

In China, a complex mix of orthodox or formal medicine (reading pulses, prescribing herbs) that was text- and theory-based; lower practices, such as acupuncture and massage, done by professionals healers; folk remedies; and religious beliefs were all tied to differing but overlapping visions of the cosmos, to interactions between the human and natural realms. Dreams themselves are an example of this mixture of high and low medicine, of the interactions of the human and natural realms, and of the slippage between illusion and reality. The paradoxical nature of dreams with regard to medicine is highlighted, for instance, in one of the best-known medical works, the *Bencao gangmu* 本草綱目 (*Systematic Materia Medica*), a compendium of many different kinds of medical texts and ideas published in the last years of the sixteenth century. It discusses dreams as a symptom of imbalance, often occurring at the same time as or caused by diseases of deficiency or excess. Having a dream meant something was wrong with the body. Dreams often were the result of invasion by pathogenic wind. Erotic dreams or dreams of having sex with demons were caused by the dangerous depletion of vital essence from nocturnal emission. Dreams were also themselves viewed as illness, and the *Bencao* provides many herbal prescriptions to treat nightmares. On the other hand, dreams often revealed the cure for the dreamer's illness. The *Bencao* lists a number of prescriptions that "came from a dream" 夢中亦醒悟也 or were given by Guanyin in a dream 夢中觀音授此. Each prescription is fabulously effective, according to the *Bencao*. Thus dreams were very real from a somatic perspective: symptoms of illnesses produced by the body but also a key to understanding the body. Sometimes doctors could diagnose a disease only by interpreting the patient's dream. Dreams enabled the dreamer to communicate with bodhisattvas, the dead, and those separated by a great distance. In representing this medical complexity, *Stone* tells us much about the way that characters in the novel, and presumably the readers of it, conceived of their lives, bodies, and mortality.

## Bao-yu and Psychology

One of the first challenges of reading *Story of the Stone* in a classroom in the West involves psychology. *Stone* has long been regarded by scholars in China and the West as presenting a high degree of psychological realism. Bao-yu is a young man who resists his father's exhortations to study and is reluctant to assume the role of eldest surviving son and some leadership of the Jia family. Instead, he seeks the genteel company of his female cousins. His interest in composing poetry is evidence of a literary bent, but his placing it above the study of the Confucian classics and his preference for feminine over masculine intellectual pursuits are perverse.

Astute readers might notice similarities between Bao-yu's behavior and classic cases of Western psychoneurosis. When Bao-yu first meets Dai-yu, he has an overwhelming sense of déjà vu. When told that she does not possess a jade like the one that hangs around his neck, he dashes it to the floor, saying that he does not want it because none of the girls has one (1.3.104). Surrounded by women, he wants to relinquish an object, perhaps phallic, that marks him as unique and powerful. His relationship with his father is filled with fear and resentment.

These pressures and conflicts remind us of traditional Freudian dilemmas. It is strange for a young man to live with his girl cousins, but in his former life too Bao-yu was an outcast—the only stone found unfit to repair the sky. The Buddhist monk and Taoist priest refer to the Stone as "that silly thing" or "absurd creature" 蠢物 (1.1.52, 54). The fairy Disenchantment says he is the most lustful person she has ever seen (1.5.145). Perhaps most like a Western concept of psychological formation is Bao-yu's alienation from the image of his "real" or whole self in the mirror and in his dreams (ch. 56), which read like a formative Lacanian experience.

Yet psychiatry is a European invention of the nineteenth century. We do not find it in China before the modern period. Chinese medicine focused on the fundamental connection and interaction between mind and body. The heart, in fact, was the organ of thinking. In Europe too before the nineteenth century, madness was diagnosed and treated by physicians as a humoral imbalance that had nothing special to do with the brain or with personal emotions or experiences. Women prone to hysteria were often treated by the removal of the uterus, the organ that made them particularly womanly and therefore emotional and difficult to control, an operation known today as a hysterectomy. In China, it was a number of factors in balance, not just the heart-mind (the Chinese word *xin* 心 is often translated as either or both), that were the locus of personality.

Cao Xueqin spent much of his life writing and revising *The Story of the Stone*. In the introduction to volume 1, David Hawkes says that his guiding principle was to translate everything, because in this novel written by a great artist with his very lifeblood everything was there for a purpose (46). Bao-yu's psychology cannot be Freudian or Lacanian or a representation of any other Western psychological schema, but it is imbued with significance and signification. Psychology or *xinli xue* 心理學 ("study of what is in the heart-mind") is a term designating Western psychological science, but similar concepts that fit under the rubric of *xinli sixiang* 心理思想 ("philosophy of what is in the heart-mind"), a category that covers epistemology, ontology, and a wide range of theories of the mind, existed in China before the Qin period (Roth 600). I suggest to students that we can use the term *psychology* in our discussion of characters in Chinese fiction, so long as we understand that, though coined in the West, it does not need to carry with it concepts of Western psychoanalysis.

The term *realism* also did not exist in China before the modern period. Mimesis in traditional Chinese aesthetics was of secondary importance, though there were art forms, particularly poetry, in which a common criterion for evaluation was that it be true to nature or life. The problem of psychological realism in Chinese literature is compounded by a preference in Chinese aesthetics for expressionism or impressionism over realism. The time-honored formulation of critical essence was, "The poem is that to which what is intently on the mind goes" 詩言志 (Owen, *Anthology* 65). Commentary on Chinese fiction, particularly in popular editions with marginal, interlineal, chapter-end comments and prefatory how-to-read essays, are littered with terms like "to make a portrait" 寫照, "[capture] the likeness of things" 肖物, "close to real" 逼真. Yet representing and "passing on the spirit" 傳神 of something was more important than "describing external likeness" 寫形, though many critical phrases involve both concepts: "completely capture the spirit and outward image" 傳神寫照 / 窮神盡像 (Rolston, *Traditional Chinese Fiction* 167). Chinese fiction, evolving from history rather than from epic, constantly needed to defend itself against the charge of being false and often did so by referring to the author's experience and discussing how well the work re-created the emotions associated with it.

So we do have a psychology of sorts — motivating forces, personal desires or fears that are expressed and unexpressed — and we have literary criteria concerning the "real" portrayal and re-creation of emotional states. Behind the psychological realism in *Stone*, however, lie considerably different conceptions of those forces, desires, and fears.

In chapter 2, we are given a reason for Bao-yu's behavior that relies on the creation of his personality independent of individual experience. We are told, through Jia Yu-cun's conversation with Leng Zi-xing, that the Jia family is in decline. Not only are they unable to economize, they are also unable to produce good sons (74). Bao-yu was born with a beautiful, lustrous piece of jade in his mouth and, when tested as an infant, showed an interest in women's things — combs, rouge — but none at all in other things, such as books and writing brushes (76). So even before we meet him, we know that he is unusual and that there is debate surrounding his nature. Yu-cun gives Zi-xing a lecture about wind and qi 氣, saying that in times of peace and benevolent reign, the negative forces that naturally abound in the world are forced to retreat. The prevailing positive forces disturb the negative, mix with them, and permeate human bodies. A profusion of mixed qi, instead of producing heroes or villains, produces eccentrics and aesthetes. Born into low classes, these people, endowed with intelligence, beauty, and a certain perversity, will become famous actors and courtesans. This mixture of essences, introduced into the body of a boy born to a wealthy family, produces a romantic eccentric (76–80). The elemental description of Bao-yu coheres with the fairy Disenchantment's characterization of him as the most lustful person in the world, suffering from "lust of the mind" 意淫 as opposed to lust of the flesh (1.5.146). Yu-cun's explanation of Bao-yu's personality follows the format of an eight-legged essay (to highlight this form, Hawkes italicizes the conjunctions that mark the different "legs"). The argument may be ironic as it is pedantic, but it is also convincing. The theory of influences of external qi and of pathoconditions determining personality is ancient, familiar, and therefore not easily dismissed.

Another way of describing Bao-yu is to say that he is born with a predisposition to be attached to the world by *qing* 情, desires, passions, emotions. This is simply his nature, not a choice or the result of a particular upbringing. His actions are not the result of unconscious, repressed desires; rather, he acts according to the elemental and material circumstances of his birth. His challenge is to work against that nature to achieve enlightened detachment.

Health in China was conceived as a balance in the dynamics of bodily processes, and illness was imbalance. Qi in Bao-yu is partly congenital and partly taken into the body through food, drink, and breath. Qi governs bodily functions as well as the emotions. Bodily changes affect emotions; emotions cause bodily changes. Abnormal or excessive emotion can affect the flow of qi and subsequently bodily functions. One of the earliest Chinese medical texts, *Huang Di's Inner Classic, Basic Questions* 黃帝內經素問, states:

> The hundred diseases are generated by the *qi*. When one is angry, then the *qi* rises. When one is happy, then the *qi* relaxes. When one is sad, then the *qi* dissipates. When one is in fear, then the *qi* moves down. In case of cold, the *qi* collects; in case of heat, the *qi* flows out. When one is frightened, then the *qi* is in disorder. When one is exhausted, then the *qi* is wasted. When one is pensive, then the *qi* lumps together. . . . When one is angry, then the *qi* moves contrary [to its regular course]. In severe cases, [patients] spit blood and there is outflow of [undigested food].
>
> (Unschuld 161–62)

Bao-yu is defined by the blend of qi in his body as much as he defines his own persona. The predisposition to passionate thoughts and feelings causes him worldly trouble (he displeases his father and thwarts family expectations) and metaphysical trouble (his attachment to the world and people is a great obstacle to his enlightenment), but he is not entirely responsible for this trouble. It is partly due to his original qi 元氣.

The dream in which Bao-yu cuts out his heart to show its purity to Dai-yu seems to come from his unconscious, yet it may also result from the exceptional qi that moves him. We know, moreover, that he has a destiny carried over from a past incarnation, a destiny that is finally revealed in dreams. Therefore just as the unconscious may explain Bao-yu, so does the constant, hidden presence of karma in his life, marked by the jade and by Dai-yu and revealed symbolically in dreams and fantasy.

Culturally construed, popular notions of medicine and illness in China often relied on sympathetic correspondences, linguistic similarities, and wordplay. The idea of linguistic signification (e.g., Grandmother Jia believes that a fire was caused by a discussion about fire [2.39.271]) might also suggest a kind of unconscious. Bao-yu lives in a world of correspondences. He is removed from a past, forgotten incarnation but also tied to it and constructed by it as its metaphors and metonymies intrude on and condition his life. *Stone* is concerned not just with the causes of emotion but also with the results of it. Bao-yu's character is interesting not just for why it is the way it is but also for what effects it has on others as Bao-yu wrestles with his passionate attachment to women, to the garden, and to beauty.

Balance and flow are two distinct but related concepts essential to the understanding of Chinese medicine and to the more quotidian aspects of Chinese culture, since Chinese medicine really is a classical scheme of knowing. In addition to the circulation and balance in the body, and between the body and the

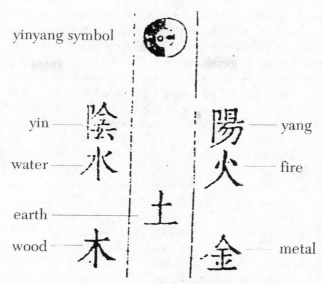

yinyang symbol

yin —— 陰

water —— 水

yang —— 陽

fire —— 火

earth —— 土

wood —— 木

metal —— 金

Fig. 1. Diagram of yin and yang and the five phases, from Zhao Xianke (1617). Thanks to Leslie Devries for the original image

universe, of blood, essence, and qi, Chinese medicine is based on a theory of systematic correspondences.[1] The health of the state functions like the health of the body (a metaphor that pervades medical discourse in China since *Huang Di's Inner Classics* of the first or second century BCE). Harmony can be disturbed by excessive desire or gluttony; by external conditions, like a change in temperature or environment; or by the invasion of evil influences or spirits. Harmony is achieved though the maintenance of the flow of blood, essence, and qi through the body—and, in the case of qi, through immediate and extended environments. Flow occurs when there is a proper balance of yin 陰 and yang 陽 and of the five phases—metal, earth, water, fire, wood—representing processes found in nature and perceived in the human body.

A syncretic worldview sees all appearances as belonging to two opposite yet complementary poles, yin and yang, which are constantly changing into and out of each other. Early thinkers in the yin-yang school considered all phenomena to be interconnected and constantly transforming—day into night into day, high tide to low to high, and so on. A similar school of thought saw the world's dynamics based on the interactions of five phases (*wuxing* 五行) or five categories of all things material and immaterial. Wood, water, fire, earth, and metal represented more than what they were named after (as in the four-elements concept in ancient Greek philosophy). Applied to the human body, five-phase theory explained the dynamic relationships and affinities of five basic bodily systems, loosely associated with liver, heart, spleen, lung, and kidney. The liver stored the blood; the heart regulated the movement of the blood and governed conscious-ness; the spleen stored and regulated energy from food; the lung regulated the qi of breath and also kept internal and external energy in their proper channels; and the kidney governed reproductive function and the stores of primordial qi, the original source of life (see Furth, *Flourishing Yin* 23). The yin-yang and five-phases schools were synthesized during the first or second century BCE and came to characterize medicine, because the body with its organs and processes functioned like the natural and social environments surrounding it (fig. 1).

The iteration of yin-yang and five-phases medical notions in *Stone* is consis-tent with diagnoses found in contemporary medical texts, but it is also employed symbolically and allegorically. Because the five-phases theory is based on pro-duction and conquest cycles, it can suggest struggle between fictional charac-ters. Fire, water, wood, metal, and earth all correspond to organs, to seasons, and to other natural phenomena, in a progression of conquering or nourishing: metal conquers wood (e.g., an ax cutting a tree), wood conquers earth (a spade digging in soil), earth conquers water (an earthen dam), water conquers fire (firefighting), and fire conquers metal (melting and molding an ax head); wood nourishes fire, fire nourishes earth, earth nourishes metal, metal nourishes water, and water nourishes wood. A popular 1851 commentary of *Stone* claims that the novel's entire structure is based on five-phases relations. Lin Dai-yu is identified with the wood humor, dangerously encountering Bao-chai's metal (or gold) phase, which has the potential to dominate her. Bao-yu, related to the earth phase and therefore positioned between Dai-yu and Bao-chai, has the po-tential to be dominated by wood or to promote metal to excess. For some critics the symbols that pair Dai-yu and Bao-yu, wood and stone, and those that pair Bao-yu with Bao-chai, jade and gold, play out their correspondences according to this medical theory.[2] Illness in *Stone* can work this way as well.

Chinese medicine is too complex to be contained by any one theoretical sys-tem, no matter how inclusive and robust. Five-phases correspondences are old and revered medical beliefs in China, but there are many others. Developments arising out of those schools of thought proliferated in the eighteenth century among literati medical practitioners, but folk and religious beliefs about medi-cine and the body were also commonly practiced, and many of those are rep-resented in *Stone*. When Bao-yu goes into a trance or becomes stupefied, his symptoms are consistent with "soul loss" (3.56.87), a condition still commonly diagnosed among Chinese immigrants in the United States, particularly those of Chinese ethnic minority descent (e.g., see Fadiman). Tradition holds that a person has two souls—a spiritual soul (魂 *hun*), which governs the higher fac-ulties of mind and heart and corresponds to yang forces, and a bodily soul (魄 *po*), which is tied to yin and governs physical senses and bodily functions (see 4.98.372).[3] The spiritual soul, light and volatile, can easily be separated from a living person. This separation can happen during sleep, be caused by fright or shock, or be the work of soul-stealing magicians, who usually employ hair or paper figures to achieve this.[4] In one popular story, soul loss occurs from a case of lovesickness (Pu; see also Chen Xuanyou). It results in a state characterized by trances and madness and leads to death. The condition is cured with a ritual known as "calling back the soul."[5] Bao-yu's fits of muzziness or delirium are caused by the bewitching of Aunt Zhao; by being frightened when Nightingale teasingly tells Bao-yu that Dai-yu is returning home to the south; or by the loss of his jade, which is repeatedly referred to as his "very soul" by characters and commentators alike. We might attribute his trances to shock or mental breakdown, but soul loss may be a more accurate diagnosis. When talking about Chinese or alternative medicine in general, it is difficult to avoid applying biomedical, Western concepts of disease. Understanding that soul loss is a possible diagnosis for Bao-yu provides us with a cultural context for the patient's situation and the mysteries of his world.

Tied to systematic correspondences is the concept of sympathetic medicine or treating like with like. In the West, the "hair of the dog that bit me" is a common example, originating with the belief that literally applying a dog's hair to the wound the same dog inflicted would help the wound heal faster. Lu Xun, a famous writer of modern Chinese literature, discusses this method still in practice as late as 1910 in China. His father was suffering from edema and a distended stomach known in Chinese as "drum tight," and the doctor prescribed eating the dried skins stretched over drums to cure the illness. The fairy Disenchantment tries to use sympathetic medicine to cure Bao-yu of his lust of the mind, introducing him to lust of the flesh in chapter 5 (146–47). This kind of thinking led to the treatment of emotional disturbances with other emotions.

In medical texts of the late sixteenth century, a relatively new category of illness began to be the topic of much discussion: emotions 情志. Traditional Chinese medicine identified seven primary emotions: anger, joy, sorrow, grief, fear, fright, and worry. (The differences between sorrow and grief, fear and fright, were of degree, and pairs were sometimes combined as one emotion.) Each emotion was tied to an organ system function: excessive anger injured the liver (wood phase), excessive fear damaged the kidney (water phase), and so on. Chinese medicine speaks of an "angry liver," "anxious heart," or "melancholy spleen." It was thought by some that when an emotion was excessive, drugs were ineffective. One could treat the emotion only with its correlative conquering or controlling emotion, according to five-phases logic: sorrow treated excessive anger, joy treated excessive sorrow, fear treated excessive joy, worry treated excessive fear, and anger treated excessive worry (Sivin). This belief is evident in characters' constant concern about the danger of Dai-yu's sadness. In chapter 19, when Bao-yu tells Dai-yu the story of magic mice, he is not just trying to cheer her up and prevent her from getting sick by sleeping too soon after eating; he is also employing the popular and formal medical treatment of using one emotion (joy-fire-heart) to counter another (melancholy-metal-lungs) (1.19.396–99).

We see the employment of emotional countertherapy in the early pages of the novel, when the narrator writes that in the contemplation of these beautiful and talented young women the reader might find relief for his melancholy:

> . . . surely my "number of females," whom I spent half a lifetime studying with my own eyes and ears, are preferable to [unofficial histories, erotic novels and "talented scholar and beautiful girl" stories]. I do not claim that they are better people than the ones who appear in books written before my time; I am only saying that the contemplation of their actions and motives may prove a more effective antidote to boredom and melancholy.                                    (1.1.50)

> 竟不如我半世親睹親聞的這幾個女子, 雖不敢說強似前代書中所有之人, 但事蹟原委, 亦可以消愁破悶.                    (1: 5)

*Stone* is often read as a chronicle of the women in Bao-yu's life. Emotional illnesses concerned primarily the male literatus suffering from melancholy and the beautiful young woman suffering from lovesickness. The reader of *Stone* suffers from the same ailments as its characters, and a contemplation of this truth can cure the readers who can understand it.

This line of inquiry aims less toward a medical anthropology than toward an aesthetics of illness and the body. The archetypes in *Stone* become a poetics of illness that, in the modern period, becomes a discourse of a national etiology: China the "sick man of Asia," modernity as a time of decadence, contamination, and infection.

## Lovesick Women: Consumption, Blood, and Karma

Emotions were dangerous. On the one hand, they were caused by the flow or blockage of qi, blood, and essence; on the other hand, they could cause such flow or blockage. Women were particularly susceptible to the harmful influences of excessive feeling, and *Stone* is a catalog of them. Alternative titles of the novel suggest this catalog. *Dream of the Red Chamber* recalls both the dwellings of rich men's daughters and the dream that Bao-yu has in which he looks into the register of the ill-fated fair, the twelve beauties of Jinling, and the two supplementary registers and reads the cryptic fates of the young women in the novel. The title *The Twelve Beauties of Jinling* is more explicit in highlighting the centrality of the fates of the women in the story. Of the twelve beauties, Lin Dai-yu, Xue Bao-chai, Qin Ke-qing (Qin-shi), Xi-feng, Adamantina, and Yuan-chun become meaningfully ill, usually chronically, and usually unto death—while the three important characters mentioned in the supplementary registers, Aroma, Skybright, and Caltrop, also have illnesses that carry karmic or structural significance. The collection of these fates and narratives of these illnesses make *Stone* read like a medical casebook, a popular genre of medical writing in the eighteenth century, but here the patients are almost exclusively female. *Stone*, like many medical casebooks of its day, found illnesses having emotional causes to be much more common in women than in men.

The source of illness in *Stone* tends to be emotion-desire (*qing*), and absence and loss enhance the affective power of *qing*. Although *Stone*, in its employment of five-phases symbolism, is more complex than its fictional predecessors, which employ primarily yin-yang correspondences in theme and structure, such as *Plum in the Golden Vase* 金瓶梅, it is similar to them in that it bases authenticity on the ability to feel emotions and associates deficiency or weakness, illustrated by illness and the frailty of the female, with a heightened intensity of emotion.[6]

Some Red Inkstone commentary asserts that a major theme of the novel is *qing bu qing* 情不情, which points to the author's ambiguous attitude toward emotion.[7] *Qing bu qing* can be defined in many ways, the first of which is "feeling for nonfeeling things," such as flowers, stones, and pictures. A second definition is "feeling without feeling [for oneself]," which indicates the breakdown between self and other—for example, feeling a character's pain so intimately that it seems as if it is one's own. This pain suggests karmic retribution: the illness and suffering of a character derive from a previous incarnation of the character, and those who sympathize most deeply were related to that person in a past life. This kind of feeling without feeling is actually an extreme form of self-indulgence. Another definition of *qing bu qing* is that of feeling too deeply and becoming unfeeling, "feeling [to the point of] not feeling," which seems to be ultimately what happens to Bao-yu.

*Qing* contributes to one of the earliest and certainly the most extensive and famous depictions of chronic illness in Chinese fiction. The first time the reader encounters Dai-yu, it is said that her mother had fallen ill and died and that the strain of caring for her mother and mourning her death was too much for Dai-yu's already delicate constitution and resulted in a severe and recurrent illness (1.2.70). This illness is karmic, related to the debt of tears, and will bring out her true identity as the Crimson Pearl Flower that the Stone watered with magic dew in chapter 1. The first description of Dai-yu in the novel, from Bao-yu's point of view, identifies her as inherently ill, like the beautiful maidens who came before her in the Chinese literary tradition: "[H]abit had given a melancholy cast to her tender face; nature had bestowed a sickly constitution on her delicate frame. . . . She had more chambers in her heart than the martyred Bi Gan; and suffered a tithe more pain in it than the beautiful Xi Shi" (3.57.102–03) 兩彎似蹙非蹙罥煙眉, 一雙似喜非喜含情目. 態生兩靨之愁, 嬌襲一身之病. 淚光點點, 嬌喘微微. 閑靜時如姣花照水, 行動處似弱柳扶風. 心較比干多一竅, 病如西子勝三分 (1: 49).[8] Dai-yu's delicate beauty is wrapped up in a cultural and literary construction of illness. Like previous beauties, she is delicate, ill, and glowing with a crimson hue, and she is bound both to her literary antecedents and to her previous incarnation as the Crimson Pearl Flower. Her identity as a medical case reveals her character as much as her character is created by it. Dai-yu suffers from consumptive heat, liver yin deficiency, lung injury, and excessive and unexpressed passion.[9] Her malady is manifested in the redness in her cheeks, loss of appetite, coughing, and expectoration of blood. The congenital or even pregenital nature, primordial qi (元氣 *yuanqi*), of her illness is described early in the novel:

> Her speech and manner already showed unusual refinement. [Everyone] also noticed the frail body which seemed scarcely strong enough to bear the weight of its clothes, but which yet had an inexpressible grace about it, and realizing that she must be suffering from some deficiency, asked her what medicine she took for it and why it was still not better. "I have always been like this," said Dai-yu. "I have been taking medicine ever since I could eat and been looked at by ever so many well-known doctors, but it has never done me any good."                                (1.3.90–91)

> 眾人見黛玉年貌雖小, 其舉止言談不俗, 身體面龐雖怯弱不勝, 卻有一段自然的風流態度, 便知他有不足之癥. 因問: "常服何藥, 如何不急為療治?" 黛玉道: "我自來 是如此, 從會吃飲食時便吃藥, 到今日未斷, 請了多少名醫修方配藥, 皆不見效."                                (1: 39)

The earthly, medical origin of Dai-yu's condition is "a deficiency of yin in the liver," the liver corresponding to the wood element. Dr. Wang prescribes something to sedate the liver, bolster the lungs (metal), and fortify the heart (fire) and spleen (earth), which have been encroached on by the hyperactive wood element of the liver (the kidneys are the fifth organ, associated with water). This condition has caused "loss of appetite, frequent dreams, and fitful sleeping in the early hours; during the daytime a tendency to take offence for no reason and a generally nervous and apprehensive attitude toward other people. Some might attribute all these to a peculiarity of temperament, but they would be mistaken" (4.83.78–79) 這病時常應得頭暈, 減飲食, 多夢, 每到五更, 必醒個幾次. 即日間聽見不干自己的事, 也必要動氣, 且多疑多懼. 不知者疑為性情乖誕 (2: 1170). These symptoms are fairly common for consumptive syndromes. Here the liver depletion causes a loss of vitality, poor appetite due to spleen malfunction, and the spitting up of blood from a disturbance of the lungs. Dai-yu's psyche is affected by her body; it is a function of her qi, not, as it may seem to readers familiar with the perspective of medical realism, of a long-term accommodation to chronic illness. The medical reading is further complicated by her karma, which we know is the true cause of both her illness and her personality (see Levy 67–101). Readers would have understood this, either intuitively or through the interlineal comments and chapter comments in widely read editions that make it clear that the doctor's diagnosis signals an early death for Dai-yu.

Dai-yu's delicate constitution, loss of appetite, and teary eyes recall her earthly origin as a delicate southerner, like that of other famous beauties of the Chinese literary tradition, and signify her heavenly origin as the Crimson Pearl Flower. The illness also situates Dai-yu among the other women in *Stone*. Some commentators read characters as types of other characters, and by extension the illnesses of such connected characters must be of a similar nature or of a kind that affects similar personalities. Even if Bao-chai's congenital tendency to overheat and Dai-yu's congenital frailty and weakness must also be read as figures of karmic retribution, in which their characters and fates are predestined, their illnesses and those of the characters who mirror or shadow them retain structural significance.

The association of Dai-yu's identity with her symptom set implicates those with similar pathologies, particularly women. Although in fiction and drama of the Ming dynasty and earlier, consumption affected men and women equally, consistent with yin-yang medical theory, in *Stone* it is a syndrome only of young women.[10] Skybright (and later Fivey) is said to be the spit and image of Dai-yu; they share similar temperaments, illnesses, and fates as well—and, of course, their sex. Dai-yu, Skybright, Fivey, and Charmante all get consumption—an illness, Lady Wang remarks, not uncommon in unmarried women (3.78.554).[11] Unmarried women are susceptible to wild swings of emotion, particularly those that are love-related, and cannot keep them in check. Illness exacerbates emotion, which is why Bao-yu tells Skybright, "[Y]ou're inclined to be quick-tempered at the best of times. Now, with so much extra heat inside you [literally, "so much fire in your liver"], you are even more inflammable!" (2.51.525) 你素習好生氣，如今肝火自然盛了 (1: 698). Skybright also fits the archetype of the beautiful, tragic, dying young maiden, is maligned by Bao-yu's mother (for sexually corrupting Bao-yu), dismissed, and sent home, where her consumption recurs and kills her—she dies of "girls' consumption" 女兒癆. Fivey, a shadow of Skybright, is beautiful, frail, and ill (5.109.179). Caltrop might also be a consumptive, suffering greatly; in some texts her illness is called dry blood consumption or simply dry blood illness. The effect of the emotional and physical outrage of being tormented by Xia Jin-gui is a flood of fiery qi forced into her liver, which leads to a drying up of the menstrual fluid. She becomes very thin and loses all interest in food (3.80.605). She is cured of this condition when the tormenting ends and she is promoted to Xue Pan's main wife (only to die soon after in childbirth).

Students often remark that Lin Dai-yu, Skybright, and other lovesick and consumptive beauties bring to mind Marianne in *Sense and Sensibility*, Catherine in *Wuthering Heights*, Marguerite Gautier in *La dame aux camelias*, or any number of heroines from Western Victorian and Romantic literature. (Nicole Kidman's Satine from the film *Moulin Rouge!* is an especially recognizable consumptive type to my students.) The metaphors and symptoms of consumption bear interesting comparative fruit, but the striking similarities of popular conceptions and metaphors of illness across oceans conceal the complex traditions that undergird them.

It is not an innovation of *Stone* to emphasize the blood-based nature of women's illnesses and the qi-based (or even essence-based) nature of male maladies, but *Stone*, along with contemporary medical texts, created separate categories of illness for men and women beyond those related to pregnancy and childbirth. As Li Shizhen wrote in his *Systematic Materia Medica* 本草綱目 of 1596, a work that every literate man in China was familiar with, "In women . . .

blood is the ruling aspect" 女子 . . . 以血為主 (卷五十二) (qtd. in Furth, "Blood" 44). The association of blood with specifically female forms of vitality is clear in classical prescriptions for the use of human blood in medicine (Furth, "Blood"). Since the Qing dynasty, when *Stone* was written, consumption was known as pulmonary consumption or dry blood consumption. It was often treated with spirit-moistening powder or stemona metal-clearing decoction and linked with a condition known as bone steaming (骨蒸 *guzheng*, so called because of a profusion of heat in the body thought to emanate from the bones), the final stage of a category of syndromes known as taxation vacuity, depletion fatigue, or wasting disorder. The popular novel followed medical practice in taking a broad category known as static congestion and assigning to it women's illnesses that were linked to blood and weakness; marked by irregular menstruation, the coughing up of blood, fever, sweating, and haptic fire; and associated with sexual frustration and suppressed passion or lovesickness.[12] Consumption was thought to be contagious as early as the Song dynasty, transmitted by consumption worms. Those who had a constitutional deficiency, engaged in excessive drink and sex, or had taxation fatigue from thought and anxiety were predisposed to invasion by these worms. It was particularly transmissible from corpses, which is why its synonyms in Chinese are corpse transmission, flying corpse, corpse influx, and demonic influx.[13] The characters in *Stone* are told to stay away from corpses, especially the corpses of those who had died from consumption (1.13.258–59; 3.78.563). As we can see, the manifestations of consumption seem similar in the East and West, but its causes were quite different.

Dai-yu's illness is depicted as relating to blood. Dai-yu coughs up blood-flecked phlegm, and the blood increases as her illness worsens (3.82.67–68, 97.340). There is also a symbolic connection between her blood and tears.[14] Tears are linked to her flushed face when she composes poems for Bao-yu on handkerchiefs on the subject of tears (2.27.39, 28.55). She has only half filled the second handkerchief when she becomes aware that her whole body is burning and her cheeks are on fire. She removes the brocade from the mirror and peers into it, seeing a face stare out at her that is "brighter than the peach-flower's hue, little imagining that what she [has] been witnessing [is] the first symptom of a serious illness," (2.34.168) 覺得渾身火熱, 面上作燒, 走至鏡台揭起錦袱一照, 只見腮上通紅, 自羨壓倒桃花, 卻不知病由此萌 (1: 457). Her karmic debt of tears is tied to her earthly consumption, which results in drying up, heat, and blood. Her karma, also the cause of taxation fatigue and lovesickness, recalls the bond between the Crimson Pearl Flower and the Stone. The ailing, lovesick maiden is weak, sexually and emotionally repressed, lonely, and ephemeral. Dai-yu thinks:

> Though here are things of burning importance to be said, without a father or mother I have no one to say them for me. And besides, I feel so muzzy lately and I know that my illness is gradually gaining a hold on me. (The doctors say that the weakness and anemia I suffer from may be the begin-

nings of consumption.) So even if I am your true love, I fear I may not be able to wait for you. And even though you are mine, you can do nothing to alter my fate.    (2.32.132)

父母早逝, 雖有銘心刻骨之言, 無人為我主張. 況近日每覺神思恍惚, 病已漸成, 醫者更雲氣弱血虧, 恐致勞怯之症, 你我雖為知己, 但恐自不能久待, 你縱為我知己, 奈我薄命何!    (1: 434)

The Red Inkstone commentary associates her with blood from the beginning. When she is first described in chapter 3, there is an interlineal comment that reads, "How lamentable! A passage where every word of every sentence is a drop of blood" 可憐! 一句一滴血, 一句一滴血之文 (35a/3.2a). Dai-yu is not unique in this condition but an exemplar. Just as she becomes the queen of the flower fairies, she is the archetype of the consumptive, suffering beauty.

Despite Dai-yu's temporary recovery because of the doctor's diagnosis and prescription, which is consistent with contemporary medical theory, the reader understands that one can cure illness but not fate (1.11.235). The narrator reminds us:

> No remedy but love
> Can make the lovesick well;
> Only the hand that tied the knot
> Can loose the tiger's bell.    (4.90.216)

心病終須心藥治,
解鈴還是系鈴人.    (2: 1254)

The implication is also that Dai-yu's illness is improper, because it is associated with uncontrolled emotion, passion, and sex, although Dai-yu has not engaged in any sexual behavior. The illness comes and goes as she becomes less and more hopeful that she will be united with Bao-yu, yet only a few of the older, wiser women in the novel, such as Grandmother Jia, suspect that desire is the root of her illness. When Grandmother Jia is given a report of Dai-yu's condition, she says:

> I simply cannot understand it. Ours is a decent family. We do not tolerate unseemly goings-on. And that applies to foolish romantic attachments. If her illness is of a respectable nature, I do not mind how much we have to spend to get her better. But if she is suffering from some form of lovesickness, no amount of medicine will cure it and she can expect no further sympathy from me either.    (4.97.343)

這個理我就不明白了. 咱們這種人家, 別的事自然沒有的, 這心病也是斷斷有不得的. 林丫頭若不是這個病呢, 我憑著花多少錢都使得. 若是這個病, 不但治不好, 我也沒心腸了.    (2: 1333)

Lovesickness was shameful because it was a disease that one should be able to control before it became the more serious bone steaming or consumption. Dai-yu is told not to worry so much, told that she is making herself ill, on at least three occasions (1.20.410, 2.32.134, 4.82.67). Consumption casts doubt on her character in the eyes of Grandmother Jia, who says, "I know that Miss Lin's peculiar temperament is in some ways attractive. But I don't think we could possibly have her as a wife for Bao-yu. Besides, I'm afraid that with such a delicate constitution she is unlikely to live to any age" (4.90.218) 林丫頭 的 乖僻, 雖也是他的好處, 我的心裡不把林丫頭配他, 也是為這點子. 況且林丫 頭這樣虛弱, 恐不是有壽的 (2: 1255). Consumption in *Stone* is constructed as a disease of women with an overabundance of repressed passion and longing, the symptoms of which cause them to be all the more desirable. It is therefore an improper illness, because although Dai-yu has no power and is not sexually active, she threatens the family name and line because of her unrestrained passion.

In medical cases consumption becomes the chaste, female counterpart of male venereal disease. It is another example of *qing bu qing*: having a disease of passion without having had sex. At the end of the novel, Zhen Shi-yin explains to Jia Yu-cun the meaning of the illness and death encountered by so many of the story's women: "The fact of the matter is that all these noble ladies to whom you refer hail from the Skies of Passion and the Seas of Retribution. Since olden times their sex has been under a natural obligation to remain pure, pure from lust, pure even from the slightest taint of passion" (5.120.372) 貴族之女俱屬 從情天孽海而來. 大凡古今女子, 那 "淫" 字固不可犯, 只這 "情" 字也是沾染 不得的 (2: 1602). *Stone* is consistent in making a shift from the sexual desire found in such late Ming works as *Plum in the Golden Vase* or *The Carnal Prayer Mat* to more subtle and more repressed emotions common in fiction of the eighteenth and nineteenth centuries.[15]

Consumption is also tied to reading and writing. Dai-yu obsessively and secretly reads drama that is forbidden because of its representation of love and desire, and she composes exquisite poetry, which she burns as a symbol that her "heart's folly" has come to an end (5.97.340). Dai-yu dies of consumption resulting from static congestion, brought on by desire, depression, and her obsession with forbidden works of fiction and drama. She created fervor among readers, with "every languishing young lady imagining herself a Dai-yu" (1.16). The suffering of the passionate woman, embodied by Lin Dai-yu, was favored over the responsible, traditional, Confucian Xue Bao-chai, who read the same plays Dai-yu read but pragmatically, self-righteously put them out of her mind. The scene in which Dai-yu dies alone after burning her poems, at the moment her beloved Jia Bao-yu marries the wrong woman, is for many readers still the most poignant in the entire book.

Dai-yu's reading was reflected in *Stone*'s female readership. There are accounts of women who died from reading the book and emphathizing with Dai-yu. One reader died from falling in love with Bao-yu. Le Jun writes about "obsessed women" in his 1794 book. He tells the story of a young woman who died from reading *The Story of the Stone*, "like all those who died from reading *The Peony Pavilion*." She obtained a copy of *Stone* from her brother's desk and could not stop reading it. She was so enthralled, she could not eat or sleep. She would shut the book and contemplate it, sighing and shedding tears. Before she could finish it, she fell ill. Fearing that the book had caused their daughter's illness, her parents burned it. As her condition worsened, she lost the distinction between dreams and reality. She would sit and mutter, "Where is Bao-yu, Bao-yu?" Her parents called in a shaman, who employed a variety of treatments, all without effect. Finally, while sitting at her desk and crying, muttering, "Bao-yu is here, Bao-yu is here," their daughter died (347).

Medical belief diagnoses these mental symptoms as the result of excessive sorrow or resentment, which can cause people to act drunk or stupid, speaking absurdities, oblivious, suffering hallucinations—but the idea of fiction's taking control of the real world is also at play here. In Cao Xueqin's novel, fiction becomes real when it should. When it resonates with the reader, stirs emotions, causes the reader to believe, then it is no longer fiction. Readers' deaths make the fiction real. In another account, Chen Yong mentions that his friend Gui Yuqian tried to dissuade him from ever reading *Stone*. Gui told of a scholar who loved *Stone* so much that he read the entire novel seven times in one month, became overwhelmed with melancholy, and died. He also said that a girl, Miss Mou, on reading *Stone* the first time, coughed blood and died. Chen replied to his friend that both cases were of overempathy, and that nothing can help those who take on the cares of others.

Young women, often overly emotional and untrained readers, were especially unable to separate fiction from reality. When they died from reading, as Dai-yu and her obsessed fans did, it was tragic but beautiful. For men to die from reading was a shameful display of attachment to middle-brow literature and also a neglect of practical concerns. Such deaths showed, for both women and men, a fundamental inability to grasp the importance of Buddhist detachment from the world and from sentiment; they also showed a disregard for the most commonly held beliefs about health and medicine. *Stone* presents cases of illnesses that can be avoided by the reader and warns of the danger of repressed desire.

## Jia Rui: Retribution, Reading, Misreading

The misreading of Jia Rui costs him his life. He is obsessed with Xi-feng, who considers him so far below her station as to be insulted by his affections. She lays various traps for him, which he eagerly falls into. He is further subjected to humiliation and pain at the hands of his grandfather for breaking curfew after being locked in a freezing courtyard overnight. His health deteriorates, and he is bedridden. The doctor prescribes ginseng, but Xi-feng denies it to him. Jia Rui remains infatuated and engages in constant masturbation, which brings his health to a crisis. At this point, a Taoist shows up saying that he can cure "retributory illnesses" (1.12.251).[16] The Chinese for this condition is *yuanye zhi zheng*

冤業之症 or, in some editions, *yuannie zhi zheng* 冤孽之症. The word *yuan* 冤 is basically a negative term referring to enemies and a Buddhist term meaning "sin," but it is also often used for love relations, especially in the words *yuanjia* 冤家, *yuanye* 冤業, and *yuannie* 冤孽, all of which may refer either to enemies or, playfully, to lovers, the usage most common in *Stone*. Love and desire, seen as the results of karmic retribution for sins in earlier lives, are the cause of harm in this life. One of the claims that Bao-yu's jade makes is that it cures *yuanji* 冤疾 ("melancholy distempers" in Hawkes's translation [1.8.189]). This reading suggests that the illness that Bao-yu's jade cures is the same from which Jia Rui suffers. Halvor Eirfring translates both as "lovesickness," but it is good to keep in mind that both also have the implications of sin and retribution (300).

The monk says that medicine cannot cure Jia Rui. Instead, he lends him a mirror, the "Mirror for the Romantic" (one of the alternative titles of *Stone*), which has a mystical background: it was created by the fairy Disenchantment herself. It is meant to serve as an antidote to the ill effects of impure thinking and rash actions, and it works through sympathetic thought. Contemplating its truth will cure the illness brought on by lustful thoughts. Jia Rui is supposed to look only at the back of the mirror, which reflects a skull, but he violates the Taoist's command and looks into the front of the mirror, which shows Xi-feng beckoning to him. He is brought into the mirror, where he has intercourse with her, after which she sees him out. He finds himself back in bed, having had a wet dream and sweating profusely. The mirror has turned itself around in his hand, showing him once more the skull. He repeats this process four times, after which demons prevent him from leaving the mirror. They drag him away screaming, "Let me take the mirror with me." He is found dead, in a puddle of icy semen on the bed (1.12.252). He dies not from lovesickness but from overstimulation, the overspending of bodily resources, a particularly male problem.

Magic mirrors have a long tradition in Chinese literature, going back at least to the Tang dynasty. They represent truth and falsehood, love and death, self-knowledge and self-deception, and so on. These themes are also common in the West—for example, the Renaissance fad for portraits that depict both the subject and the subject's reflection in a nearby mirror in a skeletal or withered version of the subject. In Buddhist and Confucian philosophy, mirrors represent the ephemerality of everything, the function of a good official, the flaws in government of an emperor. Jia Rui is given an instrument to cure an illness of desire, of mental and emotional attachment, but he refuses to use it.

This episode is believed by many to be dropped in by the author or editors from another text that is now lost. They find no relation between it and any of the major plot lines, pointing out that when the year of Jia Rui's illness is over, the narrative goes back in time to pick up the thread at the point of its divergence. But the episode is related and provides two essential keys to understanding the novel—both having to do with medicine. First, looking into the mirror, for Jia Rui, is a kind of reading that parallels reading a novel. If we are seduced by what we encounter there, it is unhealthy. The reader may sympathize with a negative role model or may become too attached to a character. Savvy readers will understand that with all fiction a detached and objective reading allows them to enjoy the constructedness of the work without literally or figuratively getting sucked in. The readers who died from reading *Stone* lacked this understanding. It was a charming but tragic naïveté in young women that led to their demise; in men, it was an unenlightened philistinism, an inability to do the most fundamental thing that educated men did—read. In each of the stories of women who died from reading *Stone*, the family immediately burns the book that caused the death. Jia Rui's family similarly tries to burn the mirror, but it is rescued by the Taoist, who then accuses the family of confusing the real with the unreal.[17] That is, the family has mistaken the proximal cause of death, the book, for the ultimate one: the excessive repression or expression of desire caused by the improper reading of fiction as truth.

The second lesson that readers should take away from the Jia Rui episode is the difference between karmic retribution (來世報 *laishi bao* or 三世報 *sanshi bao*) and worldly retribution (現世報 *xianshi bao*). The Taoist says that he can cure retributory illnesses—such as this one, which was clearly brought on by the ill-advised actions of the patient. The patient brought the illness upon himself and refuses to adhere to the prescribed course of treatment; there is no debt incurred from a previous incarnation. Fundamental to the concept of circulation and health was the notion of bodily economy. Because the body had limited resources, health was damaged by loss. Excessive bleeding and loss of essence or sexual fluids left one weak and susceptible to harmful influences from the outside. Sex in eighteenth-century Chinese fiction was generally considered dirty.[18] Smallpox, for instance, was surrounded by popular rituals that called attention to the uncleanliness of sex and of the female reproductive body. Parents were to abstain from intercourse during their child's illness, and menstruating women were to keep out of the sickroom. This ritual is observed (and violated) by Xi-feng's husband, Jia Lian, in *Stone* (1.21.424). The taboos surrounding sex are connected to the unwise expenditure by men of their essence and to the pollution surrounding the blood of women. Overspending of resources was a mistake, from the imperial level to the home to the body.[19] The Jia Rui episode is a warning about obsession and misreading: foolishly overspending his essence through an attachment to fiction, Jia Rui ends up being a spendthrift of his own corporeal reserves.

## Xi-feng: Bodily Economy and Women's Maladies

A number of scholars have discussed the theme of the mismanagement of bodily resources in other Chinese novels, notably *The Plum in the Golden Vase*, as it pertains to sexual economy, but *Stone* presents a very interesting case in Wang Xi-feng. Xi-feng is in charge of the Jia household expenses. Strict, abusive, and conniving, she breaks many taboos and laws, flirting and possibly having an affair with her nephew, Jia Rong (see Big Jiao's remark about "auntie having it off with nevvy" [1.7.183]). She brokers marriage contracts and illegally lends money at usurious rates. She also suffers from a protracted illness. She has one daughter but cannot bear more children and has a persistent loss of blood (3.72.420). Her illness reflects the Jia family economic situation, for which she is primarily responsible. In chapter 13, Qin-shi appears to Xi-feng (in a dream? as a ghost?) and tells her to economize and invest wisely for difficult times ahead. The warning goes unheeded, as Xi-feng admits before she dies (5.101.48).

Throughout the novel, we are told that the Jias are living beyond their means. They cannot afford the elaborate shows of wealth they made in the past, yet they refuse to curtail their spending. Xi-feng's blood loss mirrors the process by which both body and home are weakened by the outflow of not only cash and blood but also of morality. Her loan-sharking adds to the family shame and leads to the confiscation of property. The two parallel losses interact as well. Without sufficient funds, Xi-feng cannot obtain ginseng for her treatment, just as she once denied ginseng to Jia Rui for his illness.

If Xi-feng's illness is interesting metaphorically, her diagnosis might be more illuminating still. In addition to chronic headaches, Xi-feng suffers a miscarriage in chapter 55. She goes back to work but begins to have chronic uterine bleeding. Although the narrative tells us that in the autumn of that year she will be much improved, by chapter 72 her condition has deteriorated, with a constant flow of blood. She becomes weak, faints, is exhausted. When unjustly rebuked,

> [s]he struggled to control herself, but tears started to her eyes, and all went black before her. A sickly taste rose into her mouth and she began to vomit up quantities of bright red blood. The strength ebbed from her legs and she sank to the ground. Luckily Patience was at hand and hurried over to support her mistress as she crouched there, blood gushing from her mouth in an unstaunchable stream.                    (5.110.206)

> 一口氣撞上來, 往下一咽, 眼淚直流, 只覺得眼前一黑, 嗓子裡一甜, 便噴出鮮紅的血來, 身子站不住, 就蹲倒在地. 幸虧平兒急忙過來扶住. 只見鳳姐的血吐個不住.                    (2: 1488)

Readers may sympathize with Xi-feng, but her suffering is simply retribution. Her blood loss, barrenness, and inability to secure a future for her family are a microcosmic reflection of her bleeding of the Jia family finances and her poor planning for difficult times ahead.

The economics of illness is heightened because Qin-shi too suffers from menstrual irregularity, likely a punishment for her having an affair with her father-in-law, Jia Zhen (hinted at with the "poking in the ashes" comment of Big Jiao [1.7.183]). She believes she is dying, but Xi-feng assures her that no expense will be spared to procure for her the best medicines. In the Jia Rui episode in the next chapter, Xi-feng denies Jia Rui the ginseng that might cure his illness. The narrative returns to Qin-shi, who dies and then appears to Xi-feng, telling her to economize, to plan for the future by investing in land in order to provide for a family school and the maintenance of the ancestral shrine. Both Qin-shi's and Xi Feng's illnesses are tied to taboo and transgression.

Xi-feng's symptoms are also consistent with depletion fatigue (虛勞 *xulao* or 虛損 *xusun*) and taxation vacuity (*laoqie zhi zheng* 勞怯之症), which manifests itself particularly through the improper flow of blood.[20] Contemporary medical authorities commonly wrote that it was easier to treat ten men than one woman, saying that women were more prone to illness than men because so many of women's illnesses were blood-related. In the *New Book of Childbearing* 太產新書, a medical book published in 1793, the year after *Stone* was first published, the author writes a history of the life cycle of women in terms of blood disorders. Women in their mid-twenties are liable to have irregular periods and intermittent fevers and are vulnerable to bone steaming. By twenty-four, a woman's "sea of blood" is already in danger of depletion and attacks from cold. In addition to the usual symptoms of headache, dizziness, hot and cold sensations, and cramping, women will often suffer vaginal discharges, menstrual flooding or spotting, and protracted periods (Furth, "Blood" 49). Xi-feng is twenty-five or twenty-six when she dies (5.101.51).

Taxation vacuity is caused by sexual activity and uncontrolled emotion. It is a broad grouping of wasting illnesses. Among women, depletion fatigue usually causes pallor, shortness of breath, hot sensations, disturbed dreams and insomnia, fits of melancholy and anger. The most pronounced symptom is coughing with blood sputum, but depletion fatigue in women might also manifest itself in sterility or menstrual irregularity. In advanced cases, taxation vacuity can result in bone steaming," a life-threatening form of depletion linked by modern practitioners of traditional medicine to pulmonary tuberculosis. It is also linked to consumption in Europe, since many of the causes of consumption were thought to be emotional (Furth, *Flourishing Yin* 80–81).

Of the five fatigues that lead to taxation vacuity, three are from extreme emotion: fatigue from grief, fatigue from worry, and fatigue from striving. Since taxation vacuity and bone steaming encompass coughing blood, menstrual flooding, and other menstrual irregularities, we might see the illnesses of Dai-yu, Qin-shi, and Xi-feng as three different manifestations of an illness caused by *qing*. Dai-yu suffers fatigue from grief (for dead parents, from thwarted love), Qin-shi suffers fatigue from worry (that her taboo-breaking transgression will be found out), and Xi-feng suffers fatigue from striving (to meet the demands of her elders, to maintain a monopoly on information and power). In married and sexually active women, menstrual irregularity is more common than coughing blood, though they too become weak, emaciated, and pale. Three women characters illustrate that women's diseases are emotional and tied to blood.

Xi-feng's symptoms are caused by excessive worry. When Xi-feng tries to take over family management duties after an attack of illness, the stress causes her to relapse. The ultimate cause of her illness may be retribution, since she tempts fate by saying in chapter 15, "I've never believed all that talk about hell and retribution. If I decide that I want to do something I do it, no matter what it is"

(1.15.298; for *baoying*, read "retribution," not "damnation") 你是素日知道我的, 從來不信什麼是陰司地獄報應的, 憑是什麼事, 我說要行就行 (1: 198). Her illness, marked by blood loss and extreme anxiety, points directly to her transgression in this incarnation; it is not exclusively a karmic debt. Xi-feng, who also suffers blood loss and overemotionality, is a paired opposite of Dai-yu, who is pure and chaste rather than scheming and transgressive. This contrast highlights the broader tragedy of women in *Stone*: their proneness to violent emotion and the danger of either acting on or repressing that emotion.

Dai-yu, Caltrop, Qin-shi, Skybright, and Xi-feng all suffer from a wasting disease brought on by unrestrained *qing*, desire. Each manifests the symptom set of a consumptive who suffers from passion, grief, worry, or ambition. Of all those amorous souls waiting in the Land of Illusion at the beginning of the novel to be reincarnated in the realm of red dust, these young women waste away. They die of fatigue and taxation, according to their debts to karma or their debts to others. Their earthly retribution is still karmic, since being put on earth to suffer is part of a grand design to teach the lesson of detachment from human emotion and the suffering it causes.

Because the study of medical belief and practice is inherently interdisciplinary, looking at *Stone* though the lens of medicine reveals how intertwined the novel is with the culture in which it was produced. Because medical texts, practices, and beliefs were often based on metaphor to begin with, *Stone* likely created as much medical meaning as it borrowed. It provided readers with medical knowledge they could use to diagnose themselves. The readers may have been aesthetes and eccentrics interested in roguish fiction about consumptive beauties and thereby revealing a fanciful mixture of qi. They may have been *qing bu qing*, feeling deeply for the fictional characters of *Stone*. They may have been prone to retributory illness, unaware that the novel they held in their hands was literally a mirror for the romantic. Looking only at the surface level, they would pursue fleeting pleasure and fall ill from an excess of emotion or desire. If they were jealous or petty or seeking only wealth and power, they would also exhaust their bodily resources. But if they were able to look into the back of the mirror, to read the book as a skilled physician reads pulses, and understand this novel's warning, they might abandon their vain and frivolous pursuits and stay the deterioration of their vital forces.

NOTES

[1]Chinese blood is not the same as Western blood. Some scholars capitalize *blood* to remind readers that in traditional Chinese medicine functional systems were only vaguely connected to anatomical structures, although it is common to express them as names of organs.

[2]Zhang Xinzhi's commentary is a good example (SJPB). See Epstein's essay in this volume. Andrew Plaks discusses this approach at length in *Archetype* 49–83; see also Yim 94–97.

3 There were both refined and coarse versions of each kind of soul. In Ding Yaokang's *Sequel to the Plum in the Golden Vase*, for instance, two different spiritual souls of the same dead person get into a fight with each other.

4 About the time that *Stone* was being written, there was a pandemic of soul stealing. See Kuhn.

5 "Calling the soul" (招魂 *zhaohun,* 收魂 *shouhun,* or 叫魂 *jiaohun*) refers both to the calling away of a soul from the body, as in the soul stealing done by a wicked sorcerer, and the calling back of a soul to the body, as for example a devoted parent might do when the child's soul has been frightened away.

6 *Plum* is often thought to employ yin-yang themes, in part because its most famous commentator uses many two-term contrasts, most notably in focusing on alternating themes of cold and hot. Other commentators see more complicated, five-phases structures at work. See Scott's essay in this volume.

7 There seems to have been an attempt to rank the major characters according to the depth of their *qing* in the original versions of the final chapter. All we know now is that Bao-yu was ranked at the top of this roster, given the epithet *qing bu qing*, and that Dai-yu came second, given the epithet *qingqing* 情情 ("feeling for the feeling").

8 Xi Shi was a beauty of the Spring and Autumn Period (770–476 BCE). She was famous for her melancholy beauty, often pictured with a slight frown. Bao-yu links Dai-yu to Xi Shi by giving her the nickname Frowner. (See Dai-yu's poem on 3.64.257 and other mentions on 74.462 and 464.)

9 The Chinese syndrome *lao* does not correlate directly with consumption understood as a precursor to modern tuberculosis. Yet the implications of the English *consumption* — being consumed by an illness — as well as its cultural connotations, recalling passionate beauties coughing up blood, make it an attractive term for the translation.

10 The exception to this rule is Xiang-yun's husband, who has an illness that turns out to be consumption, which is the best of possible outcomes for him, allowing him to live for another few years (5.109.190).

11 Charmante disappears from the narrative after chapter 36, but because of the system of shadows or types, we know that she shares personality traits (she feels alone in the world, is demanding, perfectionist, beautiful, lovesick, etc.), that she will cough two mouthfuls of blood, and die of consumption (2.36.206–10).

12 On static congestion, see Zeitlin, *Phantom Heroine* 21–24.

13 Leung discusses these and other modes of transmission in her chapter on contagion in *Leprosy in China* (84–132).

14 Dai-yu also recalls the cuckoo, which weeps tears of blood as it calls listeners home, to the Land of Illusion.

15 For more on this shift, see M. Huang, *Desire* 57–86. Many works in the nineteenth century emphasized sex, disease, and emotion, and many were red-light novels.

16 A textual variant reads "cure illness resulting from lustful thoughts."

17 In some editions it is the mirror itself that speaks the reproof.

18 Note the obsession with female chastity that Matt Sommer discusses in his essay in this volume.

19 This attitude has its counterpart in the West. The Grahamites, advocates of dietary reform, denied sexual partners their semen, not unlike General Ripper in *Doctor Strangelove*, who says, "I do not avoid women, Mandrake, but I do deny them my essence."

20 Taxation vacuity was a pattern of symptoms indicating severe deficiency in qi, blood, or the organs. It included bone steaming, consumption, wasting coughs, and contagious diseases.

# Scandal in the Garden:
## *The Story of the Stone* as a Licentious Novel

### Matthew H. Sommer

## From Banned Book to Chinese Classic

Since the early twentieth century, leading intellectuals have praised *The Story of the Stone* as one of a handful of classic novels from the late imperial era, and it is now enshrined as the acme of eighteenth-century Chinese cultural achievement. But for most of the century following its publication in 1791–92, the novel was banned by Qing officials (albeit in vain). "Of all licentious books, *The Story of the Stone* is by far the worst!" ranted one nineteenth-century critic (Wang Liqi 376, 378). "It should definitely be burned!" asserted another (392). The novel appears prominently on the lists of "licentious books" (*yin shu* 淫書) proscribed and consigned to destruction by government officials—along with many other literary works now considered classics, such as *The Peony Pavilion* (*The Return of the Soul*), *The Story of the Western Wing* (*Romance of the Western Chamber*), *Outlaws of the Marsh* (*The Water Margin*), and *Plum in the Golden Vase* (*Golden Lotus*).[1] In other words, the modern reinvention of *Stone* as a great Chinese classic required occlusion of the fact that it had long been condemned as "licentious" and rejection of the standards by which it had been so condemned.

The purpose of this essay is to show the modern reader why, according to elite normative standards in the eighteenth and nineteenth centuries, *The Story of the Stone* might have been considered obscene. I show how the hero's behavior violates the standards of his day, standards that would have been taken for granted by any Qing dynasty reader—even a reader who chafed at them and savored the novel's subversive elements.

The group of eighteenth-century commentators collectively known by the pseudonym Red Inkstone famously observed that "this book cannot escape the slander of pedantic Confucians" (W. Li, *Enchantment* 236). Red Inkstone obviously anticipated and understood the orthodox criticism of the novel, even as he rejected it. In this respect he probably typifies the nonconformist aficionados who circulated the novel's manuscript privately for decades before it finally saw its way into print and who later continued to enjoy it in defiance of the censorship.

The author himself clearly knew that his novel would be judged obscene, and he sports with conventional expectations throughout the text. Perhaps the single most graphic scene in the novel is Jia Rui's death from excessive semen loss in chapter 12, when a magic mirror induces him to fantasize compulsively about making love with Wang Xi-feng. The name of this mirror is Mirror for the Romantic, and it was given to Jia Rui by a mysterious Taoist monk (1.12.251–53). In Chapter 1, we have already learned that "A Mirror for the Romantic" was an early title for *The Story of the Stone*, which was first transcribed by a Taoist monk named Vanitas (1.51). One of the arguments made by Qing critics who advocated the suppression of licentious literature was that it would provoke impressionable youths to excessive masturbation and nocturnal emission, thereby ruining their health and shortening their lives (Wang Liqi 239–40, 300, 392, 412). In other words, Jia Rui's death is a sly parody of the danger that books like *Stone* supposedly posed to youths; it suggests the author's sardonic anticipation of how his novel would be judged.

## Bao-yu's Sex Life: Innocence or Obscenity?

As every reader of the novel knows, its hero, Jia Bao-yu, has a sex life. Indeed, the main action of the novel is bracketed by two profoundly important carnal rites of passage: Bao-yu's sexual initiation in chapters 5 and 6 and the rather tardy consummation of his marriage in chapter 109.

In chapter 5, Bao-yu has a dream encounter with fairies who instruct him in the art of love. The ostensible purpose of this initiation is "to shock the silliness out of him" (137), so that he will devote his mind "seriously to the teaching of Confucius and Mencius" (146). If Bao-yu's sexual initiation actually achieved this purpose, we could skip the next 103 chapters; fortunately it has no such effect. Instead, Bao-yu awakens to discover that he has had the most famous wet dream in all of world literature. Then, at the beginning of chapter 6, he tries out what he has learned with his sympathetic chambermaid, Aroma. This episode marks the beginning of the dreamy aestheticism and sentimentality that will characterize the garden, a separate world where maturation and social responsibility are magically suspended.

In chapter 109, Bao-yu finally manages to consummate his marriage with the long-suffering Bao-chai, thereby producing a son and heir (5.109.184). This episode marks his reluctant, long overdue acceptance of the filial and social responsibilities of an adult male. He has moved out of the garden and is beginning to concentrate seriously on his studies. Soon thereafter he will pass the civil service examinations, the pinnacle of masculine achievement for the elite of his era (119.349).

What are the implications of Bao-yu's sex life? Specifically, how would the fact of his sexual maturity and experience, made explicit at the outset of *Stone*, have framed the way a Qing dynasty audience read the novel?

Wai-yee Li calls attention to the "paradoxical conjoining of innocence and experience" in Bao-yu, a paradox that the author "tries his best to sustain"; in particular, she suggests that despite Bao-yu's sexual initiation early in the novel, "his relationship with the girls in the Garden is blithely innocent" (*Enchantment* 204). Bao-yu never has genital contact with any of his cousins (leaving aside the postgarden consummation of his marriage), although he certainly does have such contact with Aroma and probably at least one other maidservant.

But we need to bear in mind that innocence, like obscenity, is a historically specific norm: its definition depends entirely on the standards of the society in question.

By the standards of elite society in the Qing dynasty, some of the most charming scenes in the garden are among the most obscene. Grandmother Jia, Lady Wang, and the other senior women do their utmost, despite frequent anxieties and doubts, to pretend that Bao-yu's relations with the girls are blithely innocent, but his sexual maturity renders this pretense untenable, as the author suggests repeatedly throughout the novel.

Bao-yu's androgyny and sentimental idealization of girls are legendary. Bao-yu does not want to grow up, and he acts out this reluctance in part through his ambiguous gender performance. He is an expert on cosmetics and other aspects of the toilet and wardrobe of young ladies. On several occasions, he is actually mistaken for a girl (his voice is mistaken for a girl's and his bedroom for a boudoir, and so on). He insists that boys, compared with girls, are coarse, impure things, "made of mud" (1.2.76). But he reserves his greatest contempt for adults of both sexes, who invariably seem corrupted by avarice, licentiousness, or both—and indeed none of the grown-ups in his enormous family can be considered much of a role model. For him, marriage—the key rite of passage in his society, marking the assumption of adult gender roles—is something to be mourned and resisted, because it is the ruin of every girl.

But none of this changes the fact, established at the start of chapter 6, that Bao-yu is sexually mature, aware, and experienced.

His chief peculiarity, often remarked by other characters, is his preference for young female company. To indulge this preference requires nonenforcement of the separation of sexes that was fundamental to the reigning Confucian ideology and standard practice in elite households. As Dore Levy notes, by the time Bao-yu moves into the garden, he is "already long past the age at which customary rules of sexual segregation should be in force" (33). In eighteenth-century China, any son of an elite family would begin life in the female quarters, in the company of his mother and sisters, his nannies and maids. But at about six years of age he would be expected to start on a centrifugal path out into the masculine, public world of education, examinations, and imperial service. Meanwhile his sisters would have their ears pierced and feet bound and would follow the centripetal path of safeguarding female chastity through cloistering. Maturation meant growing into distinct gender roles, which required separation of the sexes. Man and woman would be rejoined on marriage, as husband and wife.

In *The Story of the Stone*, the girls are indeed cloistered: their garden is a walled compound patrolled within and without by guards (the guards within are matrons), and great vigilance is maintained over who may enter or leave. Bao-yu is the only male who enters freely—let alone lives there. For him to move into the garden (a centripetal movement counter to the properly masculine trajectory) and there to idle day and night with female cousins of different surnames

*[margin, handwritten: BY's unusual status in Garden]*

(any one of whom is a potential bride, as confirmed by his eventual marriage to Bao-chai) requires that the women who have de facto responsibility for him make a very self-conscious exception to the rules. Indulging Bao-yu requires a suspension of the social maturation that would inevitably exclude him from the casual company of his cousins. But physical maturation cannot be suspended, necessitating a collective conspiracy to pretend that he is just a little boy who can still play with the girls, that he's too young to get up to mischief.

More than any other factor, this systematic, willful denial of Bao-yu's sexual maturity is what makes the novel obscene.

## *Bao-yu's Wet Dream*

The denial begins, significantly, with the notorious wet dream episode. Qin-shi takes Bao-yu into her chambers for a nap: "'Leave him to me, Grannie dear! He will be quite safe in my hands.' . . . Grandmother Jia had always had a high opinion of Qin-shi's trustworthiness . . . and was quite content to leave the arrangements to her" (1.5.125) 老祖宗放心, 只管交與我就是了 . . . 賈母素知秦氏是個極妥當的人 . . . 見他去安置寶玉, 自是安穩的 (1: 69). (This ironic comment by the author is an early clue to just how clueless the Jia matriarch is.) Qin-shi asks Bao-yu:

> "[W]here *are* we going to put you?—unless you would like to have your rest in my bedroom."
>
> A little smile played over Bao-yu's face and he nodded. The nurses were shocked.
>
> "An uncle sleep in the bedroom of his nephew's wife! Who ever heard of such a thing!"
>
> Qin-shi laughed again.
>
> "He won't misbehave. Good gracious, he's only a little boy! We don't have to worry about that sort of thing yet!" (126)

> "可往那裡 去呢? 不然往我屋裡去吧." 寶玉點頭微笑. 有一個嬤嬤說道: "那裡有個叔叔往侄兒房 裡睡覺的理?" 秦氏笑道: "嗳喲喲, 不怕他惱. 他能多大呢, 就忌諱這些個!" (70)

This dialogue introduces what we may call the Bao-yu exception to the principle of separation of the sexes. For him to sleep in Qin-shi's bed is doubly taboo: she is the wife of his nephew Jia Rong, so in addition to violating female space his choice of bed carries a strong odor of incest (note that at this time the "trustworthy" Qin-shi is apparently carrying on an affair with her father-in-law—see Hawkes's discussion [1.42]). The voice of reason speaks through the nurses, only to be dismissed with the excuse that will become familiar over the next hundred chapters: "He's only a little boy."

Bao-yu himself repeats this excuse just a few pages later, in his dream. When the fairy Disenchantment accuses him of being "the most lustful person I have ever known in the whole world" 乃天下古今第一淫人也, he protests: "Madam Fairy, you are wrong! Because I am lazy over my lessons, Mother and Father still have to scold me quite often; but surely that doesn't make me *lustful*? I'm still too young to know what they do, the people they use that word about" (145). 仙姑差了. 我因懶於讀書, 家父母尚每垂訓飭, 豈敢再冒 "淫" 字. 況且年紀尚小, 不知 "淫" 字為何物 (87).

The claim of juvenile innocence is immediately refuted on multiple levels. In the dream, Qin-shi's fairy counterpart initiates Bao-yu sexually; their dream intercourse is given corporeal effect by Bao-yu's seminal emission in Qin-shi's bed. Finally Bao-yu tells Aroma what he learned in the dream, and they begin a real sexual relationship. Elsewhere in the novel, the author is coy to the point of ambiguity about Bao-yu's sexual behavior; here, his ejaculation is as explicit as can be. Lest there be any misunderstanding, we have a witness in Aroma:

> As she was doing up his trousers, her hand, chancing to stray over his thigh, came into contact with something cold and sticky which caused her to draw it back in alarm and ask him if he was all right. Instead of answering, he merely reddened and gave the hand a squeeze.　　　(1.6.149)
>
> 襲人伸手與他系褲帶時, 不覺伸手至大腿處, 只覺冰涼一片沾濕, 唬的忙退出手來, 問是怎麼了. 寶玉紅漲了臉, 把他的手一捻.　　　(90)

This unique moment of graphic explicitness serves an important purpose: despite the author's later coyness, we can have no doubt whatsoever that Bao-yu has reached sexual maturity at the beginning of the book, well before the garden was constructed.[2]

Note that when the fairy Disenchantment expatiates on the definition and varieties of lust and accuses Bao-yu of being uniquely lustful, she is talking about the concept of yin (淫), which can also be translated as "licentious" or "obscene" (145–46). It was precisely books of this category that were prohibited by the Qing authorities. In legal texts, yin constituted a category of criminal motivation; it was the "licentious heart" that motivated rape or adultery. It is against this background that we should read Disenchantment's disquisition on lust, her warning that Bao-yu's lust of the mind is bound to be misunderstood in the real world, and her novel effort to cure him of lust through the shock of actual lovemaking. In this passage, the author is purposely toying with social and legal convention, provoking the following reaction from the Qing commentator Zhang Xinzhi: "Here the author himself frankly admits that this is a 'licentious book'" 紅樓夢面子是淫書, 作者已直認不諱 (SJPB 1: 84).

How old *is* this little boy, and what does his age signify? Bao-yu's age is a matter of considerable ambiguity, and it's not clear just how old Bao-yu is at the time of his wet dream. But when he moves into the garden, he is a "thirteen-year-old" (1.23.461), though "thirteen sui" in the original Chinese text is probably equivalent to twelve years by our reckoning. (An age calculated in the traditional unit of sui 歲 is on average one more than that calculated in years.) This is one of the few moments in the novel when he is given a precise age.

Thirteen sui was generally understood in late imperial China to be the threshold of sexual maturity. Thus, for example, the Kangxi emperor (r. 1662–1722) married Empress Xiaocheng when he was eleven (i.e., twelve or thirteen sui), and two years later a concubine gave birth to the emperor's first son (Spence, *Emperor* 119). In Qing dynasty law, people became liable for criminal acts at the age of thirteen sui, which the Qing code also specifically defined as the age of criminal liability for consenting to illicit sexual intercourse. A girl under this age was incapable of meaningful consent and could not be punished for it. The reason, according to a commentary on the Qing code, was that "in young girls of twelve *sui* and under, sexual awareness has not yet bloomed, so they still have no capacity for licentiousness." Therefore intercourse with a girl of twelve sui or under was punishable as rape, regardless of whether she had consented; but a girl of thirteen sui would be criminally liable unless she could prove coercion. In the 1720s, this standard was extended to sodomy law, so that boys too became criminally liable for consent at thirteen sui (Sommer, *Sex* 85, 125).

Therefore, when Bao-yu moves into the garden, he is at the cusp of mature sexual responsibility by contemporary social and legal standards. By chapter 49, less than halfway through the novel, he is at least fifteen sui: after listing Crab-Flower Club members, including Bao-yu, the narrator comments that "[a]part from the two young married women, the rest were all fifteen, sixteen or seventeen years old" (2.49.473) 除李紈年紀最長, 他十二個人皆不過十五六七歲 (1: 657)—"sui" in the Chinese original. The adolescent (or teenager), as an intermediate category of diminished responsibility between child and adult, is a fairly recent invention and should not be projected back to eighteenth-century China. For a son or daughter of an elite family, fifteen sui was a prime age for betrothal and even marriage; the Analects of Confucius define fifteen sui as the age when a young man should focus seriously on preparing for his career. In the classical tradition, the "capping" ceremony that formally marked the end of childhood for a young man took place after he reached the age of fifteen sui. In other words, the pretense that Bao-yu is a little boy is absurd.

## Bao-yu Moves into the Garden

A corollary to the excuse that Bao-yu is too young for sexual awareness is that he is different from other boys. In chapter 23, when the imperial concubine Yuan-chun decides that her brother Bao-yu should live in the garden along with the girls, this is her reasoning:

> Assuredly, the girls must be allowed into the garden. It should become their home. And if the girls, why not Bao-yu? He had grown up in their

midst. He was different from other boys. If he were not allowed into the garden as well, he would consider himself left out in the cold, and his distress would cause Lady Wang and Grandmother Jia to feel unhappy too. Unquestionably she should ask for him to be admitted along with the girls. (455)

何不命他們進去居住, 也不使佳人落魄, 花柳無顏. 卻又想到寶玉自幼在姊 妹叢中長大, 不比別的兄弟, 若不命他進去, 只怕他冷清了, 一時不大暢快, 未免賈母 王夫人愁慮, 須得也命他進園居住方妙. (1: 309)

Because of her rank, Yuan-chun has the power to order her father to permit Bao-yu to live in the garden, thereby violating the separation of sexes, and Jia Zheng obeys without complaint. Levy rightly emphasizes this subversion of patriarchal authority as a key moment in the breakdown of Confucian moral order in the Jia household (83). What is Yuan-chun's excuse? That Bao-yu, having grown up with girls, is "different from other boys"—an extremely vague formulation that seems to imply that he would not be a threat to female chastity because he is not subject to the same coarse impulses as other boys.

There is tremendous irony here: it is Yuan-chun who orders this violation of ritual order, yet the most extreme example in the novel of the separation of sexes is that imposed during her visit to her natal home, when she is guarded by an army of eunuchs in chapter 18. During her visit, no male family member, not even her own father, is admitted to her presence, and she must speak with the men from behind a curtain. ("Now that she was the Emperor's woman, this was the nearest to her [Jia Zheng] could ever hope to get" [362; Hawkes's amplification of the text]. But an exception is made for Bao-yu, whom she summons, embraces, and caresses. This breach of taboo rehearses her authorization of his move into the garden.

Much later in the novel (chapter 78), during a conversation with Lady Wang, Grandmother Jia reflects on Bao-yu's peculiar affinity for young female company. She rules out licentiousness as a motive:

He's a strange boy. . . . His other kinds of naughtiness I can understand; it's this passion for spending all his time with maids that I find so hard to make out. It used at one time to worry me: I thought it must be because he had reached puberty and was having experiences with them; but after watching him very carefully, I came to the conclusion that it wasn't that at all. It's very, very strange. Perhaps he was a maid himself in some past life. Perhaps he ought to have been a girl. (3.78.556)

別的淘氣都是應該的, 只他這種和丫頭們 好卻是難懂. 我為此也耽心, 每每的冷眼查看他. 只和丫頭們鬧, 必是人大心大, 知道男女的事了, 所以愛親近他們. 既細細查試, 究竟不是為此. 豈不奇怪. 想必原是個丫 頭錯投了胎不成. (2: 1094)

Grandmother Jia assumes that the normal reason a boy of Bao-yu's age would be interested in female company is for sex; she is surprised that sex did not turn out to be his motive. And yet, although she worried that when he reached puberty, he would have the same licentious impulses toward girls that other boys feel, she never restricts his access to his cousins in any way.

## Bao-yu's Unofficial Concubine

Grandmother Jia's comments are especially strange since Grandmother Jia herself gave Aroma to Bao-yu to be his chambermaid, and it is with Aroma that his sexual experience begins. Aroma, well aware that her status makes her fair game for her master, accepts his advances with equanimity:

> Aroma knew that when Grandmother Jia gave her to Bao-yu she had intended her to belong to him in the fullest possible sense, and so, having no good reason for refusing him, she allowed him, after a certain amount of coy resistance, to have his way with her.
>
> From then on Bao-yu treated Aroma with even greater consideration than before, whilst Aroma for her part redoubled the devotion with which she served him.
>
> (1.6.150)

> 寶玉亦素喜襲人柔媚嬌俏, 遂強襲人同領警幻所訓雲雨之事. 襲人素知賈母已將自己與了寶玉的, 今便如此, 亦不為越禮, 遂和寶玉偷試一番, 幸得無人撞見. 自此寶玉視襲人更比別個不同, 襲人待寶玉更為盡心.
>
> (1: 90)

Like the other maidservants in the Jia household, Aroma is a slave girl, having been sold into servitude by her parents. By tradition, a domestic female slave's master enjoyed the sexual use of her if he chose, a privilege made explicit by the legal codes of several dynasties.[3] During the Qing dynasty, the legal status of such slaves changed somewhat: by the mid–eighteenth century, a series of new laws and judicial rulings required that masters of both male and female slaves arrange timely marriages for them once the slaves reached maturity and prohibited any master from having sexual intercourse with "a married woman subordinate to his household" (Sommer, *Sex* 48). Unmarried female slaves remained sexually available, but a master who wanted to sleep with one was expected to promote her to the status of concubine (Hawkes uses the term "chamber-wife")—that is, to make her his legal secondary wife (see Sommer, *Sex* 45–54).

After Bao-yu's initiation with Aroma in chapter 6, the narrator becomes reticent about their sexual relationship, to the point that readers may wonder whether they still have one (even though Aroma typically sleeps in Bao-yu's room, to be on hand if Bao-yu wants anything during the night). But occasional clues suggest that they do continue to have sex. For example, in chapter 31, the maidservant Skybright, who is jealous of Aroma's special status, accuses her of putting on airs even though Aroma is not officially Bao-yu's concubine, only a maidservant like the rest of them:

> [Y]ou needn't think you deceive *me*. *I* know what goes on between you when you think no one is looking. But when all's said and done, in actual fact, when you come down to it, you're not even a "Miss" by *rights*. By *rights* you're no better than any of the rest of us.

我倒不知道你們是誰, 別教我替你們害臊了! 便是你們鬼鬼祟祟干的那事兒, 也瞞不過我去, 那裡就稱起 "我們" 來了. 明公正道, 連個姑娘還沒掙上去呢, 也不過和我似的.

In response, "Aroma blushed and blushed with shame," provoking Bao-yu to retort that he will formalize their relationship by promoting Aroma: "I'll make her a 'Miss' then; I'll make her my chamber-wife tomorrow, if that's all that's worrying you. You can spare your jealousy on *that* account" (2.31.111) 你們氣不忿, 我明兒偏抬舉他 (1: 419).

Aroma may not be the only chambermaid who is having sex with Bao-yu, although the author is coy on this point. Just a few pages later, Bao-yu, learning that Skybright plans to take a bath, proposes to join her in the bathtub (apparently intending to assuage her jealousy with some personal attention). She demurs:

> *Oh* no! I daren't start you off on that caper. I still remember that time you got Emerald to help you [bathe]. You must have been two or three hours in there, so that we began to get quite worried. We didn't like to go in while you were there, but when we did go in to have a look afterwards, we found water all over the floor, pools of water round the legs of the bed, and even the mat on the bed had water splashed all over it. Heaven only knows what you'd been up to. We laughed about it for days afterwards. (115)

罷, 罷, 我不敢惹爺. 還記得碧痕打發你洗澡, 足有兩三個時辰, 也不知道作什麼呢. 我們也不好進去的. 後來洗完了, 進去瞧瞧, 地下的水淹著床腿, 連席子上都汪著水, 也不知是怎麼洗了, 笑了幾天.     (422)

Through such teasing testimony, the author suggests that a great deal goes on behind the scenes.

Bao-yu's sexual relationship with Aroma should surprise no one, nor should the fact that Bao-yu considers making her his concubine. The strange thing about his relationship with her is what his mother, Lady Wang, does with it. She decides to promote Aroma to be Bao-yu's concubine but keeps the promotion unofficial and secret. It is accomplished through a sleight of hand: Lady Wang arranges to have Aroma's allowance paid out of her own income (instead of Grandmother Jia's) and raises it to the same level as those paid to Jia Zheng's concubines. But this maneuver is kept secret. At first, Wang Xi-feng and Aroma are the only ones who know; later, some of the other women in the household become indirectly aware of the promotion; but the news is never broken to Bao-yu's father, Jia Zheng. The only reason Bao-yu finds out about Aroma's "unofficial promotion to his bed" is that Aroma tells him (2.36.204).

When Lady Wang first concocts this plan, Wang Xi-feng asks the reasonable question, "Why not have her plucked and painted and make her his chamber-wife openly?" Lady Wang replies:

> First of all he is too young; secondly Sir Zheng would never agree to it; and in the third place, even if we allow a certain amount of freedom be-tween them, as long as he still thinks of her as his maid, there is some chance that he will listen to what she says, but once we make her his chamber-wife, she will feel less free to tell him what she thinks of him when he is being silly. No, I think for the moment at any rate we should leave it a little vague. We can make a more definite arrangement in two or three years' time.                                    (199)

> 那就不好了, 一則都年輕, 二則老爺也不許, 三則那 寶玉見襲人是個丫頭, 縱有放縱的事, 倒能聽他的勸, 如今作了跟前人, 那襲人該勸的 也不敢十分勸了. 如今且渾著, 等再過二三年再說.               (1: 477)

In response to this argument, the Qing critic Zhang Xinzhi comments, "See how these illicit relations, carried on in secret, are entirely the result of his mother's orders!" 見陰行苟合, 悉出母命 (SJPB 2: 566)

Much later in the novel (ch. 78), Lady Wang finally tells Grandmother Jia what she has done and explains her reasons once again:

> I deliberately kept it from everyone else, partly because if Sir Zheng had got to hear about it he would almost certainly have said that Bao-yu was too young for a chamber-wife and that having one would distract him from his studies, and partly because if Bao-yu himself thought of her as a chamber-wife, he would be less inclined to listen to her good advice and would become more ungovernable than ever.         (3.78.555–56)

> 且不明說者, 一則寶玉年紀尚小, 老爺知道了又恐 說耽誤了書, 二則寶玉再自為已是跟前的人不敢勸他說他, 反倒縱性起來.          (2: 1094)

Lady Wang's reasons for secrecy are at best absurd, at worst perverse. First, what does Lady Wang mean by claiming that Bao-yu is "too young"? Readers know that he is sexually mature, and on some level she must realize it too, since she fears he might be corrupted by one of the other maids. (This is why, for ex-ample, she immediately dismisses the maid Golden when Bao-yu makes a pass at Golden.) Lady Wang's position is paradoxical. If she means that Bao-yu is too socially immature and that a concubine would distract him from his studies, then why permit him to be surrounded by beautiful slave girls? Wouldn't they be a distraction?

It is not clear whether Lady Wang realizes that Bao-yu is already sleeping with Aroma. Does she intend that Aroma will begin sleeping with Bao-yu once Aroma is promoted? Probably not, since Lady Wang does not even plan to inform Bao-yu of the promotion. (She wants a babysitter, not a concubine!) Either way, keeping Aroma's promotion unofficial and secret will help maintain the collective denial of Bao-yu's sexual maturity—and this, I suspect, is the main reason for Lady Wang's ruse.

Second, Lady Wang's maneuver subverts her husband's authority. In the Confucian scheme, perhaps the most fundamental aspect of a father's authority is the power to arrange his children's marriages. If Jia Zheng disapproves of Aroma's promotion, then by law and custom his word should be final. Indeed, from a strictly orthodox perspective, a father's disapproval would define any sexual act as the crime of illicit intercourse, since even conjugal relations were subordinate to the imperatives of filial piety, the chief purpose of marriage being to continue the family line (Sommer, *Sex* 36–38).

Third, it may be true that Bao-yu would pay more heed to a slave girl than to a legal concubine or wife. But from a Confucian standpoint, that is a reflection of his flawed character rather than a reason to indulge him.

Because Aroma's promotion is never formalized, Aroma receives shabby treatment after Bao-yu's disappearance at the end of the novel. In chapter 120, Aunt Xue and Lady Wang discuss how to dispose of her. Aunt Xue opines:

> It's right and proper for a wife to exhibit loyalty to her husband, even when he is a true husband to her no longer. And a chamber-wife may do the same if she wishes. But Aroma was never formally declared to be Bao-yu's chamber-wife, even though in fact we know that she was. . . .
>
> I hardly think Sir Zheng would want her to remain single and make a show of faithfulness to Bao-yu. . . . He doesn't even know that she was Bao-yu's chamber-wife. He has always thought of her as just an ordinary maid, so it would seem rather absurd to him to want to keep her on.
> (5.120.364)

> 但是正配呢理應守的, 屋裡人願守也是有的. 惟有這襲人, 雖說是算個屋裡人, 到底他和寶哥兒並沒有過明路兒的 . . . 我看姨老爺是再不肯叫守著的. 再者姨老爺並不知道襲人的事, 想來不過是個丫頭, 那有留的理呢?
> (2: 1598)

Lady Wang agrees, so they force Aroma to return to her natal family and marry another man.

But by law and custom, a widowed concubine had the right to remain unmarried and to enjoy the support of her dead husband's estate. To force a chaste widow to remarry was a serious crime, and if she committed suicide in protest, those responsible could even be sentenced to death (in this respect, Qing law did not distinguish between a main wife and a concubine [Sommer, *Sex*, ch. 5]). By keeping Aroma's promotion secret and unofficial, Lady Wang wiggles out of any such risk. Aroma does in fact consider suicide: it is only her eminently practical nature and the happy chance that her husband turns out to be a decent man that dissuade her from self-destruction.

## *Scandal in the Garden*

Every effort is made to secure the walled garden from invasion by corrupt influences from outside—especially from threats to the chastity of its young female denizens. But the garden's defenses are remarkably permeable. Security breaks down repeatedly, provoking a constant undercurrent of anxiety: gates are left open, boyfriends sneak in, pornography is smuggled in, burglars climb over the walls, and so on. Whenever the senior members of the household are away from home, for a funeral or other event, the garden becomes especially vulnerable. But all this anxiety seems strangely misplaced, since the biggest security breach of all is the presence of Bao-yu, who, in the absence of parental supervision, is "free to play and idle in the Garden to his heart's content without the least fear of restraint or reprisal" (2.37.213) 單表寶玉每日在園中任意縱性的逛蕩 (1: 486).

Note that just a few pages after Bao-yu moves into the garden, his page Tealeaf gives him a supply of licentious novels and plays in hope of lifting his spirits. Tealeaf warns Bao-yu against showing these materials to anyone else and specifically against taking them into the garden; but Bao-yu promptly smuggles them in and shares them with Dai-yu (1.23.462–64). The first work he shows her is the celebrated *Romance of the Western Chamber* 西廂記 (*Story of the Western Wing*), which, like *The Story of the Stone*, was officially banned. This episode suggests one danger of allowing Bao-yu to live in the garden: as a male he has unfettered access to the outside world and can smuggle forbidden books right into his cousin's bedchamber. He is exactly what the girls are being protected against: a sexually mature male of different lineage.

This smuggling of salacious literature foreshadows the discovery in the garden (in chapter 74) of a purse decorated with pornographic images. The women in charge of the household simultaneously hush up this incident and launch a witch hunt to find out who is responsible (they assume it to be one of the maids). Their campaign gives free rein to Lady Wang's hysterical fear that one of the maids might corrupt Bao-yu. As a result, the love affair of the maid Chess is exposed, and she is dismissed; Chess later commits suicide, as does her lover.

Skybright is also rudely dismissed, and she later dies in poverty, of an illness contracted while in Bao-yu's service.

Some of the most charming scenes in the garden are among the most obscene. In chapter 19, Bao-yu visits Dai-yu in her quarters one drowsy afternoon, walks right into her bedroom while she is taking a nap, and lies down beside her. Together, they playfully argue about whether to share a single pillow.[4] She touches his cheek, he praises the fragrance of her body, she allows him to smell her sleeve, he threatens to tickle her. The scene climaxes when Dai-yu, provoked by Bao-yu's teasing, "[gets] up on her knees and, crawling over, [plants] herself on top of Bao-yu" (398) 黛玉聽了, 翻身爬起來, 按著寶玉 (267) in order to pinch his lips—only to be interrupted by none other than Bao-yu's future wife, Bao-chai.

This episode may not seem obscene to a modern reader. But in eighteenth-century China, female chastity was a deadly serious matter, especially among the elite. The whole point of separating the sexes and cloistering women was to preserve their purity. Elite females were held to a standard of chastity so strict that a woman who committed suicide to protest being touched (or even verbally propositioned) by a man not her husband would be canonized by imperial edict. A public memorial arch would be erected in her honor at state expense. Any man who provoked such suicide by touching a woman, joking with her, or making a lewd suggestion could be sentenced to death. Archives and gazetteers preserve the records of thousands of such canonizations and death sentences from the era in which *The Story of the Stone* was written (Elvin; Sommer, *Sex*, ch. 5; Theiss, *Disgraceful Matters*).

To an eighteenth-century Chinese reader, Bao-yu's wrestling match with Dai-yu would have carried an intensely transgressive and erotic charge. The couple's bedroom play goes no further than tickling and wrestling, but by the standards of the day that was already too far. We know that by this episode, our hero has been sexually active for some time, as the author reminds him (and us): earlier in the same chapter, Bao-yu observed his page Tealeaf "pressed upon the body of a girl and evidently engaged in those exercises in which Bao-yu had once been instructed by the fairy Disenchantment" (377) 卻是茗煙按著一個 女孩子, 也幹那警幻所訓之事 (254). The image of Tealeaf's having sex with the maidservant is therefore fresh in our mind when Bao-yu visits Dai-yu's bedroom. In a sense, Tealeaf's scene with the maid, observed by Bao-yu, rehearses and sets up Bao-yu's scene with Dai-yu.

The author has Bao-chai walk in just as the reader begins to wonder where the tickling and wrestling will lead. Bao-chai's interruption itself may provoke a certain thrill, given Bao-yu's parallel interruption of Tealeaf and the maid earlier in the chapter: "He made a tiny hole in the paper window with his tongue and peeped through. . . . 'Good lord!' He cried out involuntarily, and kicking open the door, strode into the study, so startling the two inside that they shook in their clothes" (377) 乃乍著膽子, 舔破窗紙, 向內一看 . . . 寶玉禁不住大叫: "了不得!" 一腳踹進門去, 將那兩個唬開了, 抖衣而顫 (254). Both interruptions illustrate the trope of voyeurism common in Chinese fiction of the sixteenth to eighteenth century: the most famous novels of that era include scenes in which some characters interrupt or spy on others who are engaged in sexual activity.[5]

The author may have intended the scene of Bao-yu in Dai-yu's boudoir to be innocent—that is, to contrast with rather than parallel Tealeaf's high jinks (just as, according to Disenchantment's taxonomy, Bao-yu's "lust of the mind" contrasts with the coarser impulses of someone like Tealeaf). Even so, the scene, constituting a radical challenge to accepted standards of propriety, would have required a redefinition of innocence. Even a reader sympathetic to such a redefinition would have felt the shock value of the scene.

Such fun and games can have consequences. In chapter 30, Bao-yu makes a pass at his mother's maid Golden while his mother is taking a nap: "'Shall I ask Her Ladyship to let me have you, so that we can be together?'. . . 'What's the hurry?' [Golden] said playfully. '"Yours is yours, wherever it may be" . . .'" —and she suggests that if Bao-yu wants "a bit of fun," he should go spy on his half brother Jia Huan, who is just then dallying with the maidservant Sunset (again, the trope of voyeurism). Suddenly Lady Wang wakes up, slaps the girl, and curses her: "'Shameless little harlot!' she cried, pointing at her wrathfully. 'It's you and your like who corrupt our innocent young boys'" (2.30.100–01). She dismisses Golden on the spot, after ten years' service, driving the girl to suicide.

Lady Wang fears Bao-yu's vulnerability to corruption by the maids:

> This was, in fact, the first time in her life that she had ever struck a maid. But the kind of "shamelessness" of which—in her view—Golden had just been guilty was the one thing she had always most abhorred. It was the uncontrollable anger of the morally outraged that had caused her to strike Golden and call her names. . . . (101)

> 王夫人固然是個寬仁慈厚的人, 從來不曾打過丫頭們一個, 今忽見金釧兒行此無恥之事, 此乃平生最恨者, 故氣忿不過, 打了一下, 罵了幾句. (412)

But she has it backward: it was Bao-yu who initiated the flirtation. She never allows herself to admit that the corrupting influence might be the innocent young boy. (How many girls would die as a result of Lady Wang's capricious prudery?) This episode contradicts Bao-yu's tenderness toward all around him: Bao-yu fails to speak up for Golden or to help her in any way—instead, the instant he realizes his mother is awake, he runs away and hides in the garden, ever his refuge from real-world responsibility.

In chapter 33, the jealous Jia Huan informs their father that Bao-yu caused Golden's suicide by trying to rape her. Huan's report, along with the embarrassing revelation of Bao-yu's intimacy with the prince of Zhong-shun's fugitive favorite, spurs Jia Zheng to beat Bao-yu to within an inch of his life. What makes Jia Huan's accusation credible to Jia Zheng is that they live in a society that encourages women to commit suicide in order to erase insults to chastity. But there is a kernel of truth in Jia Huan's lie: Bao-yu's pass at the girl led to her suicide. The implication is that his innocent antics are not so innocent after all and that in the world outside the garden such behavior can have serious consequences.

As time goes on, Dai-yu realizes that Bao-yu reciprocates her affection, and she begins to think of herself as his future wife. As her thoughts turn toward the future and the world of adult responsibility, she grows more inhibited about physical contact and tries to avoid his touch. In chapter 30, he takes her hand, but she flings him away: "Take your hands off me! We're not children any more. You really can't go on mauling me about like this all the time. Don't you understand *anything*—?" (2.30.96) 誰同你拉拉扯扯的. 一天大似一天的, 還這麼涎皮賴臉的, 連個道理也不知道 (408). (Note that this scene takes place just before his fatal flirtation with Golden.) In chapter 32, shortly before his beating by Jia Zheng, he tries to wipe the tears from Dai-yu's face, but she recoils several paces: "You'll get your head chopped off!" she says. "You really *must* keep your hands to yourself" (133) 林黛玉忙向後退了幾步, 說道: "你又要死了! 作什麼這麼動手動腳的!" (434). Much later, in chapter 92, Bao-yu comments that Dai-yu has been avoiding him, that they "almost seem to have grown apart in some way." Aroma admonishes him, "I should hope so too. . . . Now that the two of you are older, of course you must learn to be more discreet" (4.92.244) 原該這麼著才是. 都長了幾歲年紀了, 怎麼好意思還象小孩子時候的樣子 (2: 1272).

## Aroma's Warning

Aroma is the voice of reason and objectivity. She is the only character in the novel who points out that Bao-yu's presence in the garden constitutes a dangerous violation of propriety. Of course, she knows better than anyone that Bao-yu is sexually mature. She first articulates her concern in chapter 32, after hearing Bao-yu's declaration of love for Dai-yu: "She reflected with some alarm that if things between them were as his words seemed to indicate, there was every likelihood of an ugly scandal developing, and wondered how she could arrange matters to prevent it" (2.32.135) 如此看來, 將來難免不才之事, 令人可驚可畏 (1: 436).

Her opportunity comes after Bao-yu's beating by Jia Zheng. After much hesitation, she approaches Lady Wang and asks:

"... if Your Ladyship could advise me how later on we can somehow or other contrive to get Master Bao moved back outside the Garden."

Lady Wang looked startled and clutched Aroma's hand in some alarm.

"I hope Bao-yu hasn't been doing something dreadful with one of the girls?"                    (34.164)

"我只想著討太太一個示下, 怎麼變個法兒, 以後竟還教二爺搬出園外
來住就好了." 王夫人聽了, 吃一大驚, 忙拉了襲人的手問道: "寶玉難道
和誰作怪了不成?"

(455)

With this unguarded reaction, Lady Wang betrays that on some level she knows
full well what Bao-yu is capable of. Aroma assures her that no such thing has
happened—not yet:

> It's just that—if you'll allow me to say so—by now, the young master has
> grown up, and so have the young ladies who live in the Garden. More-
> over Miss Lin and Miss Bao are the young master's cousins of *different
> surname*, and even if you say they're just his cousins, there *is* after all the
> difference in sex between them. But despite that, they're together all the
> time, day and night, so the situation has become quite awkward. One can't
> help feeling uneasy. To an outsider, it just wouldn't seem consistent with
> the propriety and dignity of a great family.[6]

> 太太別多心, 並沒有這話. 這不過是我的小見識. 如今二爺也大了, 裡頭
> 姑娘們也大了, 況且林姑娘寶姑娘又是兩姨姑表姊妹, 雖說是姊妹們,
> 到底是男女之分, 日夜一處起坐不方便, 由不得叫人懸心. 便是外人看
> 著, 也不像大家子的體統.

(SJPB 2: 537–38)

Aroma emphasizes the fact that Lin Dai-yu and Xue Bao-chai are not members of the Jia lineage and therefore should be barred from direct contact with
Bao-yu. Both girls are potential brides for Bao-yu, as they all know, and Bao-chai
does eventually marry him.

Not wanting to offend Lady Wang, Aroma does not accuse Bao-yu of any
impropriety. Instead, she stresses the danger that rumors about goings-on in the
garden might harm his reputation and future career:

> They say "where nothing happens, imagination is busiest," and I'm sure
> lots of unaccountable misfortunes begin when some innocent little thing
> we did unthinkingly gets misconstrued in someone else's imagination and
> reported as something terrible. We just have to be on our guard against
> that sort of thing happening—especially when Master Bao has such a
> peculiar character, as Your Ladyship knows, and spends all his time with
> girls. He only has to make the tiniest slip in an unguarded moment, and
> whether he really did anything or not, with so many people about—and
> some of them no better than they should be—there is sure to be scan-
> dal. . . . Master Bao's reputation will be destroyed for life. . . .    (164–65)

> 俗語說的 "沒事常思有事," 世上多少無頭腦的人, 多半因為無心中做
> 出, 有心人看見, 當作有心事, 反說壞了. 只是預先不防著, 斷然不好. 二
> 爺素日性格, 太太是知道的. 他又偏好在我們隊裡鬧, 倘或不防, 前後錯

了一點半點, 不論真假, 人多口雜, 那起小人的嘴有什麼避諱, 但後來二
爺一生的聲名品行豈不完了.                                    (1: 455)

She fears that outsiders will misconstrue the unusual arrangements in the Jia
household and assume the worst. The author uses her words to anticipate once
again how orthodox opinion would view Bao-yu's presence in the garden as scandalous. The only way to solve this problem is to end the pretense that Bao-yu is
just a little boy, different from other boys, and to get him out of the garden.

Aroma's monologue is a moment of commonsense clarity unique in the novel.
It's left to a teenaged slave girl to speak the truth! Lady Wang's initial reaction
approaches enlightenment: "What Aroma had just been saying about miscon-
structions and scandals so exactly fitted what had in fact happened in the case of
Golden that for a moment Lady Wang was quite taken aback." But she quickly
recovers. Instead of removing Bao-yu from the garden, as Aroma has recommended, Lady Wang does nothing except to cede responsibility for Bao-yu's
behavior and well-being to Aroma: "I am going to place Bao-yu entirely in your
hands. Be very careful with him, won't you?" (165). This transfer of responsibility to a maidservant is an abdication of responsibility.

## Bao-yu's Homoerotic Flirtations

In addition to his relations with maidservants and girl cousins, Bao-yu engages
in homoerotic flirtation—and probably more than flirtation—with several
characters in the novel, the most important being Qin Zhong and the female
impersonator Bijou (whose real name is Jiang Yu-han).[7] With typical evasiveness, the author offers no information about actual homosexual acts, only teasing innuendo. Bao-yu's homoerotic interest may confuse the modern reader,
who is likely to conflate it with our hero's androgyny and interpret it according
to sexual categories current in our society today. This confusion may be exacer-
bated by David Hawkes's occasional use of anachronistic terms like "queer" and
"straight" in his otherwise superb translation.[8]

It is vital to understand that in eighteenth-century China, as in many other
premodern societies, male same-sex acts and relationships were understood not
in terms of the modern egalitarian polarity of sexual orientation (heterosexual vs.
homosexual, defined by the sex of one's object of desire) but rather in terms
of a hierarchy of stereotypical sexual roles (penetrator vs. penetrated) seen as
naturally corresponding to other hierarchies (such as gender, social status, and
age). To penetrate was a definitively masculine act, and to be penetrated was to
be subordinated and feminized. Typically, in same-sex relations between males,
an older, dominant partner would penetrate a younger, feminized partner—at
least that was the conventional expectation of how such acts and relationships
should be structured. From this point of view, to pursue a young male as an object of possessive desire was considered a perfectly natural part of mature male

licentiousness, although it does not necessarily follow that polite society approved of such desire. In the eighteenth century, Qing law punished consensual homosexual intercourse in exactly the same manner as consensual heterosexual intercourse outside marriage, with a beating and a term spent wearing a heavy wooden frame (known as the cangue) around the neck. This parallel in penalties suggests equal disapproval of both acts (Sommer, *Sex*, ch. 4).

Famous libertines in Ming-Qing fiction, such as Ximen Qing (of *Plum in the Golden Vase*) and Vesperus (of *The Carnal Prayer Mat* 肉蒲團 *Rou pu tuan*) sodomize their youthful pages as part of an omnivorous, insatiable sexual predation directed primarily at women. In *The Story of the Stone*, Xue Pan and Jia Lian follow this libertine pattern: both men are incorrigible lechers who pursue male as well as female sex objects. Bao-yu's homoerotic liaisons are an aestheticized, sentimentalized version of what appears gross and buffoonish in a figure like Xue Pan, whose interests are purely carnal. Such characters highlight how different Bao-yu is from the stereotypical libertine. Nevertheless, his range of erotic interest corresponds closely to Xue Pan's.

Bao-yu is clearly the dominant figure in his relationships with Qin Zhong and Bijou, in terms of social status, wealth, and age. The conventional expectation in that society would be that if Bao-yu had sex with these subordinate males, he would play the dominant sexual role as well. Sexual dominance is made almost explicit in chapter 15, when he surprises Qin Zhong having intercourse with the young Buddhist nun Sapientia: Bao-yu jumps on top of Qin Zhong, who is on top of Sapientia, and threatens to expose their affair by shouting; in exchange for secrecy, Qin Zhong promises Bao-yu "to do anything [he says]" 你要怎樣我都依你, and Bao-yu tells him to "[w]ait until we are both in bed and I'll settle accounts with you then" (299–300) 等一會睡下, 再細細的算帳. Bao-yu's proposal implies that he will extract compensation in the form of sexual service, but the author refuses to confirm or deny this obvious implication:

> As for the "settling of accounts" that Bao-yu had proposed to Qin Zhong, we have been unable to ascertain exactly what form this took; and as we would not for the world be guilty of a fabrication, we must allow the matter to remain a mystery. (1.15.300)

> 寶玉不知與秦鐘算何帳目, 未見真切, 未曾記得, 此是疑案, 不敢纂創. (1: 200)

Such teasing evasiveness is typical of how the author treats Bao-yu's sex life in general, but especially his homoerotic interests. It helps sustain the illusion of Bao-yu's innocence that he is not a libertine.

Bao-yu's attraction to Bijou is more aesthetic and sentimental than his relationship with Qin Zhong. Yet a coarser dimension is implied and at one point intrudes to deflate Bao-yu's pretentiousness. Bao-yu first encounters Bijou at a party at Feng Zi-yang's house in chapter 28. They are attracted to each other;

after a while Bao-yu excuses himself "to ease his bladder," and Bijou follows him to the toilet. It is no accident that the author arranges for them to rendezvous at the toilet, even though no sexual act is portrayed. America is by no means the only society in which men sometimes meet at public toilets for sex, and I have seen many Qing legal cases that recount acts of sodomy in such settings. (We are reminded of chapter 9, when Qin Zhong and his classmate Darling agree to meet privately in the "rear courtyard," which is a sly euphemism for the anus [1.9.208].) Bao-yu and Bijou proceed to undo their pants and exchange cummerbunds as tokens of affection; but just as they are closing up their pants, Xue Pan, who has been spying on them, jumps out and grabs them. Xue Pan assumes that he has caught them in a sexual act:

> "What are you two up to, leaving the party and sneaking off like this?" he said. "Come on, take 'em out again and let's have a look!"
>     It was useless for them to protest that the situation was not what he imagined. Xue Pan continued to force his unwelcome attentions upon them until Feng Zi-ying came out and rescued them.          (2.28.62)

> 兩個人逃席出來幹什麼?快拿出來我瞧瞧 . . . 薛蟠那裡肯依,還是馮紫
> 英出來才解開了.                                                    (1: 387)

Both the setting of this conversation and exchange at a toilet and its interruption by the unabashed Xue Pan cast ironic light on the scene and undercut the lofty tone of Bao-yu and Bijou. The author implies a rhetorical question: What does all this highbrow sentiment (Disenchantment's "lust of the mind") really boil down to, anyway?

In Bao-yu's society, as in many other premodern societies, the theater was closely associated with commercial sex work; the acting profession was considered morally and to some extent legally debased because of the stigma of licentiousness. In eighteenth- and nineteenth-century Beijing, a basic part of the commercial theater was high-end homosexual prostitution. All female roles were played by cross-dressing teenaged boys like Bijou, who were the objects of intense homoerotic fascination on the part of elite patrons, and many of these boys moonlighted as prostitutes and escorts. Some opera troupe managers made more money from renting out these boys for escort service than they did from ticket sales (Mackerras, *Rise*; Wu Cuncun).

Bijou comes from this homoerotic milieu. When his powerful admirer, the prince of Zhong-shun, installs Bijou in his palace, the boy's virtuosity on stage is presumably not the main reason he is singled out for such attention. The prince's chamberlain explains:

> His Highness says that though he could view the loss of a hundred ordinary actors with equanimity, this Bijou is so skilled in anticipating his wishes and so essential to his peace of mind that it would be utterly impossible for him to dispense with his services.          (2.33.143)

王爺亦云: "若是別的戲子呢, 一百個也罷 了, 只是這琪官隨機應答, 謹
慎老誠, 甚合我老人家的心, 竟斷斷少不得此人。"                    (1: 441)

The sexual dimension of this patronage is never spelled out, but an eighteenth-
century reader would have taken it for granted that Bijou is the infatuated
prince's catamite—hence the prince's jealousy and obsessive pursuit when Bijou runs away.[9]

The magnificent crimson cummerbund that Bijou presents to Bao-yu during
their toilet rendezvous is a gift Bijou received the previous day from another
noble admirer, the prince of Bei-jing. Later, after Bijou has fled the palace,
the prince of Zhong-shun's chamberlain comes to the Jia compound to inter-
rogate Bao-yu as to the actor's whereabouts. At first, Bao-yu denies knowing
Bijou, but when the chamberlain accuses him of wearing Bijou's cummerbund,
Bao-yu thinks, "I'd better get rid of [the chamberlain] as quickly as possible,
before he can say any more" (2.33.144) 不如打發他去了, 免的再說出別的事來
(442). It's not entirely clear what this "any more" stands for, but it appears to be
another of those points of reticence in the novel that would speak volumes if it
could. There is a great deal more to Bao-yu's relationship with Bijou than is narrated. A comment by Xue Bao-chai, who gets her information from her libertine
brother, provides confirmation: "Cousin Bao *has* been going around with that
actor" (34.157) 到底寶兄弟素日不正, 肯和那些人來往 (450).

At the very end of the novel, Aroma finds herself married to none other than
Jiang Yu-han—the former actor Bijou—who by this time has outgrown female
impersonation and become a modestly prosperous businessman. They discover
their mutual connection with Bao-yu when Yu-han finds in Aroma's trousseau
the red cummerbund he gave Bao-yu as a token of love. This discovery ce-
ments the marriage: when Yu-han shows Aroma the viridian sash that Bao-yu
gave him in exchange for the cummerbund, she is convinced that their marriage is predestined (5.120.368–69). There are important parallels between the
spouses: for one thing, both have served Bao-yu sexually or at least as an object
of erotic fascination. Also, Yu-han is a debased double for Bao-yu, just as Aroma
is one for Bao-chai—debased in terms of social and legal status, Yu-han having
been an actor, Aroma a slave and informal concubine. In Bijou's professional
femininity, we see a crude reification of Bao-yu's androgyny. The name "Yu-
han" literally means "box for the jade" (*yu* 玉 = jade, *han* 函 = box), and "*han*"
rhymes with a homonym meaning "to hold in the mouth" (含). One senses a homoerotic suggestion here of the nature of Yu-han's former role vis-à-vis Bao-yu
(the jade in question being Bao-yu, "precious jade"). The name also may refer
to the fact that Bao-yu was born with the eponymous precious jade in his own
mouth.

Bao-yu's homoerotic flirtations underscore the fact of his sexual maturity and
experience, even as the author's coy ambiguity allows the pretense of his innocence. Jia Zheng is convinced by the confrontation with the prince's chamberlain that Bao-yu has been "philandering with actors," a phrase that in Qing legal
jargon refers to the criminal patronage of male prostitutes for sodomy ("actor"

優 being synonymous with "homosexual prostitute" in legal texts).[10] This accusation is one of the two that make Jia Zheng beat Bao-yu. The other, based on Jia Huan's distortion of events, is that Bao-yu caused Golden to commit suicide by trying to rape her. Jia Zheng believes both charges, which fulfill his worst fear since Bao-yu's infancy—namely, that this son would turn out to be a libertine (1.2.76).

To Jia Zheng, Bao-yu is a libertine who pursues both female and male sex objects, both inside and outside the household. Surely, Jia Zheng will now remove Bao-yu from the garden. What does he do instead? Aside from the beating, nothing: he abdicates responsibility for the matter, and Bao-yu continues to live in the garden with the girls for dozens of chapters more. Jia Zheng is a failure as a Confucian patriarch: he spouts high-minded morality but is incapable of translating words into effective action, either in government service or in his household. In traditional terms, his most conspicuous failure is his inability to educate and discipline his son.

It is easy for modern readers to be so captivated by *The Story of the Stone*'s beauty that they miss its obscenity. But by the normative standards of elite society in eighteenth- and nineteenth-century China, this novel was unquestionably obscene. In my view, a full appreciation of *Stone* both as historical document and as pathbreaking masterpiece requires a clear understanding of why it deserved its prominent place in the lists of banned licentious books.

That *Stone* cannot compete with the notorious *Plum in the Golden Vase* in the graphic depiction of sexual acts is beside the point. The entire magnificent and complex edifice of *Stone* depends on the collective abdication of responsibility by the novel's men and on the collective conspiracy of the novel's women to pretend that a sexually mature young man is an innocent little boy. Thus the separation of sexes is waived and Bao-yu moves into the garden. Everything that follows constitutes a gross violation of Confucian moral order, prefiguring the household's ultimate crisis.

Yet this violation of moral order makes possible the main achievement of the novel: the Neverland that Bao-yu and his young female companions create for themselves in their garden refuge from the tiresome demands of social responsibility. In this way, the novel seduces readers into savoring, even celebrating, the violation of boundaries and hierarchies that frame Confucian order. The effect is far more seductive than any of the grotesque couplings detailed in *Plum in the Golden Vase*—and that is why *Stone* struck some Qing critics as an especially insidious example of the licentious novel.

## NOTES

1 For denunciation and prohibition of *The Story of the Stone*, see Wang Liqi 122, 135, 143, 162–64, 196–97, 199, 224, 375–78, 391–92, 404–05, and 424–25. Prohibitions of licentious books, plays, and songs remained in force and were reiterated throughout the

Ming and Qing dynasties. *The Story of the Stone* was listed by name starting in the first half of the nineteenth century.

2 This depiction of seminal emission anticipates Jia Rui's death, the only other scene in the novel where semen is described (1.12.250–52).

3 See Francesca Bray's analysis of the politics of reproduction in the elite household and especially her useful distinction between "social motherhood" and "biological motherhood" (351–68). Also see Susan Mann's discussion of domestic slavery in the High Qing (*Precious Records*).

4 To share a pillow (or sleeping mat) was a euphemism for sexual congress, comparable to the English "to go to bed with."

5 Note Keith McMahon's analysis of "the gap in the wall" trope in Ming-Qing fiction (*Causality*). Bao-yu's penetration of the garden may itself be considered an example of this trope.

6 This is my own translation of the passage, relying on SJPB. Hawkes translates somewhat differently: "It's just that—if you'll allow me to say so—Master Bao and the young ladies are beginning to grow up now, and though they are all cousins, there *is* the difference of sex between them, which makes it very awkward sometimes when they are all living together, especially in the case of Miss Lin and Miss Bao, who aren't even of the same clan. One can't help feeling uneasy. Even to outsiders it looks like a very strange sort of family" (164). In the HLM version, the last sentence in this passage is slightly different than in SJPB (see HLM 455).

7 See also the episode at the Jia clan school in chapter 9, in which Bao-yu and Qin Zhong become infatuated with two other boys. The portrayal of a Confucian school as a hotbed of homoerotic cruising would not have endeared this novel to Qing authorities.

8 The Chinese term that Hawkes translates as "straight"—*zhengjing ren* 正經人—in fact means "an upright, respectable person" and carries no connotation of sexual orientation whatsoever (2.47.444). See Hinsch 147–50, 196–97 (nn 32 and 35).

9 For a nonfiction account of how a Manchu nobleman in Beijing caused a scandal by installing a catamite in his household, see Sommer, *Sex* 156–58.

10 The phrase I translate as "philandering with actors"—*liudang youling* 流蕩優伶—is part of a passage translated by Hawkes as "riotous and dissipated conduct abroad leading to the unseemly bestowal of impudicities on a theatrical performer" (2.33.148).

# A Question of Taste:
# Material Culture, Connoisseurship,
# and Character in *The Story of the Stone*

## *Tobie Meyer-Fong*

In a society with abundant material goods, consumer choices become a medium through which people can express their social position or aspirations. By surrounding themselves with objects consistent with class-specific aesthetic standards, they can represent themselves as members of a particular group. Clothing, furniture, works of art, books, accessories, jewelry, foods, and houses commonly function as a status marker, but any object can. In the United States today, the upwardly mobile study wine tasting, lavish attention on home decorating, and read fashion magazines in order to associate themselves with widely recognized markers of good taste. Martha Stewart made her fortune selling taste to eager aspirants to the good life, and television programs and magazines revealing "lifestyles of the rich and famous" never want for viewers and readers eager to model their lives on those of the wealthy and notable — or to laugh at the gaudy and tasteless things with which the nouveaux riches surround themselves. Through such sources, contemporary consumers learn to distinguish between the accoutrements of good taste and markers of bad taste.

Readers who had access to *Stone* as it circulated in manuscript form would have been familiar with eighteenth-century measures of taste and conduct and thus would have been able to gauge the extent to which its characters adhered to or transgressed against prevailing standards in their consumption choices. Questions of taste and its transgression in the material realm permeate the novel and inform a broader concern about authenticity and phoniness in human relationships. Today's reader, unaware of the social context of the consumption choices made by the characters, will miss important clues as to how to evaluate their inner worth and position in the novel's elaborate social web. Clearly the Jia family benefited from their society's abundance and made decisions based on ideas about the relative value of different kinds of objects. In the absence of today's media establishment, what shaped their consumer decisions? Where did ideas and images about good taste come from in eighteenth-century China?

In eighteenth-century China, a world of unprecedented material abundance at least for the upper classes, the ability to distinguish between the good and the gauche functioned as a sign of personal quality and social status. Elegance, classicism, refinement, and understatement were read as the informed selection of the best objects. Simplicity was valued precisely because of the possibility of extraordinary quantity and lavish display. Good taste meant refraining from overindulgence. At the same time, under the influence of an expansive and monumental court culture fascinated by the exotic and extravagant, China's upper classes valued foreign, colorful, technically sophisticated, and grand things that would not have been considered in good taste by seventeenth-century consumers. Indeed, these things are now viewed as too garish by collectors who prefer their antiques to have the simple lines of artifacts appreciated by late Ming literati elites. In *Stone*, distinctions expressed through consumption choices provide readers not only with a barometer of the characters' taste in objects, clothing, and aesthetics but also with a standard by which to measure their authenticity and moral character. This essay explores the question of whether the Jias had good taste in the context of eighteenth-century China. While the Jias collectively had reasonably good taste, some Jias had better taste than others.

We first encounter the Jia family and their possessions in chapter 3, through the eyes of the newest addition to the household, Lin Dai-yu. Because of her status as an orphan and an outsider, Dai-yu is, perhaps more than any other of the novel's major characters, attuned to social distinctions and their expression through collectible objects, architecture, and clothing. She carefully studies her material surroundings for insights into social relationships, and through her observations we learn of her aesthetic discernment and about the relatives that inhabit the Rong-guo mansion's expensively appointed spaces. Her first impressions, like descriptions of household items and apparel throughout the novel, indicate that objects in the household are not only of the finest quality and most magnificent design but also of the latest fashion. She assumes a connection between these material artifacts and social standing when she observes with concern that since even the Jia family's servants are superior beings whose clothing and food are of the highest quality, as a "poor relation" she will have to adhere to rigorous standards of manners in her speech and actions or risk the scorn of her relatives and their servants (1.3.87). When she meets her relatives, she notes the fineness of their clothing, cosmetics, and jewelry and of the furnishings and artifacts arrayed in each interior space, and she modifies her behavior and physical position according to her perception of each person's status (96–97).

Contrasting the elegant and the grand, Dai-yu finds both the simple and the monumental to be part of a tasteful composite. When she enters the gates of the Rong-guo mansion, she observes the splendor and grandeur of the architecture and the high quality of the materials (88). She notes the contrast between the "smaller scale and quiet elegance" of the inner courtyard and the "heavy magnificence and imposing grandeur" of the entrance halls, further observing that in this part of the mansion, which she intuits must have once been part of the gardens, "ornamental trees and artificial rock formations, all in exquisite taste, [are] to be seen on every hand" (94) 悉皆小巧別致，不似方才那邊軒峻壯麗；且院中隨處之樹木山石皆在 (1: 42). Entering the main inner hall, an "architectural unit of greater sumptuousness and magnificence than anything Dai-yu had yet seen that day," she encounters a blue board with a golden inscription framed by imperial dragons. This item was "written for Our beloved Subject, Jia Yuan, Duke of Rong-guo" in the emperor's own hand and signed with the emperor's private seal (95). These items establish an intimate connection between the Jia household and the court, which was simultaneously an important arbiter of eighteenth-century elite standards of good taste. Clearly we are intended to see that the Jia family is both "long-established" and "highly cultivated" (1.18.358). With wealth, access to education, and close imperial connections, they have the resources needed to acquire the accoutrements that mark good taste and social status in their society. As the description of Dai-yu's arrival at the Rong-guo mansion suggests, for the Jia household both elegance and magnificence were important in the expression of good taste.

In eighteenth-century China, there were two important sources for standards of good taste: the literati and the court. Aesthetic ideas developed and promoted by the educated elites or literati had developed in the prosperous Yangzi River delta region (or Jiangnan, literally "south of the [Yangzi] River") over the pre-ceding centuries. Cities in the region, especially Suzhou, Hangzhou, Yangzhou, and Nanjing, were celebrated both as stylish contemporary fashion centers and as centers of past literati culture. Food, operas, silk, and cosmetics in Yangzi delta styles all appear in the novel, as do paintings and calligraphy by dead delta masters. Descriptions of Prospect Garden underscore the geographic and material associations between literati taste and the Yangzi delta, which was renowned for rock gardens and artificial lakes made possible by the region's extensive system of waterways. Scenes that take place in the garden suggest the primacy of the literary approach to taste and allude to the prestigious so-cial practices associated with the cultured gatherings for which the Yangzi delta was famous. The Jia family has literary as well as cultural ties to the Yangzi delta. Like the author's ancestors, the Jias had extensive personal, official, and commercial connections in Suzhou, Yangzhou, and Nanjing, which facilitated their appreciation for and consumption of objects of delta manufacture. The imperial court in Beijing emerged in the eighteenth century as a leading arbi-ter of good taste for the empire, and households like the Jias' were filled with imperially conferred artifacts. Lesser households, having the same standards of good taste and an eye to upward mobility, aspired to own objects that, even if not imperially made or gifted, manifested some of the same majestic, exotic, or splendiferous attributes as items actually fashioned for the court. In its choice of objects and in its practices, the Jia family, seeking to embody wealth, power, and cultural sophistication, upheld two standards of taste, one associated with the literati masters of the Yangzi delta region, the other with the Qing imperial court in Beijing, which itself celebrated and consumed artifacts associated with the Jiangnan mode.

Because literati taste required extensive cultural knowledge and preferred simple styles, it was difficult for the merely wealthy to emulate it. By the eigh-teenth century, however, cultural knowledge was increasingly available through published books, and refinement was increasingly challenged by advocates of conspicuous display. Thus even the newly wealthy might construct a tastefully rustic villa, and the refined might appreciate a splendid spectacle. Still, classical simplicity enjoyed a certain cachet, particularly in the aesthetic realms of music, gardening, poetry, and connoisseurship. Discussions of poetry, music, and art in

*Stone* generally reflect the primacy of an eighteenth-century understanding of literati taste as characters demonstrate their aesthetic and literary knowledge. This knowledge is particularly and positively associated with Bao-chai, Dai-yu, Adamantina, and Bao-yu. Characters like the oafish and mercenary Xue Pan embody its antithesis. Indeed, any object associated with Xue Pan, including the "little mercury-filled automata who turned somersaults when you put them down on the floor or a table," which he procured in Suzhou, can be assumed to be unspeakably vulgar, even if momentarily entertaining (3.67.311–12, 317).

The principles of literati taste appear throughout the novel, particularly in conversations about poetry, art, music, and the refined appreciation of objects, gardens, and landscape. In the eighteenth century, these areas of endeavor all embodied literati practice and thus would have been considered arenas for the proper expression of literati taste. Even casual references to objects in the household allude to literati taste. The omnipresence of real and imitation Song porcelains, such as white Ding ware or celadon Ru ware, show the family's appreciation for these conventionally celebrated styles of manufacture. More significant, the poetry games in the garden, displaying the refinement and talent of the young women involved in the Crab-Flower Club, follow established models of literati taste. The girls' drinking games, revolving around complex literary allusions, especially to canonical poets, demonstrate the cultural virtuosity and literary sophistication of the principal female characters, Dai-yu and Bao-chai especially. In sharp contrast, readers are shown the tasteless and vulgar poetry composed by Xue Pan, whose miserable efforts are consistent with his immoral character (2.28.57–59).

Dai-yu's conversation with Bao-yu about music follows central tenets of the literati mode of aesthetic discernment. Dai-yu advises Bao-yu on the setting, mood, and clothing appropriate for the learned practice of *qin* (琴 "zither") music. The terms she uses—*gentility, sobriety, dignity, antiquity, calmness,* and *exclusivity*—all represent ideals associated with literati taste and deportment. That her ideas about music are derived from her reading of an old handbook underscores the link among antiquity, text, and tastefulness (4.86.150–55). Notions of literati taste, particularly with reference to arts and antiquities, had been codified in manuals for collectors and connoisseurs in the late sixteenth and early seventeenth centuries, and many of these books and ideas continued to circulate during the eighteenth century. Music, especially zither music, resonated with the literati aesthetic. Along with chess, poetry, and calligraphy, playing the zither was considered a literati pastime. Note that the Jia household paid tribute to the four literati pastimes by naming a quartet of maids after them.

In a scene exemplifying the practice of literati-style taste, the nun Adamantina, presented throughout the novel as a person of transcendent if inconsistent and ill-fated ways, serves Bao-yu, Bao-chai, and Dai-yu tea. Her eccentricity aligns her with famous literary figures of the past: she is original, authentic, superior. She recognizes and creatively surpasses inherited and formulaic standards of taste. As Bao-yu points out, Adamantina appreciates only those who, like her, view "gold, jewels and jade as common, vulgar things" (2.41.314). Adamantina presents Bao-chai's tea in a cup inscribed by the Song dynasty literatus Su Dongpo but gives Bao-yu his in a unique drinking bowl carved from "a gnarled and ancient bamboo root in the likeness of a coiled-up dragon with horns like antlers" (314). The nun thus recognizes Bao-chai as one who appreciates literati taste and is thus entitled to consume it, but she commends Bao-yu as a fellow original: because he understands good taste, he receives something even better. She teases him about his inappropriate thirst, better suited to a mule than a connoisseur, and mocks the usually discerning Dai-yu for her failure to detect the difference between a lesser tea, made from last year's rainwater, and a more precious type, made with melted snow collected five years earlier from the branches of flowering plum trees on Mount Xuan-mu (315). The surpassing quality of tea water from melted snow seems predicated on the effort needed to obtain it and its removal from commercial circulation. The seasonal connection to both snow and plum blossoms evokes conventional literati associations with purity and separation from polluting entanglements. This water is special because it is unusual, priceless, authentic, and pure. But only a true connoisseur can appreciate its subtle distinctiveness.

Adamantina is above conventional standards of behavior (3.63.235). The nun's refusal to conform to the mundane, formal, and often empty principles of etiquette imposed by society gave her added cachet in the realm of taste, as did her rejection of money as a determinant of an object's value. In the tea party scene, Bao-yu notes that the nun refuses the return of her enameled porcelain cup of Ming dynasty manufacture because its value has been compromised by contact with the unworthy rustic Grannie Liu. He tells the nun that the cup has not lost its market value even if its circulation among lofty people can no longer be tolerated and suggests that Grannie Liu be permitted to profit from the object's sale (2.41.313–16). This episode suggests that literati taste stands aloof from the marketplace, which measures objects crassly, by their price. The true connoisseur should value objects in measures other than cash, should appreciate a cup like the one lent to Bao-chai for its inscription by Su Dongpo or a work of calligraphy for its association with a past master. Only a cretin would consider the monetary worth of a treasured possession.

The author points to the shortcomings of this mode of aesthetic appreciation. It can become stale, imitative, and constraining in the absence of authentic feeling and naturalness. In the novel, characters who demonstrate facility in the practice of literati taste are granted a certain prestige, but a higher value attaches to those who combine cultural knowledge with heart. The obsequious and pedantic "literary gentlemen" who fawn around Jia Zheng demonstrate the banality of literati taste without originality and inspiration (1.17.325–47). When Bao-yu expresses his preference for one of the less rustic pavilions in the garden, his father proclaims, "Ignoramus! You have eyes only for painted halls and gaudy pavilions—the rubbishy trappings of wealth. What can *you* know of the beauty that lies in quietness and natural simplicity?" (336) 無知的蠢物! 你只知朱樓畫棟, 惡賴富麗為佳, 那裡知道這清幽氣象? (1: 225). Jia Zheng asserts that the informed rejection of splendor in favor of simplicity is the direct consequence of study and good taste. His understanding of good taste is based on the preferences of China's literary elite and the use of cultural knowledge to exclude the merely wealthy from the sphere of good taste. The author suggests the inadequacy of this understanding when Bao-yu asks how the rustic pavilion can be natural when its naturalness is contrived.

Objects made in imperial factories or bearing the imprimatur of palace production were valued according to their royal provenance and their exclusion from normal channels of commercial exchange. Their value increased if they were gifts given directly from the court, as they were thus an expression of a direct connection between the household and the emperor. Such items are mentioned frequently in *Stone*, often in a catalog, their imperial source and extraordinary quantity marking the Jia family's high rank and social status. Special events like birthdays or the imperial concubine Yuan-chun's visit—or, less fortunately, the confiscation of the family's possessions—provide the occasion for elaborate lists of items originating in the court. There is a certain predictability to the composition of such lists: textiles, *ru-yi* scepters, rosaries made of rare wood, medallions made from precious metals bearing auspicious inscriptions, items appropriate to the scholar's studio (like inkstones), samples of the emperor's calligraphy or poetry, books, furs, and special food items, like specially flavored koumiss, a beverage associated with the central Asian frontier and by extension with the Manchu court (1.19.376).

Such lists of gifts, typical of the novel's time and social context, indicate the increasingly central role of the court as an arbiter of taste in eighteenth-century China. The Qianlong emperor frequently bestowed gifts on his favorite officials and also to commemorate his six celebrated tours of the south. Lists cataloging imperial gifts appear frequently in local histories and guides to scenic sites. On occasion, characters in the novel single out items of palace manufacture in the household for their exquisite workmanship. Twelve artificial flowers made of silk gauze and intended for use by the young women as hair ornaments were, as Aunt Xue points out, "made in the Imperial Palace, all in the latest fashion" (1.7.170). The styles of palace manufacture were widely imitated, to varying degrees of success, in commercial circles. For example, Xi-feng and Lady Wang scrutinize a pornographic purse found in the garden for clues as to its origin. When Lady Wang says that the item must belong to Xi-feng by virtue of her age and marital status, the younger woman argues that the embroidered pouch is a trashy imitation of palace embroidery and that even the tassels are clearly of the sort available for purchase "on the outside" (3.74.459). She thus distances herself from the offensive article, and Lady Wang is forced to agree that "a young woman of [Xi-feng's] breeding would not be guilty of such unseemliness" (460). In general, an imperial origin means that an object embodies fashion, excellent craftsmanship, and consummate good taste.

The emperor collected mechanical curios and clocks from overseas as well as porcelain and paintings produced in China but inspired by foreign styles and methods. Western-influenced paintings of beautiful ladies engaged in refined

Fig. 1. Leng Mei, *Renwu*. National Palace Museum cataloging number 001279

activities in garden settings made in the eighteenth-century imperial workshop by such artists as Leng Mei and Yao Wenhan reveal affinities between the court and the novel. One such painting, now in the National Palace Museum in Taipei, shows a group of beautiful women in a garden pavilion playing Chinese chess, thus fusing the representation of literati practice, the exotic use of perspective, and the visual consumption (by an imperial connoisseur?) of cultured female beauty in a southern setting. This painting also incorporates the material ex-

Fig. 2. Yao Wenhan, *Fangting caihua*. National Palace Museum cataloging number 03575

oticism of a Japanese lacquer box (fig. 1). Another scene of picnicking ladies, again from the imperial workshop, evokes for readers the novel's multilayered world of taste and consumption (fig. 2). The court's taste for novelty was shared by those with the money and connections to purchase such objects, and their possession was a mark of status beyond that obtained by ordinary wealth. Many collectors of Chinese art today see the hybrid baroque objects made in the eighteenth century as examples of tasteless excess, but in their own time these objects were an amalgamation of styles that represented the height of fashion, technical virtuosity, and cosmopolitan sophistication.

Items of foreign manufacture manifest the exotic and heterogeneous taste of eighteenth-century Chinese elites as inspired by the imperial court. Tribute silk, Japanese lacquer and damask, Kashmiri carpets, and European curios like clocks, perspective paintings, glass mirrors, and mechanical toys appear throughout the novel, pointing to the Jia family's close connection to the imperial household and to cosmopolitan good taste. The prefix "West Ocean" when describing an object signals European origins: a linen napkin, silver scissors, Bao-yu's mechanical toy boat and supposed grape wine are European imports or local reproductions of European products (3.59.138, 70.391, 57.97, 60.162). The prefix "East Ocean" describes objects of Japanese (or Okinawan) origin, attaching particularly to the then-fashionable lacquer boxes used for holding food, writing tools, or collectibles; to silk brocade and damask; and to metal products such as swords and knives. Such objects were valued for their exoticism yet fitted quite comfortably in the household. Possession of unusual foreign objects in *Stone* indicates the family's power and wealth and sets its members apart from their social inferiors. Grannie Liu's failure to understand these foreign things reveals her rustic ignorance, which is ridiculed by Xi-feng and the others. She is astonished by the sound and appearance of a mechanical clock, although it is completely ordinary to the maids, who respond to its chime with urgent concern over the mistress's imminent arrival (1.6.158). She also is described as "ignorant of the foreign mode of light-and-shadow painting." Intoxicated after her visit with Grandmother Jia, Grannie Liu attempts, with painful consequences, to shake hands with a Western-style painted portrait and then mistakes her own image, reflected in a mirror — also of foreign manufacture — for one of her neighbors (2.95.318–19).

The author often uses taste in objects to show something fundamental about a character. Granny Liu is hopelessly rustic, unaware of the exotic things that have become ubiquitous in a cosmopolitan and wealthy household. Modesty, directness, and appreciation for unadorned clothing mark Bao-chai as uninfluenced by fashion and formality, even as her extensive knowledge of painting and poetry mark her as a skilled practitioner of literati style and a person of exceptional good taste. She rejects fripperies like the floral hair ornaments of imperial manufacture and the toys brought back from Suzhou by her brother, Xue Pan. Tan-chun and Bao-yu, by demonstrating their affinity for the authentic and the original, underscore their own worth in the novel's moral calculus. Tan-chun asks Bao-yu to help her purchase a few objects with which to decorate her room. He first demurs, saying that the things for sale at temple fairs and bazaars are all ordinary. When she provides several examples of utilitarian but charming items that he previously gave her, he volunteers to have his servants help her with her purchases. She retorts, "What do the boys know about it? . . . I need someone who can pick out the interesting things and the ones that are in good taste" (2.27.36) 小廝們知道什麼. 你揀那朴而不俗, 直而不拙者, 這些東西 (1: 368). She identifies him as a person of discernment, in possession of a talent that transcends the good taste of his servants. Bao-yu, we are told throughout the novel, possesses the ability to detect what is special in the ordinary.

The bedroom of Jia Rong's young wife, Qin-shi, also illuminates the relation between objects and character. Antiquities and artwork of impossible provenance and thus of dubious authenticity fill the room with the hint of decadent sensuality (1.5.127). On such dubiousness readers of Chinese might consult Deng Yunxiang (392). The bedroom transgresses against norms of taste and behavior. Bao-yu enters the room, which Qin-shi describes as "fit for an immortal to sleep in" after he rejects an enviroment summarized by the following couplet, "True learning implies a clear insight into human activities. Genuine culture involves the skilful manipulation of human relationships" (1.5.126). The room contains artifacts said to have belonged to China's most famous beauties and voluptuaries, all associated with glamour, decadence, and the collapse of empire. Bao-yu, mesmerized and confused by its sensuality, falls into his famous dream about the fairy Disenchantment and the Land of Illusion. The transgression of the bedroom is mirrored when Qin-shi's father-in-law violates social and family protocol by sponsoring a lavish and public funeral for Qin-shi (1.13.259–65). Since the objects in the room cannot be authentic, they must be interpreted as allegorical rather than material. They point to Qin-shi's sensuality and link her moral transgressions and probable incest to the collapse of the Jia family, an event that is foretold by Qin-shi's ghost in Xi-feng's dream (1.13.255–57).

The author of *Stone* describes the Jia family and their possessions in loving detail. Indeed, the novel is a veritable catalog of the artifacts that defined elite life in eighteenth-century China, from the exotic to the everyday. In many scenes of the novel, characters make decisions about consumption and make distinctions on the basis of taste. The objects that furnish the mansion serve more broadly as metaphors for the personal relationships in it. The dispersion of the Jia family possessions over the course of the novel through accelerating theft and corruption parallels the family's declining fortunes. Even as the author creates the material context that provides his characters with a lavish and elaborately furnished setting for their interactions, he also uses taste (practiced, transcended, and transgressed) to measure the moral, aesthetic, and personal qualities of the characters. The possession of objects that embody both literati and imperial styles differentiates the Jia family from outsiders, yet a higher level of aesthetic discernment, or better taste, is associated with those members of the family—Bao-yu, Bao-chai, Dai-yu, Grandmother Jia—whom the author seems to want his readers to like best. By confronting them with taste as it operated in the realm of material objects, he calls their attention to the distinction between authenticity and inauthenticity in the personal realm, a distinction that lies at the heart of the book. Ultimately, even as the world of things provides metaphors for human transactions, we are reminded, repeatedly, that true feeling trumps the merely tasteful.

# Three Questions about *Stone*:
# Men, Riches, and Religion

*Susan Naquin*

## *Where Are the Men?*

*Story of the Stone* takes place largely in the two adjacent urban residential compounds of the extended Jia family. In the novel, as in Chinese society in the eighteenth century more generally, the world of the household is one of children, women, and servants. Men, by contrast, move constantly between the inner sphere of the family and the outer sphere of work and community. Because Cao Xueqin focused on the daily interactions of teenage children in an elite household, it is no surprise that his adult men are on the edges of the household world. Thus, although the Jia family are defined through the men and the family's fate is decided by them, only a dozen men play a significant role in the story, and most of them are rarely onstage.

The senior man of the lineage, Jia Jing, at first follows the preferred career path for elite Chinese men by passing the civil service examinations, but he apparently never serves in office and eventually chooses the life of a Taoist recluse. He lives in a temple in the suburbs and refuses to appear at family gatherings, not even on his own birthday—"I've got used to the peace and quiet of the monastery and I'm not willing to go back into your quarrelsome world again" (1.10.222) 我是清淨慣了的, 我不願意往你們那樣是非場中去鬧去 (1: 145), he maintains (see also 2.53.576–77, 3.63.242). His more conventional cousins, Jia She and Jia Zheng, rely on their noble connections rather than on the exams to secure bureaucratic appointments (1.2.74–75, 4.89.195, 96.325, 5.107.140). Jia Zheng holds office mostly in the capital. Relatively inexperienced in the problems of provincial administration, he struggles badly when appointed to such a position (5.99.22–29). Both brothers are impeached, with frightening and humiliating consequences (5.104.102–03, 105.114).

With Jia Jing outside the world of the family altogether, the burden on the other men is greater. Holding office could be demanding: even when Jia Zheng is not on an assignment, he was periodically engulfed by crises at work. The senior men are also constantly called on to represent the family at celebrations (or funerals) in their social circle. Only on major occasions do the women join them, as at the funeral of Jia Jing (3.64.248). Younger Jia men must attend to the family's affairs, but they too are often away from home for long periods. Because his father is a recluse, Jia Zhen (Cousin Zhen) is responsible for management of the Ning-guo household (2.53.557), while Jia Lian helps his father take care of their side of the family's affairs (1.2.83, 4.93.263). When it comes to plan Prospect Garden, these two take charge of surveying the land and supervising the work (1.16.318–20). When Jia Lian periodically must leave on family business, problems at home mount up, but for a younger man such travel can be a wonderful escape—as it is for Jia Qiang, who is sent to Suzhou with four male retainers to find a female theatrical troupe for the family (1.16.316).

When at home, Jia She prefers "a life of cultured ease" (1.16.319) 只在家 高臥 (1: 213), and even the more diligent Jia Zheng is "by nature a quiet, retiring man who . . . [uses] whatever leisure time he [has] for reading and playing Go" (1.4.123) 且素性瀟洒, . . . 每公暇之時, 不過看書著棋而已 (1: 66). Other Jia men relax with falconry, archery, and horse races. Xue Bao-chai's ne'er-do-well brother, Xue Pan, idle and not refined, receives a salary he doesn't need for a job doesn't he do, is rarely at home, and spends his time drinking, gambling, and going to cockfights, dog races, brothels, and the theater (1.4.118). Male servants, three or four of whom might be attached to each adult, share the lives and activities of their masters.

Although the Jia men enjoy a freedom of access to the outside world unavailable to their female relatives, in the domestic quarters of the house they are circumscribed by spatial segregation and by custom. When Lin Dai-yu arrives at the Rong-guo mansion in a closed sedan chair, her chair bearers take her no farther than inside the main gate; there they are replaced by male bearers of the Jia household, who in turn carry her only as far as an inner gate (1.3.88). Jia Zheng has various "literary gentlemen" in attendance, and they gather in his study or other outer rooms of the mansion (1.11.231, 2.33.146). Xue Pan's friends come to his study to carouse (1.26.519), and Jia She is entertained by singing girls and his "cronies and dependents" in his "own quarters" (2.53.577) 與眾門客賞燈吃酒, 自然是笙歌聒耳 (1: 728). In the inner rooms of the residential complex, married couples have private quarters where they can talk, eat, and sleep. Wang Xi-feng's conversations with her husband, Jia Lian, are frequent, frank, and affectionate (e.g., 1.23.453–54). Grown sons are obliged to visit their mothers regularly, and Grandmother Jia has a "front apartment" to which male relatives can come to pay their respects and where male servants appear on command. Jia Lian feels free to enter the quarters of Cousin Zhen in the mansion next door and to flirt with the maids there (3.64.267).

But even in the inner quarters, male-female interactions can be stiff (1.10.221, 5.103.83), and women or girls vanish on the arrival of a distant or unfamiliar male relative (2.53.557). At Grandmother Jia's various parties, held in her reception hall, her children and grandchildren participate, male and female, but her adult sons usually escape quickly, realizing that everyone will have "a chance to enjoy themselves unconstrainedly" (3.75.506; also 1.22.446, 3.54.34) 多樂一回 (2: 1055) without them. During the chaos precipitated by Bao-yu's and Wang Xi-feng's sudden demon possession, Xue Pan finds time to worry that his mother and sister might be "ogled" by "some wanton male" (1.25.501) 被人瞧見 (1: 343). Yet it is precisely in that confusion that he sees Lin Dai-yu for the first time (1.25.501), although they live in the same compound. Preserving formal distance does not prevent irregularities, however. Ogling is possible; so are trysts and love affairs in the garden and alleyways of the house. Nevertheless it is only by being treated as a child that Bao-yu has unlimited access to the private quarters of his aunts and female cousins. The construction of the garden, a separate world within a world, having small residences for all the teenagers, only facilitates irregular interaction.

Examinations, government service, family business, and socializing with peers — these are the activities that Bao-yu is expected to learn to love but that he resists, preferring "to play and idle in the Garden to his heart's content" (2.37.213) 每日在園中任意縱性的逛蕩 (1: 486). In Chinese elite culture of this period, male adulthood means study. Tutoring begins early and at home, but even pampered boys might be sent to school — in Bao-yu's case to a lineage school (1.7.179–80, 9.205–16, 4.81.44). Boys and men of well-to-do families might have a room for study in the home, as do both Bao-yu and his father (2.28.52). The goal of education is to prepare for the examinations and make a career in the world of men. Our hero's preference for poetry and games is the cause of considerable tension with his father, Jia Zheng (4.81.45–46). As Bao-yu grows older and becomes a young gentleman, he is obliged to accompany his elders on social calls, a task he detests, particularly the "visits of congratulation and condolence and the various other formal exchanges to which members of [his] class devote so great a part of their time" (2.36.194) 本就懶與士大夫諸男人接談, 又最厭峨冠禮服, 賀弔往還等事 (1: 474). Most modern readers will sympathize with the youth's preference for wearing the comfortable clothing allowed in the house and for calling only on those whom he likes (such as the handsome prince of Bei-jing).

It is Bao-yu's unwillingness to follow his father and uncles into adulthood and out of the household that drives the plot of *Story of the Stone*. The older men of the Jia family may be uninspiring examples and marginal to his boyhood world, but they are ever-present in his mind, persistent reminders of a future that he dreads but cannot escape.

## How Rich Are the Jias?

We know the Jia family are rich from the extent of their possessions and from what other people say about them. The "sleekness and luxuriance" (1.2.73) 翁蔚 涸潤之氣 (1: 26) of their mansion are discernible even from the road, and envious outsiders imagine that the rooms are "piled high with silver and gold!" (4.83.82) 銀庫幾間 金庫幾間 (2: 1173). The sources of the Jia wealth, less obvious, require reference to the background of the novel's author. Ample and secure at the beginning of the story, their wealth becomes insecure, put at risk by extravagant expenditures, lackluster accomplishments, and ineffective management.

The Jias live in the capital in two large, adjacent mansions, each having an impressive series of spacious halls and courtyards, with quarters for the family and their servants. This complex occupies an enormous block of urban real estate and is entirely walled: the few gateways are guarded to ensure the family's privacy. When we see these buildings for the first time in chapter 3 through the eyes of Lin Dai-yu (87–88), we are intended to be impressed, as she is, with the ornamental gates, balustraded loggias, resplendently painted beams and rafters, and large courtyards—a combination of "heavy magnificence" and "quiet elegance" (94). Grannie Liu, stepping into one of the reception areas, is entirely unprepared for "the bright and glittering things that filled the room" 滿屋中之物都是耀眼爭光的 and feels "transported bodily to one of the celestial paradises" (1.6.158) 如在雲端裏一般 (1: 96).

The most famous evidence of the Jia wealth is the extensive garden built on the premises (completed in ch. 17), into which young people of the household move (in ch. 23) and where they reside for much of the story. Although scholars have not been able to re-create the precise layout from the text, the garden is clearly spacious, having room for ponds and artificial hills, walkways and secluded residence halls (see Levy in this volume).

In this large compound some three hundred people live: four generations of Jias (twenty-four people) and their employees (1.6.150). The servants outnumber the masters at least twelve to one (1.3.105, 5.106.137). High-status inside maids are richly dressed and intimate with members of the family; others are attached to particular buildings or chores. Male servants attend to outside matters, especially transportation and supplies. The extended household includes long-term visitors (the occasional cousin and most notably the Jia in-laws, the Xues), most of whom are from their same social group and with whom they intermarry regularly, as well as more distant kin ("Even the Emperor has poor relations. . . . It would be strange indeed if *we* didn't have a few!" [1.16.161] 朝廷還有三門子窮親 [1: 99].) The Jias are tied by obligation to the families of their servants, to clerics whose temples they support, to their lineage school, and to dozens of actresses and nuns who reside on the mansion grounds.

The Jia wealth is manifest in their dress, food, possessions, and ready money. Cao Xueqin provides loving descriptions of the apparel of his characters (e.g., 1.3.91, 100, 2.49.479). It is made of silk, satin, brocade, and damask; varied, attractive, elaborately made, it is usually decorated with gold, pearls, or elaborate knotwork. Against the cold of winter, the Jias wear furs of sable, lynx, fox, or silks with ermine lining. Bao-yu's fragile snow cape woven of twisted peacock feathers "gleamed and glittered with gold and green and bronzy-bluish lights" (2.52.544) 金翠輝煌, 碧彩閃灼 (1: 711). The teenage children have plenty of jewelry, gold, silver, kingfisher feathers, and gems, and Bao-yu has his famous jade. The Jias eat well, and their varied and tasty food is often imported or out of season: shrimp balls in chicken-skin soup, red salted goose slices, cream cheese rolls stuffed with pine kernels, and so forth (3.62.208). Waited on by hovering servants, they eat leisurely from an endless supply of porcelain dishes.

Prospect Garden is lavishly furnished, with objects and materials whose description would be a challenge to any translator: 120 curtains of silk and satin, "flowered, dragon-spot, sprigged, tapestry, panelled, ink-splash" 妝蟒繡堆, 刻絲彈墨, 並各色綢綾大小幔子一百二十架 (1: 223); 1,200 chair covers, table drapes, valances, and tablecloths; elaborately designed wood paneling decorated with gems, gold, and mother-of-pearl (1.17.333, 223, 346). The tables, chairs, chests, and cupboards are of substantial and attractive woods, warmed by central Asian rugs, piled with striking pillows, and draped with fine silk. Ordinary utensils are made of gold, silver, porcelain, and lacquerware. Flowering plants and cut flowers are present all year round. In the private rooms of the principal family members, special objects are on display: exotic and imported goods from within and beyond the empire, antique bronzes, jade bowls, paintings, crystal bowls, delicate lacquerware, clocks. Money is dispensed readily and in large amounts, in dozens, hundreds, thousands, tens of thousands of ounces of silver at a time, vast sums to an ordinary person. Even when reduced to a mere list, the inventory made at the time of Jia She's arrest is convincing evidence of the extent of the Jias' household possessions (5.105.119–21).

Their money comes from income-generating property, principally land but also pawnshops that lend money and serve as banks (1.6.156, 2.53.563, 5.105.115). The Jias also receive payments and gifts in kind from their bailiffs. A long list, ranging from fifty catties of sea slugs to 30,000 catties of charcoal, is mentioned in chapter 53. The family also receives gifts from the emperor, but as Cousin Zhen suggests, perhaps disingenuously, "It's not that we *rely* on the money exactly," it is the honor and utility of the imperial connection (2.53.558) 咱們家雖不等這幾兩銀子使, 多少是皇上天恩 (1: 719). The presents from the imperial concubine, a daughter of the Jia house, include plenty of gold and silver (1.18.372–74).

Wealthy and powerful as they are, the Jias are not landed gentry who have made their way up the ladder of success through education and examinations and not mercantile families whose wealth comes from business or trade and is then converted into the scholar-gentry lifestyle. Instead, they represent a distinct Qing dynasty social group.

The background of the novel's author best explains the Jia wealth. Cao Xueqin was a bond servant from a banner family; his ancestors came from the northeast (Manchuria), joined the Manchu confederacy that founded the Qing dynasty in 1644, and were enrolled in the eight banners into which this conquering elite was organized. Certain of these banners were attached directly to the throne, and their bond-servant companies staffed the vast and powerful Imperial Household Agency. Some of these bond servants, as wet nurses, maids, and concubines, became quite close to the emperors; some were entrusted with the management of important and lucrative imperial household businesses. Coming from such a family (1.25–27), Cao Xueqin situated the Jias precisely in this milieu.

As the Caos had done, the Jias hold once lucrative Imperial Household–like appointments in the Lower Yangtze and host an imperial southern tour (1.16.314). Their Xue in-laws make their fortune as "Imperial Purveyors" (3.79.588) 在戶部挂名行商 (2: 1122) while their Wang in-laws serve as the emperor's agents in collecting taxes on foreign trade (1.16.314). Tribute silk, imperial-use satins, servants who were captured in inner Asian campaigns

(3.63.237–38), pearls, and furs—all in great supply in the Jia household—are goods whose production and distribution were monopolized by the imperial household and not available to most members of the Qing elite. Cao Xueqin makes no direct reference to this banner bond servant background, familiar though it would have been to readers of his time, choosing to leave blurred this explanation of the family's wealth and power (see Rawski in this volume).

Because the Jia family live "in the Emperor's shadow" (2.53.562) 天子腳下 的世面 (1: 721), their ties to the throne (like those of Cao Xueqin) are personal and close. Bao-yu's sister is selected to be an imperial concubine, and the family receive regular imperial gifts, including their residence itself. Several generations earlier, imperial service led to princely ennoblements (5.106.128), with correspondingly high social status in the banner and metropolitan world of the Qing capital. At Grandmother Jia's eightieth birthday, two days are set aside for visits from the imperial family, nobility, and high-ranking officials—the social equals and superiors of the Jias. The official positions held by the adult Jia males provide useful contacts but are nothing compared with these imperial and noble connections.

This network of influence serves most of the time as a source of power for the Jias, but those close to the throne were also vulnerable to sudden imperial displeasure as well as favor. The perils of this dependence are dramatically demonstrated in chapter 105, when charges against the Jias lead to the arrest and disgrace of Jia She, the sealing off of their home, and the shockingly brisk inventory of their possessions. Princely connections are immediately activated, the property is saved from confiscation, but the family emerge severely shaken.

This disaster is only one step in the gradual shrinking of the Jias' wealth and power, a central theme of the novel and much analyzed by scholars. It is apparent to the reader long before Jia Zheng, the family head, realizes that "We've been living far beyond our means. This recklessness was bound to lead to ruin" (5.106.138; see also 4.92.260) 已就寅年用了卯年的, 還是這樣裝好看, 竟把 世職俸祿當作不打緊的事情, 為什麼不敗呢 (2: 1439). Because of negligent management and squandered resources, income-producing properties were mortgaged or sold, and debts replaced new sources of income. Signs of this decline haunt the novel and parallel the breaking apart of the youthful garden community. The wealth of the family, like the happiness of the novel's hero and heroines, is thus both palpable and fragile, refracted through the sweet and painful memories of the author.

## What Religion Are the Jias?

People in eighteenth-century China did not identify themselves exclusively with one religion in the way that adherents of Judaism, Islam, and Christianity do. In fact, Buddhist, Taoist, and Confucian ideas and practices were much less systematized, and there was no insistence on monotheism or exclusivity. Instead, a variety of beliefs about this world and the next were widely shared. Professional clerics and some serious amateurs who were familiar with the Buddhist, Taoist, and Confucian sacred texts and expert in the respective rituals could be called on for specialized knowledge whenever needed. Religious beliefs and practices pervade *Story of the Stone*. A lame Taoist and a scruffy Buddhist monk not only provide the frame for the novel but also intervene suddenly at crucial moments in the story (1.1.47, 25.504–06).

The Jia family are often in need of a religious specialist, especially at the time of a death. For the funeral rites of the senior man in the family, Jia Jing, as well as for the beloved daughter-in-law, Qin-shi, Buddhist monks and the celibate Taoists of the Quanzhen sect are hired to chant scriptures, pray for the soul of the deceased during its transition through the underworld, and participate in the funeral procession (1.13.260–65, 14.275; chs. 63–64). A dozen young nuns (Buddhist and Taoist) are purchased by the family and brought to live in the mansion so that they can be handy for any occasion (1.17.350–51). In the same spirit of luxurious convenience, the Jias have a private religious establishment in the suburbs, the Iron Threshold Temple, whose Buddhist clerics are at their beck and call. Because coffins are stored there awaiting an auspicious day for burial, the temple is the destination for the family's elaborate funeral processions (ch. 15). A private cemetery houses their graves (3.58.122). The Buddhist Watermoon Priory is also generously patronized by the Jias, as is the Taoist Temple of the Lunar Goddess (ch. 29). The Jias have their own ancestral hall in the Ning-guo compound for the tablets and portraits of the family ancestors, a room where the most solemn rituals (which one might loosely call Confucian) are performed at the new year (2.53.568–71).

The monks, nuns, and Taoists in *Stone* are portrayed as both admirable and laughable. On the one hand, the untonsured nun Adamantina is perhaps the purest person in the novel—proud, fastidious, serious, and austere; on the other hand, the little nun Sapientia readily succumbs to Qin Zhong's passion.

Other kinds of religious specialists are brought in for special problems. Astrologers and geomancers are hired to set the timing for funerals and to locate graves; fortune-tellers are paid to calculate marriage compatibility; female shamans are enlisted to cast spells (most effectively on Bao-yu and Wang Xi-feng in chapter 28) and exorcists to counter them. In answer to problems and crises, sutras are chanted, spells recited, and the *Book of Changes* consulted. Prayers are offered readily and to a variety of supernatural powers. Specialized deities can be appealed to when needed—for example, the smallpox goddess when Wang Xi-feng's daughter is afflicted (1.21.424) or the fire god when the family stables are ablaze (2.39.271). Temporary altars may be set up at any time or place to make offerings.

Interaction with the supernatural is common in the world of the novel, and modern readers should not be too quick to term it all superstition. A belief in the power of dreams naturally pervades a story that is itself cast as a dream, a story in which the hero's dreams are unforgettable. Assumptions about fate, auspiciousness, and ill fortune are shared by all the characters. Amulets, lockets, and talismans are worn for protection, and omens are seen everywhere. Like Qin-shi, who visits Wang Xi-feng as a ghost to warn her of the family's future (ch. 13), people who have died may reappear to help, hurt, or haunt the living. Possession and exorcism are alarming but unremarkable events. As the novel progresses, the flower spirits 花神 of young girls who have died increasingly lurk in the garden, to the point that "every plant or tree [is] feared to harbor a malicious spirit" (5.102.72) 草木皆妖 (2: 1396). At the end, an elaborate Taoist exorcism must be ordered (73–76), with uncertain results.

Yet Cao Xueqin sometimes expresses a more ambivalent attitude toward this supernatural world. Jia Jing's life-prolonging exercises are scorned as "hocus-pocus," and his Taoist teachers are mocked (3.63.240). More significant, the major characters distance themselves somewhat—as educated Chinese sometimes did—from ordinary religious practice. Bao-chai, reflecting her own characteristic pragmatism, as well as a familiarity with religious literature shared by her cousins, explains, "Taoist writings and Zen paradoxes can so easily lead people astray if they do not understand them properly" (1.22.441) 這些道書禪機最能移性 (1: 298). Bao-yu makes frequent offerings, but he creates his own prayers (3.78.575), calls for reverence and sincerity above all (58.133), and denounces "the silly, senseless way in which vulgar people offer worship and build temples to gods they know nothing about" (2.43.357–59) 恨俗人不知原故混供神混蓋廟 (1: 584).

## NOTE

I became involved in this project at a conference at the University of Pennsylvania in April 2001 entitled Reading Eighteenth-Century China through *Dream of the Red Chamber*. A request from Tina Lu to answer briefly three questions of interest to me produced this essay. My thanks to those involved for their comments.

# Material Culture Matters in *The Story of the Stone*

## Ni Yibin

This essay covers a series of material cultural matters that are specific to the social context in which the scenes in *The Story of the Stone* were situated. Many of these matters were painstakingly and ingeniously dealt with in the David Hawkes and John Minford translation. For the convenience of casual readers, the translators tried their best to substitute a Western metaphor or saying for a Chinese one, so as to convey the meaning without resorting to a footnote. But further explanation of the background of the novel is needed for readers who want to appreciate the novel with its full indigenous flavor.

### Pictorial Designs with Culturally Specific Meanings

There are numerous pictorial designs in traditional Chinese culture that have been passed down through many generations and carry culturally significant messages. Cao Xueqin made extensive use of them, and they register with the knowing reader of the novel as well as with the knowing viewer of these images.

When Xi-feng, nicknamed Hot Pepper Feng 鳳辣子, makes her flamboyant entrance in the novel, she wears a fashionable wig ornamented by a gold filigree circlet framing the Eight Treasures formed by wirework and clustered pearls (1.3.91). The expression *eight treasures* (*babao* 八寶) can refer to two or three different sets of designs in Chinese decorative arts: the Eight Buddhist Emblems, the Emblems of the Eight Taoist Immortals, and a third set of miscellaneous treasures. The first is also known as the Eight Auspicious Emblems (*ba jixiang* 八吉祥), consisting of the wheel, the conch, the umbrella, the canopy, the lotus flower or bamboo, the vase, the fish, and the knot (sometimes one of these is replaced by the flaming pearl) (fig. 1). They were introduced from

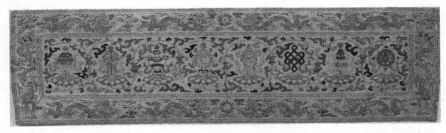

Fig. 1. Sutra cover woven in *kesi* tapestry technique featuring the Eight Auspicious Buddhist Emblems set within a border of five-clawed dragons, each in pursuit of a flaming jewel. Dyed polychrome silk yarn and gold-wrapped yarn. Qing dynasty, probably Qianlong reign (1736–95). Courtesy of Amy S. Clague

Fig. 2. Large double gourd–shaped porcelain bottle with underglaze blue decoration (1522–66).
Painted around the lower bulb are popular deities
and devotees marching with gifts for a bearded
Taoist or popular god. The scene may be an amalgamation of the Eight Taoist Immortals bearing
tribute to Shoulao and that of other legends surrounding favored gods. © Trustees of the British
Museum

Tibetan Lamaist art when the
Mongols ruled China during the
thirteenth and fourteenth centuries and became auspicious decorative elements in the following
centuries.

The second set is of objects
associated with each individual
immortal in the Eight Taoist Immortals (*an baxian* 暗八仙): the
fan of Zhong Liquan, the double
gourd of Iron-Crutch Li, the bamboo drum of Zhang Guolao, the
lotus or bamboo colander of He
Xiangu, the flower basket of Lan
Caihe, the sword of Lü Dongbin,
the castanets of Imperial Uncle
Cao, and the flute of Han Xiangzi
(fig. 2). This set of designs became
popular after the appearance of
the Eight Immortals as a decorative theme during the twelfth
century and was in vogue in the
following centuries. The Eight
Treasures design also appeared
on ingots used as gifts. Among the
ingots prepared in the Ning-guo
mansion, there were some with
this design, translated by Hawkes
as "others with patterns of auspicious flowers" (2.53.557).

Xi-feng's chignon is fastened
with five pins, the head of each
shaped as a flying *feng* 鳳 bird, from whose beak pearls are suspended on tiny
chains (1.3.91). The word *feng* in Xi-feng's name refers to the Chinese bird
that is roughly equivalent to the phoenix and in Chinese culture the noblest
in the kingdom of birds. The *feng* bird is often used as the female counterpart
of the most powerful creature, the *long* 龍 dragon (fig. 3). According to Qing
court convention, ladies from the imperial family wore nine phoenix pins; officials' wives were allowed to wear no more than five. Therefore the five pins
on Xi-feng's chignon not only echo her name but also reflect her status. Later it
is mentioned in passing that Ying-chun also has a gold filigree phoenix pin studded with strings of pearls (3.73.445).

Fig. 3. *Left*: stylized images of birds and animals were respectively used to indicate the different ranks of civil and military officials. This badge depicts a *qilin* (kylin), a mythical beast, and would have been worn by a military official of the first rank. *Right*: this Ming dynasty rank badge is woven in the *kesi* tapestry technique, giving the appearance of cut designs. This badge would have been worn on an overcoat for the court by an officer of the sixth rank, as indicated by the use of egrets as a motif. © Victoria and Albert Museum, London

When Dai-yu enters the Hall of Exalted Felicity, she sees "a long vertical scroll with an ink-painting of a dragon emerging from clouds and waves" (1.3.95). The earliest extant picture of this kind was painted by Chen Rong (active in the first half of the thirteenth century) (fig. 4). Early images of a dragon in mists and clouds were associated with Taoist transcendental practices. Later on, this kind of ink painting of dragons formed a particular genre whose purpose was to advertise its owner's status, and thus they were understood as symbolizing the saying, "waiting for the water-dropping timer to strike the hour for the court audience with the emperor," associated with the daily activity of a high-ranking official. On the one hand, the Chinese word for *tidal waves* (*chao* 潮), which were prominently represented in the painting, puns on the word for "having an audience with the emperor" (*chao* 朝). On the other hand, the dragon symbolizes the emperor. In these different ways, both phonetically and pictorially, many levels of meaning are conveyed by one image.

At Qin-shi's funeral, the prince of Bei-jing is dressed in a white formal court robe in mourning (1.15.288). The deep hem of his robe is embellished with a conventional design of gnarled rock peaks rising among buffeting crested waves and shiny flinging spray, which came to be popular first in the Ming dynasty and was exclusively a court motif in the Qing, symbolizing the unity of the country and the peace prevailing in the universe (fig. 5).

As Bao-yu is led to Qin-shi's bedroom to have a nap, his nostrils are assailed by joint-dissolving perfume, and his eyes feast on an exhibition of light erotica

Fig. 4. Dragon in clouds, painted by the Tani Buncho school of Chen Rong. Hanging scroll, ink on paper, signed and sealed. © Trustees of the British Museum

(1.5.125–27). When introducing these amorous objects and images to the reader, Cao Xueqin playfully makes references to an array of well-known femmes fatales in the history of China. On the wall hangs a scroll painting attributed to the sixteenth-century Suzhou painter Tang Yin, one of whose specialties was making pinup-like pictures of beauties for the nouveau riche merchant class in rising cities. The painting is euphemistically entitled *Begonia's Spring Slumber*,

Fig. 5. *Haishui jiangya*, design of rock peaks rising among crested waves and spray, from *Portrait of the Xiaosheng Empress Dowager*, by anonymous court artists, Qianlong period, 1751. Color on silk. Detail. © Victoria and Albert Museum, London

alluding to a Tang dynasty emperor's remark about his favorite concubine Lady Yang, who appeared half-awake at an audience with him, too exhausted from intoxication the night before to make a proper bow to the Minghuang emperor. The emperor remarked with a grin, "My lady is not completely awake yet, nor is the begonia in the garden fully awakened to a full blossom" (Hui 10–11). A poem entitled "On the Painting of Begonia Blossom and a Beauty" in Tang Yin's extant works shows that the artist did paintings with similar titles (27). Hawkes renders the content of the painting as "depicting a beautiful woman asleep underneath an apple tree" (127). His translation of *haitang* 海棠 as "apple" is tantamount, for readers in a non-Western culture, to saying that Eve gave Adam a peach instead of an apple, since the image of a young woman sitting among blossoms of begonia would evoke associations quite different from those evoked by a young woman sitting under a tree burdened by apples.

On Qin-shi's table "stood an antique mirror that had once graced the retiring room of the lascivious empress Wu Zetian" (127). Cao Xueqin includes Empress Wu's mirror here because it supposedly was a fixture in her daytime lovemaking chamber. The mirror serves as a prelude to Bao-yu's learning of the "art of love" from the fairy Disenchantment (146–47) and his experiment in that art with his closest maid, Aroma, in the next chapter (1.6.149–50). Beside the mirror lies "the golden platter on which Flying Swallow once danced for her emperor's delight" (1.5.127). Flying Swallow was a court entertainer living around 25 BCE. Her fleeting and swift dancing feats caught the attention of Emperor Chengdi (r. 32–7 BCE) of the Han dynasty, who was so besotted by her sexual charm that he made her empress after disposing of the original one. Flying Swallow's movements were so light that, according to legend, she could swirl on a crystal platter

Fig. 6. A Qing dynasty court couch or daybed. © Brooklyn Museum

held high by court ladies. Cao Xueqin may have mistaken the crystal platter on which Flying Swallow danced for a golden one. He certainly employed poetic license when he made up a "papaw that An Lushan bruised Yang Guifei's breast with" (my trans.). Historical textual sources record only that An Lushan (or An Rokhan), an eighth-century Chinese general of Sogdian and Turkish descent, once bruised Yang Guifei's breast with his powerful hand during a heated tryst with her. The bruise was so prominent that Lady Yang had to invent a piece of clothing to hide it in public.

The couch in Qin-shi's room is said to have been slept on by the fifth-century Princess Shouyang (fig. 6 shows a Qing dynasty couch), whose forehead once caught a falling plum flower, which left a five-petal mark. The colored patch on the princess's forehead set a new fashion for palace ladies to follow. Later, this makeup feature acquired the name of plum-flower patch or Shouyang patch 壽陽妝 and spread from court ladies to commoners' wives (fig. 7). In poetry on

Fig. 7. The legendary plum-flower patch on a lady's face. Anonymous painting, Yuan dynasty. Collection of the National Palace Museum, Taiwan, Republic of China

women's life in inner chambers, this makeup technique is also referred to as flower yellow 花黃 or stamen yellow 蕊黃. Because Princess Shouyang made a name for herself with this cosmetic mark, her couch was arranged among other objects associated with celebrity fashion setters and femmes fatales.

To match the royal bed, Princess Tongchang's bed curtain is fashioned out of strings of real pearls, thus known as clustered pearl net, which is part of her famously luxurious dowry, which her father, Emperor Yizong of the late Tang (r. 860–74) almost emptied the state treasury to prepare. Both the last two items were related to princesses and, some believe, were employed by the author to indicate that Qin-shi was born a princess into the family of a deceased emperor's political opponent and was later secretly adopted by the Jia family.[1]

The gauze coverlet on Qin-shi's bed is said to have been washed by Xi Shi, which is a dazzling association with another of the Four Beauties of Ancient China (the previous one was Yang Guifei). Xi Shi, born as a commoner, washed gauze by the river of her village before she was discovered by the court and became the king's favorite court lady. Even the headrest on Qin-shi's bed is linked with romance, referred to as "the double head-rest that Hong-niang once carried for her amorous mistress" (1.5.127). Hong-niang (Crimson) is the quick-

Fig. 8. A woodblock illustration, *The Western Chamber*, showing Hong-niang carrying Ying-ying's bedding and accompanying Ying-ying to Scholar Zhang's quarters

witted maid of Ying-ying, the heroine of the famous Yuan dynasty play *The Story of the Western Wing* (*Xixiang ji* 西廂記). The play was composed around a love affair between the daughter of a late cabinet minister and a poor scholar, Zhang, during their temporary stay in a monastery. When eventually Ying-ying decided to go to Scholar Zhang's lodge to consummate their love, Hong-niang helped her carry the pillow and duvet, because the scholar was too poor to have bedding suitable for a lady (fig. 8). It is cheeky of Cao Xueqin to associate the beddings in Qin-shi's chamber with the gauze washed by Xi Shi and the bridal pillow used by Ying-ying and Scholar Zhang, since both Xi Shi and Ying-ying lived more than a thousand years earlier and neither gauze nor pillow would have lasted that long — and, of course, Ying-ying is a fictional character.

## Punning Rebus Images and Other Language Games

The interpretive mechanism of expressing a message with a picture, known as pun rebus, is widely used in Chinese decorative arts (see Ni Yibin). When Grandmother Jia sees Qin-zhong, the younger brother of Qin-shi, for the first time, she hands him a cloth purse and a small statue of the Star Deity of Kui 魁星, who is an acolyte of the god of literature (fig. 9). Hawkes did not translate these two items; instead, he opted for an English expression: literary success was "in the bag" to cover them (1.8.199). In fact, the images of the two items together form a pun rebus, conveying the message, "May you be blessed by the God of Literature and lead a harmonious life" (*wenxing hehe* 文星和合), to the reader, as the Chinese text clearly spells out (1: 128).

The meaning of a pun rebus is generally conventional, easily recognized by people who speak the language and are familiar with the culture. In the message conveyed by the combination of these two gifts, the first part is both symbolic and gesturing in the sense that the act of giving a statue of the Star Deity of Kui means, "May you be blessed by this deity." The image of the deity itself is a rebus. The Chinese character *kui* for "number one" or "the star that blesses those who sit for civil-service examinations" is formed by the character for "demon" (*gui* 鬼) with the character for a bushel measure (*dou* 斗) nested in one of its long and curved strokes (fig. 10).

The second part of the message conveyed by Grandmother Jia's gift also works as a linguistic game. The embroidered cloth purse is known in Chinese as *hebao* 荷包 (fig. 11), while the Chinese expression for "living in peace and harmony" is *hehe* 和合. Because the first syllables of these two expressions make a pun, a cloth purse can be used to convey, conventionally, the message, "May you live a trouble-free life," as Cao Xueqin actually wrote: "In addition, Grandmother Jia gave Qin Zhong an embroidered purse and a figurine of Star Deity of Kui in solid gold, in order to shower him with the blessing from this god and to wish him a trouble-free life" (my trans.; Hawkes's trans. is on 1.8.199; 賈母又與了一個荷包並一個金魁星，取 "文星和合" 之意 [1: 128]).

Fig. 9. *Left:* an ink rubbing of one of the calligraphy steles at the Beilin Museum in Xi'an, *Kui-xing Kicking Up a Bushel Measure*. It is a rebus image of the Chinese character *kui* 魁, which means "coming first in the imperial civil service examinations." The rebus is made up of a *gui* 鬼 ("demon") kicking a *dou* 斗 ("bushel measure"). In addition, the demon stands on the top of the character *ao* 鳌, a sea creature whose statue was to be stepped on by the top scholar in the palace during the ceremony in which he was presented to the emperor. *Right:* Kui Xing. Made of gilded and lacquered bronze. Qing dynasty. © Trustees of the British Museum

When the imperial concubine Yuan-chun returns to the Jia mansions to have a family reunion, she bestows on Grandmother Jia, among other luxurious presents, "ten medallions of red gold with a design showing an ingot, a writing-brush and a sceptre (which in the riddling rebus-language used by makers of such objects meant 'All your heart's desire—'" (1.18.372). "All your heart's desire" is Hawkes's translation of the auspicious wish *biding ruyi* 必定如意 [1: 249], but his translation is incomplete. How is this message conveyed by the combination of

Fig. 10. The Chinese character for "demon" (*gui*) and for *kui*. The Star Deity of Kui is shaped like a devil with one of his legs kicking up a bushel measure.

Fig. 11. *Left:* an embroidered purse (*hebao* 荷包). © digitalarchives.tw. *Right:* a painting of a Manchu man wearing such a bag at his waist

a writing brush, an ingot, and a scepter? The writing brush is known in Chinese as *bi* 筆 and the ingot as *ding* 錠. The two words form *biding*, which puns on the Chinese expression for "definitely" (*biding* 必定). Furthermore, the ornamental scepter is named *ruyi* 如意, literally meaning "all your heart's desire," because its shape was developed from a back scratcher (fig. 12). Together, the three seemingly unrelated objects form a pun rebus with the message "May every wish of yours definitely come true" (*biding ruyi* 必定如意).

In the silk purses that Faithful prepares as gifts for Grannie Liu, there are also gold ingots bearing this pun rebus design (2.42.330; 1: 566). Usually, the design is incised or carved on the surface of an ingot. In Hawkes's translation we read, "ten medallions of red gold with a design showing an ingot, a writing-brush and a sceptre." Much of the cultural nuance behind the carved design is lost.

Fig. 12. Qing dynasty brush pot. Fisherman in landscape, and Liu Hai and his three-legged toad standing on a coin and scepter (*ruyi*). Made of underglaze blue porcelain. © Trustees of the British Museum

Grandmother Jia also receives from Yuan-chun "ten silver medallions with a design showing a stone chime flanked by a pair of little fish (carrying the rebus-message 'Blessings in abundance')" (1.18.372). "Blessings in abundance" translates the auspicious wish *jiqing youyu* 吉慶有餘 (1: 249). This is another common pun rebus design. The Chinese triangular chime is called *qing* 磬, and the action of striking the chime is known as *jiqing* 擊磬, which puns on the word for "blessings" (*jiqing* 吉慶); another way of expressing *jiqing* 吉慶 is through the juxtaposition of the chime *qing* with a *ji* (戟 halberd, as shown in the middle of the snuff bottle in fig. 13.) The Chinese expression for "fish" is *yu* 魚, which is a pun on the word for "abundance" (*yu* 余). The combination yields the pun rebus message (fig. 13).

In chapter 29, when Bao-yu arrives at the Taoist Temple of the Lunar Goddess for the purification ceremonies, Abbot Zhang's friends and students give him many Taoist trinkets as presents to show their appreciation in witnessing Bao-yu's legendary Magic Jade. Among these presents, there is "a tiny scepter and persimmons with the rebus-meaning 'success in all things'" (2.29.79). Again, the scepter (*ruyi* 如意) puns with the wish "all your heart's desire" (*ruyi* 如意). The fruit persimmon is pronounced *shi* 柿, and a group of persimmons may be referred to as *shishi* 柿柿, which puns on the Chinese expression for "all

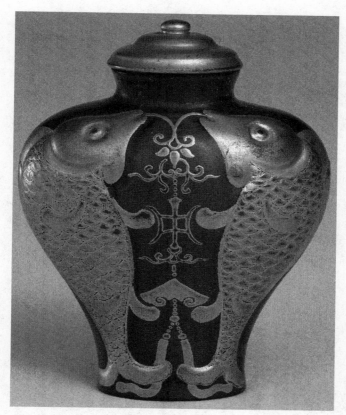

Fig. 13. The pun rebus design of the combination of the halberd (*ji*), the chime (*qing*), and fish (*yu*) on a snuff bottle, Qing dynasty. Collection of the Palace Museum, Beijing

things" or "everything" (*shishi* 事事). Thus, the image of the scepter meaning "all your heart's desire" and that of persimmons meaning "all things" form the pun rebus message "May your wishes come true in all things" (*shishi ruyi* 事事 如意) (fig. 14).

On the tray that Abbot Zhang presents to Bao-yu there is also a trinket bearing the design of quails pecking under stalks with ears of grains (2.29.79). In Chinese, ears of grains are *sui* 穗, and many of them together may be called *suisui* 穗穗, which is a pun on the expression for "year after year" (*suisui* 歲歲). The Chinese name for quail is *anchun* 鵪鶉, the first syllable of which puns on the word for "peace" (*an* 安). The combination of ears of grain and quail thus results in a pun rebus design conveying the message, "May you enjoy peace throughout the years" (*suisui ping'an* 歲歲平安) (fig. 15).

事事如意

Fig. 14. A punning rebus design of the combination of persimmons (*shi*) and scepters (*ruyi*). Courtesy of Zhejiang People's Press (*Chinese Auspicious Designs*)

On the evening of the fifteenth day of the first month of the Chinese New Year, Grandmother Jia holds a feast to entertain the whole family. Beside each table are antique porcelain vases with different flower arrangements, one of which, in Hawkes's translation of the text, is called "riches in a jade hall" (2.53.578). This arrangement is also a pun rebus design consisting of blossoms of magnolia, crab

Fig. 15. *Left:* the punning rebus design of the combination of ears of grain (*sui*) and quail (*anchun*) on a jade vase, Qing dynasty. © Victoria and Albert Museum, London. *Right:* hanging scroll. Painted in ink and colors on silk, by Lü Ji (fl. ca. 1475–1503). © Trustees of the British Museum

apple or begonia, and peony. Magnolia is *yulan* 玉蘭 in Chinese, and crab apple
or begonia are both *haitang* 海棠, the begonia also known as "*haitang* flower in
autumn" (*qiuhaitang* 秋海棠). When the two flowers combine, the first syllable
of *yulan* and the second syllable of *haitang* form the combination *yutang*, which
puns on the expression for "jade hall" or "grand household" (*yutang* 玉堂) in
Chinese. Peony has been called the flower of the rich and prestigious (*fuguihua*
富貴花) since at least the eighteenth century. The arrangement of the three
flowers — magnolia, crab apple, and peony — results in a pun rebus design with
the message "May your household be honored with prestige and enjoy great
wealth" (*yutang fugui* 玉堂富貴) (fig. 16).

Fig. 16.  School of Zhao Jiang Northern Song dynasty. Hanging scroll. Magnolia, peony, and crab
apple. Painted in ink and colors on silk. © Trustees of the British Museum

Cao Xueqin describes the game of Match My Plant in chapter 62, with participants including Periwinkle, Caltrop, Parfumée, Etamine, Nenuphar, and Cardamome. The participants are tested on their knowledge of plants and literacy through their performance in matching the names of presented plants (3.62.211). Again, the game involves knowledge that is specific to Chinese language and culture. For example, one young woman says, "I've got some Guanyin willow [*guanyin liu* 觀音柳]." Another responds, "I've got some Luohan pine [*luohan song* 羅漢松]." In this matching pair, "willow" and "pine" are different trees, while "Guanyin" and "Luohan" are different Buddhist figures. Guanyin was the name that the Chinese gave to a disciple of Amitabha Buddha–Avalokiteśvara, who was sinocised as Goddess of Mercy, while a Luohan, the Chinese name for an arhat, was a spiritual practitioner who had reached the culmination of the spiritual life. One game participant says, "I've got a peony [*mudan* 牡丹] from *The Peony Pavilion* [*mudan ting* 牡丹亭]." Another responds, "I've got a loquat from *The Story of the Lute* [*pipa ji* 琵琶記]." This pair could be said to match because there is a pun between the Chinese name for the loquat (*pipa* 枇杷) and the Chinese name for the lute (*pipa* 琵琶), both of which are pronounced *pipa*. In another round, Cardamome says, "I've got an elder-and-younger-sisters-flower [*jiemei hua* 姐妹花]." After nobody is able to match it for a while, Caltrop eventually comes up with the answer: "I've got a husband-and-wife orchid [*fuqi hui* 夫妻蕙]" (2: 859–60) (fig. 17).

Fig. 17. *Left:* a scene of the game of Match My Plant, played between two ladies on the cover of a porcelain box, Kangxi reign of the Qing dynasty. Collection of the Palace Museum, Beijing. *Right:* illustration of *dou cao*, "Match My Plant," played between two ladies, Chen Cunren and Song Qi. Gai Qi, *Honglou meng tu yong* 紅樓夢圖詠 ("Pictures on *Honglou meng,* with Encomiums")

## *Other Culturally Meaningful Objects*

In *The Story of the Stone*, Cao Xueqin not only adorns the rooms in the Jia family mansion with rare treasures created in the long history of the Chinese civilization but also clothes his characters with the most fashionable garments and feeds them all sorts of unusual delicacies.

The author's knowledge was limited to the observation of his family collection and friends' collections, the books he had access to, and the gossip he heard from his relatives and friends of noble and prestigious origins. Compared with modern scholarship based on extensive excavations, auctioned traditional works of art, and the former imperial collections, Cao Xueqin's descriptions of the luxurious things in aristocratic households were sometimes fanciful and inaccurate.

Readers of *Stone* may sometimes find it difficult to match the psychological and intellectual development of the protagonists with their age. For example, Bao-yu is described as "the thirteen-year-old heir apparent of Sir Jia of Rong-guo House" (1.23.461), while he could write a series of poems and give sophisticated comments that impressed Sir Jia's literati friends (1.17.335–46) and have a sophisticated emotional involvement with Dai-yu. In a similarly exaggerated manner, Cao Xueqin is a zealous interior designer, adorning rooms in the Jia mansions with the most extravagant works of art imaginable. Scholars take different approaches to them, but my position here is to respect his intentions. That is, I interpret the objects according to the literal meaning of their names. If Cao mentions something that could not have existed historically, I point that out, but I do not judge whether the Jia family could have owned an object or not. For example, it has been argued that in chapter 41 the Chenghua cup that Adamantina eventually gives away (2.41.312–16) had to be a Kangxi era copy because many fine copies of Chenghua cups were made in that reign. However, when Bao-yu saves the "soiled" cup by asking Adamantina to let Grannie Liu have it, he sincerely means that Grannie Liu could sell it and "live for quite a long while on the proceeds" (2.41.315). This example shows that Cao Xueqin did not think that the Chenghua teacup was a fake.

## *Jade*

In the Taoist Temple of the Lunar Goddess, among the trinkets that Abbot Zhang's friends and students present to Bao-yu are some "gold crescents and C-shaped jade pieces" (2.29.79). In the original Chinese text, "crescents" are *huang* 璜 and "C-shaped jade pieces" are *jue* 玦, both of which belong to the earliest forms shaped out of jade in China. *Huang* is basically a crescent, while *jue* is a thick ring with a gap in it (fig. 18).

The stone the Chinese call jade (*yu* 玉) includes a variety of tough and compact minerals. It was distinguished from ordinary stones six millennia ago and

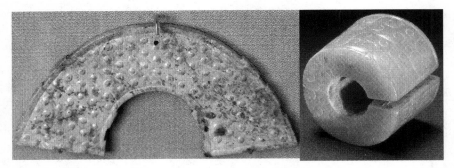

Fig. 18. *Left:* a jade *huang* piece. *Right:* a jade *jue* piece (fourth to third centuries BCE). © Trustees of the British Museum

has been held dear by the Chinese ever since. Innumerable jade objects have been unearthed in various parts of the Chinese landmass despite the fact that it is one of the most difficult materials to work with. Nowhere else in the world has a stone been so culturally defined and worshipped over such a long period of time, its influence permeating many aspects of people's lives. More than five hundred Chinese characters with the radical denoting *jade* (including the *huang* and *jue* characters) have been created. Many are names of different types and forms of jade. They all have connotations related to value, beauty, power, and riches. Confucius was said to have summarized the eleven human virtues embedded in jade—such as humanity, represented by its warm glow; wisdom, by its firm texture; moral integrity, by its edgeless shape; politeness, by its weightiness; and loyalty, by its prevailing beauty. These abstract human qualities have grown to be jade's intrinsic attributes in China. The stone has impressed the Chinese to such an extent that the Chinese vision of paradise is one bathed in the silvery glow of jade, as opposed to the golden beams in the heaven of the West.

Earliest jade products include ornaments like pendants, tools like axes, and ritual objects like shamanistic figures. During the first millennium BCE, jade began to be used to cover different parts of a deceased body, which indicates that it was believed to have supernatural power. It was worked into a variety of elaborate jewelry forms. In the last millennium, more jade was used to create sculpture, modeled after either natural forms or archaic bronzes, to embody political authority and cultural values. In late imperial China almost everybody with a decent livelihood was in possession of some jade, usually attached to the body, as a charm. It was against this background of rich connotations that Cao

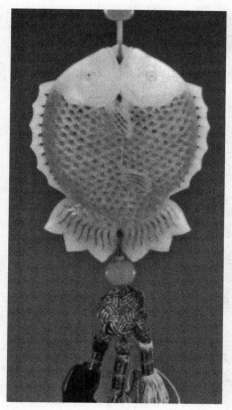

Fig. 19. Rose-colored jade perfume pendant with tassels, shaped as a double fish, Qing dynasty. Collection of the Palace Museum, Beijing

Xueqin endowed his protagonist, Bao-yu, with a magic jade in his mouth at birth.

In her first appearance in one common version of the novel, not the one Hawkes based his translation on, Xi-feng has a pair of rose-colored jade fish pendants with pea-green tassels attached to the waistband of her skirt (1.3.91 is where this text might have been). Pairs of jade carving usually embody meanings relating to love, matrimony, and harmony in life (fig. 19).

Cao Xueqin places a white jade chime suspended on a Japanese lacquered wooden frame on the long table beside a bronze tripod (*ding* 鼎) to complete Tan-chun's image as a noble lady with educated taste (2.40.292). Hawkes's translation misses the bronze *ding*, which is a crucial item for Tan-chun's extravagant yet scholarly interior plan. In seventeenth- and eighteenth-century China it was fashionable to have a dangling musical stone in a scholar's studio. The chime was shaped out of a piece of antique jade. When a conversation embarked on mundane matters such as inflation in the marketplace, the speaker would apologetically strike the stone in order to let the audience "clean their ears." Since the musical stone was also a part of the religious ensemble in a temple, its appearance in a scholar's study also served as a reminder of the scholar's unworldliness (fig. 20).

When Grandmother Jia and Grannie Liu, a relative coming from the country-side, visit Green Bower Hermitage, Adamantina "poured tea for Bao-yu in the green jade mug that she normally drank from herself" (2.41.313). From the surroundings, readers may sense that Adamantina has exquisite taste. She offers Bao-yu her own choice tea mug (*Lüyu dou* 綠玉鬥) because she recognizes and appreciates his exceptional human quality. On seeing the jade piece, Bao-yu jokingly challenges Adamantina's offer, calling it a "common old thing"

Fig. 20. A chime suspended on a frame depicted in a Ming dynasty painting (1564). Collection of the Shanghai Museum

(2.41.314). Adamantina responds by telling Bao-yu that he may not be able to find such a fine piece in his own household (fig. 21).

## Ceramics

On the first day Dai-yu enters the Rong-guo mansion, she is led to a side apartment, where Lady Wang normally spends her leisure hours. In this room, opposite the table that holds the incense-burning set, there is an identical table on which stands a stoneware vase with seasonal flowers in it (1.3.96). The author presents the vase as a Ru ware "beauty *gu*," which Hawkes renders as "a narrow-waisted Ru-ware imitation *gu*." A *gu* 觚 was a tall, slender-waisted vase with a trumpet-

Fig. 21. A jade *dou* mug, Ming dynasty. Collection of Palace Museum, Beijing

like mouth and a splayed foot ring, and, because of this shape, it was considered to resemble a beautiful woman. It was a typical Bronze Age ceremonial vessel (fig. 22).

Ru 汝 ware was one of the five famous wares in China at the turn of the first millennium, the other four being Jun 鈞, Guan 官, Ge 哥, and Ding 定. Among them, Ru ware has the fewest pieces extant (no more than a hundred) and has been treasured for its subtle bluish-green celadon glaze with a fine crackling that resembles the veins on a cicada's wing. The finest Ru ware vessels were produced for the sole use of the Huizong 徽宗 emperor of the Song dynasty (r. 1100–26), who developed an exquisite taste for art. The Percival David Foundation, housed in the British Museum in London, has many excellent specimens of this ware.

Cao Xueqin also puts a conspicuous, bushel-sized Ru ware flowerpot (*huanang* 花囊) in Tan-chun's room (2.40.292), to show the impeccably orthodox taste of a young woman who, although her mother was a concubine in the Jia family, is striving to emphasize her aristocratic identity. As a matter of fact, neither the slender-waisted *gu* nor the *huanang* flowerpot is among the surviving Ru ware vessels. So it is most likely that the author furnished his heroines' inner chambers with grand brand-names such as Ru ware, along with other famous and rare objects, in order to set the tone for his readers instead of trying to be historically accurate. Maybe it was because of the great rarity of Ru ware vessels that Hawkes made the *gu* in Lady Wang's quarters an imitation. But he did not apply the "imitation" label to the Ru ware dish in Xi-feng's outer room (2.27.29) or to the *huanang* pot in Tan-chun's room.

In Green Bower Hermitage, Adamantina first serves Grandmother Jia with a small "covered teacup of Chenghua enameled porcelain" (2.41.312). The Chenghua 成化 reign of the Ming dynasty (1465–87) was known for porcelain pieces with exquisite bodies, shapes, and decoration, especially the matching colors (*doucai* 鬥彩) decoration (fig. 23).[2] According to the first history of Chinese ceramics, published around the time of the preparation of *Stone*, a pair of Chenghua teacups cost 100,000 cash coins at the beginning of the seventeenth century, an amount that would maintain a middle-class household for a year. In the novel, Cao Xueqin pushes Adamantina's mysophobia to the extreme: the nun will throw away this expensive piece of porcelain just because Grannie Liu had a sip from it! Fortunately, Bao-yu asks Adamantina to let Grannie Liu have the teacup (2.41.315).

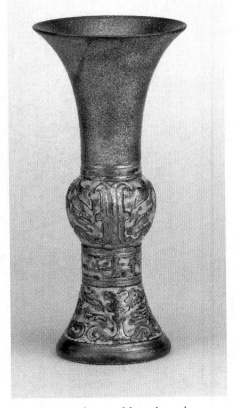

Fig. 22. A porcelain *gu* of the eighteenth century. © Trustees of the British Museum

## Food

At a banquet entertaining Grannie Liu from the country, Grandmother Jia asks Xi-feng to give Grannie Liu a dish, *qiexiang* 茄鯗, with dried eggplant as its main ingredient. The dish sounds simple, but the author gives elaborate procedures for its preparation, which have puzzled even the best translators. The first step is to immerse finely sliced, recently ripened eggplant in chicken stock. Then the slices are steamed to suck in the chicken flavor and then sun-dried. This immersion, steaming, and drying are repeated nine times before the eggplant is finally crispy and ready for use (cf. Hawkes's simplified rendition in 2.41.306–07).

Fig. 23. A cup decorated with the matching colors technique. Made in the Kangxi reign but with an apocryphal mark of the Chenghua reign (1465–1487). © Trustees of the British Museum

When Adamantina offers Grandmother Jia tea during her visit to Green Bower Hermitage, the matriarch warns the nun, "I don't drink Liuan [六安] tea" (2.41.312). Fortunately, Adamantina has done her homework for Grandmother Jia's particular taste for tea and has a perfect answer: she is serving a tea called "Old Man's Eyebrows" (*laojunmei* 老君眉). Liuan tea, a green tea from Anhui 安徽 Province, became known during the eighth century and famous during the second half of the last millennium. Because it was believed to have a cooling effect on the body according to the yin-yang theory of traditional Chinese medicine, Grandmother Jia was afraid that it would be unsuitable for her aging stomach. But Old Man's Eyebrows tea, also known as White Peony, was a specialty white tea produced in Fujian Province. It made its name by being served as tribute to the court in the eighteenth century. The tea was so called because its leaf was narrow and long and its bud had fine white hair. The color of the liquid brewed from this tea was yellowish and its taste subtle; that was why Grannie Liu found it "a bit on the weak side" (2.41.312).

After serving tea for the party headed by Grandmother Jia, Adamantina leads Bao-chai and Dai-Yu to a side room, and Bao-yu follows. The nun treats them as special guests, making tea for them with water from snow collected from the petals of plum blossoms at the Coiled Incense Temple on Mount Xuan-mu. This water is so precious that the nun has kept it underground in a "water-jar decorated with demon-face-blue kiln-transformation glaze" for five years (my trans.; Hawkes's trans. on 315). A sixteenth-century pharmacopoeia specifies that melted snow has a cooling effect on the body and is recommended for connoisseurs to make tea and cook congee, a tradition cherished by men of letters as early as the eighth century.

## Clothing

The patriarchs of Cao Xueqin's family served as commissioners of the Imperial Textile Mills in the commercial center and the most fertile land of China, in both Suzhou and Nanjing, for three generations. Likely because of this family connection, Cao Xueqin had an encyclopedic knowledge of the finest fabrics and most fashionable clothing of the time, both domestically produced or imported.

On the first encounter of Dai-yu and her relatives at the Rong-guo mansion, she is struck by Xi-feng, a fairy princess dressed more beautifully than any woman present. The satin of her bright-red fitted jacket comes from Japan and is a material worn only by the rich. Her slate-blue robe is lined with ermine, and rainbow colors are woven into the smooth blue silk fabric with the special *kesi* (緙絲) technique. Xi-feng matches her fur and *kesi* fabric with an accordion pleat sewn from imported turquoise crepe decorated with a scattered-flower pattern (1.3.91).

Xi-feng seems to adore the *kesi* fabric, the most expensive kind of decorated silk, because she also wears a slate-blue *kesi* silk cape lined with gray squirrel when receiving Grannie Liu (1.6.160) and gives Aroma a *kesi* robe of her own as a visiting home present (2.51.517).[3] Aroma's robe has a lining made of the fur from the bellies of foxes living in northeast China and is decorated with eight flower roundels. According to the dress codes of the Qing court, the wives of dukes and of the courtiers of the third rank could wear auspicious garment (*jifu* 吉服) robes adorned with eight flower roundels (fig. 24). In the novel, the design on the robe that Bao-yu wears at his first appearance (1.3.100) is none other than the eight flower roundels embroidered on Japanese damask satin in a raised manner — perhaps because he is in his early teens and the codes for children's dress overlapped with those for women. Hawkes thought that all the "eight large medallions" were "on the front" of the robe, but in fact one was on the chest, two were symmetrically arranged on either side above the deep hem, three were counterparts on the back, and the remaining two were on the shoulders.

If Xi-feng wears a fur-lined robe, Bao-yu, who has just come from outside, wears one as well. His robe is not "with tasseled borders," as Hawkes rendered it (100), but has a lining of sheepskin with tassel-like braids of wool. The special sheep used for such a lining, raised on the northern side of the Great Wall, were particularly cold-resistant. The Manchu officials treasured this sheepskin even more than sable for its insulating properties. An interesting contrast can be

Fig. 24.  The auspicious robe (*jifu*) functions as formal court wear for a woman. © Victoria and Albert Museum, London. Bequeathed by Lady Fox

drawn between Bao-yu's robe and Grandmother Jia's black crepe robe, which has a Karakul lining of pearl-like hair curls from the skin of an aborted lamb (2.42.328).

Xi-feng is presented as the fashion model in the Jia family also when she receives Grannie Liu in her own apartment (1.6.159–60). This time she wears a purplish sable forehead warmer. The warmer was semicircular and complementary to an ordinary cap, which covered the top of the head (fig. 25). It was also known as the princess hood because it was said to have been worn by Lady Wang Zhaojun of the Han dynasty (she entered the imperial harem in 40 BCE) on her journey to central Asia. Lady Wang was married to the ruler of a Xiongnu 匈奴 tribe by the Han emperor Yuan (48–33 BCE) during one of the ruler's homage trips paid to the Han court. She needed something more than an ordinary hat to keep herself warm because of the harsh weather in the northwest beyond the Great Wall. In a later chapter, Shi Xiang-yun arrives on a snowy day wearing a scarlet felt princess hood lined with golden silk on the back and embellished with a cloud design cut into the surface, accentuated by a light-yellow lining (2.49.479). The same cut-and-lined decorative technique is used on Dai-yu's red Mongolian lamb-leather boots: a cloud design cut into the surface

Fig. 25. A sable forehead warmer on a court lady. She also wears a phoenix hairpin with a string of pearls suspended from the bird's beak. Collection of the Palace Museum, Beijing

and accented with the lining of a lighter material underneath. The design on the boots is bordered with gold (478).

Cao Xueqin's family history as bond servants to the Manchu emperors may account for his acquaintance with fur of all kinds, because fur naturally appealed to the upper echelons of the nomadic Manchus. Xi-feng's peach-pink inner jacket with a sprigged design is matched by her bright-red imported crepe skirt with a "silver squirrel" lining, which could be made of either ermine or white sable (1.6.160). An overcoat worn by Jia Zhen is covered with lynx fur on the outside (2.53.565). Because lynx skin was rare and expensive, during the Kangxi reign it was decreed that only members of the imperial family and officials above the third rank could wear it. In the novel, Jia Zhen is given the hereditary title of honorable colonel of the third rank (1.13.263) and is therefore qualified to wear this fur. Xiang-yun's fur coat, a gift from Grandmother Jia, has sable's heads on the outside and long-haired black squirrel on the inside (2.49.479). Underneath, Xiang-yun wears not "a short riding-skirt," as Hawkes puts it, but a silvery pink damask satin knee-length robe with a lining of fox belly fur. Bao-yu appears with "sea-dragon's fur," which lines his Manchu-style waist-coat with buttoned-on detachable sleeves like eagle wings (481).

No material is more exotic than what Grandmother Jia refers to as "peacock gold fabric" (2.52.544). The material is said to be of Russian origin, woven with yarn made from twisted barbs of peacock feather. It was fashioned into a snow cape that glittered and gleamed like the flaunting fan tail of a peacock. The cape also had the practical virtue of being waterproof. Bao-qin's rain cape is made of a material woven from the golden-green soft feathers on a drake's head and neck (2.49.474, 485).

Some materials have a foreign name. *Duoluoni* 哆囉呢, for example, was a woolen material with a wide width, imported from the West. It is used on Li Wan's front-buttoned coat (2.49.479) and Bao-yu's aubergine gown lined with fox fur (481). Bao-chai's lotus-green "crane-profile" pelisse is knitted with imported lamb's wool (479).

In stark contrast to Xi-feng's extravagance, Bao-chai's attire reveals her austerity. Though her family, the Nanking Xue (Jinling Xue 金陵薛), according to the Mandarin's *Life-Preserver*, are so rich that "to count their money would take all day . . ." (1.4.111), Bao-chai wears fairly ordinary clothes, such as a well-worn padded jacket and padded skirt. But her mulberry-colored vest has a lining of both brown and white weasel fur, which Hawkes translates as a colored "pattern" (1.8.187–88).

In Dai-yu's eye, the maids working around Lady Wang all have better makeup and clothes than do the maids in other parts of the Rong-guo mansion. One maid wears a red silk damask dress and a black satin sleeveless jacket with scalloped borders of colored silk (1.3.97). Sleeveless jackets were often worn by maids employed in rich households, because the jackets, though ornamental, were practical for house chores. In many Chinese pictures depicting ladies with their entourage, the maids are often shown wearing a sleeveless jacket as an outer garment in contrast to their mistress's long-sleeve outer robe or dress.

Parfumée once wears a short tunic with a harlequin pattern consisting of jade-colored, deep purple, and reddish-brown lozenges (3.63.221). Wearing clothes made of patchwork materials became fashionable at the beginning of the seventeenth century, though the practice was mentioned in poems as early as the eighth century. A garment made of such material was called a paddy fields–style robe (*shuitianyi* 水田衣) in traditional China, for the patchwork pattern resembled the lined or checkered rice fields in southern parts of the country. Patchwork clothes were also worn by Chinese scholars for their association with monks' robes, which were made of materials collected from numerous households and had an antimaterialist connotation. On the Chinese stage, the paddy fields garment developed into a costume that identified the actresses wearing it as nuns—Adamantina wears one (5.109.186) (fig. 26).

Fig. 26. Two examples of a woman's garment with the paddy fields pattern. © Chinaculture.org

## Miscellaneous Cultural Issues

The clothes that the characters wear in *Stone* are not distinctively of the Qing period. Cao Xueqin's design for Bao-yu's appearance was an example of his effort to make the historical setting of the story vague, perhaps in order to avoid political persecution. In chapter 3, Bao-yu wears a gold-filigree coronet studded with gems and a golden headband in the form of two dragons fighting for a pearl over his brow (100). Such a coronet was worn by young gentlemen from upper-class families in fifteenth- to seventeenth-century China. The coronet was also worn by actors playing princes and young generals on stage.

On Xi-feng's birthday, Patience becomes upset and her clothes are in disarray because her mistress, Xi-feng, wronged her and slapped her. When she is led to Bao-yu's apartment to change her soiled clothes and redo her makeup, Bao-yu produces a porcelain box containing high-quality face powder. The box, decorated with underglaze cobalt-blue designs, was made during the Xuande reign of the Ming dynasty (1425–35), one of the most prolific periods of Chinese porcelain manufacture. These porcelains excelled in their materials, glazes, and variegated designs. In the blue-and-white box lies a row of ten elongated plantain lily buds. Pinching off one of the buds, Bao-yu explains to Patience that the powder in the bud is not based on ceruse, the common practice, but is organic, made from the seeds of garden jalap with other finest ingredients (2.44.375–76). If this is not the author's invention, the scene may well indicate that the eighteenth-century Chinese cosmetic industry had a luxurious foundation powder with crushed flower seed as its base and with pearl, cinnabar, and gold and silver foils as ingredients—to achieve a perfect combination of lightness, whiteness, rosiness, and fragrance. Patience is amazed when she empties the contents of a lily bud onto her palm. The ingenious perfumer skillfully put the foundation powder inside the bud, letting the powder absorb the sweet scent of the plantain lily petals.

At the dinner party in the reception hall in Grandmother Jia's rear courtyard on the evening of the Lantern Festival, beside each dining table is an ornamental table on which sits a porcelain dish holding a miniature landscape made out of mossy rocks adorned with snow-white Xuan pebbles (*xuanshi* 宣石) (2.53.577). Xuan stone was named after its production area, ancient Xuanzhou in Anhui Province. Rich in quartz, the mineral was white. Landscape gardeners preferred it over the more common yellow sandstone and grayish limestone. Xuan stone was widely used in private gardens in Yangzhou, Jiangsu Province, to create a highlighted setting or even a mock snowscape.

In Lady Wang's side apartment, Dai-yu notices an incense-burning set (1.3.96), which consists of a four-legged *ding* 鼎 pot, a vase for holding a bronze spatula with a rectangular blade and a pair of bronze chopsticks, and an incense container. The same arrangement is found at the dinner party during the Lantern Festival in Grandmother Jia's courtyard (2.53.577). Cao Xueqin deliberately gives a grand name to the four-legged pot for burning incense in, "*King Wen Ding*" 文王鼎—literally the "bronze vessel made for King Wen of the Zhou dynasty (1045–256 BCE)." *Ding* pots, bronze ceremonial vessels with three or four legs, developed from earthenware cooking utensils. For more than a thousand years, especially between 1600 and 200 BCE, they were regarded as symbols of the political structure of the Golden Era in the history of China. King Wen, who around 1100–1050 BCE ruled the Zhou state in what today is Shaanxi Province, was respected for his benevolence and thus held as one of the few role models for kings and emperors in China. In the twelfth century, when the Huizong emperor had a catalog of ancient bronzes compiled, a King Wen *ding* was listed in the *Illustrated Catalogue of the Antiquities of the Xuanhe Period* (*xuanhe bogu tu* 宣和博古圖). It became one of the most famous *ding* pots. According to the archive in the Imperial Household Office, in 1754, when *The Story of the Stone* was being written, Tang Ying, the official responsible for the imperial porcelain production in the manufacture center, Jingdezhen, Jiangxi Province, presented the Qianlong emperor (r. 1735–96) with an incense-burning set made of porcelain, which included a King Wen

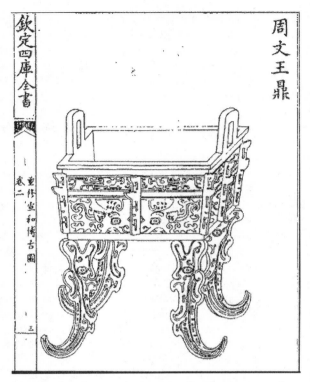

Fig. 27. A line drawing of a King Wen *ding*, from a compendium
compiled during 1107–23 of the Northern Song dynasty

*ding*, a bottle vase, and an incense container (fig. 27). Obviously Cao Xueqin
put such incense burners in the Jia mansions in order to emphasize the close
connection of the family with the imperial court and the Jia family's extravagant
way of life.

In the Jia household, chairs were not upholstered but covered with backs and
seat covers made of different fabrics, such as a silvery red brocade dotted with
flowers (1.3.96). Before upholstery was introduced to China, the Chinese used
removable lined or padded covers and cushions to make their wooden seats
more comfortable.

In Qin-shi's bedroom, the painting *Begonia's Spring Slumber*, attributed to
Tang Yin (1470–1524), is flanked by a pair of scrolls containing a poetic cou-
plet said to have been written by Qin Guan (1049–1100), whose style name,
Taixu, meaning "illusion," is the name Cao Xueqin uses for the dreamland (*taixu
huanjing* 太虚幻境) that Bao-yu enters in his nap on Qin-shi's bed (1.5.127).
Apparently the calligraphic scrolls are used to pave the way for Bao-yu's dream

Fig. 28. *Pavilion in Mountains*, by Nakanishi Koseki. School or style of Mi Fu. Painting, album leaf, ink on silk, signed. © Trustees of the British Museum

trip. Bao-yu gives Tan-chun, his half sister, a pair of calligraphic scrolls as a token of his brotherly love, and they were written by a famous calligrapher in the Chinese history, Yan Zhenqing (709–85) (2.37.214). Yan was also known as Yan Lugong, *lugong* meaning "duke of Lu" (40.292). But both the calligraphic couplet scrolls are an invention, because the practice of hanging such scrolls was not in existence in either the eighth or the eleventh century. With these impossible artifacts the author adorns the Jia residence with the aura of prestige.

The principal painting in Tan-chun's room is a hanging scroll with a landscape scene (2.40.292), supposedly by the scholar-of-ficial Mi Fu (1051–1107), alias Xiangyang, known for his unique pointillist manner of depicting mountain peaks in drifting mist characteristic of the landscape in southern China (fig. 28). But hardly any credible specimen of Mi Fu's painting has been handed down, and what we know about Mi Fu today is largely based on works by his imitators of later periods.

In the Land of Illusion, Bao-yu enters a room where, in addition to all the hallmarks of gracious living, he sees pieces of colored cotton wool on the windowsill beside spilled powder left by some woman who applied her makeup. Hawkes renders it as "some rouge-stained pieces of cotton-wool lying on the window-sill—evidently the aftermath of some fairy-woman's toilet" (1.5.138). But traditionally cotton wool was an amorous image in feminine space. When women did embroidery work, they had to cut the thread with their teeth when they finished a stitch. As a result, they often caught fabric between their teeth and needed to spit it out. As women often did their needlework near a window in order to take the advantage of the daylight, it was convenient for them to spit the wool out the window. Thus the sill became a natural place for the deposit of those bits that did not make it. Love poems made frequent reference to this image to indicate the presence of a young woman, who was either flirtatious and a good sport or melancholy and waiting to be wooed. Either type was a welcome

Fig. 29. A scene of *Heap of Honors* painted on a blue-and-white porcelain vase made in the Kangxi reign of the Qing dynasty. One can see a dais covered with white, elongated tablets behind the elderly couple. Collection of the Palace Museum, Beijing

target of the male gaze. The lyric writer Li Yu (937–78) vividly describes a flirting episode in "A Casket of Pearls":

> Leaning across the embroidered bed, she appeared so pampered,
> Indulgently chewing red silk-wool;
> With a smile, she spit it across to her dearest lover.
>
> (*Li Yu ciji* 9 [my trans.])[4]

This link between a bit of silk wool and amorous poetry gives Bao-yu a thrill when noticing the detail.

During the outing in the Taoist Temple of the Lunar Goddess, the Jia family party is entertained with popular episodes from famous plays. The full title of the second play is *Heap of Honors (Manchuang hu* 滿床笏) (2.29.80–81). The musical drama centers on the sixtieth birthday party of the great Tang general Guo Ziyi (697–781), which is attended by many of his colleagues as well as his seven sons and eight sons-in-law. All the guests hold high office and come with a court tablet, *hu* 笏. The *hu* was a narrow rectangular form made of different materials, such as jade, ivory, or bamboo, and high-ranking officials carried it when they had an audience with the emperor at court. It was both a status symbol and a tool for taking notes. At Guo's birthday party, there were so many court tablets carried to Guo's household that a large dais was set aside to accommodate them. "A heap of court tablets on the bed" became a set expression to mean the great prestige that a family enjoyed in imperial China: the heap indicated there was an unusually large number of high-ranking officials in the family and in its social circle (fig. 29). That is why Grandmother Jia feels she must show humility by saying, "It seems a bit conceited to have this second one performed," when she hears that *Heap of Honors* is among the plays chosen by the divine force (81). Since the play's theme was considered very lucky, it often appeared on furnishing and display vessels, such as a twelve-panel folding screen sent to Grandmother Jia from the Zhen family of Nanking (Nanjing) (3.71.409–10). On this large screen, the narrative scenes of Guo Ziyi's birthday party are woven into the silk fabric with the special *kesi* technique. Knowing the meaning of this story and of this design, readers will have a better understanding of the beginning of Zhen Shi-yin's commentary on the Won-Done Song, where he uses the same image to create a drastic contrast between the peak and the downfall of an aristocratic family: "Shabby huts and abandoned halls are once where the bed was heaped with official tablets" (my trans., for 1.1.64) 陋室空堂, 當年笏滿床 (1: 18).

*Stone* is a treasure house of objects reflecting the social and cultural life of eighteenth-century China, and a full appreciation of the novel calls for a matching repertoire of historical knowledge. Cao Xueqin drew on his life in an aristocratic family to fill his work with fascinating details, intermingling the fantastical and fictional with the real.

## NOTES

[1] See Xueping Zhong's essay and Tina Lu's first essay in this volume for more on this contemporary claim by Liu Xinwu.

[2] In the matching colors technique, porcelain painters outlined or half outlined designs in blue pigment directly onto the biscuit (leather-hard porcelain body). Then they

glazed and fired the generally small and delicate cups, bowls, and dishes. They filled in and added the outlined designs over the glaze with yellow, red, green, and aubergine enamel and refired them in a muffle kiln at a lower temperature. Potters first used this twice-fired technique in the early fifteenth century but perfected it in the Chenghua era.

[3] *Kesi*, which means "cut silk," derives from the visual illusion of cut threads that is created by distinct, unblended areas of color.

[4] Readers can find an English translation of the whole poem in Liu and Lo 300–01.

# IDENTITY AND INTERTEXTUALITY IN *THE STORY OF THE STONE*

## The Story of the Stone and Its Antecedents

### Mary Scott

Since *Story of the Stone* is often the first work of traditional Chinese literature modern readers encounter, they may be unable to assess both its indebtedness to its predecessors and its departures from precedent. Well-educated eighteenth-century Chinese readers, on the other hand, enjoyed *Stone*'s familiarity—its clever allusions to and appropriation of earlier texts—as well as its brilliant reinvention of the novel, by that time an established genre. Such readers must have noticed many specifically intertextual, generally structural, and broadly thematic features that *Stone* shared with earlier novels: vast length and scale, multiple symmetries, a capacious incorporation of materials from earlier works and other genres, interpenetrating mythic and mimetic registers, and a concern with issues of status and ritual correctness. At the same time, they must have been struck by *Stone*'s departures from the modes of earlier vernacular fiction, most of all in its density and range of textual reference and its self-questioning engagement with paradoxes of selfhood, consciousness, and the very nature of fiction.

By *novel*, I refer to a book-length work of Chinese fiction written between the fourteenth and twentieth centuries, not in the erudite classical language of the imperial civil service and elite literary forms but in a simpler literary language mixed with elements of the spoken vernacular. Many novels were just the kind of books that *Stone* derides as "historical romances," "erotic novels," and "boudoir romances," with formulaic plots, stereotyped characters, and lots of mediocre verse (1.1.49–50). Such books justified educated readers' disdain for vernacular fiction as a genre.

Among *Stone*'s most direct antecedents, however, were the novels that seventeenth-century readers and writers called the four marvelous books: *Three Kingdoms* (*San guo yan yi* 三國演義) (Luo Guanzhong) and *Outlaws of the Marsh* (*Shui hu zhuan* 水滸傳) (Shi Nai'an and Luo) were by that time extant in sixteenth-century versions more polished than those that circulated earlier, and *Journey to the West* (*Xi you ji* 西遊記) (Wu Cheng-en) and *Plum in the Golden Vase* (*Jin ping mei* 金瓶梅) appeared in the late sixteenth century.[1] At first glance these are very different from one another and from *Stone*, having in common only their great length, their large cast of characters, and story lines elaborated around a framework—or a scrap—of historical incident. The earliest, *Three Kingdoms*, was based on the standard historical account of the Three Kingdoms period (AD 220–80) and the dramatic and storytelling repertoire that emerged from it. *Outlaws of the Marsh* came from a skeletal account of an actual twelfth-century bandit uprising, greatly elaborated in the subsequent repertoire of plays about the Liangshan bandit heroes. *Journey to the West* was nominally based on historical records about Xuanzang, an eighth-century Buddhist priest who traveled from north China to India to seek Buddhist scriptures, but gods, demons, talking animals, and magical events predominate in it. In quite a different vein, *Plum in the Golden Vase* depicts the domestic life of an exceptionally dissipated family in exhaustive detail. The designation "four marvelous books" attests that readers saw these novels as constituting a genre or subgenre, and at least some readers took them seriously enough to provide them with an exegetical apparatus.

In particular, the seventeenth-century critic Jin Shengtan's (1608–61) critical prefaces and interlinear comments on his edition of *Outlaws of the Marsh* encouraged contemporary readers and writers to give fiction the kind of respectful close reading previously reserved for the Confucian classics, poetry, essays (including civil service examination essays), and histories. As Jin Shengtan put it, "In [*Outlaws of the Marsh*], each chapter has its principle of organization, so does each sentence and each word" (Rolston, *How to Read* 135). For Jin Shengtan, *Outlaws* was a model of prose composition, its narrative structure emerging from the interplay between repetition and contrast at every level of detail and from the assumption that every detail was subordinate to an overarching pattern. For example, in chapter 8 the hero Lin Chong buys a sword, while in chapter 12 the hero Yang Zhi is driven to sell his sword. The repetition of the sword points to the differences between these two episodes and allows readers to see these and subsequent characters not just as individuals but also as subtle variations on the loyal and righteous bandit-hero.

One example of Jin Shengtan's critical approach and terminology that resurfaces in *Journey to the West*, *Plum in the Golden Vase*, and eventually *Story of the Stone* is his attention to hot and cold details, which may highlight contrasting characterizations, mark shifts in a scene's emotional tone, or foreshadow an ebb or flow of fortune. In *Outlaws*, the famous scene of Lin Chong in the snow, in which he realizes that an erstwhile friend has betrayed him to his persecutors, ends with a fuel depot going up in flames and is followed by a scene in which Yang Zhi, in charge of overseeing the transit of valuables through bandit territory, is undone when the bandits lead the convoy into a trap by taking advantage of the porters' thirst and exhaustion on an extremely hot summer day. In these two episodes, the playing off of hot and cold settings frames both the similarities and the differences between Lin Chong and Yang Zhi. Both believe that they have been "forced to climb Liangshan [Mount Liang]," forced to join a bandit gang because corrupt petty officials drove them out of their rightful position in society, but this pairing of the two men allows the reader to make a moral calibration, comparing each against the other and assessing the other bandits whose decision to "climb Liangshan" is based on an even murkier mix of noble and base motives.

A similar interplay of hot and cold details occurs at many points in *Story of the Stone*, starting with the first chapter, when Zhen Shi-yin's dream during his nap on an endless hot summer afternoon is followed by his supper with Jia Yu-cun under the cold radiance of the mid-autumn moon, a scene that contrasts Zhen Shi-yin's warm generosity and comfortable obscurity with Jia Yu-cun's poverty, chilly self-preoccupation, and vaulting ambition. Ying-lian's abduction, the beginning of Zhen Shi-yin's reversal of fortune, takes place on the Feast of Lanterns, in the coldest season of the year. Even the naming of minor characters like Leng Zi-xing, "a touch of coldness appears" (1.3.72–83), suggests this patterning.

Jin Shengtan noted such details throughtout *Outlaws of the Marsh*, a relatively loose and episodic assembly of materials from earlier plays and stories about the Liangshan bandit gang. He went further, editing the text to enhance the patterns he found in it (Rolston, *How to Read 128*). For aficionados, commentary on fiction became a defining feature of the novel and an integral part of reading. Jin Shengtan's work encouraged other critics to write commentary, and more and more readers saw that vernacular fiction could be, like conventionally high-cultural forms, vivid and precisely descriptive, elegantly constructed, and philosophically serious. Jin Shengtan and his successors saw strong links between fiction and traditional historiography, in which dynasties rose, flourished, and fell in an endless cycle that reflected a universe that was immense and mysterious but ultimately governed by a knowable moral order.

Although *Three Kingdoms* antedates *Outlaws of the Marsh*, its most influential commentary edition comes slightly later than Jin Shengtan's version of *Outlaws*. Mao Zonggang (1632–1709?), a close contemporary of Jin's, found similar patterns of repetition, variation, and the subordination of parts to the whole in *Three Kingdoms*:

> One of the marvels of the *Romance of the Three Kingdoms* is the technique of using the guest as a foil for the host. For example, before the account of the three heroes who swear brotherhood in the peach garden

. . . comes an account of the three brothers who lead the revolt of the Yellow Turbans. The story of the oath in the peach garden is the host and that of the leaders of the Yellow Turbans is the guest.

(Rolston, *How to Read* 166)

The terms "host" and "guest," which come from the critical lexicon of Chinese landscape painting, refer to a binary comparison in which the relation between dominant and subordinate elements heightens the qualities of each, as a mountain in a painting's foreground is brought into focus by another in the background. More than a hundred years later, Red Inkstone would use the same terminology to describe aspects of the narrative structure of *Story of the Stone*, as for example in scenes in which Bao-chai is the dominant character and Dai-yu the secondary, or vice versa.

Jin Shengtan and other critics of fiction compared *Outlaws* and *Three Kingdoms* with Sima Qian's *Records of the Grand Historian* (*Shiji* 史記), a history of ancient China renowned for its dignified narrative language, for its depiction of historical characters by the gradual accumulation of details dispersed through the narrative and by contrast with other characters, and for its grand sense of how the actions of individuals shape larger historical processes. The nineteenth-century *Stone* commentator Zhang Xinzhi wrote:

The *I Ching* [*Yi Jing* 易經 "Classic of Changes"] has the following passage: "When a minister murders his lord or a son murders his father, this is not due to the events of a single morning and evening. The ultimate causes lie in the gradual development of circumstances." . . . The entire text of [*Story of the Stone*] is an elaboration of just this concept of gradual development.

(Rolston, *How to Read* 326; trans. of *I Ching* quotation in Wilhelm 393)

For many critics and ordinary readers during the past seven centuries, the best vernacular novels surpassed all other forms in their depiction of the cumulative consequences of individual actions over time. These novels explored some of the same philosophical questions that had concerned poets, historians, and philosophers of earlier times: the nature of fate, the relation between the actions of individuals and the larger patterns of history, the demands of family and friendship, the nature of the self, the proper means and ends of self-cultivation, and the conflict between duty and desire. The novel's great length allowed it to explore these questions in a context of changes almost as minute and imperceptible as those of real time. This is why some commentators of fiction turned to the hexagram patterns of the *Classic of Changes* to elucidate the slow, subtle shifts in configurations of character and incident in long works.

Red Inkstone, who clearly read Jin Shengtan's *Outlaws* commentary and commentary versions of the other "marvelous books," including Zhang Zhupo's

commentary on *Plum in the Golden Vase* and various seventeenth-century commentaries on *Journey to the West*, often note places where *Stone* borrows an
incident or develops a theme from them. A century later, Zhang Xinzhi made
the same point: "The [*Story of the Stone*] grows out of [*The Journey to the
West*], takes a trail blazed by [*Plum in the Golden Vase*], and takes its spirit from
[*Outlaws of the Marsh*]" (Rolston, *How to Read* 327). Even without the help
of a commentator, these borrowings are easy to see. *Outlaws of the Marsh*, like
*Stone* and *Journey to the West*, begins with a mythical stone, a magical stone
tablet that, when it is unearthed and opened, releases 108 malign stars that
take human form as the members of the Liangshan bandit gang. Chapter 18 in
*Journey to the West*, in which the Monkey King rescues a maiden from a forced
marriage to a pig demon, is a parodic retelling of an episode from *Outlaws of
the Marsh* in which Sagacious Lu rescues a young girl from a forced marriage
to a bandit.

One of the clearest textual borrowings is the account of the Stone's origins
(1.1.47–48), which closely resembles the description of the birth of the Monkey
King in the first chapter of *Journey to the West*:

> There was on top of that very mountain an immortal stone, which mea-
> sured thirty-six feet and five inches in height and twenty-four feet in cir-
> cumference. The height of thirty-six feet and five inches corresponded to
> the three hundred and sixty-five cyclical degrees, while the circumference
> of twenty-four feet corresponded to the twenty-four solar terms of the
> calendar. On the stone were also nine perforations and eight holes, which
> corresponded to the Palaces of the Nine Constellations and the Eight
> Trigrams. Though it lacked the shade of trees on all sides, it was set off
> by epidendrums on the left and right. Since the creation of the world, it
> had been nourished for a long period by the seeds of Heaven and Earth
> and by the essences of the sun and the moon, until, quickened by divine
> inspiration, it became pregnant with a divine embryo. One day, it split
> open, giving birth to a stone egg about the size of a playing ball. Exposed
> to the wind, it was transformed into a stone monkey endowed with fully
> developed features and limbs. Having learned at once to climb and run,
> this monkey also bowed to the four quarters, while two beams of golden
> light flashed from his eyes to reach even the Palace of the Pole Star.
>
> (Wu Cheng-en, *Journey* 1.1.68)

In *Journey to the West*, this image of a stone bursting with power and possibility is developed as an emblem of the protagonist's potential for self-realization,
the Buddhist category of mind. *Tower of Myriad Mirrors* (*Xiyou bu* 西游补),
*Journey*'s brief and brilliant seventeenth-century sequel, further develops the
idea of passionate emotion and attachment (*qing* 情) as both a means and a
barrier to enlightenment, linking the stone with the mirror, which has ancient

origins in China as a metaphor for the mind—both the enlightened, reflective mind and the dazzled, deluded mind. In *Story of the Stone* as in *Journey to the West* and *Tower of Myriad Mirrors*, the stone is identified with mind, with consciousness itself. It exists in a vast, orderly space-time that is not just knowable by human consciousness but also coextensive with it. The mirror as a figure for the egoless mind that merely reflects what passes before it has a textual history reaching back at least to the exchange of poems in the eighth-century Zen Buddhist text *Platform Sutra of the Sixth Patriarch* (*Liuzu tanjing* 六祖壇經), a classic account of the experience of enlightenment with echoes in both *Journey to the West* and *Story of the Stone* (Yampolsky 130). The mind-mirror that can be either a precious jade or a clouded, unpolished stone is one of the many images of doubleness that inform *Story of the Stone*.

Zen Buddhism has a long tradition of comparing the mind to a playful, inquisitive, and easily distracted monkey. Bao-yu is explicitly compared to a monkey at several points in *Story of the Stone*, and his courtyard dwelling in Prospect Garden, with its prominent mirror and extravagant collection of curiosities, recalls the eponymous novel's Tower of Myriad Mirrors in which the Mind Monkey is imprisoned. The conception of Bao-yu as a character owes a good deal to both *Journey's* and *Tower's* model of the Monkey King, with his impulsive nature, egoism, and undisciplined, restless intelligence. Sun Wukong, "monkey awakened to vacuity," is on a spiritual journey, depicted in *Journey* as an expedition from Chang'an to India, across immense heavenly and earthly spaces, to procure Buddhist scriptures. Jia Bao-yu's spiritual journey is as protean and peripatetic as the Stone itself, but instead of extending itself through space as the Monkey King's journey does, it folds in on itself as the labyrinthine Prospect Garden, itself a mirror of the fairy Disenchantment's garden, which provides both the site and the means for Bao-yu's awakening from desire and worldly illusions.

The other great sixteenth-century "marvelous book," *Plum in the Golden Vase*, launched a new stage in the long novel's development, in which the focus shifted from larger-than-life historical and mythological figures toward ordinary domestic life. *Plum's* intricately detailed fictional world is woven in a frame that was originally one of the tales in *Outlaws of the Marsh*: Pan Jin-lian's attempted seduction of her brother-in-law, the Liangshan bandit Wu Song; her murder of her husband, Wu Da-lang, in order to marry her lover, Ximen Qing; and Wu Song's eventual murder of Pan Jin-lian. Most of *Plum*, however, takes place in the home and garden of a numerous and well-to-do family, where the passionate excesses of Ximen Qing, the master, and the jealous competition among his wives eventually lead to the family's downfall. In both novels, the garden's splendor and decay mark the family's prosperity and decline. Such garden settings were common in romantic plays and in the boudoir romances that *Stone* derides, but the degree to which the Ximen garden is simultaneously richly mimetic and charged with symbolic power is unparalleled in Chinese literature—until Prospect Garden.

Like the garden of the Jias, Ximen Qing's lust- and intrigue-ridden garden is a microcosm of the empire, and its disorder reflects the corruption that permeates society. In both novels, society's distemper is portrayed through the neglect of rituals, through insubordinate or inappropriately favored servants, and through transgressions against the propriety of family relationships. Disorder in family and social relationships is often portrayed through the device of intimate objects — a fan, a tiny shoe, a pearl, a purse embroidered with an erotic picture — lost or stolen in the garden by one character to be discovered by another, setting in motion a series of romantic trysts kept or discovered, and concomitant accusations, punishments, and attempts at blackmail.

Note the close resemblance between the funeral of Qin-shi (Qin Ke-qing) (*Stone*, chs. 14–15) and the funeral of Li Ping-er (*Plum*, chs. 62–63; see Plaks, *Four Masterworks* 55–182). Red Inkstone specifically point out that *Plum* was the model here for *Stone*. In both novels, an inappropriately grand funeral for a woman with a junior position in the household's rank order makes an open secret of an illicit sexual relationship between that woman and an elder male of the family. In *Plum*, Ximen Qing contrives his sworn brother's death and then takes Li Ping-er, his brother's widow, as his sixth wife; in *Stone*, Jia Zhen carries on an affair with his daughter-in law, Qin-shi, that ends with her illness and death. At both funerals, the man's inordinate grief as well as his immoderate expenditure on lavish coffin boards and purchase of official rank for the deceased suggest that this transgressive relationship is a trope for disruptions of family hierarchy and correct ritual order in general. In *Stone*, this reading is supported by the poem on Qin-shi in the fairy's register (1.5.135) and by Red Inkstone's comments on *Stone*'s account of Qin-shi's death from illness, which suggest that the death was originally depicted as a suicide committed out of shame at the affair's discovery.

*Plum*'s use of doubled characters also influenced *Stone*. Ximen Qing's family and their neighbors and rivals, the Qiaos, whose surname means "false," foreshadow *Stone*'s mutually reflecting stories of the Jia ("illusory") family and their counterparts, the Zhen ("real") family, who in an extended joke about their non-fictionality appear in the novel only in secondhand accounts instead of live, onstage. Dai-yu and Bao-chai, a complementary pair of young women, are blended together in Bao-yu's dream of ideal love (ch. 5) as the fairy Disenchantment's little sister Two-in-One, whose counterpart in Bao-yu's waking life is Qin-shi. This multiple doubling of the women in Bao-yu's life (e.g., Aroma and Skybright are shadows of Bao-chai and Dai-yu, respectively) owes a good deal to Zhang Zhupo's explication of the doubling of female characters Pan Jin-lian and Li Ping-er in his notes on *Plum*. In both novels, the two most important women characters, taken together, are emblematic of the limitless nature of male desire. As Wai-yee Li has pointed out, the elusive, ambiguous, divine woman as both the object of desire and the representation of the endlessly receding goal of enlightenment has deep roots in the classical poetic tradition, which considerably antedates this motif's appearance in fiction (*Enchantment* 3–46).

*Plum in the Golden Vase* emerged from a prosperous social world infatuated with the theater and preoccupied with the competing claims of individual feeling and the constraints of conventional morality. In *Plum*, unlike *Outlaws* and *Three Kingdoms*, we find depictions of play performances and direct quotations from contemporary plays and songs, which often function as an ironic commentary on the novel's plot and characters (Hanan). Like *Plum*, *Story of the Stone* is riddled with references to plays and often quotes directly from them, but, unlike *Plum*, *Stone*'s characters are aware to some degree of those texts' significance in their own lives.

Members of the Jia family visit a Taoist monastery where plays are performed for their entertainment and for the entertainment of the gods (2.29.80). The plays, chosen randomly from slips of paper in a pot, are *The White Serpent* (*Baishe ji* 白蛇記), a play about the heroic founding emperor of the Han dynasty; *A Heap of Honors* (*Manchuang hu* 滿床笏), an auspicious play about a famous general whose family has been distinguished by high rank and many honors; and *The South Branch* (*Nanke meng* 南柯夢), a story about a man who wins fame, official position, and love, only to awake and realize that it was all a dream. Grandmother Jia is pleased at the first two, but when she falls silent after the third, readers glimpse the Jia family's past, present, and future in the sequence of play titles.

Nearly all the plays mentioned in *Stone* were familiar to eighteenth-century Chinese audiences, and favorite scenes from most of them were included in *Zhui bai qiu* 綴白裘 ("White Embroidered Fur Robe"), a well-known eighteenth-century dramatic anthology. Some scholars point to the fairy Disenchantment's dramatic song suites (1.5) as supporting evidence for Red Inkstone's comment that *Stone* itself was originally imagined as a play rather than as a novel. The novel in any case contains hundreds of references to and quotations from various kinds of plays, including lively, humorous genre pieces, elegant romantic dramas, and the conventionally auspicious plays performed at birthdays and other celebrations. Play references feature commonly in riddles and other verbal games in the text, and like these other jeux d'esprit, they function as little mirrors scattered through the text that simultaneously reflect both their immediate context and larger patterns of signification in the novel.

The Jias love to watch plays performed by their own troupe of actors. Many of *Stone*'s characters are devoted and knowledgeable playgoers, some are actors, and some are conceived according to the roles of the traditional theater: Bao-yu is a young scholar (*sheng* 生); Bao-chai, Dai-yu, and all the young women are female romantic leads (*dan* 旦); Wang Xi-feng is a *hua dan* 花旦 (a beautiful, high-spirited, often somewhat immodest young woman); Grandmother Jia is an old *dan* (a respectable older lady); and Xue Pan is a clown (*chou* 丑). Chapters are constructed around stock dramatic scenes or types: Chapter 9, for example, in which Tealeaf sets off a brawl in the Jia family schoolroom, is a variation on the classic big-commotion scene (*da nao* 大鬧) common to many plays, and the portrait of Doctor Zhang, who diagnoses Qin-shi's illness in chapter 10, is a version of a standard dramatic set piece featuring a doctor who recites an arcane-sounding medical prescription full of double entendres.

Another common play device that migrated from theater to fiction is the plot that turns on the fate of a talismanic object like a fan, handkerchief, or other love token — a device reflected in such famous play titles as *The Precious Sword* 寶靈刀, *The Peach-Blossom Fan* 桃花扇, and *The Wooden Hairpin* 荊釵記. (Such talismans are important in *Plum* as well.) Bao-yu's jade is matched at first with Bao-chai's golden lock-amulet, a pairing that is then briefly brought into question by a competing pair of tokens: the golden kylin Bao-yu is given at the Taoist temple and Shi Xiang-yun's smaller golden kylin (2.29.81). Bao-yu's jade, the quintessential significant object, is exhibited as a wonder, clouded over, nearly destroyed, lost, found, and finally returned to its origins, providing an opportunity at each turn of the tale to give new insight into Bao-yu's relations with other characters and his developing (though at the end of the novel still imperfect) understanding of himself.

Plays that focus on a young man who becomes a monk to embark on a quest for enlightenment were a subgenre particularly relevant to *Stone* (Q. Li 44–46). A pivotal quotation from a play is the aria "Zhishen at the Monastery Gate" (*Lu Zhishen zuinao wutaishan* 魯智深醉鬧五台山) (1.22.435), based on an episode in *Outlaws of the Marsh*, in which Lu Zhishen, an impetuous and often violent righter of wrongs done to others, takes refuge — much against his own inclinations — in a community of monks who are horrified by his heedlessly drunken, meat-eating disregard of their order's rules. Paradoxically, he becomes an enlightened monk by the end of his life, illustrating the Buddhist insight that those who experience the full extremes of human passions may achieve enlightenment more readily than those who follow a more conventional path to it.

This spiritual transformation through intense life experience makes Lu Zhishen a prototype for Jia Bao-yu, different as the two characters may seem at first. Lu Zhishen's aria clearly foreshadows Bao-yu's eventual departure from his family:

> Naked and friendless through the world to roam.
> I ask no goods, no gear to take away,
> Only straw sandals and a broken bowl,
> To beg from place to place as best I may.   (1.22.435)

> 沒緣法, 轉眼分離乍. 赤條條, 來去無牽掛, 那裡討, 煙蓑雨笠卷單行？
> 一任俺, 芒鞋破砵隨緣化.
> (1: 294)

The quotation also moves the action forward by rounding out the characterizations of Bao-yu, Bao-chai, and Dai-yu. The occasion is Bao-chai's fifteenth birthday, and Bao-chai — who has just demonstrated her diplomatic skills by requesting several plays that she knows Grandmother Jia will enjoy—chooses this one. At first Bao-yu expresses scorn for "noisy plays" (435), as many *Outlaws of the Marsh* plays were. Bao-chai, who is knowledgeable to the point of pedantry on many topics, explains the musical form, recites the aria for him, and brings him around to appreciating the beauty of its lyrics and music. Bao-yu reveals himself as an enthusiastic but hasty and volatile judge, while Bao-chai is calm, scholarly, superior, older-sisterish.

As usually happens in scenes involving Bao-yu and either of his two favorite cousins, Dai-yu's response is quite different from Bao-chai's. Having already rebuffed Bao-yu's cheerful efforts to please her with his choice of plays, Dai-yu takes offense when Xi-feng and Xiang-yun point out her resemblance to one of the little actresses. She takes out her anger on Bao-yu, who is so hurt that he writes imitations of passages from the Taoist philosopher Zhuangzi and the Zen classic *The Platform Sutra*, in which he renounces Dai-yu, Bao-chai, and womankind in general. When Bao-chai and Dai-yu discover his scribblings and, amused, quiz him on them, he is convinced that they are closer to enlightenment and more insightful than he will ever be—a wonderfully ironic foreshadowing of the fact that it is he, not they, who will renounce the world and embark on a mendicant's life.

The first major scene in the following chapter is organized around Bao-yu and Dai-yu's flirtatious exchange of quotations from *The Western Chamber* 西廂記, a fourteenth-century play that is one of the most eloquent evocations of romantic love in the Chinese tradition, about a pair of young lovers who enter a passionate relationship without their parents' knowledge. In testimony to how much passionate love troubled this society, in which female chastity and deference to elders were cardinal virtues, *The Western Chamber* has a long history of being both celebrated and condemned. Jin Shengtan listed it along with *Outlaws of the Marsh* as one of the "six works of genius" (Rolston, *How to Read* 125), but that Bao-yu feels he must hide his copy from his parents and cousins shows that it was generally seen as unsuitable for young readers.

This scene shows Bao-yu and Dai-yu in the springtime of young love, just after Bao-yu and his sisters and cousins have moved into Prospect Garden. In its turn, this chapter of *Story of the Stone*—known in its many theatrical versions as "Dai-yu Buries the Flowers"—has become a famous romantic scene in Chinese literature. As if to underline the double meaning of the word *chun* 春 ("springtime" but also a euphemism for erotic love), Bao-yu has smuggled several racy novels and plays into the garden. These set the tone for Bao-yu and Dai-yu's conversation, in which he identifies himself and Dai-yu with Scholar Zhang and Cui Ying-ying (Oriole), the famous lovers of *The Western Chamber*.[2]

After Bao-yu is summoned elsewhere, the chapter concludes with a scene in which Dai-yu overhears lines from an aria from *Peony Pavilion* 牡丹亭. Written in the latter part of the sixteenth century, *Peony Pavilion* is the best known of the late-sixteenth-century playwright Tang Xianzu's four dream plays, all of them concerned with the power of passion and with illusion. Dai-yu's identifica-

tion with the romantic heroine of *Peony Pavilion*, Du Li-niang, who dies of love
for Liu Meng-mei, a handsome young man she knows only through his portrait,
and who then is restored to life through the power of their love, marks Dai-yu
as a person who will be undone by an excess of feeling. She hears premonitions
of her own early death in the lines:

> Because for you, my flowerlike fair,
> The swift years like the waters flow. . . .    (1.23.466)

則為你如花美眷. . . .
似水流年    (1: 316)

This self-identification seems sentimental, almost maudlin, but in chapter 98
Dai-yu does in fact die young and full of grief and longing, and, unlike Du Li-
niang, she does not come back to life to consummate her love. Dai-yu is one of
many characters in vernacular fiction who embody extreme desire and longing.
As Martin Huang (*Desire*) and others have pointed out, the problem of the
degree to which an individual's emotion should be subject to the constraints
of family duty and social morality increasingly became the focus of fiction, and
indeed almost came to define fiction, from the late sixteenth century on.

Chapters 23 and 98 form a symmetrical pair: the first opens the idyll of garden life, and the second brings the idyll to its inevitable close. One of the lines
from *Peony Pavilion* in chapter 23 points to chapter 98:

> Here multiflorate splendour blooms forlorn
> Midst broken fountains, mouldering walls. . . .    (466)

原來是 姹紫嫣紅開遍,
似這般, 都付與斷井頹垣.    (316)

The long transition from chapter 23 to chapter 98 is marked by recurrent
references to *The Western Chamber* and *Peony Pavilion*. These are a counter-
point to Dai-yu and Bao-yu's tempestuous encounters and to Dai-yu's persistent self-identification with both Cui Ying-ying and Du Li-niang despite the
mounting evidence that because of her emotional and physical fragility the family elders are less and less inclined to marry her to Bao-yu. References to *The
Western Chamber* and *Peony Pavilion* also figure in the portrayal of Dai-yu and
Bao-chai's growing friendship, culminating in chapter 42, when Bao-chai gently
reproves Dai-yu for revealing her knowledge of these unladylike texts in her
poems and Dai-yu humbly accepts the reproof.

*Stone*'s ending can even be understood as an ironic inversion of the dramatic "grand reunion" (*da tuanyuan* 大團圓), the conventional happy ending
in romantic comedy that, by reuniting the main characters and resolving the
complications of the story, made any transgressive dimensions in the play's plot

conform to the conventional norms of marriage. In the novel, the "grand reunion" comes in the middle rather than at the end, and the second half of the narrative is marked by the steady decline of the family's wealth, happiness, and standing in the world. The gathering of characters in the Roster of Love originally planned as *Stone*'s conclusion would have been a version of the "grand reunion," but since many of the characters are dead, scattered, unhappily married, or ruined by that point, the scene would have functioned more as an elegy than as a resolution.

In modern Chinese, vernacular novels are usually called "chapter novels" (*zhanghui xiaoshuo* 章回小說), because they are organized in chapters that simulate sessions of oral storytelling. These chapters often have titles in the form of roughly parallel couplets and begin with a poem and the storyteller's characteristic opening, "The story is told that. . . ." Chapters generally end, as *Stone*'s chapter 1 does, on a calculated note of suspense: "If you wish to know what further calamity this portended, you will have to read the following chapter" (1.1.66). Narrator's asides — often poems — and formulaic ways of handling narrative transitions mark the vernacular novelist's self-conscious adoption of the persona of a teahouse storyteller as narrator, which, as Andrew Plaks (*Four Masterworks*) and others have noted, allows for ironic triangulations among the narrator, the reader, and the characters, in which the narrator's often moralistic summations of events need not be taken as the last word.

*Story of the Stone* adapts this set of conventions freely, using storytellers' tags at times but more sparingly and in a more fluid and ironic way than earlier fiction does. The omniscient, emotionally detached teahouse narrator is transformed in *Stone* to a narrator, the Stone itself, who acknowledges the limits of what a narrator can know. The reader does not find out, for example, exactly how Bao-yu "settles accounts" with Qin Zhong (1.15.300), because Wang Xi-feng, fearing that Bao-yu's jade will be stolen, has taken it for safekeeping under her pillow. The Stone, not having witnessed the night's events, declines to speculate.

Vernacular novels typically have a round or square number of chapters, sometimes as few as ten or sixteen, but the marvelous books have a hundred chapters (like *Journey to the West* and *Plum in the Golden Vase*), 110 (some versions of *Outlaws*), or 120 (like *Three Kingdoms* and other versions of *Outlaws*). In its first published version, *Story of the Stone* had 120 chapters, which suggests that the editors of the unfinished eighty-chapter manuscript versions were guided not just by whatever fragmentary original draft they may have had but by the example of the marvelous books. The editors also followed a general model of narrative balancing through symmetry, the principles of which were articulated with particular clarity in Zhang Zhupo's commentary on *Plum in the Golden Vase*, especially the principle of karmic retribution that suffuses Chinese traditional narratives of all kinds.[3]

The relative banality of the balancing episodes in the last forty chapters of *Stone*, when the last forty are compared with the first eighty, shows that the editors worked competently but not always brilliantly to meet a set of generic expectations. Note the obvious symmetry in chapter 120's methodical resolution of the stories of Jia Yu-cun, Zhen Shi-yin, Ying-lian, and the Stone from chapter 1. Another example is the balanced placement of Bao-yu's initial dream visit to the Land of Illusion (ch. 5), in which he finds the fairy Disenchantment's registers incomprehensible, against his later dream visit to what now appears to him as the Domain of Truth in which all is revealed (ch. 116). Similarly, Qin-shi's inordinately grand funeral (chs. 14–15) is placed close to the beginning of the book and just before the construction of Prospect Garden, while Grandmother Jia's ritually inadequate and badly managed funeral (ch. 110) appears close to the end of the book and not long after the garden's fall into haunted ruin. Such symmetries imply a notional center, which Plaks (*Archetype*) and others locate in the joyous winter scenes of Prospect Garden and the celebration of the New Year (chs. 53 and 54), before marriage, misfortune, scandal, and death begin to thin the garden dwellers' numbers.

Following traditional fiction commentators, Plaks has articulated a reading of *Stone* based on the symmetries, correspondences, and complementarities that register at every turn of the narrative. Among the complementarities that shape particular scenes in the novel, he notes movement and stillness; union and separation; fastidious purity and earthy vulgarity, as for example in the scenes that show the nun Adamantina and the old country woman Granny Liu (*Archetype* 55 and appendix 2). Other complementarities are heat and cold, including both the literal heat and cold of the seasons and the waxing and waning of worldly favor and fortune; inside and outside, as in the interspersing of garden scenes with scenes set in the world outside; or movement and stillness, as when the tumultuous schoolroom scene in chapter 9 is followed by a quietly resentful conversation between Jia Huang and his mother and whispered concerns about Qin-shi's illness in chapter 10. The length of such a list reminds us to consider any detail or scene in *Story of the Stone* as part of an overall pattern of repetition and variation.

For readers today, the Chinese vernacular novel is remarkable for its integration of mythic and mimetic narrative registers. *Three Kingdoms*, for example, invokes a cosmic context for human history in the wizardry of the loyal prime minister Zhuge Liang, and *Journey to the West* moves freely between a geographically plausible journey from the city of Chang'an to the holy places of India and the fantastic spaces of heaven. *Stone*'s frame tale — Nü-wa's rejection of the Stone as she repairs the vault of heaven, the Stone's fated encounter with the Crimson Pearl Flower, its sojourn in the world under the auspices of the lame Buddhist and scabby Taoist, and Vanitas's redaction of the chronicle inscribed on the Stone — is the most elaborated example of this feature, but *Outlaws of the Marsh* is also framed by a story about a stone, in this case a stone tablet that releases malign bandit star-spirits to wreak havoc on the human world.

In *Story of the Stone*, the interpenetration of the quotidian and the fantastic suggests that the distinction between truth and illusion is subjective and relative. This idea goes back to the philosopher Zhuangzi's account of awakening from a dream about a butterfly, uncertain whether he dreamed of the butterfly or the butterfly dreamed of him (Watson, *Chuang-tzu* 49). Variations on the theme that pleasure, honors, and riches are but a passing dream recur in many early classical language stories, which were in turn the inspiration for such great dramatic works as the late-sixteenth-century playwright Tang Xianzu's four dream plays. The theme also finds expression in the *Heart Sutra*'s 心經 assertion that the essential nature of phenomenal experience is emptiness, an insight that finds expression in the great vernacular novels' depiction of the tendency in all human endeavors and institutions, however glorious and powerful, to decline and disappear with passing time. The *Heart Sutra* is quoted in full in chapter 19 of *Journey to the West*, but it is also a subtext in *Three Kingdoms*, *Outlaws of the Marsh*, and especially *Plum in the Golden Vase* and *Story of the Stone*. In both *Plum* and *Stone*, a richly colored, almost painfully tangible account of a family's domestic life and of the web of social connections that link the family to imperial power and bureaucratic authority gives way in the end to images of catastrophe, erasure, and the blank whiteness of mourning and death. Worldly phenomena fade into nothingness, as the text acknowledges its own fictionality by coming to an end.

*Stone* is a canonical text in the presently ordained Chinese literary pantheon, yet it is also countercanon, because its recontextualization of existing texts—from Confucian, Buddhist, and Taoist philosophical texts to popular opera and storytelling—situates the reader in an implicit polemic between orthodoxy and critique. When Bao-yu complains that he is bored by the orthodox classic Mencius, for example, we must locate ourselves somewhere between our sympathy for a young boy's short attention span and boredom with moral abstractions and the cultural and parental imperative to study a text required for the civil service examinations. Similarly, when Bao-chai chastises Dai-yu for immodestly revealing her familiarity with the romantic play *The Western Chamber*, we situate ourselves somewhere between Bao-chai's austere Confucian standards for female behavior and Dai-yu's romantic identification with the play's heroine.

The long vernacular novel's history began to be written during the New Culture movement of the early twentieth century as part of a larger project of vernacularizing the written language to accommodate the aspirations of the new Chinese nation-state and locating in the great works of Chinese vernacular fiction an indigenous counterpart to the European realist novel. At first, both Chinese and Western scholars often emphasized the social-historical and auto-biographical dimensions of vernacular fiction and minimized its mythic and fantastic qualities as blemishes on an otherwise exemplary realism. They also dismissed the traditional fiction critics' emphasis on formal rhetoric, largely because of its associations with the examination essay form, the much criticized eight-legged essay, which twentieth-century political reformers denounced as a straitjacket for many generations of Chinese intellectuals. Traditional fiction critics expressed their understanding of texts in the language of traditional religious and social values, especially the filial piety and obedience that were the hallmarks of Confucian teaching and the Buddhism quietism and fatalism that, in the reformers' view, were antithetical to their hopes of transforming Chinese society.

More recent critics have tried to read traditional vernacular literature on its own terms, guided by the comments of earlier generations of Chinese readers and the particulars of Chinese cultural history rather than by the history of narrative in the West. No single reading of these complex texts can ever be sufficient, but our understanding of them can be greatly enriched by exploring the differences between the realist readings and the traditional critics' readings as well as by the realization that each generation of readers will read them anew.

## NOTES

[1] *Outlaws of the Marsh* has also been known by the English titles *Water Margin* and *All Men Are Brothers. Journey to the West* is also known as *Monkey. Plum in the Golden Vase* is also known as *The Golden Lotus*.

[2] For more on these plays in *Stone*, see Ling Hon Lam's essay in this volume.

[3] For more on retribution, see Andrew Schonebaum's essay in this volume.

# Dreams, Subjectivity, and Identity in *Stone*

## *Tina Lu*

Imagine a reader at the end of the eighteenth century picking up a printed volume of *The Dream of the Red Chamber*. What did she think that title meant? She certainly did not think it referred to a specific dream, even though dreams play an obvious and important role in the novel's plot—especially in chapter 5, when Bao-yu visits the Land of Illusion and the fairy Disenchantment, and in chapter 56, when he dreams of his double, another boy named Bao-yu. Although dreams figure importantly in traditional Chinese literature, the sheer number and richness of them in the novel are remarkable.

Even a comparatively minor dream, like that in chapter 98, richly rewards close reading. Having just learned of Dai-yu's death, Bao-yu collapses into a faint and encounters a man who sends him back to life in a very unusual way: "the man took a stone from within his sleeve and threw it at Bao-yu's chest" (4.98.373) 袖中取出一石, 向寶玉心口擲來 (2: 1350). Is this dream a special conduit to the Nether World, where Dai-yu has gone? Or does it reflect some special connection between the cousins that has now been severed by her death? Bao-yu's dream echoes an earlier dream of Dai-yu's, in which Bao-yu responds to her demand for his heart by opening his chest and literally removing his heart. Or is the realm of dream not supernatural at all but simply psychological, foreshadowing Sigmund Freud's idea that dream expresses what can find no voice in waking? The heart is of flesh, but Bao-yu's essence is stone, and the contrast between stone and flesh has much the same connotation in Chinese as in English. Whether Bao-yu is being restored to himself or leaving some human nature behind remains ambiguous, but the dream in chapter 98 expresses something of that dynamic.

Each of these readings coheres, making it impossible to reduce dream either to supernatural or to psychological. In chapter 5, Bao-yu is introduced to sexuality by Disenchantment's sister Two-in-One, who combines the physical charms of Dai-yu and Bao-chai but bears Qin-shi's childhood name. Two-in-One is part of a magical world but also an expression of Bao-yu's subconscious desires and fears. Here and elsewhere, there is no way to reduce dream either to supernatural or to psychological.

To an eighteenth-century reader, dream possessed a broad range of meaning, extending beyond literal dream to involve subjectivity and identity. These three concepts are inseparable not just in the novel but also in the culture as a whole.

Even the waking portions of the novel have a dream-like feel. Although some aspects of everyday life with the Jias are treated with precise and scrupulous care, details are often withheld. Alone among all the plays and fiction of its day, *The Story of the Stone* never situates itself in either time or space, an omission that would have been glaringly obvious to a contemporary reader. The Jia family lives neither in Beijing nor in Nanjing but in some unearthly, dreamy amalgam of the two capitals. In summer their surroundings are lush and green, just as we would expect for Nanjing, but the novel's winter scenes are filled with mention of snow and cold weather paraphernalia, the furs, snow capes, and portable braziers that were necessary in Beijing's harsh climate. We never find out the name of the emperor, or his dynasty, and because of that vagueness, we do not even know the Jias' ethnicity. Although they engage in some Manchu practices—they eat dairy products, the boys practice archery, the girls and boys of the family are raised together—the Jias inhabit some nebulous space between Manchu and Han.

We never even have a clear sense of how old the cousins are for most of the novel: they are something like children, in the adults' treatment of them, but at the same time they are of marriageable age. Bao-yu and Dai-yu are allowed many of the familiarities of children, even as they possess the sensibilities of adults. In short, they are adolescents, but that category did not exist in premodern China, where teenagers would simply have been considered marriageable adults. Even if there were some small liminal space between physical maturity and marriage, it certainly would not have lasted for years and years. Whatever other purposes such indeterminacy serves—to rise above politics by not defining the Jias' ethnicity, to further narrative by not specifying the characters' ages—it also contributes to the novel's oneiric feel.

In the mid–eighteenth century, the dream of the novel's alternative title would have intimated a sense of nostalgia. The great Ming dynasty's collapse in 1644, more than a century before *Stone* was written, a fall first to disorganized bandits and then to the Manchus of the far northeast, had seemed almost inconceivable, and a profound reevaluation of virtually every facet of Ming life ensued. Everyone agreed that with the fall of the dynasty the world as they knew it had ended, replaced by something entirely different.

Many people, among them some of the most influential writers of the day, felt deep nostalgia about the passing of the old world, which was strongly associated with a splendor that was sensual, unsustainable, and even slightly louche. Perhaps the single greatest focus of yearning for that bygone past was the pleasure quarters of the great cities of Jiangnan (especially Suzhou, Hangzhou, and Yangzhou, all located on the lower Yangzi delta), where beautiful courtesans entertained brilliant men of the elite in poetry games and conversations about erudite subjects. These demimondaines were among the most educated women of their age, but at the same time they were tragic beauties, to be pitied just as much as they were admired, since of course their profession placed them outside any family network. After the fall of the Ming dynasty, pleasure quarters were never again so central; even though the sex trade returned, courtesans distinguished by education and talent never reappeared. Elite culture itself seemed to undergo a transformation, into something much more morally earnest and sincere—even sanctimonious—about Confucian values. To many, the splendors of the past had been replaced by a diminished present that might be more upright but was certainly dingier.

Memories of the Ming world were often referred to as dreams, to demonstrate their existence only in the mind. The long life of the seventeenth-century memoirist Zhang Dai was broken in two by the dynasty's fall: the first half rich and splendid, filled with every material and sensual pleasure, the second marked by suffering and poverty. Both his volumes of meticulously detailed memories featured "dream" in their titles: *Dream Reminiscences of Taoan* (*Taoan mengyi* 陶庵夢憶) and *Dream Searching for West Lake* (*Xihu mengxun* 西湖夢尋).[1]

Cao Xueqin, whose family became wealthy because of its connections to the Kangxi emperor, was not racked with nostalgia for the previous dynasty. But nineteenth-century readers did not know who he was, and for many of them the novel as a whole spoke to Ming nostalgia. These readers even saw a hint in the novel's obsession with red: Zhu, the surname of the Ming royal house, means "carmine."

The very idea of dream, therefore, was infused with connotations of nostalgia. Even though *Stone* is told in the present, we are given so many intimations of what will happen to the characters in the future that each moment of the present becomes nostalgic. In premodern times, family attachments of the sort that bind Bao-yu to his sisters and female cousins were by nature temporary, doomed to dissolution, as each of the young women would be expected to marry out. Every gathering is tinged by something of the proleptic sadness Dai-yu herself expresses, albeit in a parodic, quasi-humorous manner: "since the inevitable consequence of getting together was parting, and since parting made people feel lonely and feeling lonely made them unhappy, ergo it was better for them not to get together in the first place" (2.31.109–10) 人有聚就有散, 聚時歡喜, 到散時豈不冷清? 既清冷則生傷感, 所以不如倒是不聚的好 (1: 418).

The nostalgia of the novel is partly for the vanished glories of the Cao family, partly for the passing of any childhood. But it also taps into a powerful cultural undercurrent of feeling for the lost dynasty. The main objects of yearning for the Ming—tragic poetic beauties, refined pleasures, profligate splendor, and unsustainable wealth—should sound familiar to any reader of *Stone*. In fact, some scholars have observed that Bao-yu's relationship with his female cousins—the many parties and meetings of the poetry club where Bao-yu is the only male surrounded by talented beauties—structurally mimics the gathering in which one male client is entertained by a flock of gifted courtesans. This is not to say that Bao-yu is like a visitor to a brothel or that his cousins and sisters are like prostitutes but rather to point out that the novel harnesses extra energy and resonance from a nostalgia that already existed in the culture.

Another meaning of dream to an eighteenth-century reader is more familiar to us. As twenty-first-century consumers of pop culture, we are all aware of the clichéd ending, especially common in television and film, in which a character realizes that everything that preceded was dream. That move was an important part of the repertoire in premodern China too. Sometimes dream signified a different realm from waking, as different as the contents of a book are from a scene in which that book rests on a nightstand, for example. Nowhere in Chinese literature are these diegetic registers deployed more skillfully than in the opening chapters of *Stone*, which are a virtuosic play on different frames of reality, one nested in another.

The novel begins on the mythological plane, with the rock left over from the goddess Nü-wa's repair of the heavens. The rock is taken by a monk on a trip; then we read the inscription carved on it, which is the novel itself, beginning with a man named Zhen Shi-yin, who in turn dreams of the same monk and a Taoist talking about the rock's incarnation as a minor deity, Divine Luminescent Stone-in-Waiting, in love with the Crimson Pearl Flower. By page 53, we have been told about a love affair between a rock and a flower, by a monk and a Taoist who are being dreamed by someone whose story is recounted in a carving on the rock that earlier was with the monk and the Taoist. Confusion is an appropriate response to this Möbius strip of an introduction.

The Stone's existence connects these different frames and shows how they are related, since the Stone exists on each plane of reality: Bao-yu, "the precious jade," is at once the extra rock left over from Nü-wa's repair of the heavens, the boy born into the Jia family (to whom Zhen Shi-yin's friend Jia Yu-cun is related), the jade that is mysteriously in the boy's mouth when he is born, and the Divine Luminescent Stone-in-Waiting whose dew watered the Crimson Pearl Flower. Each instantiation of the Stone is framed by a different device: the contrast between the contents of a book with the reader's frame of existence (which introduces the entire novel, the inscription), the contrast between the contents of a conversation with the speakers' frame of existence (which is how the romance between the two minor deities is cordoned off), and finally the contrast between dream and waking (which points to the dream in which Zhen Shi-yin meets the monk and Taoist again at the frontier of Illusion).

This last contrast was the most common way in the Chinese literary tradition to nest one narrative in another. By the mid–eighteenth century, writers had been using dreaming for more than a thousand years as a device to set one reality off from another. In chapter 29, Grandmother Jia mentions *The South Branch* 南柯記, a seventeenth-century play by Tang Xianzu based on a late-eighth-century story. In both play and story, a dissolute named Chunyu Fen is summoned to a mysterious land whose king offers him his beautiful daughter in marriage. Chunyu and his wife are happily married and raise many children together. Twenty years later, his wife dies, and the king sends his son-in-law back home, where Chunyu finds everything looking exactly as it had when he left—down to his own body still slumbering on the veranda. In short, the whole twenty years were a dream. But there is no precedent in Chinese literature for the complication we find in the first few chapters of the *Stone*.

Most of the novel, of course, inhabits a single frame of reality, where Bao-yu is a more or less normal young boy whose family expresses remarkably little interest in why he was born with a jade in his mouth. Still, the Jias' reality never absolutely trumps the others. Sometimes we are made aware that the main events of the novel have allegorical significance from the perspective of the five elements (where Dai-yu, whose last name means forest, is wood, Bao-yu stone, and Bao-chai metal). Whenever the monk and the Taoist appear, they hint that the novel's whole dense fabric of reality—the physical surroundings of the Jia mansion, the psychological complexities of the family members' interpersonal interactions—is ultimately an illusion. Dreams are essential to this perception, as in Bao-yu's dream in chapter 5, in which he follows the fairy Disenchantment into the Land of Illusion.

This particular meaning of dream, that what appears real is nothing but a figment of the imagination, has more than literary history behind it; it is very much a part of Buddhist doctrine, which teaches that perceived reality is not real at all but a construction of the mind. Some scholars have suggested that Chinese fiction itself began, a millennium after other genres had been flourishing, only after the introduction of Buddhism, since it is in the very nature of stories that what seems real is not or that what appears to be reality might stand for something else.

In the Lotus Sutra, perhaps the single most influential Buddhist scripture in East Asia (which circulated widely in Chinese translation, 妙法蓮華經, from the fifth century on), the Buddha tells a parable about a father who lures his sons from a burning house with the promise of toys and decorated oxcarts. When the boys do as he asks, the father follows through with his promise. The idea of expedient means (in Sanskrit, *upāya*) illustrated by this parable, that any method, even one that is initially deceptive, to lead people to the truth is acceptable, has implications for narrative: a fiction that prevaricates on the surface might be truth at a deeper level. Dream, in the sense of an illusory reality, might serve as a poetics of fiction. It is no paradox, then, that *Stone*, a psychologically realistic novel whose physical details are so precise that the novel is an invaluable source for historians of the eighteenth century, should regularly use dream to refer to its own illusory nature.

Though the novel ends with Bao-yu's enlightenment, the novel's use of Buddhism in its narrative arc is more literary than religious. Multiple diegetic levels or frames of reality find a parallel in the Lotus Sutra's structure: the Buddha tells a parable that might then feature a character who in turn describes another, equally richly inhabited reality. The pattern of emerging from one frame of understanding into another—Buddhist enlightenment, that is—is much more important than the actual content of that new understanding. To apply this principle to the novel, although Greensickness Peak is more real than the Jia mansion, we are less interested in what takes place on it.

That goes some ways to explaining why actual Buddhist practice in the novel is not particularly sympathetic, and the content of Buddhist doctrine is relatively unimportant. Adamantina, the young lay nun from a good family, comes off as more priggish than pious; her desire for purity excludes the kindly Grannie Liu's overtures but allows the presence of Bao-yu, a young, single man. (To an eighteenth-century reader, her friendship with Bao-yu would have edged into the lascivious.) Bao-yu and Dai-yu's exchange of gathas in chapter 22 does not seem notably different from any number of other poetic exchanges between the two and displays the same emotional dynamic: Bao-yu's clumsy enthusiasm matched by Dai-yu's desire to prove herself his superior. We are probably better off considering the structural influence on *Stone* of Buddhist teachings rather than their theological content.

In the last few decades of the Ming Dynasty, dreams stood in not for memory or the illusory nature of reality but for subjectivity, what a philosopher might call mind. Mary Scott's essay in this volume touches on the influence Tang Xianzu's play *The Peony Pavilion* 牡丹亭, also known as *The Return of the Soul* 還魂記 (1598), had on the novel. Dream is a vital part of the play's exposition: it practically becomes a synonym for the power of passion. This connotation of dream—meaning passion or, more broadly, subjectivity—was the most important one at the time of the writing of *Stone*.

The novel's most significant dream, in chapter 5, performs a function very similar to that of Du Li-niang's dream at the beginning of *Peony Pavilion*; I suspect that the presence of a dream so early in the text is yet another way in which the novel is indebted to the play. Both dreams mark the emergence of a sexual awareness from which there is no return. After chapter 5, without Bao-yu's necessarily having done anything in the waking world, we must understand his behavior as that of a fully sexualized being. Romance and sexuality are central in both *Stone* and *The Peony Pavilion*, and yet both texts largely steer away from explicit content; these two dreams serve as a repository for sexuality, a place where it can be expressed and yet is localized away from the rest of the text.

In a play, this constellation of dreams, subjectivity, and identity has everything to do with the stage. Staging, playacting, and imagination all deal with the relation between surface and reality. Cao Xueqin loved the theater, and as Scott explains there are many ways in which the novel is more indebted to the play than to other novels. There is even a fragment of play embedded in the novel (notably in a dream), when Disenchantment introduces Bao-yu to a song cycle in chapter 5 that retells the events of the novel. (Chinese drama was all sung, and the song-and-dance suite "A Dream of Golden Days" appears to be the libretto of a play. It is entirely possible that these are songs that Cao Xueqin wrote for the play he originally envisioned and that he included in the novel that took its place.)

Reality, the dream suggests with a play that restages the novel, is a function of genre. In chapter 5's dream, Bao-yu encounters poetic rebuses that tell the fates of his sisters and cousins. Fiction seems to invite questioning in a way that the poems of the rebuses and songs do not. (It is no coincidence that in the Chinese tradition, the theme of "it was all a dream"—namely, texts that undo themselves at the end by declaring all that has transpired was a dream—is strongly associated with fiction. In the exception that proves the rule, Tang Xianzu's plays, dreams are actually *real*.)

Drama and poetry in Chinese were more strongly associated with a single, named author than was fiction, and the prose of novels sometimes reads as if it were close cousin to the paratext with which novels were surrounded in every premodern edition. *Stone* comments on itself; it is tentative, changeable; there even seem to be two versions of a few events—the novel's ending, also Qin-shi's death. In fact, the seeming incontrovertibility of the rebuses and song cycle is one reason that later critics had more faith in them than in the actual denouements of the characters that took place in the 120-chapter version.

In both *Stone* and *Peony Pavilion*, mirrors, like dreams, are a figure for individual subjectivity, since the evanescent image on a mirror is something only the viewer can see. One of *Stone*'s alternative titles is *Dream*; another is *A Mirror for the Romantic* (*Fengyue baojian* 風月寶鑑). Some scholars have suspected that *A Mirror for the Romantic* was originally written by Cao Xueqin as a freestanding, much shorter work, and that parts of that novella were later shoehorned into the text we have now. For the English reader, the title might seem to valorize romance, but the mirror is involved in one of the most moralistic episodes of the novel. In chapters 12 and 13, Jia Rui, an impoverished distant relative of our Jias, conceives an unrequited passion for Wang Xi-feng, who proceeds to torture him with no more concern for his well-being than a cat shows for a mouse. The scabby-headed monk appears and gives Jia Rui a magical mirror that Jia Rui on no account is to flip over. The side of the mirror that the monk offers shows a skeleton; the flip side shows the beautiful Xi-feng, beckoning Jia Rui to join her in all sorts of lascivious acts. Jia Rui, already weakened and ill, falls prey to temptation and before long has masturbated himself to an early grave. In *The Story of the Stone*, the mirror, self-pleasuring, and subjectivity are all parallel. Jia Rui's mirror represents not a space of personal liberty but a trap constructed by his own mind.

What happens when dream meets mirror? In Chinese, Jia Bao-yu's name is a homophone for "fake precious jade." If Bao-yu is false, there must be a real version of him—and indeed there is, a kind of mirror reflection of our protagonist: Zhen Bao-yu, "real precious jade," is the scion of a family the equal of the Jias in status and wealth but resident in the other capital. The doted-on favorite of his grandmother too, Zhen Bao-yu, so we are told, not only looks like our Bao-yu, but also rejects all thought of studying and prefers to spend his time with the young women of the household. (The two families are perfect matches as well. The Zhens have a daughter chosen to be an imperial concubine, and they too face the emperor's disfavor and are later restored.)

In chapter 56, four women from the Zhen household visit and tell Grandmother Jia all about their Bao-yu. She is amused by the resemblance, but our Bao-yu is distressed. What is the relation between these two doppelgängers? Do they belong to the same world, or, as their names indicate, is one somehow false (*jia* 假) and the other real (*zhen* 真)? It is through dream that Jia Bao-yu works out his relation to Zhen Bao-yu: he finds himself in a garden that looks just like his own, staffed by maids that look like the family's own Patience, Aroma, and Faithful. Much to his dismay, the maids rebuff him, treating him as an intruder—even as an impostor. Finally, he finds living quarters that look like his own Green Delights, where a maid is teasing her master over his fondness for his cousin. He overhears that boy complaining:

> I heard Grandmother say that there is another Bao-yu in the capital who is exactly like me, but I didn't believe her. I've just been having a dream in which I went into a large garden and met some girls there who called me a "nasty creature" and wouldn't have anything to do with me. I managed to find this Bao-yu's room, but he was asleep. What I saw was only an empty shell lying there on the bed. I was wondering where the real person could have got to.
>
> (3.56.86)

> 我聽見老太太說, 長安都中也有個寶玉, 和我一樣的性情, 我只不信. 我才作了一個夢, 竟夢中到了都中一個花園子裡頭, 遇見幾個姐姐, 都叫我臭小廝, 不理我. 好容易找到他房裡頭, 偏他睡覺, 空有皮囊, 真性不知那裡去了.
>
> (1: 775–76)

The other Bao-yu is recounting a dream that resembles almost to the last detail the dream that our Bao-yu is having. One way to think of this moment is to compare it with the novel's opening, as a nested narrative: here, Bao-yu is dreaming of another Bao-yu explaining his dream of another Bao-yu.

In the late Ming, the privacy of the mind, as exemplified by dream, was a kind of freedom. But in the eighteenth century, dream has turned into a trap, not unlike the mirror that kills Jia Rui. When the other Bao-yu recounts his dream, we are close to an infinite loop, as if Cao Xueqin has set two mirrors face-to-face, each reflecting the other ad infinitum. But the symmetry is not exact: the other Bao-yu ought to have dreamed of a boy who related a dream in which he overheard another boy relating a dream, and so on. Instead, the other Bao-yu's dream ends when he encounters "an empty shell" (in Chinese, a *pinang* 皮囊, or "sack of skin," quite a chilling image).

There are not two mirrors but only one. After the two Bao-yus confront each other in our Bao-yu's dream, the other Bao-yu is summoned by his father. Our Bao-yu calls after him, both in the dream frame and in his bed, as he sleeps, whereupon Aroma awakens him. Confused by his dream, our Bao-yu wakes, and Aroma comforts him by pointing to the mirror at the foot of his bed. After all, Grandmother Jia warns young people—whose souls aren't fully formed yet—against allowing themselves to cast reflections in mirrors too frequently. The maid Musk blames the mirror for Bao-yu's dream: "you must have been looking at yourself in it before you dropped off to sleep" (3.56.87) 自然是先躺下照著影兒頑的 (1: 776). As these characters share folk beliefs about mirrors, we learn that to them a reflection in a mirror assumes some of the identity of a person, leaving less identity for the person. The reflection is a simulacrum, not merely a fake but a thief, robbing the original of some of its reality.

We might think of this moment not as nested narratives or a recursive loop but as two subjectivities in competition: Who is dreaming of whom? Which Bao-yu is the original and which the reflection? The question recalls the most famous dream in Chinese literature, that of the philosopher Zhuangzi, who lived in the fourth century BCE. Zhuangzi dreamed that he was a butterfly, and when he woke up, "he didn't know if he was Zhuang Zhou who had dreamt he was a butterfly, or a butterfly dreaming he was Zhuang Zhou" 不知周之夢為蝴蝶與, 蝴蝶之夢為周與 (Watson, "Discussion" 49).

In *The South Branch*, all the experiences of a lifetime were a figment of the dreamer's mind. But Bao-yu is not Chunyu Fen the dreamer; he is but one of Chunyu's children, a figment of imagination. In the duel of subjectivities with the other Bao-yu, our Bao-yu is nothing but an empty shell, a figment of the other Bao-yu's mind, the "fake precious jade."

NOTE

[1] For more on Zhang Dai, see Spence, *Return*.

# The Capillaries of Power:
# Hierarchy and Servitude in *The Story of the Stone*

## *Christopher Lupke*

A fascinating dimension of *The Story of the Stone* is the elaborate depiction of the retinue of individuals that makes up the Jia family's servant staff. Of particular note in this network of characters are several maids assigned to serve various prominent characters in the family; of these maids, three stand out for the amount of detail invested in their depiction, the sympathetic tone that the narrator employs in their portrayal, and the fact that they are present thoughout the novel: Aroma, chief maid of Bao-yu; Patience, Xi-feng's chief maid; and Faithful, the only remaining close servant of Grandmother Jia. They are characters of first-order complexity occupying a place on a stage comparable to that of the characters who belong to the Jia family, a family that derives its high rank from military accomplishments of past generations but now is enmeshed, mainly through Jia Zheng, in official society and aspires to be considered a part of the literati. A number of other maids are given prominent roles, and some feature in subplots in the novel. These include Caltrop, a kidnap victim of high-class origin; other maids of Bao-yu, such as Skybright; of Bao-chai, such as Oriole; and of Dai-yu, such as Nightingale and Snowgoose. These supporting characters, as well as the tragic Er-jie, not a maid but a woman subjected to near servitude and even degredation, supplement the main narrative skein in colorful ways.

One might assume before reading *Stone* that these various servants are in effect slaves who work for the landed gentry family that the Jias collectively constitute and that this enslavement will entail ill treatment, even physical and psychological abuse. But their situation is not exactly like this. These servants were not compelled by force to serve the Jias; rather, they were purchased from their families (or were house-born). Generally they are not abused, though there was abuse of servants in the social reality of China at the time. That said, there are two fundamentally different social planes in *Stone*, that of the elite and that of those who tend to their needs. The two differ in every respect—in their life choices, education, the expectations placed on them, the way they speak, their dreams and hopes, and even the clothes on their back. This difference marks the stratification by which the servant class was denied access to the power, prestige, and wealth of the landlord class and denied the social mobility accorded to male members of the elite who could enhance their families' conditions by competing in civil service examinations. But the servants in the novel do not contest this unequal distribution of power. In fact, they sometimes support it more than do their masters. There is great empathy and much sharing of sentiments between the Jia family and their servants.

Some of this empathy may stem from the fact that the Jias are of bond-servant heritage, descendants, as Evelyn Rawski notes in this volume, of Chinese prisoners of war from generations ago. Perhaps the Jia family recognize in their contractually obligated servants some of the subjugation that their ancestors previously experienced under the Manchus. There is always a slight insecurity in the Jia family toward their social superiors—the royals to whom Yuanchun, their prized daughter, has been betrothed as imperial concubine. William T. Rowe observes that by the time of *Stone* many bond-servant families had achieved elite status, become active in official life, and no longer incurred any of the debasement their ancestors experienced during and just after the Manchu conquest.[1] Slaves—or indentured servants, as many of the maids in the novel are—came from pariah families, though obtaining slaves from commoner families did occur.[2]

Through a detailed character reading of several of the maids, I demonstrate how servants reinforce the social hierarchy, how they act to maintain the status quo. I also give examples of how relationships among family members become intertwined with those of the maids, blurring the boundary that stands between them. I provide illustrations of the realistic characterization of maids and discuss how they function as structuring devices, both to communicate necessary information to the reader without the intrusion of the narrator and to serve as conduits for motif symbols, reminding the reader of events that occurred many chapters before. Maids also work as vehicles for the myriad subplots that keep the reader engaged over the course of a work of such epic proportions.

Early in *Stone*, the narrator makes clear that Aroma will be a major character in the novel. Originally a maid of Grandmother Jia, she was handpicked by the matron of the Jia household to serve as Bao-yu's chief maid because of her "tried and conspicuous fidelity" (1.3.106) 心地純良 (1: 51). But from the outset Bao-yu asserts his own mischievous and amorous personality over her by changing her name from Pearl to Aroma. The translation of "aroma" from the Chinese *xiren* 襲人 loses some of the dimensions of the original. *Xiren* is not a generic scent but connotes the smell of flowers and literally means "to invade," suggesting something sensual and perhaps even seductive; it is in any case assailing. Her character is complex and paradoxical. Although in the first volume of the translation we are led to believe that she may be receptive to Bao-yu's precocious sexual curiosity, she turns out to be a no-nonsense enforcer of the orthodoxy that would have Bao-yu adhere to proper behavior. The reader would not normally think that adherence to social norms and established hierarchies is a message inculcated from the bottom—that is, through a maid. But time and time again in the novel, and in many different ways, Aroma so instructs. In order to convince Bao-yu of the necessity to behave, she often argues that his recklessness will hurt the ones he cares for—his closest maids—rather than himself. That reminder usually works.

The reader gets a first real glimpse of Aroma at the beginning of chapter 6, just after Bao-yu's allegorical and erotic dream. We learn that the relationship between Aroma and Bao-yu will be an unusual one, for after some questioning from the young woman, Bao-yu simply transfers to her what he has learned in his dream. Thereafter, they forge an affectionate bond. This muted sexual bond is not typical of prescribed behavior in eighteenth-century China. When maids are about to return home for a visit, they are always reminded of the rules: they must use their own bedding and toiletries, avoid contact with others, and have two interior rooms to themselves (2.51.518). The novel strives to be as realistic as possible, cataloging the details of everyday life among the landed gentry—details of social relationships, issues of money, personality conflicts, and various mundane concerns—yet both fantasy and sexual innuendo supplement the realism so readers will read on. The unusual and the taboo add spice to matters that are routine. The relationship of servant with benefits that Bao-yu enjoys with Aroma is one example. In the scene where Aroma feigns sleep in order to coax Bao-yu to bed with her (1.8.198), the sexual side of their relationship is underlined. But despite her devotion to Bao-yu, or perhaps because of it, Aroma endeavors at different turns and in different ways to set him on the straight and narrow path of a young Confucian scholar—and possible civil servant.

In chapter 19, Aroma is called home by her mother to participate in a family gathering. This sort of request was common for young, female servants working in a family of great wealth. They were sold into the employ of the wealthy family for an agreed-on number of years. When the stipulated period of service was over, they returned to their own family, most likely for a marriage betrothal. Therefore both Bao-yu and Aroma know that eventually they must go their separate ways. But where particular economics and the affections that could develop from close proximity came into play, it often happened that a maid was brought into the family in a permanent fashion, through concubinage. This route was impossible for males, since daughters were traditionally married out of the family while sons took their wives into the family. In a society, like China's, that valued the perpetuation of the male line, there were additional provisions made beyond the principal marriage: male children often took one or more concubines.

Being a chamber wife, which comes up regularly in *The Story of the Stone*, was a kind of concubinage. It occured when the personal maid of a given male (or another maid in the household) was deemed a good enough match for her status to be upgraded from servant to a second or third wife. She became his concubine, inferior to this principal wife but complementary to her and (at least in theory) not in competition with her. How these relationships played out in real life ranged from the ideal cases of complete harmony to out-and-out domestic warfare. Since we know that Bao-yu is indulged well beyond what is reasonable even for a family of such means as the Jias' and that he is closely attached to Aroma, it is reasonable to assume that she may one day become his chamber wife. But this arrangement is uncertain until a contract has been made, and Aroma uses that uncertainty as leverage. In chapter 19, she makes the veiled threat that she can leave the Jias and return home for good. She reminds Bao-yu that there are rules governing the rights of indentured servants and that the Jia family has the reputation of treating its servants justly. But the narrator reveals that it is not her intention to leave the Jias or the service of Bao-yu. She simply wants Bao-yu to behave: he must reform his speech to conform to that befitting a young male; he must give the appearance of liking his studies; and he must stop playing with women's clothing, makeup, and lipstick. Her demands on Bao-yu reinforce orthodox forms of heterosexual, masculine Chinese behavior (1.19.385–89).

This austere side of Aroma's personality, which increases with each passing chapter, balances the amorous side. Aroma demonstrates through various machinations and psychological manipulations her desire to see Bao-yu conform to the patriarchal and patrilineal values of traditional China, even though in this conventional framework people like her were far down on the hierarchical chain. Continually reminding Bao-yu what the proper path should be, she becomes his superego. Although she has responsibilities for and power over other, lesser maids, she is beneath members of the Jia family and their peers. Yet she is able by her wits and proximity to exert power over Bao-yu. She uses that power to fortify the social hierarchy. She may hope someday to become an official concubine of Bao-yu, which would elevate her in class, but she cannot hope to become his principal wife, as Dai-yu and Bao-chai do. The scene in which Nanny Li, Bao-yu's former wet nurse, bullies Aroma shows that Aroma's power is limited. Bao-yu's relationships with women exist on completely different social planes that seldom interfere with one another. Immediately after Aroma's threat and his anxious discussion with her, Bao-yu seamlessly moves to playful banter with Dai-yu, a woman who is on a par with him socially and might become his principal wife; all thoughts of Aroma for the moment have been left behind (1.19.393). The possibility that Bao-yu and Dai-yu (or Bao-yu and Bao-chai) could become engaged is completely compatible in eighteenth-century China with his simultaneous relationship with Aroma. In any case, by the end of the chapter Bao-yu has already forgotten Aroma's entreaty to act like a man (397–99).

As the novel progresses, the depiction of Aroma's character becomes more embroidered and nuanced, and the paradox that Aroma is seductive and emotionally tied to Bao-yu yet at the same time the dispassionate critic of his social behavior continues. The two roles coexist and are not in conflict with each other. A change in her professional status in the Jia household enhances the custodial aspect of her persona. Aroma was originally part of Grandmother Jia's vast phalanx of servants, but we learn that Lady Wang, Bao-yu's mother, has taken a proprietary interest in the young woman. Meanwhile Aroma becomes increasingly impatient with Bao-yu's incorrigible ways. She threatens to return to the service of Her Old Ladyship, then expresses displeasure at Bao-yu's cavorting (1.21.418, 422). She again threatens to leave him when he is caught wheedling lipstick from Grandmother Jia's chief maid, Faithful (1.24.469). But Aroma's position is never in question, for near the end of the first volume of the translation a visitor judges his importance in Bao-yu's eyes by the fact that it is Aroma who serves him (26.513). Yet she uses comfort and cajolery to soothe Bao-yu rather than direct confrontation (2.29.87–92). When she remonstrates with him about his excesses, be they amorous, humorous, or furious, she points out that the ones who will be blamed for his intemperance are the servants:

> Her Old Ladyship will be really angry if the two of you are still at daggers drawn on the day of the festival, and that will make life difficult for *all* of us. Why not put your pride in your pocket and go and say you are sorry, so that we can all get back to normal again?                    (2.29.92)

> 你們兩個再這們仇人似的, 老太太越發要生氣, 一定弄的 大家不安生.
> 依我勸, 你正經下個氣, 陪個不是, 大家還是照常一樣, 這麼也好, 那麼
> 也 好?                                                          (1: 405)

Aroma, at all times loyal to Bao-yu, manipulates him not for the sake of control but rather to protect him from himself. That she is a stabilizing force in his life does not go unnoticed by Lady Wang. The young woman exhibits surprising wisdom for her age and social station. After Bao-yu is nearly beaten to death by his father, Aroma tells Lady Wang that the whipping did Bao-yu some good, and Lady Wang agrees (2.34.136). At this point in the novel, Lady Wang assumes that one day Aroma will become Bao-yu's chamber wife but feels it would be premature to make that arrangement formal now. She promotes the young maid in position and pay and moves her employment to her own account and out of the jurisdiction of Grandmother Jia, all without the matron's knowledge (2.36.204). Aroma now answers directly to Lady Wang and not to Her Old Ladyship. Through Aroma, Lady Wang can better control, or at least curb, Bao-yu's behavior. Aroma proves loyal in this new role and thereafter appears more detached emotionally from Bao-yu. She no longer permits herself the "affectionate intimacies" she once did with Bao-yu (3.77.548). She increasingly furnishes reports to Lady Wang on his behavior (4.96.331). In one instance there is the suspicion that she relays to Lady Wang his exact conversations with other maids (3.77.538). But Aroma is never explicitly depicted by the narrator as a spy; she is always seen in a sympathetic light.

Despite her allegiance to Lady Wang, Aroma can be deceptive if she feels the deception serves the higher goal of harmony in the family and the emotional stability of Bao-yu. In one incident, for example, Sunset, a minor maid, steals a bottle of perfume from Grandmother Jia to give to Jia Huan, Bao-yu's ne'er-do-well half brother. Bao-yu offers to take the blame for Sunset. Patience, Xi-feng's chief maid, supports this suggestion, because if Sunset and Jia Huan are involved, Huan's sister, Tan-chun, could get into trouble. Aroma agrees to go along with the plan even though she first warns that Lady Wang will be upset when she hears about the theft (3.61.178–79).

While appreciating the fact that *Stone* reveals much about the world of rigid hierarchy in China of the eighteenth century, we must not forget that we are reading a literary work that must be faithful to certain formal expectations — continuity, trajectory, closure — in order to succeed aesthetically. Aroma plays an important structural role in this regard. As the narrative progresses, she worries more and more about her future. She imagines what it would be like to live as a chamber wife to Bao-yu with Dai-yu as his principal wife. She worries that Dai-yu's temperamental behavior may lead to her suffering a tragic fate similar to that of Er-jie or Caltrop (4.82.58–61). She has gradually come to respect Bao-chai, Bao-yu's other potential intended, and feels that Bao-chai's equanimity is more conducive to her and Bao-yu's well-being in such a triangular relationship (96.329). For her part, Bao-chai has long held Aroma in high esteem although the maid is "uneducated" (1.21.417). This concern over destiny sheds light on the character of Aroma and provides a road map to her hopes and desires. Ultimately, however, her worries have no material bearing on what happens to her in the novel: Aroma is eventually betrothed by her parents to a local businessman. Bao-yu's disappearance from the novel circumvents the problem of his formal relationship with Aroma, and although the maid is reluctant to accept the marriage proposal out of loyalty to Bao-yu, she acquiesces out of respect for her parents. When she meets the businessman in the final chapter of the novel (5.120.368–69), it is revealed that he is the stranger to whom Bao-yu gave her sash in so cavalier a manner earlier in the novel (2.28.62). This coincidence allows the narrator to intervene and remind the reader that all is predestined. Aroma's fate was presaged in the register of female characters in the novel that Bao-yu read in chapter 5 (133). Beyond the cultural issue of predestination, so dominant in Chinese thought (both philosophical and popular), is the textual fact that the resolution of this maid's fate gives the novel a palpable sense of continuity and the feeling that the novel can now conclude because all loose ends have been tied together.

Aroma is not the only important maid in the work. Another is Patience, the chief servant of Xi-feng, who is already in a triangular marriage with Xi-feng and Jia Lian. Patience illustrates that the latitude that may be afforded to maids in service to their masters and mistresses is not unique to Aroma. Patience too is a person of power and acumen. To get an idea of her influence, consider Xi-feng, niece of Lady Wang and principal wife of Jia Lian. Xi-feng is one of the most powerful women in the Jia domestic array. She comes from a wealthy family, is married to the oldest grandson of Grandmother Jia, and is niece to the wife of Jia Zheng, who as a government official of high rank commands a prestige even greater than that of his older brother and mother, the matriarch. But Xi-feng is more than the sum of her familial relations; she is intelligent, assertive, and at times ruthless. She is given the task of running the domestic finances early in the novel, and she does so with dispatch. That she finally fails has less to do with her than with larger issues of family income from various properties, issues that are beyond the scope of the narrative. For Patience to contend with Xi-feng, as she does on many occasions, is something no other servant in the household dares to do. Only her elders in the family will confront her. Even her husband, Jia Lian, an indolent and licentious lout, chooses indirect means of dealing with her. But Patience, because she is so capable and loyal, can speak her mind to Xi-feng.

The scene in which Patience discovers that Jia Lian has been having an affair behind Xi-feng's back reveals much about this maid's personality as well as about the curious relationship between these three characters (1.21.427–30). Although disgusted, Patience agrees to maintain the charade of Jia Lian's innocence but uses the information to keep Jia Lian in line. When Xi-feng comes on the scene, she makes a snide remark regarding Patience's sexual propriety vis-à-vis Jia Lian. Patience, angered, slams down the door blind in Xi-feng's face as Xi-feng enters the room. This retaliation shows that Patience is not afraid to face Xi-feng, confident that it will not be held against her, because her bond with her mistress is built on trust and the appreciation of her abilities. Patience at times defends Xi-feng to others in the family who insinuate that Xi-feng is not handling the finances well. Patience has confidence in Xi-feng, for her mistress is intelligent, sharp-witted, and good with numbers, even if she can be judgmental, harsh toward the staff, and extremely jealous.

The relationship Patience has developed with Xi-feng is an unusual one by Chinese standards. Can a maid ingratiate herself so much as to adopt a "scornful" tone toward her mistress, as Patience does when she sees that Xi-feng does not realize when others are trying to manipulate her (2.36.196)? More surprising is that Xi-feng does not even notice this behavior so audacious for a maid. Patience and Xi-feng have grown so close that they form a team. In light moments, such as when Xi-feng and Faithful banter and get into a food fight, Patience is eager to join the fray. Xi-feng, for all her harshness to underlings when she feels they deserve it, can be indulgent, open, and even intimate with senior maids whose capability, she feels, is beyond question.

The rapport between Xi-feng and Patience carries over into discussions about the family finances. Xi-feng, put in charge of the household budget, enlists Patience's help. In this task, Patience has no compunction about scolding Xi-feng, and when Xi-feng points out that Patience uses the familiar "you" to address her instead of the more formal "madam," Patience retorts that Xi-feng can slap her face if she wishes. She's done it before (3.55.65). This sort of exchange would be more characteristic of blood sisters in traditional Chinese culture. We really see the power of Patience on display when it comes to the ways in which money is allocated by Xi-feng. The first inkling of trouble comes when Aroma confronts Patience about the household finances (2.39.262–63). Patience downplays a delay in the disbursement of monthly allowances among the maids by explaining that Xi-feng has lent the money out for the purpose of gaining some interest on it. We learn from this explanation that Patience is privy to Xi-feng's usurious methods. But doubt is also cast in our minds about the wisdom, ethics, and security of such dealing, and this doubt is sustained as the narrative proceeds. We are led to suspect that Xi-feng is putting the maids' allowances at risk and that Patience is implicated (2.43.352). But Patience never breaks with Xi-feng over finances, remaining steadfast to the end. When Xi-feng dies, she pawns her own belongings to ensure that her mistress has a proper funeral (5.114.261).

Despite the easy relationship that Patience enjoys with Xi-feng, she is intelligent enough to know when to hold her tongue. When Jia Lian is caught cheating on Xi-feng and Patience is defamed and struck by her mistress and even her master, she flees and promises to commit suicide. Subsequently comforted by others in the family, she regains her composure, but the episode provides this insight into her character: in an emotional calamity such as this, she does not persist in her assertive but ever loyal rapport with Xi-feng; she withdraws as any maid would. When Jia Lian establishes Er-jie in a separate house outside the family compound as a wife on a par with Xi-feng and this scheme is revealed to Xi-feng, Patience knows enough to maintain absolute silence. Joker confesses that he helped his master, Jia Lian, find a place for Er-jie. While interrogating Joker, Xi-feng turns to Patience at times to make comments. The narrator observes that Patience "dared not reply" (3.67.327). Later, when Er-jie is living in virtual incarceration in the Jia compound, Patience extends her some sympathy by feeding her on the sly. When Xi-feng catches wind of this assistance and scolds Patience, Patience again dares not reply (3.69.362). The power of Patience has been accumulated only through years of dutiful service and sagacious behavior; she has earned Xi-feng's trust and respect. But when Xi-feng is pushed to extremes, Patience minds her place, neither retorting nor making light of Xi-feng's fury. She remains quiet and waits for it to subside.

The third most important maid in the novel is Grandmother Jia's servant Faithful. Like Aroma and Patience, Faithful possesses sterling qualities: she adheres to propriety and tact, is generous and good-natured, and, true to her name, is dedicated to a fault. Grandmother Jia states that Faithful "is better than all you grandchildren" (2.39.261). Bao-chai observes in the same passage that Faithful epitomizes all the attributes that a maid should. Faithful is protective of Grandmother Jia and able to keep track of the matron's myriad belongings. Without Faithful, Grandmother Jia would be taken advantage of. As a result, Faithful is the only one who can talk back to Her Old Ladyship. Not even her own sons, Lady Wang, or any of the other senior residents of the Jia mansion can do that. Grandmother Jia will actually listen to what Faithful has to say. In Chinese, Faithful's name, *Yuanyang* 鴛鴦, connotes a mutually faithful married couple, but Faithful is willing to sacrifice any conjugal life for Grandmother Jia. Thus if Grandmother Jia will permit things from Faithful that she will not from others, Faithful never abuses that privilege. But we cannot forget that she is a servant. Her needs, even when it comes to momentous occasions such as the death of her mother, often go unmet. Grandmother Jia quips, at this difficult time for her beloved maid, that she simply cannot let Faithful return home (3.54.23–24).

Jia She, a dissolute son of Grandmother Jia, takes a fancy to the young maid, hoping to take her as a concubine (2.46.406). Jia She has a reputation of preying on young, attractive members of the servant class; having conquered them, he loses interest in them. Because he is the oldest son in the clan, it is assumed that he will prevail with Faithful, and he dispatches his wife, Lady Xing, to set up the match. Their only concern is that the close bond between servant and the old mistress might present an obstacle. Lady Xing therefore goes to her daughter-in-law, Xi-feng, first, to figure out a way to persuade the maid to agree to the match. Lady Xing, certain that Faithful will prefer being a chamber wife to a maid, eventually broaches the subject directly with Faithful. Here it should be noted that in the text Lady Xing and Xi-feng refer to maids as essentially no more than "slaves" (2.46.412).[3] The term *indentured servants* is more accurate. But was it really possible for a maid, whether slave or indentured servant, to exercise free will? In *Stone*, the answer is both yes and no. In some cases, servants, particularly certain trusted maids, had considerable autonomy and power. But often they had none and were subjected to abuse. They usually had little control over their own destiny—for example, when it came to the selection of a marriage partner. But in traditional Chinese society, people, whether servants or not, whether male or female, normally could not choose whom to marry. *Stone* makes this issue a central conflict—consider the betrothal of Dai-yu or Bao-chai to Bao-yu. Characters above them, such as the imperial concubine, cannot choose, nor below them, such as several servants. That being said, some characters, if they put up resistance and have the support of a powerful master or mistress, can thwart an unwelcome advance. Faithful is the best example of this success in the novel.

She confides in her childhood peers, Patience and Aroma, and each suggests ways to foil Jia She's desire. Faithful, however, decides to use no stratagem; she will simply profess her loyalty to Grandmother Jia in the following manner, which becomes a defining moment for her in the narrative:

> As long as Her Old Ladyship lives, I shall stay with Her Old Ladyship. And when all's said and done, even when the old dear goes to her rest, there are still the years of mourning. There would be no question of his taking a concubine with his mother just dead. And by the time the period of mourning is over—well, anything might have happened. I'll just have to wait and see. If I get really desperate, I can always shave my hair off and become a nun; or failing that, there's always suicide. *I* don't mind going through life without a man. Glad to keep myself clean.    (2.46.416)

> 老太太在一日, 我一日不離這裡, 若是老太太歸西去了, 他橫豎還有三年的孝呢, 沒個娘才死了他先納小老婆的! 等過三年, 知道又是怎麼個光景, 那時再說. 縱到了至急為難, 我剪了頭髮作 姑子去, 不然,還有一死. 一輩子不嫁男人, 又怎麼樣? 樂得乾淨呢!    (1: 620)

Fortunately for Faithful, when Grandmother Jia learns of the plan, it sends her into a fury. Jia She has attempted all sorts of ways to win over Faithful, including enlisting the help of several of her relatives. But she is adamant and eventually, and publicly, brings her case before Grandmother Jia. Of course, the old woman is livid and vents her wrath on her son and daughter-in-law. Remember that at the start of the novel Her Old Ladyship parceled out all her trusted maids to her adored grandchildren, reserving only Faithful for herself. Most of the prominent maids in the novel came from Grandmother Jia's stable of servants. She therefore feels that although her family members maintained the appearance of propriety, underneath they were plotting against her. Grandmother Jia, the most venerated person in the household, summarily rejects Faithful's proposed betrothal to Jia She as a concubine. There is nothing for Jia She to do but accept the decision, although he does so grudgingly. Faithful's loyalty to Her Old Ladyship has been rewarded.

Later in the novel, Faithful organizes an eighty first birthday for her mistress, doing so in austere Buddhist fashion, which includes copying a sutra. She contends that her loyalty to Grandmother Jia and place in her servitude are a matter of karma (4.88.178–79). In chapter 110, when Grandmother Jia passes away, Faithful wishes that her funeral be one befitting such a grand lady. By this time, however, funds are depleted and the funeral is not up to the standard that Faithful hoped. Her loyalty remains steadfast, and, true to her word in earlier chapters, she hangs herself so that she can leave the corporeal world with her mistress. She is viewed by the other characters and by the narrator as a paragon of virtue. In fact, she is the epitome of uprightness, and her upholding of orthodox morality would gain her the accolades bestowed on the most upstanding of women in traditional China.

These three maids are notable for their model behavior and the considerable power they wield behind the scenes. They are no threat to the established moral order, because they have been inducted into it themselves. They reinforce that order from the bottom up, functioning as the mortar between the bricks, as it were. One of the most interesting paradoxes of *The Story of the Stone* is that much of the work of achieving the exalted traditional ideal of social harmony in the novel is engendered by these and other maids in the household. Although Aroma, Patience, and Faithful are the most prominent, other maids in *Stone* are significant as well. Dai-yu's Nightingale and Snowgoose assist in preserving or restoring harmony among those they serve. Skybright has a sparkling personality and sharp tongue. Several maids embellish the narrative by leavening the text with intricate subplots. The plight of Skybright offers a cautionary tale to maids who, despite being decent and responsible, might be a little too acerbic. Bao-yu's "youngest and least sensible" page Tealeaf (1.9.211) is a bad influence on the main characters yet advances the narrative. It is Tealeaf who introduces Bao-yu to the *Story of the Western Wing* (*Western Chamber*) and other books banned from the garden (1.23.462–63). Tealeaf thus plays a vital role in the link among Bao-yu, Dai-yu, the exposure or contamination of Dai-yu to these corrupting romances, and the deep melancholy she feels as a result. The maids Crimson and Scribe inadvertently start rumors about Bao-yu's engagement that are damaging to Dai-yu (4.89.207–09). Oriole, Bao-chai's trusted maid, plays an important role in the cohesiveness of the narrative, adding to the notion that Bao-yu and Bao-chai's marriage is predestined. She is the first to recognize that the inscription on Bao-yu's jade talisman mysteriously corresponds to that on Bao-chai's locket (1.8.189). Later she knots tassels for Bao-yu and takes the opportunity to enumerate the lofty qualities of her mistress (2.35.189–93). The verb *to knot* 結 in Chinese is the same as the verb *to marry*, a connection captured by the English phrase "tie the knot." Near the end of the novel, when the marriage between Bao-yu and Bao-chai has taken place, Oriole reminds Bao-yu of that episode, to suggest that she foretold their union (5.118.334). By this time, she has been put in charge of Bao-yu's day-to-day needs. In sum, as players who reveal information, convey knowledge to others, maintain or restore harmony, act out on occasion and add flair to the story, expose family members to things they might otherwise not encounter, and serve as devices for making the novel cohere, the maids in this long narrative cannot be underestimated.

The power of maids is a noteworthy element of *Stone*, but it has its limits too. Maids suffer evil because of their lower station in life. When Caltrop, a woman of scholar-gentry origin, is kidnapped early in the novel, knowledge of her origin is lost. She is given to Xue Pan as a chamber wife (1.16.308), which many in the family lament as a waste of a genteel young lady. Caltrop always presents herself well in company and exhibits breeding, though she is now regarded as of the servant class. It is difficult to say whether the author saw her breeding as a result of early nurture or of innate nature. Her high-class origin shows in her ability to compose elegant and sophisticated poetry (2.48.452). Caltrop is an example of how someone of the servant class can be mistreated, brutalized, and even put in mortal danger, as she is by Xue Pan's depraved wife Jin-gui (see 3.79.593–606). Her fate is telegraphed in the cryptic poem Bao-yu finds in the second register of women found in chapter 5—between the leading ladies, as it were, and the maids (1.5.133). That she is placed in this intermediate register reflects the ambiguity of her position in the novel as a noblewoman whose social status has been lost. Her demise at the hands of Jin-gui (whose name means "cassia") is predicted, but fortunately she is rescued by Bao-chai, who takes her in as a maid. Caltrop has something of a reconciliation with Xue Pan after he repents his dissolute ways (5.120.362). But she dies in childbirth (373).

The fate of Er-jie also shows the inhumanity that exists in the Jia household, an element of the character of Xi-feng that cannot go ignored despite the broader, sympathetic depiction of her. Er-jie is not a servant, but the subplot that details her plight demonstrates that even people who are not servants can be badly abused by a wealthy family. Er-jie is duped into being installed as a parallel primary wife by the licentious Jia Lian, husband of Xi-feng. The contrast between the way the Er-jie episode unfolds and how a man like Jia She takes a chamber wife illustrates the difference between a triangular relationship of husband, principal wife, and chamber wife, which is socially acceptable, and that between a husband and two principal wives, which is not acceptable and not common in Qing society. The second principal wife is a challenge to the authority of the first and a humiliation as well. When Xi-feng learns about Er-jie, therefore, the reader knows that the arrangement will not stand. The episode also shows the complexity of Xi-feng's character: This ambiguous figure in the novel can be charming and charismatic, sensitive and understanding, humorous and witty but also bitter, jealous, vicious, and vindictive. She is a study in contrasts, a character who is different things to different people and never dull.

Er-jie is treated sympathetically throughout the affair, and there is an almost prurient fascination with her slow torture and ruin. Her story, beginning with Jia Lian's seduction of Er-jie, developing through her installation in the home outside the family compound, continuing with the clearly iniquitous arrangement of her taking residence in the garden, and ending with her gruesome demise after a bloody miscarriage, presents the Jia mansion at its worst. Xi-feng, humiliated by the public revelation of Jia Lian's chicanery, chooses methodical revenge over instant rage as a way to settle scores. The servant staff react either with petrified silence in the face of Er-jie's engineered annihilation or, as Autumn does, play a facilitating role in it. The only exception is Patience, who attempts to give aid to Er-jie but is caught in the act and duly punished. Afterward, Patience does not dare interfere. The author uses Er-jie's tragic story to expose the underside of life in an elite family with great wealth, prestige, and the desire to be considered scholar-gentry despite their military background.

The relations between servant and master in *The Story of the Stone* are complex and intriguing. The lives of servants and members of the landlord family become entangled. A superb example of this class commingling is that of Aunt Zhao and her children. Aunt Zhao, once a mere maid, is taken as a chamber wife by Jia Zheng, the father of, among others, Bao-yu, Jia Huan, and Tan-chun. Although only the half brother and sister of Bao-yu, Jia Huan and Tan-chun are, by virtue of the patrilineal structure, legitimate members of the Jia clan. That their mother is a former maid casts a lingering shadow on the children, particularly Jia Huan. He is one of the least sympathetic characters in the book, a fact attributed to his feelings of inferiority as a concubine's son (1.20.406–08). Tan-chun, by contrast, is beloved and accepted as an equal both to Bao-yu and to her sisters and cousins. (The names of females of her generation all contain the character *chun* 春, which marks them as same-generation relatives.) She becomes an indispensable assistant to Xi-feng in managing the household accounts, approaching her job with the utmost efficiency and exactitude. She even takes her biological mother to task for expecting favoritism (3.55.50–52). In the same passage Tan-chun admits that she views her mother as a servant in the household and considers Lady Wang, Jia Zheng's principal wife, her true mother. Although Tan-chun is cold to her mother, others wonder whether she will be treated as a peer of her sisters, immediate cousins, and Bao-chai and Dai-yu (61). She is the embodiment of how difficult it can become to separate servant and master, given the intimacy of human interaction, the passage of time, and the natural bonds that can form between the two. What in one generation began as a clear distinction, a second generation may be unable to discern.


NOTES

[1] See Rowe's discussion of debasement and servitude in "Social Stability."

[2] I am indebted to Susan Mann for explaining this distinction and for many insights on the issue of gender made in her work *Precious Records* (esp. 37–44). Mann uses some examples from *Stone* to illustrate what was occurring in Qing society.

[3] For more on status of slaves, see Rawski in this volume.

# "Enlightenment through Feelings": Poetry, Music, and Drama in *The Story of the Stone*

## I-Hsien Wu

Among the wealth of human experiences and the historical and philosophical complexities portrayed in *The Story of the Stone*, "enlightenment through feelings" (or "awakening through love") is the most difficult lesson for Bao-yu to learn and the most important for the reader to comprehend. It is a paradox that calls for disenchantment through enchantment, detachment through attachment, and disillusionment through idealistic fascination. For Bao-yu to understand the shortcomings of love and the illusory nature of human existence, he must first blindly devote himself to his beloved girls and firmly believe that they will always surround him with the same devotion. Only through this immersion in emotions, the novel tells us, can one recognize the truth: that passion has its limitations and the glorious human world is only a great void.

In the novel, this path to transcendence is highlighted by the use of poetry, music, and drama. The poems the hero reads, composes, and reflects on reveal his psychological states. The music he listens to communicates beyond spoken words and written texts. The aural and visual immediacy of drama shakes and transforms his belief system. Carefully examining the activities of reading, writing, listening, and viewing, *Stone* creates an intricate journey in which poetry, music, and drama are seamlessly integrated into the narrative. The attentiveness to these genres, however, is a result of historical development. For centuries in the Chinese tradition, poems were a standard part of prose fiction, musical activities were written into stories of various lengths, and dramatic texts and performance practices repeatedly left their marks in the language of the novel. In *Stone* this integration reaches its artistic peak, particularly in constituting Bao-yu's interiority. This essay begins with a general introduction to Chinese poetry; continues with reviews on *Stone* poetics, musicality, and dramatics; and ends with an analysis of how these genres merge to create a chronicle of the hero's emotional awakening.

## Poetry: General Introduction

At the time *Stone* was written, poetry was composed mainly in classical Chinese, in which each individual word is represented by one monosyllabic character and the occasional words of more than one syllable are written with as many characters as there are syllables. The poetic meter was primarily syllabic, based on the number of syllables (and therefore number of characters) in a line. The pattern of tones was also an important part of traditional poetic metrics. Chinese is a tonal language. Modern standard Mandarin Chinese has four tones:

the high-level tone ($\bar{a}$), the rising tone ($\acute{a}$), the dipping tone ($\check{a}$), and the falling tone ($\grave{a}$). Classical Chinese may have had more than four. In poetry, these tones are categorized into two groups: even tone, which is basically the equivalent of the modern high-level and rising tones, and oblique tone, which contains the others. Some verse forms in classical Chinese poetry require strict tonal sequencing in each line; others are more flexible. The following illustration is a reading of the first poem in *Stone*, a quatrain in seven-syllable lines. Under the Chinese originals are transliterations of the characters (with tone marks), a word-by-word gloss of the Chinese, and David Hawkes's English translation (1.1.49; 4). Note that the traditional Chinese poetic language rarely uses tense markers, pronouns, or prepositions. There is no distinction between singular and plural, and sentence subjects are often omitted. These elements are supplied by the translator according to the context. The rhyming is *aaba*, one of the two major patterns for classical Chinese quatrains (the other is *abcb*).

| 無 | 材 | 可 | 去 | 補 | 蒼 | 天 |
|---|---|---|---|---|---|---|
| wú | caí | kě | qù | bǔ | cāng | tiān |
| no | talent | can | go | repair | blue | sky |

Found unfit to repair the azure sky

| 枉 | 入 | 紅 | 塵 | 若 | 許 | 年 |
|---|---|---|---|---|---|---|
| wǎng | rù | hóng | chén | rùo | xǔ | nían |
| vainly | enter | red | dust | as | these | years |

Long years a foolish mortal man was I.

| 此 | 系 | 身 | 前 | 身 | 後 | 事 |
|---|---|---|---|---|---|---|
| cǐ | xì | shēn | qían | shēn | hòu | shì |
| this | is | body | before | body | after | affair |

My life in both worlds on this stone is writ:

| 倩 | 誰 | 記 | 去 | 作 | 奇 | 傳 |
|---|---|---|---|---|---|---|
| **qìan** | **sheí** | **jì** | **qù** | **zùo** | **qí** | **chúan** |
| ask | who | record | go | make | marvelous | account |

  Pray who will copy out and publish it?

  The first two lines of this poem state the core theme of the novel: the story of an abandoned mythic stone's journey through the mortal world. Traditional readers often interpret these lines as an echo of the confessional prologue, the author's lament for his failed ambitions, but this autobiographical approach has been questioned repeatedly, because very little is known about the author, even though we have a lot of information about his family. The expression "red dust" (紅塵 *hongchen*) in line 2 is not only the keyword of these two lines but also a central theme of the novel.[1]

  The quatrain also addresses the metafictional aspect of the novel. The second half of the poem questions the notion of writing, raising the issues of plot, narration, and circulation. In these two lines the Stone declares its multiple roles: it is the hero ("My life"), the narrator ("is writ"), and the record bearer ("on this stone"), and indeed the story is experienced by the Stone, narrated by the Stone, and written on the Stone. The Stone's greatest concern is transmission, which is completely beyond its control: "who will copy out and publish" its marvelous account? The term *qichuan* 奇傳 in addition to its literal meaning, "marvelous account," can be interpreted as an inversion of *chuanqi* 傳奇, referring to Tang dynasty (seventh- to ninth-century) short stories written in classical languages by literati authors, a significant genre in the development of Chinese fiction. *Qichuan* might also refer to one of the generic terms for the literati novel, *qishu* 奇書 ("marvelous book"), which would not have been used because of the rhyme. In any case, the Stone's consideration is answered and elaborated immediately after the poem: persuaded by the internal author's (the Stone's) statement on writing and reading, the internal reader Vanitas turns himself into the copyist and brings the manuscript from the mythic realm to the mortal world, where the novel is subjected to a series of reinterpretations and editions. Evidently the novel regards itself as a work in flux: as soon as the process of circulation begins, the text takes on a life of its own, a life completely beyond the control of the original author.

## *Poetry: In* Stone *and Earlier Fictions*

Almost all the important verse forms in classical Chinese poetry can be found in *The Story of the Stone*: the quatrain (the poem discussed above), regulated verse (the chrysanthemum poems in ch. 38), the ballad (Dai-yu's poem on fallen blossoms in ch. 27), *ci* song lyric poetry (the willow floss song lyrics in ch. 70), and linked verse (in chs. 50 and 76). There are also vernacular song lyrics (the won-done song in ch. 1), lantern riddles (a collection can be found in the last part of ch. 22), and drinking games (one is depicted in the second half of ch. 40) that involve poetic languages. This array of verse forms and their frequent appearance make *Stone* an encyclopedic volume on classical Chinese poetry and demonstrate the place of verse in premodern Chinese prose fiction.

Incorporating poetry in prose narrative had long been a tradition in Chinese literature. When examining usage of poetry in the premodern Chinese novel, scholars usually begin with the Tang dynasty short stories, in which poems are regularly inserted, often providing windows to the inner world of the characters amid the largely objective narration. In one of the most celebrated Tang tales, "The Story of Ying-ying" 鶯鶯傳, by Yuan Zhen (779–831), Student Zhang falls in love with Cui Ying-ying (Oriole), whom he encounters in a monastery. At first Ying-ying rejects him, but eventually she gives in, only to be abandoned by him. In the end each of them marries someone else. In this short story several poems are inserted. Ying-ying writes three quatrains: one is sent to Zhang as an invitation to a nocturnal meeting, and two are written to express her feelings after their separation. While her first poem reflects the social convention of poetic exchange popular at this historical time, her other two poems reveal her psychological state as a deserted lover. There is one more quatrain in the story, written by Zhang's friend Yang Ju-yuan, who summarizes and laments the love affair; these lines function as a remark of the internal reader. There is also a long poem of thirty couplets written by Yuan Zhen, titled "Encounter with an Immortal," which follows the poetic conventions and compares Ying-ying and Zhang's story to a romance between a fairy and a mortal man.

The use of poetry in vernacular short stories became standardized in format as early as the Song dynasty and flourished in the Ming dynasty. These stories typically begin with one or more poems that initiate the narration, summarize the plot, or provide the moral of the tale. The stories usually also end with poems of similar functions. The number and roles of poems inserted in the main body of the text are expanded considerably after the Tang dynasty; some of the poems are descriptive, commenting on characters, scenery, objects, and so on; some are written by the characters as emotional expressions or exhibitions of talent; some narrate, extending, repeating, connecting, and commenting on the story line.

These characteristics of poetry in short stories can also be found in all the celebrated full-length novels of premodern China. In *Stone*, more than two hundred poems are inserted. Continuing the tradition, these poems allow the narrator to describe and comment (such as the verses on Bao-yu and Dai-yu's appearance in ch. 3 and the quatrain in ch. 1 that laments the hardship of the creative process). Poems written by the characters give insight into their minds and their talent. Dai-yu's "Autumn Window: A Night of Wind and Rain"

秋窗風雨夕 in chapter 45 expresses her nocturnal grief for the season of lone-liness, and Bao-chai's poem on willow floss reveals her aspiration: "When the strong wind comes he will whirl us upwards / Into the skies" (3.70.388) 好風頻借力, 送我上青雲 (2: 972). In addition, the poems in *Stone* often function as prophecies: the fates of the young women are written in verse (ch. 5), and many other poems, such as the lantern riddles in chapter 22, tell the destinies of their authors.

  *Stone* also reflects the social aspects of poetry. The poetry composition at the imperial concubine's homecoming (ch. 18) mirrors the practice of writing celebratory poems under the emperor's decree. The creation of linked verses by collective effort is portrayed twice in the novel—one time as the climax of a garden gathering at Snowy Rushes Retreat (ch. 50), one time as betraying a morbid sensitivity at Concave Pavilion (ch. 76). The Crab-Flower Club shows a practice popular among the literati: from its initial establishment to the poetry competitions (the crab-flower poems in ch. 37, the chrysanthemum poems in ch. 38, the linked verses in ch. 50, and the willow floss lyrics in ch. 70) to its reorganization (ch. 70). Another aspect of the late imperial literati culture is shown by the poetry club: Bao-yu and his cousins assume pen names to sign their poems and address one another. Li Wan serves as the president, Ying-chun as the proctor, and Xi-chun as the copyist, but Dai-yu, Bao-chai, Tan-chun, and Bao-yu (and later Xiang-yun) become the main poet-competitors. At the club meetings, they compose poems on the same subjects, usually set to the same rhymes, within a time limit. When finished writing, they comment on one another's work, and the president usually makes the final judgment. These activities demonstrate poetry as a social practice that was part of the literati life; more important, they reflect the rise of women's poetry clubs among the elite families of late imperial China.

  Even though the novel does not systematically explore theories of poetry, prosody is mentioned on many occasions, particularly when the characters comment on one another's work. In chapter 48, when Caltrop applies herself to making verses, the novel explains the basics of regulated verse, which includes eight lines in a poem and involves rules such as tonal balance and parallelism. The structure is given in Dai-yu's words:

> In Regulated Verse there are always four couplets: the "opening cou-plet," the "developing couplet," the "turning couplet" and the "conclud-ing couplet." In the two middle couplets, the "developing" and "turning" ones, you have to have tone-contrast and parallelism. That's to say, in each of those couplets the even tones of one line have to contrast with oblique tones in the other, and *vice versa*, and the substantives and non-substantives have to balance each other. . . .    (2.48.456–57)

> 不過是起承轉合, 當中承轉是兩副對子, 平聲對仄聲, 虛的對實的, 實的對虛的.    (1: 645)

Dai-yu's "Celebrating the Chrysanthemums" 詠菊 in chapter 38 is a good example of this verse form. The following analysis is shown in couplets to accommodate the English translation, which rearranges word order (2.38.251; 512).
Words with more than one syllable in Chinese are shown with hyphens, and
their English translations are underlined.

[The opening couplet:]

| 無 | 賴 | 詩 | 魔 | 昏 | 曉 | 侵 |
|---|---|---|---|---|---|---|
| *wú-* | *lài* | *shī* | *mó* | *hūn* | *xiǎo* | *qīn* |
| restless | | poem | demon | down | morning | attack |

| 繞 | 籬 | 欹 | 石 | 自 | 沉 | 音 |
|---|---|---|---|---|---|---|
| *rào* | *lí* | *qī* | *shí* | *zì* | *chén* | *yīn* |
| surround | fence | lean | stone | self | deep | sound |

Down garden walks, in search of inspiration,
A restless demon drives me all the time;

[The developing couplet:]

| 毫 | 端 | 蘊 | 秀 | 臨 | 霜 | 寫 |
|---|---|---|---|---|---|---|
| *háo* | *dūan* | *yùn* | *xiù* | *lín* | *shūang* | *xiě* |
| brush | tip | contain | elegance | facing | frost | write |

| 口 | 齒 | 噙 | 香 | 對 | 月 | 吟 |
|---|---|---|---|---|---|---|
| *kǒu* | *chǐ* | *qín* | *xīang* | *dùi* | *yùe* | *yín* |
| mouth | teeth | hold | fragrance | toward | moon | recite |

Then brush blooms into praises, and the mouth
Grows acrid-sweet, hymning those scents sublime.

[The turning couplet:]

| 滿 | 紙 | 自 | 憐 | 題 | 素 | 怨 |
|---|---|---|---|---|---|---|
| *mǎn* | *zhǐ* | *zì* | *lián* | *tí* | *sù* | *yùan* |
| full | paper | self | pity | compose | long | grief |

| 片 | 言 | 誰 | 解 | 訴 | 秋 | 心 |
|---|---|---|---|---|---|---|
| *pìan* | *yán* | *sheí* | *jǐe* | *sù* | *qīu* | *xīn* |
| piece | word | who | understand | tell | autumnal | heart |

Yet easier 'twere a world of grief to tell
Than to lock autumn's secret in one rhyme.

[The concluding couplet:]

| 一 | 從 | 陶 | 令 | 評 | 章 | 後 |
|---|---|---|---|---|---|---|
| *yī* | *cóng* | *Táo* | *lìng* | *píng-* | *zhāng* | *hòu* |
| since | from | Tao | prefect | remark | | after |

| 千 | 古 | 高 | 風 | 說 | 到 | 今 |
|---|---|---|---|---|---|---|
| *qīan* | *gǔ* | *gāo* | *fēng* | *shūo* | *dào* | *jīn* |
| thousand | ancient | high | demeanor | speak | to | now |

That miracle old Tao did once attain;
Since when a thousand bards have tried in vain.

The rhyme scheme is *aabacada*. Both the developing couplet and the turning couplet observe parallelism: noun pairs with noun ("brush" with "mouth," "elegance" with "fragrance"), verb pairs with verb ("contain" with "hold," "write" with "recite"), and so on. These two couplets also loosely follow the rule of tone contrast. For example, *suyuan* ("long grief," oblique tone, oblique tone) is contrasted with *qiuxin* ("autumnal heart," even tone, even tone). The name Tao in the last couplet refers to Tao Qian (365–427), a beloved poet who associated chrysanthemums with his high-minded life in reclusion. This poem triumphs in the chrysanthemum poetry contest for its originality. The developing couplet "Then brush blooms into praises, and the mouth / Grows acrid-sweet, hymning those scents sublime" is particularly appreciated by the judge. This treatment of chrysanthemum reveals not only Dai-yu's poetic talent but also her devotion, melancholy, and self-esteem: she is the restless writer searching for inspiration day and night; she has a world of grief to tell in the frosty autumn moonlight; and she sees herself as the embodiment of chrysanthemum portrayed by Tao Qian, which is elegant, fragrant, and above the turbulent secular world.

In addition to the fundamental technicalities, *Stone* explores the broader aesthetics of poetry composition. First, it repeatedly emphasizes the imaginary aspect of writing, that poetry is more about the mind than about facts and events. In chapter 37, when Li Wan suggests white crab blossom as the subject for the poetry club's first meeting and Ying-chun questions how they can write poems on the flower if they have not seen it, Bao-chai replies that looking at the object is completely unnecessary: "The ancients used a poetic theme as a vehicle for whatever feelings they happened to want to express at that particular moment. If they'd waited until they'd *seen* the objects they were supposed to be writing about, the poems would never have got written" (2.37.221) 古人的詩賦, 也不過都是寄性寫情耳. 若都是等見了作, 如今也沒這些詩了 (1: 491). Second, originality is highly valued. When Xiang-yun proposes chrysanthemum as the theme for the second poetry competition, Bao-chai modifies the hackneyed seasonal topic by making verb-object and concrete-abstract titles: "The combining of narrative and lyrical elements in a single treatment makes freshness and greater freedom" (2.37.236) 賦景詠物兩關著, 又新鮮, 又大方 (1: 502). Later Li Wan applauds Dai-yu's triumph in the treatment of the chrysanthemum theme: "The titles themselves were original, and—particularly in their treatment of the subject—these are three highly original poems" (2.38.254) 題目新, 詩也新, 立意更新 (515). Similarly, when praising Dai-yu's "Songs for Five Fair Women" 五美吟, Bao-chai states, "Whatever subject one chooses for a poem, . . . it is important that one's treatment of it should be original. If one merely plods along in the footsteps of earlier poets, it doesn't matter how fine the language is, the lack of originality will prevent it from being a really good poem" (3.64.258) 作詩不論何題, 只要善翻古人之意. 若要隨人腳蹤走去, 縱使字句精工, 已落第二義 (2: 893). Originality is considered even more important than formal regulations of poetry, as Dai-yu explains to Caltrop: "[I]f you've got a really good, original line, it doesn't matter all that much even if the tone-contrast and parallelism are wrong" (2.48.457) 若是果有了奇句, 連平仄虛實不對都使得的 (1: 645). In Caltrop's learning process, the importance of studying first-rate poetry is emphasized—Dai-yu lists Wang Wei's (?–761) pentasyllabic poems in regulated verse, Du Fu's (712–70) regulated verse heptasyllabics, Li Bo's (aka Li Bai, 701–62) heptasyllabic quatrains, and works of Tao Yuanming (the alternative name of Tao Qian), Xie Lingyun (385–443), Ruan Ji (210–63), Yu Xin (513–81), and Bao Zhao (?–466) (2.48.457–58). The first three on this list are poets of the Tang dynasty, the golden time in Chinese history that produced a canon of highly regarded poetry. The rest of the poets are from earlier times and manifest aesthetics of different eras. Since Dai-yu is the most talented and most productive poet in *Stone*, her choice reflects the author's taste, which is manifest not only on this list but also throughout the novel.

Finally, poetry in the Chinese tradition extends far beyond the textual sphere of the highbrow. Poetic expressions often become part of the everyday vocabulary of both the educated and the underprivileged. This aspect of poetry is vividly captured in *Stone*. The prince of Bei-jing observes about Bao-yu to his father that "the young phoenix was worthy of his sire" (1.15.289) 雛鳳清於老鳳聲 (1: 192), a line originally from a poem by Li Shangyin (813–58), but Grannie Liu, an uneducated poor widow, also quotes a saying based on a poem: "A prince's door is like the deep sea" (1.6.153) 侯門深似海 (93), which is from Cui Jiao's (ninth-century) quatrain "To the Departed Maid" 贈去婢: "Once you entered the prince's door, like the deep sea, / From that time I became a stranger to you" 侯門一入深如海, 從此蕭郎是路人 (*Quan tang shi* 2: 1278). Poetry, therefore, is not limited to the elites but is a shared mode of expression.

## *Music*

Music, like poetry, was an important aspect of the literati culture in premodern China. In *Stone* musical activities can be observed as slices of the elite-aristocratic life. Rituals are always accompanied by music, as in Qin-shi's funeral (ch. 13), Yuan-chun's homecoming as an imperial concubine (ch. 18), and the New Year's sacrifice at the Jia ancestral hall (ch. 53). Music is entertainment, either as a game or as a performance: at Feng Zi-ying's party, each guest is asked to sing a song about a girl who is upset, glum, blessed, or content (ch. 28); when Grannie Liu tours Prospect Garden, Grandma Jia has an instrumental ensemble positioned in the pavilion at the pond, explaining that the music will sound even better with the reflection of water. This performance is described in cheerful tones: "[I]n the cold, clear air of autumn, the ululation of flutes rising above a drone of pipes and organs came stealing through the trees and across the water, ravishing the hearts and minds of those who heard it" (2.41.308) 只聽得簫管悠揚, 笙笛並發. 正值風清氣爽之時, 那樂聲穿林度水而來, 自然使人神怡心曠 (1: 550). Listening to such fine music for the first time, Grannie Liu is so delighted that she moves her hands and feet vigorously, which Dai-yu makes fun of by quoting the passage in the *History Classic* about the animals dancing to the music of the ancient sage-king Shun (2.41.309).

More important, in *Stone* music is associated with poetry—not only in terms of meter and tones but also in the poetic language and activities that create musical performances. In chapter 76, at the evening banquet for the Mid-Autumn

Festival, Grandma Jia sends a message to a solo flute player to perform from a distance. While the first piece "steals like a balm over the soul, soothing and dissolving all earthly griefs and cares" (3.76.509) 凡心頓解, 萬慮齊除 (2: 1058), the second piece in slow tempo brings down the blissful gathering:

> Then, silencing them once more, the sound of the flute concealed in the cassia-bushes below came stealing into their ears, this time more plaintive even than before. Indeed, this time the combination of the flute's melancholy with the effects of nocturnal stillness and ghostly moonlight induced a feeling of such overpowering sadness in the listeners that they turned their backs on it and sought, with talk and somewhat forced laughter, to escape it. (3.76.510–11)

> 只聽桂花陰裏, 嗚嗚咽咽, 裊裊悠悠, 又發出一縷笛音來, 果真比先越發淒涼. 大家都寂然而坐. 夜靜月明, 且笛聲悲怨 . . . 眾人彼此都不禁有淒涼寂寞之意. 半日, . . . 才忙轉身陪笑, 發語解釋.
> (2: 1059; the English and Chinese versions differ slightly)

The flute's melancholy is a recurring motif in classical Chinese poetry and prose. The language of this section on the flute is a sound reminder of the famous "The First Poetic Exposition on Red Cliff" 前赤壁賦, by Su Shi (1037–1101), which describes a nocturnal boat trip to the historical battleground:

> One of my companions played the flute, accompanying me as I sang. The notes were resonant and low, as if expressing some deep wound, as if yearning, as if sobbing, as if declaring some discontent. The after-echoes trailed away, attenuating like a thread but not breaking off. Such notes made the dragons dance as they lay sunken in their dark lairs, and caused women who had lost their husbands to weep in their lonely boats. (Owen, *Anthology* 293)

> 客有吹洞簫者, 倚歌而和之, 其聲嗚嗚然, 如怨如慕, 如泣如訴; 餘音裊裊, 不絕如縷; 舞幽壑之潛蛟, 泣孤舟之嫠婦.

The vertical flute on Su Shi's boat, as explained by the player, mourns the passing of history as well as of an individual lifetime. The excursion, however, ends on a cheerful note, as Su and his guest finally agree that the natural world is an infinite treasure available for them to enjoy. The flute at the Jia family banquet, however, signals that the happy festivity has ended. When Grandma Jia opens her eyes, she sees most of the chairs at her table empty and says with a sigh, "We'll end the party now" (3.76.511), which signals the collapse of the aristocratic household. The significance of the music does not stop here. Dai-yu and Xiang-yun are among those who leave the banquet early, but they are tempted to compose linked verses about the mid-autumn night with the touch of the same flute. The music not only provides the background but also enters their composition. With the change of musical ambiance, their lines move from "The sounds of music everywhere pulsate" 匝地管弦繁 to "The sounds of music softly terminate" 更殘樂已諼, and finally conclude with "Where, moon-embalmed, a dead muse lies in state" (3.76.516, 519, 522) 冷月葬詩魂 (2: 1064, 1066, 1069). The chilling fantasy, accompanied by the morbid sound, points to Dai-yu's death.

Chapters 86–87 highlight the *qin* 琴, a plucked string instrument of the zither family that is associated with the aesthetics of the premodern literati, the idea that music is fundamentally about virtue and morality (fig. 1): "'The essence of Qin,' replied Dai-yu, 'is restraint. It was created in ancient times to help man purify himself and lead a gentle and sober life, to quell all wayward passions and to curb every riotous impulse'" (4.86.154) 黛玉道: 琴者, 禁也. 古人制下, 原以治身, 涵養性情, 抑其淫蕩, 去其奢侈 (2: 1215). The most prestigious musical instrument in the Chinese tradition, the *qin* is almost always played solo — in private or shared with one or two close friends who are true music lovers; it is intended never for entertainment but for spiritual and intellectual cultivation. As illustrated in the novel, playing the *qin* requires a special environment ("seek out a quiet chamber, a studio with distant view, or upper room; or some secluded nook 'mong rocks and trees, on craggy mountain top, by water's edge" 必擇靜室高齋, 或在層樓的上頭, 在林石的裏面, 或是山巔上, 或是水涯上), a specific time ("Let the weather be clear and calm, a gentle breeze, a moon-lit night" 再遇著那天地清和的時候, 風清月朗), and the player's perfect mental and physical condition, attire, and fingering techniques ("Poise Breath and Blood in Perfect Harmony. Your Soul may now commune with the Divine and enter into that mysterious Union with the Way" 氣血和平, 才能與神合靈, 與道合妙, "And before you think of playing, be sure to dress in a suitable style — preferably in a swansdown cape or other antique robe" 若必要撫琴, 先須衣冠整齊, 或鶴氅, 或深衣, "Assume the dignified manner of the ancients, a manner in keeping with the chosen instrument of the sages. Wash your hands. Light the incense. Sit on the edge of your couch. Place the Qin on the table before you, and sit with your chest opposite the fifth fret. Raise both hands

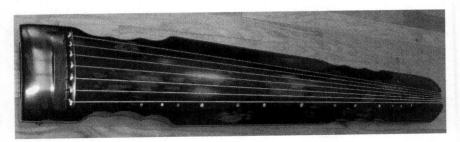

Fig. 1. A *qin*. © Andrew Schonebaum

slowly and gracefully. You are now ready, in body and mind, to begin" 要如古人的像表，那才能稱聖人之器．然後盥了手，焚上香，方才將身就在榻邊，把琴放在案上，坐在第五徽的地方兒，對著自己的當心，兩手方從容抬起，這才心身俱正）(4.86.154–55; 2: 1215).

This discourse on the *qin* quotes several sources, including *Discussions in the White Tiger Hall* 白虎通義, by Ban Gu (32–92), which states that *qin* means "restraint"; "The Qin Music" 琴操, attributed to Cai Yong (132–92), which argues that the *qin* was created "to help man purify himself and lead a gentle and sober life, to quell all wayward passions and to curb every riotous impulse" 禦邪僻，防心淫; and *Music Reminiscent of Antiquity* 太古遺音, compiled by Yang Lun 楊倫 (sixteenth to seventeenth century), which lists fourteen suitable occasions to play the *qin*. Beyond these fragmentary quotations, Dai-yu's speech is largely taken from a passage in Yang Biaozheng's (sixteenth-century) *Miscellaneous Notes on Playing the Qin* 彈琴雜說, with only a few minor changes. This is the only instance in the 120-chapter *Stone* that quotes a source to such extent.

Through Bao-yu and Dai-yu's conversation, the characteristics of *qin* handbooks are also explained. Generally, for each piece, the title and a textual description precede the music itself. The *qin* notation is in tablature, which indicates pitch by performance technique. *Qin* tablature looks like a combination of partial Chinese characters written vertically, so Bao-yu calls it an esoteric text in confusion. Several *qins* hang on the wall of the Jia family's main library, but none of them is fit to play—the musical instrument has sadly become merely a symbolic ornament. But for Dai-yu, the *qin* is about communicating feelings (fig. 2). The anecdote she mentions, "To play a Rhapsody of Hills and Streams and share its inner meaning with a fellow music-lover" (4.86.153) 高山流水,

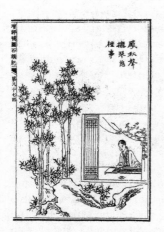

得遇知音 (2: 1214), refers to the legend of Bo Ya and Zhong Ziqi, in which Zhong never fails to understand the meaning of Bo Ya's music. When Zhong dies, Bo Ya splits his *qin* and never plays again, because there is no one left in the world worth playing for.[2] In chapter 87, touched by the tender memories attached to the objects that mark the development of her relationship with Bao-yu and responding to the poems Bao-chai sends her, Dai-yu composes four stanzas set to an air for the *qin*. As she combines music and poetry as embodiment of her sorrow, she subverts the convention of the *qin*: it is no longer about restraint but about expression.[3]

Indeed, ultimately, music communicates emotions. In chapter 93, Jiang Yu-han's singing reminds Bao-yu of a passage from the chapter

"On Music" 樂記, in the *Liber Ritualis* (also known as *The Book of Rites* or *Liji* 禮記, a Confucian classic): "Feeling stirs within and is embodied in sound. When that sound is fashioned by art, music is born" 情動於中, 故形於聲. 聲成文, 謂之音, to which Bao-yu concludes, "Poetry conveys feeling, but music strikes to the very core" (4.93.266) 詩詞一道, 但能傳情, 不能入骨 (2: 1288). The novel tells us that the immediacy of sound is often stronger than written text. Therefore, when music and poetry are combined, the power of expression can be overwhelming, as in Bao-yu's journey of enlightenment.

## Drama

All premodern Chinese dramas are essentially musical dramas, consisting of arias to be sung and spoken parts to be performed in recitative, mannered speech, or plain prose. The lyrics, many of them first-rate poetry, are usually set to preexisting melodies called "tune patterns" 曲牌. The musical aspect of premodern Chinese drama is so strong that even the reading texts of traditional plays included the tune pattern titles for the arias even though there might have been no expectation that the reader would sing them.

The rise of the premodern Chinese novel is closely related to drama. Preexisting dramatic works on the same topics influenced the writing of *Romance of Three Kingdoms*, *Outlaws of the Marsh* (*The Water Margin*), and *The Journey to the West*. More than a dozen dramas, either as text or as performance, are mentioned in the domestic setting of *Plum in the Golden Vase*. In *The Story of the Stone*, drama is a recurring theme. The novel not only reflects drama as a social convention but also examines and reworks the genre to make it an integral part of the narrative. In the Jia family, drama is an indispensable part of celebration. In chapter 19, Bao-yu drifts away from Jia Zhen's New Year's party because he can't bear the spectacle and high volume of the day's repertoire. In chapter 54, during the Lantern Festival, dramatic excerpts are performed with two types of flute as accompaniment. Stages of different sizes are built into the house, but temporary stages are also constructed for occasions. The family keeps its own troupe, a group of twelve young actresses originally purchased to perform at Yuan-chun's homecoming. Owning a family troupe was common among the aristocratic families in late imperial China, even though the custom was banned by imperial edicts. The Jia family enjoys the privilege but sometimes, for variety, will hire professional troupes to perform at the house.

Like poetry, dramas can also function as prophecy in *Stone*. In chapter 18, for example, excerpts from four dramas are chosen to be performed for Yuan-chun: "Shi-fan Entertains" 豪宴, from *The Handful of Snow* 一捧雪; "The Double Seventh" 乞巧, from *The Palace of Eternal Youth* 長生殿; "The Meeting of the Immortals" 仙緣, from *The Han-dan Road* 邯鄲記; and Li-niang's death scene from *The Return of the Soul* 牡丹亭 (1.18.371). These performances imply, respectively, the decline of the Jia family, the death of Yuan-chun, the delivery of the jade by Zhen Bao-yu,[4] and the death of Dai-yu. In chapter 22, to celebrate Bao-chai's birthday, a small stage is set up in the courtyard in Grandma Jia's apartment, and a troupe of child actors hired to perform. To please Grandma Jia, Bao-chai repeatedly selects "noisy plays" from the repertoire (1.22.435). When Bao-chai asks for *Zhi-shen at the Monastery Gate* 魯智深醉鬧五臺山, Bao-yu can't help criticizing her choice. She explains the musical character of the piece she has chosen and recites the lyrics for him. The aria "Clinging Vine" 寄生草, a piece about leaving the secular life to join the religious world, about parting and loneliness, like many other songs and poems in the novel, is an omen of Bao-yu's destiny.

The most important dramas in *Stone* are *The Western Chamber* (also known as *The Story of the Western Wing* 西廂記) and *The Return of the Soul* (also known as *The Peony Pavilion* 牡丹亭). Inspired by "The Story of Ying-ying" and later literary works based on it, *The Western Chamber* was written by Wang Shifu (1250–1300), a dramatist in the Yuan dynasty (thirteenth to fourteenth century), when China was under Mongolian control. Created in *zaju* 雜劇 style, the dominant dramatic genre in thirteenth- to fifteenth-century northern China, it is the favorite love comedy in traditional Chinese drama.[5] *Return of the Soul*, written by Tang Xianzu 湯顯祖 (1550–1616), tells the story of Bridal Du (Du Li-niang), who falls in love with a young man in her dream and subsequently dies of longing but also returns to life because of love. The arias sung by Bridal Du and her lover in the dream sequence are particularly admired for their lyrical intensity.

*The Western Chamber* and *Return of the Soul*, considered the favorite romances in the Chinese dramatic tradition, have enjoyed unparalleled popularity and given rise to numerous sequels, parodies, revisions, and adaptations, both on stage and in print. Their amorous content and language, however, were often considered improper and even dangerous, particularly for impressionable youths vulnerable to the lure of passion. Curiously, in *Stone* it is not the performative aspect but the textuality of drama that is problematized. As shown in the novel, it is completely acceptable to enjoy a love scene on stage with other family members, but drama is not allowed to be read as text in private. Therefore when Tealeaf brings Bao-yu the play books, he has to warn the young master not to bring them into the garden and not to let anyone know (ch. 23); when Dai-yu finds Bao-yu reading *The Western Chamber*, he hides it and lies (ch. 23); and when Bao-chai realizes that Dai-yu has been reading these dramas in private (ch. 40), she gives her a stern lecture, concluding, "[L]et us avoid like the plague those pernicious works of fiction, which so undermine the character that in the end it is past reclaiming" (2.42.334) 最怕見了些雜書, 移了性情, 就不可救了 (1: 568).

Indeed, in opposition to public performance, private reading was often associated with the construction of sentimental interiority, which could easily corrupt the reader and lead to forbidden paths. There were stories of readers pining away under the influence of *Return of the Soul*. The tragedy of Feng

Xiaoqing, the young poetess who was sold to a man with a jealous first wife, is probably the most celebrated account. Depressed and distressed, Xiaoqing found solace in reading *Return of the Soul* and emulated Bridal Du. Soon after Xiaoqing's death, her persona was intertwined with that of the dramatic heroine in the popular imagination and embodied in plays, tales, paintings, and art-works. *The Western Chamber* and *Return of the Soul* also inspired love stories of various kinds, including that of Bao-yu and Dai-yu. Reading and listening to these works elevates their feelings for each other from childlike intimacy to sentimental youthful love, which is the first step to enlightenment through feelings.

## Enlightenment through Feelings

Bao-yu's journey of awakening is a long one. His dream voyage to the Land of Illusion in chapter 5 represents his earliest opportunity to attain enlightenment, and poetry, music, and drama are the main vehicles used in the effort to disenchant him. First, the fairy Disenchantment gives him the prophetic verses on the ill fates of the young women, but it is the reader, not the character, who is enlightened. Second, the performance of the song-and-dance suite "A Dream of Golden Days," which Disenchantment opposes to the musical dramas of the mortal world, is arranged. The lyrics of the suite are extensions of the earlier prophetic verses, performed as songs rather than presented as texts. The addition of music is designed to express and communicate something that words have failed to articulate, and music is believed to be such an important mechanism that Disenchantment finds it necessary to make special arrangements—she verbally explains her composition and brings Bao-yu the libretto. Ironically, although Bao-yu finds the singing captivating, the suite does not please him. Disenchantment's music fails to convey the divine prophecy because it is different from the musical drama of the mortal world. Bao-yu, after all, is familiar only with the fixed roles and set tunes found in the works of earthly composers. To him, an outsider, the poetic, musical, and dramatic languages of the mythic realm are meaningless.

As Bao-yu continues on his spiritual journey, he moves into Prospect Garden, the Land of Illusion in the human world. The process of enlightenment begins in chapter 23, which depicts the first incidents of the garden life. For Bao-yu, the removal into the garden is "utterly and completely satisfying" (1.23.460) 再無別項可生貪求之心 (1: 311), and he immediately composes four seasonal poems celebrating his state of contentment. The narrator characterizes these poems as "a fairly accurate impression of the mood and setting of those carefree days" 卻倒是真情真景 (312), creating an illusion of permanence—that the hero has lived in the garden for years and the poems are records of the garden life—even though the relocation has just taken place and the life described in the poems is merely a projection of his imagination, alluding to the garden motifs often described in classical poems, tales, and dramas. According to the principles of poetry mentioned elsewhere in the novel, these poems express only what Bao-yu feels at that particular moment, his total satisfaction in the ideal world.

The satisfaction is surprisingly short-lived; soon the hero begins to feel restless. Welling from within, without any external stimulation, a lack strikes him, consuming his blissful and childlike freedom. To entertain his restless young master, Tealeaf brings in an assortment of books that Bao-yu has never heard of, including the tales of Flying Swallow and her sister, Empress Wu, and the Jade Ring Concubine (Yang the Prized Consort). Most of the titles on the list are pornographic, but it is the chaster volumes of love that initiate the hero into the realm of romance.

The first love story the novel confronts is *The Western Chamber*, which Bao-yu secretly shares with Dai-yu as a reading. The story gives them the vocabulary to communicate passion. Right after Dai-yu finishes the drama, Bao-yu blurts out without thinking, "How can I, full of sickness and of awe, withstand that face of yours which kingdoms could o'erthrow" (1.23.464) 我就是個 "多愁多病身," 你就是那 "傾國傾城貌" (1: 315), quoting the drama they just read. Fully aware of the source and its flirtatious connotation, Dai-yu is offended, but they reconcile quickly, and she quotes another line to tease him back, "Of silver spear the leaden counterfeit" (465) 是個銀樣鑞槍頭 (316), revealing her own recognition of the drama and subsequently her acknowledgment of love. Awakening to feelings can be intuitive, but articulating them takes practice. In chapter 26 they try again. Bao-yu overhears Dai-yu quoting from the same drama, chanting to herself, "Each day in a drowsy waking dream of love" (1.26.516) 每日家情思睡昏昏 (354). This time the exercise ends with Bao-yu's quoting, "If with your amorous mistress I should wed, / 'Tis you, sweet maid, must make our bridal bed" (517) 若共你多情小姐同鴛帳, 怎捨得疊被鋪床 (354), whose erotic implication goes overboard and ends their role-playing session in Dai-yu's tears and another anxious, garbled apology from Bao-yu. Communication of feelings is difficult, but the couple's practice at communication is not fruitless. In the following chapters, Bao-yu and Dai-yu work to reach mutual and mature understanding. No longer quoting the drama, their dialogues begin to shape a romance of their own, which is more profound than the story of *The Western Chamber*.

Even more shocking and more dramatic is listening to *Return of the Soul*, which takes place when Dai-yu passes by the Pear Tree Court and overhears a rehearsal. The section describing the event highlights a complex junction of psychology, music, literature, and a unique experience of awakening. When Dai-yu hears "the languorous meandering of a flute and the sweet modulation of a girlish voice" (1.23.465) 笛韻悠揚, 歌聲婉轉 (1: 316), her mind advances dramatically with the progression of two arias, both from the most celebrated scene of *Return of the Soul*, "The Interrupted Dream" 驚夢. She first hears two phrases from the aria *zao luo pao*, Bridal Du's lines lamenting the beautiful springtime and her own beauty passing without being appreciated: "Here multiflorate splendour blooms forlorn / Midst broken fountains, mouldering walls.... And the bright air, the brilliant morn / Feed my despair. / Joy and gladness have withdrawn / To other gardens, other halls" 原來姹紫嫣紅開遍, 似這般都付與斷井頹垣 ... 良辰美景奈何天, 賞心樂事誰家院. The first phrase of the aria moves her strangely and stops her footsteps. With the second phrase, she "unconsciously nodded her head and sighed" 不覺點頭自嘆. "'It's true,' she thought, 'there is good poetry even in plays. What a pity most people think of them only as entertainment. A lot of the real beauty in them must go unappreciated'" (1.23.466) 心下自思道: "原來戲上也有好文章. 可惜世人只知看戲, 未必能領略這其中的趣味" (1: 316). After this thought she immediately regrets her inattention, which has caused her to miss some of the singing. She focuses on the music again, but the song has changed to a different aria, which is sung by Bridal Du's lover. Listening to the first phrase, "Because of you, my flower-like fair, / The swift years like the waters flow" 則為你如花美眷, 似水流年, she is moved "to the depth of her being" 心動神搖, and listening to the second phrase, "I have sought you everywhere, / And at last I find you here, / In a dark room full of woe" 你在幽閨自憐 she thinks, "It was like intoxication, a sort of delirium" 如醉如癡 (316–17). Finally she cannot even remain standing and collapses onto a rock.

Listening to these arias brings several poems to the heroine's mind. The first two appropriate the image of a red leaf on flowing water and fallen flowers: one by Cui Tu (fl. 9th century), "Relentless the waters flow, the flowers fade" 水流花謝兩無情, and one by Li Yu, the emperor-poet of the southern Tang dynasty, "The blossoms fall, the water flows, / The glory of spring is gone / In nature's world as in the human one" 流水落花春去也, 天上人間. The second, actually an aria from *The Western Chamber*, perfectly summarizes the intertextual relation among poetry, drama, garden, and romance: "As flowers fall and the flowing streams run red, / A thousand sickly fancies crowd the mind" (1.23.467) 花落水流紅, 閑愁萬種 (1: 317).[6] These poems set the tone of Dai-yu's existence. Unlike the seasonal splendor that moves Bridal Du to passion, spring in Prospect Garden has passed its prime, even though Bao-yu and the girls have just moved in. The falling flowers in the physical and textual gardens define Dai-yu's self-knowledge. Through her acts and through her writing, the narrative repeatedly reinforces the connection. The most famous example is her poem on burying fallen blossoms at the end of chapter 27, in which Dai-yu compares herself to the flowers at the end of the season, "As petals drop and spring begins to fail, / The bloom of youth, too, sickens and turns pale. / One day, when spring has gone and youth has fled. / The Maiden and the flowers will both be dead" (2.27.39) 試看春殘花漸落, 便是紅顏老死時. 一朝春盡紅顏老, 花落人亡兩不知 (1: 371).

This poem on burying fallen blossoms is an outburst of her accumulated emotions. It is also a response to the dramas Dai-yu has just read and listened to, and her chanting gives Bao-yu a chance to duplicate her experience outside Pear Tree Court. As he listens to her, he is subjected to stages of emotional transformation similar to what she underwent listening to the actresses. Overhearing her chanting and contemplating the loss of her flowerlike fairness, he is struck with anguish and plunges into deeper grief when he applies her inevitable departure to the other girls, himself, and the garden. His inconsolable grief leads to a moment of confrontation, ending with his heartfelt statement to Dai-yu, "If I were to die now, I should die with a grievance, and all the masses and exorcisms in the world wouldn't lay my ghost. Only when you explained what your reason was for ignoring me should I cease from haunting you and be reborn into another life" (2.28.44) 就便死了, 也是個屈死鬼, 任憑高僧高道懺悔, 也不能超生, 還得你申明了緣故, 我才得托生呢 (1: 375). The young couple, both overwhelmed and transformed by the power of poetry combined with the immediacy of sound, are again on the same plane of awareness: not only of each other's feelings but also, more significantly, of the ephemeral nature of beauty.

Dai-yu laments the transient nature of their paradise, but the novel pushes Bao-yu to transcend further. At the end of chapter 36, to make further amends for his absence during Dai-yu's enchanted encounter with *Return of the Soul* arias, the novel positions him beyond the written text again, and the dramatic immediacy forces him to redefine his notion of feelings and completely change his self-consciousness. This powerful event begins as a late-night conversation between Bao-yu and Aroma, in which he challenges the Confucian notion that "a scholar dies protesting and a soldier dies fighting" (2.36.205) 文死諫, 武死戰 (1: 480) and describes his ideal death:

> Now *my* idea of glorious death would be to die now, while you are all around me; then your tears could combine to make a great river that my corpse could float away on, far, far away to some remote place that no bird has ever flown to, and gently decompose there until the wind had picked my bones clean, and after that never, never to be reborn again as a human being—that would be a really *good* death.                    (2.36.206)

> 比如我此時若果有造化, 該死於此時的, 如今趁你們在, 我就死了. 再能夠你們哭我的眼淚流成大河, 把我的屍首漂起來, 送到那鴉雀不到的幽僻之處, 隨風化了, 自此再不要托生為人, 就是我死得得時了.    (1: 481)

His language is poetic, lyrical, and eccentric. It is drenched with feeling. He does not desire worldly reputation; all he wants is the tears of the girls, because he considers himself the master of Prospect Garden. This notion of glorious death, however, is immediately proved to be an idle fantasy. The morning right after he makes the statement, after reading *Return of the Soul* two or three times, he begins to realize the incompleteness of drama as text and decides to visit Pear Tree Court and ask the actress Charmante to sing the arias for him. It is not clearly stated in the narrative, but the song cycle that Bao-yu wants to hear, which begins with "In these quiet courts the floating gossamer," leads to exactly what Dai-yu hears outside Pear Tree Court. The novel, then, gives the hero access to the heroine's experience of music.

Unexpectedly, Charmante is unfriendly to him, behaving as if his very presence is distasteful to her. Her rejection of his request not only denies him access to Dai-yu's experience but also disproves his assumption that Charmante is just like the other girls in the garden and shakes his confidence that they all adore him as he adores them. But this denial, which he considers the most embarrassing moment in his life, is only the beginning of a harsh lesson. Charmante totally ignores him when Jia Qiang shows up. Witnessing the intimacy between her and Jia Qiang, which is as intense as the love story in *Return of the Soul* and as dramatic as Bao-yu's own relationship with Dai-yu, Bao-yu becomes deeply fascinated and bemused and finally realizes there is no place for him in this couple's world. Leaving Pear Tree Court, given the opportunity and the ability for self-criticism, he returns to his quarters and confesses to Aroma, "[T]hat stuff about all of you making a river of tears for me when I die: I realize now that it's not possible. I realize now that we each have our own allotted share of tears and must be content with what we've got" (2.36.210) 昨夜說你們的眼淚 單葬我, 這就錯了. 我竟不能全得了. 從此後只是各人各得眼淚罷了 (1: 483). This thought brings him sorrow, but the lucid self-knowledge signals his new stage in life — knowing that each person, including him, has a destined share of feelings and relationships.

As the most "lustful" person in the world (1.5.145), as Disenchantment calls him, Bao-yu has a naive initial understanding of love, believing that he can enjoy all the friendship and company of the girls while he dedicates all his romantic feelings to Dai-yu. He projects his feelings onto others, unaware that what he considers mutual is often one-sided. His idea of glorious death is actually self-indulgent, blind, and narcissistic. The lesson in Pear Tree Court clearly and coldly reveals that, although the hero is the master in his little sector, the House of Green Delights, he cannot claim Prospect Garden as his own. After the Pear Tree Court incident, he realizes how shallow and limited his vision is, that he has a "small capacity but a great self-conceit" (2.36.210) 管窺蠡測 (1: 483), as his father has said. When the garden world denies his importance, his belief system and the value of his entire existence are put in question. He has to reposition himself in the cosmos, even if it is only in his little version of the cosmos. This reflective and self-critical moment is a magnificent milestone in Bao-yu's journey of awakening through love, the purpose of his trip to the mundane world.

While the hero acknowledges his limited vision and denies his fantasy, the novel reveals the double meaning of "enlightenment through feelings": it is awakening to love and experiencing love's enchantment, exactly what Dai-yu and Bao-yu do; but it is also acknowledging the inadequacy and the subjective nature of love, which is what Charmante demonstrates to the hero, a lesson he can never learn from Dai-yu. Only by recognizing the shortcomings of feelings can he move on and transcend them and continue to other modes of enlightenment. Although the Pear Tree Court experience constitutes such a crucial moment of awakening, it is clear that the author never considered it the hero's final destination. Bao-yu's awareness of his position in the world of human relationships, however, becomes part of his character. As shown in chapter 78, in which Bao-yu contemplates Skybright's death, Bao-chai's departure, the banishment of the five maids, and Ying-chun's forthcoming marriage, he senses that their happy gathering has come to an end. Time has proved how foolish was his wish for all the girls' tears: not only because they have their own centers of life but also because they cannot remain in the utopian garden forever. Skybright and the other maids are sent away largely under the accusation that they have reached womanhood, and marriage is an even worse tragedy in the hero's eyes. But he tells himself that it is useless to fret about it, because he still has his own share of relationships: "I'll go and enjoy Dai-yu's company for a while; and after that, I've still got Aroma to go back to. It looks as if we three will soon be the only ones left " (3.78.564) 不如還是找黛玉去相伴一日, 回來還是和襲人廝混, 只這兩三個人, 只怕還是同死同歸的 (2: 1100). This humble belief in Dai-yu's love and Aroma's devotion shows that his journey of enlightenment is still incomplete, for Dai-yu will die after she pays her debt of tears and Aroma will leave him to marry an actor. Bao-yu has more mileage to cover before his ultimate gesture, when he cuts off all human attachments and becomes a monk.

Only life itself can put the hero on this route. The Pear Tree Court episodes illustrate the blindness of love and the limitations of poetry, music, and drama. What Bao-yu witnesses is more piercing than what he reads and listens to, because at center stage is life itself rather than art's imitation or representation of it. When he steps into the court, he enters the situation and becomes an insider by personally experiencing rejection and denial—and here lies the shortcoming of Dai-yu's *Return of the Soul* experience: although the music and lyrics move Dai-yu and change her profoundly, she remains outside the court and is never able to transcend her love. The disillusionment Bao-yu experiences is about life itself and cannot be classified under any specific discipline; it is a series of momentary and partial experiences that adds up to completeness, irreplaceable by any other form of expression or instruction. Here the narrator casts doubt on the value of reading again and confirms his position that the transcendental reader (exemplified by Vanitas in ch. 1) exists only in the mythic realm. Literature, whether voiced through poetry, music, or drama, even if written with the author's blood and tears, cannot compete with life's immediacy.

## NOTES

[1] See the discussion of "red" in the introduction to part 2 of this volume.

[2] This legend is discussed in the appendix to volume 4 of *Stone*.

3 In chapter 90, instead of playing Zhong Ziqi to Dai-yu's Bo Ya, Bao-yu ends up as the ox in the expression *dui niu tan qin* 對牛彈琴 ("play the *qin* for an ox"), which John Minford translates using the English saying "cast pearls before a swine" (4.86.156).

4 The episode of Zhen Bao-yu's delivering the jade is known only because of a comment in the Red Inkstone commentary. No such episode occurs in the novel as we now have it.

5 *Zaju* originated as a short variety play (the literal meaning of *zaju*) in the eleventh century, and during the Yuan dynasty it developed into a four-act dramatic form in which songs alternate with dialogue. *Zaju* also features a wedge, a flexible, self-contained scene that usually appeared between acts. Each act had its own musical key, and only the leading actor sang.

6 The last aria that Dai-yu remembers is from the very beginning of *The Western Chamber* and is sung by the heroine. On why Dai-yu cannot see herself as Ying-ying in the end, see Waltner.

# Making Sense of Bao-yu:
## Staging Ideology and Aesthetics

*Maram Epstein*

One of the most challenging aspects of reading *The Story of the Stone* as a window onto the social values of eighteenth-century China is making sense of Bao-yu. Comments by other characters in the novel suggest that Bao-yu does not conform to the conventional expectations of how a son in an elite family should behave. But for all his father's disappointment with Bao-yu's lack of interest in fulfilling his role as scion of a wealthy and politically prominent family, it is equally clear that Bao-yu exemplifies an aesthetic and emotional refinement that is highly admired in the fictional world of the novel and indeed by most of its readers. Sequels and commentaries to the novel, however, show that Bao-yu's positive qualities notwithstanding, many readers felt uneasy about his more self-indulgent and decadent aspects, felt that the young man needed to be more serious, more studious, and, well, just more conventional.

As is true of so many aspects of the richly polysemous *Story of the Stone*, the characterization of Bao-yu captures tensions between opposing ideological values concerning the shifting priorities between self-expression and societal stability. Representing one side of the debate is the spontaneous Bao-yu, who tries to avoid the formal interactions demanded by Confucian ritual; on the other side is his father, Jia Zheng, who is uncomfortable attending informal social gatherings but negotiates highly ritualized formal interactions with great ease. *Stone* uses a complex aesthetic and symbolic vocabulary to explore the clash between the ritualized Confucian self, the foundation of social stability, and the authentic, expressive self. The construction of the authentic self, while superficially similar to what we might consider modern individualism, such as psychological and emotional interiority, is an exploration of the individual not as an autonomous and self-interested entity but as a dynamic subject who comes into being through intense emotional and aesthetic relationships. Many of Bao-yu's qualities that may strike modern readers as queer, and I mean *queer* in the broadest terms possible, are markers of his authentic nature. His ambiguous gender and sexuality are very much part of his resistance to the ritually proper social roles his father would have him assume.

To understand Bao-yu, we must first appreciate the way that orthodox ritual norms informed family life in traditional China. Instead of being a preserve of the private, the family was conceptualized as a microcosm of the larger political and social order that was organized according to Confucian rituals. Central to the Confucian system is the delineation of the five relationships: between emperor and subject, between parent and child, between husband and wife, between older sibling and younger sibling, and between friends. With the exception of friendship, these relationships are hierarchical and, in that each has a distinct superior and inferior position, parallel. Bao-yu treats his maids as friends, but his dealings with them should conform to the emperor-subject or master-servant (slave) relationship. Ritual protocols were used to choreograph both daily contact between family members and large gatherings, such as the reception for the imperial concubine in chapter 18, for which the entire Jia household assembles according to rank, birth order, and sex. Although family rituals superficially appear equivalent to notions of etiquette—for example, children were expected to stand when a family elder entered the room—Confucian ethics had embedded ritualism into the cosmic order. Breaches of ritual could lead to serious cosmological imbalances. Natural disasters, especially flooding, are still read as a sign that China's leadership has engaged in improper policies. Status differences in traditional China were based on a complex matrix of age, birth order, social class, gender, and social network: it is for this reason that the seating order at banquets must be negotiated so that it best reflects the relative status of each person. In each relationship but friendship, the socially inferior person signals his or her relative low status through language (the use of polite terms of address, difficult to capture in English), acts of solicitude (such as serving food to an elder), and bodily demeanor.

Traditional Chinese family life in elite households was marked by a high degree of formality. When Bao-yu gets off his horse and stands, bowed slightly, to make way for his father's literary friends as a demonstration of respect to them and to his father, or when he refers to another member of the family by his or her rank (e.g., referring to his mother as Her Ladyship when talking to a third person), he is behaving as a young man should in an elite family. The first time readers see him, Bao-yu follows ritual protocol perfectly when he rushes in to greet his grandmother, ignoring Dai-yu, whom he has never met, and then leaves to pay a visit to his mother in her apartment (1.3.101). Only after he has paid a formal visit to those most ritually important to him does he acknowledge Dai-yu's presence. Practically every aspect of elite social life was informed by ritual, including the daily visits children and their spouses made to parents, terms of address, and styles and colors of clothing as determined by sumptuary laws.

A cornerstone of ritual governing gender was the separation of men and women. Women belonged to the inner sphere of the household; men could enter the inner sphere, but more properly belonged to the outer sphere of public affairs. Women were not to leave their quarters; when they did, they were chaperoned and shielded from direct contact with this outer male world. Thus, when Dai-yu travels north to join the Jia family after the death of her mother, the curtained palanquin in which she is carried is a symbolic extension of the sequestered women's quarters in which she grew up (ch. 3). Gardens, although structurally inside the household, are an ambiguous space between the inner (female) and outer (male) spheres. By the eighteenth century, many works of fiction idealized the enclosed garden as an aestheticized space in which social formalities could be relaxed. Despite the fascination with gardens as a setting for informal gatherings, they never completely lost their hint of transgressive potential. That Bao-yu lives with his unmarried female cousins in Grand Prospect Garden is a fantasy possible in literature but shockingly transgressive in practice. The reputations of families and individuals were tied to how well these social rules were observed (or how well the appearance of their being observed was kept up), but in addition maintaining proper ritual order was linked to the preservation of the political and cosmic order.

The hierarchical relations foundational to traditional Chinese social order are based on the cosmological superiority of yang over yin. In metaphysical discourse, yin and yang are mutually complementary and interdependent forces. Yang is associated with the sun, the male, brightness, fire, heat, originating activity, regulatory power, life, health, and the like. Yin is associated with the moon, the female, darkness, water, cold, passive receptivity, mutability, death, ghosts, illness, and so on. The processes of natural generation and regeneration are dependent on the free and endless mixing of these two energies. But Confucian ethical discourse fixed the regulatory function of yang and the unstable fertility associated with yin in a social matrix in which the yang position (ruler, parent, elder, male) is dominant over the yin position (subject, child, younger, female). When properly controlled, yin serves to support and regenerate the yang metaorder. When yin is not regulated, it is so inherently unstable that it contains the potential for transgression and subversion. At the core of the Confucian vision is the belief that ritual practices are necessary to maintain the cosmic and sociopolitical order. For example, floods, a sign of yin excess, were historically tied to loss of order, such as an emperor's excessive attachment to his harem. In *The Story of the Stone*, the small flood in Bao-yu's courtyard residence is a consequence of the impropriety of his flirting with his mother's maid Golden (ch. 30).

Gender is a vital component of yin-yang symbolism. Confucian discourse naturalizes the hierarchical relation between yang and yin by pointing to the constancy and power of the sun and the comparatively weak and mutable presence of the moon. By the late imperial period, this superiority of the sun over the moon was commonly used as an analogy to explain the natural superiority of men over women and to justify the unequal social practices of polygamy, whereby a man could take many female partners but a woman could have only one male partner in her lifetime. Bao-yu clearly enjoys his privileged social position as the one male at the center of a constellation of women who orbit him, yet he inverts this natural order when he proclaims that women are superior to men (1.2.76, 20.407–08). His ambiguous gender and sexuality, pointing to an inversion of the proper moral and natural order, are markers of his authentic nature.

Bao-yu rebels against the normative expectations for boys also in his disdain for orthodox learning. Education was an essential component of elite life; sons in elite families were expected to devote themselves to studying the five Confucian classics, *The Book of Poetry, The Book of History, The Spring and Autumn*

*Annals*, *The Book of Rites*, and the *Book of Changes* (equally well known by its Chinese title, the *I Ching*), as well as the Four Books of the neo-Confucian curriculum, *The Confucian Analects*, *The Mencius*, *The Great Learning*, and *The Mean*. (Neo-Confucianism was a twelfth-century synthesis of Buddhist, Taoist, and Confucian ideas that became adopted as state orthodoxy in the fourteenth century. Whereas classical Confucianism was most concerned with behavior, neo-Confucianism followed Buddhism in focusing on the interior self and the control of emotions and desires.) Education was first and foremost conceived of as a moral process; most Confucian thinkers believed that the raw material of human nature needed rigorous training to achieve its full ethical potential. By the eighteenth century, study of the Confucian classics as a route to self-improvement had been eclipsed by the need to prepare for the civil service examination. This preparation involved memorizing the Four Books and the mastery of a highly structured writing form called the eight-legged essay (its eight sections were written in parallel prose). Success in the examination system was a prerequisite for appointment as an official. There was widespread acknowledgment that this educational system did not prepare examination candidates in the practical skills they would need to serve as officials, but its defenders pointed to the ways the curriculum fostered a culture of self-discipline and moral reflection. Indeed, the faith in the merit-based examination system as capable of identifying the most talented men in the empire was so strong that the system was not abolished until 1905. Despite the strict quotas limiting the number of successful graduates, the prestige of being an official was so great that, for most families that could afford to educate a son, study for the examination system was the preferred, if not the only legitimate, occupation for young men. As reflected in the pep talks Lady Wang and Li Wan give their sons before their sons depart to take the examination for the first time, success on the examination was viewed as the best way a son could repay his family's emotional and financial investment in him (5.119.336–37). Although Bao-yu is clearly highly educated, he scorns the type of learning associated with the examination system. His interest is in those forms of literacy linked to aesthetics and self-expression.

In contrast to Bao-yu's rejection of many of the behaviors and beliefs normatively associated with elite male socialization, his young nephew Jia Lan, the son of Li Wan, exemplifies the ideal son. Jia Lan is studious, respectful of the generational and gender differences in the household, and obedient to and solicitous of his widowed mother. An example of Lan's propriety is his refusal to join the family's mixed-sex New Year's party until he is expressly invited by his grandfather, Jia Zheng (1.22.446). In a narrative cliché common to popular literature, Jia Lan's virtuous behavior is rewarded when he passes the official examination while still a teenager (5.119.349).

Bao-yu's worldview clashes most with that of his father, Jia Zheng, whose personal name Zheng 政 literally means "governance," a close cognate of the word *zheng* 正 ("orthodoxy" or "correct"). Jia Zheng spends much of his time in the outer male sphere of the scholarly library, the imperial court, and official office. Although he admits to the lack of intimacy in highly formal gatherings, such as when he greets his oldest daughter, the imperial concubine, from behind a screen (1.18.362), he seems much more at ease in interactions scripted by ritual. His informal interactions with family members at more intimate gatherings are painfully awkward (1.22.446–47). Zheng conforms to orthodox norms of behavior but is revealed to be a parody of correctness in his inability to deal with events that do not fit into a ritual script. The impracticality of his fastidiousness in the official realm shows when he cannot set a moderate limit on the customary payments, known as squeeze, that were part of the business of running a magistrate's yamen. As a result of his refusal to get involved in the compromises demanded by actual official engagement, he is impeached and loses his office when his servants siphon off too much of the grain tax (5.102.77).

Nowhere is the clash between Jia Zheng's orthodox views and Bao-yu's resistance to them clearer than in their attitudes toward textual knowledge. For Jia Zheng, education is synonymous with the morally didactic process of examination preparation. For Bao-yu, the only education that matters is aesthetic literacy. In one of the many ironic juxtapositions in the novel, Bao-yu gives himself over to playing in the garden and organizing the poetry club immediately after his father is sent off as commissioner of education (2.37.216). Jia Zheng recognizes the cultural value of poetry as a marker of taste but has no personal interest in it. The only occasions during which he is interested in poetry are when he leads his literary retainers through the garden in order to name the various sites (ch. 17) and, later, when the Board of Rites puts out an order to commemorate all persons of merit and he and his retainers compose poetry to celebrate the heroic woman warrior Fourth Sister Lin (3.78.565). Jia Zheng takes a certain pride in Bao-yu's outstanding poetic abilities yet sees this kind of literacy as far inferior to the more practical and morally edifying Confucian curriculum.

The schoolroom scene in chapter 9 illustrates Bao-yu's resistance to his father's pragmatic values. It is significant that the episode appears in the ninth chapter: the number 9 is the numerological equivalent of yang. This chapter is the first exploration of the yang-associated theme of Confucian education at the exclusively male setting of the school. Its details make much of Bao-yu's ritual progress from the female-associated inner quarters of the household to the outer male sphere of the school. Not surprisingly, Bao-yu uses the school setting to deepen his romantic friendships with other boys rather than study. Traditional commentaries to the novel point to this scene as an illustration of Jia Zheng's failure to educate his son.

Another area in which Bao-yu falls short of ritual ideals is in his performance of filial piety, the duties and obligations a child owes his or her parents and the most important aspect of Confucian ritualism. Bao-yu lapses in filial respect when he flirts with Golden in front of his mother (2.30.100) and when he lies about his friendship with the actor Bijou to his father and the steward of the prince of Zhong-shun. These breaches of propriety are shocking. As Lady Wang makes clear, Bao-yu's sexual interest in her servant carries hints of incest, since Golden "was almost like a daughter" to her (2.32.139). Moreover, no matter how he feels about his former wet nurse, Nannie Li, Bao-yu should treat her with the respect due a mother figure. His lack of concern for her along with the way he indulges every whim of his maids leads to her frequent outbursts when she feels her authority and social privilege are being threatened (see 1.20.400–01).

But that Bao-yu resists the prescriptive paradigm of how a son in an elite family should behave and that this resistance sometimes has negative consequences do not answer the question of how he was understood in an eighteenth-century Chinese context. Chinese culture was never so monofaceted that it could be equated with Confucian ritualism. Both the Red Inkstone commentary and the popularity of the novel (in terms of readership and the numbers of sequels and commentaries it inspired) demonstrate that many readers identified with or at least felt sympathetic to Bao-yu's free and poetic nature. As a literary creation, Bao-yu gave voice to a widespread frustration with the social expectations for elite men. His relationships with his maids and cousins gave life to many eighteenth-century fantasies about companionate marriages between equally talented men and women. Much of his attraction for readers was precisely his wholehearted pursuit of an identity that lay outside the prescribed official and ritual order.

Even though *The Story of the Stone* conforms to many of the conventions of realism, it is not a realistic text. Bao-yu is very much the product of an aesthetic movement that had its roots in a sixteenth-century critique of the hegemonic ritual order. This cult of sentiment (also translated as "the cult of passion") began as an attack on orthodox neo-Confucian values. Li Zhi was perhaps the most famous intellectual associated with the cult of sentiment writers. Although his views were too radical to make them truly representative of sixteenth- and seventeenth-century intellectual history, they anticipated many representative Qing developments. Moreover, he was given pride of place in the history of Chinese literary aesthetics, in that a number of influential commentaries to works of vernacular fiction and drama that defended the literary value of these marginal genres were attributed to him (falsely). The characterization of Bao-yu reflects many of Li Zhi's ideas.

Among the many intellectual and political trends of which Li Zhi was critical was the overly bookish approach to learning promoted by the state orthodoxy (de Bary). In his critique, the rote learning promoted by the existing educational system excelled at producing bookworms who could reproduce texts they did not understand and could manipulate ritual forms but were ineffectual when confronting real problems, such as combating the corruption and bureaucratic paralysis that had overtaken the Ming court. Cao Xueqin's characterization of Jia Zheng seems the perfect illustration of Li Zhi's parody of the learned but incompetent scholar-official. Li Zhi followed the great philosopher and statesman Wang Yangming in promoting practical learning and unity of thought and action in place of a traditional neo-Confucian emphasis on textual study, intense introspection, and self-discipline. Wang Yangming had argued against the existing educational curriculum of one standard that fit all in favor of a flexible curriculum that took individual differences into account. Li Zhi pushed this concept of a relative rather than absolute standard even further by making the subjective a standard of moral truth. Mainstream neo-Confucian thought had followed Buddhism in being suspicious of the emotions, believing that individual consciousness is a subjective filter that distorts a person's ability to apprehend objective reality. In contrast, Li Zhi argued that emotions were the basis of the authentic self. His authentic self, unlike the ritualized self, valued the qualities of being true to oneself and of the spontaneous expression of emotion.

Li Zhi attacked those scholar-officials who mastered the orthodox norms in order to get ahead in the system. He dismissed the current generation of officials as useless: "[A]ll they understand is bowing and saluting; they sit squarely all day as if they were molded of clay" (Epstein 77). At its worst, ritual became a hypocritical performance based on a false external standard that masked a person's true self, such as when officials pretended to be virtuous in order to hide their greed and ambition. In a tone of disdain that was echoed 150 years later by the fictional Jia Bao-yu, Li Zhi wrote:

> Since people are false, there is nothing that is not false. In this way, if you use false speech to talk to a false person, the false person will be pleased; if you tell false matters to a false person, the false person will be pleased; if you discuss false writings with a false person, the false person will be pleased. If everything is false, everyone will be pleased.          (77)

In place of what he described as an artificial, externally derived moral standard, he promoted the innate childlike heart, a concept that is central to his definition of the authentic. According to Li Zhi, the childlike heart has a natural and spontaneous understanding of the good and can be taken as a true source of authentic morality. In one of his most radical pronouncements, he rooted his definition of the good and the authentic in desires:

> Liking goods, liking sex, study, personal advancement, accumulating wealth, buying more land and property for their descendents, searching for auspicious sites with which to bless their children — all the things that order life and are productive, all these things that everyone practices, acknowledges, and speaks of as good — these are the authentic.
>
> (78; also see de Bary 200)

The ideas of Li Zhi were radical in his time. He was reviled by his conservative contemporaries, was jailed for spreading dangerous ideas (he committed suicide while in jail), and was blamed by one of the most influential seventeenth-century historians for disseminating irresponsible views that had contributed to the fall of the Ming dynasty in 1644. Despite this, many of his philosophical and aesthetic views became incorporated into the mainstream of eighteenth-century intellectual history. Key among these were his ideas about relativism and the importance of the subjective and the emotions as a foundation of authentic self-expression. The sensibilities of the spontaneous and childlike Bao-yu resonate strongly with Li Zhi's ideas of the authentic (e.g., 4.82.51–52).

A favorite rhetorical strategy Li Zhi employed was to take concepts viewed negatively by mainstream orthodox thought and invest them with positive connotations. He transformed desire, anathema to mainstream neo-Confucian thought, into the basis for moral action. This kind of oppositional rhetoric reverberates through *Story of the Stone* and indeed through much of seventeenth- and eighteenth-century fiction. Cult-of-sentiment writers championed as markers of authentic purity those concepts that were devalued in mainstream orthodox thought. In the view of such writers, to be outside the traditional structures of power was to be more authentic; in this sense, women, children, and the uneducated rustic were innately more authentic than male literati.

Because of the way Chinese aesthetics makes use of yin-yang symbolism, a vast vocabulary became associated with the depiction of the authentic in literature. Bao-yu's more peculiar traits emphasize his authentic nature. In addition to their primary meanings of dark and light, female and male, yin and yang had accrued a vast range of associative meanings: cold and heat, inner and outer, intimacy and ritual formality, illness and health, ghosts and the living, dreaming and waking, nature (or wilderness) and civilization, and so on. Yin and yang terms are analogically linked, so that to invoke one quality evokes others. The playing off of yin against yang is central to the structure of many texts. One of Cao Xueqin's achievements in *Stone* is the complexity and richness of his deployment of these overlapping symbolic vocabularies.

Grand Prospect Garden can be thought of as a fantastic, cult-of-sentiment mise-en-scène of yin-associated values and aesthetics. Social interactions in the garden are determined by spontaneous feelings rather than by duty and ritual hierarchy. Bao-yu shows the greatest respect and regard not for the elders in the family but for the young women he likes best, including the maids. Ritual demands that he pay daily visits to his parents, but he does everything he can to avoid contact with his father. The oppositional quality in the sentimental arrangement of relationships in the garden can perhaps best be seen in his eagerness to serve Patience, the maid of his cousins Jia Lian and Wang Xi-feng (2.44.375). No matter how much empathy he feels for Patience and no matter how much she appreciates his acts of kindness, she is only a maid. Moreover, it is highly inappropriate for him to come so physically close to Lian's concubine, since she might give birth to Lian's heir. Bao-yu has no interest in maintaining order or decorum in the garden; instead, it is a place where each of the young women he favors can give full expression to her emotions, no matter whether she feels delight, longing, or peevishness. In his encouraging Skybright to tear up valuable fans for the pleasure of hearing them rip, we see him as a connoisseur of other people's emotions (2.31.116).

Bao-yu and his cousin Dai-yu are emblematic of cult-of-sentiment values. The aesthetics promoted in that cult are linked to yin: the feminine, nature, beauty (as opposed to function and duty), emotions, intimacy, illness, and the erasure of boundaries (remember that maintaining hierarchical boundaries is a core function of ritual). Life in Grand Prospect Garden is dedicated to the pursuit of beauty; the rhythms of the garden are based on the natural world; and the network of relationships in the garden is structured by emotions, not by propriety. Beauty and its appreciation are central: all the inhabitants of the garden are beautiful, and all have exquisite taste.

Bao-yu, the only male allowed into the garden, is strikingly feminine. From his first birthday, when he chooses rouge, jewelry, and other objects associated with women, he shows his identification with the feminine (1.2.76). Those characters in the novel, male and female, who personify the cult of sentiment are feminized by it. The men to whom Bao-yu is drawn, notably Qin Zhong, the prince of Bei-jing, and the actor Bijou (1.7.177, 1.14.287, 2.28.61), are described as femininely beautiful, emotionally sensitive, and unconventional in their behavior. (The Red Inkstone commentary glosses Qin Zhong's name 秦鐘 as "the seeds of sentiment" [*qing zhong* 情種].) Note that Bao-yu is drawn not to all women, only beautiful young women. With the exception of Wang Xi-feng and Qin Ke-qing, he takes no interest in mature or married women. He idealizes young women as purer, more intelligent, and more emotionally authentic than men. This conceptualization of the feminine is as much available to men as it is to women. By the eighteenth century, it was well established that young male leads in fiction and drama should be as beautiful as young women. One of the motifs of romantic fiction is that the scholars and their lovers are equally beautiful and talented. But Bao-yu does go further than most eighteenth-century fictional protagonists in his rejection of the masculine values associated with the world of officialdom and in his appropriation of the feminine.

Since gender roles are so culturally specific, it bears repeating that the terms *masculine* and *feminine* carry different valences in eighteenth-century China than they do in contemporary United States society. The Chinese values governing appropriate gender behaviors were less biologically based than United States norms; instead, they mirrored the hierarchical symmetry of yang and yin. Women were confined to inner quarters, where they were hidden from men, and expected to follow the lead of male members of their households. For their part, men could circulate freely in the outer realms associated with education, government, trade, and warfare. Because of the value placed on intellectual and aesthetic achievements in elite culture, there was a bias against athleticism in men. As can be seen in *Stone*, cultural refinement is associated with physical delicacy; conversely, the physical strength of a character such as Xue Pan marks his brutishness.

A character's sex does not predetermine his or her gender in *Stone*. Wang Xi-feng is extremely beautiful but has many masculine attributes—for example, the ambition that consistently places her in a position of power over men and takes her and her business interests outside the household. Given the connection between masculinity and ethically corrupt behavior in *Stone*, her desire for success and power is neatly counterpoised against Bao-yu's lack of ambition. Her combination of yang ambition in a yin body is the mirror of his yin sensibilities housed in a male body (Yee, "Counterpoise").

By eighteenth-century standards, Dai-yu is the most feminine character in the novel; she is also the most representative of the cult of sentiment. Ethereally beautiful, she evokes the stunning but ephemeral beauty of spring blossoms. The most talented of the poets in the garden community, she shares Bao-yu's contempt for traditional, career-based learning. Impatient with the social pretenses demanded by normal etiquette and manners, she is ruled by her emotions. Modern United States readers might find her instability to be a flaw, but traditional Chinese readers were drawn to her emotional honesty and spontaneity. Unlike the cold and reserved Bao-chai, whom some commentators dismiss as hypocritical in her shows of deference to family elders, Dai-yu embodies the authentic and aesthetic ideals heralded by the cult of sentiment.

Illness is associated with constructions of the authentic because of the way it accentuates the uniqueness and transience of beauty. Being ill makes a character more sensitive to the moment and therefore heightens the affective power of his or her emotional expressions; it also evokes pity in others. Like spring blossoms, the most delicately beautiful of the young women, Lin Dai-yu, Qin Ke-qing, and Skybright, are fragile and prone to illness. Bao-chai looks robustly healthy but gives off an intoxicating, cold fragrance as a side effect of the medicine she takes. Bao-yu and Qin Zhong, the two most beautiful and sensitive young men in the family, share the young women's propensity to a weak constitution. In the polyvalent semiotics of *Stone*, although illness can be read negatively as suggesting a fundamental loss of order and health, in the cult of sentiment it carries the positive connotations of being delicate, sensitive, and expressive.[1]

Bao-yu's sexually ambiguous relationships with Qin Zhong and Bijou are consistent with the cult of sentiment. Since what matters is the ability to conform to cult-of-sentiment values in terms of taste, physical beauty, unconventionality, and sensitivity, a person's sex is less important than a person's affect. Biological males enter Bao-yu's affective world as easily as women, so long as they share his philosophical and aesthetic values. Male same-sex relationships are common in eighteenth-century Chinese texts, which treat them as parallel to heterosexual relationships, in that the male object of desire is younger, less well educated, and more beautiful and frail than the socially and sexually dominant male partner (Vitiello). In this context, the hint of a sexual connection between Bao-yu and Qin Zhong is not unusual. In fact, a sexual relationship between adolescent boys would have been less troubling to the Jia family than Qin Zhong's sexual relationship with Sapientia, the young nun who was a frequent and longtime visitor in the Jia household (1.15.299–300).

The gender play in *Stone* is also a common feature of cult-of-sentiment aesthetics. Bao-yu's girlishness is balanced by Wang Xi-feng's mannish ambition and the boyishness of Shi Xiang-yun, who delights in wearing boys' clothing. Bao-yu orders the actress Parfumée, who specializes in playing male roles, to dress as a young man and change her name to the foreign-sounding "Yelü Hunni" (3.63.236). The cousins Shi Xiang-yun, Li Wan, and Tan-chun quickly follow suit and refashion their actresses as foreign young men. Judging from commentaries and sequels to the novel, traditional Chinese readers enjoyed the gender play in *Stone*. In conventional Chinese theater, troupes were all men or all women, which meant that it was not unusual for young men, such as Bijou, to specialize in playing romantic female leads and for actresses to play men. This practice spread into narrative prose. Traditional Chinese vernacular fiction is filled with female knights-errant, some who dress as women and others who dress as men, as well as men who are beautiful, vulnerable, and emotive. In the eighteenth and nineteenth centuries, this kind of gender play was a standard motif in fictional texts. The more complex the inversions, the richer the aesthetic pattern.

Gender play is just one aspect of an aesthetic that prizes illusion and loss of boundary. Doubling is another. Even though Jia Bao-yu is presented as unique, from the very beginning of the novel readers are made aware that he has an identical other, Zhen Bao-yu, who also has a precious jade and also proclaims to all who will listen that women are superior to men. All boundaries in *Stone* are shown to be permeable. Characters from the mythic frame story repeatedly enter the mimetic world of the novel; Qin Ke-qing moves between life and dreamed reality in chapter 5. At times the division between self and other dissolves. Not only can Bao-yu anticipate how other people feel, he also has an uncanny ability to feel with them. Watching an actress scratch a character over and over again into the dirt of the garden, he becomes concerned that she might catch cold during a sudden downpour. In turn, she mistakes him for a young woman and remarks that he too must be getting wet. "Her words made him suddenly aware that his body was icy cold, and when he looked down he saw that he was soaked" (2.30.104) 一句提醒了寶玉，"噯喲" 了一聲，才覺得渾身冰涼 (414). Shortly after Dai-yu moves into the Jia household, she and Bao-yu develop "an understanding so intense that it was almost as if they had grown into a single person" (1.5.124) 便是寶玉和黛玉二人之親密友愛處，亦自較別個不同，日 則同行同坐，夜則同息同止，真是言和意順，略無參商 (1:68); the two are so close they can finish each other's sentences. Eventually they meet in a shared dream, and he literally erases the physical boundary of his body by cutting open his chest to show her his heart (4.82.65, 83.76).

This fascination with the permeability of boundaries inverts the ritual injunction to fix and stabilize identity by defining the distinctions between things. The concept of the rectification of names, a core Confucian teaching, spells out the need to define social roles. Confucius explained a well-run society in the following terms: "Let the ruler be a ruler, the subject a subject, the father a father, the son a son" (*Analects* 12.11.114). Confucian ritual establishes distinctions so that everyone is clear about how he or she fits in the social hierarchy. Life in Grand

Prospect Garden, however, resists the injunction to maintain order and a stable identity. In chapter 49, the population of the garden explodes with the arrival of more cousins, including Bao-qin, whose beauty temporarily eclipses that of Bao-chai and Dai-yu, and everyone becomes casual and careless in their use of kinship terms:

> The Garden's society was now larger and livelier than it had ever been before. . . . Apart from the two young married women [Li Wan and Xi-feng], the rest were all fifteen, sixteen or seventeen years old. Most of them were in fact born in the same year, several of them in the same month or even on the same day. Not only Grandmother Jia and Lady Wang and the servants, even the young people themselves had difficulty remembering who was senior to whom, and soon gave up trying, and abandoned any attempt at observing the usual formalities of address.          (2.49.473–74)

> 此時大觀園中比先更熱鬧了多少 . . . 敘起年庚, 除李紈年紀最長, 他十二個人皆不過十五六七歲, 或有這三個同年, 或有那五個共歲, 或有這兩個同月同日, 那兩個同刻同時, 所差者大半是時刻月分而已. 連他們自己也不能記清誰長誰幼, 併賈母, 王夫人及家中婆子丫鬟, 也不能細細分晰, 不過是 "弟" "兄" "姊" "妹" 四個字隨便亂叫.          (1: 657)

Confusion about the identities of the characters in the garden becomes even more pronounced in chapters 62 and 63, when the garden bursts into a riot of activity to celebrate all the overlapping spring birthdays.

In the cult of sentiment, this proliferation of like-minded characters is a positive sign of the power of sentiment to transcend the boundaries of the individual, but from a ritual perspective the erasure of boundary and identity is dangerous. At Bao-yu's birthday party, social and architectural distinctions both dissolve (ch. 63). Early in the chapter, one of the older servingwomen chastises Bao-yu for his disrespect toward his mother and grandmother in addressing their maids by their personal names (3.63.220). He likewise disrespects crucial physical barriers when he has the garden gates opened in order to invite his female cousins to his private party long after they should have retired.

The relaxation of social rules during Bao-yu's party might seem playful, but only if one ignores the growing concern expressed in this section of the narrative about thefts, losses, breaches of security in the garden, and the breakdown of order as the actresses and maids increasingly assume the privileges of the masters. The blurring of identities becomes very serious business in the tangled knot of incestuous relationships surrounding the You sisters in chapters 64–66. That Jia Zhen, his son Jia Rong, and their cousin Jia Lian are sleeping with the sisters, who are their sisters-in-law and cousins, is worsened by the fact that the family is in mourning for Zhen's father, Jia Jing. Chinese mourning rites demanded that children abstain from eating, drinking, sex, and even social contact while mourning parents. Though many families did not carry out the prescriptions for mourning to the fullest extent, the many breaches of propriety in these chapters are so flagrant that even the servants express their disgust.

The decadence and danger of the cult of sentiment are most clearly revealed in these chapters. As the fairy Disenchantment warned in chapter 5, love (synonymous with "sentiment" in Chinese) is so closely related to lust that the two can become indistinguishable. Her goal in staging Bao-yu's dream is to teach Bao-yu that love is an "illusion" (*jia* 假, a homophone for the Jia surname 賈) so that he can "shake himself free of its entanglements" and devote himself to the moral teachings of Confucius and Mencius (1.5.146). The veneer of sentiment is stripped from the depictions of lustful desire in chapters 60–69, leaving an unadorned picture of incest, betrayal, and murder. Even the beautiful Wang Xi-feng, who until this point has been able to mask her more underhanded dealings, is shown in her full cruelty and cunning.

It is no coincidence that this crack in the aesthetic surface of the cult of sentiment occurs in the chapters in the sixties. Six (*liu* 六 in Chinese) is the numerical equivalent of yin; nine is the numerical equivalent of yang. The chapters in the sixties make use of yin-yang numerology to explore the threat of yin run amok. It is significant that Cook Liu 柳 and Liu 柳 Xiang-lian suddenly step into the spotlight: their presence points to the sixness of bribery, theft, death, suicide, and murder—in short, of the breakdown of the social order. Note that chapter 6 features the jarring entrance of Grannie Liu 劉 into the novel. Chapter 5 is thematically the most important in the novel, because it is here that Jia Bao-yu enters his illusory dream of red chambers, but in chapter 6 he tries to actualize the lesson in his waking life by initiating Aroma into the arts of love.

The chapters having the number 6 form a chain of signification in the novel that highlights orthodox values, especially a concern about the dangers of desire. Chapter 12 (6 × 2) presents a stark picture about the dual-sided nature of desire. Unlike Bao-yu's sentimental lesson in chapter 5, Jia Rui's encounter with desire becomes a matter of life and death. Jia Rui pursues Wang Xi-feng and falls deathly ill after she repeatedly entraps him. The Mirror for the Romantic is given to him by a Taoist, possibly one of the two mysterious religious figures who appear at regular intervals throughout the novel to restore Bao-yu's jade during moments of crisis. The mirror, parallel to the young woman Two-in-One given to Bao-yu in chapter 5, is the two faces of desire. One side of the mirror, a terrifying image of a skull, can bring Jia Rui enlightenment; the other side shows Xi-feng luring her victim to his death. Chapters 17 and 18 (6 × 3) pick up the thread of Bao-yu's dream from chapter 5. It is in these chapters that Bao-yu reencounters his dream while touring the garden. He experiences déjà vu when he approaches Prospect Hall, the main building in the garden. "The sight of this building and its arch had inspired a strange and unaccountable stir of emotion in Bao-yu which on reflection he interpreted as a sign that he must have known a building somewhat like this before" (1.17.343) 寶玉見了這個所在, 心中忽有所動, 尋思起來, 倒像那裡曾見過的一般, 卻一時想不起那年

月日的事了 (1: 229). He reenters his dream world in chapter 36 (6 × 6) as a succession of young women in the garden watches him sleep (2.36.201), and You San-jie heads to this same Land of Illusion after her love-induced suicide in chapter 66 (3.66.306). This sequence of chapters containing 6 addresses the dual nature of lust/sentiment. Romantic passion (*qing* 情) is the ultimate expression of the emotions celebrated by cult-of-sentiment writers. But because of its connection to sexual desire (*yu* 欲), *qing* was treated with great suspicion in neo-Confucian (Buddhist-influenced) thought. Bao-yu's iconic jade 玉 (*yu* in Chinese, a pun on *yu* ["desire"]) figures prominently in this chain of signification. His jade is the physical manifestation of his subjective consciousness; when Bao-yu loses his jade, he quite literally loses his mind. The centrality of the jade, which is polished to a mirror-like sheen, is reflected in the large polished stone that stands at the entrance to Green Delights. During the Lantern Festival, when each of the riddles refers to some aspect of the person posing it, Bao-yu's riddle refers to a mirror (1.22.449). This chain of signification connects his precious jade to the Mirror for the Romantic, which is meant to bring Jia Rui, and indeed everyone else around him, to an enlightened understanding of the self-destructive potential of desire.

Just as yin themes are explored in the chapters containing 6, yang themes inform certain of the chapters containing 9. Bao-yu begins his formal education at the all-male environment of the clan school in chapter 9; he is not enrolled again in the family school until chapter 81 (9 × 9); and he and Lan leave home to take the official examination in chapter 119. Chapter 27 (3 × 9) marks the rapid shift in season from spring to summer (the *yang* season). The temperature in chapter 29 becomes oppressively hot, and the entire family, including the women, leaves the Rong-guo mansion to find respite from the heat at a local Taoist temple. At the temple, Xi-feng and Jia Zhen give vent to sudden bursts of anger (a hot emotion associated with yang). A final example of yang numerology occurs in chapter 99, an episode that is unusual in that it is focalized through Jia Zheng's perspective. It enumerates his trials serving as an official in the capital.

*Stone* also uses five-phases symbolism (Plaks, *Archetype* 61–68).[2] Bao-yu's characterization, and indeed the entire garden world, is informed by it. The five phases (also commonly referred to as the five elements) are a development of yin-yang thinking and are a key cosmological concept in Chinese metaphysics. Through a complex system of associative terms, the five phases organize the cosmos into a coherent, dynamic, and interconnected totality. Mapped onto the elements of earth, water, wood, fire, and metal are the four seasons, the five directions, the five major organs of the body, the five colors, the five major offices of government, and so on. Chinese medicine is based on the five-phases system; illness occurs when the body is out of harmony because it is either blocked or circulating too quickly, or because it suffers from excess or deficiency of any one element. Each element generates the element that follows: as winter precedes spring, water nourishes plant growth, which then feeds fire, and so on. A simple schema representing the five phases might look like the one in figure 1.

north
water
black
winter
kidney

| west | center | east |
|------|--------|------|
| metal/gold | earth | wood |
| white | yellow | green |
| autumn | spleen | spring |
| lung | | liver |

south
fire
red
summer
heart/mind

Fig. 1. The five phases

The use of five-phases periodicity in *Stone* is intertwined with the cult of sentiment, in that the novel foregrounds a social world based on natural dynamic rhythms instead of on an idealized ritual code. Once readers become aware that Lin Dai-yu's family name means "woods," that the Dai in her name refers to a green-black color, and that her passions are quite heated, they see that she fits the schema as a spring-summer character. Dai-yu is physically delicate but has intense energy. Her most celebrated scene is her "farewell to the flowers" as spring turns to summer and she attempts to protect the fallen blossoms by sweeping them into muslin bags (2.27.38–39). Much of the poetry associated with her points to her ephemeral nature: as wood burns hot but then turns to ash and then smoke, she too will vanish into thin air. Complementing Dai-yu is Xue Bao-chai: her family name Xue 薛 is a homonym for "snow" 雪, and the *chai* in her name is a gold hairpin. "Snowy" Bao-chai can be mapped onto the fall-winter quadrant of the five-phases schema. She is physically robust but does not do well in the heat; moreover, she has strikingly white skin and is temperamentally cool. She is introduced into the narrative during a cold winter scene that is punctuated by heavy snow; it is during this scene that Bao-yu becomes intoxicated by her cold aroma. Dai-yu, who had been inseparable from Bao-yu until this point, is literally left out in the cold (ch. 8). Wang Xi-feng also fits in the five-phases schema. Her iconic red color and nickname "Peppercorn" suggest her association with summer. Her dominant personality traits, anger and ambition, are linked to fire in that they are easily sparked, flare up quickly, and consume everything in their path. Xi-feng becomes a dominant character during the hot spell in chapter 29, when she seems to be everywhere in the temple while everyone else wilts under the oppressive heat. Her associative range extends into fall, the killing season, as seen when she borrows a knife and manipulates Jia Lian's new concubine, Autumn, to drive their shared rival, You Er-jie, to death in chapter 69. Significantly, You Er-jie commits suicide not by hanging herself but by swallowing gold. As the season turns toward winter, Xifeng disappears from the narrative focus.

Bao-yu occupies the center of the schema. His jade symbolizes the earth element. As the microcosm of the emperor, he must center the symbolic system through appropriate action, but he refuses this responsibility. At the center of the schema, he has no seasonal identity but moves freely between Dai-yu and Bao-chai and their shadows as their seasonal moment arrives. *Shadow* is a term used in Chinese fiction criticism to describe secondary characters that are modeled after a primary character. Two of Dai-yu's most important shadows are the delicately beautiful maids Skybright and Crimson (in Chinese, Lin Hong-yu 林 紅玉 ["Woods Red-Jade"]), while the plump and sensible Aroma and the maid Musk are shadows of the aromatic Bao-chai. The major events in Grand Prospect Garden are organized around a calendar as the family gathers to celebrate birthdays and seasonal moments. Much like traditional picture albums that feature iconic scenes depicting the pleasures of each season, the cousins' colorful banquets and gatherings follow the energies of the seasonal cycle.

The architecture of the garden residences reflects each character's elemental identity. Dai-yu's Naiad's House is hidden by the "hundreds and hundreds of green bamboos" that surround it (1.17.330); in contrast, "not a single tree" grows in Bao-chai's All Spice Court, only fragrant plants and herbs (339). Although Bao-chai's All Spice Court is larger and grander than Dai-yu's Naiad's House, it is much farther from Green Delights. Distance indicates each young woman's degree of intimacy with Bao-yu. Spectacularly beautiful maiden crab blossoms surround Bao-yu's residence. According to folklore, this type of apple tree came from the Land of Maidens (345). A huge polished stone, an architectural rendering of his jade, stands at the entrance to his House of Green Delights ("green" 青 is pronounced *qing*, a pun for "sentiment" [*qing* 情]). The interior of Bao-yu's residence is filled with clever trompe l'oeil details that illustrate how he is at the center of the Buddhist world of illusion (*jia*) explored in the novel.

One of the reasons *Story of the Stone* is such a masterpiece is that it can be read on many different levels. Readers who enjoy it for the story of the love triangle among Bao-yu and his two beautiful cousins have as rewarding a reading experience as those who are attuned to the novel's aesthetic structuring. For twenty-first-century readers used to the conventions of realism, the minutiae of daily life in an elite eighteenth-century Chinese family as well as the creation of psychologically complex characters are convincing evidence that the novel is realistic. The novel does in fact provide reliable information about Chinese culture and history. By embodying so many different meanings, Bao-yu is a literary construct around whom is spun a densely woven symbolic and aesthetic pattern. His characterization gives readers insight into the often contradictory desires of eighteenth-century Chinese to enjoy a life dedicated to the pleasures of the authentic self yet at the same time to maintain a stable domestic, social, and cosmological order. Although Bao-yu is not a realistic depiction of a son in an elite family, it is possible that young men like him did exist and that he and his young female cousins inspired readers. His character captured a widespread frustration with a social and ritual code that emphasized formality over self-expression and duty over intimacy. Grand Prospect Garden was the perfect escapist fantasy, distracting readers from the grueling rigors of examination preparation and its likely disappointments and from the demands made on both men and women to sacrifice their own pleasures and interests for the sake of their families. Who under such conditions would not enjoy reading about a life dedicated to beauty, poetry, passionate emotions, and the spontaneous celebration of the moment?

Finally, what about the queerness of Bao-yu's gender and sexual identities? Because modern readers are so culturally attuned to questions of gender and sexuality, these aspects of his character have particular significance for them. But traditional readers were not troubled by such ambiguity: it was long established as a literary sign of having an authentic nature. Of a piece with his own delicate physical beauty, Bao-yu's femininity and appreciation of other beautiful people, both male and female, accentuate his emotional purity, sensitivity, and refined aesthetic taste. In this sense, Bao-yu is an embodiment of the cult of sentiment.

NOTES

[1] For more on traditional views of illness, see Andrew Schonebaum's essay in this volume.

[2] Some readers may be familiar with the five elements because they are the organizational concept behind the Pokémon figures.

# Truth and Fiction in the Translating of *The Story of the Stone*

## *John Minford*

The story of how a literary masterpiece acquires a new life in translation sometimes makes for interesting reading. One thinks of the wonderful English version of Rabelais by Sir Thomas Urquhart, who is said to have died laughing
at the restoration of Charles II; of Edward Fitzgerald's *Rubaiyat of Omar
Khayyam*;[1] of the incomparable (despite its occasional coyness) Proust of C. K.
Moncrieff; of Arthur Waley's *Genji* and *Monkey* (the latter written in defiance of
the blackout during the Blitz). In the case of the classic Chinese novel *Honglou
meng* or *Shitou ji*, its English rebirth has something of the quality of the many-
layered tale of origins embedded in the very first chapter of the novel itself.[2] A
whole book has been written recently in Chinese about the novel's French incarnation, about the originator of that project, André d'Hormon and the Cercle
de Royaumont, and his collaborators, Li Tche-houa (Li Zhihua) and Jacqueline
Alézaïs (Zheng). But little has been written about David Hawkes and his equally
remarkable achievement. The late Stephen C. Soong, a prominent Hong Kong
critic and translator, published a delightful literary study in 1976 of the first volume of *Stone*, wittily entitled *Honglou meng xiyou ji* 紅樓夢西遊記 ("*The Story
of the Stone*'s Journey to the West") (Lin Yiliang). A short essay of mine refers in
some detail to some of the marvels of Hawkes's translation ("Pieces").[3]

## *A Family Enterprise*

The present fragmentary narrative is in part based on an interview conducted
in Oxford ten years ago, on 7 December 1998 by Connie Chan Oi-sum (299–

335), partly on the translator's own published writings,[4] partly on my correspondence and conversations with him over the years, and partly on my own memories. It can be supplemented by reference to the series of four notebooks that Hawkes kept during his years working on the novel, which have been published in a facsimile edition in Hong Kong (Story . . . *A Translator's Notebooks*).

As his student, apprentice, and ultimately collaborator, beginning more than forty years ago in 1967, when I was an undergraduate and we first read the novel's opening ten chapters together at Oxford, I find it hard not to be affected by the strong personal ties that bind us, ties which in part stem from the enormous debt we both owe to this magical work of literature. As his friend and son-in-law, I welcome this opportunity to pay tribute to a man who as well as being a great scholar, teacher, and translator, has also been an inspiring and guiding influence in my life.

In this whole story (as in the novel itself) it has never been easy to separate truth and fiction. Life and art have constantly intertwined. Something of this can be seen in the dedications of the five volumes of the published Penguin Classics translation. The first volume ("The Golden Days," in 1973) was dedicated to Dorothy and Jung-en—Dorothy Liu (née Cheng) and her husband, Liu Jung-en. Dorothy, who died in 2008, taught Chinese for many years at London University's School of Oriental and African Studies. From the inception of the translation project in the early 1970s, she was constantly available (often at the end of the phone) as an informant to Hawkes while he worked his way through the novel's first eighty chapters. Her daughter, Tao-Tao, still teaches Chinese at Oxford and was indeed my own very first instructor of Chinese in the summer of 1966 (she subsequently sat in on our *Stone*-reading classes). The second volume ("The Crab-Flower Club," in 1977) was dedicated to R. C. Z., Professor R. C. Zaehner, David's friend, a great authority on Indian and comparative religion and fellow of All Souls College, Oxford, who had died three years earlier.[5] (David also became a fellow of that distinguished college after his retirement from the Oxford chair of Chinese.) I still remember the excitement caused by Zaehner's review in the *Times Literary Supplement* of Robert Pirsig's counterculture novel *Zen and the Art of Motorcycle Maintenance*. For me, this dedication testified to the shared broadness of interest and sympathy of these two great Oxford scholars and to their gift for bringing together rigorous scholarship and new and challenging currents of thought, a gift I came to value highly in David and in all of his work as teacher and translator. From volume 3 onwards, all of the *Stone* volumes were dedicated to members of the family: volume 3 ("The Warning Voice," in 1980) to Jean, David's wife; my own volume 4 ("The Debt of Tears," in 1982) to my wife, Rachel (David and Jean's daughter); and my volume 5 ("The Dreamer Wakes," in 1986) to our four children. (Incidentally, all of these volume titles were invented by the translators.) So just as the Chinese *Stone* was itself a family novel, with various family members joining in, in more or less helpful ways, so too the combined five-volume translation was a family undertaking.[6]

While we are on the subject of the "family enterprise," I am often asked how I came to play the part of Gao E. Here are David's own words:

> I'd just about got to the point where I'd signed on to do this, to do the whole novel for Penguin Classics, when John came back from I don't know where (he was living a very rambling life, here and there, doing this that and the other thing, and had dropped out of academic life at one stage), and said "Oh I've decided what I want to do with my life, I want to translate *Honglou meng*." I thought, poor guy, I've just cornered the market for the next twenty years, it seemed really tough. So I thought about it, and thought, I don't know, it's going to take me umpteen years to do the whole thing and when all's said and done there are certain differences between the first 80 chapters and the last 40—whatever you think. So I thought it could be useful. Suppose I drop dead after doing 80 chapters, it'd be nice to have someone to carry on. . . . I felt at the same time, if he was doing it, we were in a way close enough for me to share things with him to some extent; and yet we were different people. . . . We decided we would be quite autonomous. We were in liaison, but we were working pretty much independently of each other.    (Chan Oi-sum 335)

I have kept the very first letters that David wrote to me on the subject from the Oriental Institute in Pusey Lane, Oxford, in early 1970, and I still remember the excitement with which I read them:

> Betty Radice [editor at the time of Penguin Classics] read the McHugh-Kuhn translation of HLM over Christmas. [She had, I believe, been put on to it by Arthur Cooper, an old friend of David's, translator of Li Bo and Du Fu.] She is completely bitten by the novel (even in that disguise), and anxious that I should undertake the translation. She also leapt at the idea of the sort of collaboration with you I suggested when we met.    (20 Jan.)

> I am sending you my translation of Chap. 1. I hope, after reading it, you won't decide that you want nothing more to do with the whole business! Whatever you decide, I should like it back eventually, though there is no tearing hurry. If you are interested I can send you my proposals for dealing with some of the names in the book.    (6 Feb.)

Betty Radice, a superb editor of the old school (and herself a gifted translator of Latin), was not only responsible for commissioning the translation: she remained closely involved in the ongoing progress of the Penguin *Stone* until she retired from Penguin some ten years later. In 1976 she read my first chapters (of vol. 4) with enormous care, making numerous (often highly critical!) comments in colored pencil. Before I left England for Australia in 1977, I went to meet her in London, and I still remember how at the end of our meeting she bade me farewell on the steps of the Penguin office with the words, "Read Bunyan! Read Swift!" She was deeply concerned that I should make a determined effort to acquire a passable English prose style and not "let the side down."

To complete the story of my own involvement, that departure of mine to Australia in 1977 was prompted by an extraordinary chain of events in which *Stone* played a vital role. Professor Liu Ts'un-yan was then in charge of Chinese studies at the Australian National University. He was a longtime aficionado of the novel (and himself a novelist) and knew of the translation work in progress (by then, vol. 1 had appeared). He wrote to David early in 1976, "in Chinese characters about a millimeter high," suggesting that David's "exalted disciple" might be interested in traveling to the antipodes to pursue further studies (letter from Hawkes to Minford, 17 May). I did, and for over three years Liu Ts'un-yan became what the Germans so aptly call my *Doktor-Vater*, guiding my reading and nursing the translation through its gestation and remaining to this day another benevolent father figure (after all his name means "perpetuation of benevolence").

## The Way to the Stone: Extracts from an Interview

But I am already far ahead of myself. To go back to the very beginning: "What, you may ask, was the origin of this translation?"

To answer this question, we must ask another: How did David Hawkes begin studying Chinese in the first place? I shall allow his own words to speak, doing no more than add one or two headings. What we have here are some of his recollections of the steps that would eventually lead him to undertake the *Stone* project in 1970.

In the 1998 interview, he begins by talking about how he first became interested in the study of Chinese, in the years immediately before World War II, during which he had been involved with the teaching of Japanese to code breakers in Bedford:

> There was a very popular book by Lin Yutang called *The Importance of Living*, which everyone was reading in about 1938–39. . . . I think it was before the war even, when I was still a schoolboy. During the war I was doing Japanese in Intelligence. . . . But I didn't want to do Japanese academically. You couldn't, they didn't teach Japanese at Oxford in those days. I was getting interested in oriental things. I think I must have read one or two translations. I read Waley's *Monkey*, a few things like that, while I was in Bedford during the war. . . . At the end of the war, because I was a civilian, I got out very quickly in 1945, and I could go to Oxford in the last term of the year, beginning in October 1945. I said, can I keep my scholarship and transfer to Chinese. I didn't even know if they'd say yes, but they said yes, you can. And so I came back in October 1945. There was

only one teacher [E. R. Hughes], and I was the only student! It was very lonely! There were some more who came later. By the time I graduated there were only about five or six of us studying.

Hughes was an old missionary originally. He was a nice old man, who'd come to academic life very late in life really. He was getting pretty old. He was near retirement age. There was a professor of Chinese between the wars called Soothill. All these people—the few people teaching Chinese in England at that time—were what they call Old China Hands. Either they were old missionaries, or they'd been in the foreign service—you know, consuls and that sort of thing. . . . Hughes was a disappointed man, because they never suggested he should be the next professor. They made him a reader. . . . One thing he succeeded in doing before I came was to persuade the University to have an honors school of Chinese. And in fact the first person who got an honors degree in Chinese was Gladys Yang. That's the wife of Yang Xianyi. Gladys Taylor she was then, she came of a missionary family. . . . The old scholars in Oxford were very suspicious of [Chinese]. . . . Hughes's new honors school was all *Wu Jing Si Shu* [the Five Classics and Four Books of the Confucian tradition]. The very first thing I had to do was to read *Da Xue* [recites the opening of *Da Xue*]. . . . Then after that you read some little bits of things: little bits of *Lunyu*, *Shu Jing*—can you imagine it! I mean, it was just ridiculous! A little bit of *Shi*, a bit of *Guo Feng*, a bit of *Da Ya*. I mean no one can understand what it means. And then we had to read some of *Yi Jing*, and some of *Li Ji*—two books of *Li Ji* I think. And then we read . . . *Daodejing*, and the *Tianxia* chapter of Zhuangzi, which is very very difficult to read . . . we didn't know about Chinese literature at all![7] Anyway, that was what the degree course was like. . . . And I was very determined to try and go there if I possibly could. . . .

### Chen Yinke

By the time I graduated, that was in December 1947, Hughes had decided to retire. He was still around, but he was going to retire. And they appointed a new professor. They wanted to get a very famous professor in Leiden [Duyvendak]. . . . One of the good things Hughes did [earlier], when he realized that he had no chance to become professor himself, he agitated to get a good Chinese scholar—I mean a *Chinese* Chinese scholar. He got them (in 1937 I think) to appoint Chen Yinke from Lingnan University, the old Lingnan when it was in Guangdong. And he accepted. Officially Chen Yinke was professor of Chinese at Oxford for about seven years. But he never came. He said now that there's a patriotic war against Japan, I don't think I should leave my country. He was a very honorable man in this way. But he said, may I come at the end of the war. And they said, OK, fine. But by the end of the war, he was losing his sight. So it was agreed, he said, I'll come to England, and have the operation (it was a detached retina). He came to England, and had the operation, and unfortunately afterwards was blind. So he never came to Oxford.

## Wu Shichang

When I graduated I got to know Wu Shichang [Wu Shih-ch'ang] quite well. He came [to Oxford] on his own, of course; his family was back in China. And he was a very progressive man. He was friends with Guo Moruo and people like that.[8] He was a very considerable scholar as well. With a wide range of interests. In addition to his *Honglou meng* studies, he was also a good scholar, interested in *jiaguwen* ["oracle bones"] and things like that. When he first came he had lodgings, B & B lodgings in Iffley Road. About half a mile down the road from here. . . . As soon as I graduated I started having some lessons with him. I used to go to his house. I read some Tang *shi* ["poetry"] with him. As well as that I tried to read some *baihua* ["vernacular"] on my own: one of Lu Xun's stories and a chapter or two of *Shuihuzhuan* [*Outlaws of the Marsh*].

## Beida, Hu Shi, Empson, Arrival in Peking

Because I wanted to get to China, I'd saved up enough for the passage. Everyone went by boat in those days. The cheapest passage was 89 pounds, from Southampton to Hong Kong. The voyage took one month. I was writing letters about this all the time. I wanted to go to Beijing University. In those days there were three Peking universities. They were Tsing Hua and Yenching—they were both outside the city. I thought it would be much more interesting to be inside the city. I wanted to go to what they called in those days Guoli Beiping Daxue. (It was Beiping then). And I was writing letters and never getting any reply. In the end I was helped to go there by William Empson, the poet, who was teaching there. He was the only foreigner there, at Beida [Chinese abbreviation for Beijing University]. There were very few foreigners in Beijing at the time. He was there with his wife and his two little sons. . . . At that time the Beida *xiaozhang* ["president"] was Hu Shi—he became *xiaozhang* some time in 1946 or 1947. I think he had been ambassador or something in Washington, and on his way to take up the post at Beida he had passed through Oxford, where he was given an honorary degree. I remember seeing him outside the [Oxford University] divinity school, or wherever it was they'd been giving him his degree. Some Chinese friend said, "Oh, there's Hu Shi!" But I never met him. Wu Shichang gave me letters of introduction—for example, I had a letter of introduction to Qian Zhongshu, who was living in Shanghai then.[9]

Empson had once been into the office of the *xiaozhang* and he saw several of my letters lying around, probably unopened, I don't know. Hu Shi never bothered about his correspondence. He used to boast about it, that he never bothered with letters. . . . I didn't know Empson. I didn't know anything about him at all. I think I might have read one of his poems once in an anthology. But he saw these letters and thought, this is terrible, this poor young man is trying to get to China and Hu Shi's not even opening his letters. So he started things moving. So anyway, when the *lunchuan* ["steamship"] got to Dagu or whatever it's called [the port for Tientsin (Tianjin)], I was called to the purser's office on the ship, and they said, "There's a message for you." It was from Mrs. Empson, Hetta Empson, saying please come and stay with us until you've got somewhere else to go to. . . . The next day I joined my Chinese friends—I think they were going to Tsing Hua. Of course we went on the train from Tientsin to Beijing. Beijing *chezhan* ["railway station"] at that time was full of refugees, people sitting on the ground with bundles and children, saying please help me. It was a bad time then. Just the year before, in 1947, they—the Guomindang—had compulsorily evacuated a lot of students from Shenyang and Changchun, and just dumped them down in Beijing, and sort of forgotten about them. I think there had been a big demonstration that turned into a riot just the summer before. Anyway, they were met by a lorry. In those days you had great big tin trunks. I had two trunks, and a bicycle as well. So we all got on this lorry, and I put my trunks and the bicycle on it. They said they'd give me a lift, which was very kind of them. And so they took me, they found the address, of this very narrow little *hutong* ["alley"], the lorry could just about go down it. And then they took out my bicycle and trunks and set me down, and I met the Empsons. They were living in an old house.

**Beijing University**
I don't know if you know about the old Beijing University? Have you ever been to Beijing? Of course, I wouldn't know it now. I can go around it in my dreams—I mean, as it was fifty years ago. Then of course it was a walled city. [Draws a map.] In the old days the north part was just like a box. . . .

The old Beijing University was in Shatar. . . . If you talk about Beijing University nowadays, Beida, they think of it being outside the walls. . . . All these places around here were to do with *qiren* ["Manchu bannermen"] or the palace. In fact the oldest part of Beiping *daxue* was the old *Guozi Jian* ["Imperial Hall of Classics"]. All the other parts were very seedy new buildings. There was a *Hong Lou* ["Red Building"], funnily enough! [Laughs.] It was where the Japanese used to torture people in the basement during the war. It's said that Mao Zedong was librarian there once, but I don't know if he really was. There was *Hong Lou*, and *Hui Lou* ["Gray Building"], and *Bai Lou* ["White Building"]. . . . And a very very big dusty campus in the middle called *Minzhu Guangchang* ["Democracy Square"]. The hostels were all over the place. The Empsons were living quite near the university. It was quite an old place, probably a Manchu's residence at one time. Everywhere was *ping fang* ["one-story buildings"] of course, this whole part. The only tall buildings were down in the consular area, the banks and so on. When you went through the *hutongs* it was very dusty. And there were just gray walls on either side. Off the big roads, that is. You don't see anything, just walls and gates. . . . If you went up on top of Coal Hill and looked down, it looked like a forest, because you could see all the trees in the courtyards. . . . The hostel I stayed in, after staying with the Empsons for about three weeks, was in Dongchang *hutong*. . . . It wasn't an old building, it wasn't a *ping fang*. It was called the *yanjiusheng sushe* ["postgraduate students hostel or dormitory"]. . . . It was actually a two-story prison that had been built by the Japanese for Chinese officers. It was like a prison inside. You know what prisons are like, upstairs they have a sort of gallery . . . that you can look through, with a rail. . . . You can look right down from top to bottom and you see the cells all around. They were little cells, about from there to here [gestures], just big enough for a bed, and a table and a little chair. Barred windows and everything. So that was the hostel, and there were about—well, half of them were Chinese, and then there were these Indians. The Indians included Amit Tagore, who was the great-nephew of Rabindranath Tagore. . . . And there were a whole lot of other Indians from Santiniketan studying Buddhism. . . . Anyway, I went and lived in this hostel.

**On First Reading *The Story of the Stone***

I'd heard about *Honglou meng* from students in Oxford. . . . I think a friend, maybe Qiu Ke'an, showed me a copy of this great novel, so I'd heard about it. I think I tried to read the first chapter, and it was very difficult. Actually the beginning of *Honglou meng*, if you're not familiar with either *baihua* or modern *wenyan*,[10] is quite difficult, because it's written in a very strange style to start with, that first chapter. . . . I struggled through about a page, I think! [Laughs.] But anyway, people talked a lot about *Honglou meng*, Chinese students, and I thought well, I'll try and read it. So what I did, through a Chinese friend of the Empsons, a lady the Empsons knew, they found an unemployed—I don't know what he was, I think he'd been a government clerk in Hebei. He wasn't from Beijing, he came from outside. He hadn't got a job, he was living on his wife; they were very very poor. He was a sort of a *lao xiansheng*, a very old-fashioned man. He always wore a *changpao* ["long gown"] all through the year. Everyone used to wear a *changpao* in the winter; you wore a *mianpao* ["padded gown"], everyone did, just to keep warm. But you never did in the summer, unless you were a shopkeeper or something like that. But he was very old-fashioned. He used to come round, every day I think. I spent quite a lot of money on having lessons. He couldn't speak a word of English, and I don't think he'd taught language before either; but with the help of some Chinese friend I bought a copy of *Honglou meng*, and

342   TRUTH AND FICTION IN THE TRANSLATING

we used to sit side by side, and we'd read it—he'd read it—read it out loud—and then start explaining it; and I didn't understand what he said, but I could see what he was talking about. So it was a sort of direct method gone mad, if you like! I wouldn't suggest it as an ideal way of learning, but it's the way I chose. I thought of it as a way of learning. I wanted to read the novel, having heard about it. . . . Gradually I found it did work, actually; I didn't understand a lot of what he said first of all, he was just talking away all the time. He didn't speak real *Beijing hua* [Beijing dialect], he probably spoke with rather a funny sort of accent. I expect I never learned proper Pekinese.

## Teachers at Beida

None of the teachers at Beida, well very few, spoke anything like even *Putonghua* [Mandarin Chinese]. They were practically all southerners. I went to some classes by Yu Pingbo, and I could hardly understand a word he said![11] He was from Zhejiang, I think. There were one or two who spoke very very good *Beijing hua*—Luo Changpei for example. I went to Luo Changpei's class; he was a *qiren*, he was a friend of Lao She.[12]

Yu Pingbo was famous, but I didn't even know that at the time! I didn't know anything about all this scholarship. I was trying to learn Chinese. I was a sort of *pangtingde* ["auditor"], I was going to classes and listening, and I suppose the classes I followed most religiously and learnt most from were in *wenzixue* ["philology"]. I went to classes by Tang Lan [a historian of the ancient periods]. There were only a few people who went to them. Particularly after *jiefang* ["liberation"] (I don't know any other way to call it, whatever you think about it) you had to be careful what you said. . . . But in the case of *wenzixue*, if you were talking about *Shuowen jiezi* [the early dictionary of etymology], you can't really go too far wrong. As long as you don't get too much into anthropology and that sort of thing. I was very interested, and I used to go to quite a lot of lectures. Officially, I did "Li Sao" [the opening poem in *The Songs of the South*] as my special subject when I was graduating in Oxford. . . . I had to register myself as an "advanced student," so I put down the *Chuci* [*Songs of the South*]. I started trying to translate. I did quite a bit of translating, actually, from *Chuci*. Not very literary translation, just translating the words for myself. Trying to find out what it meant. . . . The only person who was lecturing on it was called You Guoen. I didn't care for him very much, I didn't like him as a person. He was rather a creepy sort of person really. . . . I used to go to various classes on Chinese literature, history of literature. There was someone called Zhao Xilu, I remember. Lin Geng was interesting. He was someone who spoke very beautiful *Beijing hua*. . . . He was lecturing on *Nanbeichao wenxue* [the literature of the Southern and Northern Dynasties]. . . .

## *On Translating* The Stone

David was always insistent that what he was embarking on was a *novel* in translation, a book that lovers of literature might find enjoyment in, not a text for scholars to pore over and dissect. He himself was a voracious reader of literature in several languages. I remember that over the period when he was settling in to this great project, he was reading and rereading many favorite works of classic English fiction, including the novels of George Meredith and Henry James. He immersed himself in the findings of *hongxue* ("Redology") and even attended the first *hongxue* conference in Madison, but "I felt by the end of it that I'd really had enough of *hongxue* to last me for two lives. It's very interesting. But a lot of it isn't relevant to translating." As for translation theory or principles of translation, he had no time for them either:

> I don't know whether I've got any principles. . . . I thought that what I'd like to do was a translation where I didn't have to think about academic considerations, scholarly considerations. I'd just think about how to present this book—this was Penguin, after all—in such a way that I did the whole of it but at the same time it was enjoyable for the English reader, if possible. They could get some of the pleasure out of it that I had got myself.[13]

## *Envoi*

I recall David saying to me on one occasion in his study at 59 Bedford Street: "We're just doing this for the hell of it!" Not because we had received some large grant (we never did); not because the translation fitted into some grand scheme of things (it never did). We were doing it because we had to, because we had both been well and truly bitten by the book, it had come along and changed our lives.

It seems most apt to conclude these hastily compiled jottings with some words from the novel itself. First, from the passionate (and superbly translated) "younger brother's" preface, in which Tangcun quotes Cao Xueqin:

> I might lack learning and literary aptitude, but what was to prevent me from turning it all into a story and writing it in the vernacular? In this way the memorial to my beloved girls could at one and the same time serve as a source of harmless entertainment and as a warning to those who were in the same predicament as myself but who were still in need of awakening.
>
> (1.21)

雖我未學, 下筆無文, 又何妨用假語村言, 敷演出一段故事來, 亦可使閨
閣昭傳, 復可悅世 之目, 破人愁悶, 不亦宜乎?                    (2)

And then from the closing pages of the novel:

> Perhaps my fellow humans whom the realm of life has ensnared may find in this tale an echo, . . . a reflected light to quicken their own aspirations. . . . [And yet] it was really all utter nonsense! Author, copyist and reader were alike in the dark! Just so much ink splashed for fun, a game, a diversion!                                                    (5.120.374–75).[14]

> 或者塵夢勞人, 聊倩鳥呼歸去, 亦未可知. . . . 果然是敷衍荒唐! 不但作者不知, 抄者不知, 並閱者也不知. 不過遊戲筆墨, 陶情適性而已!
> (1604)

Above all, let me leave you with some verse. It was here that David truly came into his own, bringing to bear not only his huge learning in the field of Chinese poetry but also his creative ingenuity and his own lyrical impulse. Often he would walk down to his vegetable plot in the afternoon to puzzle over some intractable rhyme. What strikes most readers (Chinese and non-Chinese) as the novel's hardest element, the way in which classical poetry and the writing of poetry in a wide variety of modes and meters form an integral part of plot and characterization, in David's hands become sheer delight. My example comes from the first chapter, which condenses so powerfully and memorably the novel's message.

> Pages full of idle words
> Penned with hot and bitter tears:
> All men call the author fool;
> None his secret message hears.    (1.1.51)

> 滿紙荒唐言,
> 一把辛酸淚!
> 都雲作者癡,
> 誰解其中味?    (7)

## NOTES

This essay was completed in late 2008 and read by David Hawkes in 2009, a few months before his death in July of that year.

[1] See the excellent account by Dick Davis in his introduction to the *Rubaiyat*.

[2] See the gentle spoof in chapter 1 (51). For an account of the forerunners of the Penguin *Stone*, see Minford, "Slow Boat," about the translators Bencraft Joly, C. C. Wang, Kuhn, and others. More recently, there is a full account in my introduction to the reprint of Joly's translation by Tuttle, Vermont. It was later discovered that the early missionary

Robert Morrison (1782–1834) was the first (before Thom, Bowra, and others) to translate (but never publish) a section of the novel. See Chan Oi-sum.

3 A large number of articles have appeared in various Chinese journals, but these tend
to focus either on minor inaccuracies or on such orientalist arguments as "Where Has
the Red Gone?" Exceptions to this superficial coverage are Laurence Wong's doctoral
thesis and Fan Shengyu's doctoral thesis. There is a brief and slightly misleading study of
Hawkes and his work in Zhang Jinghao and Chen Kepei (285–311).

4 Most of these can be found conveniently collected in Hawkes, *Classical*. They include "*The Story of the Stone*: A Symbolist Novel" and "The Translator, the Mirror and
the Dream: Some Observations on a New Theory."

5 In a letter from Oxford dated 29 November 1974, David wrote, "Robin Zaehner died
very suddenly (on the street) last Sunday." Zaehner wrote in his book *Our Savage God*,
"This tragi-comic charade is bound together by a golden cord of mysticism" (210). The
words could so easily have been written about *Stone*.

6 Cyril Birch, in his "Tribute to David," echoes this idea: "David did more than just
translate a great novel. We can see that he embraced the whole ethos of the *Dream*, even
to the extent of converting the project into a genuinely family enterprise. . . ."

7 The works reffered to are *Da Xue* 大學 (*The Great Learning*), *Lunyu* 論語 (*The
Analects*), *Shu Jing* 書經 (*Classic of History*), *Shi[jing]* 詩經 (poems from the *Book of
Songs*), *Guo Feng* 國風 ("Airs of the States" from *Book of Songs*), *Da Ya* 大雅 (Major
Odes of the Kingdom from *Book of Songs*), *Yi Jing* 易經 (*The Classic of Change* or *Book
of Changes* aka *I Ching*), *Li Ji* 禮記 (*Book of Rites*), *Daodejing* 道德經 (Tao Te Ching),
*Tianxia* 天下 (part of the *Zhuang Zi* 莊子 [Chuang Tz'u]).

8 Guo Moruo was a Chinese author and government official in the People's Republic
of China. He produced a popular translation of Goethe's *Sorrows of Young Werther*
(1922). He was the first president of the Chinese Academy of Sciences. On the eve of the
Cultural Revolution, Guo recanted his entire literary career, declaring that all his publications deserved to be burned. This act saved him from the ignominy of persecution that
soon was inflicted on nearly all the ranking writers and artists of the nation.

9 Qian Zhongshu was a scholar and writer widely known for his satirical novels, including *Fortress Beseiged* (1947).

10 *Wenyan* means "classical Chinese," and *Stone* is written in what some call "modern
*wenyan*" — something between classical Chinese and the modern vernacular.

11 Yu Pingbo was a famous essayist, poet, historian, and *Stone* scholar. See Xiaojue
Wang's essay in this volume for more on him and Mao Zedong's campaign against his
work on *Stone*.

12 Lao She was an influential writer, perhaps most famous for his novel *Camel Xiangzi*
(aka *Rickshaw Boy*) and the play *Teahouse*.

13 Many of these excerpts from the interview are quoted in my foreword to the facsimile edition of David's *Translator's Notebooks*.

14 David held the last forty chapters in high esteem and shared my view that most
probably Gao E was telling the truth, and he and Cheng Weiyuan had found some scraps
of an original ending and were just doing their best as editors.

# The Story of the Stone and Its Visual Representations, 1791–1919

## Shang Wei

Like many dramas and novels of the early modern era (1550–1919), *The Story of the Stone* (also known as *Dream of the Red Chamber*) was accompanied by woodblock illustrations when it first appeared in print in 1791. But it proved to be much more than an illustrated novel: in the centuries that followed, paintings, murals, peep shows, and decorative artifacts that featured characters and scenes from *Stone* became part of the lived environment of Chinese men and women. In other words, instead of being a mere textual phenomenon, *Stone* took on a new life through visual renditions at different levels of remove from the text.

The *Stone* phenomenon is constantly changing, and no one text entitled *Stone* can account for the scope of influence and popularity that this work enjoyed in the nineteenth and twentieth centuries. Even a cursory examination of the pictorial renditions of *Stone* confronts us with a variety of visual experiences facilitated by the social, cultural, and technological changes in nineteenth-century and early-twentieth-century China: the widespread use of new technologies in art, the infiltration of European painting methods and concepts into the leisure entertainments of urban and rural audiences, the flourishing of regional styles and brands in the visual and performing arts in the new age of commercialization, the frequent intersections of high and low culture and thus the constant shifting and blurring of the boundary between them, the rise at the end of the nineteenth century of what might be described as mass culture in an embryonic form, and finally the irrepressible fascination with the art of illusion making, which is best captured in a series of murals inside the Forbidden City. The diverse visual renditions of *Stone* that proliferated during this period provide a prism for examining trends in visual culture as well as the evolving roles that these versions of the novel played in shaping those trends.[1]

## Visualizing the Dream

As in most woodblock editions of novels and dramas, the *Stone* illustrations fall into two categories: scenes and portraits. The scenes are either descriptive or narrative, presenting moments from the novel; the portraits are of main characters, usually full-length and with or without a setting.[2] The earliest illustrations of *Stone*, those included in Cheng Weiyuan and Gao E's 1791 movable type edition, however, lie somewhere in between.[3] The twenty-four pictures, each occupying one full page (half folio), the opposite page (the other half of the folio) bearing commentary verses, are narrative by nature, depicting the characters in action. But the pictures retain some defining features of portraits, as each focuses on one character, his or her name printed in the folding area between the two half folios. Unlike in most woodblock portraits of the time, the characters lack identifiable individuality. Although sophisticated in design, the pictures are poorly carved; yet as the earliest *Stone* illustrations, they set a precedent for later visual renderings of the novel. For instance, the series begins with an image of the Stone, Jia Bao-yu's previous form of existence in the mythic realm reincarnated as a piece of precious jade to be worn around his neck as a talisman. This image anticipates the opening scene in Gai Qi's picture album, first printed in 1879, and a few other illustration series. In the 1791 edition, Bao-yu is portrayed as wearing the ethnic Han-style hairdo, which deviates from the textual depiction of him in the novel, but it became the norm for *Stone* illustrations that followed. This same series also presents Lin Dai-yu accompanied by a parrot, an image that was often reproduced, with variations or significant adjustments, in later illustrations of *Stone*.[4]

## Portrait Illustrations

Even a cursory look at the portrait-type illustrations of *Stone* raises questions about their relation to the text. Far from visual auxiliaries dependent on the written text, they work in the inherited tradition of woodblock illustration while generating their own images, motifs, and scenes through reproductions and modifications in an unfolding sequence throughout the novel.[5] Typically a portrait takes on a life of its own when a character of the novel is given an iconic image or posture that lends itself to variations and rerenderings. For instance, it did not take long for the image of Lin Dai-yu to become associated with the motif of talking to her parrot, a motif already common in the portraits of beautiful ladies.

Book illustrators of the time often duplicated or modified earlier illustrations in their visual renditions of a novel. This tendency was facilitated by the increasing use of photolithography toward the end of the nineteenth century. As a result, there emerged a sequence of the same images in continuous metamorphosis over time—especially portrait illustrations. A sequence of lithograph illustrations published in 1889 appropriates the image of Xi-luan, a minor character who makes only a transitory appearance in chapter 71, from the picture album published by Dianshi Studio (*Dianshi zhai* 點石齋) eight years before, altering her look and facial expression and filling in the empty space behind her with a wood frame of furniture displaying rocks, bonsai, and flower vases. On the opposite page, a verse lamenting her tragic fate with a melancholy tone replaces the one from that earlier album marveling at her unrecognized charm and beauty. Then, when Wu Yue produced a set of letter paper decorated with lithographic portraits of seventy-two female characters from *Stone* in 1914, he largely replicated the 1889 series, including the portrait of Xi-luan. Instead of the poem from 1889, however, he resorted to Dianshi Studio's 1881 album, copying its commentary verse on Xi-luan in the upper left corner of the picture

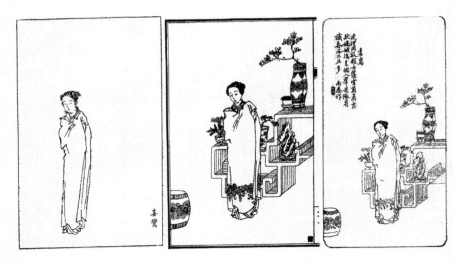

Fig. 1. *Left*: Xi-luan, from *Zengke* Hongloumeng *tuyong* 增刻紅樓夢圖詠, a large-scale album of the pictures of *Stone* characters published by Dianshi Studio in 1881, lithograph. *Center*: in *Zeng-ping buxiang quantu Jinyuyuan* 增評補像全圖金玉緣, 1889, lithograph. *Right*: in Wu Yue's portrayals of *Stone* characters, 1914, lithograph

and adding his signature (fig. 1). In this case, cutting and pasting are the dominant modes of visual reproduction of the images of *Stone* characters.

These portraits often carry a verse inscription on the same or facing page, which comes from the accumulated poems by the literati readers of the time who commented on the main characters or incidents of the novel. These verses fulfill many functions: marking off certain scenes or moments in the novel as essential to the representation of the characters, reinforcing images with emotional intensity and symbolism, and forming a sequence of derivative texts that frame the visual perceptions and renditions of *Stone* characters for years to come. Some verses are said to be responses to the *Stone* illustrations or paintings instead of to the novel itself. These cases demonstrate how the portraits and the writings on the portraits engage each other in a productive dialogue that moves them both further away from the text of *Stone*.

The illustrations in the Wang Xilian commentary edition of *Stone* (printed in 1832) are exceptional in that each portrait is paired with an image of a plant or flower on the facing side of the folio that comments on the personality of the character portrayed. The plant or flower often carries rich symbolic meaning acquired through a long tradition of lyric poetry and folklore. In the two portraits shown in figure 2, Wang Xi-feng is matched with a flower called "flower of jealousy," otherwise known as skullcap, while You-Shi, the mother of Jia Rong and wife of Jia Zhen, is paired with "smiling flower" (*michelia figo*), to reveal

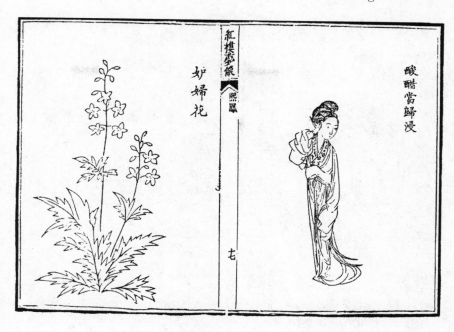

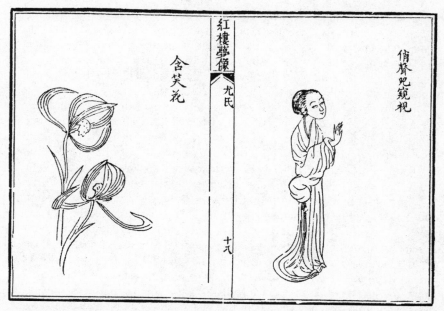

Fig. 2. Wang Xi-feng and You-Shi in the 1832 Wang Xilian commentary edition of *Stone*, wood-block print

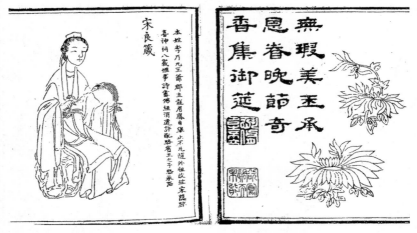

Fig. 3.  A female portrait from the 1832 edition of *Flowers in the Mirror*, woodblock print

their respective personalities and dispositions. This format is closely related to the 108 portraits contained in an 1832 edition of *Jinghua yuan* 鏡花緣 (*Flowers in the Mirror*) (Li Ruzhen), a novel influenced by *Stone*. With only four exceptions, they depict all the female characters from the novel, each paired with a page of flowers, plants, or artifacts such as jade, mirrors, screens, musical instruments, and bronze vessels that bear written inscriptions as an introduction to and comment on the subject of the portrait (fig. 3). The *Stone* portraits in the Wang Xilian commentary edition follow a similar model, though they are less sophisticated in design and rather crudely executed.

Despite the substitution of the commentary verses with flowers and plants, the image of each character contained in Wang Xilian does carry a short inscription in its upper-right corner, quoting not from *Stone* but from *Xixiang ji* 西廂記 (*The Story of the Western Wing*, a Yuan dynasty romance of unrivaled popularity [Wang Shifu, *Xinkan*]). As readers of I-Hsien Wu's essay in this volume know, Bao-yu and Dai-yu often cite the arias and dialogues from *Western Wing* in their daily communications, and the same strategy of transtextual appropriation is extended to the character portraits of this particular edition of *Stone*. Echoing the encoded meanings of the flowers, these quoted lines and phrases generate yet another perspective on the characters through transtextual references.[6] This practice dates to earlier times. A female reader reportedly listed the names of all the main characters of *Stone* on the surface of a fan and then ascribed a line or phrase from *Western Wing* to each name as a comment (Ni Hong, *juan* 4, 2–4). The portraits in the Wang Xilian commentary edition give a visual form to the verbal game, replacing names with images while retaining the same textual references to the play — another example of the cut-and-paste mode in the visual rendition of *Stone*.[7]

The portraits were often grouped together at the beginning of a text instead of distributed throughout. They thus could stand alone and so were only one step away from the emergence of independent picture albums, such as *Hongloumeng tu yong* 紅樓夢圖詠 ("Pictures and Poems on *Dream of the Red Chamber*"), compiled by the students and followers of Gai Qi (1773?–1828). Printed as an independent volume in 1879, it comprises fifty portraits, distinct from the preexisting *Stone* illustrations for their elaborate elegance reminiscent of literati-style paintings of beautiful ladies, especially those made by Tang Yin and Qiu Ying of the Ming dynasty. This album opens with an exquisite portrayal of Precious Stone and Crimson Pearl Flower — Bao-yu and Dai-yu in the forms of their previous existence in the mythic realm — that recaptures the flavor of literati-style landscape painting through woodblock technology (fig. 4). A visual equivalent to the framing narrative of the novel, this picture predisposes the audience to see the two protagonists and the trajectories of their lives through the lens of allegory and metafiction. It is fittingly accompanied by two poems on the next three pages reflecting on the framework of the novel and Cao Xueqin's achievement of literary immortality. Composed by one of Gai Qi's admirers in 1833, the second poem is followed by a long colophon of a personal, retrospective account of Gai Qi and his illustrations, which serves as a preface to

Fig. 4. The opening scene in Gai Qi's *Hongloumeng tu yong*, woodblock print; the album was made in the early nineteenth century and published in 1879.

the album. There is a complex interplay of words and images throughout the volume, as the fifty-six portraits are supplemented and corroborated by seventy-four inscriptions.

## Narrative Illustrations

Like portrait illustrations, illustrations of specific incidents from *Stone* are sometimes bound together in a separate section at the beginning of the work instead of prefacing or being inserted into the chapters that contain those incidents. As Robert Hegel has observed, separate fascicles of illustrations to novels were reminiscent of albums of paintings bound in butterfly style. Often, in an extant copy, "the fascicle containing the illustrations in late Ming novels may be well worn whereas the text seems scarcely to have been opened, much less given extensive use" (*Reading* 200). Evidently the visual or graphic could take priority over the textual, although this preference does not necessarily suggest the autonomy of visuality achieved at the expense of text. Like the portraits, these illustrations often carry their own written inscriptions, which contextualize the images. Even when a picture album is perceived to be independent of the text of *Stone*, some basic knowledge about the novel is still necessary for comprehension, although contemporary viewers might have obtained this knowledge from many sources, including operas, storytelling, and other intermediary forms, instead of directly from the novel. A few comprehensive collections of *Stone* illustrations make clear the artists' ambition to offer a graphic synopsis of the novel in its entirety. For instance, the 1884 lithographic edition of the novel under the title *Zengping buxiang quantu Jinyu yuan* 增評補像全圖金玉緣 ("The Destination of Gold and Jade with Added Commentaries and Supplemental Pictures") contains 116 portraits and 240 narrative illustrations. Each chapter carries two illustrations, representing the two major scenes of the chapter, duly indicated in each chapter heading in the form of a couplet. Each illustration includes a one-line caption copied from half the chapter heading. So organized, these illustrations constitute a complete pictorial sequence that closely parallels the unfolding narrative of the novel.

But if these narrative illustrations are meant to retell the stories of *Stone*, they do so in more than one way. In less comprehensive illustration series, as exemplified by some late-nineteenth-century lithographic editions, rather than a fixed two illustrations per chapter, usually two or more scenes are shown in a single image. Greater variation is evident in the 230 color paintings made by Sun Wen and Sun Yunmo from 1867 to 1903, which did not become widely known until recently. The number of illustrations per chapter in this volume ranges from one to more than thirteen, and each illustration has a distinct compositional scheme and framing device. The painters have more to say visually about some chapters than about others, but even when they capture one chapter in an illustration, they do more than show its content. To portray Jia Rui's sexual adventure and its consequences in chapter 12, Sun Wen (Sun Yunmo is

Fig. 5. Illustration for chapter 12 of *Stone*, by Sun Wen and Sun Yunmo, ink and color. © Lüshun Museum, Dalian

believed to have made more contributions later in the album) divides the visual space into three interrelated sections through the markers of walls, fences, and architecture, thereby allowing a sequence of events to be displayed simultaneously: Jia Rui appears in each section, moving from his midnight adventure in the right lower corner of the painting to his death in his living chamber (invisible to the audience), while the Daoist, who appears in the background to the upper left corner, descends from the sky to reclaim the magic mirror, which Jia Rui's parents blame for his demise (fig. 5). So conceived, this painting becomes a sequence condensed on one page, thereby taking the narrative function of the visual medium to its limits. It also achieves the dramatic effect of simultaneity inaccessible to the written medium.

### Scenes in *Stone* Illustrations

Occasionally the Suns' illustrations are concerned more with space than with action, and they are thus more descriptive than narrative. For instance, following a series of illustrations of the tour through Prospect Garden made by Bao-yu, Jia Zheng, and a group of literati protégés in chapter 17, a piece offers a glimpse into the internal space of the House of Green Delights, Bao-yu's future residence in the garden. Cao Xueqin describes the house:

> Its interior turned out to be all corridors and alcoves and galleries, so that properly speaking it could hardly have been said to have *rooms* at all. The partition walls that made these divisions were of wooden panelling exquisitely carved in a wide variety of motifs: bats in clouds; the "three friends of winter"—pine, plum and bamboo, little figures in landscapes, birds

and flowers, scrollwork, antique bronze shapes, "good luck" and "long life" characters, and many others. The carvings, all of them the work of master craftsmen, were beautified with inlays of gold, mother-o'-pearl and semi-precious stones. In addition to being panelled, the partitions were pierced by numerous apertures, some round, some square, some sunflower-shaped, some shaped like a fleur-de-lis, some cusped, some fan-shaped. Shelving was concealed in the double thickness of the partition at the base of these apertures, making it possible to use them for storing books and writing materials and for the display of antique bronzes, vases of flowers, miniature tray-gardens and the like. The overall effect was at once richly colourful and, because of the many apertures, airy and graceful.

The *trompe-l'oeil* effect of these ingenious partitions had been further enhanced by inserting false windows and doors in them, the former covered in various pastel shades of gauze, the latter hung with richly-patterned damask portières. The main walls were pierced with window-like perforations in the shape of zithers, swords, vases and other objects of virtù.

The literary gentlemen were rapturous:

"Exquisite!" they cried. "What marvellous workmanship!"    (1.17.346)

只見這幾間房內收拾的與別處不同, 竟分不出間隔來的. 原來四面皆是雕空玲瓏木板, 或 "流雲百蝠," 或 "歲寒三友," 或山水人物, 或翎毛花卉, 或集錦, 或博古, 或萬福萬壽. 各種花樣, 皆是名手雕鏤, 五彩銷金嵌寶的. 一榥一榥, 或有貯書處, 或有設鼎處, 或安置筆硯處, 或供花設瓶, 安放盆景處. 其榥各式各樣, 或天圓地方, 或葵花蕉葉, 或連環半璧. 真是花團錦簇, 剔透玲瓏. 倏爾五色紗糊就, 竟系小窗, 倏爾彩凌輕覆, 竟系幽戶. 且滿牆滿壁, 皆系隨依古董玩器之形摳成的槽子. 諸如琴, 劍, 懸瓶, 桌屏之類, 雖懸於壁, 卻都是與壁相平的. 眾人都贊: "好精緻想頭! 難為怎麼想來!"
(1: 231)

The literary gentlemen's exclamations of praise can be readily extended to Cao Xueqin himself, as his deft depiction of the interior layout and architectural details of the house is just as exquisite and demonstrates as much a sense of craftsmanship. Sun Wen rises to the occasion by matching Cao's words with the virtuosity of his visual depiction. Instead of seeking to reproduce what is described in chapter 17 of the novel, he creates a space that feels labyrinthine because of the uncertainty of trajectory and orientation (fig. 6). The main hallway is flanked by the partitioned foyer on the right and a built-in cabinet on the left, displaying antiques on its top shelf. From the hallway is a door leading to yet another room in the background, but all we can see are objects in an alcove. The visitors, who occupy the foreground, are shown not heading to the hallway but engaged in conversation. Their wandering tour has no clear indication of direction. Indeed, Sun Wen provides no visual cue for navigating this crowded

Fig. 6. Illustration for chapter 17, from Sun Wen's and Sun Yunmo's picture album on *Stone*. © Lüshun Museum, Dalian

interior space of irregular layout. The foyer, which is exposed to an outdoor scene, contains a lobby that seems to lead elsewhere, while the orientation of the main hallway is obscured by screens, cabinets, and bookcases holding books, ceramics, jades, and bronze vessels.

As Cao Xueqin's description suggests, a space so constructed serves no other purpose than to display the art and objects it contains. Even the interior becomes an exhibit, as exemplified by the wooden frame of the foyer, which contains decorative designs, paintings, and works of calligraphy and is exquisitely pierced by apertures in a variety of motifs. The antiques and paintings showcase the range of the art collection of this elite family, and each is a reminder of the time to which it belongs: the ancient bronze vessels, the paintings of the Song-Yuan literati style in black and white. These artifacts and paintings not only serve as the objects of representation but also constitute the integral components of Sun Wen's art of book illustration, both enriching and complicating its own stylistic profile.

In comparison, Wang Zhao's 1888 picture album depicting *Stone* is more consistently concerned with landscape, both physical and mental. His employment of the technology of lithography, which was first introduced to China by Western missionaries in 1826 and became widely used in the publication of periodicals and magazines from 1876 forward, enables Wang to reproduce nuances, fine lines, shadings, and textures not possible even in the most delicate style of woodblock illustrations.[8] Almost all the scenes in this series (as shown in the sixty-four extant illustrations) are depicted from above, at a forty-five-degree angle, and there are no close-ups; the human figures, modest in scale, are only a small part of the scene, their actions and facial expressions hardly distinguishable. Wang Zhao often uses trees, rocks, architecture, gates, screens, and other types of furniture as framing devices to organize space, and the scenes so organized lend themselves to a wide range of interpretations. In the scene representing Jia Rui's fateful obsession with Wang Xi-Feng that leads to his demise, the round gate reveals what is hidden behind the walls but also contains a scene so exquisitely framed as to suggest a picture within the picture: a dreamland that offers a glimpse of Jia Rui's fantasy (fig. 7). Likewise, the picture that depicts Bao-yu's visit to Dai-yu best captures the ambiance of Dai-yu's residential quarter, which is noted for, among other things, its surrounding bamboo grove and meditative if not otherworldly aura (fig. 8). Inspired by literati-style landscape paintings, Wang deliberately uses empty space in his composite illustrations throughout the album to suggest lingering mist or a mysterious haze that hovers in the air, giving an illusory, dreamlike quality to his rendition of the everyday environment in all its tangible materiality.

## From Popular Culture to Mass Culture: The *Stone* Phenomenon in Transition

I have shown the main forms of *Stone* illustrations and their variations through selected examples from the period. I also touched on a few related issues: the relation between written and graphic media, recurring patterns in the making of *Stone* illustrations, and print technologies. During the final years of the nineteenth century and the early decades of the twentieth, the wide use of lithography ushered in the age of mass production and consumption of visual culture, leading to the proliferation of periodicals and magazines. With the new print technology came new commercial enterprises, including a Shanghai-based advertisement industry that targeted middle-class urban women, and in these emerging visual genres the images of *Stone* characters were dramatically refashioned.[9] Lithography gave rise to photography, which in turn fueled mass culture with new resources and possibilities. Shanghai courtesans, who drew much public attention by taking their names from *Stone* characters, could be found posing for the cameras with an idyllic garden as backdrop, presumably Grand Prospect Garden, which by then had become a popular name for modern cinemas, theaters, parks, and residential complexes in Shanghai as well as a widely recognized trope for modern Shanghai at large (C. Yeh, *Shanghai Love* 149).

But before the dawn of modern mass culture, *Stone* had already found its way into the fabric of regionally based popular culture, and paintings and related visual genres had brought the novel into intimate contact with the common people. The willow-green style (*Yangliu qing* 楊柳青) of New Year's festival prints, a popular folk style originating in Hebei (literally, *Yangliu qing* refers to a complex of popular print workshops near Tianjin), was familiar to thousands of peasants as well as urbanites in the Qing, and peep shows remained widely appealing in the early decades of the twentieth century. Iconic images of *Stone*

Fig. 7. A scene from chapter 12 of *Stone*, in Wang Zhao's *Hongloumeng xiezhen*; lithograph

characters were prominent in card games and other forms of leisure entertainment; they also became fashionable in embroidery and home decoration. Familiar scenes from the novel were depicted on lanterns, lampshades, and the lower hems of women's capes. On the streets of Beijing during the final decades of the Qing and the early republic era, *Stone* characters were painted on the windows of carriages passing by, while ladies strolled around wearing scenes

Fig. 8. Lin Dai-yu's residential quarter, depicted by Wang Zhao, 1888; lithograph

from the novel on their sleeves (see Wang Shucun 198–235). The circulation of these visual products was largely regional, primarily because of restrictions in production and distribution. Therefore depictions of *Stone* images and scenes varied according to the locality. This variation persisted even when metropolis-based and nationally distributed mass media became a dominant force in visual production and reproduction.

## Grand Prospect Garden and Its Visual Reconstructions

Grand Prospect Garden, the primary setting for the novel, figures prominently in many *Stone* illustrations and paintings. That illustrators should concern themselves with depicting the garden should come as no surprise, as the text itself often invites readers to visualize the garden from a painter's perspective. The narrator first mentions its design in chapter 16, and the following two chapters allow readers to tour the recently constructed garden first along with Bao-yu, Jia Zheng, and a group of literary gentlemen and then with Yuan-chun. Bao-yu not only composes a poem describing each scenic spot and residential site but also gives each a name (although not all are adopted), thereby claiming co-authorship, if not ownership, of the garden. We get another extended tour of the garden when Granny Liu visits it, and her visit in turn leads Xi-chun, Bao-yu's youngest female cousin, to embark on an even more ambitious project in chapter 42: to capture a panorama of the garden in one prodigious painting. Her announcement of her intent prompts Bao-chai to dictate a long list of stationery, pigments, and utensils she thinks Xi-chun will need to have at her disposal, including twenty large coloring brushes and twenty small coloring brushes, ten face liners, four boxes of oyster-shell white, two hundred leaves of red powder gold, four superfine silk strainers, twenty catties of light charcoal, and one three-drawer chest. In her usual teasing tone, Dai-yu predicts that it will take Xi-chun two years to complete her proposed painting.

Cao Xueqin seems more interested in what his characters have to say about pictorial representation of the garden than in Xi-chun's painting. Dai-yu offers Xi-chun advice on the overall design, drawing on the models of literati-style landscape paintings and court-style architecture paintings. Bao-chai suggests that Xi-chun save time and energy by working from the architectural designs produced for the construction of the garden and put in the human figures only after the garden structure has been accurately laid out. These comments suggest different ways of viewing and representing the garden that anticipate the debates in which painters, illustrators, and publishers would engage in the years to come.

### Mapping the Garden: Methods and Technologies

The woodblock prints and paintings of the time chose many ways of visualizing Grand Prospect Garden. One method was to juxtapose all its residential and

Fig. 9. Grand Prospect Garden, from the 1832 Wang Xilian commentary edition of *Stone*, *Zeng-ping butu*

scenic sites on a flat space with no perspective depth, using trees, rocks, and architecture to divide the scene into distinct and self-contained units. This strategy enabled illustrators to display all sorts of activities occurring in each unit simultaneously, a device that would have been impossible to achieve through the written medium. Inscriptions added on gates or rocks or words inserted in adjacent empty space could turn the illustration into a map that gave an overall view of the garden and identified each site or structure by name (fig. 9). Not without precedent in the woodblock prints of local gazetteers, city journals, tourist guides, and in various styles of landscape painting, this elaborate, encompassing view of the garden would provide future artists and book illustrators with a blueprint for constructing their own imagined garden while allowing them to make whatever adjustments they saw fit in that framework (fig. 10).[10]

Not all depictions of the garden aim at capturing a panoramic view; some take the audience inside and explore its spatial depth through deft manipulation of perspective and vanishing points. These techniques were often employed in peep shows, known as West Lake lens (西湖鏡 *Xihu jing*) or West Lake scene (西湖景 *Xihu jing*), a visual art form that is said to have been introduced to China late in the Kangxi reign (1662–1723) and that became popular in streets and urban entertainment quarters in the following years.[11] Because

Fig. 10.  Grand Prospect Garden rerendered in the 1884 lithographic edition of *Zengping buxiang quantu Jinyuyuan* printed by Shanghai Tongwen shuju (*top*) and in the 1925 lithographic edition of *Stone* by the same publishing house (*bottom*)

they originated in Europe, these lenses are also known in China as occidental lens (西洋鏡 *Xiyang jing*) or occidental scenes (西洋景 *Xiyang jing*). They
displayed images of exotic objects, nude women, erotic pictures, and notable
architecture and scenic spots in Europe and China (including West Lake in
Hangzhou). Sometimes scenes from popular theater and vernacular fiction were
included, and the visual presentations were usually accompanied by storytelling
and singing. *West Lake lens* refers to a variety of optical devices that changed
over time. The simplest type consisted of a cabinet or box with peepholes to allow a person to view a series of pictures arranged in sequence inside and pulled
into view one at a time by a string controlled by the operator or performer. In
some cases, mirrors were placed inside the cabinet so that a viewer could see
reflections of an image from different angles. More sophisticated devices employed a convex lens, magnifying glass, or telescope to present the image and
to produce a visual sensation that transfixed audiences of the time. A member
of the Korean envoy who journeyed to Beijing in the first half of the nineteenth
century was so enchanted by the West Lake lens that he compared it to the legendary immortal's bottle gourd said to contain an omniscient view of the Daoist
fairyland: "Reflected in the mirrors set on the side wall inside the cabinet, the
images so close to us appear as if they were ten li [five kilometers] away, while
such a tiny item like a piece of hair or feather is magnified to the size of roof
beams; the clouds and fog lingering in the sky are so vivid as to be mistaken as
real. All this is due to the employment of a telescope" (Sŏng U-Jŭng 227). Such
an exotic optical instrument granted him a vision that he deemed to be magical,
well beyond the ordinary experiences of mortal eyes. In a story, Li Yu (1610–
80), a prolific writer of great wit and ingenuity, once described the telescope in
terms of an immortal's eyes.[12]

Prospect Garden is a recurring subject in the popular art of the West Lake
lens. In the show, the telescope and convex lenses facilitated the creation of
a picture rich in perspective depth and illusion. A variety of court paintings
produced in the early and mid Qing are notable for their extensive use of what
is called the linear method, a Chinese term for the European technique of
perspective drawing (Nie Chongzheng, *Xianfahua*; Wu Hung, "Beyond Stereotypes"). The employment of perspective drawing in the pictures designed for
the West Lake lens demonstrates how rapidly this European method spread
beyond the imperial court. Although the governing principles of traditional Chinese garden design stress the importance of segregating the space into interconnected subsections through the use of walls, rocks, trees, architecture, and
winding paths, these polychrome woodblock prints, attributed to the workshops
in Peach Flower Village (*Taohua wu* 桃花塢) near Suzhou in the lower Yangzi
delta, construct a landscape of open space of unusual depth, in which all the
prolonged straight lines of the roads and the roofs of the buildings converge on
one remote vanishing point near the center of the scene (fig. 11). Landscapes
so conceived were not limited to peep shows; they became widespread through
many popular styles of painting in the nineteenth century. Even the images of

Fig. 11.   An image of Prospect Garden used in the peep shows of the Qing period. Woodblock print in color

Prospect Garden featured in New Year's woodblock prints of the willow-green style are sometimes rendered in a similar way, although that style originated in the rural areas near Tianjin in north China.

How is Prospect Garden envisioned in the arts patronized by royalty? Wu Shijian, who served as academician reader-in-waiting during the Guangxu reign, wrote the following note to one of his verses included in *Qing gongci* 清宮詞 ("Poetry on the Court of the Qing"): "Imperial Consorts Jin and Zhen ordered the painters in the Imperial Academia [*Ruyi guan* or Ruyi Studio] to produce a painting on Prospect Garden and had it handed over to court officials, when it was done, for comments in poetic form" (17). Some scholars believe this note refers to a painting found in a scrap basket in the compound of a former prince's mansion near Triumphant Gate in the 1940s or early 1950s (fig. 12).[13] Despite a lack of supporting evidence to help identify its sponsors and painters, the painting's connection to the royal family is indisputable.

Large in size (362 cm × 137 cm) and lustrous with color, the painting portrays Prospect Garden on a scale and with a magnificence reminiscent of the imperial Summer Palace (*Yihe yuan* 頤和園), which was restored to its past glory during the same period, after having been savaged by British and French troops in 1860. The vision of the garden is organized as a series of architectural units, receding from All Spice Court (*Hengwu yuan* 蘅蕪苑) in the foreground through Concave Pavilion (*Aojing guan* 凹晶館) to the distant Smartweed Loggia (*Liaofeng xuan* 蓼風軒) and Autumn Studio (*Qiushuang zhai* 秋爽齋). This

Fig. 12. *Grand Prospect Garden*, ink and color (originally without title). Collection of the Palace Museum, Beijing

progression from right to center left is counterpoised by the two stone steps leading to a remote view of yet another pavilion at the top of a cliff in the upper right of the painting. Instead of presenting a bird's-eye view, the painter depicts the garden at eye level and involves viewers with techniques that evoke a strong sense of penetration into depth; even the architectural details of the distant towers and pavilions can be discerned with no difficulty. Instead of a picture of a vague fantasy, this painting presents with astonishing visual fidelity and clarity a convincing pictorial report of a garden of royal magnitude.

Although such a painting appeals to us with its uncompromising visual realism, a close look at the characters in it reveals something else. Following the linear perspective method already popular in the court paintings of the Qing dynasty, it has 173 human figures gathering in five major buildings (each of the main characters appears in several sites simultaneously), enjoying themselves in leisure activities described in more than six chapters of the novel. This juxtaposition of disjunctive scenes, given in the novel as an unfolding narrative sequence, conjures up a vision of an eternal paradise blissfully removed from the human temporality, and yet this fantasy land is rendered with such visual fidelity that it appears so tangible as to be within reach.

## Reconstructing the Garden: Real and Unreal

Efforts to represent Prospect Garden through visual media have been complicated by widespread rumors that Cao Xueqin based it on a real, historical garden. Yuan Mei, a leading literary figure of the time, claimed that Garden of Contentment (*Suiyuan* 隨園), his residential garden in Nanjing, provided the actual model for Cao Xueqin's *Stone*, as it used to be the estate of the Cao family, despite the fact that it had changed hands at least once before Yuan Mei's time.[14] Prince Gong's Palace (*Gongwang fu* 恭王府), located next to Shicha Hai at the center of Beijing, is also said to be the model for Cao Xueqin's imaginary garden, but it seems far more likely that this palace was modeled on Prospect Garden.[15] The quest for *Stone's* sources ends up revealing instead more about the novel's sweeping influence.

Scholars, artisans, and architects have long been interested in producing models of Prospect Garden through written and graphic media. The first three-dimensional model of the garden dates to 1919, but the earliest large-scale one was produced by leading architects at Qinghua University (including Liang Sicheng) in 1963; fifteen square meters in size, it consists of more than 140 buildings, bridges, terraces, and corridors (Gu Pingdan 192–200). More drawings of the garden and even floor plans of the architecture of the Jia household have been created since then, but consensus is yet to be reached on such questions as the exact location of the pond inside the garden.[16] A more fundamental question remaining to be answered is, Does Cao Xueqin's literary description of Prospect Garden and of the architecture of the Jia mansion lend itself to an accurate pictorial or three-dimensional replication, given the defining differences between written and visual media and the fact that Cao himself, deliberately or not, often left details on space, proportion, and distance rather vague or even self-contradictory?

It would take a leap of faith to move from a three-dimensional model to an actual reproduction of the garden in the real world, but that is precisely what occurred in the 1980s, when *Stone* was made into a thirty-six episode television series. The shooting site, located in Xuanwu District, Beijing, has since become a theme park open to the public, with all the usual and unusual entertainment and services expected of a tourist destination. Its success led to the construction of many similar parks in Shanghai and other major cities, through joint ventures of local governments, private developers, and investors undertaken in the name of commercializing national and local cultural heritage. Such a re-created garden is undeniably solid, but it would take something more than physicality to make what Cao Xueqin intended to be an equivalent to the Land of Illusion in the human realm.

## Illusion and Fantasy: The Mural Paintings in the Palace of Eternal Spring, the Forbidden City

Located on the west side of the Forbidden City, the Palace of Eternal Spring (*Changchun gong* 長春宮) is one of the six residential compounds occupied by empresses, imperial consorts, and concubines. Originally built in 1420, it housed many eminent residents, including Empress Dowager Cixi, who took lodgings in the main chamber and the flanking halls for most of the Tongzhi reign and did not move out until 1885. The powerful empress was emotionally attached to the palace and played an important role in reshaping it. The palace compound underwent many adjustments over the years in architectural layout and functions. The noticeable additions made to it in the last decades of the

Qing included a stage and, on the walls of its four corners, eighteen large paintings that depict scenes from *Stone*. Unlike the many paintings, calligraphy, and other treasures collected and displayed in the Forbidden City, which since 1925 has been a national museum, these murals were not given the attention they deserved until recently.

A brief examination of the murals highlights the importance of visual media in shaping the *Stone* phenomenon; it reveals the ambiguities and inconsistencies in the imperial approach to *Stone*; the blurring of the boundary between high and low cultures, especially with reference to court paintings; and finally the unquenchable fascination with the arts of illusion making in architecture, interior decoration, and paintings both inside and outside the palace.

## Murals, Stage, and Bao-yu's Invitation

The eighteen murals on *Stone* in the Forbidden City have suffered considerably from years of exposure to sunlight and extreme temperatures, but most of their images are clear enough for identification. No inscriptions were included, but some of the paintings feature writing on embroidered silk banners, horizontal boards, calligraphy scrolls, and other media, and this writing provides valuable clues to aid interpretation. Preliminary research has shown that well-known scenes from *Stone* appear in these murals: a drunken Shi Xiang-yun lies down on a rock (ch. 62), Bao-chai chases butterflies with her fan (ch. 27), four beauties enjoy fishing (ch. 81), and other characters are featured in banquet scenes (chs. 38, 62–63) (see Zhou Ruchang, "*Honglou*" 14–16; Hu Wenbin, "Zhi"). But because a number of scenes are rendered in ways rarely encountered in other *Stone* paintings and illustrations, some scholars wonder which edition of the novel was used as the textual source (Hu Wenbin, "Zhi"). It is possible that these paintings were not based on any specific textual source but are instead takeoffs of *Stone*, used in a visual extravaganza to give form to the illusionary Prospect Garden. The dreamlike landscape and its alluring variations on the walls open an imaginary window to the garden that seems far away and otherworldly yet so close.

Who are the sponsors of these murals? According to Wu Shijian, the imperial consorts Jin and Zhen once commissioned a painting or paintings of Prospect Garden (presumably with Empress Dowager Cixi's approval), and some scholars argue that he was perhaps referring to the *Stone* paintings on the wall of the Palace of Eternal Spring. The available evidence, however, points to Cixi as the driving force behind this project. The murals were likely painted during the 1884 renovation of the compound done in celebration of her fiftieth birthday. Several of the paintings carry words of blessing for longevity that suit the occasion perfectly.[17]

The painters of the murals are unidentified. They may have come from an art studio near the Gate of Earthly Peace (*Di-an men* 地安門) (Zhou Ruchang, "*Honglou*" 15). The work may have been done by two professional artists, one known as Old Painting Studio (*Gucai tang* 古彩堂), who was said to have apprenticed in a Buddhist portrait studio located in the Eastern Street of the Drum Tower (*Gulou dong dajie* 鼓樓東大街), the other called Chen Number Two (*Chen Er* 陳二), who specialized in landscape painting (Wang Zhongjie). The employment of professional painters from outside the imperial court in the execution of this enormous project underscores the social and cultural flux of the time. Indeed, the visual proliferation of the *Stone* did not always support the hierarchy of high over low culture. More often than not, the migration of aesthetic forms, ideas, techniques, artifacts, and artists connected otherwise disparate social spaces. Court paintings were often commissioned from professional painters outside the Forbidden City, and court painters were often hired from professional workshops or studios.[18] Although the imperial patrons' intentions were inevitably reflected in the themes and designs of these projects, it became increasingly more difficult to distinguish what are usually called court paintings in form and style, simply because they were not always executed by painters in residence at the court.

Although the visual quality of these mural paintings has deteriorated, visitors today may still fall under their magic spell. It is noteworthy how the painters take into account the architecture of the palace in conceiving and executing their works, effectively transforming the compound into part of the imaginary world of *Stone*. In the northwest corner of the compound is a mural that features Bao-yu's visit to a Buddhist convent called Moon in the Water (a Buddhist term signifying illusion), generating the elaborate illusion of an extended corridor that leads straight toward a wall with a landscape painting flanked by a parallel couplet. Bao-yu appears at the end of the corridor, gazing at the young woman who is walking toward us while looking halfway back. With extra care the painters smoothed the transition from reality to illusion: we are not far away from Bao-yu, walking along a real corridor that appears to merge seamlessly into the one painted on the wall (fig. 13). The mural fulfills two purposes simultaneously: it serves as an open invitation to the illusory world painted on the wall, and it casts doubt on the boundary between real and unreal by integrating the corridor of the compound into its design.

Framed by the mural paintings, the compound also features a space for theatrical performance on the southern side of the courtyard, which further blurs the line between reality and illusion (fig. 14). The southern hall already contained a small indoor theater when Cixi moved into the living chambers on the opposite side. In preparation for the celebration of her fortieth birthday in 1874, an additional structure was added to provide a more spacious outdoor stage, allowing her to enjoy operatic performances in the courtyard or from the porch of the main chambers (Liu Chang, Zhao Wenwen, and Jiang Zhang). The combination of the *Stone* murals and the stage transforms the compound into such an enchanting place that one visitor was prompted to compose verse, reiterating the dialectics of reality and illusion so marvelously epitomized in the novel:

Fig. 13. One of the eighteen murals on *Stone* from the Palace of Eternal Spring in the Forbidden City. Collection of the Palace Museum, Beijing

Fig. 14. The complex of Eternal Spring, viewed from the stage on the south side of the courtyard. © CRIENGLISH.com

Eternal spring lingers in the winding corridors and multiple passages,
All the paintings feature the characters from *Dream of the Red Chamber*.
Leaning against the carved railings, I gazed fixedly at them, pondering—
How lively they are, both the real and the unreal!

迴廊複道亘長春,
幅幅紅樓夢裏人.
徒倚雕闌凝睇想,
真真幻幻兩傳神.　(Yang Pengyu 166)


## Li Yu and His Influence

No one better exploits the Qing fascination with illusionistic murals than Li Yu
(1610–80), a comic writer and versatile mind, in his description of the murals
on the four walls of his drawing room in his celebrated *Xianqing ouji* 閑情偶寄
("Casual Expressions of Idle Feeling"). After years of contemplation and careful
planning, he invited four famed painters to implement his design: the expansion of flowering trees intertwined with fog over the walls created the illusion
of an open garden view in the confines of the room. To enhance the intricate
play of real and unreal, Li Yu placed a few parakeets on a short copper perch
driven into one of the walls. The birds were hardly distinguishable from the
painted leaves and flowers. When invited guests arrived, according to his account, they were immediately impressed by the lifelike effect of the murals
but were amazed when the birds began turning their heads and spreading their
wings as if they were about to come down from the painting. Li Yu took much
pleasure in his guests' shock and confusion: "[T]hey were all struck dumb and
changed their countenances, wondering whether the paintings were made by
the magic touches of an immortal" (184–85).

　Li Yu was so dedicated to the art of illusion that he rarely missed an opportunity to apply it. A self-styled interior decorator and designer, he emphasized
the importance of framing devices in creating what he described as unintended
pictures. A fan-shaped, movable window was exquisitely built on a roaming boat
to turn the outside landscape that happened to fall in its frame into a delightful painting. With the sensibility of a modern cameraman, he staged the scene
outside the window of his residential hall in Nanjing with great deliberation: a
pot of flowers was so situated that the pot was hidden from the viewers, at the
right distance for the window to frame their entire visual field. This was craftsmanship that erased their own traces. When the outside view was not appealing enough to be a picture, Li Yu suggested painting flowers, rocks, and birds
on paper and then attaching the images to the back of a fan-shaped window
(fig. 15). Fascinated by craft and technical details, he offered detailed instructions on how to produce a window suitable for this purpose without compromising its normal function.[19] He loved the challenge of producing a landscape
painting so realistic that it would be taken for an outside scene contained by
the window (fig. 16). In the years that followed, Li Yu became an important

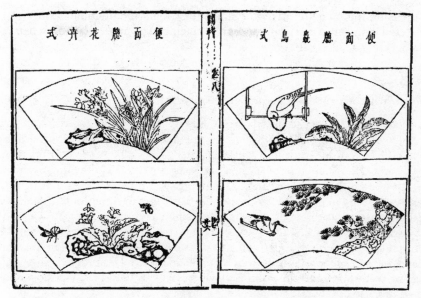

Fig. 15. Paintings on the fan-shaped windows proposed by Li Yu in his "Causal Expressions of Idle Feeling"

Fig. 16. Paintings Li Yu suggested to paste on the back of the windows to compensate for the lack of a pleasant outside view

source of inspiration for interior design in the Qing era, and his influences were reflected in the taste and preferences of Manchu royal families (see Hay, *Sensuous Surfaces* 23, 306, 326).[20]

## Illusionistic Murals and Imperial Fascinations

Illusionistic paintings and murals are conspicuous features of the royal art and architecture of the eighteenth and nineteenth centuries, such as in Prince Gong's Palace. Known for its exquisite garden, said to be modeled in part on the Prospect Garden of *Stone*, the palace is also distinguished by the elaborate design of its residential complex, architecture, and ornaments. According to a study published in 1941, Tower of the Way Revealed in Apparition (*Xianfa lou* 現法樓),[21] which has long disappeared, contained a grotto or cave: at the end of an intriguing indoor labyrinth made of narrow, twisting corridors, one might be startled by an emerging apparition: "an ornamental façade, made to represent a building of two storeys, from which one issued into a large room whose ceiling was painted to represent sky." Following is a lively description of the indoor garden, ornamental facade, and ceiling murals:

> Here, at the back, was a mount of piled rock, running up through both storeys, and simulating an external arrangement, but built altogether indoors. The composition as a whole was meant to give the illusion of a bamboo grove in the open air, with a pavilion in the centre, and caves beyond; and this was contrived by painting the sides of the room in perspective, and then framing them with a *lang-tzŭ* or gallery that was half real and half merely drawn upon the walls. Above was the "sky"; beyond was painted a grove of bamboo. The columns of the gallery were real, however, and bore a real roof, on top of which was a viable passage connecting with the second storey of the central, free-standing pavilion.    (Ch'ên and Kates 37)

The observers conclude by describing what they saw as a garden "rather amazingly, that has moved into the house." Apparently the illusion evoked on the walls and ceilings of the building "was, on the whole, successful" (37–38). Li Yu, who provides a lively description of the murals on the walls of his living room, might not have had access to these painting techniques, but his design showed similar experimentation.

Prince Gong's Palace has a precedent in the Lodge of Retiring from Diligent Service (*Juanqin zhai* 倦勤齋, hereafter the Lodge of Retirement) inside the Forbidden City, which was completed in 1776, the year when the construction of Prince Gong's Palace was launched (38n108).[22] The overall design of the Lodge of Retirement, which includes floor-to-ceiling murals of an outdoor garden, palace and tower roofs, pine trees, and blue sky framed by a painted bamboo fence, not only offered immediate stimulus for the design of the indoor

Fig. 17. Trompe-l'oeil murals on the ceiling and north and west walls of the Lodge of Retirement in the Forbidden City. Collection of the Palace Museum, Beijing

garden and illusionistic murals in Prince Gong's Palace but also helps explicate the *Stone* murals in the Palace of Eternal Spring.

In 1771, Emperor Qianlong issued an edict to construct a complex called Tranquillity and Longevity (*Ningshou gong* 寧壽宮) in the northeastern part of the Forbidden City, in anticipation of his retirement in 1795 after ruling the empire for sixty years. Both an integral part of the imperial palace and its miniaturization, this complex of 6,400 square meters comprises grand halls for official ceremonies and meetings, bedroom chambers, gardens, theaters, and other structures for religious and everyday functions. At the north end of the complex stands the Lodge of Retirement, whose interior space "offers visual surprises at every turn," as "wood is transformed into bamboo lattice, bamboo is re-formed into sculptured reliefs, mirrored screens become doors and walls become paradisiacal gardens" (Berliner 12). Left in disrepair for many years, the Lodge of Retirement was not open to the public until recently, when it was successfully restored.[23]

On the west side of the Lodge of Retirement, a narrow hallway leads to the grand theater hall, with trompe-l'oeil murals covering the ceiling and the north and west walls. The 4.37-meter-high ceiling features an expansive mural depicting clusters of pink and violet wisteria blossoms (fig. 17). Rendered three-dimensional with highlights and shadows, the flowers appear to be descending from a painted bamboo trellis; a few clusters stretch over the edge and hang down in the blue sky portrayed on the wall of the room. The illusion of being

Fig. 18. The indoor theater and the murals on the north and west walls of the hall, in the Lodge of Retirement. Collection of the Palace Museum, Beijing

outdoors is further enhanced by painted wisteria and lattice that leave gaps through which to see the blue sky far above. According to Nie Chongzheng, this mural may have been painted by Guiseppe Castiglione, one of Emperor Qianlong's favorite court painters, known in China as Lang Shining. Painted on silk mounted on the walls, it was probably made for another palace building but later removed to the Lodge of Retirement (Nie Chongzheng, "Architectural Decoration"). In addition to the ceiling murals, the paintings on the western and northern walls of the hall warrant special attention, as they extend the outdoor scene to include an extensive view of the imperial palace with convincing details (fig. 18). A moon-shaped gateway leads to a palace garden, where a crane, the symbol of longevity suitable for the Lodge of Retirement, greets us with a friendly gesture—not unlike Bao-yu's gazing toward viewers with a glance in one of the murals in the compound of the Palace of Eternal Spring (fig. 19). The enticing outdoor view is composed of deep blue sky, palace and pavilion roofs, walls, flying magpies, and mountains in the background, but it is delicately framed by a painted speckled bamboo lattice fence that reaches to the ceiling. A magpie perches on the fence, accentuating its three-dimensionality: the fence is both an object of representation and a framing device for the entire mural.

Further examination of the murals in the Lodge of Retirement discloses two elements closely associated with the art of illusionistic murals in the imperial palace: a door or gateway as an invitation to the world of illusion; a stage as a space dedicated to illusion making. To the north of the indoor theater is a

Fig. 19. The moon-shaped gate painted on the north wall has its exact mirror image, a real moon-shaped gate made of the speckled bamboo fence, on the south side of the wall across the hall of the Lodge of Retirement.

moon-shaped gate painted on the wall that has its mirror image — a real moon gate of the same size and shape and made of the speckled bamboo fence — on the south side of the hall. Facing the stage is the seat the emperor would occupy while he watched the performance; next to the hall are stairs that lead to the upper story, where the emperor would rest after the performance. On the upper story, he is greeted by a beautiful lady who gazes out from behind a door curtain, yet a closer look shows that she is just the central figure of another mural (fig. 20). On either side of the painted doorway is a painted side table

Fig. 20. The painting on the wall of the second story depicts a lady emerging from behind a door curtain in the Lodge of Retirement. Collection of the Palace Museum, Beijing

holding antiques, books, and a stone chime, with two literati-style paintings occupying the space above, paintings that represent the paintings on the wall as
the painted wallpaper represents itself. These paintings become the equivalents
to and substitutes of the objects themselves, constituting a self-contained world
without referents, a world that opens its doors to all visitors.

Near the doorway is a painted Western-style clock that points permanently to
11:18, either in the morning or at night, but this detail seems to spoil the game
of illusion, gesturing toward a temporality that the painting cannot possibly capture. Painting by its nature deals only with a frozen moment — in this case, the
moment when the enigmatic lady is about to emerge from behind the door. The
addition of the clock is thus an ironic spin on the visual game that both engages
and perplexes its audience.

The stage in the center of the hall is an enchanted site, like the outdoor stage
in the compound of the Palace of Eternal Spring surrounded by the *Stone* murals as its backdrop. In both cases, the murals are inseparable from the art of
theater. Wu Hung's study of the theater hall in the Lodge of Retirement reveals
yet another intricate connection: "[T]he stage and the murals must have been
designed and conceived as parts of a larger illusionistic entity: a bamboo fence,
exactly like the painted fence in the mural, enclosed the back stage" ("Beyond
Stereotypes" 320). This connection recalls the intriguing relation between the
two moon gates in the theater hall, raising the question of where reality ends
and illusion begins.

Characterized as mimetic and perspectival, the European Renaissance mode
of visual perception and representation is usually associated with realism and the
positivism of the rising scientific culture in the modern West. In the court arts of
the Qing, however, this mode does not lead to any secure grasp of what is called
reality; instead, it becomes a means to explore the intersections and interplay of
the real and unreal. Paradoxically, the murals of the Lodge of Retirement depict
both the outdoor view of the imperial palace and the interior private room with
great realism yet invite observers to leave behind the concrete, material world.[24]
The observers are treated not as passive onlookers of a spectacle but as participants in an illusion-making project whose ultimate artistic triumph depends on
their active collaboration.

The ingenious use of mirrors in the Lodge of Retirement suggests yet another connection with the murals on *Stone* in the Palace of Eternal Spring and
with the visual experiences represented by *Stone* itself. Moving west toward the
theater inside the lodge via a narrow hallway, one passes, on the right, a bedroom meant for the emperor. Two large mirrors reflect the embroideries and
the screen partitions on the opposite wall. According to the experts responsible
for the recent restoration of the lodge, the mirrors are

> most likely imported from Europe, each [measuring] 195 × 86 cm; they
> are both inserted into *zitan* frames that sit on wooden stands, decorated
> with inlaid designs of birds and flowers, and appear to be classical Chinese
> single-panel standing screens. . . . The one towards the front of the build-

ing, . . . appearing to be a standing screen, is in fact a door that leads to the western side of the building.

Believing that Emperor Qianlong was involved in the design of the lodge, Nancy Berliner commented, "Set within a Chinese frame and playing with visual foolery, this European mirror provides the entrance to a further series of grander European- and Chinese-inspired visual tricks in the western side of *Juanqin zhai*, all hinting at this emperor's sense of humor" (24).

Although no mirrors are depicted in the murals that feature the scenes from *Stone* in the Palace of Eternal Spring, these paintings are noted for their deft manipulation of what may be called mirror images. The painted corridor in the mural that depicts Bao-yu's visit to the Convent of Moon in the Water can be seen as an extension of the corridor that leads viewers to the front of the mural, but it is also the reflection of that corridor. Unlike the mirror on the door disguised as a screen inside the Lodge of Retirement, the painted corridor recalls the painted moon-shaped gate that mirrors the gate on the other side of the hall—an illusion sure to tantalize visitors. We are invited not only to follow Bao-yu but also to join him and even identify with him, as he inhabits a world parallel to ours. In fact, as we view the mural, it can hardly escape our attention that we are standing right on the spot that is occupied by Bao-yu inside it.

Before Emperor Qianlong's lodge was under way, Cao Xueqin had already explored many of the disorienting and illusionistic possibilities of mirrors, including the dressing mirrors widely used by the well-to-do families of the day. In chapter 41, Grannie Liu, a visitor from the countryside, at first fails to recognize her reflection in a Western-style mirror she encounters inside the Jia household. Once she realizes her error, she makes another mistake by fearing that she is trapped inside the mirror, wondering aloud, "[H]ow do I get out of here?" 這可怎么出去呢? She fingers the mirror's carved surround:

Suddenly there was a loud *clunk*! which so frightened the old woman that for some moments she rolled her eyes in terror. The mirror was in fact a kind of door. It had a West Ocean mechanism by which it could be opened or closed, and Grannie Liu, in feeling around it, had accidentally touched the spring which had made the mirror slide back into the paneling, revealing the doorway underneath.                                             (2.41.320)

一面用手摸時, 只聽 "咯噔" 一聲, 又嚇的不住的展眼兒. 原來是西洋機括, 可以開合, 不意劉姥姥亂摸之間, 其力巧合, 便撞開消息, 掩過鏡子, 露開門來.                    (Cao and Gao, *Hongloumeng* [1972] 2: 505)

Elaborating on both mirrors and doorways as visual tropes, chapter 56 gives an intriguing spin to a number of the issues at the core of the novel. Asleep in front of a dressing mirror in his bedroom, Bao-yu dreams of entering a parallel world, where he meets for the first time his counterpart, Zhen Bao-yu (literally, "Real or Authentic Precious Jade"). Each addresses the other as Bao-yu, and

Fig. 21. The main chamber of Palace of Eternal
Spring, once occupied by Empress Dowager Cixi.
© CRIENGLISH.com

each assures the other that their encounter is not a dream. As Bao-yu awakens,
he is heard calling his own name while pointing to the mirror, which he mistakes
for the doorway by which the other Bao-yu just exited. One of his maids cites
Grandmother Jia's theory about mirrors and dreams: "[W]hen you're young your
soul isn't fully formed yet, and if you're reflected in mirrors too often, it can give
your soul a shock which causes you to have bad dreams. Fancy putting your
bed right in front of that great mirror!" (3.56.87) 小人魂不全, 有鏡子照多了,
睡覺驚恐作胡夢. 如今倒在大鏡子那裡安了一張床 (1: 776). Grandmother Jia's
explanation, apparently expressing the common wisdom of the time, applies to
many, young and old, who are attracted and puzzled by their images in mirrors.

In the compound of the Palace of Eternal Spring, there is an additional *Stone*
mural, painted on silk and fixed to the wall of the main living chamber; it shows
a lady touring a scenic spot in a deer carriage attended by her maids (fig. 21).
The silk is believed to have been mounted during the Qianlong reign. Some
scholars suggest that the lady depicted is Grandmother Jia touring Prospect
Garden, but the deer carriage is a vehicle only for the immortals, so the scene is
of a Daoist fairyland that invites residents of the room to fantasize. Surrounded
by the painting of this Daoist utopia as well as by scenes from *Stone*, Cixi, who
once lived in this room, could have easily transported herself into a dream world
and imagined herself in the company of the fictional characters of the eternal
youth, in keeping with the name of the compound.

## Coda: A Political Interpretation

The discourse of illusion, which seems to have been renewed in the Qing, is
multifaceted and rooted in diverse religious and literary traditions.[25] Cixi's insatiable impulse toward illusion and fantasy lends itself to political and historical
judgments often issued in hindsight. She was fond of *Stone* and is said to have

left commentary in red ink on a hand-copied manuscript that was prepared especially for her.[26] She did not hesitate to turn her residential quarters into an enchanted site framed by the murals of *Stone* scenes and characters, even while some of her loyal officials were still trying to protect the general public from being contaminated by the novel. This contradiction helps explain why the official prohibition of what was deemed obscene literature, including *Stone*, was not successful.

Empress Dowager Cixi is also known for elaborate self-fashioning through photography and other visual media, in which she often dressed as Guanyin (Avalokiteśvara), the goddess of mercy, and on a few occasions as the wife of a fisherman, while assigning the role of husband to poor Li Lianying, her favorite eunuch.[27] This penchant for role-playing can be traced back to Emperors Yongzheng and Qianlong, whose portraits show them in a variety of roles they claimed for themselves, from recluse, hunter, fisherman, and Daoist to European aristocrat (Wu Hung, "Emperor's Masquerade"). The role-playing is obviously not without political significance, as an emperor had long been expected to assume multiple roles—to be, for example, a Confucian, Daoist, and Buddhist at once. But the game of self-fashioning went beyond politics and public life. Yongzheng, for instance, would present himself as Dongfang Shuo stealing peaches in fairyland or as Li Bai chanting poetry. Cixi was therefore a true follower of an imperial tradition, a tradition she brought up-to-date by embracing new visual media and technologies, including photography.

In his *Gudong suoji* 古董瑣記 ("Miscellaneous Notes on the Past"), published in 1926, Deng Zhicheng, an eminent historian, wrote, "[Empress Dowager Cixi] enjoyed reading fiction and was able to recite from memory some passages of these works. She had intimate knowledge of *Stone* and often compared herself with Grandmother Jia" (*juan* 6, 24–25). In this retrospective, allegorical reading, Cixi's projection of herself into *Dream of the Red Chamber* and her identification with the matriarch of the declining Jia family seem to presage the downfall of the empire over which Cixi presided:

> Not surprisingly, three years after her death, the Qing Empire came to the end of its fortune. Moreover, the Summer Palace [which was rebuilt and expanded under Cixi's rule] and Grand Prospect Garden seem to add radiance to each other despite the distance in time. Thus, the mournful *Dream of the Red Chamber* more than sums up the 260-year history of the empire. This is truly astonishing. (24–25)

Focusing on the garden, Deng notices its analogy with the imperial Summer Palace. Cixi's lavish spending in the restoration of the Summer Palace did not prevent it from falling into desolation, and thus the palace ends up sharing the same destiny with the fictional garden in *Stone*. According to Deng, the 260-year history of the Qing Empire and the fortune of the Jia family converged, both fading from view.

NOTES

I want to thank Jonathan Hay, Robert Harrist, David Rolston, and Sara Kile, who read an early draft of this paper and offered many invaluable suggestions for improvement. My appreciation also goes to Yin Ji'nan and Pan Jian'guo, for their advice on some of the subject matter I address in this essay.

1 For the major sources of *Stone* paintings and illustrations, see the following collections: Hong Zhenkuai; *Guben Hongloumeng chatu huihua jicheng*; *Hongloumeng banke tulu*; Wang Shucun.

2 For a critical survey of Chinese portraits in the early modern era, see Vinograd.

3 Although the main text of this edition was printed in movable type, the illustrations that went with it were carved on wooden blocks.

4 For more on this influence, see Zhang Hui 323–24. Note that parrots are a recurring trope in the romances and "portraits of beautiful ladies" (*meiren tu* 美人圖) of the Qing, and this trope can be traced to literary and visual genres of the earlier periods. See I. Wu.

5 For more on woodblock and lithographic illustrations in premodern and early modern China, see Hegel, *Reading*; Hay, "Painters"; and E. Wang.

6 *The Story of the Western Wing* features the love of Student Zhang and Cui Ying-ying, her maid Crimson serving as a messenger between the two. The inscription in the upper right corner of Wang Xi-feng's portrait quotes from a couplet in an aria sung by Crimson, as she, under Ying-ying's order, delivers to Student Zhang a medicine prescription (actually a note agreeing to a rendezvouz) to help cure his lovesickness: "Cassia flowers sway their shade in the dead of night; / Vinegar soaks the one who 'ought to return'" (Wang Shifu, *Xinkan* [see vol. 2, act 4, of the 1498 edition of the play]; for the English translation, see Wang Shifu, *Story* 214–15). The aria from which these lines derive is characterized by its heavy use of puns on the names of Chinese herbs. The second line, which is cited on the portrait of Wang Xi-feng, contains two instances of wordplay: vinegar is known for its pungent flavor while being widely employed in literature as registering the emotion of jealousy or envy; "ought to return" can be read as a noun designating *angelica polymorpha*, which is often used as medicine, as suggested in Crimson's following explanation, to "vivify the blood." When this line is appropriated to describe Wang Xi-feng, it highlights her jealous disposition while offering the prescription to heal the menstrual problems that in the end ruin her health. Likewise, the portrait of You-Shi cites one line from Crimson when she spies on Student Zhang, who is in despair after being rejected by Ying-ying: "I'll wet the paper window and make a hole, / And with silenced voice peep inside" (vol. 2, act 1; for the English translation, see Wang Shifu, *Story* 193). In a few later editions, the words "silenced voice" are mistaken as "a sweet voice." The illustrators of the Wang Xilian commentary edition deliberately chose "a sweet voice" in correspondence with the image of "smiling flower" on the accompanying page to You-Shi's portrait.

7 The pairing of the name of each *Stone* character with a line from *Western Wing* was later extended to a card game, the rules of which are laid out in a how-to manual called *Honglou renjing* 紅樓人鏡 ("A Mirror for the Characters from *Dream of the Red Chamber*"), compiled by Tan Guanghu. The enactment of the game in a real-life setting is vividly depicted in chapters 33 and 34 of *Haishang chentian ying* 海上塵天影 ("The Shadows of Earth and Heaven in Shanghai"), a 1905 novel set principally in Shanghai (Zou Tao).

[8] On the history of lithography in nineteenth-century China, see Pang, *Distorting Mirror* 40–42.

[9] For the Shanghai commercial posters of *Stone* characters and scenes produced in the early republic era (1910–39), see Zhang Yanfeng 21, 22, 64, 72, 75, 77.

[10] Some of the visual constructions of Prospect Garden in the nineteenth century drew their source of inspiration from the literati paintings and woodblock illustrations of private gardens and estates that thrived in the seventeenth century and remained popular in the nineteenth. One may compare some nineteenth-century visual renditions of the garden with their contemporary paintings on estates and gardens as represented by Zhou Xian's *Thatched Cottage of Fan Lake*. On Zhou Xian, see Erickson.

[11] For a brief description of the peep shows, see Dikötter 251–52.

[12] For an English translation of Li Yu's "A Tower for the Summer Heat," see *Tower* 3–40.

[13] For more information about this painting, see Hong Zhenkuai 218–21; Zhu Min.

[14] Yuan Mei's claim is refuted by his contemporaries and those who came afterward. For more on this topic, see Zhou Ruchang and Zhou Yueling 18–23. See also Levy's essay in this volume.

[15] Zhou Ruchang is a strong supporter of the hypothesis that Prospect Garden is modeled on Prince Gong's Palace. For more of his and other scholars' writings about this subject, see Zhou Ruchang and Zhou Yueling 24–293.

[16] More studies on this and related subjects can be found in Gu Pingdan; Hu Wenbin, "*Tianlai*"; Guan Huashan; and Huang Yunhao.

[17] Scholars do not agree about when these murals were executed. Jiang Shunyuan suggests 1879 as the date (91), but Liu Chang and Wang Shiwei hold that they were most likely painted after 1897. In either case, it would be difficult to imagine the execution of these murals without Cixi's support or permission.

[18] The imperial academy of arts (*Ruyi guan* 如意馆), which served as the home of court painters, was well established in the early Qing dynasty, but after the Qianlong reign it gradually deteriorated, despite efforts to reverse this trend by Empress Dowager Cixi. See Nie Chongzheng, *Qingdai*.

[19] For more on Li Yu's experiments with devices of visual manipulation, see Sieber.

[20] Li Yu's fascination with the art of illusion making was shared by other literati and semiliterati in the remaining years of the Qing. Shen Fu, a man of letters who made a living as a clerk and by running a small business, provides a vivid account of the pleasure he took in miniature gardens and interior decoration. In chapter 2 of his *Fusheng liuji* 浮生六記 (*Six Records of a Floating Life*), he describes how he "found much delight in pruning miniature potted trees to make them look like real ones" (56). In the art of designing miniature gardens, he fully indulged himself: "To make a miniature mountain, pile up some dirt, then place stones on it and plant flowers and grass here and there. The fence in front of it should be of plum trees, and the wall behind it should be covered with vines, so that it will look just like a mountain even though there is no mountain there" (60). This hobby allowed him to explore the ways "to show the real amidst an illusion" and "create an illusion amidst reality" (60, 61).

[21] The name of the tower derives from the Buddhist tradition that buddhas and bodhisattvas reveal themselves to worshippers to preach the true way.

[22] The owner of the palace during this period was the notorious Heshen, not Prince Gong. With Emperor Qianlong's trust and indulgence, Heshen enjoyed unparalleled

power over both domestic and international affairs, but he was executed by the succeeding Jiaqing emperor in 1799, immediately after Qianlong's death. One of the charges brought against Heshen was that he deliberately modeled his luxurious garden complex on Qianlong's Palace of Tranquillity and Longevity, of which the Lodge of Retirement was an important component—a crime that warranted capital punishment. The illusionistic murals in Prince Gong's garden and the Lodge of Retirement both have their precedents in Yuanming Yuan, an imperial garden whose construction was initiated by Emperor Kangxi, who ruled the Qing from 1662 to 1723. The east part of Yuanming Yuan consists of European palaces and gardens, known as the Chinese Versailles, which were designed and built in the reign of Emperor Qianlong and includes what is called *Xianfa qiang* 線法牆 ("the perspective wall"), on which were mounted a dozen oil paintings of central Asian towns and scenery rendered in the European method of perspective. Seen from afar, these paintings evoke the illusion of exotic scenery extending indefinitely into the open horizon. Some scholars argue that these paintings took as their models the stage designs and decorations of the Italian theaters as exemplified by the opera house in Vicenza designed by Andrea Palladio. It is said that in 1760 General Zhaohui brought a beautiful Aqsu woman, later known as *Xiangfei* 香妃 ("the fragrant lady") for Emperor Qianlong after his successful military conquest of Turkestan, and the Perspective Wall was designed to quench her nostalgia for her home town in Aqsu in western Xinjiang. For more on the Perspective Wall and its source of influences, see Tong Jun 78–80; see also Young-tsu Wong 64–65.

[23] For a comprehensive introduction to the lodge, see Berliner; Wu Hung, "Beyond Stereotypes" 319–22.

[24] For more on the motif of the painted murals and its further development in the literary discourse of the Qing, see Zeitlin, *Historian* 183–202.

[25] This discourse is often derived from the rich tradition of Buddhism (Zeitlin, *Historian* 183–202).

[26] See Xu Ke 3767–68. The copyists of this particular edition of the novel, who left their signatures on the inner margin of the pages, include Lu Runxiang, a palace graduate.

[27] For more on Cixi's fascination with and self-representations through photography, see Pang, *Distorting Mirror* 81–85; Rojas 1–30.

# Sequels to *Stone*: Polygamous Harmony and the Theme of Female Talent

*Keith McMahon*

## Polygamous Harmony

After appearing in published form in 1791 and 1792, *The Story of the Stone* immediately began spawning sequels. The novel struck a deep chord. Many readers valued the sublimely tragic ending, but others, frustrated, felt an irresistible urge to repair the damage. They loved the portion of the novel in which Bao-yu and his female cousins and maids enjoyed daily life in Grand Prospect Garden. Starting in 1796 and continuing into the twentieth century, authors wrote sequel after sequel that extended that happiness into harmonious adulthood. A short summation of how they turned the sadness to happiness tells us a great deal about the society in which the original novel took place. Sequel authors had Bao-yu marry *both* Dai-yu and Bao-chai (or their reincarnated versions), and marry not only them but also a number of other cousins, women, and maids who were part of the original grand gathering. Harmonious polygamy, in short, became their answer to the original novel's unresolved problems. Bao-yu was turned into an ideal model of manhood in traditional China, the benevolent polygamist.

A brief look at the names and dates of the sequels will give an idea of the quick succession in which they were published. The first appeared in 1796 and was called *The Later Story of the Stone* (後紅樓夢 *Hou Honglou meng*), by Xiaoyaozi. It was closely followed by others with titles like *Revisiting the Silken Chambers* (綺樓重夢 *Qilou chongmeng* [c. 1797]), by Wang Lanzhi; *Sequel to Story of the Stone* (續紅樓夢 *Xu Honglou meng* [c. 1797–98]), by Qin Zichen; *Return to Story of the Stone* (紅樓復夢 *Honglou fumeng* [c. 1799]), by Chen Shaohai; *New Sequel to Story of the Stone* (續紅樓夢新編 *Xu Honglou meng xinbian* [1805]), by Haipu zhuren; *The Resolution of Story of the Stone* (紅樓圓夢 *Honglou yuanmeng* [1814]), by Mengmeng xiansheng; *The Story of the Stone Revisited* (紅樓夢補 *Honglou meng bu* [1819]), by Guichuzi; *Patching the Story of the Stone* (補紅樓夢 *Bu Honglou meng* [1820]) and *The Sequel to Patching the Story of the Stone* (增補紅樓夢 *Zengbu Honglou meng* [1824]), both by Langhuan shanqiao; and *The Illusion of the Story of the Stone* (紅樓幻夢 *Honglou huanmeng* [1843]), by Huayue chiren. *In the Shadow of the Story of the Stone* (紅樓夢影 *Honglou meng ying* [1877]) was the only novel in Chinese history up to that time that we can verify was by a woman, Gu Taiqing (1799–1877), and it departs in significant ways from the male-authored sequels. No other sequels appeared until the early 1900s, when authors began to incorporate contents reflecting China's interaction with modernized Japan and Western nations. In this essay I consider only the ones before the 1900s, because they hardly refer to the West at all and thus describe a cultural sphere that is still quite self-contained. They were all written as continuations of *The Story of the Stone* from either chapter 97, in which Dai-yu died, or from the final chapter 120.

The sequels have three main strategies for repairing what went wrong in the original novel. They reform Bao-yu by turning him into an upright and straightforward young man with only a trace of the excessive sensitivity of his previous self; they modify the character of Dai-yu (or her equivalent) and allow her to ascend to the position of strong main wife in the polygamous family; and they resolve the complex problems that led to the failure of the love affair between Bao-yu and Dai-yu. The attainment of polygamous harmony crystallizes all three of these strategies and characterizes the main plot of all but one of the sequels published between 1796 and 1877 (the exception ends with a monogamous marriage). A great many other novels of the Ming and Qing (1368–1911) end in a similar way—that is, with the triumph of the polygamous man as hero of both family and of the world of imperial politics. In most of the sequels, the polygamist hero and his many wives behave chastely, but in two of them, as in many Qing novels, sex between the polygamist and his wives plays a major role. Despite the dominance of the polygamous man, however, the sequels share what might seem a paradoxical feature with the original novel, that of female talent and the presence in general of strong and remarkable women. In these and other novels of the Qing dynasty, the polygamous man loves women of extraordinary talent, in some cases women who play dominant roles both at home and abroad. The women are wise, virtuous, and solid, but they are also unjealous, tolerating one another and willingly sharing themselves with their husband, Bao-yu.

Since polygamy is a backdrop to both the original *Story of the Stone* and the sequels, it is important to understand its features in Chinese society. From ancient times, men of wealth and privilege had many wives, though such men probably never amounted to more than ten percent of the population (a guess, as we lack accurate data): maintaining a polygamous household required a level of wealth and power available only to the few. The emperor and his empress and consorts were the primary model of polygamy in China, since polygamy had a ritually purposive function in both defining the greatness of the man and ensuring the birth of sons and thus successors to the throne. In the polygamous family, only one of the wives was the primary or main wife. Marriage to her was typically contracted with an eye for the social, political, and financial benefits of both the man's and the woman's families. The other wives were concubines and at a distinctly lower level than that of the main wife. The chief reason for taking a concubine was to have a son if the main wife failed to bear one. But men typically took concubines for pleasure as well. The women usually lived in the same house as the man but in separate chambers (unlike African or separatist Mormon polygamy, for example, in which each woman occupies a separate house). The distinction in status was marked by such things as the fact that concubines could be easily divorced while main wives could not. Concubines daily paid their respects to the main wife. Sons of concubines belonged to the main wife, especially if they were the firstborn and therefore primary heirs. Concubines could be former prostitutes and might return to prostitution if they were dismissed or widowed. Main wives aged along with the husband, and some concubines did too, but new concubines were typically in their teens and twenties. By law, concubines could never replace the main wife, though Chinese history is filled with both fictional and nonfictional cases in which the affection of a man for his concubine compelled him to break this rule. As for number of concubines, emperors had thousands (Emperor Wu of the Western Jin, who lived from 236 to 290, had more than ten thousand), but usually men had one, two, or several (statistics are hard to come by, since concubines were listed in family genealogies only when they had sons).

In *Stone*, Bao-yu is a kind of prepolygamist. That is, both society in general and his family in particular expected him to take concubines. Polygamy was a common and natural form of marriage in well-off families. In effect he already has a concubine, the maid Aroma (though she is not called one), his first sexual partner and a constant companion through much of the novel. Chinese history is filled with stories of jealous rivalry between main wife and concubines and between concubines themselves. In the novel, however, such problems arise not because of Bao-yu's relationship with Aroma but because Bao-yu loves two women who are of the same social class as he, Dai-yu and Bao-chai, and who therefore cannot both marry the same man. He loves Dai-yu more, but his elders choose Bao-chai as his wife. He loves her too, for that matter, as well as Aroma, Parfumeé, and a number of other young women. But it would be difficult to imagine the author or authors of *Stone* allowing him to marry all of them as a way of ending the novel. Such a marriage could occur only in the kind of fiction that *Stone* makes fun of, the so-called beauty-scholar romances. These formulaic stories, filling the literary landscape in the Ming and Qing, were about a young man who meets and happily marries the woman of his choice and in many cases two or more such women and their maids as well. *Stone* adheres more closely to orthodox reality, in which elders frowned on deep love between two people: a son should always be primarily attached to his parents and the larger family, whose interests take precedence over his attachment to wife or concubine. As ancient books of ritual dictated, if parents disapproved of a son's wife or concubine, the son was obliged to expel the woman from the household. Sequel writers instead followed the beauty-scholar romances and created stories in which self-determined love between the young did not interfere with the larger familial harmony.

Reforming Bao-yu was the first way in which the sequels repaired the original novel, because many readers felt that he was effeminate, spoiled, and degenerate. The Bao-yu of the sequels is still highly cultured but firmer and more focused. He is goal-oriented, no longer lacking the desire to study and seek an exemplary career. He may become a high official or a valiant martial hero.

He stays proper and avoids decadent people such as actors and playboys. He doesn't lick women's lip rouge and no longer acts like a clinging little boy. In a few cases he participates in the birth and early rearing of one of his children, as if further to demonstrate his improvement on the traditional father who is aloof from such things. According to the *Analects* of Confucius, "A gentleman keeps aloof from his son" (141–42 [16.13]). Like Bao-yu's father, Jia Zheng, fathers are traditionally distant and strict with sons, not intimate. In the sequel *In the Shadow of the Story of the Stone*, Gu Taiqing creates a Bao-yu who in one scene holds his baby son while one of his female cousins remarks, "Look how far he has come. He has even learned how to hold a baby!" (更能幹了, 練的會 抱孩子了 [1: 75]).

Although he is sexually proper in most of the sequels, in two the reformed Bao-yu becomes a sexually masterful polygamist, thus echoing the heroes of a large body of erotic fiction in the Ming and Qing. The implication of *Revisiting the Silken Chambers* and *The Illusion of the Story of the Stone* is that the original Bao-yu lacked the ability to be a capable polygamist—that is, he was not a man who could attract and handle multiple wives and sexually satisfy them to the point that they were glad to be his cowives. The new Bao-yu no longer goes crazy because he is torn between his two cousins. In *Revisiting the Silken Chambers*, the new Bao-yu is a precocious young man who as an adolescent already knows what sex is all about. It is the most explicitly erotic of all the sequels. He is reborn as Xiao-yu 小鈺, who has five wives by age sixteen, including the reincarnation of Dai-yu. Before his marriage he has sexual relations with numerous young women, often prepubescent girls so that they will not get pregnant. He learns special sexual techniques from a nineteen-year-old female acrobat, then practices them with a group of twenty-four maids. He embodies a correction of two kinds of polygamists who appeared in earlier fiction. One is the profligate, like Ximen Qing in the sixteenth-century erotic novel *Plum in the Golden Vase*, who was unable to control jealous rivalry among his women and who was finally done in by one of them. The other is the original Bao-yu, who failed to be a confident master of polygamous sex.

The other erotic sequel, *The Illusion of the Story of the Stone*, is milder in tone. It is the women, especially Dai-yu, who encourage and manage the polygamy. Bao-yu never initiates, never appears sexually aggressive. In traditional Chinese polygamy, especially as practiced by emperors, the chief worry of advisers and moralists was that the polygamist would favor one woman to the detriment of the household or the whole empire. Dai-yu assumes the role of managing Bao-yu's relations with his wives and thereby eliminating jealousy. In methodical fashion, she has him distribute measured fractions of his heart to each of his wives. Dai-yu receives what she labels as the innate and pure heart that he possessed before birth, a heart that signifies that their love was predestined. The other women receive portions of his postbirth heart, which is divided ten ways—Bao-chai belongs to this group and gets only two portions (only one sequel favors Bao-chai over Dai-yu). With this clearly defined arrangement, each woman accepts her portion and no one tries to upset the balance.

## The Theme of Female Talent

The theme of female talent is central to understanding both the original novel and the sequels that turn Dai-yu into a strong main wife. The theme has a long history in China but was especially prominent since the late Ming (late sixteenth century to the first half of the seventeenth). In its most sublime and heroic form, it features women acting valiantly and independently, even if that means sacrificing themselves and dying. It takes numerous forms in both fiction and reality. In real life, there were famous female writers, some of whom were prostitutes or concubines, whom male writers and scholars adored and whose works these men often anthologized. In a society that frowned on talented and educated women, some families nevertheless prized highly educated wives, mothers, and daughters. Such women gave their households a certain cachet. The image of the talented woman embodied an exceptionalism that signaled a critique of decadence and corruption, especially among men. Bao-yu's theory of muddy men and pure-as-water women (1.5.146) is an expression of this critique, which also suggests that women are morally superior to men. Bao-yu is not the only male in the Ming and Qing to express this opinion.

The theme of female talent came to the fore in times of social turmoil and dynastic decline, such as prevailed at the end of the Ming dynasty. Biographers wrote of exceptional women, and writers of poetry, fiction, and drama portrayed them in works that the authors of *Stone* and its sequels knew and referred to, especially the late-sixteenth-century play *Peony Pavilion*, by Tang Xianzu. The heroines outshone their male counterparts in moral valor and fortitude. One kind of heroine was inherited from the ancient past, the woman who uses martial arts to carry out acts of justice. If her father was wrongly accused and murdered, for instance, and she had no brothers to rely on (or if her brothers lacked the courage), she would exact vengeance herself and murder her evil enemy. Another common type from the ancient past was the woman who disguised herself as a man. She appeared in both male- and female-authored narratives, in which she cross-dressed in order to leave home and engage in social and political arenas as an equal of men. During her cross-dressing outings she often met her future mate, whom she married in the end after she returned to female dress. In female-authored narratives, returning to female dress and the role of wife and mother could mean a traumatic loss of independence. In any case the heroine was a strong and dynamic character, as capable as men if not more so. Examples of female talent in *Stone* are Bao-chai, Dai-yu, and other brilliant young women who have poetic and artistic ability but no way of demonstrating it except in the narrow confines of a home of lackluster men.

The sequels re-create these women but remove their pain. Sometimes the women do not remain helplessly restricted to home. In *Return to Story of the Stone*, Bao-chai is a general who participates in the defeat of pirates; in *Resolution of Story of the Stone*, Dai-yu helps Bao-yu quell bandits. These two sequels echo other Ming and Qing novels in which women act in similar ways. Dai-yu is the most prominent example of female talent in the sequels: a new woman, fuller in flesh and happier in spirit, no longer bitter or prone to making cutting remarks. In *The Later Story of the Stone*, she is Bao-yu's soul mate and the capable and strict manager of his polygamous household. In this and other sequels she conforms to the traditional model of the empress who drafts concubines for her husband and in so doing ensures that they are smart and virtuous. She is unjealous and tolerates no jealousy among the other wives. Under her rule, the women carefully manage their living quarters and follow the rules of visitation with Bao-yu so that no one will monopolize him. In *The Illusion of the Story of the Stone*, she says that in the past they were selfish and private in their love but now must share themselves openly and fairly with all others (52–53), hence her division of his heart into distinct mathematical portions. She is particularly concerned that Bao-chai might think Dai-yu is monopolizing Bao-yu. Even though Bao-chai gets only two portions of his postbirth heart, Dai-yu's goal is that the three of them become one heart. Eventually all three sleep together in the same bed each night—a practice that was probably rare in reality, unless the man was with women of rank lower than that of the main wife.

## Resolving the Irresolvable

Resolving the irresolvable is the third strategy that the sequels employ, to exacting and in some cases farcical lengths. One usually irresolvable issue is a man's wish for easy and unproblematic access to women. In the erotic sequel *Revisiting the Silken Chambers*, we see the hypernormalization of sexual promiscuity. Bao-yu becomes a leader of women who gains their intimacy and allegiance by demonstrating a masterful understanding of their bodies and their sexuality. He repeatedly helps them with ablutions, illness, their first menstruation, and their first experience of sex, for which they are all extremely grateful. No other Chinese novel portrays a man who devotes so much energy to facilitating the bodily and sexual education of women. The distance between him and them collapses. In effect he ventriloquizes the female. He engineers their wishes, which are his wishes to begin with. The original Bao-yu empathized with women and tried to understand them, but he was still an outsider. In *Revisiting the Silken Chambers*, Bao-yu stages women's agency for his own pleasure. In a later sequel, *Patching the Story of the Stone*, Bao-chai describes the author of *Revisiting the Silken Chambers* as an aberrant man who has lost all sense of humanity.

Another way to resolve the irresolvable is to make open and pragmatic what could not be so in the original novel. In *The Illusion of the Story of the Stone*, women openly express their love for someone and their enjoyment of sex. After Bao-chai tells Dai-yu how much she loves her, Dai-yu says that she loves Bao-chai as much as Bao-yu loves Bao-chai. Dai-yu and Bao-yu talk about a night during which they made love twice: she climaxed first, felt his essence inside her, and then both fell into a deep sleep. Such language would have been impossible in the world of the original novel; it is possible only in an erotic novel, which excites the fantasies of the male author and readers. In another scene, Bao-chai facilitates the love affair between a younger female cousin, Xi-luan, and Dai-yu's brother, Qiong-yu 瓊玉 (a newly invented character in the novel). Like Bao-yu and Dai-yu in the original novel, Qiong-yu and Xi-luan fall in love but cannot express their feelings to each other or anyone else. In the original novel, words like "I love him" or "I love you" cannot be uttered. Feelings are blocked; impasses always occur; people are not free to express their emotions except in indirect ways. "I love you" is not a customary set of words in premodern Chinese society, where elders arrange marriages and where reticence and reserve govern behavior in marriage and romance. But Bao-chai now manages to get Xi-luan to admit that she "loves" 愛 Qiong-yu, a declaration that opens the way to setting up the marriage between the two (132). Sequels like this resolve what *Stone* was unable to resolve because it was too realistic and too pessimistic.

*Return to Story of the Stone* presents a contrasting case of resolving the irresolvable, in which normative boundaries separating male from female simply vanish. Unlike the erotic sequels, in this one an atmosphere of chaste and suffused intimacy prevails in which Bao-yu, reborn as Meng-yu 夢玉, is all "sentiment" (情) and no "lust" (色) (287). When he is with his wives and maids, "he is not even aware that he is male and they are female. As far as he is concerned, someone else's body is mine, and mine is someone else's. . . . Even if one of the women is sponging herself or taking a bath, he comes and goes as he pleases, and no one minds" (並不知自身是男, 他人是女. 覺得他的身子就是我的身子, 我的身子就是他的身子. . . . 那怕遇着擦身洗澡呢, 大爺來就來, 要去就去, 聽其自然 [287]). This is another outlandish attempt by a sequel to create seamless harmony between polygamist and wives. Meng-yu hugs one woman, assists another with her shoe, and, in an echo of his former mischief, licks the rouge off someone else's lips. But no one is jealous, because although Meng-yu has twelve wives, he is fair to everyone and blends in as if everyone were of one gender. It is significant that the author's younger sister wrote a preface to *Return to Story of the Stone* in which she stated that the book was appropriate for both male and female readers. She was alluding to the fact that orthodox society frowned on educated women's reading novels. But in fact educated women in the Qing had long been avid readers of fiction and drama, and by the early nineteenth century *The Story of the Stone* was considered appropriate reading material for women. The portrayal of chaste intimacy in *Return to Story of the Stone* is a sign of the rise of female readership.

The reversal of family decline and the theme of female talent play central roles in Gu Taiqing's *In the Shadow of the Story of the Stone*, but in other respects her sequel couldn't be further from works like *Return to Story of the Stone*, *Revisiting the Silken Chambers*, and *The Illusion of the Story of the Stone*. She creates a polygamous Bao-yu married to Bao-chai, Aroma, and two others (the author herself was a concubine), but not to Dai-yu, whom the author does not return to life. Unlike the reinvested hero of all the other sequels, Bao-yu is a melancholy figure who, though successful in the examinations, forever misses Dai-yu and other favorites who are no more. The author avoids the passionate optimism and idealized resolution of the irresolvable of the other sequels.

Although a number of the sequels were republished in the nineteenth century and thus must have had a reliable readership, none was very popular, and none will probably ever be translated into a foreign language. They simply are not up to the quality of the original. The sequels flatten the subtlety and sublimity of *Stone* by making its original themes and intentions balder and more explicit. They have Bao-yu become a polygamist instead of abandoning his family to become a monk. His "mind lust" in the original novel (1.2.76) made of him a man who despised men who were vulgar and brazen in their lust for women. In the sequels, mind lust turns practical and fulfills itself in a way that erases the problems of jealousy, rivalry, and hurt feelings that would normally occur in a polygamous household. Inability to express oneself inspired some of the most beloved scenes in *Stone*, but in the sequels people have no problem asking for and getting what they wish. Women in *Stone* who suffered from oversensitivity and inferior status in the sequels either find ways to escape those problems or turn into new women who live with those problems as if they were not problems. In sum, the sequels impose transparency where it could not have existed originally. They collapse the separate worlds of natural and supernatural, for example, by making the dead come back to life and characters travel between the two. They elide the boundaries between male and female and eliminate the contradictions that normally occur between men and women. *Revisiting the Silken Chambers* engages in a farcical usurpation of female agency, in which Bao-yu makes scores of women want to consort with him. The female subject becomes transparent to the male.

Ever since the earliest records of polygamy in Chinese history, female jealousy and rivalry have been constant features. Women plotted against each other, murdered rivals and rivals' offspring, and did all they could to restrict their husband's access to other women. Men were callous and dissolute in their choice and expulsion of women, though they could also become hopelessly captivated by one woman, a woman who succeeded in monopolizing the man's emotions. The sequels help us read the *Story of the Stone* in the light of the cultural inheritance of the practice of polygamy in China. They are significant in their attempt to erase the traumatic edges of both polygamous relationships and exclusive love between two people. The theme of female talent is a sign of the attempt to bridge the gap between polygamy, long a bastion of male privilege, and the love of one partner only, which favors individual choice and can provide more power to the woman. Perhaps male authors felt guilt and the need to justify themselves because of what they knew to be the woman's fundamental dislike of the man's polygamous privilege. What else can it mean when a male author who idealizes polygamous marriage constructs a harmony that is ruled and managed by women? Perhaps a talented main wife is a jealous woman in disguise—that is, dressed up in virtue and managerial talent as a substitute for her jealous temper. In a perverse way, the male author who idealizes polygamous harmony acknowledges the power of the woman's anger by handing her the role of directing and managing his polygamy. He fantasizes her agreement with his polyamorous desires by having her promote them for him. Whatever our interpretation may be, the sequels to the *Stone* are examples of how profound and troublesome works of art vex readers and compel them to create ways of abridgement and simplification, even if that effort means creating works that the original author would have disdained and rejected.

NOTE

A modified version of this essay appears in chapter 2 of my *Polygamy and Sublime Passion: Sexuality in China on the Verge of Modernity* (Honolulu: U of Hawaiʻi P, 2010).

# The *Stone* Phenomenon and
# Its Transformation from 1791 to 1919

## Shang Wei

This essay is concerned not with *The Story of the Stone* per se but with the *Stone* phenomenon. The novel, especially after its publication in 1791–92, gave rise to numerous commentaries, anecdotes, sequels, and imitations and became the core of a matrix that generated a sequence of derivative texts. At the same time, *Stone* was subject to constant rerenderings in various forms (such as selections and simplified or abridged versions) and also adapted into a broad range of genres and media (illustrations, paintings, story picture books, plays, and various subgenres of regionally based storytelling and singing). This phenomenon was constantly evolving, ever growing, more elusive, and much larger than any specific text called *Stone*.

Focusing on the period from 1791 to 1919, I consider how the *Stone* phenomenon took shape and evolved, what the driving forces were behind the self-reproduction and transformation of *Stone*, what role technologies and media played in shaping and reshaping it, how it was made accessible to people of different social and cultural status, and finally what those people did with *Stone*. This approach is different from a study of the historical reception of *Stone*, which presupposes a stable and definitive text to be received, interpreted, and reinterpreted over the course of time. Nor is it restricted to the category of studies of popular culture, as *Stone* offers a perfect lens through which to examine the intersections and mutual influences of high and low cultures. The boundary line between high and low was in fact constantly shifting in the reproduction, transmission, appropriation, and consumption of *Stone*. Moreover, the *Stone* phenomenon survived the turbulent changes in the final decades of the nineteenth century and the early twentieth century, with the assistance of modern media and technologies. On the one hand, *Stone* constituted part of the rising mass culture associated with urban entertainments, magazines, modern commercial publishing, and popular professional writers. On the other hand, it became strongly entrenched in the literary canon after the May Fourth Movement (1919) because of the modern intellectuals' quest for an equivalent tradition to the modern European novel, thereby raising a large question about tradition and modernity. Seen from this perspective, the *Stone* phenomenon becomes a converging point of the social, cultural, and technological changes that define and redefine early modern and modern China.

Despite its affinity with the established traditions of Chinese literature (as Mary Scott discusses in this volume), *Stone* on the whole is experimental by any conventional standard—an avant-garde work of the time, so to speak. Like several of its contemporary novels written by high-minded literati of cultivated taste, including *Rulin waishi* (儒林外史 "The Unofficial History of the Scholars,") it first circulated in limited quantity as hand-copied manuscripts among a small circle of relatives and friends. Although the literati hardly embraced the vernacular novel as a respectable literary genre, *Stone* gradually gained critical acclaim among the educated elite, and the publication of Cheng Weiyuan and Gao E's 120-chapter edition was a landmark event, turning the novel into an instant best seller across the kingdom. Few other novels in early modern China experienced such a drastic reversal in fortune. While most of the literati novels of the time transmitted in hand-copied form remained obscure or were entirely forgotten, in the final decades of the eighteenth century *Stone* acquired fame well beyond the world of the elite.

What explains *Stone*'s popularity among the general public? Related to this question is a more basic one: How many people then were educated enough to be able to read the novel? The short answer is, not many. Although there was a large literate or semiliterate population in Qing China, the number of readers capable of reading *Stone* was probably low, given the novel's complexity, length, and encyclopedic scope. Literacy is of course an important factor for the popularity of a novel, but one must take into account the specific ways a novel is read and made accessible to the reading public. Many who claimed to have read *Stone* may have only skimmed through it or read an abridged or simplified version. The general public acquired some knowledge about *Stone* through the mediation of oral or dramatic performances, visual representations, and verbal games.[1] The popular reception of *Stone* therefore is inseparable from the appropriation and reproduction of the novel. Rich in content and comprehensive in its inclusion of literary and nonliterary genres, *Stone* lends itself to a wide range of uses. Aspiring writers often resort to it as an inexhaustible sourcebook for their own work; some readers consult it as a comprehensive compendium of language and knowledge; others cite it as a reference point for representing or making sense of reality; still others find in its endless account of drinking verses and poetry parties a repertoire of verbal games to be reenacted in their leisure time.

*Stone* appeared in print in time to benefit from a number of unfolding social transformations. The second half of the eighteenth century witnessed a rapid growth in population and an increasing literacy rate. Even a conservative estimate indicates that the general population increased from 143 million in 1741 to more than 300 million in 1794, with an average annual increase of over 3.2 million, and this trend accelerated in the following century. Literacy rates grew as education and print culture became more widespread. By the end of the nineteenth century, as one historian calculates, one-third or even one-half of school-age males acquired some basic or practical literacy through private and charitable schools.[2] According to a study on the New Territories of Hong Kong in the late Qing and early republican era, "alongside the varied corpus of written materials there existed in both town and country an equally extensive body of ancillary writing whose importance for villagers, citizens, and researchers alike lies in the fact that it created the cultural environment in which Chinese lived" (Hayes 103).

Commercial publishing was gradually geared toward the growing reading public from the mid–eighteenth century onward. Publishers were keener than ever to reach readers of modest means. Books were printed and sold at lower costs than before, while the development of book-lending businesses in cities also increased the circulation of books among the general public. When *Stone* was transmitted in hand-copied form, each copy was said to cost several dozen taels of silver, but the constant reprints after 1791 in Beijing and many other cities made the novel more affordable for book buyers, lowering the price to less than two taels for a printed copy.[3]

The literati remained the dominant force in the creation of literature, including vernacular fiction, but in the eighteenth and nineteenth centuries the word *literati* became ambiguous, its application so varied in terms of status, career, and mentality. Literati could no longer be considered as belonging to one social group. Learning and literary achievement could identify them, as could official pedigree and post. But from the 1750s to the 1850s, few men of letters received the public recognition they had been promised. Many who had successfully secured an official pedigree failed to win an official appointment, and there were over a million civil licentiates who had no official post or the financial means to claim an elite status. An increasing number of educated men dutifully took the civil service examinations year after year but had little hope of obtaining even the lowest-level degree. In this period, the civil service examinations were a major factor in the increase of educated men who were no longer recognized as the cultural elite, much less as members of the ruling class. These were both potential producers and consumers of literary culture, and their presence defies the simple demarcation of high and low cultures or elite and popular cultures.

The mid–eighteenth to mid–nineteenth century witnessed a surge of regional culture in the forms of theater, storytelling, and singing. Of over three hundred subgenres of local theater that have survived to the twentieth century, more than half can be traced to this period. Storytelling and singing thrived in Beijing, Yangzhou in the lower Yangzi delta, and other cities during the final decades of the eighteenth century. Set primarily in wine houses, teahouses, and theaters, these performances were part of the expanding urban consumer culture, but they also peppered surrounding rural areas. Derived mainly from existing written sources, including such well-known novels as *The Romance of the Three Kingdoms*, *Outlaws of the Marsh* (*The Water Margin*), and *Stone*, performances in local theaters and stories told to the public were vital in consolidating the popularity of these works by adapting them to forms accessible to highly diverse regional audiences.

Although commercial publishing in the lower Yangzi delta was interrupted by the Taiping Rebellion in the 1850s and early 1860s, readers continued to read and comment on the versions of *Stone* in circulation, and reprints and new editions emerged in 1859.[4] New printing technologies (including lithography) in the 1880s, the booming of mass media (represented by newspapers and magazines) from then on, and the gradual transformation of Chinese cities and society at large in the age of modern capitalism gave an additional boost to *Stone's* popularity among the general public. The novel appeared in new formats, and in the second decade of the twentieth century it appeared with modern punctuation. Moreover, *Stone* lore infiltrated various aspects of urban life, ranging from fashion to leisure entertainment. Such modern issues as the nation-state and science and technology found their way into sequels and other works bearing the marks of the novel's influence, while *Stone* itself was often adapted to new circumstances.

## Textual Production, Reproduction, and Stone Lore

In the opening chapter of *Stone*, Cao Xueqin describes his novel as created through a process of constant revision and the consideration of many titles. In this account, *Stone* has no textual stability; it is contingent on the continuous intervention of readers turned commentators and editors—despite its putative celestial origin and its association with monumental permanence as engraved on a divine stone. Cao challenges his readers how to interpret a novel that remains indefinite and fluid. He also anticipated what would become of his unfinished novel in later years, for *Stone* has indeed been subject to greater transformations and adjustments since his death.

*Stone* has a complex textual history. The early hand-copied versions, each containing a portion of the comments made by the Red Inkstone Studio (*Zhiyan zhai*), a few members of Cao's inner circle, are considerably different. Published in 1791 and slightly modified in 1792, Cheng Weiyuan and Gao E's 120-chapter edition of the novel was so immensely popular that it became the main if not the only edition known to most readers, consigning the Red Inkstone Studio commentary manuscripts to oblivion. But this edition did not escape the textual mutation that the hand-copied manuscripts had experienced. Although texts bearing the title *The Story of Stone* or *Dream of the Red Chamber* continued to emerge in hand-copied form, some said to be vastly different from all previous versions, printed editions were altered too. The novel was adapted, translated, and abridged, and it gave rise to many sequels and imitations. Even when the main text of the novel was unchanged, *Stone* was almost always framed and reframed by a staggering number of paratexts—prefaces, commentaries, annotations, character genealogies, chronologies, and appendixes of various sorts—that together constituted an ever-growing lore whose influence on readers can hardly be overestimated.

The sheer length of the 120-chapter edition invites abridgment and abbreviation. From 1805 to 1809, when Liang Gongchen served as the education commissioner in Anhui Province, a licentiate in Anhui was said to have put together an abridged version called *Hongloumeng jieyao* 紅樓夢節要 ("The Essence of *Dream of the Red Chamber*") and handed it over to publishers (Liang Gongchen, *bian 4, juan 4*: 12–13). Compiled by Sha Yizun, a handy volume entitled *Hongloumeng zhaihua* 紅樓夢摘華 ("Selected Jewels from *Dream of the Red Chamber*") was published in 1868. It consists of only sixteen short episodes, which are followed by an attachment of several lyrics taken from the novel.[5] In his preface to the volume, the compiler explained his rationale:

> It seems insufficient to sum up *Dream of the Red Chamber* with a dozen of the selected sections from it, given the enormous length of the original. However, can you name other parts of the novel that surpass them in linguistic virtuosity and writing style? Scholars often gather together to discuss learning and exchange opinions on certain subjects. They will surely obtain the upper hand on these occasions if they spend time studying these selections carefully, and indeed, they could not benefit more even if they learn by heart hundreds of other texts. I wrote these few sentences in the preface so that beginners will know the right route to follow.
>
> (Yisu, *Hongloumeng shulu* 173–74)

Obviously Sha Yizun was addressing his fellow literati, especially entry-level students. His justification of the need for such an anthology demonstrates that *Stone* had become a fashionable topic for discussion in literati circles.

Other compilers had other audiences in mind. A devoted reader of the novel, Hasbuu (in Chinese, Hasibao) spent more than six years translating *Stone* into Mongol (his preface is dated 1847). Hasbuu took the liberty of editing the text to produce a forty-chapter edition highlighting the love story of Bao-yu and Dai-yu, thus reducing the novel to a manageable scale for both his audience and himself, for he admitted that his learning was unequal to the task of rendering the entire novel. His version also contains commentary as a way of offering guidance for readers beyond the literati community. In his preface, he stakes an exclusive claim to the Mongol version of the novel, describing it as his own *Little Stone* in contrast with Cao Xueqin's original (Zhu Yixuan 768–833).

From the late sixteenth century on, editor-compilers often assumed the role of commentator as well, and their work significantly shaped commercial print culture. The covers or title pages of vernacular fiction often featured their names in large type, and a novel without commentary was hard to sell. Sometimes the attached remarks were mistakenly included in the text of the novel during the process of transcription and printing, erasing the boundary between commentary and text. The effect of the commentaries on readers of the past is hard to gauge, but we can guess, from our own reading experience, that the voice of a commentator could be distracting as well as engaging, intimidating as well as enlightening.

No previous novel had generated so much commentary as *Stone*. Commentaries accumulated, as new ones responded to earlier ones, and more and more readers were encouraged to join the ongoing conversation, but the growing volume of commentary also invited mockery and criticism. In an essay serialized in the 1907 and 1908 issues of *Xiaoshuo lin* 小説林 ("The Forest of Fiction"), a magazine known for carrying fiction in installments, Yu Mingzhen dismissed the existing commentaries as shoddy and outworn, as having nothing to commend themselves. He then laid out his plan to remove them all from the printed edition of the novel while granting readers space to indulge themselves in making remarks. Widened page margins would provide them with a chat room for voicing their opinions on *Stone*. Despite the limits of printing technology, readers were invited to participate in the derivative discourse surrounding the novel.

Yu's plan was conceived in the early twentieth century, when lithography and letterpress became common printing methods. *Stone* was appearing in smaller fonts than the woodblock types and with narrower page margins. The accumulated commentaries were in fact soon to be stripped from the printed edition of the novel. The first edition of *Stone* with modern punctuation, made by Wang Yuanfang, came out in 1921. Although Wang preserved Cheng Weiyuan's preface, his edition began with a scholarly essay on the novel by Hu Shi, a modern intellectual, and all the conventional remarks that had framed and punctuated the earlier printed editions were eliminated. This elimination was part of the larger change in commercial publishing in the early decades of the twentieth century.

That poetry offered readers another means for engaging with *Stone* should come as no surprise: poetry was the most respected literary genre in the premodern and early modern eras, and it also occupied a conspicuous position in plays and vernacular fiction. Like the vernacular novels of the Ming and Qing, *Stone* makes frequent use of various genres of classical poetry in conveying characters' monologues and the narrator's comments; revealing the inner world of characters; delineating the natural scenery and details of clothes, furniture, and architecture; and evoking the ambience of the residential garden. Poetry also features in the everyday communications and leisure entertainments (from dramatic performances to card games) depicted in the novel. It invites readers to decipher its hidden meanings, for even an insignificant lantern riddle may cast light on the personality and fate of its composer and readers.

Readers employed poetry to comment on *Stone* as narrator-commentators or to speak on behalf of the characters. The first-person point of view, which had been cultivated in the lyrical tradition, was especially compelling in consolidating emotional engagement with the novel's characters. Long poetry sequences on *Stone* usually fall into one of two categories: they either present a series of sketches of and comments on the characters or recapture the novel's scenes and events.

Because character study was immensely popular, readers of *Stone* commented on the personalities and mental states of the characters as if they were real people, like their own acquaintances. The emotional engagement was such that even a debate on the merits of a character could bring friends to blows. Poetry facilitated the discourse. "A Hundred Songs on *Dream of the Red Chamber*," composed by Ling Chengshu, for instance, contains lyrics about the life and fate of the characters in the novel. Huang Changlin's two hundred quatrains on *Stone* is more ambitious, evaluating two hundred characters. In another series, by Zhou Shu, the heading of each poem indicates that the poem is mourning or mocking a particular character. The speaker's tone and perspective vary: some verses are playful or ironic; others identify so closely with a character as to become a statement from the character. As is typical in classical poetry, the first-person singular pronoun is absent, allowing the poet to shift perspective with little difficulty. Some poems engaged in imaginary dialogue with a character and explored alternative scenarios.

The longest example of the type of poetry sequence that recapitulates scenes or events of *Stone*, composed by Lin Xiaoji and others and published in 1889, consists of 240 topics and 360 poems. *Stone* was both a convenient subject and a rich source to help Lin display his literary talents, as he realized how difficult it was to distinguish himself in a time of overproduction in classical poetry. He did nothing less than systematically rerender the novel in the form of poetry. This poetic version of *Stone* differs from the original not only in form and mode of expression but also in the way it is organized. Lin Xiaoji divided the novel into representative scenes and captured them in a series of verses with prefaces and other attached materials. The novel was thus reorganized and literally transformed into an anthology of poetry. When narrative gives way to lyrical musing, plot continuity becomes secondary if not entirely irrelevant. Since each of these poems elaborates a selected moment of *Stone*, it can be appreciated independently and becomes portable. Other poetry sequences on *Stone* are less systematic and comprehensive; they are random assemblages of scenes from the novel, including such memorable moments as Dai-yu burying the petals of fallen flowers and Bao-yu mourning Skybright's premature death. Their authors, reducing this novel of great length and complexity to a few of its components, joined contemporary book illustrators and playwrights in repackaging *Stone*. A number of the poetry sequences were inspired by visual representations of *Stone*; some were composed as inscriptions or colophons for a specific set of illustrations or paintings on fans.

Women readers, who were of elite families and who often received a decent education in classical literature, are notable among those who commented on *Stone* through poetry. With its lively and sympathetic portrayal of female characters and its embracing of nearly all the classical genres, including poetry, *Stone* can be credited for kindling women readers' interest in the vernacular novel. Even before the printed edition emerged, some women had already gained access to hand-copied manuscripts and recorded their impassioned responses. Female readers' fascination with *Stone* was enhanced by the publication in 1818 of *Jinghua yuan* 鏡花緣 ("Flowers in the Mirror"), another literati novel that is visibly influenced by *Stone* and also has gentry women among its characters (Li Ruzhen). This novel appeared as a new wave of women's literature was gathering momentum, the previous wave having ebbed in the second half of the seventeenth century. Compared with their predecessors in the late Ming, female writers of the nineteenth century were less diverse in family background, education, and experience. Most were not courtesans or Buddhist nuns but from elite families and who married gentlemen with degrees and official titles. But their literary horizon was broader than their predecessors', as they extended their creativity to such genres as drama and the string ballad. The string ballad was a popular narrative form of prosimetric that became irrevocably associated with women and their literary life. Gu Chun (1799–c. 1877, often referred to by her sobriquet Taiqing), an accomplished Manchu writer, broke new ground by composing *Shadow Dream of the Red Chamber* (紅樓夢影 *Honglou meng ying*), one of the sequels to *Stone* and possibly the first vernacular novel written by a woman. Gentlewomen's poems on *Stone* are part of both women's literature and *Stone* discourse from the late eighteenth century through the nineteenth century. These authors were sympathetic to the female characters and often brought a personal perspective to bear on their judgment of the novel in general. Occasionally they described how they had indulged in reading *Stone* by the light of a midnight lamp, and they loved to prolong the pleasure of solitary reading by sharing their poems with their female friends, male relatives, and family acquaintances. Most of these gentry women were formally or informally associated with a reading group. *Stone* was transmitted in the circles of Yuan Mei, Chen Wenshu, and other literary luminaries, who were known for mentoring female disciples. Readers can find more on this subject in Ellen Widmer's *The Beauty and the Book*.

Poetry composition in premodern China was not limited to verbal articulation and textual production; instead, it was a part of social practice and thus often a collective if not necessarily public activity. Widmer points out that the game of matching poems on *Stone*-related topics was widespread in the late eighteenth and early nineteenth centuries and that its participants included female poets. A poetry contest on four episodes from *Stone* was once held in the manner of a civil service examination. All the participants' names were concealed, but when it turned out that the winner was a woman, the organizer of the contest replaced her with a civil official so as not to embarrass the male competitors (138). Although some women poets were reluctant to become visibile beyond their coterie, their poems on *Stone* often found their way into print. Wang Zhang, another woman from a gentry family, left behind four quatrains, each on one character from *Stone*, and her husband, Qiu Weiyuan, composed a hundred more in her memory. At the urging of his colleagues, Qiu dispatched their works along with a notice to solicit responses from twenty of his friends and acquaintances. The resulting anthology was published in 1898, and a sequel was soon issued, containing poems on *Stone* by yet another dozen or more authors from Guangdong, Fujian, Shanghai, Tianjin, Taiwan, Japan, and other places (Yisu, *Hongloumeng shulu* 297–301). Stimulated by a woman's poetry, this anthology encapsulates the dynamic of a larger community at work in facilitating the discourse around *Stone*.

More scholarly discourse on *Stone* assumes the form of annotations or treatises. The term *Redology* (紅學 *hongxue*), literally "Learning of *Dream of the*

*Red Chamber,"* was coined as a lighthearted parody of the disciplines in literati scholarship and the curriculum of the civil service examinations in the Guangxu reign (1875–1908) (Li Fang). Even before that term emerged, self-described experts had already produced a large corpus of auxiliary texts to assist readers and fuel the discussion among fans of the novel. Of these works, *Guidelines for Reading* Dream of the Red Chamber (讀紅樓夢綱領 *Du Hongloumeng gang-ling* ), by Yao Xie (also known as Meibo), stands out as a scholarly compendium on the novel. It has three categories of entry. The first are entries concerned with the characters in the novel; they are arranged according to the social status and genealogy of the characters and provide detailed information about their personalities, appearances, and the terms by which they are addressed. The second is divided into several subcategories: entries on *Stone*'s chronologies and its representation of dreamland, cities, residential mansions, objects, art, and writings. The third contains discourses on miscellaneous subjects as well as summaries of the existing interpretative and scholarly works on *Stone*. Wang Xilian, whose commentary edition was among the most frequently reprinted versions of the novel in the late Qing, was perhaps the first to describe *Stone* as an encyclopedia. Similar observations had been made about *Outlaws of the Marsh* (*Water Margin*) and *The Plum in the Golden Vase*, but *Stone*'s account of elite life and culture is more comprehensive, and its frame of reference overlaps little with those of the earlier novels. Yao Xie's *Guidelines* is an effort to contribute to and summarize *Stone* lore, and its upgraded modern equivalent is *Hongloumeng da cidian* (紅樓夢大辭典 "The Encyclopedia of *Dream of the Red Chamber*"), published in 1990, which organizes the critical literature about the novel into these categories: objects and household utensils, architecture, the art of garden design, foods and cuisine, medicine, appellations, official titles, ceremonies and institutions, customs, seasons and festivals, religions and superstitions, poetry and verses, plays and performances, music, visual arts, entertainments, historical personas, and geography (Feng Qiyong and Li Xifan). Each of these categories has developed into a subfield in the growing scholarship on *Stone*. Recipes based on those used in the novel fulfill a less lofty but more practical function, appearing on restaurant menus.

The dynamics of the growing discourse on *Stone* found its most compelling manifestation in the form of fiction sequels. A number of earlier novels enjoyed an eventful afterlife, undergoing reincarnations in the middle of the seventeenth century, but none has generated as many ensuing narratives as *Stone*. In 1796, only five years after the Cheng-Gao edition was published, the first fully fledged sequel was published, *Hou Hongloumeng* (後紅樓夢 "The Later Dream of the Red Chamber"). Four more appeared in the next ten years. By 1824, another four were in print. After the slowdown in pace during the second half of the nineteenth century, the production of *Stone* sequels revived at the beginning of the twentieth century and has since become an industry assembly line. Several dozen titles have been churned out, and the number is growing (see M. Huang, *Snakes' Legs*; Widmer, *Beauty*, chs. 6 and 7).

Most of these sequels begin where the 120-chapter edition ends or begin after chapter 97, in which Dai-yu dies. Few authors of these sequels disclose their identity. *Later Dream of the Red Chamber*, for example, claims to have been composed by Cao Xueqin at the urging of Bao-yu, the male protagonist of *Stone*. The author proves this claim by referring in a preface to a letter Cao Xueqin received from his mother.

The production of *Stone* sequels is often shaped by conflicting pulls: a sequel must justify its existence by answering the need to continue the narrative, but that very continuation may undercut its effort to make its own ending the definitive one. This paradox is compounded by another: a sequel that provides *Stone* with a happy ending of reconciliations and family reunion may open up a new front of controversies by radically recasting the character and fate of a few female protagonists. In one version, Dai-yu returns to life with newly acquired skills and confidence for managing her inherited family estate in Beijing (*Later Dream*, by Xiaoyaozi); in another, Bao-chai becomes a general noted for her command of troops in the defeat of pirates (*Another Dream*, by Chen Shaohai). In both, Wang Xi-feng, who figures prominently in *Stone*, is put to shame. Once the production of continuing narratives is set in motion, it is difficult to halt. Sequels beget more sequels, and each claims to be the only legitimate continuation of, or supplement to, the parent novel. The authors of *Stone* sequels, acutely aware of the ongoing competition, showed their disdain in prefaces or other attached texts for the existing sequels. Equally partisan, the characters of their novels, having read the rival texts, expressed their opinions about them. The plots of sequels were conceived in response not only to *Stone* but also to other sequels. Competition thus becomes part of the narrative. The proliferating sequels capture the dynamics of the expanding, cross-regional community of the reading public, as most were composed and commented on by men and women of different origins and published by different publishing houses, and most were reprinted in several different cities. By the middle of the nineteenth century, *Stone* had become the core of a large matrix for textual production and reproduction. The derivative discourses it generated were diverse in form and enormous in output.

## Elite Concerns and Official Censorship

An assessment of *Stone*'s transmission and reception in the mid and late Qing requires addressing the subject of official censorship, for *Stone* was, as Cao Xueqin anticipated, condemned not long after it appeared in print. Although the cultural elites of the time praised the novel, their praise often carried a defensive overtone. Even those impressed by the narrative art of the novel sometimes expressed concern that the novel might be morally hazardous. Elite readers were far from agreeing about *Stone*'s values and influences. Some felt certain that the novel could not harm them, but they were not so certain about impressionable younger readers and about less sophisticated audiences exposed to the novel through visual representations, storytelling and singing, and theatrical performances.

Censorship of obscene fiction, bawdy songs, and vulgar plays, which goes back to the Yuan dynasty, reached its peak in the Qing era. Imperial edicts issued the same message with regard to *Outlaws of the Marsh* and a few earlier novels, which were already proscribed in the late Ming for their treatment of rebellion. One of the earliest cases of official censorship of *Stone* was initiated by Liang Gongchen, when he served as the provincial education commissioner in Anhui from 1805 to 1809. Dismayed that no systematic measures had been taken to dampen the public craze for the novel, he decided to take the matter into his own hands:

> When I was education commissioner in Anhui Province, a licentiate degree holder, who was quite good at writing, once secretly compiled a book called *The Essence of Dream of the Red Chamber* and passed it on to publishers and had it printed. Once I found this out, I deprived him of the degree and set the woodblocks on fire. Those who were on the spot were struck with awe. It is too bad that no one followed suit in other places. Mr. Yu Yannong once said in earnest: "*Dream of the Red Chamber* is an extreme instance of heretical ideas and evil deeds. Even more detestable is that all it does is trash the Manchus. I once thought of submitting a request for an official prohibition on the novel, but I have held myself back because I was afraid that I might not be able to phrase the proposal appropriately." What he said here resonated with me deeply. There are all fictional characters in this book, except the author Cao Xueqin himself. But Cao paid his own dues by being subjected to poverty and died an old licentiate with unfulfilled aspirations, leaving behind no offspring and winning no sympathy at all—this is probably divine retribution for composing an obscene book.                                      (*bian* 4, *juan* 4: 12–13)

This passage expresses some of the charges that the conservative officials brought against the novel: it corrupted readers' minds and derailed their morals with fantasy and illusion while feeding anti-Manchu sentiment by tapping into what was then widely regarded as court scandals and gossip. Liang Gongchen's account also sheds light on the ultimate limitation of censorship. Liang in his solo campaign against *Stone* seems to count more on divine retribution than on official action.

*Stone* and its fiction sequels were mentioned in a report of banned books by the administration of Suzhou District in 1837. Seven years later, the education commissioner of Zhejiang Province compiled a similar list of the fiction and dramas to be prohibited. The most vigorous campaign against obscene fiction was launched by Ding Richang, largely during his service as governor of Jiangsu Province. Immediately after assuming this post in February 1868, Ding submitted a memorandum to the imperial court, urging a greater effort be made by all the provincial administrations to regulate fiction and plays. With imperial endorsement, he issued a specific order on 5 June to district and county officials stressing the importance of cultivating virtue and maintaining social order in the wake of the Taiping Rebellion, which had devastated the local community and social stability. Attached is a list of 233 banned titles, including songbooks and short plays, as well as *Stone* and its sequels. Ding Richang issued another order with an additional thirty-four titles six days later, and yet another order to prohibit theaters from staging lewd plays. The casual mixture of male and female audiences at performances, he wrote, posed a threat to the local order and individual morality. In a follow-up report, Ding cited the magistrate of Shanyang County for his meritorious service in confiscating more than fifty copies of each banned book and more than two hundred songbooks. He claimed that his campaign achieved a decisive victory, destroying several thousand books in Suzhou and Changzhou Districts alone (Wang Xiaochuan 121–31).

The censorship of *Stone* and other obscene fiction may paint a dark picture of the age as one of "oriental despotism." One might naturally consider the prohibition of fiction and drama an example of literary inquisition primarily concerned with "seditious" books. In such an account, both censorship and inquisition mark ruthlessness of an authoritarian regime. But some questions arise: What was the driving force for initiating and reinforcing the censorship? How did the censorship work, if it ever did? And how effective was it in containing *Stone*'s popularity?

The Qing authorities rarely enforced the prohibitions on licentious fiction and drama with the same rigor as they did in their prosecution of "treason by books." Generally speaking, literary inquisition, politically motivated, was a top-down process initiated by the court, and to succeed it required the cooperation of local governments. By contrast, the effort to ban indecent literature usually took the form of a loosely organized, bottom-up campaign, beginning with concerned local officials requesting an endorsement by the imperial court. Literary inquisition sometimes also proceeded as a campaign, especially from 1773 to 1782, when *Siku quanshu* 四庫全書 ("The Comprehensive Collection of the Four Treasures"), a court-sponsored compilation, was under way, but more often it focused on individual cases, targeting one author or a group of authors. An inquisition normally concluded with the execution of the guilty author or authors, their family members and relatives, depending on the gravity of the case, and the destruction of all their works, regardless of content. Official bans on fiction and drama often focused on categories of works instead of individual authors, and the punishments issued to those responsible for the composition, publication, and circulation of banned works were much less severe. The central authorities took extreme measures to seize "seditious" books, which were normally published through private venues, but when it came to fiction and drama, local officials found themselves in a delicate position, because they had to deal with the formidable forces of commercial publishing.

Circulated in large quantities through the book market, such novels as *Outlaws of the Marsh* and *Stone* were much more difficult to contain than an anthology, and their elimination was virtually impossible. Furthermore, any effort to regulate the book market could easily backfire: a local government might cause an undesirable public disturbance. Even someone as zealous as Ding Richang cautioned his subordinates not to interfere with the routine functioning of the book market:

> You should set up a deadline for all the bookstore owners to submit the forbidden books and woodblocks in their possession. The department in charge of this matter will pay each owner the total sum of money for the books being handed over and then assemble all the copies for destruction. As before, you are warned not to use this as an excuse for creating disturbance by dispatching the government agents to seize books from the bookstore owners directly.                    (Wang Xiaochuan 121)

According to Ding, the bookstore owners would be financially compensated for the books they surrendered to the local government; it is not clear what punishment they would face if they failed to cooperate. The local officials also knew better than to encourage bookstore owners and customers to inform on one another: accusations, fueled by personal vengeance, would spiral beyond their control. Thus, despite their duty to investigate and prosecute cases of licentious fiction, officials were often reluctant to act when such texts came to their attention.[6]

In their struggle to contain the proliferation of *Stone*, officials had the conservative regional gentry as allies. These gentlemen were the unofficial leaders of local society, respected for their cultural prestige, economic power, and political connections. They exercised their influence over communities, lineages, and schools in ways the authorities could not. In response to the censorship campaign championed by the administration of the Suzhou District, Yu Zhi, a gentleman from Wuxi, Jiangsu Province, drafted a compact in 1837 to ban obscene books, and it was signed by the owners of sixty-five commercial publishing houses. Many of his other writings are village compacts, school regulations, family instructions, and morality books, each closely tied to a specific social institution or practice. Yu Zhi contributed to Ding Richang's 1868 campaign against licentious literature inasmuch as his lists of banned fiction and songbooks were incorporated into Ding's lists (Wu Shicheng 14–15; Che Xilun; Chen Yiyuan, "Ding Richang de keshu"). Other gentry sprinkled their writings with anecdotes about the dangers of licentious literature. A young woman who became delusional after reading *Stone* cried over the novel her parents burned: "Why did you throw my Bao-yu and Dai-yu into the fire?" She died soon afterward. Young men did not fare better. A young male reader of *Stone* from Suzhou became distraught and began to behave preposterously: he established Dai-yu's spirit tablet in his room and offered sacrifices to it twice a day, then wandered off in search of the Land of Illusion. It took the family months to track him down. No one suffered more than the author of *Stone*; it was said that Cao Xueqin was subjected to merciless torture in hell. The drama of retribution and justice thus prevailed in the end.

It is difficult to assess the effect of such discourse on the general reading public, although the combination of the official campaigns in Suzhou District (1837), Zhejiang Province (1844), and Jiangsu Province (1868) may have temporarily stemmed the tide of *Stone* sequels in the lower Yangzi delta. But Ding Richang's campaign fell short of its stated goal. Only a few years after he initiated his crackdown on bawdy drama and fiction, Chen Qiyuan described it as a failure, because "too many literary men enjoyed reading *Stone*" (200). Ironically, Ding Richang used to be one of them: he wrote a favorable preface, an epilogue, and more than two hundred pieces of commentary on Huang Changlin's "Two Hundred Poems on *Dream of the Red Chamber*" in 1841, when he was eighteen (Chen Yiyuan, "Ding Richang, Qi Rushan"). Ding's zeal seemed misplaced in the eyes of his fellow bureaucrats, who responded to his campaign with amusement or disbelief. *Stone* was so popular in the circle of government officials and the royal house that its devoted readers included Emperor Qianlong and the Empress Dowager Cixi, who was said to have written comments in the margins of its pages (Zhao Liewen; Xu Ke 3767–68). Visual media were another way the *Stone* phenomenon infiltrated the court culture of the Forbidden City: produced in the Guangxu reign (1875–1908), the mural paintings in the Palace of Eternal Spring featured scenes from *Stone*. Manchu princes too were exposed to the novel's growing influence through youth books (子弟書 *zidishu*), drum ballads, regional operas, and other forms of performance. By the end of the nineteenth century, *Stone* had loomed so large in the public imagination that no other novel could match its appeal across the boundaries of gender and social class.

## Stone *and Regional Cultures*

The rise of highly diversified regional cultures in the eighteenth and nineteenth centuries reshaped the empire's social dynamics. New performance genres emerged, while existing regional traditions, which had largely been obscure and geographically isolated, began to gain national visibility as people migrated and their local traditions were spread and blended. Though deeply rooted in regional dialects, tunes, and performance styles, forms of theater evolved over time as they traveled along the trade routes and transcended their humble origins by drawing large crowds in Beijing and other faraway cities. Peking opera and a few other styles even won the patronage of the royal house and the official elites. Storytelling and singing were geographically and socially less mobile by comparison, but like most genres of regional theater, they retained such a firm grip on their audiences that elite influence hardly reached the audiences without resorting to these popular forms of entertainment. New agents and players were ushered in, and the lines of demarcation were redrawn between center and periphery and between elite and popular cultures. In this changing cultural landscape, the debates among the established elites grew less consequential, and the driving forces for cultural production and consumption came from elsewhere.

*Stone* appeared in print in time to tap into the boom of local theater and oral performance of literature; its adaptation helped connect it to audiences otherwise beyond its reach while also enhancing its popularity across the empire through cultural migration and interaction. Written records show that by the middle of the twentieth century, nearly thirty subgenres of regional theater and performance literature had featured stories from *Stone*. In remote regions, illiterate audiences could access the repertoire of *Stone* through the performance of their familiar regional genres. This was a cultural scene fundamentally different from the one into which Cao Xueqin was born; he would have been shocked to hear his characters speaking and singing onstage in so many different tongues.

Before *Stone* appeared in the burgeoning regional theaters, it was first rendered in Kun-style opera. Like all other subgenres of Chinese theater, the Kun style began as a local form but gradually developed into a national one embraced by the cultural and official elites of various regions. In the seventeenth century and first half of the eighteenth, no other style approached Kun opera in epitomizing elite taste and distinction. In *Stone* itself, Kun-style opera is an integral part of the Jia family's celebration of festivals and birthdays. Bao-yu, in his dream visit to the Land of Illusion in chapter 5, watches a theatrical performance of *Dream of the Red Chamber* (or *Dream of Golden Days* in David Hawkes's translation), composed by the fairy Disenchantment, while reading the manuscript of her libretto. This piece assumes the music mode of the Kun style, although it follows none of the existing suites of tunes and songs. *Stone* also makes frequent use of the theatrical devices of the Kun style: the metafictional frame, signature objects and props, and organization of narrative space and scenes.

A year after the publication of the Cheng Weiyuan and Gao E edition, Zhong Zhenkui, a man of letters versed in the Kun style, composed in that musical mode a short scene, "Burying Flowers," based on chapters 26 and 27 of *Stone*. In 1796, he read *Later Dream of the Red Chamber* and found its happy ending more suitable and composed a play that drew on both *Stone* and its sequel. Other playwrights followed suit (A Ying, *Hongloumeng xiqu ji* 5–118). Wan Rong'en incorporated into scene 5 of his *Destinies of the Awakened Stone* (published in 1803) the lyrics of all fourteen songs of *Dream of Golden Days* from Cao Xueqin's original with no significant modification (119–230). The most ambitious project was undertaken by Chen Zhonglin in the nineteenth century, a work of enormous proportions that falls into the category of desktop play, meant primarily for reading and not stageable without revision by professional musicians (523–804). Before Chen's play was published, Wu Gao wrote a play accompanied by notes on the music, which actors often consulted (431–84). Much less ambitious than Chen Zhonglin, Wu Gao was fascinated by what he saw as the most potent moments of the novel. Lyrical instead of narrative, its scenes consist of a few arias to be performed at private gatherings in the gardens or parlors of elite families. A play so conceived fits well the mode of anthology making used by contemporary publishers in the compilation of selections from *Stone*. It also illustrates how in Kun-style opera (and in other theatrical modes as well) a few highlights were staged from a shared repertoire for one occasion instead of a play in its entirety.

When Cao Xueqin lived, the Kun style was dominant in theater because of the unfailing appreciation and sponsorship of the literati, but by the year of his death, it was in decline, unsustained by the socioeconomic infrastructure. The burgeoning of local theaters coincided with the rise of professional troupes, which, unlike the private troupes kept by the elite families, were based in cities and toured nearby regions. During the same period, commercial theaters and teahouses gradually became the main venues for theatrical performance, attracting a large and diverse audience from both city and countryside. The elites did not approve of the rising tide of local operas, dismissing them as cacophonous strumming. But their mockery and criticism did not dampen the public enthusiasm for the regional theaters, which flourished outside the zone of influence of the elites. Only occasionally did Cao Xueqin present a glimpse of one of the bustling regional operas—for example, the Yiyang style in chapters 19 and 22 of *Stone*. Here is a description of such performances in Jia Zhen's compound:

> The plays they were performing turned out to be very noisy ones: *Dinglang Finds His Father*, *Huang Bo-yang and the Ghostly Army*, *Monkey Makes War in Heaven*, and *The Investiture of the Gods*. All of them, but especially the last two, seemed to involve much rushing in and out of supernatural beings, and the sound of drums and cymbals and blood-curdling battle-cries, as they whirled into combat across the stage with banners flying and weapons flashing or invoked the names of the Buddha with waving of burning joss-sticks, was positively deafening. It carried into the street outside, where the passersby smiled appreciatively and told each other that only a family like the Jias could afford theatricals that produced so satisfying a volume of noise. (1.19.376)

> 誰想賈珍這邊唱的是 "丁郎認父," "黃伯央大擺陰魂陣," 更有 "孫行者大鬧天宮," "姜子牙斬將封神" 等類的戲文, 倏爾神鬼亂出, 忽又妖魔畢露, 甚至於揚幡過會, 號佛行香, 鑼鼓喊叫之聲遠聞巷外. 滿街之人個個都贊: "好熱鬧戲, 別人家斷不 能有的." (253–54)

The sarcastic tone of this passage registers Cao's attitude toward a style that originated in Yiyang, Jiangxi, in the Ming dynasty and became widespread in Beijing and other regions in the mid–eighteenth century. He could not have anticipated that his novel would be adapted to such a mode of cacophonous strumming.

When the decline of the Kun style became evident toward the end of the eighteenth century, *Stone* took on a new life in the booming regional operas. Compared with most contemporary literati novels, which were seldom rendered in any theatrical form during the nineteenth century, *Stone* was constantly re-incarnated in regional opera. Although each new form had its own local source, these operas shared a growing repertoire among themselves. *Stone*, the product of an literati author's imagination, had already been filtered into some regional operas during the Jiaqing (1796–1820) and Daoguang (1821–50) reigns.

No prosimetric form of storytelling and singing played a more important role than youth books (*zidishu*) in disseminating *Stone* stories among Man-chu and Han audiences in northern China. Emerging in the Qianlong reign (1736–96), youth books were originally performed in Manchu but gradually shifted to Mandarin Chinese. Popular in Beijing and the northeastern region of the empire, this genre began to disintegrate into subgenres at the end of the Qing. More than four hundred youth books have survived, and nearly forty of them are concerned with *Stone* (Hu Wenbin, *Hongloumeng zidishu* 2). One of the most comprehensive explications of *Stone* is entitled "Destinies of Dews and Tears." Based on chapters 96–98 and 104 of *Stone*, it traces the se-quence of events (including Dai-yu's death and Bao-yu's wedding) leading up to Bao-yu's ultimate redemption. The story lines are unaltered but streamlined and simplified considerably. The author enters the characters' internal world and speaks on their behalf. "Destinies" emphasizes contrasts, discoveries, and unexpected turns; its frequent use of reiterative locutions and parallel lines heightens the melodrama and sentimentality, leaving little room for ambiguity and ambivalence. Neither terseness nor restraint is characteristic of a youth book piece.

Youth books had a southern rival in string ballads, which originated in Su-zhou. Although not always written by female authors, string ballads were typi-cally performed by female actors (but works composed by the gentlewomen of the mid Qing were usually read instead of performed), and it is no surprise that Dai-yu became an important figure in the string ballad works. In one account, the audience was moved to tears by a performance. Sometimes the texts them-selves reveal the location as well as the commercial nature of the performance. One particular piece called *Dream of the Red Chamber* begins with a brief preview of the stories to be told, but the announcement also carries an implicit compliment or blessing to all the stores and restaurants near the performance site, with their names deftly inserted into the lines of the opening verse (Yisu, *Hongloumeng shulu* 366). It is not difficult to find the place on a Qing dynasty map of Suzhou.

String ballads are read as literature as often as they are received through performance. Many were transmitted in print and hand-copied manuscript. The first printed edition of *Stone* string ballads appeared in an anthology in 1886 (Ma Rufei). A few men of letters composed string ballads on *Stone* and had them published in magazines and journals. Chen Diexian wrote a long string ballad about *Stone* entitled "Shadows of Peach Blossom" (*Taohua ying* 桃花影) and had it published in 1900. It was serialized under the title "Shadows of Xiao-Xiang Rivers" (*Xiao-Xiang ying* 瀟湘影) in *Women's World* (*Nüzi shijie* 女子世界), a magazine targeting a female audience, in 1914. Zou Tao included several string ballads on *Stone* in his novel *Haishang chentian ying* 海上塵天影 ("The Shadows of Earth and Heaven in Shanghai").

Many *zidishu* stories were written by known authors and circulated in handwritten and printed forms. From the Qianlong reign onward, Hundred Copy Zhang (Baiben Zhang) became a household name by selling hand-copied *zidishu* in the temple or street fairs held regularly in Longfu Temple, Huguo Temple, and other places in Beijing. Zhang's family business lasted for generations, and many extant *zidishu* works concerning *Stone* bear on their covers the trademark "Hundred Copy Zhang without bargains," along with the store addresses and the catalogs of the titles available for customers to choose from as well as prices for the items on sale. Years later, woodblock editions of *zidishu* texts appeared in Shenyang, Kaiyuan, and Beijing, where some small diners sold or lent *zidishu* copies in addition to serving steamed buns (Hu Wenbin, *Hongloumeng zidishu* 2).

The exuberance of regional cultures persists in the age of modern cosmopolitanism, new technologies, and mass media. Though tempered and compromised in many ways, regional theater gained a new life through film. The cinematic renditions of *Stone* can be traced to an obscure short film, *Dai-yu Buries the Flowers* (*Dai-yu zanghua* 黛玉葬花), made in 1929, featuring the title scene performed by Mei Lanfang, a leading actor of Peking opera who was also known for his performance of the Kun-style opera repertoires. The late 1950s and early 1960s witnessed a surge of musical and operatic films in the People's Republic of China, including *Dream of the Red Chamber* (1962) in the form of Yue-style opera, a genre that originated in Zhejiang Province. This film has been so popular that the image of Dai-yu portrayed by Wang Wenjuan has become the standard by which to measure other actresses' performance in that role, and so far few have passed the test.

## Stone *Remade: Mass Media, Urban Culture, and Modern Ideologies*

We cannot assess the scale and depth of social and cultural changes by looking only at a few selected and often retrospectively recognized historical events, yet those events can give us a general impression of what a different age the period from 1840 to 1919 was. The first Opium War, a military intervention of British troops in 1840, led to the construction of foreign establishments in major coastal cities, such as Shanghai. The war reshaped China's geopolitical, economic, and cultural scene. The damage inflicted by the British empire was compounded by the thirteen years of the Taiping Rebellion (1851–64), which devastated the lower Yangzi delta, the economic and cultural center of the Qing. The abolition of the civil service examination in 1905 marked the end of an institution that for a thousand years had served as the cornerstone of the elite hegemony. The republican revolution of 1911 brought the dynastic history to an end and ushered in the republican era. Finally, the May Fourth Movement of 1919 led to a wholesale rejection of traditional Chinese culture in the name of democracy and modern science.

These markers of modern Chinese history indicate the new circumstances under which *Stone* was received and reproduced. Not all the social and cultural changes were registered in the new reception of *Stone*. Men of letters continued to engage the novel in the ways their predecessors did; the same kinds of sequels and imitations were churned out. *Stone* proved as malleable as before. Mao Dun, one of the first major modern writers, compiled an expurgated edition, obliterating sexual scenes in ways that Yu Zhi and other regional gentlemen of the previous century would have applauded. But despite this continuity, new directions were taken. When first-person narrative gained increasing currency in fiction writing in the early decades of the twentieth century, under the influence of European novels, Yu Xuelun wrote *Lin Dai-yu's Notes* (*Lin Daiyu Biji* 林黛玉筆記), in which he rewrote and reorganized part of *Stone* from Dai-yu's perspective; it was given a new title, *Lin Dai-yu's Diary* (*Lin Daiyu Riji* 林黛玉日記), when it was reprinted in 1936—a testament to the importance of the diary form in the making of modern Chinese fiction.

No city better exemplifies the radical changes that modern China experienced than Shanghai in the second half of the nineteenth century, and it was in Shanghai that *Stone* found a new home and contributed to the making of a unique hybrid culture. The devastation of the lower Yangzi delta by the Taiping Rebellion forced many of the regional gentry to take refuge in Shanghai, where they sought to restore their inherited cultural tradition while adapting to the commercial enterprises and foreign establishments in the age of European colonialism and capitalism. Shanghai witnessed the birth of a new generation of men of letters, who were associated more closely with the emerging mass media and publishing business than with the civil service examinations and office holding. The publication and circulation of newspapers, periodicals, and magazines set a new rhythm for urban life, and the mixture of information and diverse genres in the new media reflected the heterogeneous population of the metropolis. The surge of Shanghai as a brave new world of business and sensual adventure provided ample stimulus for narrative and fantasy. In numerous pieces of fiction and nonfiction, Shanghai was compared with Grand Prospect Garden—a mirage that defied the most daring human imagination to capture its otherworldly allure and magnificence. A 1924 novel entitled *Haishang da-guanyuan* 海上大觀園 ("The Grand Prospect Garden in Shanghai"), by Wumu Shanseng, featured Silas Aaron Hardoon, a businessman who made a fortune from the opium trade and real estate dealings. His utopian garden of thirteen hectares, completed in 1910, comprised eighty buildings, twelve terraces, eight pavilions, eight ponds, and ten courtyards. Hardoon did not name his garden after the garden in *Stone*, but in the eyes of the novelist no other comparison could capture the awe it evoked in its beholders.

Stone prevailed in the most unlikely places—for example, in the brothels of Shanghai, where both courtesans and their patrons made use of the novel in negotiating their relationships and fashioning their identities. Courtesans appropriated the names of *Stone* characters—mostly female characters but occasionally Bao-yu—in their self-representation. They staged the Peking opera version of *Stone* in urban theaters. Once a courtesan, after marrying a well-known actor of the Peking opera, managed a commercial theater she named after Prospect Garden. *Stone* was providing both the framework and the sources for their role-playing as well as for their strenuous if often futile efforts to make sense of the world of red dust in which they were caught. City guides and tabloids followed suit, offering the courtesans an alternative stage for gaining publicity (see C. Yeh, *Shanghai Love*, ch. 3; McMahon, "Fleecing").

If the courtesans chose from *Stone* a female role to play, men of letters, who often were their patrons, had to make Bao-yu their model—for example, in writing fiction or autobiography. The earliest novel so composed is Yu Da's *Qinglou meng* 青樓夢 ("Dream of the Green Chamber"), dated 1878 and set primarily in Suzhou instead of Shanghai. Portraying its male protagonist as a reincarnation of Bao-yu allows the novelist to describe his amorous adventures in the guise of romance, but the narrative is fraught with so many fantasies and clichés of conventional scholar-and-beauty fiction that it reads more like a parody of *Stone*, whether or not the intention was parody. Zou Tao, who arrived in Shanghai in 1880 and lived there for forty years, produced many works—biographies, city guides (which include biographies of Shanghai courtesans based to a large extent on his personal contacts with them), and a novel called *The Shadows of Earth and Heaven in Shanghai*. Following both *Stone* and *Flowers in the Mirror*, the novel represents the worldly ordeals of nearly three dozen heavenly fairies in Shanghai and other places. A few female characters go abroad to study Western science and philosophy. Su Yunlan, who was driven into prostitution, manages to learn some English and establishes a girls' school in a Shanghai garden, where she and her fellow courtesans enjoy poetry parties as *Stone* characters did in Prospect Garden.[7]

Chen Diexian was an author noted, among other things, for his consistent effort to rejuvenate *Stone* narrative through fiction and autobiography, but he went further than many of his predecessors in that rewriting *Stone* for him became mixed up with enacting its plots in his own life. His novel *Destiny of Tears* (*Leizhu yuan* 泪珠缘) was conceived in the mode of *Stone* and set in the households of a few prestigious families. Its male protagonist is a modern Bao-yu who indulges himself in aimless amorous activity. A man of feeling capable of empathy and sensibility, he shares Bao-yu's trademark universality of affection and takes comfort, again like Bao-yu, in the company of women as he resists facing the world of brutal inheritance disputes, endless machinations, and mutual destruction. A similar motif is found in Chen's autobiographical fiction *The Money Demon* (黄金祟 *Huangjin sui*), which was composed in literary Chinese, and "The Koto Story," which reshuffles elements in *The Money Demon*. *The Money Demon* shows the inevitable erosion of love by domestic politics and money and ends up questioning the sustainability and even the possibility of the romance it evokes. In an age of ruthless social and economic changes, Chen's narrative of unrestrained sentimentality is itself a gesture of farewell to a vanishing way of life to which he hopelessly clung. But Chen was himself part of his society's modernization. He began as a cultural entrepreneur by participating in the publication of newspapers and magazines, including a newspaper pointedly named *Prospect View* (*Daguanbao* 大觀報) and a magazine called *Women's World*, where yet another of his works of autobiographical fiction, *A Short Account of Him* (他之小史 *Ta zhi xiaoshi*), was published in installments in 1914–15. His involvement in the burgeoning mass media facilitated the circulation of his passions and his writings at a pace once unimaginable, thereby giving an additional stimulus to his penchant for self-expression. Chen Diexian's cultural entrepreneurship gave way to an industrial one, as he became so dedicated to the production of tooth powder that his success in controlling the national market left him with no time for and perhaps no interest in fiction writing. In this way, his literary career ended.

*Stone* is a novel of great scope and complexity. In its sympathetic and ever fresh portrayal of women, it addresses a range of issues, from love, gender, and marriage to family in ways unprecedented in Chinese literature. Its evocation of the world of femininity forces readers to see women from a perspective that differs from that of a Confucian society. The male protagonist, the product of two opposing cosmic forces, the benign humors and the cruel and perverse humors, is locked in irreconcilable conflict and thus cannot be either wholly good or wholly bad. At the center of the novel is his rite of passage as he seeks self-knowledge through all available means. This personal journey highlights different aspects of Chinese culture in all their charm and intriguing complexity, but it also registers weary discontentment with tradition. Rarely traveling except in dreams, experiencing the world only through empathy and imagination, Bao-yu refuses to grow up and reaches enlightenment as a consequence of disillusionment. His journey is interwoven with the gradual decline of his family in the epic fashion reminiscent of the fall of a dynasty, with all its grandeur and sense of irreversibility.

Is *Stone* a modern novel, and if so, modern in what sense? The intellectual discourse on *Stone* has not been confined to high culture, because the modern state and intellectuals instilled in the general public modern ideas, in what they claimed to be a top-down movement of enlightenment. The mass culture of the twentieth century in China cannot be fully comprehended without taking into account this movement. As May Fourth discourse defined Chinese modernity, traditional fiction as a genre gradually lost its legitimacy. Writers like Zhang Henshui continued to write traditional chapter novels, but their work, which remained popular among urban readers in the 1930s and 1940s, became marginalized in the literary histories written in accordance with the May Fourth viewpoint. May Fourth scholars did not give up their attempt to redeem *Stone* in the light of what they saw as the universal model of European modernity. Like Liang Qichao and Wang Guowei, they saw *Stone* and a few other novels of the Ming and Qing eras as exceptions to the norm in the tradition of Chinese literature. Detecting in *Stone* qualities associated with European novels and modernity, they integrated it into their teleological account of Chinese modernity.

The *Stone* phenomenon persists in the early modern and modern eras through textual production, reproduction, and appropriation, but it also penetrates the fabric of everyday life. In recent decades, *Stone* has become ever more closely associated with modern media and technologies, and in the age of visual culture and global capitalism it is also inseparable from coordinated commercial enterprises and market operations, for better or worse. With all the changes modern China is experiencing, *Stone* remains relevant, as it too continues to change.

## NOTES

I would like to thank Ellen Widmer, Lydia Liu, and David Rolston for their helpful comments on the draft version of this essay.

[1] For a critical introduction to the visual renditions of *Stone* in this period, see my essay *"The Story of the Stone* and Its Visual Representations" in this volume.

[2] Rawski's estimate ("Economic and Social Foundations") is disputed by a few contributors to Johnson, Nathan, and Rawski, and scholars have not reached consensus on how to define and measure literacy in early modern China. See Brokaw, *Commerce* 560–70, 527–28.

[3] In his 1791 preface to the first print edition of *Stone*, Cheng Weiyuan offered the following account of the novel as it was transmitted in hand-copied form: "Each time when busybodies produced a manuscript copy of the novel, they immediately put it in temple-market and raised its price as high as several dozen taels of silver, and thus the novel spread very quickly" (4.385; see *Chengjiaben Hongloumeng* 1: 1–2). Carefree Wanderer wrote in his preface (dated before 1796) to *Later Dream of the Red Chamber*, "Cao Xueqin's *Dream of the Red Chamber* has long been popular among readers. Each hand-copied copy cost several dozen taels of silver" (Xiaoyaozi 1). Mao Qingzhen's account is slightly different: "After the celebration of Emperor Qianlong's eightieth birthday, the Beijing edition [that is, Cheng Weiyuan and Gao E's 120-chapter edition] began to spread in the Jiangsu and Zhejiang regions, each copy costing several dozen taels of silver. However, repeated reprints over time have lowered the price for each copy to less than two taels" (qtd. in Yisu, *Hongloumeng juan* 357–58).

4 At least two extant editions of *Stone* can be dated to 1859. Both were entitled *The Illustrated Dream of the Red Chamber* 繡像紅樓夢 (*Xiuxiang Hongloumeng*), but they differ in format (see Yisu, *Hongloumeng shulu* 41–42). One was published anonymously; the other was printed by Wuyun lou and distributed by Guanghua tang (see Hegel, "Niche Marketing" 254–55, 265). Despite the Taiping Rebellion, readers continued to read and produce written commentaries on *Stone*. For instance, Yao Xie (Meibo) wrote the preface to his *Du Hongloumeng gangling* in 1860.

5 Some extant hand-copied manuscripts contain only the poems selected from *Stone*—for example, *Hongloumeng shichao* 紅樓夢詩鈔 ("Selected Poems from *Dream of the Red Chamber*"), compiled by Recluse of a Red-Leaf Village; *Honglou zadiao* 紅樓 夢雜調 ("Miscellaneous Poems from *Dream of the Red Chamber*"); and *Honglou jiazuo* 紅樓夢佳作 ("Fine Pieces from *Dream of the Red Chamber*") of 1852. These anthologies were the result of the widespread literary practice of matching, imitating, or parodying the verses in *Stone*. They also demonstrate the efforts by literati readers to whittle *Stone* down to a convenient anthology form at a much reduced scale.

6 On official censorship, see Brokaw, Introduction 17–20; Chan Hok-lam; Brook; and Guy.

7 For other late Qing sequels to *Stone*, such as Wu Jianren's *The New Story of Stone* (*Xin Shitou ji* 新石頭記) (1908), see D. Wang, *Fin-de-Siècle Splendor* 271–74.

# *Stone* in Modern China:
# Literature, Politics, and Culture

## *Xiaojue Wang*

"Yesterday . . . Lin Daiyu wore a blue satin gown trimmed with pearls; she was riding in a four-wheeled carriage drawn by black horses, with her coachman dressed in a gray crepe-de-Chine jacket and a black-rimmed straw hat" (C. Yeh, *Shanghai Love* 3). Thus reported *Entertainment* (*Youxi bao* 遊戲報), a leading newspaper in late-nineteenth-century Shanghai. On 4 May 1899, *Entertainment* ran a full-page article about the biannual Shanghai horse race, with a close-up of Lin Dai-yu, a top-ranking courtesan in the foreign settlements who had assumed the name of the heroine of the classical Chinese novel *The Story of the Stone*.[1] While the courtesan version of Dai-yu was out riding a horse-drawn carriage, dressed in the latest fashion, dashing through the Shanghai Concession, the turn-of-the-century variation of Bao-yu was sitting in an aerial car that flew in the sky like a big bird on a trip to central Africa for a safari. This science fiction reincarnation of Bao-yu was presented by Wu Jianren, a prominent late Qing dynasty writer, in his innovative utopian science fiction novel *Xin Shitouji* 新石頭記 (1908; "New *Story of the Stone*").

Such endorsement of the leading characters of *Stone* attests to the tremendous popularity that Cao Xueqin's classic novel enjoyed and to how it continues to grip the literary and cultural imagination of modern China. In the heteroglossia of late Qing literature, there appeared various rewritings of *The Story of the Stone*, especially in the genre of depravity fiction, in which the tragic romance between Bao-yu and Dai-yu was recast and restaged in the late imperial opera or courtesan quarters. In these fictions, erotic and monetary desires, the contest between love and lust, are played out. Chen Sen's *Pinhua baojian* 品花寶鑑 (1849; "A Precious Mirror for Judging Flowers") and Han Bangqing's *Haishanghua liezhuan* 海上花列傳 (1894; "Sing-Song Girls of Shanghai") are good examples. While Chen Sen rewrote *Stone* into a homosexual romance set in the opera world of female impersonation and dubious gender identity, Han Bangqing reimagined Prospect Garden (*Daguan yuan* 大觀園) in his panoramic portrayal of Shanghai's courtesan culture. At the inception of modern Chinese literature, these works of mimicry not only take up themes and conceptual frames from *Stone* but also probe the moral anxiety and the politics of eroticism that the original work only touched on. With audacious innovations and experiments, this body of literature, as David Der-wei Wang maintains in his study of late Qing fiction, signifies the advent of modernity in Chinese literary history (*Fin-de-Siècle Splendor* 13–52).

In twentieth-century Chinese literature, instead of composing sequels to or rewriting *Stone*, writers embraced the novel's family structure and used it to criticize the deficiency and moral hypocrisy of the traditional familial hierarchy and emphasize the urgency of social and cultural transformation. *Stone*'s influences are to be found in a wide range of works by writers of disparate cultural and political agendas: Ba Jin's *Jia* 家 ("Family") advocates antitraditional new cultural and moral values informed by the May Fourth New Culture Movement; Zhang Henshui's *Jinfen shijia* 金粉世家 ("Old Grand Family"), a popular family saga and social critical drama, marks one of the best literary contributions by the popular culture school Mandarin Ducks and Butterflies; *Moment in Peking: A Novel of Contemporary Chinese Life* is a modern English version of *Stone* written by Lin Yutang, the renowned mediator of Eastern and Western cultures. In this opus magnum written during his sojourn in the United States, Lin brings the ups and downs of a number of distinguished families in the ancient capital Beijing to bear on significant social and cultural mutations from the late Qing dynasty to the Chinese republican era.

In other terrains of representation, visual and performance cultures in particular, *Story of the Stone* remained one of the most popular sources throughout the modern age. Excerpts of the novel have been adapted for practically every type of regional opera and later for film (including opera film) and television dramas across mainland China, Taiwan, Hong Kong, and other Chinese-speaking communities. The 1987 Chinese Central Television Station (CCTV) adaptation of *Stone* has remained the classic version, although in recent years, major mainland Chinese TV stations have planned to remake it. As part of these efforts, a variety of reality television shows and pageant competitions emerged, allowing people to participate in selecting their ideal candidates to portray Bao-yu, Dai-yu, and Bao-chai.

Having given this brief outline of the afterlife of *Stone* in literature and popular culture, I turn to the field of *Stone* study in twentieth-century China as it relates to cultural transformations in the Chinese age of modernization. Investigation of *Stone* criticism is the best way to grasp not only the appreciation of *Stone* in modern times but also the drastic cultural and historical change of twentieth-century China. In examining the interpretation of and research on this late-eighteenth-century masterpiece conducted by three twentieth-century intellectuals, I seek to delineate how the work of these modern Redologists reflected their cultural pursuits and registered intriguing configurations of Chinese aesthetic and political modernity.[2] Wang Guowei's *"Hongloumeng pinglun"* 紅樓夢評論 (1904; "A Critique of the *Dream of the Red Chamber*") was written at the beginning of Chinese modernity; Yu Pingbo's *Hongloumeng yanjiu* 紅樓夢研究 (1952; "Studies on *The Dream of the Red Chamber*") was published after the mid-twentieth-century Chinese divide, which triggered a series of socialist political purges in the People's Republic of China from the 1950s to the 1970s, culminating in the Cultural Revolution; and Eileen Chang's (Zhang Ailing's) *Honglou mengyan* 紅樓夢魘 (1976; "The Nightmare of the Red Chamber") was the last seminal work completed by this legendary woman writer during her diasporic years in the United States.

# Wang Guowei

At the end of the nineteenth century, Wang Guowei, an erudite scholar of the late Qing and early republican periods, completed his treatise on *Stone*. It makes a significant contribution to the study of *Stone*, which has been examined from many perspectives: literary, linguistic, historical, economic, political, religious and philosophical, culinary, sartorial, medical, botanical, horticultural, architectural, and art-historical. In the early twentieth century, in addition to the literary and interpretive tradition of commentary, the *Suoyin* 索引 school focused on dark imperial or Manchu secrets inherent in the novel, and the *Kaozheng* 考证 school sought meaning in the novel through textual and evidential research. These two schools were the prevailing approaches to the work.[3] Wang Guowei's *Stone* treatise, written in elegant classical Chinese, is distinct from all these studies in that it is the first piece of literary criticism to employ Western aesthetic and philosophical discourses to interpret a traditional Chinese novel.

Wang Guowei is considered the first scholar to systematically introduce Western aesthetic theory to China. Drawing on both classical Chinese sources and Western philosophical thought, German aesthetic theory in particular, his *Stone* critique exemplifies a new approach to literary criticism. Unlike the traditional commentary-style literary elucidation and criticism characterized by random remarks, it takes the form of a logically structured systematic exposition of the subject matter. It deals with the ontological, aesthetic, and ethical aspects of the novel, beginning with the notion of *yu* ("desire") as the prime cause of suffering in human life. According to Wang, insatiable desire drives people from one goal to another, and only art provides a way to transcend this endless pain. He introduced Immanuel Kant's theory of beauty, particularly of the beautiful and the sublime as two essential categories of aesthetic discourse. Art, in its aesthetic disinterestedness, provides a way for the aesthetic subject to be emancipated from the relations of interest.

For Wang, *Stone* is the best achievement of Chinese art in exploring the essence of life and freeing people from the bondage of desire. Bao-yu not only is created as the protagonist but also marks the prime theme of the novel. In its transformation from a piece of stone left behind in the Goddess Nü-wa's mission of mending the sky into a piece of jade in the mortal and material world, Bao-yu (the name means literally "a precious piece of jade") and his jade (*yu* 玉) serves as a pun on *desire* (*yu* 欲) and therefore symbolizes the desire of human life. By leaving the material world, one can be liberated from the perpetual drive of desire. Xi-chun and Nightingale, Dai-yu's maid, and Bao-yu leave the world in different ways. Whereas Xi-chun and Nightingale decide to spend the rest of their lives a monastery after they endure pain and misfortune, Bao-yu abandons the secular world on the basis of his knowledge of life through observation of the sufferings of others. One can easily see here the influence of

Arthur Schopenhauer on Wang. Wang considers the religious way to emancipation the lesser, the artisitic way the greater.

A key concept for Wang is the tragic. He believes that *Stone* is the one and
only work of tragedy in Chinese literature and art, because traditionally Chinese
writers create happy endings for their works. Tang Xianzu's play *Mudan ting* 牡
丹亭 (1598; *Peony Pavilion*) reincarnates its heroine, and Hong Sheng's play
*Changsheng dian* 長生殿 (1688; "The Hall of Longevity") reunites the couple
in the end. Only two works in Chinese literature run counter to tradition by
ending with anguish: Kong Shangren's play *Taohua shan* 桃花扇 (1699; "Peach
Blossom Fan") and Cao Xueqin's *Stone*. However, in distinguishing a forced
calamity from an autonomous one, Wang emphasizes that *Peach Blossom Fan's*
calamity is political and historical, dealing with sovereignty, whereas *Stone's* is
philosophical and literary, dealing with the universe. The tragic romance between Bao-yu and Dai-yu is depicted as rooted in the fundamental order of the
human world, not caused by any particular scheme or evil individual. Therefore
*Stone*, capturing the genuine spirit of Aristotelian tragedy, is the perfect work of
tragedy in Chinese literature.

Pondering Aristotle's and Schopenhauer's notions of tragedy in the light of
Kant's aesthetic sublime, Wang comes up with his own concept of the tragic
sublime. He suggests that the tragedy of *Stone* creates a channel of catharsis,
thus separating readers from their worldly entanglements and uplifting them
into the state of the sublime. He selects the episode that describes Dai-yu's reaction on learning of the upcoming wedding of Bao-yu and Bao-chai (4.96.87)
to illustrate his point.

The work of tragedy, which according to Schopenhauer is the highest form
of art, also opens a path toward the ultimate goal of ethics. Wang asks, Is not
emancipation from the eternal torment of desire the highest ideal? In search of
a subjectivity beyond interpersonal and social networks to transcend the worldly
order, Bao-yu may defy Confucian ethical principles, but his search serves the
cause of a greater ethics. In defining this alternative transcendental state, Wang
turns to German philosophy, particularly Schopenhauer's theory of desire and
emancipation, as well as to the Buddhist and Taoist traditions for illumination.
According to Schopenhauer, the best solution to the fundamental problem of
life, which is the drive of desire, lies in the suspension or denial of one's will to
live. Wang keenly perceives the affinity among Schopenhauer's concept, the
Buddhist nirvana, and the Taoist absolute void. When the mind is liberated
from all illusions and fetters of desire, one is able to achieve emancipation, the
ultimate goal of ethics. Wang interprets this poem in *Stone* as portraying the
purity of emptiness:

> The disillusioned to their convents fly,
> The still deluded miserably die.
> Like birds who, having fed, to the woods repair,
> They leave the landscape desolate and bare.    (1.5.144)

看破的, 遁入空門;
痴迷的, 枉送了性命. ——
好一似食盡鳥投林,
落了片白茫茫大地真乾淨!　(86)

Wang concludes his examination of *Stone* with a further reflection on art, in response to previous *Stone* studies as well as to Kantian aesthetic theory. Chinese Redology uses the biographical approach: Who is the author? Is the story based on the author's life? Drawing on Schopenhauer's theory of art and artistic creativity, Wang maintains emphatically that art as a form of pure knowledge exists prior to any experience of empirical reality. He reproves both the *Suoyin* and *Kaozheng* schools for not only rejecting art as an autonomous realm but also ignoring major issues the novel explores, such as the notion of desire and the new subjectivity.

Reconsidering Kant's aesthetic discourse, Wang finds that it neglects creative subjectivity, a neglect that ultimately leads to the repression of other human capacities. In the Kantian discourse of the aesthetic, particularly that of the sublime, what is formulated is the joy of reason in the midst of the experience of transcendence. The Enlightenment's theorization of the sublime reflects the ambition to construct an empirical anthropology and to highlight the centrality of a human being as a subject of reason. This theorization differs from Wang's idea of emancipation. With its emphasis on reason and rationality, Kantian human freedom can be realized only by an enlightened subject of reason. According to Wang, however, it is the negation of the subject that enables emancipation and the overcoming of the insatiable desire and sufferings of human life. In his embrace of the Taoist and Buddhist notion of the void and absolute emptiness, Wang shows his affinity with Schopenhauer.

The Enlightenment discovery of the individual and of the emancipation of people from social, historical, and religious constraints may thus become a new enslavement of the individual, the negation or even death of the subject. The dark vision advanced by Wang emerged from a particularly bleak situation in modern Chinese history. Since the Opium War in the mid–nineteenth century, the Chinese Empire had undergone a series of military and diplomatic failures that resulted in humiliating treaties. The advent of the modern era in late Qing China was marked by confusion and uncertainty, frustration and disenchantment.

Chinese intellectuals attempted to revitalize Chinese cultural tradition in this distressing encounter with the West. Wang's *Stone* study constructively appropriates Western thought to revisit Chinese tradition in an age of decline. It not only adopts a modern analytic perspective to examine a classical Chinese novel but also provides a critical meditation on modern discourse itself, particularly on German aesthetic philosophy. In this regard, Wang's Redological work poignantly captures the spirit of his age and best reflects the zeitgeist of Chinese cultural rethinking and rejuvenation at the threshold of Chinese modernization.

Critics have observed that Wang's *Critique* and other critical writings created for literature and art an independent and autonomous territory instead of accepting their utilitarian function, be that didactic or political (Ye Jiaying; Bonner). This new realm of the aesthetic provided a way to revive the cultural essence and foster modern citizenship. Wang was not alone in this regard: Liang Qichao, one of the leaders in Emperor Guangxu's Hundred Days' Reform (1898), proposed to forge a new literature to redeem the nation after the failed political reform; Cai Yuanpei, who studied philosophy in Germany and later became the president of Beijing University, cultivated a modern Chinese nation by means of aesthetic education.

This newly championed artistic autonomy should not be mistaken for escapism from political and social engagement.[4] Wang's conception of art is informed by his concern with the crisis confronting China in a time of domestic chaos and foreign economic and military encroachment. As the traditional culture was facing annihilation during the clash between East and West, he selected a literary classic as the object of his critical meditation, to come to terms with worldly pain and suffering and to formulate his notion of the aesthetic realm as a way of overcoming political and historical exigencies. Although he was strongly influenced by Western philosophers such as Kant and Schopenhauer, his primary concerns differed considerably from theirs. It is against the backdrop of a collapsing order that Wang ponders the existential and cultural situation. Pursuing meaning in a time of crisis, his *Stone* critique goes beyond literary criticism and philosophical inquiry.

If Wang expresses his reservation about Kantian optimism in the faculty of reason, he is also aware of the pitfall in Schopenhauer's pessimistic denial of one's will to live. In this dark vision of nothingness and void, the death of the subject looms large. When China entered the twentieth century, particularly the time of Chinese enlightenment as represented by the May Fourth New Culture Movement with its agenda of radical antitraditionalism, the Chinese cultural essence was charged with hindering national survival and cultural rejuvenation. Wang became increasingly distressed about the decline of tradition. On 2 June 1927, he drowned himself in a pond of the Imperial Summer Palace, located in a western suburb of Beijing.

His suicide is a compelling and disputed event of twentieth-century Chinese cultural history. There have been many theories about his death and his ambiguous suicide note: "After fifty years of living in this world, the only thing that has not yet happened to me is death; having been through such historical turmoil, nothing further can stain my integrity" 五十之年, 只欠一死. 經此事變, 義無再辱! (qtd. in Liang Qichao 95). There is speculation that by sacrificing his life, Wang Guowei, a political conservative, showed his loyalty to the last Chinese empire, the Qing dynasty. Chen Yinque, a historian of the twentieth century and Wang's colleague at Tsinghua University in Beijing, refused to attribute Wang's death to Qing loyalism. In an essay in memory of Wang,

Chen argued that with his self-destruction, Wang asserted his loyalty to Chinese cultural tradition rather than to any particular dynasty and represented the Chinese intellectual mentality characterized by "thoughts of freedom, spirits of independence" (218).

David Der-wei Wang, in his reflection on the enigma of Wang Guowei's death, pushes Chen's argument a step further and emphasizes that Wang was concerned with the preservation of all cultures threatened by the storm of modernization, not merely with Chinese traditional culture at the advent of the modern age: "Is it possible that Wang killed himself to express not so much belated Qing loyalism as an anticipatory mourning for all cultures, ancient and modern, on the verge of self-destruction?" (*Monster* 225). In David Wang's view, Wang Guowei occupies a more modern position than most of the self-proclaimed literati of his time, for he realizes the trap of modernity and regards modern temporality as "something more than the staged realization of enlightenment, revolution, and corporeal transcendence" (225).

With Wang Guowei's death, the annihilation of the aesthetic subject takes on yet another poignant implication. His suicide testifies to the dilemma of a modern Chinese subjectivity in the time of Chinese enlightenment and modernization. How could tradition be preserved? Would modernization deliver on its promise to solve the predicament of history and humanity? Reexamining the legacy of the age of reason, many critics have argued that the one-dimensional dependence on reason and rationalism and the Enlightenment's promotion of the teleological notion of progress have serious limitations. At the beginning of the Chinese modern age, Wang saw the incompatibility between the Enlightenment's boundless optimism about reason and progress and the bleak vision of disjunction and uncertainty that entails the death of modern subjectivity. His suicide points not only to the demise of traditional culture but also to the self-destruction of the modernization project, which will result in a "desolate and bare landscape" (1.5.144) that Wang had envisioned in his interpretation of *Stone* twenty years earlier.

## Yu Pingbo

At the beginning of the twentieth century, amid the chaos caused by a collapsing cultural tradition and the confusion caused by Westernization in China, Wang defined *Stone* as a book about suffering and about desire and its renunciation. With the end of his life, he anticipated the menace looming in the Chinese modern age. During the mid-twentieth-century socialist modernization, this eighteenth-century classic work was, in an uncanny way, again propelled into the limelight. The year 1949 witnessed the advent of Communist rule on mainland China and the retreat of the nationalist government (or Kuomintang [KMT]) to Taiwan. China was divided into different political and cultural entities—the mainland, Taiwan, Hong Kong, and overseas—a division that caused the diaspora of millions of Chinese people. At the peak of the dynamic socialist construction in mainland China, *Stone*, a work of fiction that couldn't be more detached from socialist reality, unexpectedly became the catalyst for the first wave of political campaigns against intellectuals in the realm of culture and ideology.

In September 1952, Yu Pingbo, an essayist, poet, historian, and literary critic, published a Redology anthology that included revised parts of his *Hongloumeng bian* 紅樓夢辨 (1923; "Explicating *The Dream of the Red Chamber*") and some articles. In May of the following year, *Wenyi bao* 文艺报 ("Literary Gazette"), the leading literary journal in the newly founded People's Republic of China, published a series of review articles praising Yu's book and his *Stone* research. In the first few years of the young socialist state, *Stone* study seemed to occupy a safe niche far from political and social reality.

The situation changed dramatically in 1954. Yu Pingbo's *Stone* study was rebuked in every corner of socialist China, and this rebuke launched the first major purge against intellectuals left over from the pre-1949 "old evil society" of the KMT regime who had remained in mainland China. More strikingly, the nationwide Criticize Yu Pingbo Campaign was instigated by Chairman Mao Zedong himself.

It all started when Li Xifan and Lan Ling, two graduates of Shandong University, wrote a paper criticizing Yu Pingbo's recently published *Stone* research. They submitted their paper to *Literary Gazette*, which was not interested in publishing it, in early 1954. Nine months later, it appeared in *Wenshizhe* 文史哲 ("Philosophy, History, and Literature"), a journal of Shandong University. It is not difficult to understand why an article written by two young college graduates challenging a prominent scholar in the field of classical literature received little attention from principal literary periodicals. But Mao Zedong saw it as the perfect opportunity to attack bourgeois intellectual authorities.

On 16 October 1954, he issued to the members of the Central Political Bureau, "My Letter on the Study of *The Dream of the Red Chamber*." In it he extolled the article by Li and Lan as initiating "the first serious bombardment against the erroneous views of a so-called authoritative writer in the field of study of the *Dream of the Red Chamber*" 這是三十多年以來向所謂 "紅樓夢" 研究權威作家的錯誤觀點的第一次認真的開火 ("Guanyu *Hongloumeng*") and reprimanded *Literary Gazette* for ignoring and obstructing this revolutionary effort. Thereafter, every academic and cultural institution in mainland China had to criticize capitalistic idealism as represented by Yu Pingbo's studies of *Stone*.

One may wonder why, in the intense time of actualizing his socialist modernization project, Mao took a personal interest in a piece of literary criticism. But literature for him had never been an autonomous field, a place only for the expression of individual opinions; he considered it a battleground of no less importance than politics. In a series of lectures delivered in Yan'an in 1942, later known as "Talks at the Yan'an Forum on Literature and Art" ("Zai Yan'an wenyi zuotanhui shang de jianghua" 在延安文藝座談會上的講話), Mao stated that literature and art should serve the purpose of politics and revolution and asserted the party's control over all cultural activities. The Yan'an talks were made the official doctrine of literature of socialist China in 1951, by Zhou Yang, who was regarded as the Chinese Andrei Zhdanov, the cultural commissar of the Stalin era.

Mao used a difference of opinion about how to interpret a work of classical literature to establish the rule of Marxist dialectical materialism and historical materialism in academic research, taking over the field of literature and art from intellectual authorities like Yu Pingbo, who were informed by capitalist subjective idealism. Instead of residing in the secluded ivory tower of academia, the interpretation of classical literature became an essential part of the socialist transformation and construction. The 1954 *Stone* controversy was therefore a serious political confrontation between Marxist and capitalist ideologies, and it shaped all subsequent campaigns in Chinese academia, culminating in the Cultural Revolution.

Since the goal was to eradicate all remnants of capitalism in the field of thought, the attention of the campaign soon shifted from Yu Pingbo to his mentor, Hu Shi, the foremost Chinese intellectual and the father of the New Redology.[5] Under the influence of his doctoral adviser, John Dewey, Hu Shi, a leader in the May Fourth New Culture Movement, advocated that Chinese scholars use a scientific methodology, particularly pragmatism, in their academic research. In his 1921 treatise "Textual Research on *The Dream of the Red Chamber*," Hu Shi identified Cao Xueqin as *Stone*'s author and applied historical pragmatism as a critical method, thus providing a new point of departure for *Stone* study. His famous phrase "Be bold in hypothesis but cautious in seeking proof" 大膽的假設, 小心的求證 became the watchword of this new methodology. He wrote, "I have always attempted to set aside preconceptions, to persevere in the aim of seeking proof, and to let proof act as my guide, to lead me to the correct conclusions" 我在這篇文章裡, 處處想撇開一切先人的成見; 處處存一個搜求證據的目的; 處處尊重證據, 讓證據做嚮導, 引我到相當的結論上去 ("*Hongloumeng* kaozheng" 575). Yu Pingbo followed Hu Shi in espousing the method of historical-biographical positivism and promoting the relevance of facts, textual evidence, and historical documentation to literary criticism. In his seminal work of *Stone* research, entitled *Explicating* Dream of the Red Chamber, Yu advanced his theory of *Stone*'s authorship. He claimed that only the first eighty chapters were written by Cao Xueqin; the last forty were written by Gao E. Yu thereby came to be known, along with Hu Shi, for establishing a new field in Redological studies, the *Kaozheng* school.

By charging that Hu Shi's bourgeois idealist standpoint in *Stone* study had "poisoned the minds of young people for the past thirty years" 毒害青年三十餘年 ("Guanyu *Hongloumeng*"), Mao established the Marxist-Leninist criteria of literary criticism. On various occasions, he presented himself as an avid reader of *Stone*. Condemning the capitalist idealist interpretation, he urged his party comrades to read this novel "at least five times, as I did," in order to understand its true spirit ("Guanyu zhexue"). For Mao, *Stone* was a work of Chinese history rather than a work of art. The *Kaozheng* school's overemphasis on meticulous textual evidence obscured the main subject matter. In one talk on philosophy and class struggle a couple of years before he launched the Cultural Revolution, he gave his own interpretation of *Stone*. He paid particular attention to the fourth chapter, in which the natures of the four grand families (Jia, Shi, Wang, Xue) are portrayed, considering that portrayal the major theme of the novel. In his reading, the theme of *Stone* was not love or desire but antifeudalist class struggle: "severe class struggle, with the (sacrifice) of dozens of lives" "紅樓夢" 裡階級鬥爭很激烈, 有好幾十條人命 ("Guanyu zhexue" 549). Only from the perspective of class struggle could one understand *Stone* and Chinese history at large.

By the spring of 1955, the Criticize Yu Pingbo Campaign had turned to Hu Shi and then to leaders of cultural and propaganda departments of the Communist Party, Hu Feng in particular. Ultimately, the *Stone* controversy expanded to the nationwide Antirightist Campaign in 1957, aimed at the entire Chinese intelligentsia. At the peak of Hu Shi criticism, Yu Pingbo had to write a confessional article to denounce Hu Shi. Entitled "To Break with the Reactionary Thought of Hu Shi," it was published in *Literary Gazette*, the same journal that promoted his *Stone* study a couple of years earlier. While hundreds of thousands were suffering from the contamination of Hu Shi's ideas, Hu Shi himself could satisfy his intellectual curiosity only by reading reports in his Manhattan apartment about his own purge. The former leader of the May Fourth revolution half a century earlier was now engaged in socialist political radicalism through *Stone*, an eighteenth-century literary classic.

Ironically, the political confrontation between Marxism and bourgeois idealism popularized *Stone*. The campaign against Yu Pingbo resulted in a great increase of readers of *Stone* in socialist China. Between 1958 and 1962, 140,000 copies were printed, and *Stone* become the most sold book after *Selected Works of Mao Zedong*, a success that Yu Pingbo, in the dreadful years of the purge triggered by his *Stone* research, would never have expected. In 1989, when the Tian'anmen incident ended the first wave of socialist reform after the Cultural Revolution, Liu Zaifu, the director of the Institute of Chinese Literature of the Chinese Academy of Society Sciences, was forced to leave mainland China. *Stone* was the only book he took with him. During his exile, he completed his *Stone* reading and wrote *Hongloumeng wu* 紅樓夢悟 ("Illuminations on *Dream of the Red Chamber*"). In the world of *Stone*, he found his "spiritual homeland and native soil" 我從背包裡掏出 "紅樓夢" 說: "故鄉和祖國就在我的書袋裡" (3).

## Eileen Chang (Zhang Ailing)

During the campaign against Hu Shi on the other side of the Pacific, Hu Shi, who was in New York, wrote a letter to the novelist Eileen Chang (Zhang Ailing) who had recently left mainland China and arrived in the United States. Hu

Shi reviewed Chang's novel *Yang ge* 秧歌 (1954; "The Rice-Sprout Song").[6] He praised her literary talent and observed that the novel had a "lifelike atmosphere" and a "realistic or natural artistic quality" 平淡而近自然的境界, the same remark Hu had used thirty years earlier in his appreciation of Han Bangqing's courtesan novel *Haishanghua liezhuan* 海上花列傳 (1892; "Sing-Song Girls of Shanghai").[7] Interestingly, both Hu Shi, who promoted this much-neglected and underestimated novel, and Chang, who translated the Wu-dialect parts of *Sing-Song Girls* into Mandarin Chinese, highly valued this late-nineteenth-century novel for its ability to accurately convey the "realistic or natural artistic quality" of *Stone*.

A descendant of an illustrious family in late imperial China and an important Chinese writer of the twentieth century, Chang won her literary reputation in wartime Shanghai under the Japanese occupation (1942–45). Her writings are marked by dedication to sensuous, feminine, and material details and insight into human frailty and historical contingency; they are permeated by her famous aesthetics of desolation. After Japan's surrender at the end of the Second World War, especially after the Communist regime canonized all literature and art along the line of socialist realism, she was virtually erased from mainland Chinese literary history, in part because of her noncommittal political position. In 1952 she left Shanghai for Hong Kong and eventually for the United States, where she spent the rest of her life. Although recent decades witnessed the resurrection of her work, first in Taiwan, Hong Kong, and overseas sinophone communities and eventually in the PRC, the writer herself never returned to mainland China.

In 1963, Chang, who often noted the influence of *Stone* and *Sing-Song Girls* on her writing, undertook her own research on *Stone*, a mission to which she devoted the next ten years of her life. In 1976, the Crown Press of Taipei published her last major work, a study of *Stone*, which she playfully named *The Nightmare of the Red Chamber*. In her years in the United States, where she attempted to make a new start as a writer of English fiction, why did she put aside her own literary creation and dedicate an entire decade to Redological research? In her solitude after the death of her second husband, the American scriptwriter Ferdinand Reyher, why did she choose to delve into the world of *Stone*? In what ways do *Stone* and her *Stone* reading bear on her work? An exploration of these questions will not only provide a deeper look into Chang's aesthetic world but also offer a better vision of *Stone*'s influence on the artistic and literary topography of modern China.

*Nightmare* is composed of seven articles: "The Incomplete *Dream of the Red Chamber*," "Episodes in *Dream of the Red Chamber*," and five close readings of the novel. Chang attributes her *Stone* study to her thorough familiarity with the novel: "When I read different editions, even the slightest difference in the usage of words would jump out at me instantly" 不同的本子不用留神看，稍微眼生點的字自會蹦出來 (*Honglou mengyan* 6). Impressed by the sophistication and profundity of her study, Zhou Ruchang, a contemporary leading Redologist, maintained that only Eileen Chang could be called Cao Xueqin's soul mate ("Zi bi" 222).

In her preface to *Nightmare*, Chang notes that her study of *Stone* is a scrutiny between the lines and among various editions, a practice that she compares with walking a labyrinth, assembling a jigsaw puzzle, reading a detective story, or following multiple possibilities, as in *Rashomon*. Her research combines hermeneutic and philological methods. Like *Suoyin* scholars, she spends pages examining the minute details of clothes, shoes, and jewelry of Bao-yu, Dai-yu, and other characters, in order to unveil their ethnic origins and expose the hierarchical distinctions between Manchu and Han Chinese in eighteenth-century China. Like *Kaozheng* scholars, she also does meticulous textual analysis and edition comparison. While she accepts Hu Shi and Yu Pingbo's conclusion regarding *Stone*'s authorship, her study focuses more on critical examination of the uneven literary quality of Gao E's forty-chapter sequel.

But Chang's research differs significantly from both major Redology schools. Her *Suoyin* reading never lingers on obscure political allegories or dynastic secrets. What Chang seeks to uncover are aesthetic nuances and cultural implications buried or overlooked in the novel's detailed account of everyday life. Rich in imagination and sensitivity, her *Kaozheng* interpretation deviates from the objective, scientific, and cautious mode proposed and practiced by Hu Shi. Her Redological pursuit is uniquely marked by her perspective as a woman writer. Her approach is literary rather than scholarly. In the field of *Stone* study, she is often regarded as a quasi-Redologist, just as in modern Chinese literature, she eluded canonization, occupying an ambiguous position between mainstream May Fourth enlightenment literature and the Mandarin Ducks and Butterflies type of middle-brow fiction substantially informed by the Chinese vernacular tradition, of which *Stone* is an important part.

Chang is a fiction writer, not a scientist. It is precisely because her *Nightmare* is not just a scholarly monograph that her *Stone* interpretation is such an interesting pursuit. It is a complex of layered articulation of materialist history and human nature. Her undertaking antedated her Redologist research. In her early teens, she was captivated by *Stone*, so much so that she couldn't resist the temptation to write her own modern version. Composing a few chapters under the title "Modern *Dream of the Red Chamber*," this teenage girl fabricated a twentieth-century Prospect Garden much along the lines of late Qing dynasty *Stone* fantasy—in particular, of Wu Jianren's *New Story of the Stone*.

In modern Chinese literature, Chang is the quintessential practitioner of *Stone*'s artistic sophistication and the finest interpreter of its interwoven relation between quotidian existence and historical pathos. Her novella *The Golden Cangue* (1943) is an example. *Cangue* is considered by C. T. Hsia in his 1961 study *A History of Modern Chinese Fiction* the "greatest novelette in the history of Chinese literature" (398). The story unfolds in the framework of a family saga, depicting a declining aristocratic family trapped in the historical transition from the imperial to the republican era. Chang excels in conveying the sensuous and decadent texture of life. The indulgence in palpable details of domestic life—fabrics, colors, grains, flavors, and ornaments—may seem pointless at first, but it is precisely through this abundance that she registers the interpersonal dynamics of social life and plumbs the depths of psychology.

Clothing exists as a social as well as a material condition. In *Nightmare*, Chang notes that although the author of *Stone* pays great attention to the clothes and ornaments of his characters, he makes an exception for Dai-yu. Throughout the entire 120 chapters, there are only two moments that depict Dai-yu's clothes, and the depictions are minimalist, her garments described as timeless, beyond any fashion. In Chang's reading, this absence encapsulates Dai-yu's character as pure and celestial, never contaminated or restrained by worldly criteria.

The poetics and politics of fashion also lie at the center of Chang's literary imagination. In her "Chronicle of Changing Clothes" she provides a fascinating meditation on various changes in Chinese clothing from the Qing dynasty to the republican era, considering fashion part of society and history.[8] Her fictional work is filled with perceptive remarks of the relations between corporality and identity, sentience and materiality. In *The Golden Cangue*, describing Cao Qi-qiao's suffocation in the old-fashioned Jiang family into which she is taken to be the wife-cum-maid of an invalid son, Chang writes, "[Qi-qiao] stared straight ahead, the small, solid gold pendants of her earrings like two brass nails nailing her to the door, a butterfly specimen in a glass box, bright-colored and desolate" (537) 她睜著眼直勾勾朝前望著, 耳朵上的實心小金墜子像兩隻銅釘把她釘在門上——玻璃匣子裡蝴蝶的標本, 鮮艷而淒愴 (*Jinsuo ji* 151). The moral and psychological degradation is captured in this uncannily splendid yet morbid image. Thus Chang presents her modern Prospect Garden, a paradise lost in the changes of the twentieth century.

Chang's work pays attention to spectral characters stranded in the fissures of changing times and disparate cultures. Saturated with a sense of loss, her aesthetics of desolation conveys the dialectic of worldly desire and its renunciation, which, as Wang Guowei emphasizes at the last moment of the collapsing Qing dynasty, constitutes the central theme of *Stone* (102–03). Looking back at the Chinese modern age, Chang observes, "our age plunges forward and is already well on its way to collapse, while a bigger catastrophe looms. The day will come when our culture, whether interpreted as vanity or as sublimation, will all be in the past. If 'desolate' is so common a word in my vocabulary, it is because desolation has always haunted my thoughts" (D. Wang, Foreword) 個人即使來得及, 時代是倉促的, 已經在破壞中, 還有更大的破壞要來. 有一天我們的文明, 不論升華還是浮華, 都要成為過去. 如果我最常用的字是 "荒涼," 那是因為思想背景裡有這惘惘的威脅 (E. Chang, Preface). In her consideration of the human condition in historical contingency, be it the vanishing imperial epoch, the Japanese invasion, or the Communist revolution, this writer of the aesthetics of desolation appreciates Wang Guowei's emotional and intellectual investment in his *Stone* interpretation at a time when, with the onslaught of modernization, uncertainty persists and catastrophe looms.

At the beginning of the twentieth century, as economic reform accelerated, socialist China once again became ecstatic over the promise of modernization and progress. At this juncture, a cinematic work was adapted from *Sing-Song Girls of Shanghai*, the late Qing bona fide successor of *Stone*. The film, *Haishanghua* 海上花 (1998; *Flowers of Shanghai*), was directed by Hou Hsiao-hsien with his longtime collaborator Zhu Tianwen, both of whom are from Chinese families who immigrated to Taiwan at the 1949 division. Zhu Tianwen, a writer often regarded as a fin de siècle disciple of Eileen Chang, used Chang's Mandarin translation of *Sing-Song Girls* for the screenplay. Claustrophobically obsessed with the facade of social life and the ephemerality and frailty of human affection, the film went against the grain of the prevailing optimism about modernization and globalization. This dissonance, with its inquiry into desire and disillusionment, provides a timely, perceptive reflection on modernity in its dark, decadent aesthetics.

NOTES

[1] For more on late Qing courtesan culture, see Hershatter; Henriot.

[2] The term *Hong xue* 紅學 ("Redology") refers to the study of *Dream of the Red Chamber*.

[3] For a detailed discussion of the New Redology of the early twentieth century, see Edwards, "New *Hongxue*."

[4] For a detailed analysis of this artistic autonomy, see Wang Ban, esp. ch. 1.

[5] For a detailed account of the 1955 Criticize Hu Shi Campaign, see Grieder.

[6] *The Rice-Sprout Song* is the first novel Chang wrote after she left mainland China and arrived in Hong Kong in the 1950s. It was written in Chinese and published in 1954 in Hong Kong. Chang rewrote it in English, and it was published by Charles Scribner's Sons in the United States in 1955. The version she sent to Hu Shi was the Chinese one.

[7] For Hu Shi's letter to Chang, see E. Chang, "Yi Hu Shizhi"; for Hu Shi's article on *Sing-Song Girls of Shanghai*, see his preface to Han Bangqing. This remark was originally proposed by Lu Xun.

[8] This essay was titled "Chinese Life and Fashions" in the English-language journal *Twentieth Century*. Chang later rewrote it in Chinese ("Gengyi ji").

# *The Story of the Stone* on Television

## *Xueping Zhong*

In 2007, if anyone googled or *baidu*'ed Chen Xiaoxu, at least 4,730,000 pages would appear.[1] Who was Chen Xiaoxu? Why did her death in 2007 generate so much public interest in China? The answer is in part that Chen played Lin Dai-yu, a major female character in the thirty-six-episode television miniseries of *Stone* made in 1987, in part that she led a rather unusual life after playing that role until her untimely death.[2] Two decades after her portrayal of Dai-yu, the development of a celebrity-and-fashion-obsessed youth culture in China turned Chen into a legendary figure (despite the fact that her portrayal of Dai-yu was not particularly well received initially). Relevant to this essay is that the netizens' outpouring of responses to her death and their commemoration of her helped bring forth tales and memories about the making of the 1987 version of the *Stone* TV series. These responses and commemoration dovetailed, interestingly enough, with the publicity and controversy, in 2007, over the remaking of *Stone* into another television series. Twenty years since the showing of the first miniseries, we find that in the age of television (and now also of the Internet), this classical novel continues to capture the imagination of the populace.[3] The death of Chen Xiaoxu and the controversy over the making of *Stone* into another television series were not the only *Stone*-related public phenomena in the new millennium. They reflect a collective fascination with *Stone*, a fascination that may be as much about contemporary Chinese society and culture as about, if not more than about, this classical novel.

This essay focuses on the 1987 miniseries, the first large-scale (PRC-made) television adaptation of the novel *The Story of the Stone*.[4] I examine aspects of its production decisions and textual representations and also explore some of its cultural, gender, and ideological implications. I first offer a brief narrative about the background of the making of the 1987 version of *Stone*, specifically the historical context of the 1980s in which the emergence of television industry and television culture echoed the elite-originated culture fever movement. I consider formal and narrative aspects of the miniseries and highlight a few points of contention that indicate the complex legacy of this novel and unique place it occupies in Chinese culture in its seemingly infinite possibilities for reinterpretation. Finally, in reference to the production of yet another television adaptation of the novel, I suggest that in some ways the novel may be more relevant than ever in today's China. This relevance is ironic, because most of those who engage in scholarly or televisual reinterpretation of the novel are oblivious to these famous lines from it: "Pages full of idle words / Penned with hot and bitter tears / All men call the author fool / None his secret message hears" (1.1.51) 滿紙荒唐言, 一把辛酸淚. 都雲作者痴, 誰解其中味 (7).

That this miniseries was made in the 1980s is important. Writing about the decade in China, scholars have paid close attention to what is known as "high culture fever," a movement in which intellectuals, in their response to the call for thought liberation and in their revolt against what they perceived to be the negative and underlying causes of the Cultural Revolution (1966–76), initiated debate on a range of issues, all in the loosely defined domain of culture.[5] Many looked to the West for ideas; others moved to reexamine China's past in search of cultural roots. The stated aim of both was to enlighten (reenlighten) the masses. The key issues of this movement have preoccupied Chinese intellectuals throughout the century-long development of modern China. The movement was marked by debate about the problems of traditional Chinese culture and the need to enlighten the masses; an explosion in literary writing, a phenomenon referred to by many as the second literary renaissance — second to the May Fourth period (1915–27); and renewed interest in Western thought and ideas. The high culture fever was also marked by intellectuals' newfound authority in meaning production.

But scholars have had little to say about the simultaneous development of such popular cultural forms as television and print media. In retrospect, one can argue that these forms emerged and developed along the lines of the "new enlightenment" of the 1980s, despite the fact that they may have appeared more mainstream than many literary works.

Indeed, throughout the 1980s all cultural forms — literature, film, theater, television, and print media — enjoyed equal opportunity treatment: intellectuals used them all to convey their ideas. In fact, the cultural elite welcomed the introduction of television into China, feeling it was yet another step toward modernization, a vehicle for transmitting their ideas, much as the left-wing intellectuals of the 1930s welcomed film as a medium for conveying progressive ideas.[6] The production of the six-episode television essay (for a lack of a better term to describe the genre) of *River Elegy* 河殇 in 1986 is an example of the use of television to enlighten (that it was banned after its first episode shows that the government was worried about the potential political power of this medium). The lack of market forces and the thought liberation initiated by the Communist Party (though the party did crack down on debates it thought had gone too far) explain the fluidity at the time and why most television dramas produced in the 1980s were adaptations of either classical novels or modern literary texts.[7] Like filmmaking in the 1930s, television was considered by the cultural elite to be a new means for conveying their ideas.[8]

According to Wang Fulin, a director, the interest in making *Stone* a television drama emerged during his first trip to the United Kingdom in the early 1980s, a time when China had opened up to the West and when the cultural elite was eager to learn from the West. Visiting the BBC television station, he learned about the BBC's adaptations of Shakespeare and other authors of literary classics such as Charles Dickens and Leo Tolstoy into television series. Wang then made the connection between television drama and Chinese literary classics. Coincidentally, the Chinese Central Television Station (CCTV) was beginning to explore producing the kind of television series Wang envisioned.[9] As the only director in the three-member drama department at the CCTV, he became the natural choice for directing the first Chinese television *Story of the Stone*.[10] But the making of the miniseries was to involve far more than the director. Unlike filmmaking, in which directors loom large, in the making of television dramas scriptwriters are equally if not more important. The televisual adaptation of *Stone* had not only three scriptwriters but also a group of advisers: twenty well-known scholars of *Stone* studies, cultural figures, and officials.[11]

In 1983, after a succession of seven day-long discussion meetings convened by the directors of the CCTV, the writing of the script began. The decision was reached that the adaptation should stay faithful to the first eighty chapters but not to the last forty (*Hongloumeng 87* 12). It was also decided that the adaptation should emphasize the realism of the novel, showing how the novel functioned as an encyclopedia of China's "feudal" society and showing how the decline of the Jia family and their associates reflected the class struggle of the time (3–4). These directives indicated a return to social realism (as opposed to the socialist realism promoted by the Chinese Communist Party during the Mao era) in post–Cultural Revolution China.[12] Although members of the advisory board represented different schools of interpretation, the foregrounding of *Stone*'s social dimension harks back to the idea that culture, be it popular or avant-garde, should enlighten the masses. This decision was followed by the selection of actors, their training courses on the novel in seclusion, the building of a Prospect Garden in Beijing, and the shooting of the miniseries.[13]

When the series was first aired, it was said to have emptied streets. According to Wang Fulin, many bookstores around the nation quickly ran out of copies of the novel. Since then, the miniseries has had about seven hundred reruns. It generated heated debate and discussion, in both scholarly journals and popular magazines. The *Journal of* Stone *Studies* 紅樓夢研究 devoted more than 150 pages of its fourth issue in 1987 to the TV series. About forty scholars, critics, television professionals, and viewers participated in a symposium on the series. The production, broadcast, and reception of the series were a major cultural event and showed a society at a crossroads of change. Especially significant in the larger historical context was the tension between the need to foreground the realism of the novel and the inevitable presence of the novel's sentiments of *xu huan* 虛幻 ("illusion and disenchantment").

The *Stone* miniseries consisted of thirty-six episodes, each episode running about forty-five minutes; therefore much of the novel had to be compressed, disregarded, or changed. Almost thirty of the episodes were based on the first eighty chapters, so the scriptwriters took great liberties with the last forty. Most scholars of the novel objected, especially to the last six episodes. But anyone familiar with the history of *Stone* studies and the popular interest in *Stone* would know that any choice an adaptation made to end the narrative would meet with criticism and create controversy.

The first challenge facing the series was to translate to the screen the exquisite description of complex human relationships. This challenge was not met: the visual representations are conventional and predictable, lacking the novel's layered narrative texture. What gets translated in televisual terms is only the extravagant lifestyle of the Jias and their associates.[14] We see family meals, family gatherings on various occasions, poetry contests among the young women and Bao-yu, the building of Prospect Garden in preparation for Yuan-chun's visit and the homecoming itself, the celebration of Grandmother Jia's birthday, and the wedding of Tan-chun. The producers clearly took great care in staging the wealth and power of the rich: to celebrate such lavishness but also to indicate its illusory nature. How successfully this double meaning was conveyed continues to be a matter of debate.

More relevant to this discussion is the narrative structure of the series, which gives a modern reading of *Stone*. While the novel is known, and treasured by many, for its unparalleled, brilliant representations of characters; for its exquisite and folkloric quality both; for its detailed descriptions of the everyday life in the Jia households; and for its sense of illusion, pessimism, and disenchantment, the 1987 *Stone* miniseries negotiates these qualities into a realist and melodramatic show about how these rich families live, thrive, and decline in ways that reflect the negative nature of their society. Despite the use of various formal elements, such as visual cues, a voiceover that brackets the miniseries with two key lyrical passages from the first chapter, and songs and music, it is the narrative structured around Prospect Garden that captures the novel's social criticism. This criticism is rooted in Buddhist and Taoist sentiments, which, carrying a sense of unreality and illusion, are difficult for a televisual representation to convey.

Therefore the series is organized in a way more straightforward than that of the novel. It downplays the first several chapters of the novel, especially chapter 5, which contains an elaborate description of Bao-yu's dream, including songs that foretell the fate of the major female characters. The series scales back the fantastic quality, the thing that makes the novel fascinating to many readers. Yet the series does make use of the lyrics from the songs of "A Dream of Golden Days" 紅樓夢十二支 in chapter 5.[15] Though the drama downplays Bao-yu's visit to the Land of illusion, that it structures much of its narrative around Prospect Garden can be seen as a way of alluding to that land.

The use of Prospect Garden, in other words, is a major negotiation strategy of the series. In the novel as well as in the TV drama, the garden has many implications. Its origin speaks not only of the family's wealth but also of the family's connection with power: Yuan-chun, after her promotion to imperial concubine, is given the opportunity to visit her family. Much of episodes 10 and 11 is devoted to her homecoming, which culminates with a prolonged montage of processions, greeting rituals, fireworks, meals, and poetry competition. During this visual feast, Yuan-chun's sadness and loneliness are conveyed: her required formality with her family, the stiffness of the entire event, the detached manner in which Yuan-chun watches the extravaganza playing out in front of her. From time to time, the camera cuts to close-ups to show that her heavily made-up face hardly ever smiles. But her talent and education are evident during the poetry competition she presides over.[16]

The narrative link between Yuan-chun and the garden is established when she issues the decree that all her unmarried female relatives and Bao-yu should move to live in the garden. The decree prevents Jia Zheng, Bao-yu's father, from forbidding Bao-yu to reside in the garden. From episode 10 to episode 35, when the garden is ransacked and destroyed and Yuan-chun dies and Jia Zheng falls out of favor, the series does a good job conveying decline. At the beginning, scenes of life in the garden are bathed in warm light to indicate the carefree existence of the young inhabitants within. As the series goes on and the underlying decay of the family's financial situation begins to surface, the visual representations of the garden change. There are falling petals, a frequently used image in traditional Chinese poetry to symbolize the coming to an end of something beautiful; an increasing use of bluish lighting; more frequent shots of the closed gate to the garden and of various locked doors to quarters of the young women. The gate and doors suggest imprisonment.

What eventually happens in and to Prospect Garden in the series moves the story in the direction of social realism. In the later episodes, reality catches up with the young people, master and servant alike. Scenes of sunny and outdoor daylight give way to night searches and assaults. The camera follows Bao-yu and his anxious attempts to find out what has happened to the female servants who are the first to suffer from the violence that eventually falls on this once tranquil garden of maidens. By situating him in the garden instead of in his dream, as in the novel, the series places him in reality, and he becomes witness to the sadness, pain, and death of both servants and relatives—including Dai-yu, whom he loves. By directly dramatizing his affinity with and sympathy toward women, especially when he wishes to help them but cannot, the series realizes the novel's criticism of a society in which women suffer. The young women die (Dai-yu in episode 33), are married off unhappily (Ying-chun and Tan-chun in episodes 30 and 32), or run off to become a nun (Xi-chun in episode 34) or a prostitute (Shi Xiang-yun in episode 36; this change in the series generated heated criticism).[17]

For the major female characters, the series follows the book more closely when it uses the registers found in the Land of Illusion. Its strategy is to match the lines in them and the songs in the novel with how the fate of each woman unfolds on the screen.

Many critics did not like Chen Xiaoxu's portrayal of Dai-yu, but Dai-yu is a difficult character to represent. In the novel this talented young woman has a mind of her own, but for modern readers she can be too sensitive, whiny, frail, and fussy, too prone, in today's language, to depression, which is more or less how she appears, unfortunately, in the TV series. The series deliberately downplays the triangle among Bao-yu, Dai-yu, and Bao-chai. It is no accident that the first song—"Jinling, Twelve Beauties, the Main Register" 金陵十二釵正冊—in chapter 5 tells about the three of them and that the second song is about Bao-yu and Dai-yu. The series omits the first song and associates the second with Dai-yu alone.[18] When the triangle is deemphasized, Dai-yu's sadness and expressions of loneliness seem groundless, no more than a secluded young woman's mental problem. The series also has Dai-yu die before and without knowing of Bao-yu's wedding to Bao-chai, so that Dai-yu's deathbed moment becomes less meaningful. In the novel, Dai-yu dies on the day of the wedding. But many scholars have expressed dissatisfaction with the last forty chapters of *Stone*, including the coincidence of Bao-yu's marriage and Dai-yu's death. So what the TV series represents is not necessarily a worse alternative to Gao E's continuation of Cao Xueqin's eighty chapters.

The novel names Dai-yu's lodgings Xiaoxiang House 瀟湘館 ("Naiad's House" in Hawkes's translation). This reference to bamboo echoes her association, implied in her register in chapter 5, with the vegetable world and with the sentimentality of mottled bamboo.[19] The series repeatedly shows her sitting at her desk in a room decorated in a bamboo theme. Bamboos surround her courtyard. She is often dressed in blue, and her room is lit with cold blue light. When the camera cuts to the exterior of her quarters, the bamboos are shown in blue moonlight and waving in the wind, giving a sense of sorrow and loneliness. But this visualization fails to capture the symbolic meaning of bamboo in traditional literati aesthetics: it was admired for its uprightness; it also stood for pride and an unwillingness to bend. Again, such simplification makes Dai-yu appear too easily offended and too sentimental.

The TV series does a better job of conveying Dai-yu when it utilizes lyrics from the novel and turns them into songs to go with two key moments in her story: one is when she reads *The Story of the Western Wing* (*The Western Chamber* 西廂記) with Bao-yu, the other is when she buries fallen petals. The words from the novel, accompanied by music, give depth to her representation. The Dai-yu-related register is the "Second Song: Hope Betrayed" 枉凝眉, and it reads as follows:

> One was a flower from paradise,
> One a pure jade without spot or stain.
> If each for the other one was not intended,
> Then why in this life did they meet again?
> And yet if fate had meant them for each other,
> Why was their earthly meeting all in vain?
> In vain were all her sighs and tears,

In vain were all his anxious fears:
All, insubstantial, doomed to pass,
As moonlight mirrored in the water
Or flowers reflected in a glass.
How many tears from those poor eyes could flow,
Which every season rained upon her woe?    (1.5.140)

一個是閬苑仙葩,
一個是美玉無瑕。
若說沒奇緣,
今生偏又遇著他;
若說有奇緣,
如何心事終虛化?
個枉自嗟呀,
一個空勞牽掛。
一個是水中月,
一個是鏡中花。
想眼中能有多少淚珠兒,
怎經得秋流到冬盡,
春流到夏!    (882)

This song tells about Bao-yu and Dai-yu and their fate never to be together despite their love for each other. In the TV series, however, it is used as if it were about Dai-yu only. Lines from this register are transported into a song that is played a few times throughout the drama—an attention that most of the other characters do not receive. In the drama, the song does not occur until after the young women and Bao-yu move into Prospect Garden and after the first celebratory atmosphere gives way to such visual cues as falling petals on the ground and stream. The song plays when Dai-yu discovers the book that Bao-yu is reading and she begins reading it too. The camera cuts between her reading the book, her being observed by Bao-yu, and their reading it together (fig. 1). In choosing this moment for the first play of the song, the series shows that it understands that the song is about the two of them.

Dai-yu's sadness is further conveyed in a poem attributed to Dai-yu when she decides to bury the petals before they are blown into dirty water and stained. The series turns much of the poem into a song and plays it as she buries the fallen petals:

The blossoms fade and falling fill the air,
Of fragrance and bright hues bereft and bare.
Floss drifts and flutters round the Maiden's bower,
Or softly strikes against her curtained door.

花謝花飛花滿天,
紅消香斷有誰憐?

Fig. 1. Bao-yu and Dai-yu read *Story of the Western Wing*. From the 1987 TV series (*left*) and from the 2010 TV series (*right*). © Sina.com

游絲軟系飄春榭,
落絮輕沾撲繡簾。

Three hundred and three-score the year's full take:
From swords of frost and from the slaughtering gale
How can the lovely flowers long stay intact,
Or, once loosed, from their drifting fate draw back?

一年三百六十日,
風刀霜劍嚴相逼,
明媚鮮妍能幾時,
一朝飄泊難尋覓。

Blooming so steadfast, fallen so hard to find!
Beside the flowers' grave, with sorrowing mind,
The solitary Maid sheds many a tear,
Which on the boughs as bloody drops appear.

花開易見落難尋,
階前悶殺葬花人.
獨倚花鋤淚暗灑,
灑上空枝見血痕。

And then I wished that I had wings to fly
After the drifting flowers across the sky:
Across the sky to the world's farthest end,
The flowers' last fragrant resting-place to find.

願儂此日生雙翼,
隨花飛到天盡頭.
天盡頭,
何處有香丘?

But better their remains in silk to lay
And bury underneath the wholesome clay,
Pure substances the pure earth to enrich,
Than leave to soak and stink in some foul ditch.

未若錦囊收豔骨，
一抔淨土掩風流。
質本潔來還潔去，
強於污淖陷渠溝。

Can I, that these flowers' obsequies attend,
Divine how soon or late *my* life will end?
Let others laugh flower-burial to see:
Another year who will be burying me?

爾今死去儂收葬，
未卜儂身何日喪？
儂今葬花人笑痴，
他年葬儂知是誰？

As petals drop and spring begins to fail,
The bloom of youth, too, sickens and turns pale.
One day, when spring has gone and youth has fled,
The Maiden and the flowers will both be dead.    (2.27.38–39)

試看春殘花漸落，
便是紅顏老死時。
一朝春盡紅顏老，
花落人亡兩不知！    (370–71)

I quote the lyrics extensively here to indicate that without the music and these words (shown as subtitles on the screen) that accompany the images of Dai-yu walking in the garden alone with a small hoe, carrying an embroidered cotton bag in which she puts the fallen petals, and placing the bag in the ground and burying it, her actions would appear maudlin. Like the novel (in ch. 27), the series places this moment shortly after the young women move into the garden (episode 12), as a narrative explanation for the rest of Dai-yu's behavior. Her sadness and deteriorating health are related to her sense of hopelessness. The burial motif in this song-poem foreshadows Dai-yu's death, and the song conveys a sense of disenchantment and doom. But because Dai-yu is not placed in the complex narrative of a romantic triangle, after this scene she is portrayed mainly as a young woman who is oversensitive, small-minded, and prone to throwing temper tantrums for no reason.

The story of Wang Xi-feng, another important beauty found in the main register, is better integrated into the televisual narrative. Many critics considered her to be the most successfully portrayed character of the series. Wang Xi-feng, like the garden, helps provide structure to the entire narrative. She enhances both the drama's realist orientation and its melodramatic flavor. The success of her representation has less to do with the development of her character. In the novel, Wang Xi-feng comes to be entrusted with managing the finances of Rong-guo household. Being a married woman, she does not get to reside in Prospect Garden, but as a woman in a position of power she has freedom of movement, mobility, like Bao-yu. Her role as household manager makes her another focus in the telling of the decay of the rich and powerful. Deng Jie was praised for her portrayal of this key character, who has beauty, cunning, and the ability both to please whomever she wants and destroy without mercy those who cross her. Episode after episode shows how she deals with her adversaries, how she punishes. In episode 6, when she is in charge of organizing an elaborate funeral for Qin-shi (Qin Ke-qing) of the Ning-guo household, she gathers a hundred servants and proceeds to issue orders in the most severe manner. In episode 5, she schemes to punish a young male relative who was foolish enough to try to seduce her. In episodes 25–27, she invites her husband's concubine, whom he has secretly married, to live with her—only for the purpose of making the woman suffer. This treatment leads to the concubine's untimely death. Is Wang Xi-feng a conniving shrew with no other intended meaning?

If, in creating Bao-yu, Cao Xueqin suggests that a man may feel affinity with and sympathy for women, the author at the same time has no illusions about relationships between women in an oppressive patriarchal society. In Wang Xi-feng we encounter a woman who can oppress other women. But throughout the novel, young women, both daughters of the family and servants, suffer at the hands of older women. Cao Xueqin shows that women are themselves products of the patriarchal society. The TV series dramatizes this reality. Yet it seems to take particular relish in the dark side of Wang Xi-feng. There is a disproportionate amount of time given to Xia Jin-gui, who is even worse than Xi-feng. A minor character whose presence in the novel puzzles some critics to begin with, Xia Jin-gui in the series has an entire episode (30) to be a coldhearted shrew, to mistreat her mother-in-law, persecute servants, cause Caltrop's death, constantly pick fights, and throw herself on the ground and roll around while wailing insults. In at least two episodes, when Xia Jin-gui's side of the story is told, one cannot but wonder what the significance is for the series to pay so much narrative attention to a character who turns out to be everybody's nightmare.

Toward the end of the series (episodes 35–36), the producers changed Xi-feng's death. They put Xi-feng in jail and had her die there. Then a long shot showed her body, wrapped in straw mats, dragged through snow in the wilderness. It is unclear what this unexpected choice means.[20] Could it be that instead of criticizing the society through representations of flawed characters, the series unconsciously took relish in blaming the women for their downfall? The complex message conveyed in the main register regarding the fate of Wang Xi-feng is reduced to her being a terrible woman. Accompanying this scene is a song whose lyrics are lifted from the "Ninth Song: Caught by Her Own Cunning" in chapter 5 of the novel:

> Too shrewd by half, with such finesse you wrought
> That your own life in your own toils was caught;
> But long before you died your heart was slain,
> And when you died your spirit walked in vain.

Fall'n the great house once so secure in wealth,
Each scattered member shifting for himself;
And half a life-time's anxious schemes
Proved no more than the stuff of dreams,
Like a great building's tottering crash,
Like flickering lampwick burned to ash,
Your scene of happiness concludes in grief;
For worldly bliss is always insecure and brief.    (143)

機關算盡太聰明, 反算了卿卿性命。
生前心已碎, 死後性空靈。
家富人寧, 終存個家亡人散各奔騰。
枉費了, 意懸懸半世心;好一似, 蕩悠悠三更夢。
忽、喇喇似大廈傾, 昏慘慘似廳將盡。
呀!一場歡喜忽悲辛。嘆人世, 終難定!    (85)

The series uses not this complete song, only the first several lines, which blame the woman. Yet the complete song situates her in the larger context of society's game of illusory power. As in the disproportionate role of Xia Jin-gui, the series falls short in its negotiation with the novel, failing to capture the novel's more complex way of conveying social criticism.

The ending of the series generated the most criticism. Possibly the producers themselves did not quite know how to end it. In the last episode, after Bao-yu is released from jail—the series completely changes the story line from all existing *Stone* versions by having the entire Jia family put in jail—he wanders about. After a brief reunion with Aroma, he is found on the road with no apparent direction. While Bao-yu's wandering may echo the novel, the series invents too much. Bao-yu meets Shi Xiang-yun, who, to the anger of many critics, is now a prostitute; then he meets, in the snow, a procession in which Jia Yu-cun is locked up in a cage on his way to some kind of exile.[21]

But when it does end, interestingly enough, the series uses words from the novel. The scriptwriters took Zhen Shi-yin's commentary of the "Won-Done Song," which appears at the beginning of the novel, to function, at the conclusion, as a statement about the ironic nature of the human condition and also as a warning to the masses. It also completes the circle of the lines taken from chapter 1: "Pages full of idle words / Penned with hot and bitter tears / All men call the author fool / None his secret message hears." Although the producers avoided the novel's play with what is real and what is not, those "pages full of idle words" continue to enchant both intellectuals and the general public.

More than twenty years since the series, Chinese people show tremendous interest in this novel. In those years, they have witnessed periodic public debate over how to interpret and represent the novel in television and other media. Liu Xinwu, a former writer who became a self-taught scholar of the novel, gave a series of lectures on CCTV in 2005. He reinterpreted the meaning of the twelve beauties in such a way that he caused an uproar. He was criticized for reading too much into the text and for misleading the reading public. The criticism was so intense that the television station canceled the lectures before all of them were aired. Unperturbed, Liu had his lectures published. In 2007, he returned to the CCTV's lecture forum with more of his different interpretations.

In 2007, a controversy over the remaking of another televisual *Stone* series erupted. The director, Hu Mei, a woman known both for her fifth-generation filmmaking experience and for directing a series of hit television dramas, openly disagreed with the choices of actors and actresses and quit. Li Shaohong, another fifth-generation female director and also known for a number of films and hit television dramas, took over.[22] The final product aired in 2010. The making of this drama generated heated debate, expressed mostly on the Internet. Today, if anyone googles or *baidu*'s Hongloumeng or Chen Xiaoxu, one finds images of the characters from both the 1987 version and the new version. They are very different, and that difference is symptomatic of what has happened, socially, economically, culturally, and ideologically, in the last twenty years in China. The emphasis on glamour in the new version of *Stone* is indicative of the cultural logic and cultural production that have become increasingly governed by the market, by the consumer culture, which ironically is aligned more, not less, with the hegemony of wealth and power. The novel, of course, speaks against that hegemony:

> Men all know that salvation should be won,
> But with ambition won't have done, have done.
> Where are the famous ones of days gone by?
> In grassy graves they lie now, every one.

> 世人都曉神仙好,
> 惟有功名忘不了!
> 古今將相在何方?
> 荒冢一堆草沒了。

> Men all know that salvation should be won,
> But with their riches won't have done, have done.
> Each day they grumble they've not made enough.
> When they've enough, it's goodnight everyone!

> 世人都曉神仙好,
> 只有金銀忘不了!
> 終朝只恨聚無多,
> 及到多時眼閉了。

> Men all know that salvation should be won,
> But with their loving wives they won't have done.
> The darlings every day protest their love;
> But once you're dead, they're off with another one.

世人都曉神仙好,
只有妓妻忘不了!
君生日日說恩情,
君死又隨人去了。

Men all know that salvation should be won,
But with their children won't have done, have done.
Yet though of parents fond there is no lack,
Of grateful children saw I ne'er one.   (1.1.63–64)

世人都曉神仙好,
只有兒孫忘不了!
痴心父母古來多,
孝順兒孫誰見了?   (17)


NOTES

[1] *Baidu* 百度 is a major search engine in China. If anyone *baidu's* her today, about 3,720,000 pages would appear.

[2] After playing Dai-yu, Chen never acted again and went into business instead. When she was diagnosed with breast cancer, she allegedly refused treatment. Shortly before she died, she became a Buddhist nun.

[3] After the 1987 television adaptation, more varied adaptations or *Stone*-related dramas appeared on television, including the thirty-episode *Yueju* 越劇 TV miniseries (of the same title) (2002), the thirty-episode miniseries *Cao Xueqin* 曹雪芹 (2003), and the twenty-one-episode miniseries *Honglou yatou* 紅樓丫頭 ("Honglou Maids") (2003). The latest version was a fifty-episode miniseries whose production included a nationwide auditioning for the roles.

[4] Unlike theatrical and filmic adaptations of *Stone*, the particularities of the television medium make large-scale adaptations possible.

[5] This revolt started with the Chinese Communist Party's own definition of the Cultural Revolution as ten years of turmoil that wrongly persecuted many people and with the party's initiation of thought liberation. Writers and scholars were the most active participants in the revolt. These culture intellectuals explored what had contributed to the destruction of the Cultural Revolution. They echoed the May Fourth Movement (1915–27), during which intellectuals questioned the value of traditional culture and argued for an urgent need to enlighten the masses. On the culture fever of the 1980s, see J. Wang, *High Culture Fever*; X. Zhang; Tonglin Lu; and Zhong.

[6] On filmmaking in the 1930s and 1940s in China, see Pang, *Building*; Zhang Zhen; Yingjin Zhang, *Cinema*; and Clark.

[7] Examples of classics adapted are *The Story of the Stone* and *Journey to the West* (*Xiyou ji* 西遊記); examples of modern works adapted are *Four Generations Living under One Roof* (*Sishi tongtang* 四世同堂), by Lao She, and *Times Idled Away* (*Cuotuo suiyue* 蹉跎歲月), by Ke Yunlu 柯雲路.

[8] In the 1980s, the term *intellectual* in Chinese was generally used to refer to writers, literary critics, scholars (of literature, history, philosophy, and political theory), filmmakers,

magazine editors, journalists, and producers of television programs. Intellectuals were culturally oriented, and it was assumed that they spoke from a shared position. Since the 1990s, there has been disagreement among intellectuals over the direction of China's path to modernization. On this change, see Wang Hui.

[9] The Chinese television industry went through major structural changes in the 1990s. Chinese television stations were responsible for producing their own programs—whether news, dramas, or other types—and CCTV was one of the main producers of dramas. The first Chinese television drama was made in 1958, but until the late 1970s few people had access to television. It was not until after the Cultural Revolution that television took on the function of a popular medium. Television stations first showed old films, then imported foreign dramas. See J. Hong.

[10] There were other forms of adaptation of *Stone. Dai-yu Burying Flowers* (*daiyu zanghua* 黛玉葬花) was a Peking opera performed by Mei Lanfang, an actor famous for playing young female roles. There was also a Shaoxing 紹興 opera version of *Stone*. Films included *The You Sisters* (*Honglou eryou* 紅樓二尤) and *The Story of the Stone* (based on the Shaoxing opera's rendition of the tragic love between Bao-yu and Dai-yu).

[11] The advisory board consisted of such luminaries as Wang Kunlun, Wang Zhaowen, Zhou Ruchang, Shen Congwen, Wu Zuguang, Zhong Dianfei, Qian Zhongshu, and Yang Xianyi (Yang Hsien-yi). Wang Kunlun, head of the board, was the author of *Honglou renwulun* 紅樓人物論 ("On Characters in *The Story of the Stone*"), which is considered the first book to study the characters in *Stone*. Zhou Ruchang was the leading representative of the contemporary *Kaozheng* 考證 school of Redology 紅學. Yang Hsien-yi was the cotranslator (with his wife, Gladys Yang) of *A Dream of Red Mansions* (Peking: Foreign Langs., 1978–80). Many of these scholars gave lectures during the three-month training session.

[12] See Berry; Clark. *Social realism*, defined along the lines of critical realism in nineteenth-century European literature, revealed social ills. *Socialist realism* stressed the positive aspects of lives of workers, peasants, and soldiers while casting class enemies in a negative light.

[13] There are two Prospect Gardens in China, one in Shanghai, the other in Beijing. Construction on the one in Beijing began in 1984, and that garden was opened to the public as a tourist site in 1989.

[14] Examples are episodes 10 and 11, which focus on Yuan-chun's homecoming visit.

[15] The songs used are "Second Song: Hope Betrayed" 枉凝眉 (140), "Ninth Song: Caught by Her Own Cunning" 聰明累 (143), and "Epilogue: The Birds into the Wood Have Flown" 飛鳥各投林 (144).

[16] For studies of women's education in premodern China, see Mann, *Precious Records*; Ko, *Teachers*.

[17] In the novel it is Adamantina who is forced into prostitution. That Shi Xiang-yun becomes a prostitute and that she and Bao-yu meet is not totally made up; early notes on a manuscript of the novel contained such content. It is likely that the producers of this miniseries, in their alteration of what happens in the last forty chapters, made use of commentary on a manuscript that some Redologists believe once existed.

[18] The scriptwriters felt that to focus on the triangle would have been "truly a misunderstanding" (*tianda de wuhui* 天大的誤會) of the novel (*Hongloumeng* 87 2).

[19] Mottled bamboo is associated with a legend regarding the consorts of Emperor Shun, who were said to have died in the Xaioxiang region, today's Hunan Province. The

consorts cried so much that their tears mottled bamboo. In the novel, Dai-yu is nick-named *xiaoxiang feizi* 瀟湘妃子 because she weeps a lot.

[20] Perhaps they took the reference to snow in chapter 5 too literally. In any case, their portrayal of Xi-feng's death does not follow the hints in the first eighty chapters that she would be divorced.

[21] Some Redologists argue that Xiang-yun's becoming a prostitute and Bao-yu's chance meeting with her may not be a total invention by the TV series producers. They argue that the author may have intended a fate for the Jia clan and their relatives more dire than the one that was written.

[22] "Fifth-generation" refers to a group of (mainly) Beijing Film Academy graduates who made experimental films in the 1980s. Among them are Zhang Yimou, Chen Kaige, and Tian Zhuangzhuang.

# Bao-yu Goes to High School

*Mary Ellen Friends*

## What's in a Name?

"Is it Te*lem*achus or Tele*mach*us?" The Deerfield Academy freshman class had embarked on its annual epic journey through the *Odyssey*, and a seasoned teacher wanted to know whether her intern had steered students in the right direction. I smiled, put my head down, and continued my history prep. Humor lay not in the question itself; after all, the Greek teacher said the pronunciation was *this* while the university professor claimed it was *that*. What made me smile was that the same question had been posed in this very humanities office the year before. A short but animated discussion ensued while I resisted the urge to say, "Is it Li Bo or Li Bai? Is it tom*a*to or tom*ah*to?" In point of fact, I liked the spirit of the discussion. Years earlier, it had been something of a personal victory when *Star Trek* introduced the character Data, and I finally could convince students to pronounce the word with a long vowel. With regard to the novel under discussion in this volume, moreover, I am grateful to know that *The Story of the Stone*'s author has a surname pronounced "Ts'ao" and that I should not refer to him as if he were a female of the bovine persuasion. Like my colleagues in the English department, I want to know how to properly acknowledge a character of fiction or history, not just because it gives me confidence in the classroom but also because it familiarizes the unfamiliar and helps make history and literature come alive. I may smile as the department of history repeats itself, but I too will revisit a name in a novel as many times as is necessary for it to give full meaning to the tale.

Names ought to be keys to understanding a text, but they can be obstacles to learning if we buy into the notion that they are exotic or difficult to learn. Let's begin with the hard truth: many high school students of literature, and not a few of their teachers, get so intimidated by the plethora of seemingly difficult-to-pronounce names in *The Story of the Stone*, they never undertake to read the novel at all. Deliberating over a the name of a character in the *Odyssey* is one thing, they think, but working through *Stone*'s hundreds of names, many of them related by family or meaning, is another monster altogether. One need only list the three central characters — Bao-yu, Dai-yu, and Bao-chai — to scare off timid readers, or point out the parallels between Jia Bao-yu and Zhen Bao-yu to alarm the hardy. But is the difficulty of names ever a good excuse not to read great literature? My own high school teacher did not seem to think so when he assigned Dostoevsky's *The Brothers Karamazov*. Karamazov and Samsonov, Fyodorovitch, Mussyalovitch, and Vassilyevitch do not strike me as easier names to pronounce than Jia, Lin, Wang, and Zhen. Even if the final name on that second list leaves some readers in the dark, translator David Hawkes stands ready in the opening pages of the Penguin edition to light the way. In a single, succinct paragraph and a five-hint list under the heading "Note on Spelling," he reduces the perceived difficulty of pronunciation by ninety percent. More adventuresome readers may go on to read the explanations on syllables, initial consonants, and vowels that follow in the next two pages, but Hawkes's short list goes a long way toward eliminating hard-to-pronounce names as an excuse not to read the book.

As teachers of young students, we may even come to understand the challenge of names in *The Story of the Stone* not as an obstacle to learning but as an opportunity to help our students mature. I remember fighting the good fight in a world cultures class not so many years ago, when students reading Achebe's *Things Fall Apart* suggested we call the main character OK instead of Okonkwo. In this proposed revision of the text, the ill-fated youth Ikemefuna became Ike, Ezinma became Zee, and so on. Frustrated though I was by their cavalier approach to the novel, I had trouble articulating the importance of calling characters by their names, until Achebe himself helped me out. In his short essay "The Author as Teacher," he writes passionately on a point he feels is "fundamental and essential to the appreciation of African issues by Americans":

> Africans are people in the same way that Americans, Europeans, Asians, and others are people. Africans are not some strange beings with unpronounceable names and impenetrable minds. Although the action of *Things Fall Apart* takes place in a setting with which most Americans are unfamiliar, the characters are normal people and their events are real human events. (21)

These words helped me in the particular teaching of *Things Fall Apart*, but they also inspired my teaching of Asian Civilizations, Modern China, and Great East

Asian Books. After reading Achebe's essay, I stopped apologizing in my history classes for the fact that Xuanzang the monk and Xuanzong the emperor both lived in the Tang dynasty or that Koxinga was an enemy rather than a duplicate of Kangxi. In my literature class, too, I took Achebe's lead and insisted we call a jade a jade. A student in the room understood my larger point immediately. He pointed out that while the *Stone* protagonists Bao-yu and Dai-yu share a syllable in their names, those names are far easier to distinguish on the printed page than were the names of two students, Alex (male) and Alex (female), who were taking the class. The epiphany was a minor one, to be sure, but it was just what we needed to begin viewing the *Stone* names as normal instead of difficult and unpronounceable. What is more, once we got in the habit of saying characters' names aloud in discussions, and once we insisted on using characters' proper names rather than pronouns or other indefinite references, those characters became familiar and not exotic. In a few class periods, the fictional beings that peopled the *Stone* were not obstacles in the form of names but instead were intriguing teenagers and young adults, undergoing real human events and having some of the same concerns that consumed the intellectual and emotional energy of the modern teenagers sitting in class. Having broken the name barrier, my students were now free to investigate the wealth of both local and universal themes that lay ahead.

In *Stone*, breaking the name barrier not only reduces false exoticism, it also allows the teacher of younger students to selectively and incrementally introduce the layers of meanings inherent in the names. *Bao-yu* ("Precious Jade") deserves early explanation, of course; the young protagonist is, after all, an avatar of the Stone on which the story is written, and he simultaneously wears the precious jade on a cord around his neck. But the significance of his surname, *Jia*, a pun on *jia*, meaning "fictitious" (44), can wait until students are engaged in the novel and ready to discuss Bao-yu's world as a land of illusion. Similarly, Dai-yu and Bao-chai in this scenario are free to remain young women whose names happen to be Dai-yu and Bao-chai until the day a student picks up on the fact that each bears a portion of Bao-yu's name and guesses there is a connection to be made between the females and their male cousin. The key here is to resist the temptation to tell all to the students lest they feel the novel is inaccessible unless interpreted by an expert in the field.

There are points in the novel where the meanings of names really do help illuminate the text. My students understand Zhen Shi-yin's role in chapter 1 more fully, for example, when they've read a bit from Dore Levy's *Ideal and Actual in The Story of the Stone* and learn that his name puns the phrase "true matters concealed" (14). They also gain insight into *Stone*'s rich wordplay when they investigate name meanings in chapter 5. We work together with the appendix to volume 1 (528–29) to unpack the meanings of the pictures, especially as they relate to characters' names. I have students use one half of the board to sketch the picture of Xue Bao-chai and Lin Dai-yu described on the bottom of page 133 (this is usually something of a fun disaster) while classmates use the board's other half to break down the names: Lin = forest (written as two trees), Dai = eye black (eyeliner) + homophone of "belt," Yu = jade. For Xue Bao-chai, Xue = homophone of "snow," Bao = "Precious," and Chai = hairpin. This simple exercise provides a good break for students, and it reduces the intellectual confusion they might have felt when they read the chapter on their own. The diagrams help demystify Bao-yu's dream experience, get all students on the same page (so they know more than does Bao-yu himself), and provide groundwork for the larger discussion of the chapter's pivotal role in the book.

In the course of this exercise, it is virtually inevitable that at least one student will discover the links between Bao-yu's name and the names of his two cousins. The name syllables are right there on the board (but the anxious teacher might even give a nudge in the right direction, if necessary). Students will be inspired by this lead in a number of ways. They may inquire into the meaning of Bao-yu's surname (if they do not know it already), they may connect the painting's merging of Bao-chai and Dai-yu into the dream character Ke-qing ("Two-in-One"), or they may ask to look at one or two other chapter 5 portraits or songs in detail. This method of student discovery admittedly takes longer than would a straight lecture, and it almost guarantees that the class will not cover every important element of the chapter, but it opens students' eyes to the reality that, without ever having studied Chinese, they can learn what's in a name and discover deeper meaning in the text. They may have forgotten that their freshman teacher told them Telemachus means "faraway fighter," but they will remember the meanings of names they hunt down on their own.

Two final notes on names in *Stone*. I try to be sympathetic to students who wilt at the novel's sheer number of names, yet we encounter only a fraction of those names in the twenty-six chapters of volume 1 that we read for class. At the end of the Penguin edition, Hawkes provides a list of characters, and he includes in that list necessary cross-references. He also offers two family trees to help readers keep things straight. I find photocopying the name list and family trees useful; my students can then keep the documents at hand while they read instead of interrupting the flow of the reading by continually flipping to the back of the book. Some students go on to make their own diagrams of relationships, but most find the printed documents help enough by the second week of reading.

If students continue to sigh over too many names (but they rarely do), I remind them of a telling scene in Peter Shaffer's *Amadeus*. The emperor of Austria has just finished listening to *Abduction from the Seraglio*, and he comes onto the stage to offer his critique. After some hesitation and a quick word with his director of opera, the emperor declares the opera has "too many notes." Mozart, aghast, replies, "I don't understand. There are just as many notes, Your Majesty, as I require—neither more nor less." The emperor insists he's right and adds this ridiculous double-edged compliment: "Your work is ingenious; it's quality work. And there are simply too many notes—that's all. Just cut a few, and it will be perfect."

Mozart's reply to the emperor regarding the number of notes in his opera might be Cao Xueqin's reply to a reader who wants him to cut a few characters from his literary masterpiece: "Which few did you have in mind, Your Majesty?" In the end, *The Story of the Stone*'s rich and varied cast of characters contains just as many names (neither too many nor too few) as the author requires to both bring Bao-yu's mundane world to life and help us understand its illusory nature.

## The First Days

From a high school student's perspective, some assigned novels start out slowly. "Just get through the first fifty pages," a high school senior might tell a younger peer, "and you'll find it really picks up." Such advice is generally not sound, but it is particularly dangerous if applied to *Stone*. Readers who hurry through even the first chapter in pursuit of a plot will find they are lost. At the very least, they will discover too late that they have been missing half the point of the novel, for they will have not seen the narrative frame that makes this the story of the Stone in the first place. A reader or teacher who does not take time with the first chapter also forgoes opportunities to explore topics such as Chinese conventions in fiction writing, Cao Xueqin's particular brand of humor, Buddhist concepts of enlightenment, and the syncretic relation among Chinese Buddhist, Taoist, and Confucian ideas. A teacher aware of the wealth of lecture and discussion possibilities will want to approach the novel's opening pages slowly and with great care.

One problem with a slow approach, however, is that we simply do not have time. If *Stone* is part of a world literature course, or even if it is in the sort of great East Asian books course I teach as a high school senior seminar, there are only so many days a teacher can carve out of the curriculum for even the greatest of Chinese novels. My own teaching schedule gives me approximately three hours of class meeting time divided into four classes each week, and I am allowed to assign a maximum of fifty minutes of homework for each of those four weekly classes. If we linger longer than a day on chapter 1, we will not even get Bao-yu and the young women into the garden before we need to move to a different book.

The second problem with starting too slowly is that students will disengage from the text. My students appreciate the Nü-wa myth and the colorful monk and Taoist, but they also want to get to the mansions and meet the novel's main characters. To be frank, these young readers, while interested and bright, read *Stone*'s first few chapters in a manner analogous to that of the Taoist Vanitas when he reads the Stone's inscription for the first time. They suspect the chapters are of "some consequence," but they are not convinced the ideas in them "would make a very remarkable book" (1.1.49). Lectures on the layers of meaning do not necessarily convince them otherwise; in fact, feeding students straight information about Chinese culture, belief systems, and history is an endeavor that almost always yields diminishing returns. Hardworking, enthusiastic teachers who want their students to see the full meaning and structure of the novel as it is laid out in the first twenty pages run the risk of turning a great adventure into a three- or four-week chore.

When I began teaching *The Story of the Stone*, I found the words of a favorite Grateful Dead song running through my head: "Well, the first days are the hardest days. . . ." It seemed obvious that everything hung in the balance of the first few days. If I did not give enough background or explanation from the outset, students would get lost on the path from Stone to dream to kidnapped daughters to dead mothers to the Ning-guo and Rong-guo households. If I gave too much, students would get bored or frustrated by the perceived difficulty of the text. I am embarrassed to admit it, but it was not until I actually got into the classroom and started teaching that I found the middle path. Students themselves let me know what was difficult or interesting about the reading, and I learned to take my cues from them.

I begin a four-week study of *Stone* with a full-class introduction to the novel that draws on information from Hawkes's introduction, essays by authors whose work appears in this volume, and Jonathan D. Spence's overview of the novel in his *Search for Modern China* (106–11). I generally give students the Spence piece for their reference, and I find they particularly enjoy tracking the six elements of eighteenth-century elite life Spence outlines in his essay.[1] This day of introduction is my opportunity to make sure students have a fair sense of the novel's overall structure and a general understanding of why both common English-language titles of this book — *The Story of the Stone* and *The Dream of the Red Chamber* — are of great help in understanding major themes. The reading for night 1 is chapter 1, and my month of self-discipline begins on class day 2.

The month I share *Stone* with students is one of self-discipline because it involves a lot of letting go. Like most serious high school teachers, I learn what I can about the books I will bring to class. I am eager to share the connections I have made and tease out the threads I already know will run through the story. But I need to remember that students, too, have great ideas. They do not need much in the way of Chinese cultural background to appreciate the Stone's dissertation to Vanitas, the play of illusion and truth, and the mundane ambitions of young scholars like Jia Yu-cun. If I am to give students the time and space they need to discuss the reading, I must limit my role to that of navigator. It is my responsibility to make sure students generally know what is happening in the text (such briefing may take as long as ten minutes per class in the first few days), and it is my right to direct the discussion when I feel we absolutely need to cover a particular point in a particular chapter. But students need class time to dig into one or two topics in depth. I sometimes have to repeat Levy's insight as a mantra, "On one level . . . no analytical explanation is needed, and none will serve" (1), but more often I am surprised and delighted by the observations and astute connections students make when they are given freedom to talk about literature among themselves.

This student-centered approach to learning is known in some circles as the Harkness method, though it is broader and more fluid than the name implies. It is a pedagogy often associated with schools such as Philips Exeter Academy, and it is outlined beautifully by Nita Pettigrew:

> The teachers task, then, is to listen to [the student] dynamic, to be an informed and open-minded witness to her students' explorations—and to be genuinely interested. In English, as in every other discipline, each student comes to the assigned problem with his own store of knowledge and experience. Ninth graders will read *Julius Caesar* with a very different perspective than seniors do. So we let the students lead the way. They make the observations; they raise the questions. When the teacher is focused on *how* the student is making meaning, the student is empowered to explore those issues that capture her imagination. The students can feel the teacher's respect for their ideas; their learning environment is nurturing and safe, and the emphasis is on their own thinking process: an "answer" is merely one solution to a problem, on result of a thoughtful process.                                                    (44)

The "Aha" moments of a student-centered classroom that Pettigrew describes are ones I have had again and again in teaching *Stone*, but I could not have experienced them if I had fully choreographed each lesson.

The writer who reminded me to let students make their own way through *Stone* was Cao Xueqin himself. He does this first through the character Vanitas. Vanitas does not understand the value of the Stone's story the first time he reads it; he needs to criticize the story, engage in a debate with it as a medium, and then read it all again. Only then, and only because he as "approached Truth by way of Passion," does he become enlightened (1.1.51). Bao-yu too will have to make his way through the whole story on his own, as we learn in chapter 5. His teacher, the fairy Disenchantment, repeatedly spells out truth for him in the form of pictures, poems, and songs. Like many healthy adolescents on the receiving end of a lecture, he glazes over and grows bored. "Silly boy!" sighs the fairy. "You still don't understand, do you?" (145). In these scenes, and in others throughout the text, Cao lets us know that truth comes not in an instant or because our teacher hands it to us in a lesson. It comes, instead, through the reader's personal, critical engagement with the text and (especially for younger readers) through articulating the experience of Bao-yu's passionate story.

## The Golden Days

I have test-driven a number of selected chapter sets from *Stone*, but I find class is most successful when we read straight through volume 1. This solution may strike an outsider as lazy (or cheap, since it means I do not have to buy all five volumes for each student), but it really is the best deal for the teacher who both wants to create a student-centered learning environment and feels the need to provide some daily structure and background. As a bonus, the straight-through approach opens avenues of fun, and it can even tempt students to a long-term commitment to the text.

This approach to *Stone* reveals authorial cadence, and it establishes a pace in the classroom conducive to the abilities and interests of my students. This is not to say that selecting famous or plot-furthering scenes is not a viable option. I teach Arthur Waley's *Monkey* rather than Anthony Yu's translation of *Journey to the West*, for example, to give high school students the "there and back again" quality of the adventure without fully compromising Buddha's message that truth must be experienced to be learned—and here is yet another plea by a Chinese author to let students do the bulk of the learning (Wu Ch'eng-en [Waley] 8.78; Wu Cheng-en [Yu] 1.8.184). I feel comfortable using the selected-chapter version, because students love Monkey and Pigsy enough to ask for Yu's version later in the year.

When I taught a selected-chapter version of Murasaki Shikibu's *Tale of Genji*, however, I ended up photocopying "The Broom Tree" chapter Edward Seidensticker left out of the pared-down text (the 1976, not the 1983 edition). "The Broom Tree," my students decided, was their favorite chapter, because it was the one that most fully resonated with their lives. Teenagers of both genders freely admitted to sitting around on rainy nights talking with same-gender peers about who was hot and who was not, about what they looked for in a mate or what they wanted in a date. That laughter-filled, semiconfessional class made them sympathetic to Genji, and it made them willing to embrace less familiar or more sophisticated aspects of the protagonist's personality later on. The next year, I ordered the full Seidensticker translation, and I received two summer e-mail messages from students who proudly announced that they had finished the text.

With the hope that students will finish *Stone* on their own, I assign consecutive chapters from volume 1. It is also my feeling that in a world where teenagers spend weekend hours bouncing around from favorite scene to favorite scene of a dozen movies, a teacher could do worse than reintroduce the idea that authors in any time-oriented medium design their masterpieces to be experienced at a certain pace and with particular variance of experience. The most breathtaking aspects of Prospect Garden, my students discover, are not laid out in full view for visitors to absorb all at once. They are around a bend or just beyond a hill, skillfully placed so even those familiar with the landscape happen on them and thus appreciate them more fully.

The straight-through approach not only maintains the integrity of the original story but also makes it easier to adopt a student-centered approach to learning. Once we have officially begun to read, this teacher promises to use less than half of each class lecturing or posing content-oriented questions (Pettigrew 45). In that ten-to-twenty-minute slot I may give a minilecture on Manchu rule in a predominantly Chinese society, show slides from a Web site on the novel's main characters, or read passages from an essay on the Chinese civil service exam. I may end my teacher-centered portion of class by posing a question that turns discussion over to students, or I may save my talk until the end of class and allow students to dig into the reading right away. Whatever I decide, students come to class knowing they will have time and space to lambaste Xue Pan or debate Xi-feng's culpability in Jia-Rui's death.

Occasionally students become so involved in debate or are working so hard on their own to figure out whether Disenchantment really wanted Bao-yu to understand the songs that I shut down the projector, close my computer, and save the *PowerPoint* for another day. This is a luxury I have with the straight-through approach: an important-scenes approach to *Stone* would not allow it. I would need to show that slide show in that class period so students could make the leap to the next set of chapters. I would also spend precious class time lecturing to fill in gaps or otherwise explain plot or theme developments in the chapters we did not read. Students in my class, eager to know how the book ends, often spend a class reading passages from later chapters and asking me the fate of certain favorite characters, but the bulk of class time is still in their hands, and they still leave the course knowing the value of their experience with the novel.

## When I Think Back

Every group of students is different, and each year brings new opportunities while confirming that old lesson plans are out-of-date. There is nevertheless consistency in success and failure in a class on *Stone*, especially when one is handing the novel out to teens. High school students want images but not ones that try too hard to re-create the story. They are interested to know that this book is full of autobiographical and biographical elements; they are bored stiff with an essay on authorship. Although they think it's cool to connect with Chinese culture, they are ultimately most interested how the novel resonates with their lives.

One of my first bad teaching ideas in the month-long course on *Stone* was to show a film version of the novel. Some high school students may love the 1977 film starring Brigitte Lin (*Dream*), but mine rolled their eyes at the too-sweet romance scenes, and they dissolved into giggles when characters started singing. They were disappointed by the absence of many supporting characters, and they spent so much time criticizing each scene, they failed to notice certain conventions of behavior and style I had hoped would help them more fully envision the book. I remembered, too late, how sophisticated teenagers are with regard to film. I had also not taken into account that the movie might undermine some of my foundational points about the need for a rich cast of characters and about Cao's particular authorial flow. Teachers of high school students know that our young charges almost always light up at the prospect of a movie during class time, but my choice suited their interests so poorly, they were relieved to stop watching the film.

What seems to work better for high school students is a combination of still images and scenes from a film that does not even want to be *The Story of the Stone*. Students particularly liked Dream of the Red Chamber: *An Experience in Traditional Chinese Aesthetics*, a Web site of paintings by An Ho. These twelve beautiful interpretations of women in the novel are accompanied by helpful paragraph-long descriptions of each character. Students also appreciated the watercolors in "Red Chamber" from the comics on the *China-on-site* Web site, and they liked images of traditional-style paper cuts I incorporated into a *PowerPoint* slide show. Finally, they loved watching scenes from *Raise the Red Lantern*, a film I chose for three reasons: it is easy to acquire, it is cinematographically beautiful, and it has terrific rooftop and indoor shots that give students a sense of a traditional Chinese mansion. The total collection of images lets students sharpen their mental images of characters and scenes without hijacking and replacing those images, and it raises good questions—for example, questions about eighteenth-century Chinese fashion and traditional color symbolism.

Another decidedly poor choice I once made was to assign a long excerpt from Hawkes's introduction to volume 1 for the first night of reading. I had had trouble deciding which of his many wonderful explanations to offer, so I gave students many. Unsurprisingly, my teenagers did not care much about the nitty-gritty of authorship because they had not yet met the author. They were mildly interested in the idea that Cao modeled his female characters on women he knew, but again, they had not yet encountered the characters. It was not that my students could not handle the analysis. They were perfectly capable of working through any scholarly excerpt I sent their way. It was simply a case of too much too soon, and the mistake cost me dearly in terms of their interest in my first year teaching the book.

I now introduce our study of *Stone* with a class-long mix of lecture, reading, and discussion. It includes but is not made up exclusively of Hawkes's words. We might read in class from Levy's book, Yu's *Rereading the Stone*, and C. T. Hsia's "Dream of the Red Chamber" in his *Classic Chinese Novel*, but I tend not to assign these works for homework. By and large, younger students need the homework time for reading the novel if they are to make substantial progress through the book in a month.

My students read, keep journals, and write papers not unlike those assigned to college undergraduates. Sometimes, however, it is fun to break up the reading with a nonpaper, nonreading assignment. One that works particularly well for younger readers of *Stone* is to have them cast three characters from chapters 6 and 7 for both a movie and a play version of the book. The homework directions go something like this:

> You are a rising star in the filmmaking industry, and your big break has finally come. Martin Scorsese is directing his last great epic film, *The*

*Dream of the Red Chamber*, and, unbelievably, you have a shot at the job of casting director, both because of your natural talent and because you've convinced your boss of your familiarity with the novel. Through luck and a little string-pulling, you've managed to secure a morning meeting with Scorsese himself next Tuesday. Your task is to come up with a dream team of three actors or actresses to fill three important roles in the upcoming film. You have complete freedom in determining which three roles to cast, but you know it is important to choose well to show your skill and versatility in casting. Most important will be the fit you make between roles and actors. After all, the job will not be yours unless you make a successful pitch at Tuesday's meeting. You must convince Scorsese that you understand the characters you cast and know how best to make his film great.

Quite by chance, our school's drama instructor has also contacted you recently to tell you that she too will be directing *Dream*, although her production is a three-act play. You are obviously quite busy, but you tell her you'll do your best to offer casting suggestions. It won't be hard, you think, to suggest real people from the Deerfield community to fill the same three roles you're preparing for Tuesday's meeting. As time and interest permit, you will help our director cast her play.

Note: You have an assistant to help you with visuals. Submit names and roles to me by Monday evening (for example, as Disenchantment, Meryl Streep and Mrs. Curtis [our head of school]), and I'll construct a slide presentation.

This short assignment not only encourages students to think carefully about characterization in *Stone*; it also makes them understand characters in terms of both actors on a stage and real people they know. My students tackled the assignment with enthusiasm, and the class in which we unveiled choices was great fun. We avoided hurt feelings in the community by establishing rules of polite discourse before students shared their picks, but we had some belly laughs nonetheless. One student later declared it was the "most fun assignment" he had completed that year, and virtually all the students in the class acquired the semiregular habit of adding real actors to their cast of characters as they continued reading the book.

A somewhat different but almost equally appealing class activity for adolescent readers links contemporary music with *Stone*. The idea for this came to me as I prepped for the class that would follow the chapter 9 assignment. We had already discussed Confucian academic expectations as they led to the civil service examination, and I needed a prompt for a discussion that would eventually get us to Yu's analysis of Bao-yu's relationship with his father (*Rereading* 179–86). The rather irreverent solution was to open class with Paul Simon's "Kodachrome," a song that begins with the lines "When I think back on all the crap I learned in high school / It's a wonder I can think at all." Students had a rich time discussing what Bao-yu did in fact learn while at the clan school. They started with peer pressure, bullying, bribery, and sex, and they moved on quite naturally to the fact that Jia Zheng both wasn't and was getting what he asked for by sending Bao-yu to school. Class did end with a messy debate about the applicability of the song's second verse ("If you took all the girls I knew when I was single / And brought them all together for one night"), but we had bridged our gap, and I could begin the next day's class on a high academic note.

In the end, I try to respect my high school students both by assuming they are intellectually capable of analyzing *The Story of the Stone* and by remembering that they are adolescents. A course that features Cao Xueqin's great novel includes reading (twenty to thirty-five pages per night), journal work, short essays, and a final research project. It asks every student to grapple with theories by experts in the field, and it requires each member of the class to engage in class discussion. At the same time, it attempts to arrive at that central point in learning where academic challenge is synonymous with fun; where what we read for school is the same as what we read for pleasure; and where the teacher, the novelist, the writers of scholarly articles, and the students all contribute to the experience at hand.

NOTE

[1] Spence's six categories are family structure, politics, economics, religion, aesthetics, and sexuality.

# Bao-yu's Multimedia Classroom: Reading, Performance, and the Vicissitudes of the Voice from *The Story of the Stone* to Its Film Adaptations

*Ling Hon Lam*

## Bao-yu's Multimedia Classroom

To wake up a class dissipated in afternoon drowsiness, the desperate literature teacher ends up pulling the same old trick: calling on a student endowed with the loudest voice to read aloud a passage from, say, chapter 23 of *The Story of the Stone*. Hardly sharing the character's excitement about reading literature in this episode, the students at least find themselves under a sonic attack that makes them a class again. The trick doesn't last: patience soon thins out during a pointless, if not monotonous and hypnotic, recitation. The voice finally stops, and students are given time to digest the passage in the hope that someone will come up with something to say. The result is usually a class shattered into silent individuals, each lost in baffling text. The last resort now for the teacher is the magic word *multimedia*, the nostrum for a generation that has quit reading. A film clip depicting the reading scene in chapter 23 is shown, and attention is regained—but attention to what? The audiovisual detour seldom leads back to the written word. The audience is rallied to other media, and the failure to engage students in a literary text is magnified rather than alleviated by the multimedia solution.

Yet this pessimistic classroom scenario errs not so much in maintaining the centrality of literature as in assuming the existence of a stable boundary between literature and other media. Juxtaposing a literary text and multimedia is pedagogically effective not because multimedia entertains otherwise impassive students—such entertainment is self-defeating, as it does not draw students to literature—but because a literary work, especially one as sophisticated and encyclopedic as *Stone*, itself constantly involves or crosses over into other media, thus opening the ground for intermedial experience (Wolf 36). Chapter 23 of the novel is not simply what we read aloud or silently in class; it reflects on which mediating format induces sound or silence, and on what social meanings are imparted to the audience by various media and reading practices. Engaging chapter 23 alongside its modern media renditions, therefore, is to consider what we ourselves have been doing and experiencing in our multimedia classroom and society at large. Conversely, modern adaptations of the story across media boundaries foreground the conjunction and disjunction between media, a concern already expressed in Cao Xueqin's eighteenth-century novel.

To many modern readers, the novel tells of the tragic love, in a feudal family, between Bao-yu and Dai-yu. Love seems celebrated here as a quintessential quality inherent in the characters and ultimately as the transcendental message of the whole story. But chapter 23, a pivotal moment in the novel when Bao-yu and Dai-yu move into Prospect Garden with their amorous feelings awakened, gives us quite a different picture. Here we are shown that Dai-yu is not initiated into love until she is exposed to romantic drama. She cannot even enjoy romantic drama by watching its performance until she silently reads (*kan* 看) a printed copy of the play *The Western Chamber* that Bao-yu smuggles into the garden (1.23.462–65). The feudal family does not suppress the idea of romantic love: everyone in the household may attend the performance of romantic plays commissioned inside the family compound (e.g., chs. 18 and 54). But reading the texts of those plays is prohibited. This peculiar rule is clearly articulated in chapter 51, in which Dai-yu remarks, "Even if, as well-bred young ladies, we may not read the books in which they are to be found, we've all watched plenty of plays. Every three-year-old child is familiar with these stories" (2.51.514)。這兩首雖於史鑑上無考, 咱們雖不曾看這些外傳, 不知底里, 難道咱們連兩本戲也沒有見過不成? 那三歲孩子也知道, 何況咱們? Li Wan agrees and adds that it is acceptable to learn love tales from storytellers, performances, or temple oracles, as long as one does not *read* those stories. "It's not as if we ourselves had read the lyrics of *The Western Chamber* and *The Peony Pavilion*, licentious books we would be afraid to glance over" 況且又并不是看了西廂, 牡丹的詞曲, 怕看了邪書 (1: 691).[1]

In other words, at issue is not love as quintessential quality or transcendental content but the differences among the media through which a story is presented, each medium affecting the construction of community and individual interiority in a different way. The distinction made here is between an oral performance of opera, for listening, and a printed copy of opera, for silent reading. Whereas the voice turns listeners into an audience, silent reading has each reader enter his or her own private world and as a result shatters the unity of the audience (Ong 74). That division makes reading a play more dubious than having it performed. Listening to a play performed with one's family fosters a sense of community; reading it silently (in secret) generates an individual interiority that may threaten the community. Recent studies acknowledge the emergence of solitary leisure reading as an effect of the flourishing print culture in late imperial China, but they have reservations about whether the practice of silent reading ever developed as in early modern Europe (Lowry 58). It is argued that vocalization or auditive reading, descended from the traditional way of learning Confucian classics, was still the norm of reading texts in general during the era of print (McLaren 168). That characters in *Stone* constantly read in silence almost without exception (Lam 390–91) and that silent reading and oral performance of the same dramatic texts are painstakingly distinguished in the novel (358–82) open a neglected dimension of reading practices in eighteenth-century China.

The disjunction between performance and reading, between orality and ocularity, and between individual and community is laid out in chapter 23. But the end of the chapter complicates these dichotomies, because after learning to appreciate romantic plays through her silent reading, Dai-yu overhears a rehearsal of another romantic opera, *The Peony Pavilion* (aka *The Soul's Return*). The narrator reminds us that up to this point "she has never ever been interested in seeing plays" (*suxi buda xi kan xiwen* 素習不大喜看戲文 [1: 316]).[2] Back in chapter 18, Dai-yu attended the performance of the scene "Departure of the Soul" (*Lihun* 離魂), extracted from *The Peony Pavilion* (371), but was unresponsive to it. Yet this time the experience of silent reading alters the way she listens. She is now totally absorbed in the performance, as if using her ears in place of her eyes to closely read a piece of writing (*wenzhang* 文章), as if the voice, mediated by silent reading, has turned into a text. We no longer have a clear-cut opposition of orality versus literacy; rather, in the wake of silent reading facilitated by print (Yung 12–20), performance itself is textualized, ears function as eyes, and listening becomes conducive to the construction of interiority (Mazzio; Chandler 156–63). The seemingly natural alignment between orality and collectivity, or between silent reading and individuality, is therefore subject to synesthetic displacement in the intermedial situation (Lam 383–98).

This interplay between performance and reading and between orality and ocularity, as dramatized in chapter 23 of *Stone*, comes to the forefront when the novel itself is visualized or vocalized in modern mass media. The scene of Dai-yu's silent reading, a pivotal moment in many *Red Chamber* film adaptations, reveals how subjects and communities have been generated, as in the eighteenth-century novel, through mediations of the voice.[3] These adaptations deal with the scene of silent reading in subtly different manners, each revealing a distinct intermedial culture specific to its own geopolitical context in modern Chinese history. In this essay, I discuss how the tension and circulation between the voice and silence central to chapter 23 was the primary issue when the novel crossed over to the silver screen the first time, in 1924. Then I focus on three *Red Chamber* films, made in 1944, 1962, and 1977 (all available on DVD and, except for the 1962 version, with English subtitles), tracing the vicissitudes of the technologically mediated voice in the modern medium of film and the transformations of social meanings assigned to silent reading, vocalization, and performance at various historical junctures. The point of the comparison is not to judge which adaptation is the best or whether the novel's plot or characterization was faithfully followed; the point is to show how the very operation of adapting across media boundaries demonstrates every time the profound reflection provided by the novel on the ramifications of intermedial encounter.

## 1924: Listening to a Silent Opera

Chapter 23 of the novel played a role in both the modernization of Peking opera and the formation of early Chinese cinema in the 1910s and 1920s. In 1915, Mei Lanfang, the famous female impersonator, was struck by the fact that *The Story of the Stone*, popular as it was, could not be seen onstage. Although a dozen operatic adaptations of the novel appeared during the late eighteenth and nineteenth centuries, they were almost never performed, existing as desktop plays. In collaboration with the drama critic Qi Rushan and the playwright Li Shikan, Mei turned chapter 23 of the novel, plus a small segment from chapter 27, into a six-scene Peking opera: *Dai-yu zanghua* 黛玉葬花 ("Dai-yu Buries Flowers"). With an innovative approach to historical costume and stage setting (Mei, *Wutai* 290–302; Qi Rushan 113–14; He Xishi; Qi Song; Goldstein 122–23), the adaptation represents Mei's effort to integrate Peking opera into modern visual culture (Pang, *Distorting Mirror* 157–58). In the play's final and longest scene, Dai-yu (played by Mei Lanfang himself) silently reads *The Western Chamber* and then overhears *The Peony Pavilion* (Qi and Li 98–104). On 3 November 1924, the Hong Kong filmmaker Lai Man-wai of China Sun Motion Picture asked Mei to perform in a short documentary (Lai 8). Mei chose to present, among four other plays, the two scenes of flower burial and reading *The Western Chamber* from *Dai-yu Buries Flowers*. This documentary is one of the earliest opera films but unfortunately is no longer extant.

That this first *Red Chamber* movie was a silent film based on an operatic adaptation adds layers to the tension between silently reading and listening to opera in the novel. In early Western cinema, silent films frequently drew on opera not just for story lines but also for general models of narrative, spectacle, and spectatorship (Theresa). The first Chinese films on historical record—the eight opera documentaries made by Fengtai Studio from 1905 to 1909—testify to a direct, intimate relation between Chinese cinema and opera theater (Pang, *Distorting Mirror* 141–48). Although silent film exhibitions were usually accompanied by sound that ranged from live music or music on phonograph to live spoken commentary (Camper 369; Marks 72–74), the accompanying sound as extrinsic to the image track underlined the nature of early film as a mute medium (Mei, *Wo* 17). The issue of silent reading vis-à-vis listening in *The Story of the Stone* was therefore rearticulated in the first film version as the paradoxical coupling of silent film and operatic voice.

In his memoir *My Life in Film*, posthumously published in 1962 (*Wo*), Mei Lanfang described almost four decades later the lost film that he never had a chance to see. He concentrated on the problematic of silence:

> As to filming *Dai-yu Buries Flowers* . . . on the theatrical stage, this play mainly relies on singing and recitation to express emotion. . . . When the play was adapted into silent film, however, singing and reciting were deleted. What else could be used to express emotion? Nothing but those slow movements and quiet facial expressions.

Subtle bodily movements and facial expressions that communicate inner thoughts, Mei further noted, are undetectable on theatrical stage but effective in film (19). At first glance, Mei seemed to abide by the form of silent film and address solely the visual-spatial aspects of performance. He especially emphasized the use of a real garden in Beijing as the film setting—it enabled the actor to stride forward slowly, with the camera following, and an occasional

《黛玉葬花》　（民新影片公司出品　1924 年）

Fig.1. "Can You Hear Me Now?" A still from *Dai-yu Buries Flowers*
(1924), in *Dazhong dianying* 大眾電影 249 (1961): 15

pause could highlight his countenance, probably in close-up (15) — unlike the empty, symbolic theatrical stage typical of Peking opera, where one could walk only in circles (18–19). But in Mei's account, the intended effect of these slow movements and quiet facial expressions was aural as well as visual. They were aimed to "make the audience feel as if they were listening to the singing, even though it was a black-and-white silent film," to convey the melancholic feeling in the inaudible songs (16). Silence on-screen did not revoke but evoked the absent voice (fig. 1).

It has been argued that Italian singing in its excess and extremity aspires to what is beyond sound — the silence of death. This affinity between operatic voice and silence explains why silent film became the unlikely ally of Western opera (Grover-Friedlander). Visiting the same paradox from the other direction, Mei's silent opera aspired to the acoustic of vision. Recoiling from deathly silence, the inaudible singing that Mei invited us to imagine functioned to exorcise the ghostliness of silent films or, in Theodor Adorno and Hanns Eisler's words, "to spare the spectators the unpleasantness involved in seeing effigies of living, acting, and even speaking persons, who were at the same time silent" (50). The anxiety in silent film about the living dead who speak without a voice does not disappear after the advent of sound; synchronized speech and music in sound cinema conjure up rather than expel specters. A case in point is the 1944 *Red Chamber* film.

## 1944: The Vocal Hand of Opera in a (Horror) Movie Theater

Between 1924 and 1944, at least four *Red Chamber* films were made—a Cantonese talkie made in 1936 was also named *Dai-yu zanghua* (the English title was *Farewell, Flowers*) (Huang Shuxian 80)—but none survived. The earliest extant *Red Chamber* film is the 1944 production, which was named after the novel and directed by Bu Wancang in occupied Shanghai. The famous actress and singer Zhou Xuan played Dai-yu, and Yuan Meiyun, who started her career as a Peking opera singer but turned to film acting after 1933, cross-dressed as Bao-yu. It had been more than a decade since the first Chinese talkie was made, in 1930, and yet, despite the technological breakthrough that gave opera film new leverage, the production of opera film in Shanghai, the center of the Chinese film industry, stagnated in the 1930s and 1940s—for various political and economic reasons, such as the Japanese occupation of Shanghai after 1937, which led to Mei Lanfang's retirement as a form of resistance (Gao 90–93). The 1944 adaptation *The Dream of the Red Chamber* is not an opera film but a full-length black-and-white feature.

Unlike Mei's *Dai-yu Buries Flowers*, which covered only one small episode, Bu Wancang condensed the entire novel into a two-hour film by narrowing it down to Bao-yu and Dai-yu's ill-fated romance. Starting with Dai-yu's arrival and ending with Bao-yu's departure after her death, Bu's film is structurally more streamlined than its two lost predecessors, which have similar themes, made in 1927 (Du 146–49; Chen Dingxiu). Though criticized in 1944 for being too reductive to do the complex story justice (Mai 171–72), Bu's version established the basic model for later adaptations to come (A. Wong, "Honglou meng" 141), which seldom go beyond Bu's scope. The romantic emphasis led Bu to make pivotal the episode of Bao-yu and Dai-yu's silent reading of *The Western Chamber*.

Interestingly, Bu relocates the moment of Dai-yu's overhearing *The Peony Pavilion* to an earlier point in the film. By having the listening scene precede and qualify the silent reading, he shows that he is rethinking the role of the voice, given recent developments in sound technology. As a sound film recording on location and on a sound stage, his adaptation apparently cannot tolerate

Fig. 2. Zhou Xuan subvocalizes as Lin Dai-yu (1944).

the silence of reading in the novel. Mei Lanfang evoked inaudible singing to fill the uneasy void in 1924; synchronized music and voice along with a series of vocalizing gestures perform a similar function in the 1944 film. First there is a burst of background music at the moment Dai-yu discovers the copy of *The Western Chamber* lying on the ground. Then a close-up of Dai-yu reading the book shows that the actress is subvocalizing, moving her lips without making audible sound (fig. 2). Finally, unlike Bao-yu and Dai-yu in the novel, who effortlessly memorize and recite what they have silently read, both Yuan Meiyun and Zhou Xuan in the film must consult the book and read off the page when in their conversation they cite a couple of lines.

These subtle variations introduced by the 1944 film are ambiguous in their implications. On the one hand, the sound film gives the act of reading a new voice that restores the sense of communality between characters and between the filmic world and the audience. On the other hand, the voice no longer comes from the human body; it is a leftover in precarious status, lingering over the printed page. Such detachment of voice from body, at times dramatized in the 1930s Chinese sound films (Zhang Zhen 308–09, 319–28), is underscored in the 1944 adaptation at the end of the reading scene. Seeing that Bao-yu is being lured away by Bao-chai, Dai-yu turns her back to the camera and, in a striking gesture unconceivable in the novel, throws her copy of *The Western Chamber*

Fig. 3. The book along with the voice washed away (1944)

into the river. The camera pans right, following the forsaken book in the running stream, until a wipe replaces the shot with the ensuing indoor scene, cutting in toward the left. The background music, substituting for Dai-yu's voice,
is gone the moment the book disappears from the screen. The furious Dai-yu
therefore discards not only the book but also her voice along with it (fig. 3).
The synchronized music as Dai-yu's disposable voice ironically reveals "an un-
bridgeable gap [that] separates forever a human body from 'its' voice . . . so
that even when we see a living person talking, there is always some degree of
ventriloquism at work" (Žižek 92; also see Adorno and Eisler 51).[4]
    The disembodied female voice as a symptom of sound cinema at once reca-
pitulates and modifies the mediated, privatized voice experimented with in Cao
Xueqin's novel. Two years after the end of World War II, Zhang Ailing (Eileen
Chang), the famous wartime Shanghai writer whose indebtedness to and scholarship on *Stone* is well known, gave a vivid depiction of the ambiguous nature of
this woman's voice in her short tale "A Splendid Romance":

> That woman's voice [of Shaoxing opera] is a tranquilizer for the anxious
> modern people, and therefore now prevails everywhere from city to coun-
> try. That singing voice is so fleshy that you can even stroke it with your

hand. The horror of this era is just like watching a horror movie, and the audience in darkness holds this woman's hand fast for consolation.

(E. Chang, "Huali" 104)

The pervasive presence of the woman's voice from the local Shaoxing opera evokes the immediacy of community. This voice even turns into a tangible entity — the extended body of the woman. We can almost imagine that the female voice in the air is incarnated as a mythical matriarch whose body, covering the entire nation, hovers over our heads so that we can reach out and feel her. Yet Zhang Ailing fragments this body by localizing the voice in a movie theater, and the fleshy incarnation of the voice turns out not to be the body as a whole but a fetishized hand alone. Thrown into a modern world that looks like a horror movie, people in the audience are separated from one another by the darkness in the theater, a source of fear dating from the beginning of commercial exhibition at the turn of the century (Gunning 14). What one can rely on to overcome this horrific isolation is the female voice of opera singing heard in the dark: it is like a woman's hand found conveniently next to one's seat. One is promised a reconnection to some sort of community through a voice-hand that metonymically implies a living, intact body. But would it be another bad joke of a horror movie that what one holds fast to as a last resort turns out to be a dismembered hand and that what one hears is no more than a spectral, disposable voice that belongs to no body?

Intact and severed, ruptured and rearticulated, the cinematic voice in Bu Wancang's 1944 film adaptation and in Zhang Ailing's tale sways between the normative voice evoking community and the private voice in the eighteenth-century novel. This indeterminacy points to the paradox underlying the modern nation as an imagined community — a communal entity dreamed up by isolated individuals who can imagine themselves joined with others only through mass media. At the geopolitical level, the same ambiguity informed the relation of those Shanghai "collaborators" (including Bu and Zhang) to the edifice of Pan-Asianism (Fu 38–48), which contained both the redemptive aspiration to unite peoples across territories and Japan's imperialistic drive to subsume others to hierarchical divisions (Duara 110).[5] Uttering in a cinematic voice the schizophrenic split between inclusion and exclusion, the 1944 *Dream of the Red Chamber* itself suffered both acceptance and rejection at the whim of the Japanese patronage. Though the film came out with sky-high production values from the China Film Company (Zhonghua dianying 中華電影), headed by Kawakita Nagamasa, the leading film distributor from Japan who promoted Sino-Japanese affinity through cinema ("Guangrong zhi ye"; Tsuji 31–44; Shimizu 212–19, 261–63), the Japanese authorities cut short the showing of the film in Shanghai for the odd reason that it went too deep in portraying "animosity" ("Diren patan 'enyuan'").

Only thanks to the figure of the modern movie theater in the sound film era did the vocal hand of opera, with its ambiguous promise, become possible.

It is no accident that Zhang Ailing, whose acquaintance with film culture informed her wartime essays and stories (Lee 276–80), also wrote seven reviews in English of twelve Chinese films made in occupied Shanghai in 1943. Her postwar career was largely defined by her screenplays written in Shanghai and Hong Kong between 1947 and 1962. One of the screenplays she wrote for Hong Kong's Motion Picture and General Investment Company (MP and GI) was *Dream of the Red Chamber* (Sima 120; Law 144–45).

## 1962: Zeroing in on a Spurious Tableau

This screenplay of Zhang Ailing was never executed. She finished the first draft by 28 January 1962, but in early March, MP and GI aborted the project after their major competitor, Shaw Brothers, announced they were making their own film adaptation (Zhou Fengling 61, 66). And yet, the Shaw Brothers film turned out to be completely overshadowed by another *Red Chamber* film, released in November. *The Dream of the Red Chamber*, directed by Cen Fan, would become a classic in Chinese film history. The color film is based on a 1958 Yue opera play produced by the Shanghai Yue Opera House, starring the famous actresses Xu Yulan and Wang Wenjuan. Thanks to the aesthetics of Yue opera, which is a local species of Chinese opera using exclusively female actors, the play enhances the romantic and sentimental orientation that we saw in the 1944 film adaptation (J. Jiang, *Women* 240–50).[6] The stage performance was brought to Hong Kong in 1960, and its popularity catalyzed the coproduction of the film version by Shanghai Haiyan Studio and Hong Kong's King Sum Film Company two years later (*Hongloumeng huabao* 2). Eclipsing the other early extant *Red Chamber* opera films—the Cantonese opera film *Dai-yu zanghua* (the English title is *Substituted Bride*), made by Fengming dianying 鳳鳴電影, and the Huangmei opera film *The Dream of the Red Chamber*, made by Shaw Brothers, released respectively in July and August 1962—the Yue opera film was critically acclaimed and broke Hong Kong's box office record.

This 1962 Yue opera version was a product of the heyday of mainland opera film, an ideological apparatus quickly embraced by the newly born People's Republic of China. From 1953 to 1960, a total of seventy-one opera films were made by the state-run studios. The year 1960 witnessed the record-high annual production of fifteen opera films, followed by a sharp downturn to four in 1961 (Gao 290–97), a clear index showing the impact of the failed Great Leap Forward (1958–60), which resulted in the largest famine in human history and claimed about thirty million lives. Aggressive collectivization was reversed after January 1961, and Liu Shaoqi, then the PRC chair, mitigated the crisis with moderate economic policies. In 1962 the annual output of opera film rose back to twelve. It was in this historical interstice that the mainland–Hong Kong coproduction of the Yue opera film was made possible. Hong Kong's input concentrated on the provision of imported celluloid film, camera equipment, and supplies for set construction and makeup, all of which were in shortage given the material conditions in mainland China during the early 1960s (Cen 59).

To Xu Jin, who wrote both the Yue opera play and film versions, the "Reading *The Western Chamber*" episode encapsulates character development and holds dramatic tension (Afterword 161–62). A flier that advertised the film's premiere at Hong Kong's Astor Theater on 22 November 1962 endorsed his view with a still that featured Bao-yu and Dai-yu reading the play. Although saturated with music and singing, the Yue opera film highlights the visual aspect of the scene. If the 1944 talkie introduced voice into the act of silent reading, the 1962 opera film went in the opposite direction. The overhearing of *The Peony Pavilion*, which the 1944 talkie relocates to precede the silent reading scene, is omitted from the 1962 film. Instead, the 1962 film inserts before this scene a scene of vocalization (not found in the original Yue opera play), in which Bao-yu, played by the cross-dressed Xu Yulan, is forced by his father to study the Confucian classics for the civil service examinations. Sitting upright in the study against the background of a dauntingly large bookcase, Bao-yu recites aloud the didactic message from the book but, soon feeling weary and bored, rubs his eyes. Reading aloud therefore is related to pedantry and indoctrination, which Bao-yu finds unbearable. In the following scene of silent reading in a secret corner of the garden, background music, as in the 1944 film, rises to express Dai-yu's excitement. But new elements are introduced: a couple of close-ups show the contents of the book in Dai-yu's hands, hence underscoring the media specificity of the opera film. The novel never describes the copy of *The Western Chamber*, and the reader needs no physical description—nor do opera theatergoers, who readily accept that the prop in an actor's hand is no more than a bunch of blank sheets bound together. But in 1956, the opera film art director and critic Han Shangyi argued that the film camera created a new desire in the viewer: "For instance, if a John Doe is reading a letter, the spectators would subconsciously want to see the letter close up; if a Tommy Atkins goes into a forest, the spectators would also like to see the scenery" 張三看一封信, 觀眾會下意識地想看這封信的 "特寫"; 李四進入森林, 觀眾也想看看森林的景色. It is because, Han explained, unlike a Chinese opera theater, which makes use of symbol, suggestion, and imagination, film relies on and has resources for concretely representing a three-dimensional world by optical means (46).

Much of the then-contemporary discussion was devoted to reconciling the "symbolic" representation of opera and the "realistic" representation of film, yet Han's observation calls attention to a more critical phenomenon—namely, that spectators are induced to identify with the characters by seeing through their eyes (or, more precisely, through the eye of the camera), which is precisely what the camerawork of the 1962 film does in the silent reading scene. First, a medium long shot tracks in as Dai-yu, sitting beside Bao-yu in the garden, starts browsing *The Western Chamber* with great eagerness. Second, a point-of-view shot, which is also the first close-up of the book, shows the open pages of the printed text Dai-yu is supposedly eyeing. Third, a close-up shows Dai-yu turning the page, to reconfirm that the previous close-up was from her perspective.

Fourth, a pan starts with Bao-yu's close-up and follows his gaze to the right, leading us back to Dai-yu, who is still absorbed in her reading. Fifth, to take Dai-yu's viewpoint again, the camera cuts to the second close-up, of the book, yet this time what is revealed is not the play text but an illustration to the play that depicts a young couple, the immortalized lovers Student Zhang and Oriole in *The Western Chamber*, standing together in a garden (fig. 4, top). Sixth and finally, the illustration dissolves back into a long shot of the garden scene with the images of Bao-yu and Dai-yu superimposed on those of Student Zhang and Oriole (fig. 4, bottom).

Fig. 4. *Top:* second close-up of the book (woodblock). *Bottom:* dissolution and superimposition (1962)

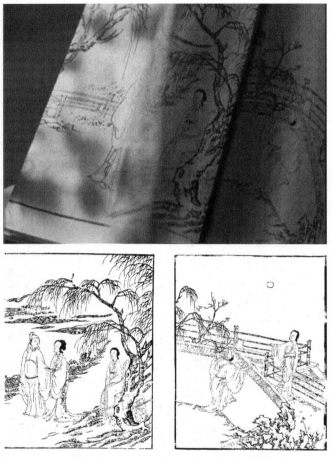

Fig. 5. A split-second revelation (*top*), and the original illustrations to the 1616 edition of *The Western Chamber* (*bottom*)

This six-shot sequence establishes a delicate network of gazes guiding the spectators, through Dai-yu's eyes, first to the play text and then to the illustration. The core of the scene is therefore the visual appearance of the physical copy of the play, not the play's abstract romantic message. In contrast, the camera work is simpler in the 1944 version: a medium shot of Dai-yu picking up the book; a one-second take of its plain cover, which has only the book title on it; a long shot of Dai-yu stepping aside to read; a thirteen-second take of Dai-yu subvocalizing in close-up; and, finally, a panning shot of Bao-yu walking toward Dai-yu to disrupt her reading. No eye-line match is stressed, except for the fleeting shot of the book cover. The focal point here is not the characters' gaze but Zhou Xuan's lips seductively moving in resonance with the background music.

By the techniques of dissolving and superimposing, the 1962 film suggests that Dai-yu and Bao-yu are replicas of the romantic couple depicted in the illustration. The visual representation of what Dai-yu silently reads does not isolate the individuals but rather serves as a tableau that prescribes the positions for the audience members to identify with and shapes their interrelations to one another accordingly. Silence no longer shatters but generates new communality by way of dramatic iconography. If in the 1944 adaptation voice is smuggled back in to sustain a precarious sense of community, in the 1962 version it is the visual image that gains the power of a collective icon asserting identification among spectators, character, and illustrated figures. This iconic film image of Bao-yu and Dai-yu reading *The Western Chamber* would linger in public memory and decorate quotidian life (in the form of calendar posters, for instance), even during the time when the film was banned in mainland China after Jiang Qing, in response to limited previews in late 1962, denounced it as "a clandestine friend of the property class" (*zichan jieji de mimi zhiyin* 資產階級的秘密知音) (Cao Hongpei 27).

To the otherwise smooth process of iconographic identification there is an underside of nonidentification in the physical copy of the play itself. The first close-up of the book displays the printed text of *The Western Chamber*, the second an illustration, supposedly from the same copy—supposedly, because the continuity editing and the unspoiled physical look lead viewers to believe so. Judging by the typography, the open pages of the text shown in the first close-up are from the late Ming woodblock edition of *The Western Chamber* compiled by He Bi in 1616. This edition was discovered and a facsimile of it published in 1961; therefore it was available as a prop for the film. But the illustration in the second close-up (fig. 4, top), despite its early-seventeenth-century woodblock style, is nowhere to be found in He Bi's or any other edition of the play. The picture shown on-screen is a forgery planted in the facsimile. Closer scrutiny of the second close-up shows that as Dai-yu turns the page, two preceding illustrations to the right are fleetingly revealed, and they match perfectly the original pictures found in the frontispiece of the 1616 edition (fig. 5). In a magician's sleight of hand, when the page is completely turned over, what is shown is a picture that cannot be found in the 1616 edition and therefore should not have been there.

The spurious picture was carefully done in the style of the genuine illustrations, especially in its representation of human figures, willow trees, and railings. Why did the filmmakers bother to create this fake image? Because the 1616 edition has no illustration that depicts the two lovers, Student Zhang and Oriole (Cui Ying-ying), really *being together*. Either one of them is absent or a high wall or vast space separates them. The only exception is the picture to the left that the second close-up barely shows before the page is turned: the couple are standing close enough to hold hands (fig. 5, bottom left). Yet, instead of really bringing the lovers together, this illustration heralds their separation by capturing the moment when Oriole is seeing off Student Zhang, whom the young woman's mother forces to depart. To the right, we can see the maid Crimson beside a chariot, waiting to escort Oriole home; to the left, willow branches hang, a classical symbol of bidding farewell. In short, the 1616 edition illustrates isolation rather than togetherness, an emphasis that is reversed by the spurious picture in the 1962 film. The spurious picture, while keeping many elements of the original picture, removes the chariot and the maid, giving the impression that the couple can stay together as long as they like. As a product of its times, when romantic relationship bore the risk of coming too close to petit bourgeois sensibility and had to justify itself in the name of antifeudalism, the spurious picture omits the strongest expression of passion in the original picture—the couple's holding hands before the separation—by having the two figures stand side by side without touching. The togetherness made present here is not private, for the young couple, but public, for the viewing public to participate in the identification of a widely circulated icon. Talking about her stage experience as Dai-yu in the scene of reading *The Western Chamber*, Wang Wenjuan celebrated the love between the characters in refutation of feudalistic oppression but ended with a disclaimer that "at the same time I have to avoid propagating unhealthy petit bourgeois sentiments and the malignant effects objectively incurred" (71). Both the stage production and the film adaptation were in congruence with the way the theme of love was handled in the first seventeen years of the Communist regime (1949–66): libidinal energy was channeled to fuel revolutionary zeal, but amorous feelings had to be kept in check (Liu Jianmei 162–92).

But why was the image of the maid deleted from the frame if the theme was communal togetherness and not private intimacy? In making silent reading communal, the 1962 film adaptation ironically models the communal on a couple who exclude any intrusion by a third party. This exclusion of the broader audience—a retreat from extreme collectivism after the devastating failure of the Great Leap Forward—is further confirmed by the film's implicit aversion to the voice, which is quite surprising, given that it is an opera film. Vocalizing a text in the film is identified with indoctrination. It is the vocalization of *The Western Chamber* by Bao-yu, who sings aloud one of its arias and alarms Dai-yu for its improper implication, that destroys the magical moment of being together. The sequence ends in a way almost opposite to that of the reading scene in the 1944 film version: in 1944, a furious Dai-yu shocks the audience by throwing away the book that embodies her voice; in 1962, the couple simply sit down, putting an end to their quarrel by resuming their perusal of the cherished copy of the play. What keeps them together is the silence of the printed text and woodblock illustration; what causes trouble between them is the voice.

## 1977: Switching the Usual Suspect

How a third party can be incorporated into silent reading and how the voice may become problematic would be further tackled in the 1977 Hong Kong Shaw Brothers production, a Huangmei opera film version directed by Li Hanxiang and titled *Jinyu liangyuan Honglou meng* 金玉良緣紅樓夢.[7] The official English title is still *The Dream of the Red Chamber.* In the 1970s, Hong Kong outgrew industrialization and turned into a multifaceted economy; this change coincided with significant improvement in social welfare (Tay 32–33). The second half of the decade, especially the year 1976, saw huge growth in the box office figures of Hong Kong cinema (Chen Qingwei 13–14, 17). In 1977–78, there were five *Red Chamber* films made by Hong Kong and Taiwanese studios scrambling for this expanding market. It was also the prime time of traffic between Hong Kong and Taiwanese cinema. Li Hanxiang traveled back and forth between Hong Kong and Taiwan in his early career (Huang Ren et al. 28–43; E. Yeh). Among his 1977 film stars were the Taiwanese actresses Brigitte Lin (Lin Qingxia, cross-dressed as Bao-yu) and Sylvia Chang (Zhang Aijia, playing Lin Dai-yu). The exchange between Hong Kong and mainland Chinese film culture, interrupted for a decade, started to revive in that year, right after the end of the Cultural Revolution. Among the first signals of this reconnection, the 1962 mainland–Hong Kong production reasserted its authority when it was reexhibited in Hong Kong theaters and greeted by an enthusiastic audience. In the crowd was Li Hanxiang, who found inspiration in the 1962 classic for his own film adaptation (He Siyin).

Taiwanese competitors accused Li Hanxiang of plagiarizing the 1962 mainland production (Huang Ren et al. 26). But Li actually entered into a sophisticated dialogue with the Yue opera film version, especially in his treatment of the "Reading *The Western Chamber*" scene. Like the 1962 film, Li precedes the scene with the father's admonition for Bao-yu to study the Confucian classics. But instead of showing Bao-yu's painful toil of vocalizing the classics, the 1977 version cuts to the scene in which Bao-yu and Dai-yu have been reading *The Western Chamber.* This quick shift humorously presents the youngsters' leisure reading as a mischievous response to the father's imperative to study. More important, by skipping Bao-yu's recitation of the classics, Li Hanxiang dissociates vocalization from indoctrination and heralds a new social meaning attributed to the voice.

The influence of the 1962 Yue opera film is most obviously acknowledged in the several shots of woodblock illustrations in the reading scene from Li Hanxiang's Huangmei opera film version. These tribute shots are multiplied to the extent that Dai-yu and Bao-yu in the 1977 film seem to be reading a comic book rather than literature. In three shots, five illustrations are shown, all from the 1620s Ling Chucheng woodblock edition. (To be more precise, the copy used in the film is the *Huike chuanju* 彙刻傳劇 edition, compiled by Liu Shiheng and first published in 1919, which reproduces the illustrations to Ling Chucheng's edition. Liu's edition was reprinted several times in the twentieth century and is easily available.) The first two shots repeatedly show the same illustration in which Student Zhang is kneeling to ask Oriole to go to bed with him. As if to model after the bedchamber setting of the woodblock picture, Li Hanxiang transplants the entire scene of silent reading from the corner of the garden

Fig. 6. Invisible wall of privacy (1977)

to Bao-yu's room. Ironically, the woodblock picture of intimacy contrasts with what is happening between Dai-yu and Bao-yu: each holding one volume of *The Western Chamber*, they are too occupied by their reading to be physically intimate. Their distance is underlined when Dai-yu, lying on a chaise, pulls away from Bao-yu in order not to let him see what she is reading, even though both are reading the same play (fig. 6). In the second shot, the camera zooms out and shows that an open volume with the same picture, which suggests love-making, is lying on the table with other volumes of the play. It looks as though the young couple have finally put down the books to do something else after viewing that arousing picture. Here we glimpse the possibility that the director is sliding into the *fengyue* 風月 ("soft-core porn") genre that his other movies had established since his 1972 hit *Legends of Lust* (*Fengyue qitan* 風月奇譚) (Yau Ching). But no—the camera tilts up and reveals the couple just sitting in separate chairs and reading in silence. So there is no sexual relationship, indeed.

This scenario seems to suggest that through silent reading, Dai-yu and Bao-yu are too withdrawn into their private selves to act out the illustration and to be really together. But the third shot gives this normative alignment of individuation and silent reading an intriguing twist. A different pair of illustrations depict scenes that precede the lovemaking one, in which Oriole's maid, Crimson, is sent by Madam Zheng to visit Student Zhang, who has been sick in bed for days. Crimson provides a thematic transition to the next shot, which shows two maids walking in the garden. Panning to the left, the camera follows them until they walk past Dai-yu and Bao-yu, who now find themselves out in the garden but still reading *The Western Chamber* when the maids pass by (fig. 7). In contrast to the 1962 film, in which communality is undercut by purging the maid image from the woodblock illustration, Li Hanxiang's version innovatively embeds the act of silent reading in the public realm, signaled by the presence of the maids

Fig. 7. The maids pass by (1977).

both in the illustrations and in the garden scene. The panning shot of the garden, imitating the format of traditional Chinese hand-scroll landscape painting, which horizontally unfolds from right to left (Wu Hung, *Double Screen* 57–59), further emphasizes the spatial continuity between the maids and the reading couple.

This kind of hand-scroll panning shot has frequently been cited by Chinese critics as a quintessentially "Chinese" cinematic technique, in that it draws on traditional aesthetics. These critics find that the 1962 film fails to provide a hand-scroll vision because its shots of the garden are only fragmentary (Jiang Jin, "Lun Xingshi mei" 32, 39; Lin Niantong 41–47). Without essentializing the national aesthetics of Chinese cinema (defined by a certain privileged traditional painting genre and format), we should understand the different styles found in the 1962 and 1977 film versions in terms of their different usage of picture and ultimately different framing of community. The fragmentary garden shots actually bear out the 1962 film's exclusive focus on a single book illustration—a format by definition incompatible with the hand-scroll or "panoramic" continuum (Burkus-Chasson 374)—and on the couple in the picture from which the maid has been ousted. In contrast, the 1977 film integrates the multiple illustrations into a hand-scroll panning shot in order to put the maids back into the continual space shared by the reading couple. Silent reading therefore turns both private and public. It is public precisely because the community sanctions an invisible wall of privacy so that others may come and go without disturbing the silent reader. Individuals now engage in their reading outright in their sitting room and in open space. Reading romantic plays in silence has become an open secret rendered transparent in broad daylight.

But the performance itself is taboo. In the 1977 film, Dai-yu and Bao-yu do not mind letting maids see them reading *The Western Chamber*. Yet Bao-yu must wait until the maids have left and no other people are around before he bursts out singing lines from the play. The paradox in the novel—namely, that performance of the text is allowed whereas reading the text is not—has been reversed. Now it is the performance culture that plays the usual suspect. In the next scene, in Bao-yu's room when Bao-yu has the opera actor Jiang Yu-han perform an aria without knowing that it is overheard by the maid Aroma behind the screen, Aroma immediately comments on the impropriety of fraternizing with an actor. In the novel, Bao-yu's problem is not so much his friendship with an actor as his alleged involvement in the actor's flight from his powerful patron (ch. 33). The relocation of Jiang's performance at Bao-yu's place in the 1977 film shifts our attention from the actor's flight to performance itself. In the novel, Jiang's singing occurs in a drinking game at Bao-yu's friend's in chapter 28 and has little to do with Bao-yu personally. Aroma's comment on actors cannot be found in the novel but came from the Yue opera play and film versions. Since Jiang never performs in the Yue opera play and film, her comment there is not a response to performance at all (Xu Jin, *Yueju* 23–24). The 1977 film recontextualizes these elements to put the scandal of performance per se into sharp focus. Li Hanxiang's adaptation thus comes closer to our contemporary situation, in which a public performance or film screening is more susceptible to censorship than a printed text is. The voice here no longer makes any ambiguous promise to unify individuals in their separateness (as seen in the 1944 film); neither does it wield the authority of state indoctrination for collectivism (as seen in the 1962 film). Instead, the voice turns secretive and retreats from public ears, foreshadowing the advent of Walkmans, iPods, and home theaters with 5.1 surround sound.

Chapter 23 of *The Story of the Stone* has been a provocative site for experimentation and reflection on the transmuted nature of the voice in the history of twentieth-century Chinese media and society. Several modern film adaptations of the novel show how the presence or absence of the voice conjures up diverse and ambiguous ways for us to imagine community and individuality. The multifarious effects of vocalization and silent reading does not deny media specificity but subjects it to the fluidity of intermedial encounter in a certain historical time and space. In this essay I have offered three geopolitical contexts we may map on three film adaptations: occupied Shanghai under the shadow of pan-Asianism, post-1949 Shanghai (coupled with Hong Kong) in the transient period of economic reform on the eve of the Cultural Revolution, and late-1970s Hong Kong (coupled with Taiwan) rising as a capitalist society. On a more general horizon, we should recognize that all three films address the issue of divergence and convergence of media, an issue that is always at the heart of the eighteenth-century novel. The novel's insight into intermedial encounters turns out to be most relevant to our understanding of the construction of modern subjects and communities.

NOTES

[1] The translated sentence, with slight modification, was taken from Cao and Gao, *Dream* (1978–80) 2: 168. David Hawkes unfortunately gives this statement the opposite meaning and makes Li Wan uncharacteristically open-minded: "And even if one knows them from books, it can hardly be said that to have read a few lyrics from *The Western Chamber* or *The Soul's Return* [*Peony Pavilion*] is tantamount to reading pornography" (2.51.515). Hawkes has to make an interpolation (just "a few" lyrics) to tone down the suspicious nature of the plays. Nevertheless, his rendition contradicts the understanding, widely shared by the characters in the novel, that reading such plays automatically opens one to the accusation of reading pornography.

[2] Preserved in all the early manuscript copies and in the first printed edition of 1791, this crucial line is omitted from Hawkes's translation, which follows the inferior reading of a reprint (465). The technical term *xiwen* means "southern drama" and must not be literally read as "play texts." The phrase *kan xiwen* 看戲文 can only mean "seeing plays" instead of "reading plays." It would be absurd to say, "Dai-yu has never been interested in reading plays"; the fact is, she has just read *The Western Chamber* with great interest. Before that, she had no chance to read a play, simply because no copy was handy until Bao-yu smuggled one into the garden. The phrase makes sense only when we understand *kan xiwen* as "seeing plays": the Jia household provided ample opportunities to see plays, but Dai-yu has never been interested in seeing them.

[3] I call these adaptations *Red Chamber* films because most are named after the novel's alternative title "The Dream of the Red Chamber," and none adopts the title "The Story of the Stone," which Hawkes keeps for his translation of the novel. I have identified thirty films released at theaters, five television films, and eleven TV serial dramas based on the novel. The latest *Red Chamber* film, in two parts, is based on a Kun opera production and debuted at UNESCO in Paris in June 2012.

[4] This ventriloquism effect is even more pronounced in such later films as the 1962 and 1977 versions of *The Dream of the Red Chamber*. Whereas the dialogues in the 1944 film were recorded on location or a sound stage and were therefore simultaneous with the action, better technological control over synchronization allowed the 1962 and 1977 films to record the sound in a separate, postshooting operation. The voice was therefore detached from and imposed after the fact on the filmed image of the body that was actually mute. The 1977 film went further, dubbing the dialogue and singing with voice artists. Despite or precisely because of the advancement of synchronization, the voice disowns the body on-screen.

[5] The charge of collaboration with Japan would dog Zhang after 1945 and recently resurfaced because of the controversy in China over Ang Lee's film adaptation of her novella *Lust, Caution*.

[6] *Yueju* 越劇 is a local opera form that originated in the Zhejiang countryside around the mid–nineteenth century and developed in Shanghai at the turn of the twentieth. It gradually came to use actresses only after 1923; by 1938, male actors had virtually disappeared from its stage. Under state sponsorship, Yue opera reached its zenith during the 1950s and early 1960s and was considered second only to Peking opera, before it succumbed to attacks for its bourgeois romantic elements after 1964 (Jiang Jin, *Women* 26–59, 181–96).

[7] Huangmei opera, or *Huangmei diao* 黃梅調, originated in Huangmei County, Hubei Province, in the late eighteenth century but entered the cities with increasing sophistication only in the wake of 1926. The Huangmei opera film became a significant genre after the 1955 mainland production *Tianxian pei* 天仙配 ("Marriage with a Heavenly Fairy"). In the hands of Li Hanxiang, starting with his 1959 Shaw Brothers masterpiece *Jiangshan meiren* 江山美人 ("Kingdom and the Beauty"), the genre enjoyed great popularity in Hong Kong and Taiwan till the end of the 1970s.

# *The Story of the Stone* and World Literature

## *Haun Saussy*

Many readers will first encounter *The Story of the Stone* in translation as part of a survey course on world literature. What is world literature, and what does this work have to do with it? How is the work deformed or reframed by being so included?

Of course, when this novel was completed in the 1750s and first printed in the 1790s, it was not launched into any arena known as world literature. The phrase *world literature* came into common use following the publication of Goethe's *Conversations with Eckermann* (1836), in which the aged poet confided to his friend that "the age of world literature is near, and everyone must now work to hasten its approach" (Eckermann 224). As it happens, Goethe was stimulated to think of a globe-spanning interchange of literary texts by his reading of a Chinese novel, *Yu Jiao Li* 玉嬌梨, which had recently been translated into English.[1] He found this book remarkable for the way that "external nature is always associated with the human figures," "an infinite number of legends . . . are constantly introduced into the narration," and its characters exhibit behavior "more clear, pure, and decorous" than in a European novel (qtd. in Weissbort and Eysteinsson 203). Not only exotic customs but also a distinctive style and fictional technique made this Chinese novel a revelation for its German reader: more than just a means of armchair travel, world literature is an exploration of unanticipated art forms.

Marx and Engels saw in the phenomenon of world literature an indication of the unification of the world by trade and capital markets:

> The bourgeoisie has through its exploitation of the world market given a cosmopolitan character to production and consumption in every country. . . . The intellectual creations of individual nations become common property. National one-sidedness and narrow-mindedness become more and more impossible, and from the numerous national and local literatures there arises a world literature. (38–39)

Free trade would soon have its armies, dispatched to break down "national one-sidedness" in the Opium Wars and many further conflicts; but literary cosmopolitanism advanced through translators and a small number of writers who, like Byron, Scott, Goethe, and Hugo, qualified as international superstars. Whereas Goethe, Marx, and Engels spoke prophetically of the pooling of the different literary heritages in a single world literature to come, the disparity between national literary traditions and the awareness of world literature was uppermost for Georg Brandes in 1899: "A few writers out of many thousands, a few works from hundreds of thousands, are part of world literature. Everyone has the names of such writers and works on the tip of the tongue: the *Divine Comedy* belongs not to Italy alone, nor *Don Quixote* to Spain" (62). Differences of language and taste, the unavailability of translations, and the limits on any reader's attention mean that world literature will always be a selective category.

David Damrosch proposes, sensibly, that "works become world literature by being received into the space of a foreign culture" (282) — in this case, by being received into ours. Such reception makes a difference. For thirty or forty years now, *The Story of the Stone* has been read widely outside China through its English, French, German, and other translations. Translation creates expectations different from those when the work is read by China specialists or in a context framed by the milieu in which it originated: the work comes before the public as literature, as something inherently worth reading. Presenting it as historical or cultural source material implies no such claim. When the novel appears on the reading list of an undergraduate class or when someone recommends it to a friend, it enters a new category. No longer a member of the set that includes *The Story of the Western Wing*, *The Outlaws of the Marsh*, *The Journey to the West*, and *The Peony Pavilion* and no longer a member of the set that includes *Three Ways of Thought in Ancient China*, *The Legal Code of the Qing Empire*, and *China's Examination Hell*, it now keeps company with *The Tale of Genji*, *Old Goriot*, *The Magic Mountain*, and *Things Fall Apart*.

To incorporate *Stone* into such a series is to assert that it has comparable virtues. The reader is invited to evaluate it for style, characters, plot, conceptual depth, astuteness of design, vividness of description, verisimilitude, and meaning — as if it were no embarrassment to apply universal standards of judgment. (Indeed the greatest compliment one can offer a work of literature is to read it without special context.) Interpretation creates bases for comparison. When David Hawkes, in his introductory comments to volume 1 of *Stone*, outlines the bases of a Freudian reading ("Bao-yu is an almost clinical picture of the kind of child whom old ladies refer to in lowered voices as 'a very strange little boy'" (32), the gesture is double: it advances a claim both for the importance of the novel (that it anticipated Freud; that it thereby resembles other masterworks, by Sophocles, Shakespeare, Leonardo da Vinci; that it offers insights into universal human nature) and for the importance of the interpretation (that Freudian theory applies not only to Western literary works but also to works from alien times and places). Hawkes's other main contribution to the interpretation of the novel, his essay "*The Story of the Stone*: A Symbolist Novel," similarly extends the reach of "symbolism," making it no longer an artistic movement centered in 1880s Paris but a general characterization of literary works from any time and place, even as the term prepares the reader for claims about the novel's design and meaning. To read the work as disguised autobiography puts it in another series: Cao Xueqin now rubs shoulders with Marcel Proust and Richard Wright. To read it as the portrait of an age classes it with *The Human Comedy* and *A Dance to the Music of Time*. To see it as microcosmic allegory brings in epics: *The Divine Comedy*, *The Faerie Queen*, and *Paradise Lost* (see Andrew Plaks's *Archetype and Allegory in* The Dream of the Red Chamber, a pioneering comparative analysis with structuralist features). World literature, as an act of judgment and classification tells us what company the novel keeps — or, to be more precise, it creates that company and leaves us to draw the consequences.

The very use of the word *novel* to describe *Stone* puts us on the path of judgment and classification. Like *world literature*, *novel* too is a culturally specific term and can have misleading implications. At present, in the English-speaking world, only specialists know much more about *xiaoshuo* 小說 and *monogatari* 物語 than the fact that both terms are often translated as "novel." But in English, *novel* suggests a form that rose out of journalism, commerce, and relaxed political control (see Watt). Most European languages use a term cognate to our *romance*, a word with specific and quite different histories and connotations, giving long-form fiction a genealogy that goes back to medieval tales of love and chivalry. One illusion to which scholars of European literature are prone is the idea that the novel, emerging out of various parallel developments in the languages of Europe between 1600 and 1700, spreads over the next few centuries to become the dominant literary form in all quarters of the world, the characteristic literary form of modernity. To this model one must oppose the fact of fiction's polygenesis: not only do *xiaoshuo* and *monogatari*, to take only the Chinese and Japanese versions of long fiction, arise many centuries before the putative rise of the novel in Europe, but they also first appear in competition with quite different complexes of genres, styles, and formats (history writing, poetry, scholarly commentary, anthologies). Still other civilizations have their versions of long fiction. The comparative study of the novel must look on all these rivals with an open mind, and beyond them consider folktales, epics, sagas, mythology, and even riddles: world literature properly understood includes these forms and more. *The Story of the Stone*, with its inveterate love of mimicry, contains in itself the makings of a world history of literature from a Chinese point of origin, incorporating dozens of genres and modes. Therefore this work is an excellent place to begin questioning the story of European literary expansion and eventual global dominance.

Since the 1980s, debates about the canon have redrawn the boundaries of world literature. Students have heard about the obsolescence of "dead white males." They are aware that membership in a canon does not follow from a pure judgment of quality and that judgments are based on criteria that are themselves the objects of debate in a culture. Places in the canon are open for competition, and in the United States, where multiculturalism is inflected by the politics of ethnicity and identity, some of the interest in *Stone* doubtless derives from the notion that it is the Chinese contender for the title of major work of world literature. Under multiculturalism, novels "represent": they have constituencies, though ones undreamt of by their authors.

There is no need to be wholly cynical about multiculturalism: it can also create and guide curiosity. Students may open *Stone* seeking to learn, or to confirm what they know, about China. They need to know that it depicts not China per se or China in the light of eternity but a highly specific social stratum and time in China, heightened and colored for the purposes of art. Once this caveat about taking works of fiction too literally is made, the novel can be explored as an "encyclopedia of feudal culture" (to quote a description by one of its Chinese critics; for the phrase, see Mao Zedong, "Guanyu zhexue" 556–67; He Jianxun 113). Students may already conceive of Chinese culture as hierarchical and organized around a strong family; *Stone* gives them all they need to see how conflicts in such a society emerge and play out. They may know something about Confucianism, Buddhism, or Taoism: characters in the novel, and the work's overall thematic structure, concretize these ways of life. It is best for teachers not to be specialists in this material (if they are, there may be advantages to keeping their light under a bushel). That the world literature course is not set up as a course in history, ethnography, or comparative ethics allows the background information to be treated as secondary; exploration of narrative, character, dialogue, authorial voice, interrelations of media, and similar issues can and should be primary. Goethe enjoyed *Yu Jiao Li* too much to take it as nothing more than a report on Chinese customs, and his example is worth emulating.

Always a compromise between the vastness of the subject and the limited time available, the world literature course will never include all five volumes of the Hawkes and Minford *Stone*. For years, classroom needs were served by the one-volume abridged version by C. C. Wang (Cao and Gao, *Dream* [1958]), but little can be learned from it about the work's artistic properties. A reasonable compromise is to teach volume 1 of the Hawkes translation. It does not bring the story to its end—but, as some may argue, neither does the whole five-volume set. Volume 1 only begins to sketch the relations among Bao-yu, Dai-yu, and Bao-chai, which are amply and delicately chronicled in the middle volumes. Many episodes that take place outside the Jia family compound and introduce a grittier and wider perspective on the society of the time come later. But volume 1 introduces the fantastic frame story and shows it repeatedly invading the realism of the inner story; it presents the main members of the Jia family; it includes the set-piece accounts of Ke-qing's death and burial and thus motivates the building of the garden. It sets out the social critique implicit in the depiction of Jia Yu-cun, the ambiguity in the role of Wang Xi-feng (whom American students usually find delightful rather than coarse and overreaching), and above all the Bao-yu problem. Students who read only as far as chapter 18 will be well embarked on the novel, though many surprises are in store for them. When we teach this novel well, curiosity will drive students to follow up with volumes 2 to 5 over the summer vacation—and to remember *The Story of the Stone* not as an example of Chinese or Asian fiction but as an absorbing and captivating part of their lifetime literary experience.

NOTE

[1] Also known as *Shuangmei qiyuan* (雙美奇緣 "The Unusual Marriage of a Pair of Beauties"), one of the best known and most representative works in the "talented scholar and beautiful maiden" genre mocked by the Stone in chapter 1 (49).

# NOTES ON CONTRIBUTORS

**Maram Epstein** is associate professor of Chinese and East Asian languages and literatures at the University of Oregon. She is the author of *Competing Discourses: Orthodoxy, Authenticity, and Engendered Meanings in Late-Imperial Chinese Fiction*.

**Mary Ellen Friends** teaches Asian history and culture at Deerfield Academy.

**Charlotte Furth** is professor of history emerita at the University of Southern California. She is the author of *A Flourishing Yin: Gender in China's Medical History, 960–1665*.

**Martin Huang** is professor of East Asian languages and literature at the University of California, Irvine. He is the editor of *Male Friendship in Ming China* and the author of *Negotiating Masculinities in Late Imperial China*.

**Ling Hon Lam** is assistant professor of East Asian studies at Vanderbilt University. His research interests are Ming-Qing drama and fiction, women's writing, sex and gender, history of sentiments, nineteenth- and twentieth-century media culture, and critical theories. His forthcoming book is titled "From Dreamscapes to Theatricality: The Spatiality of Emotion in Early Modern China."

**Dore J. Levy** is professor of comparative literature and East Asian studies at Brown University. She is the author of *Chinese Narrative Poetry: The Late Han through T'ang Dynasties* and *Ideal and Actual in* The Story of the Stone.

**Tina Lu** is professor of Chinese literature at Yale University. She is the author of *Persons, Roles, and Minds: Identity in* Peony Pavilion *and* Peach Blossom Fan *and* Accidental Incest, Filial Cannibalism, and Other Peculiar Encounters in Late Imperial Literature.

**Christopher Lupke** is associate professor of Chinese at Washington State University. He has edited *The Magnitude of Ming: Command, Allotment, and Fate in Chinese Culture* and *New Perspectives on Contemporary Chinese Poetry*.

**Keith McMahon** is professor in the Department of East Asian Languages and Cultures at the University of Kansas. He is the author of *Misers, Shrews, and Polygamists: Sexuality and Male-Female Relations in Eighteenth-Century Chinese Fiction*, *The Fall of the God of Money: Opium Smoking in Nineteenth-Century China*, and *Polygamy and Sublime Passion: Sexuality in China on the Verge of Modernity*.

**Tobie Meyer-Fong** is associate professor of history at Johns Hopkins University. She is the author of *Building Culture in Early Qing Yangzhou* and has recently finished a book about the cultural and social impact of the Taiping Rebellion. She is a coeditor of the journal *Late Imperial China*.

**James Millward** is professor of history at Georgetown University. He is the author of *The Silk Road: A Very Short Introduction*; *Eurasian Crossroads: A History of Xinjiang*; and *Beyond the Pass: Economy, Ethnicity, and Empire in Qing Central Asia, 1759–1864*. He coedited *New Qing Imperial History: The Manchu Summer Palace at Chengde*.

**John Minford** is professor and head of the Asian Studies China Centre at the Australian National University. With David Hawkes he translated *The Story of the Stone*. He has also translated Sun Zi's *The Art of War* and Pu Songling's *Strange Tales from a Chinese Studio*.

**Susan Naquin** is professor of history at Princeton University. She is the author of *Peking: Temples and City Life, 1400–1900* and the coauthor of *Chinese Society in the Eighteenth Century*.

**Ni Yibin** taught English linguistics in the Department of English and Chinese art and culture in the University Scholars Program, National University of Singapore. He is the author of *Symbols, Art, and Language from the Land of the Dragon: The Cultural History of a Hundred Chinese Characters*.

**Evelyn S. Rawski** is university professor at the University of Pittsburgh. She is the author of *The Last Emperors: A Social History of Qing Imperial Institutions* and coauthor of *Chinese Society in the Eighteenth Century*.

**Haun Saussy** is university professor in comparative literature at the University of Chicago. He is the author of *The Problem of a Chinese Aesthetic* and *Great Walls of Discourse and Other Adventures in Cultural China* and coeditor of *Chinese Women Poets: An Anthology of Poetry and Criticism* (with Kang-i Sun Chang) and of *Sinographies* (with Eric Hayot and Steve Yao).

**Andrew Schonebaum** is assistant professor of Chinese literature at the University of Maryland. He has just finished a book titled "Novel Medicine: The Curative Properties of Chinese Fiction."

**Mary Scott** is professor in the Department of Humanities at San Francisco State University. She is working on a translation of *Pin hua bao jian*, a novel about men who play female roles in nineteenth-century Beijing theater.

**Meir Shahar** is associate professor of Chinese studies at Tel Aviv University. He is the author of *Crazy Ji: Chinese Religion and Popular Literature* and *The Shaolin Monastery: History, Religion, and the Chinese Martial Arts*.

**Shang Wei** is Du Family Professor of Chinese Culture at Columbia University. He is the author of *Rulin waishi and Cultural Transformation in Late Imperial China* and a contributor to *The Cambridge History of Chinese Literature*.

**Matthew H. Sommer** is associate professor of Chinese history at Stanford University. He is the author of *Sex, Law, and Society in Late Imperial China*. His second book, close to completion, is *Polyandry and Wife Selling in Qing Dynasty China: Survival Strategies and Judicial Interventions*.

**Xiaojue Wang** is assistant professor of Chinese literature and culture at the University of Pennsylvania. She is currently working on a book titled "Modernity with a Cold War Face: Reimagining the Nation in Chinese Literature across the 1949 Divide."

**I-Hsien Wu** is assistant professor of Chinese language and literature at the City College of New York. Her research interests are Ming-Qing fiction and drama, modern Chinese literature, Chinese music theory, and modern ethnomusicology. She is working on a book-length study on *The Story of the Stone*, titled "The Journey of the *Stone*: Rites of Passage and Literary Inquiry in *Dream of the Red Chamber*."

**Xueping Zhong** is professor of Chinese literature and culture at Tufts University. She is the author of *Masculinity Besieged? Issues of Modernity and Male Subjectivity in Chinese Literature of the Late Twentieth Century* and *Mainstream Culture Refocused: Television Drama, Society, and the Production of Meaning in Reform-Era China*.

# WORKS CITED

In general, printed books in the late imperial period consisted of a number of separately bound volumes (*ce* 冊), but books had their own internal divisions, *juan* 卷, which often did not correspond with their physical divisions. Books in the Ming and Qing were commonly divided into a certain number of *juan*, a term that connotes "roll" and derives from the time when a roll of stitched-together strips of bamboo was the standard form for books. *Juan* is most often rendered into English as "fascicle," "scroll," "chapter," or "volume," which is misleading, as there were often multiple *juan* in one physically bound "book."

## *Print Editions of* The Story of the Stone

Cao Xueqin. *Zengping buzhu quantu Shitou ji* 增評補註全圖石頭記 [*The Story of the Stone*, Illustrated Throughout, Supplemented with Portraits, and Newly Annotated]. N.p., 1886.

BJPP - Cao Xueqin and Gao E. *Bajia pingpi Hongloumeng* 八家評批紅樓夢 [*The Story of the Stone*, with Comments by Eight Commentators]. Ed. Feng Qiyong 馮其庸 et al. Beijing: Wenhua Yishu, 1991.

HLM - Cao Xueqin 曹雪芹 and Gao E 高鶚. *Honglou meng* 紅樓夢 [*Dream of the Red Chamber*]. Ed. Zhongguo yishu yanjiuyuan "Honglou meng" yanjiu suo. 2 vols. Beijing: Renmin Wenxue, 2002.

Cao Xueqin and Gao E. *Hongloumeng* 紅樓夢. 4 vols. Beijing: Renmin Wenxue, 1972.

SJPB - Cao Xueqin and Gao E. *Honglou meng sanjia pingben* 紅樓夢三家評本 [*Dream of the Red Chamber*, with Annotations by Three Commentators]. Annotated by Huhua zhuren 護花主人 [Wang Xilian 王希廉], Damou shanmin 大某山民 [Yao Xie 姚燮], and Taiping xianren 太平閒人 [Zhang Xinzhi 張新之]. 4 vols. Shanghai: Guji, 1988.

Cao Xueqin and Gao E. *Jingjiao quantu qianyin pingzhu Jin yu yuan* 精校全圖鉛印評註金玉緣 [The Affinity of Gold and Jade, Finely Collated, Fully Illustrated, Lead Type, Annotated, and Commented]. Taipei: Guangwen, 1991.

Cao Xueqin and Gao E. *Zeng ping bu xiang quan tu Jin yu yuan* 增評補像全圖金玉緣 1884. [The Affinity of Gold and Jade, Fully Illustrated, Corrected, with Added Commentary]. 1st ed. Beijing: Beijing tu shu guan, 2002.

## *Translations of* The Story of the Stone

Cao Xueqin. "A Burial Mound for Flowers." Trans. H. C. Chang. *Chinese Literature: Popular Fiction and Drama*. Ed. Chang. Edinburgh: Edinburgh UP, 1973. 383–404. Print. Excerpts from ch. 23.

———. *Hung lou meng; or, The Dream of the Red Chamber: A Chinese Novel*. Trans. H. Bencraft Joly. Hong Kong: Kelly, 1892. Print. Chs. 1–56.

────. "*Red Chamber Dream.*" *From the Fourteenth Century to the Present Day.* Trans. and ed. Cyril Birch. New York: Grove, 1972. 201–58. Print. Vol. 2 of *Anthology of Chinese Literature.* Excerpts from chs. 63–69.

Cao Xueqin 曹雪芹 and Gao E 高鶚. "A Burial Mound for Flowers" and "One Smear Wang." *Dream of Red Towers.* Trans. Victor H. Mair. *The Columbia Anthology of Traditional Chinese Literature.* Ed. Mair. New York: Columbia UP, 1994. 1020–35. Print. Excerpts from chs. 23 and 80.

────. *A Dream of Red Mansions.* Trans. Gladys Yang and Yang Hsien-yi [Yang Xianyi]. 4 vols. Beijing: Foreign Langs., 1978–80. Print.

────. *A Dream of Red Mansions: An Abridged Edition.* Trans. Gladys Yang and Yang Hsien-yi. Boston: Cheng, 1999. Print.

────. *Dream of the Red Chamber.* Trans. and ed. C. C. Wang. New York: Twayne, 1958. Print.

────. *Red Chamber Dream.* Trans. B. S. Bonsall. U of Hong Kong Libs., n.d. Web. 19 Feb. 2011.

────. *The Story of the Stone.* Trans. David Hawkes and John Minford. 5 vols. Harmondsworth: Penguin, 1973–82. Print.

## *Criticism and Resources*

A Ying 阿英, ed. *Hongloumeng xiqu ji* 紅樓夢戲曲集 [A Collection of the Plays Adapted from *Dream of the Red Chamber*]. Beijing: Zhonghua, 1978. Print.

Achebe, Chinua. "Teaching *Things Fall Apart.*" *Approaches to Teaching Achebe's* Things Fall Apart. Ed. Bernth Lindfors. New York: MLA, 1991. 20–24. Print.

Adorno, Theodor, and Hanns Eisler. *Composing for the Films.* London: Continuum, 2007. Print.

Ba Jin 巴金. *Jia* 家 [Family]. Beijing: Renmin Wenxue, 1986. Print.

Berliner, Nancy, ed. *Juanqinzhai in the Qianlong Garden, the Forbidden City, Beijing.* London: Scala, 2008. Print.

Berry, Chris, ed. *Perspectives on Chinese Cinema.* London: BFI, 1991. Print.

Birch, Cyril, ed. *Anthology of Chinese Literature: From the Fourteenth Century to the Present Day.* New York: Grove, 1972. Print.

────. "Tribute to David." *A Birthday Book for Brother Stone.* Ed. John Minford. Hong Kong: Chinese UP, 2003. 8. Print.

Bonner, Joey. *Wang Kuo-wei: An Intellectual Biography.* Cambridge: Harvard UP, 1986. Print.

Brandes, Georg. "World Literature." Damrosch, Melas, and Buthelezi 61–66.

Bray, Francesca. *Technology and Gender: Fabrics of Power in Late Imperial China.* Berkeley: U of California P, 1997. Print.

Brokaw, Cynthia. *Commerce in Culture: The Sibao Book Trade in the Qing and Republican Periods.* Cambridge: Harvard UP, 2007. Print.

────. Introduction. Brokaw and Chow 3–54.

Brokaw, Cynthia J., and Kai-Wing Chow, eds. *Printing and Book Culture in Late Imperial China.* Berkeley: U of California P, 2005. Print.

Brook, Timothy. "Censorship in Eighteenth-Century China: A View from the Book Trade." *Canadian Journal of History* 23.2 (1988): 177–96. Print.

Burkus-Chasson, Anne. "Visual Hermeneutics and the Act of Turning the Leaf: A Genealogy of Liu Yuan's *Lingyan ge*." Brokaw and Chow 371–416.

Cai Yuanpei 蔡元培. "Shitou ji suoyin" 石頭記索引 [Key to *Story of the Stone*]. Yisu, *Hongloumeng juan* 319–23.

Camper, Fred. "Sound and Silence in Narrative and Nonnarrative Cinema." *Film Sound: Theory and Practice*. Ed. Elisabeth Weis and John Belton. New York: Columbia UP, 1985. 369–82. Print.

Cao Hongbei 曹紅蓓. "Yueju dianying: Diandao zhongsheng 'xiao *Honglou*'" 越劇電影: 顛倒眾生 "小紅樓" [Yue Opera Film: The Little "Red Chamber" That Infatuated the Audience]. *Zhongguo xinwen zhoukan* 16 Oct. 2006: 26–27. Print.

Carlitz, Katherine. "Desire, Danger, and the Body: Stories of Women's Virtue in Late Ming China." Gilmartin, Hershatter, Rofel, and White 101–24.

Cen Fan 岑範. Interview. "Fang *Huangshan lei*, *Qunying hui*, *Honglou meng* deng xiqu yingpian de daoyan Cen Fan" 訪 "荒山淚" "群英會," "紅樓夢" 等戲曲影片 的導演岑範 [Interview with Cen Fan, the Director of *Huangshan lei*, *Qunying hui*, and *Honglou meng*]. *Wutai yu yingmo zhi jian: Xiqu dianying de huigu yu jiangshu* 舞台與影片之間: 戲曲電影的回顧與講述 [Between Stage and Screen: Accounts of Opera Films in Retrospect]. Ed. Zhao Jingbo 趙景勃 and Ran Changjian 冉常建. Beijing: Zhongguo Wenlian, 2007. 48–68. Print.

Chan, Bing C. *The Authorship of* The Dream of the Red Chamber *Based on a Computerized Statistical Study of Its Vocabulary*. Hong Kong: Joint, 1986. Print.

Chan Hok-lam. *Control of Publishing in China, Past and Present*. Canberra: Australian Nat. U, 1983. Print.

Chan Oi-sum, Connie. "*The Story of the Stone*'s Journey to the West: A Study in Chinese-English Translation History." MA thesis. Hong Kong Polytechnic U, 2001. Print.

Chandler, James. "Moving Accidents: The Emergence of Sentimental Probability." *The Age of Cultural Revolutions: Britain and France, 1750–1820*. Ed. Colin Jones and Dror Wahrman. Berkeley: U of California P, 2002. 137–70. Print.

Chang, Eileen 張愛玲. "A Chronicle of Changing Clothes." *Written on Water*. Trans. Andrew F. Jones. New York: Columbia UP, 2005. 65–78. Print.

———. "Gengyi ji" 更衣記 [Changing Clothes]. *Liuyan* 流言 [Written on Water]. Taipei: Huangguan, 1991. 67–76. Print.

———. "The Golden Cangue." *Modern Chinese Stories and Novellas, 1919–1949*. Ed. Joesph Lau et al. New York: Columbia UP, 1981. 530–59. Print.

———. *Honglou mengyan* 紅樓夢魘 [The Nightmare of the Red Chamber]. Taipei: Huangguan, 1976. Print.

———. "Huali yuan" 華麗緣 [A Splendid Romance]. *Yuyun* 餘韻 [Aftersound]. Taipei: Crown, 1987. 97–111. Print.

———. *Jinsuo ji* 金鎖記 [The Golden Cangue]. Hong Kong: Nü shen, 1983. Print.

———. Preface. *Chuanqi* 傳奇 [Romance]. 2nd ed. E. Chang, *Zhang* 6.

———. *The Rice-Sprout Song*. Berkeley: U of California P, 1998. Print.

———. "Yi Hu Shizhi" 憶胡適之 [Remembering Hu Shi]. *Zhang kan* 張看 [Viewed by Eileen Chang]. Taipei: Huangguan, 1991. 141–54. Print.

———. *Zhang Ailing quanji* 張愛玲全集 [Complete Works of Eileen Chang]. Vol. 5. Taipei: Huangguan, 1996. Print.

Chang, H. C. *Chinese Literature: Popular Fiction and Drama*. Edinburgh: Clark, 1973. Print.

Che Xilun 車錫倫. "Qing Tongzhi Jiangsu chajin 'xiaoshuo changben pian mu' kaoshu" 清同治江蘇查禁小説唱本片目攷述 [A Study of the Lists of Prohibited Fiction and Songbooks Made by the Administration of Jiangsu Province in the Tongzhi Reign]. *Su wenxue congkao* 俗文學叢攷 [Studies of Popular Literature]. Taipei: Xuehai, 1995. 149–82. Print.

Chen Diexian 陳蝶仙. "The Koto Story" [*Zhenglou ji* 箏樓記]. Chen Diexian, *Money Demon* 279–84.

———. *Leizhu yuan* 涙珠緣 [Destiny of Tears]. Hangzhou: Daguanbao guan, 1900. Print.

———. *The Money Demon* [*Huangjin sui* 黃金祟]. Trans. Patrick Hanan. Honolulu: U of Hawai'i P, 1999. Print.

———. *Ta zhi xiaoshi* 他之小史 [A Short Account of Him]. *Nüzi shijie*. Print.

Chen Dingxiu 陳定秀 et al. "*Honglou meng* benshi" 紅樓夢本事 [Synopsis of *The Red Chamber Dream*]. *Honglou meng zhuanhao* 紅樓夢專號 [Spec. issue on *The Red Chamber Dream*]. Ed. Gan Yazi 甘亞子. Shanghai: Peacock Motion Picture, 1927. 1–12. Print.

Ch'ên, H. S., and G. N. Kates. *Prince Kung's Palace and Its Adjoining Garden in Peking*. Beijing: Vetch, 1940. Print.

Chen Qingwei 陳清偉. *Xianggang dianying gongye jiegou ji shichang fengshi* 香港電影工業結構及市場分析 [Structure and Marketing Analysis of the Hong Kong Film Industry]. Hong Kong: Dianying Shuanzhoukan, 2000. Print.

Chen Qitai 陳其泰. *Tonghuafengge ping Honglou meng jilu* 桐花鳳閣評紅樓夢輯 [Comments Transcribed from *The Story of the Stone* Commented by the Master of the Mangrove Phoenix Studio]. Ed. Liu Caonan 刘操南. Tianjin: Tianjin Renmin, 1981. Print.

Chen Qiyuan 陳其元. *Yongxian zhai biji* 庸閒齋筆記 [Miscellaneous Notes of the Idle Studio]. Beijing: Zhonghua, 1989. Print.

Chen Sen 陳森. *Pinhua baojian* 品花寶鑑 [A Precious Mirror for Judging Flowers]. Taipei: Guangya chuban gongsi, 1984. Print.

Chen Shaohai 陳少海. *Honglou fumeng* 紅樓復夢 [Return to *Dream of the Red Chamber*]. Beijing: Beijing Daxue, 1988. Print.

Chen Xuanyou 陳玄祐. "The Departed Spirit." *From Antiquity to the Tang Dynasty*. Ed. John Minford and Joseph S. M. Lau. New York: Columbia UP, 2000. 1032–34. Print. Vol. 1 of *Classical Chinese Literature*.

Chen Yinque 陳寅恪. "Qinghua daxue Wang Guantang xiansheng jinian beiming" 清華大學王觀堂先生紀念碑銘 [Inscription on the Monument to Mr. Wang Guantang at Tsinghua University]. *Chen Yinque wenji* 陳寅恪文集 [Selected Works of Chen Yinque]. Vol. 3. Shanghai: Shanghai guji, 1980. 218. Print.

Chen Yiyuan 陳益源. "Ding Richang de keshu yu jinshu" 丁日昌的刻書與禁書 [Ding Richang's Projects of Book Publication and Prohibition]. Chen Yiyuan, *Gudai* 117–137.

———. "Ding Richang, Qi Rushan yu *Hongloumeng*" 丁日昌, 齊如山與紅樓夢 [Ding Richang, Qi Rushan, and *Dream of the Red Chamber*]. Chen Yiyuan, *Gudai* 108–16.

———, ed. *Gudai xiaoshuo shulun* 古代小說述論 [On Premodern Chinese Fiction]. Beijing: Xianzhuang, 1999. Print.

Chen Yong 陳鏞. "Chusanxuan congtan" 散軒叢談 [Collected Essays of Chusanxuan]. Yisu, *Hongloumeng juan* 349–50.

Cheng Weiyuan 程偉元. "*Honglou meng* xu" 紅樓夢序 [Preface to *Honglou meng*]. Yisu, *Hongloumeng juan* 31.

*Chengjiaben Hongloumeng* 程甲本紅樓夢 [The Cheng jia Edition of *Dream of the Red Chamber*]. Beijing: Shumu wenxian, 1992. Print.

Chou, Ju-hsi, ed. *Art at the Close of China's Empire*. Tempe: Arizona State U, 1998. Print.

Clark, Paul. *Chinese Cinema: Culture and Politics since 1949*. Cambridge: Cambridge UP, 1987. Print.

Clunas, Craig. *Superfluous Things: Material Culture and Social Status in Early Modern China*. Honolulu: U of Hawai'i P, 2004. Print.

Cohen, Myron L., ed. *Asia: Case Studies for the Social Sciences: A Guide for Teaching*. New York: Sharpe, 1992. Print.

Confucius. *The Analects*. Trans. D. C. Lau. Harmondsworth: Penguin, 1979. Print.

Dale, Corinne H., ed. *Chinese Aesthetics and Literature: A Reader*. Albany: State U of New York P, 2004. Print.

Damrosch, David. *What Is World Literature?* Princeton: Princeton UP, 2003. Print.

Damrosch, David, et al. eds. *The Longman Anthology of World Literature*. 6 vols. 2nd ed. New York: Pearson, 2008. Print.

Damrosch, David, Natalie Melas, and Mbongiseni Buthelezi, eds. *The Princeton Sourcebook in Comparative Literature: From the European Enlightenment to the Global Present*. Princeton: Princeton UP, 2009. Print.

Davis, Dick. Introduction. *The Rubaiyat of Omar Khayyam*. Trans. Edward Fitzgerald. London: Penguin, 1989. 1–41. Print. Penguin Poetry Lib.

Davis, Paul, et al., eds. *The Bedford Anthology of World Literature*. 6 vols. New York: Bedford–St. Martin's, 2003. Print.

de Bary, William Theodore. "Individualism and Humanitarianism in Late Ming Thought." *Self and Society in Ming Thought*. Ed. de Bary. New York: Columbia UP, 1970. 145–247. Print.

de Bary, William Theodore, et al., eds. *Sources of Chinese Tradition*. 2 vols. 2nd ed. New York: Columbia UP, 2000–01. Print.

Deng Yunxiang 鄧雲鄉. *Honglou fengsu tan* 紅樓風俗譚 [On Social and Cultural Life in *Dream of the Red Chamber*]. Beijing: Zhonghua, 1987. Print.

Deng Zhicheng 鄧之誠. *Gudong suoji* 古董瑣記 [Miscellaneous Notes on the Past]. Shanghai: Saoye Shanfang, 1926. Print.

Dikötter, Frank. *Exotic Commodities: Modern Objects and Everyday Life in China*. New York: Columbia UP, 2006. Print.

Ding Yaokang 丁耀亢. *Xu Jin ping mei* 續金瓶梅. Taipei: Tianyi, 1975. Print.

"Diren patan 'enyuan,' jing jinying 'Honglou meng'" 敵人怕談 "恩怨," 竟禁映 "紅樓夢" [The Enemy, Afraid of Mentioning "Animosity," Bans the Screening of *The Dream of the Red Chamber*]. *Jinri dianying* 今日電影 10 Dec. 1944: 3. Print.

*Doctor Strangelove; or, How I Learned to Stop Worrying and Love the Bomb*. Dir. Stanley Kubrick. Columbia Pictures, 1964. Film.

Dong Yue 董說. *A Tower of Myriad Mirrors* [*Xiyou bu* 西遊補]. Trans. Shuen-fu Lin and Larry J. Schultz. Ann Arbor: Center for Chinese Studies, U of Michigan P, 2000. Print.

*The Dream of the Red Chamber*. Dir. Lin Han-hsiang. Perf. Brigitte Lin. Celestial (IVL), 1977. DVD.

Dream of the Red Chamber: *An Experience in Traditional Chinese Aesthetics: Paintings by An Ho and Furniture by Henry Lautz*. Oglethorpe U Museum of Art, n.d. Web. 14 Dec. 2007.

Du Zhijun 杜志軍. "Zaoqi *Honglou meng* dianying yanjiu de jinliang: *Honglou meng tekan* de faxian ji qi yiyi" 早期紅樓夢電影研究的津梁: 紅樓夢特刊的發現及其意義 [Toward the Study of Early Films of *The Dream of the Red Chamber*: The Discovery of *Special Issue on The Dream of the Red Chamber* and Its Significance]. *Honglou meng xuekan* 紅樓夢學刊 July 2003: 139–52. Print.

Duara, Prasenjit. "The Discourse of Civilization and Pan-Asianism." *Journal of World History* 12.1 (2001): 99–130. Print.

Dudbridge, Glen. *Legend of Miaoshan*. Rev. ed. Oxford: Oxford UP, 2004. Print.

Eagleton, Terry. *The English Novel: An Introduction*. Oxford: Blackwell, 2005. Print.

Eckermann, Johann Peter. *Gespräche mit Goethe in den letzten Jahren seines Lebens*. Leipzig: Brockhaus, 1885. *Internet Archive*. Web. 6 Sept. 2011. Entry 31 Jan. 1827.

Edwards, Louise P. *Men and Women in Qing China: Gender in* The Red Chamber Dream. Honolulu: U of Hawai'i P, 2001. Print.

———. "New *Hongxue* and the 'Birth of the Author': Yu Pingbo's 'On Qin Keqing's Death.'" *Chinese Literature: Essays, Articles, Reviews* Dec. 2001: 31–54. Print.

Eifring, Halvor. "The Psychology of Love in *Story of the Stone*." *Love and Emotions in Traditional Chinese Literature*. Ed. Eifring. Leiden: Brill, 2004. 271–324. Print.

Elliott, Mark C. *The Manchu Way: The Eight Banners and Ethnic Identity in Late Imperial China*. Stanford: Stanford UP, 2001. Print.

Elvin, Mark. "Female Virtue and the State in China." *Past and Present* 104.1 (1984): 111–52. Print.

Embree, Ainslie T., and Carol Gluck, eds. *Asia in Western and World History: A Guide for Teaching*. New York: Columbia UP, 1997. Print.

Epstein, Maram. *Competing Discourses: Orthodoxy, Authenticity, and Gender in Late Imperial Chinese Fiction*. Cambridge: Harvard U Asia Center, 2001. Print.

Erickson, Britta. "Zhou Xian's Fabulous Construct *The Thatched Cottage of Fan Lake*." Chou 67–93.

Fadiman, Anne. *The Spirit Catches You and You Fall Down*. New York: Farrar, 1997. Print.

Fan Shengyu 范聖宇. *Honglou meng guankui yingyi, yuyan yu wenhua* 紅樓夢管窺: 英譯, 語言與文化 [Looking into *Honglou meng*: English Translations, Language, and Culture]. Beijing: Zhongguo Shehui Kexue, 2004. Print.

Feng Qiyong 馮其庸 and Li Xifan 李希凡, eds. *Hongloumeng da cidian* 紅樓夢大辭典 [The Encyclopedia of *Dream of the Red Chamber*]. Beijing: Wenhua Yishu, 1990. Print.

Feng Qiyong 馮其庸, et al., eds. *Bajia pingpi Honglou meng* 八家評批紅樓夢 [*The Story of the Stone* with Comments by Eight Commentators]. Beijing: Wenhua Yishu, 1991. Print.

Feuerwerker, Albert. "Chinese Economic History in Comparative Perspective." Ropp, *Heritage* 224–41.

*Flowers of Shanghai*. Dir. Hsiao-hsien Hou. 3H Productions, 1998. Film.

Fu, Poshek. *Between Shanghai and Hong Kong: The Politics of Chinese Cinemas*. Stanford: Stanford UP, 2003. Print.

Furth, Charlotte. "Blood, Body, and Gender: Medical Images of the Female Condition in China, 1600–1850." *Chinese Science* 7–8 (1986–87): 43–66. Print.

———. "Concepts of Pregnancy, Childbirth, and Infancy in Ch'ing Dynasty China." *Journal of Asian Studies* Feb. 1987: 7–35. Print.

———. *A Flourishing Yin: Gender in China's Medical History, 960–1665*. Berkeley: U of California P, 1999. Print.

Gai Qi 改琦. *Hongloumeng tu yong* 紅樓夢圖詠 [Pictures of and Poems on *Dream of the Red Chamber*]. Shijiazhuang: Hebei Meishu, 1996. Print.

Gao Xiaojian 高小健. *Zhongguo xiqu dianying shi* 中國戲曲電影史 [History of Chinese Opera Film]. Beijing: Wenhua Yishu, 2005. Print.

Gilmartin, Christina K., Gail Hershatter, Lisa Rofel, and Tyrene White, eds. *Engendering China: Women, Culture, and the State*. Cambridge: Harvard UP, 1994. Print. Harvard Contemporary China Ser. 10.

Gimm, Martin. "Manchu Translations of Chinese Novels and Short Stories: An Attempt at an Inventory." *Asia Major* 3rd s 1.2 (1988): 77–114. Print.

Goldstein, Joshua. *Drama Kings: Players and Publics in the Re-creation of Peking Opera, 1870–1937*. Berkeley: U of California P, 2007. Print.

Graham, A. C., trans. *Chuang-tzu: The Inner Chapters*. 1981. London: Unwin, 1986. Print.

The Grateful Dead. "Uncle John's Band." *Workingman's Dead*. Warner Bros. Records, 1970. LP.

Grieder, Jerome. "The Communist Critique of *Hunglou meng*." *Harvard Papers on China* Oct. 1956: 142–68. Print.

Grover-Friedlander, Michal. *Vocal Apparitions: The Attraction of Cinema to Opera*. Princeton: Princeton UP, 2005. Print.

Gu Pingdan 顧平旦, ed. *Daguan yuan yanjiu* 大觀園研究 [Studies on the Grand Prospect Garden]. Beijing: Wenhua Yishu, 1981. Print.

Gu Taiqing 顧太清. *Honglou meng ying* 紅樓夢影 [In the Shadow of *Dream of the Red Chamber*]. Beijing: Beijing Daxue, 1988. Print.

Guan Huashan 關華山. *Hongloumeng zhong de Jianzhu yanjiu* 紅樓夢中的建築研究 [A Study of the Architectures in *Dream of the Red Chamber*]. Taipei: Dayuan Caise Yinshua, 1984. Print.

"Guangrong zhi ye" 光榮之頁 [A Page of Glory]. *Honglou meng: Huaying xinpian tekan* 紅樓夢: 華影新片特刊 [*The Dream of the Red Chamber*: Spec. issue on Zhonghua dianying Company's New Movie]. Shanghai: Zhonghua Dianying Gufeng Youxian, 1944. N. pag. Print.

*Guben Hongloumeng chatu huihua jicheng* 古本紅樓夢插圖繪畫集成 [A Comprehensive Collection of Illustrated *Dream of the Red Chamber*]. 6 vols. Beijing: State Lib., 2001. Print.

Guichuzi 歸鋤子. *Honglou meng bu* 紅樓夢補 [*The Dream of the Red Chamber* Revisited]. Beijing: Beijing Daxue, 1988. Print.

Gunning, Tom. "Weaving a Narrative: Style and Economic Background in Griffith's Biograph Films." *Quarterly Review of Film Studies* 6.1 (1981): 10–25. Print.

Guy, Kent. *The Emperor's Four Treasures: Scholars and the State in the Late Ch'ien-lung Era*. Cambridge: Council on East Asian Studies, Harvard U, 1987. Print.

Haipu zhuren 海圃主人. *Xu Honglou meng xinbian* 續紅樓夢新編 [New Sequel to *Dream of the Red Chamber*]. Beijing: Beijing Daxue, 1990. Print.

Han Bangqing 韓邦慶. *Haishanghua liezhuan* 海上花列傳 [Sing-Song Girls of Shanghai]. Taipei: Heluo tushu, 1980. Print.

———. *Sing-Song Girls of Shanghai*. Trans. Eileen Chang and Eva Hung. New York: Columbia UP, 2005. Print.

Han Shangyi 韓尚義. "Xiqu yingpian de bujing xingshi" 戲曲影片的布景形式 [Forms of the Set in Opera Film]. *Zhongguo dianying* 中國電影 Nov. 1956: 46–48. Print.

Hanan, Patrick. "Sources of the *Chin P'ing Mei*." *Asia Major* ns 10.2 (1963): 23–67. Print.

Hart, Lorenz. "Falling in Love with Love." *Rodgers and Hart: A Musical Anthology*. Milwaukee: Leonard, 1984. 42–44. Print.

Hawkes, David. Rev. of *The Art of Chinese Poetry*, by James J. Y. Liu. *Bulletin of the School of Oriental and African Studies* 26.3 (1963): 672–73. Print.

———. *Classical, Modern, and Humane: Essays in Chinese Literature*. Hong Kong: Chinese UP, 1989. Print.

———. *A Little Primer of Tu Fu*. London: Clarendon, 1967. Print.

———. "*The Story of the Stone*: A Symbolist Novel." Hawkes, *Classical* 57–68.

———. The Story of the Stone: *A Translator's Notebooks*. Ed. Liu Ching-chih. Hong Kong: Centre for Lit. and Trans., Lingnan U, 2000. Print.

Hay, Jonathan. "Painters and Publishing in Late Nineteenth-Century Shanghai." Chou 134–88.

———. *Sensuous Surfaces: The Decorative Object in Early Modern China*. London: Reaktion, 2010. Print.

Hayes, James. "Specialists and Written Materials in the Village World." Johnson, Nathan, and Rawski 75–111.

He Bi 何璧, ed. *Ming He Bi jiaoben bei Xixiang ji* 明何璧校本北西廂記 [The Northern Version of *Western Chamber,* Redacted by He Bi of the Ming]. By Wang Shifu 王實甫. Shanghai: Shanghai guji shudian, 1961. Print.

He Jianxun 何劍熏. "Lun Honglou meng de zhuti sixiang" 論紅樓夢的主題思想 [On the Main Themes of *Honglou meng*]. *Zuojia chubanshe bianji bu* 作家出版社編輯部 [Discussions on the *Honglou meng* Question: An Anthology]. Ed. *Honglou meng* wenti taolun ji 紅樓夢問題討論集. Vol. 2. Shanghai: Guji, 1955. 107–25. Print.

He Siyin 何思穎. Interview. *Honglou yimeng di er ji: Zhuimeng* 紅樓一夢第二集: 追夢 [One Dream in the Red Chamber, Episode 2: In Pursuit of Dream]. China Central Television, 30 Apr. 2007. Web.

He Xishi 何希時. "Mei ju *Dai-yu zanghua* suotan" 梅劇黛玉葬花瑣談 [Trivia about Mei's Drama *Dai-yu Buries Flowers*]. *Jingju tanwang lu sanbian* 京劇談往錄三編 [The Third Installment of Records of Old Anecdotes about Peking Opera]. Ed. Zhongguo renmin zhengzhi xieshang huiyi Beijing shi weiyuanhui Wenshi ziliao weiyuanhui 中國人民政治協商會議北京市委員會文史資料委員會. Beijing: Beijing, 1990. 573–76. Print.

Hegel, Robert. "Niche Marketing for Late Imperial Fiction." Brokaw and Chow 235–66.

———. *Reading Illustrated Fiction in Late Imperial China*. Stanford: Stanford UP, 1998. Print.

Henriot, Christian. *Prostitution and Sexuality in Shanghai: A Social History, 1849–1949*. Trans. Noel Castelino. Cambridge: Cambridge UP, 2001. Print.

Hershatter, Gail. *Dangerous Pleasures: Prostitution and Modernity in Twentieth-Century Shanghai*. Berkeley: U of California P, 1997. Print.

Hightower, James R. Rev. of *The Art of Chinese Poetry*, by James J. Y. Liu. *Journal of Asian Studies* 23.2 (1964): 301–02. Print.

Hinsch, Bret. *Passions of the Cut Sleeve: The Male Homosexual Tradition in China*. Berkeley: U of California P, 1990. Print.

Hong, Junhao. *The Internationalization of Television in China: The Evolution of Ideology, Society, and Media since the Reform*. Santa Barbara: Praeger, 1998. Print.

Hong Zhenkuai 洪振快, ed. *Hongloumeng guhua lu* 紅樓夢古畫錄 [A Catalog of the Paintings on *Dream of the Red Chamber*]. Beijing: Renmin Wenxue, 2007. Print.

*Hongloumeng 87 ban dianshi juben* 紅樓夢 87 版電視劇本 [The Script of the 1987 Version of the *Stone* TV Series]. Ed. Jiang Hesen 蔣和森. Beijing: Zhongguo dianying 中國電影出版社, 1987. Print.

*Hongloumeng banke tulu* 紅樓夢版刻圖錄 [A Collection of the Woodblock Prints of the *Dream of the Red Chamber* Illustrations]. Yangzhou: Guangling Guji Keyinshe, 1999. Print.

*Hongloumeng huabao* 紅樓夢畫報 [*Dream of the Red Chamber* Pictorial]. Hong Kong: King Sum Film, 1962. Print.

Hsia, C. T. Rev. of *Archetype and Allegory* in Dream of the Red Chamber, by Andrew Plaks. *Harvard Journal of Asiatic Studies* June 1979: 190–210. Print.

———. *The Classic Chinese Novel: A Critical Introduction.* New York: Columbia UP, 1968. Print.

———. *A History of Modern Chinese Fiction.* Bloomington: Indiana UP, 1999. Print.

Hu Shi. "*Hongloumeng* kaozheng" 紅樓夢考證 [Textual Research on *Dream of the Red Chamber*]. *Hu Shi wencun* 胡適文存 [Selected Writings of Hu Shi]. Taipei: Yuandong Tushu, 1953. 575–620. Print.

———. Preface. *Haishanghua liezhuan* 海上花列傳序言 [Sing-Song Girls of Shanghai], by Han Bangqing. Taipei: Guangya, 1984. 8. Print.

Hu Wenbin 胡文彬, ed. *Hongloumeng zidishu* 紅樓夢子弟書 [A Collection of the Youth Books of *Dream of the Red Chamber*]. Shenyang: Chunfeng Wenyi, 1983. Print.

———. "Tianlai jingwu xin—liuge daguanyuan moxing ji" 添來景物新—六個大觀園模型記 [Six Models of the Grand Prospect Garden]. *Hunqian mengying Hongloumeng* 魂牽夢縈紅樓夢 [The Lingering Dream of the Red Chamber]. Beijing: Zhongguo, 2000. 240–41. Print.

———. "Zhi yin liude fengliu ji" 只因留得風流跡 [The Traces of the *Dream of the Red Chamber*]. *Hongloumeng yu Beijing* 紅樓夢與北京 [*Dream of the Red Chamber* and Beijing]. Xi'an: Shaanxi Renmin, 2008. 96–98. Print.

Huang Changlin 黃昌麟. *Hongloumeng erbai yong* 紅樓夢二百詠 [Two Hundred Poems on *Dream of the Red Chamber*]. Shizhu Shanfang, 1917. Print.

Huang, Martin W. "Author(ity) and Reader in Traditional Chinese Xiaoshuo Commentary." *Chinese Literature: Essays, Articles, Reviews* 16 (1994): 41–67. Print.

———. "Boundaries and Interpretations: Some Preliminary Thoughts on *Xushu*." M. Huang, *Snakes' Legs* 19–45.

———. *Desire and Fictional Narrative in Late Imperial China.* Cambridge: Harvard UP, 2002. Print.

———. *Literati and Self-Re/Presentation: Autobiographical Sensibility in the Eighteenth-Century Chinese Novel.* Stanford: Stanford UP, 1995. Print.

———, ed. *Snakes' Legs: Sequels, Continuations, Rewritings, and Chinese Fiction.* Honolulu: U of Hawai'i P, 2004. Print.

Huang Ren 黃仁 et al. *Yongyuan de Li Hanxiang jilian zhuanji* 永遠的李翰祥紀念專集 [Li Hanxiang Forever: A Memorial Collection]. Taipei: Jinxiu, 1997. Print.

Huang Runhua 黃潤華. *Quanguo Manwen tushu ziliao linahe mulu* 全國滿文圖書資料聯合目錄 [Union Catalog of Manchu-Language Materials in the People's Republic of China]. Beijing: Shumu, 1991. Print.

Huang Shuxian, ed. *Hong Kong Filmography, Vol. 1: 1913–1941.* Hong Kong: Hong Kong Film Archive, 1997. Print.

Huang Yunhao 黃雲皓. *Tujie Hongloumeng jianzhu yixiang* 圖解紅樓夢建築意象 [An Illustrated Study of the Architecture in *Dream of the Red Chamber*]. Beijing: Zhongguo Jianzhu Gongye, 2006. Print.

Huayue chiren 花月痴人. *Honglou huanmeng* 紅樓幻夢 [The Illusion of *Dream of the Red Chamber*]. Beijing: Beijing Daxue, 1990. Print.

Hui Hong 惠洪. *Leng zhai yehua* 冷齋夜話 [Nocturnal Notes of the Cool Studio]. Beijing: Zhonghua, 1988. Print.

Hummel, Arthur W., Jr. *Eminent Chinese of the Ch'ing Period.* Washington: GPO, 1943–44. Print.

Idema, Wilt, and Lloyd Haft. *A Guide to Chinese Literature.* Ann Arbor: Center for Chinese Studies, U of Michigan, 1997. Print.

Ji Cheng 計成. *The Craft of Gardens* [*Yuan Ye* 園冶]. Trans. and ed. Alison Hardie. Introd. Maggie Keswick. New Haven: Yale UP, 1988. Print.

Jiang Jin 姜今. "Lun Xingshi mei" 論形式美 [On Formal Beauty]. *Dianying yishu* 電影藝術 3 (1963): 32–40. Print.

Jiang, Jin. *Women Playing Men: Yue Opera and Social Change in Twentieth-Century Shanghai.* Seattle: U of Washington P, 2009. Print.

Jiang Shunyuan姜順源. *Gugong jianzhu jiemi* 故宮建築解密 [The Secrets of the Architectures in the Forbidden City]. Beijing: Zijincheng, 1995. Print.

Jin Shengtan 金聖嘆. *Jin Shengtan pi ping Shui hu zhuan* 金聖嘆批評本水滸傳 [Jin Shengtan Comments on *Outlaws of the Marsh*]. 2 vols. Changsha: Yuelu Bookshop, 2006. Print. Critical Eds. of the Four Famous Works 四大名著批評本.

Johnson, David, Andrew J. Nathan, and Evelyn S. Rawski, eds. *Popular Culture in Late Imperial China.* Berkeley: U of California P, 1987. Print.

Keightley, David N. "Early Civilization in China: Reflections on How It Became Chinese." Ropp, *Heritage* 15–54.

Kessler, Lawrence D. *K'ang-hsi and the Consolidation of Ch'ing Rule, 1661–1684.* Chicago: U of Chicago P, 1976. Print.

Keswick, Maggie. *The Chinese Garden: History, Art, and Architecture.* New York: Rizzoli, 1978. Print.

Kierkegaard, Søren. *Fear and Trembling.* Trans. Sylvia Walsh. Cambridge: Cambridge UP, 2006. Print.

Ko, Dorothy. *Every Step a Lotus: Shoes for Bound Feet.* Berkeley: U of California P, 2001. Print.

———. *Teachers of the Inner Chambers: Women and Culture in Seventeenth-Century China.* Stanford: Stanford UP, 1994. Print.

———. "The Written Word and the Bound Foot: A History of the Courtesan's Aura." Widmer and Chang 74–100.

Kuhn, Philip A. *Soulstealers: The Chinese Sorcery Scare of 1768.* Cambridge: Harvard UP, 1990. Print.

Lai Shek, ed. *The Diary of Lai Man-wai.* Trans. Ma Sun. Hong Kong: Hong Kong Film Archive, 2003. Print.

Lam, Ling Hon. "The Matriarch's Private Ear: Performance, Reading, Censorship, and the Fabrication of Interiority in *The Story of the Stone.*" *Harvard Journal of Asiatic Studies* Dec. 2005: 357–415. Print.

Langhuan shanqiao 嫏嬛山樵. *Bu Honglou meng* 補紅樓夢 [Patching *Dream of the Red Chamber*]. Beijing: Beijing Daxue, 1988. Print.

———. *Zengbu Honglou meng* 增補紅樓夢 [Sequel to Patching *Dream of the Red Chamber*]. Beijing: Beijing Daxue, 1988. Print.

Law Kar. "The Cinematic Destiny of Eileen Chang." Trans. Stephen Teo. *Transcending the Times: King Hu and Eileen Chang.* Ed. Law. Hong Kong: Provisional Urban Council of Hong Kong, 1998. 141–46. Print.

Lawall, Sarah, et al., eds. *The Norton Anthology of World Literature*. 6 vols. 2nd ed. New York: Norton, 2003. Print.

Le Jun 樂鈞. "Chi Nüzi" 癡女子 [Obsessed Young Woman]. Yisu, *Hongloumeng juan* 347.

Lee, Leo Ou-fan. *Shanghai Modern: The Flowering of a New Urban Culture in China, 1930–1940*. Cambridge: Harvard UP, 1999. Print.

Leung, Angela. *Leprosy in China: A History*. New York: Columbia UP, 2008. Print.

Levy, Dore J. *Ideal and Actual in* The Story of the Stone. New York: Columbia UP, 1999. Print.

Li Fang 李放. "Baqi hualu" 八旗畫錄 [Notes on Paintings under the Eight Banners]. Zhu Yixuan 51.

Li Ki 禮記. *Liji* [*Book of Rites*]. Trans. James Legge. New York: University, 1967. Print.

Li, Qiancheng. *Fictions of Enlightenment:* Journey to the West, Tower of Myriad Mirrors, *and* Dream of the Red Chamber. Honolulu: U of Hawai'i P, 2004. Print.

Li Ruzhen 李汝珍. *Jinghua yuan* 鏡花緣 [Flowers in the Mirror]. Beijing: Renmin wenxue, 1996. Print.

Li, Wai-yee. *Enchantment and Disenchantment: Love and Illusion in Chinese Literature*. Princeton: Princeton UP, 1993. Print.

———. "Full-Length Vernacular Fiction." Mair, *Columbia History* 620–58.

———. "The Late Ming Courtesan: Invention of a Cultural Ideal." Widmer and Chang 46–73.

Li Yu 李漁. *The Carnal Prayer Mat* [*Rou Pu Tuan* 肉蒲團]. Trans. Patrick Hanan. Honolulu: U of Hawai'i P, 1996. Print.

———. *Li Yu ciji* 李煜詞集 [Collected Ci Poems by Li Yu]. Shanghai: Guji, 2009. Print.

———. *A Tower for the Summer Heat* [*Shier lou* 十二樓]. Trans. and ed. Patrick Hanan. New York: Columbia UP, 1992. Print.

———. *Xianqing ouji* 閑情偶寄 [Casual Expressions of Idle Feeling]. Hangzhou: Zhejiang Guji, 1992. Print. Vol. 3 of *Li Yu quanji* 李漁全集 [The Complete Works of Li Yu].

Liang Gongchen 梁恭辰. *Beidong yuan bilu* 北東園筆錄 [Notes Made in the Northeast Garden]. 1867.

Liang Qichao 梁啓超. "Wang Jing'an xiansheng muqian daoci" 王靜安先生墓前悼詞 [Eulogy for Mr. Wang Jing'an]. *Zhuiyi Wang Guowei* 追憶王國維 [In Remembrance of Wang Guowei]. Ed. Chen Pingyuan and Wang Feng. Beijing: Zhongguo guangbo dianshi, 1997. 95–97. Print.

Lin Niantong 林年同. *Zhongguo dianying meixue* 中國電影美學 [Chinese Film Aesthetics]. Taipei: Yinchen Wenhua, 1991. Print.

Lin Xiaoji 林孝箕 et al. "Honglou shijie" 紅樓詩借 [Poems Aided by *Dream of the Red Chamber*]. Excerpts. Yisu, *Hongloumeng juan* 531–34.

Lin Yiliang 林以亮 (Song Qi 宋淇). *Honglou meng Xiyou ji* 紅樓夢西遊記 [*The Story of the Stone*'s Journey to the West]. Taipei: Lianjing, 1976. Print.

Lin Yutang 林語堂. *Moment in Peking: A Novel of Contemporary Chinese Life*. New York: Day, 1939. Print.

Ling Chengshu 凌承樞. "Hongloumeng baiyong ci" 紅樓夢百詠詞 [A Hundred Songs on *Dream of the Red Chamber*]. Yisu, *Hongloumeng juan* 460–75.

Liu Chang 劉暢 and Wang Shiwei 王時偉. "Cong xiancun tuyang ziliao kan Qingdai wanqi Changchungong gaizao gongcheng" 從現存圖樣資料看清代晚期長春宮改造工程 [The Late Qing Reconstruction Plans for the Palace of Eternal Spring as Seen from the Extant Materials]. *Gugong bowuyuan yuankan* 故宮博物院院刊 [Palace Museum Journal] 4 (2005): 190–206. Print.

Liu Chang 劉暢, Zhao Wenwen 趙雯雯, and Jiang Zhang 蔣張. "Cong Changchungong dao Zhongcuigong" 從長春宮到鍾粹宮 [From the Palace of Eternal Spring to the Palace of Zhongcui]. *Zijincheng* 紫禁城 [The Forbidden City] 175 (2009): 14–23. Print.

Liu, James J. Y. *The Art of Chinese Poetry*. Chicago: U of Chicago P, 1962. Print.

———. *Chinese Theories of Literature*. Chicago: U of Chicago P, 1975. Print.

Liu Jianmei. *Revolution plus Love: Literary History, Women's Bodies, and Thematic Repetition in Twentieth-Century Chinese Fiction*. Honolulu: U of Hawai'i P, 2003. Print.

Liu, Wu-chi, and Irving Yucheng Lo, eds. *Sunflower Splendor: Three Thousand Years of Chinese Poetry*. Bloomington: Indiana UP, 1990. Print.

Liu Xinwu. *Honglou wangyue: Cong Qin Keqing jie du Hong lou meng* 紅樓望月 [*Red Chamber's* Full Moon]. Taiwan: Shuhai, 2005. Print.

Liu Zaifu 劉再復. *Hongloumeng wu* 紅樓夢悟 [Illuminations on *Dream of the Red Chamber*]. Beijing: Sanlian, 2006. Print.

———. *Reflections on* Dream of the Red Chamber. Trans. Shu Yunzhong. Amherst: Cambria, 2008. Print.

Lowry, Kathryn. *Tapestry of Popular Songs in Sixteenth- and Seventeenth-Century China: Reading, Imitation, and Desire*. Leiden: Brill, 2005. Print.

Lu, Tina. *Accidental Incest, Filial Cannibalism, and Other Peculiar Encounters in Late Imperial Chinese Literature*. Cambridge: Harvard U Asia Center, 2009. Print.

Lu, Tonglin. *Misogyny, Cultural Nihilism, and Oppositional Politics: Contemporary Chinese Experimental Fiction*. Stanford: Stanford UP, 1995. Print.

Lu Xun. "Fuqin de bing" 父親的病 [My Father's Illness]. *Lu Xun quan ji* 魯迅全集 [The Complete Works of Lu Xun]. Vol. 2. Beijing: Renmin Wenxue, 2005. 294–300. Print.

Luo Guanzhong 羅貫中. *Three Kingdoms* [*San guo yan yi* 三志演義]. Trans. Moss Roberts. Berkeley: U of California P, 2004. Print.

Mackerras, Colin. "The Drama of the Qing Dynasty." *Chinese Theatre from Its Origins to the Present Day*. Ed. Mackerras. Honolulu: U of Hawai'i P, 1984. 92–117. Print.

———. *The Rise of the Peking Opera, 1770–1870*. Oxford: Clarendon, 1972. Print.

Mai Ye 麥耶. "Honglou meng ji qita" 紅樓夢及其他 [*The Dream of the Red Chamber* and Others]. *Zazhi* 雜誌 13.4 (1944): 171–75. Print.

Mair, Victor. *The Columbia Anthology of Traditional Chinese Literature*. New York: Columbia UP, 1994. Print.

———. ed. *The Columbia History of Chinese Literature*. New York: Columbia UP, 2001. Print.

Mair, Victor, et al., eds. *The Hawai'i Reader in Traditional Chinese Culture*. Honolulu: U of Hawai'i P, 2004. Print.

Mann, Susan. "Learned Women in the Eighteenth Century." Gilmartin, Hershatter, Rofel, and White 27–46.

———. *Precious Records: Women in China's Long Eighteenth Century*. Stanford: Stanford UP, 1997. Print.

Mao Dun 茅盾, ed. *Jieben Hongloumeng* 潔本紅樓夢 [A Clean Version of *Dream of the Red Chamber*]. Shanghai: Kaiming, 1935. Print.

Mao Qingzhen 毛慶臻. *Yiting kaogu zaji* 一亭考古雜記 [Yiting's Miscellaneous Notes Reflecting on the Antiquities]. 1892. Print.

Mao Zedong 毛澤東. "Guanyu *Hongloumeng* yanjiu wenti de xin" 關於 "紅樓夢" 研究問題的信 [A Letter on the Study of *The Dream of the Red Chamber*]. *Mao Zedong xuanji* 毛澤東選集 [Selected Works of Mao Zedong]. Vol. 5. Beijing: Renmin, 1977. 134. Print.

———. "Guanyu zhexue wenti de jianghua" 關於哲學問題的講話 [Speech on Philosophical Issues]. *Mao Zedong sixiang wansui* 毛澤東思想萬歲 [Long Live Mao Zedong Thought]. N.p., 1969. 548–61. Print.

Marks, Martin. *Music and the Silent Film*. New York: Oxford UP, 1997. Print.

Marx, Karl, and Friedrich Engels. "Manifesto of the Communist Party." *Selected Works in One Volume*. New York: Intl., 1968. 35–63. Print.

Mazzio, Carla. "The Melancholy of Print: *Love's Labor's Lost*." *Historicism, Psychoanalysis, and Early Modern Culture*. Ed. Mazzio and Douglas Trevor. New York: Routledge, 2000. 186–227. Print.

McLaren, Anne E. "Constructing New Reading Publics in Late Ming China." Brokaw and Chow 152–83.

McMahon, Keith. *Causality and Containment in Seventeenth-Century Chinese Fiction*. Leiden: Brill, 1988. Print.

———. "Fleecing the Male Customer in Shanghai Brothels of the 1890s." *Late Imperial China* 23.2 (2002): 1–28. Print.

Mei Lanfang 梅蘭芳. *Wo de dianying shenghuo* 我的電影生活 [My Life in Film]. Beijing: Zhongguo Dianying, 1984. Print.

———. *Wutai shenghuo sishinian* 舞台生活四十年 [Forty Years Onstage]. Beijing: Zhongguo Xiju, 1987. Print.

Mengmeng xiansheng 夢夢先生. *Honglou yuanmeng* 紅樓圓夢 [Resolution of *Dream of the Red Chamber*]. Beijing: Beijing Daxue, 1988. Print.

Miller, Barbara Stoler, ed. *Masterworks of Asian Literature in Comparative Perspective: A Guide for Teaching*. New York: Sharpe, 1993. Print.

Minford, John. Foreword. Hawkes, Story of the Stone: *A Translator's Notebooks* x–xv.

———. "Pieces of Eight: Reflections on Translating *The Story of the Stone*." *Translating Chinese Literature*. Ed. Eugene Eoyang and Lin Yao-fu. Bloomington: Indiana UP, 1995. 178–203. Print.

———. "The Slow Boat from China: The *Stone's* Journey to the West." *Komparative Philosophie: Begegnungen zwischen östlichen und westlichen Denkwegen.* Ed. Rolf Elberfeld et al. München: Fink, 1998. 171–80. Print.

Minford, John, and Robert H. Hegel. "*Hong-lou meng.*" Nienhauser 1: 752–56.

Ming, Feng-ying. "Baoyu in Wonderland: Technological Utopia in the Early Modern Chinese Science Fiction Novel." *China in a Polycentric World: Essays in Chinese Comparative Literature.* Ed. Yingjin Zhang. Stanford: Stanford UP, 1998. 152–72. Print.

Moretti, Franco, ed. *The Novel: Volume 1: History, Geography, and Culture.* Princeton: Princeton UP, 2006. Print.

Murasaki Shikibu. *The Tale of Genji.* Trans. and abr. Edward G. Seidensticker. New York: Vintage, 1976. Print.

———. *The Tale of Genji.* Trans. Edward G. Seidensticker. New York: Knopf, 1983. Print.

Nabokov, Vladimir. *The Annotated* Lolita. Ed. Alfred Appel. New York: McGraw, 1970. Print.

Naquin, Susan. *Peking: Temples and City Life, 1400–1900.* Princeton: Princeton UP, 2000. Print.

Naquin, Susan, and Evelyn Rawski. *Chinese Society in the Eighteenth Century.* New Haven: Yale UP, 1987. Print.

Nattier, Jan. "The Heart Sutra: A Chinese Apocryphal Text?" *Journal of the International Association of Buddhist Studies* 15.2 (1992): 153–223. Print.

Ni Hong 倪鴻. *Tongyin qinghua* 桐陰清話 [Pure Talks under the Shadow of Wutong Trees]. Shanghai: Saoye sanfang, 1941. Print.

Ni Yibin. "The Anatomy of Rebus in Chinese Decorative Arts." *Oriental Art* 49.3 (2003–04): 12–23. Print.

Nie Chongzheng 聶崇正. "Architectural Decoration in the Forbidden City: Trompe-L'Œil Murals in the Lodge of Retiring from Hard Work." *Orientations* 26.7 (1995): 51–55. Print.

———. *Qingdai de gongting huihua he huajia* 清代的宮廷繪畫和畫家 [The Court Paintings and Court Painters in the Qing]. *Qingdai gongting huihua* 清代宮廷繪畫 [The Court Paintings of the Qing Dynasty]. Ed. Gugong Bowuyuan 故宮博物院. Beijing: Wen Wu, 1992. 1–24. Print.

———. *Xianfahua xiaokao* 線法畫小攷 [A Study of the Linear Perspective Method]. *Gugong bowuyuan yuankan* 故宮博物院院刊 [Palace Museum Journal] 3 (1983): 85–88. Print.

Nienhauser, William H., Jr., ed. *The Indiana Companion to Traditional Chinese Literature.* 2 vols. Bloomington: Indiana UP, 1986–98. Print.

Norman, Jerry. *Chinese.* Cambridge: Cambridge UP, 1988. Print.

Ong, Walter J. *Orality and Literacy: The Technologizing of the Word.* London: Routledge, 1988. Print.

Owen, Stephen, trans. and ed. *An Anthology of Chinese Literature: Beginnings to 1911.* New York: Norton, 1996. Print.

———. "Cao Xueqin." Lawall et al. 146–48.

————. "Omen of the World: Meaning in the Chinese Lyric." Dale 71–102.

————. *Readings in Chinese Literary Thought.* Cambridge: Harvard UP, 1992. Print.

Owen, Stephen, and Kang-i Sun Chang, eds. *The Cambridge History of Chinese Literature.* 2 vols. Cambridge: Cambridge UP, 2010. Print.

Pan Zhonggui 潘重規. *Hongxue lunji* 紅學論集 [Collected Works of Redology]. Taipei: Sanmin, 1991. Print.

Pang, Laikwan. *Building a New China in Cinema: The Chinese Left-Wing Cinema Movement, 1932–1937.* New York: Rowman, 2002. Print.

————. *The Distorting Mirror: Visual Modernity in China.* Honolulu: U of Hawai'i P, 2007. Print.

*Peter Shaffer's* Amadeus. Dir. Milos Forman. Perf. F. Murray Abraham. Thorn EMI Video, 1984. Videocassette.

Peterson, Willard, ed. *The Ch'ing Dynasty, Part 1: To 1800.* Cambridge: Cambridge UP, 2001. Print. Vol. 9 of *The Cambridge History of China.*

Pettigrew, Nita G. "The Art of Listening." *Lion's Eye. Philips Exeter Academy.* Philips Exeter Acad., n.d. Web. 23 Feb. 2011.

Pirsig, Robert. *Zen and the Art of Motorcycle Maintenance: An Inquiry into Values.* New York: Morrow, 1974. Print.

Plaks, Andrew H. *Archetype and Allegory in* The Dream of the Red Chamber. Princeton: Princeton UP, 1976. Print.

————. *The Four Masterworks of the Ming Novel: Ssu Ta Ch'i Shu.* Princeton: Princeton UP, 1987. Print.

————. "The Novel in Premodern China." Moretti 181–216.

*Plum in the Golden Vase* [*Jin Ping Mei* 金瓶梅]. 3 vols. Trans. David Tod Roy. Princeton: Princeton UP, 1997– . Print.

Pu Songling 蒲松齡. "Precious" [A "Bao" 阿宝]. *Strange Tales from Make-Do Studio* [*Liaozhai Zhiyi* 聊齋誌異]. Trans. and ed. Dennis Mair and Victor Mair. Beijing: Foreign Langs., 1989. 116–24. Print.

Qi Rushan 齊如山. *Qi Rushan huiyilu* 齊如山回憶錄 [Qi Rushan's Memoir]. Beijing: Baowentang, 1989. Print.

Qi Rushan 齊如山 and Li Shikan 李釋戡. "Dai-yu zanghua" 黛玉葬花 [Dai-yu Buries Flowers]. *Mei Lanfang yanchu juben xuanji* 梅蘭芳演出劇本選集 [Anthology of Mei Lanfang's Play Texts]. Ed. Zhongguo Xijujia Xiehui 中國戲劇家協會. Beijing: Yishu, 1954. 89–104. Print.

Qi Song 齊崧. "Mei Lanfang de *Dai-yu zanghua*" 梅蘭芳的黛玉葬花 [Mei Lanfang's *Dai-yu Buries Flowers*]. *Lun Mei Lanfang* 論梅蘭芳 [On Mei Lanfang]. Taizhong: Zhuanji Wenxue, 1978. 173–79. Print.

Qin Zichen 秦子忱. *Xu Honglou meng* 續紅樓夢 [Sequel to *Dream of the Red Chamber*]. Beijing: Beijing Daxue, 1988. Print.

Qiu Weiyuan 邱煒爰. "*Hongloumeng* fenyong jueju" 紅樓夢分詠絕句 [Quatrains on *Dream of the Red Chamber*]. Yisu, *Hongloumeng shulu* 297–301.

*Quan tang shi* 全唐詩 [Complete Tang Poems]. 2 vols. Shanghai: Shanghai guji, 1986. Print.

*Raise the Red Lantern.* Dir. Zhang Yimou. Perf. Gong Li. 1991. Razor Digital Entertainment, 2006. DVD.

Rawski, Evelyn S. "Economic and Social Foundations of Late Imperial Culture." Johnson, Nathan, and Rawski 3–33.

———. *The Last Emperors: A Social History of Qing Imperial Institutions.* Berkeley: U of California P, 1998. Print.

"Red Chamber." *Comics.* China-on-site.com, n.d. Web. 14 Dec. 2007.

Rojas, Carlos. *The Naked Gaze: Reflections on Chinese Modernity.* Cambridge: Harvard U Asia Center, 2008. Print.

Rolston, David L., ed. *How to Read the Chinese Novel.* Princeton: Princeton UP, 1990. Print.

———. *Traditional Chinese Fiction and Fiction Commentary: Reading and Writing between the Lines.* Stanford: Stanford UP, 1997. Print.

Ropp, Paul S. "The Distinctive Art of Chinese Fiction." Dale 103–28.

———, ed. *Heritage of China: Contemporary Perspectives on Chinese Civilization.* Berkeley: U of California P, 1990. Print.

Roth, Harold D. "Psychology and Self-Cultivation in Early Taoistic Thought." *Harvard Journal of Asiatic Studies* 51.2 (1991): 599–650. Print.

Rowe, William T. "Social Stability and Social Change." Peterson 493–502.

———. "Women and the Family in Mid-Qing Social Thought: The Case of Chen Hong-mou." *Late Imperial China* 13.2 (1992): 1–41. Print.

Saussy, Haun. "Women's Writing before and within the *Honglou meng.*" Widmer and Chang 285–305.

Schonebaum, Andrew. "Dreams of World Literature: *Honglou meng* in the West, 1829–1929." The Story of the Stone *and* The Tale of Genji *in East Asia: Media, Gender, and Cultural Identities.* Ed. Haruo Shirane and Shang Wei. New York: Columbia UP, forthcoming.

Shahar, Meir. *Crazy Ji: Chinese Religion and Popular Literature.* Cambridge: Harvard U Asia Center, 1998. Print.

Shang Wei. "The Literati Era and Its Demise, 1723–1840." Owen and Chang 2: 245–342.

Shen Fu 沈復. *Six Records of a Floating Life* [*Fusheng liuji* 浮生六記]. Trans. Leonard Pratt and Chiang Su-hui. New York: Penguin, 1983. Print.

Shi Nai'an 施耐庵 and Luo Guanzhong 羅貫中. *Outlaws of the Marsh* [*Shuihu zhuan* 水滸傳]. Trans. Sidney Shapiro. Beijing: Foreign Langs., 2001. Print.

Shimizu Akira 清水晶. *Shanghai sokai eiga watakushi-shi* 上海租界映画私史 [A Private History of Cinema in Shanghai's Foreign Concessions]. Tokyo: Shinchōsha, 1995. Print.

Sieber, Patricia. "Seeing the World through *Xianqing ouji* (1671): Performance, Visuality, and Narratives of Modernity." *Modern Chinese Literature and Culture* 12 (2000): 1–43. Print.

Sima Xin 司馬新. *Zhang Ailing zai Meiguo: Hunyin yu wannian* 張愛玲在美國: 婚姻與晚年 [Eileen Chang in America: Her Marriage and Late Years]. Shanghai: Shanghai Wenyi, 1997. Print.

Simon, Paul. "Kodachrome." *There Goes Rhymin' Simon.* Warner Bros. Records, 1973. LP.

Sivin, Nathan. "Emotional Counter-therapy." *Medicine, Philosophy and Religion in Ancient China: Researches and Reflections.* Aldershot: Variorum, 1995. 1–19. Print. Variorum Collected Studies Ser.

Smiley, Jane. *Thirteen Ways of Looking at the Novel.* New York: Knopf, 2005. Print.

Sommer, Matthew H. "The Penetrated Male in Late Imperial China: Judicial Constructions and Social Stigma." *Modern China* 23.2 (1997): 140–80. Print.

———. *Sex, Law, and Society in Late Imperial China.* Stanford: Stanford UP, 2000. Print.

Sŏng U-Jŭng 成祐曾. 茗山燕詩錄 [Mingshan's Poetry Recording of His Trips to Yan]. *Yonhaengnok chonjip* 燕行錄全集 [The Complete Record of the Written Accounts of the Journeys to Beijing]. Ed. Im Kijung 林基中. 東國大學校, 2001, vol. 69.

Spence, Jonathan D. "Ch'ing." *Food in Chinese Culture: Anthropological and Historical Perspectives.* Ed. K. C. Chang. New Haven: Yale UP, 1977. 259–94. Print.

———. *Emperor of China: Self-Portrait of K'ang-hsi.* New York: Vintage, 1974. Print.

———. *Return to Dragon Mountain: Memories of a Late Ming Man.* New York: Viking, 2007. Print.

———. *The Search for Modern China.* New York: Norton, 1999. Print.

———. *Ts'ao Yin and the K'ang-hsi Emperor, Bondservant and Master.* New Haven: Yale UP, 1978. Print.

Su Shi 蘇軾. "The First Poetic Exposition on Red Cliff" ["Chibi fu" 赤壁賦]." Owen, *Anthology* 293.

Sun Wen 孫溫. *Quanben Hongloumeng* 全本紅樓夢 [Picture Book of *A Dream of Red Chambers,* by Sun Wen of the Qing Dynasty]. Ed. Lushun Museum. Trans. Han Dan. Beijing: Zuojia, 2007. Print.

Taku, Ashibe 芦辺拓. *Murder in the Red Mansions* [*Koromu no satsujin* 紅楼夢の殺人]. Tokyo: Bungei Shunju, 2004. Print. Trans. into Chinese as *Honglou meng sharen shijian* 紅樓夢殺人事件.

Tan Guanghu 譚光祜, ed. *Honglou renjing* 紅樓人鏡 [A Mirror for the Characters from *Dream of the Red Chamber*]. *Lidai jiuling daguan* 歷代酒令大觀 [A Comprehensive Collection of Drinking Verses through the Ages]. Ed. Yu Dunpei 俞敦培. Wulin: Zuijing Shuwu, 1925. Juan 4, 12–17. Print.

Tang Xianzu 湯顯祖. *The Peony Pavilion* [*Mudan ting* 牡丹亭]. Trans. Cyril Birch. Bloomington: Indiana UP, 2002. Print.

Tang Yin 唐寅. *Tang Bohu quanji* 唐伯虎全集 [Complete Works of Tang Yin]. Beijing: Zhongguo shudian, 1988. Print.

Tay, William. "Colonialism, the Cold War Era, and Marginal Space: The Existential Condition of Five Decades of Hong Kong Literature." *Chinese Literature in the Second Half of a Modern Century.* Ed. Pang-yuan Chi and David Der-wei Wang. Bloomington: Indiana UP, 2000. 31–38. Print.

Theiss, Janet. *Disgraceful Matters: The Politics of Chastity in Eighteenth-Century China.* Berkeley: U of California P, 2004. Print.

————. "Managing Martyrdom: Female Suicide and Statecraft in Mid-Qing China." *Nan Nü* 3.1 (2001): 47–76. Print.

Theresa, Rose. "From Méphistophélès to Méliès: Spectacle and Narrative in Opera and Early Film." *Between Opera and Cinema*. Ed. Jeongwon Joe and Theresa. New York: Routledge, 2002. 1–18. Print.

Tolstoy, Leo. *Anna Karenina*. 2nd ed. Trans. Louise Maude and Aylmer Maude. Rev. ed. Ed. George Gibian. New York: Norton, 1995. Print. Norton Critical Ed.

Tong Jun 童雋. "Beijing Changchunyuan xiyang jianzhu" 北京長春園西洋建築 [The European Architectures in the Garden of Eternal Spring in Beijing]. *Yuanming yuan* 圓明園. Vol. 1. Ed. Zhongguo Yuanming yuan xuehui choubei weiyuanhui 中國圓明園學會籌備委員會. Beijing: Zhongguo Jianzhu Gongye, 1981. 71–80. Print.

Torbert, Preston M. *The Ch'ing Imperial Household Department: A Study of Its Organization and Principal Functions, 1662–1796*. Cambridge: Council on East Asian Studies, Harvard U, 1977. Print.

Tsuji Hisakazu 辻久一. *Chūka den'ei shiwa: Ichi heisotsu no Nitchū eiga kaisōki, 1939–1945* 中華電影史話: 一兵卒の日中映画回想記 [Historical Accounts of China Film Company: A Soldier's Memoir on Sino-Japanese films, 1939–1945]. Ed. Shimizu Akira 清水晶. Tokyo: Gaifūsha, 1998. Print.

Tu, Weiming. "The Continuity of Being: Chinese Visions of Nature." *Confucian Thought: Selfhood as Creative Transformation*. Albany: State U of New York P, 1985. 35–50. Print.

Tu Ying 涂瀛. "Huo wen" 或問 [Various Questions]. *Honglou meng sanjia ping ben* 紅樓夢三家本. 4 vols. Shanghai: Guji, 1988. 49. Print.

Unschuld, Paul U. *Huang Di Nei Jing Su Wen: Nature, Knowledge, Imagery in an Ancient Chinese Medical Text*. Berkeley: U of California P, 2003. Print.

Vinograd, Richard. *Boundaries of the Self: Chinese Portraits, 1600–1900*. London: Cambridge UP, 1992. Print.

Vitiello, Giovanni. "Exemplary Sodomites: Chivalry and Love in Late Ming Culture." *Nan Nü: Men, Women and Gender in Early and Imperial China* 2 (2000): 207–57. Print.

Volpp, Sophie. "The Literary Circulation of Actors in Seventeenth-Century China." *Journal of Asian Studies* 61.3 (2002): 949–84. Print.

Waltner, Ann. "On Not Becoming a Heroine: Lin Dai-yu and Cui Ying-ying." *Signs* 15.1 (1989): 61–78. Print.

Wang Ban. *The Sublime Figure of History: Aesthetics and Politics in Twentieth-Century China*. Stanford: Stanford UP, 1997. Print.

Wang, David Der-wei. *Fin-de-Siècle Splendor: Repressed Modernities of Late Qing Fiction, 1848–1911*. Stanford: Stanford UP, 1997. Print.

————. Foreword. E. Chang, *Rice-Sprout Song* vii–xxv.

————. *The Monster That Is History: History, Violence, and Fictional Writing in Twentieth-Century China*. Berkeley: U of California P, 2004. Print.

Wang, Eugene Y. "The Rhetoric of Book Illustrations." *Treasures of the Yenching: Seventy-Fifth Anniversary of the Harvard-Yenching Library Exhibition*

*Catalogue*. Ed. Patrick Hanan. Cambridge: Harvard-Yenching Lib., 2003. 181–217. Print.

Wang, Fulin 王扶林. "The Origin of the Adaptations into Television Dramas of the Four Classical Novels by CCTV" [*Yangshi paishe* Honglou Meng *deng sida mingzhu de qiyin* 央視拍攝紅樓夢等四大名著的起因]. SINA Corporation, 1996. Web. 20 June 2012. <http://blog.sina.com.cn/wangfulinblog>.

Wang Guowei 王國維. "*Hongloumeng* pinglun" 紅樓夢評論 [A Critique of *The Dream of the Red Chamber*]. *Ershi shiji Zhongguo xiaoshuo lilun ziliao* 二十世紀中國 小說理 論資料 [Critical Materials on the Chinese Novel by Twentieth-Century Chinese Scholars, Volume 1, 1897–1916]. Ed. Chen Pingyuan and Xia Xiaohong. Beijing: Beijing UP, 1989. 96–115. Print.

Wang Hui. *China's New Order: Society, Politics, and Economy in Transition*. Ed. Theodore Huters. Cambridge: Harvard UP, 2003. Print.

Wang, Jing. *High Culture Fever: Politics, Aesthetics, and Ideology in Deng's China*. Berkeley: U of California P, 1996. Print.

———. "The Poetics of Chinese Narrative: An Analysis of Andrew Plaks's *Archetype and Allegory* in The Dream of the Red Chamber." *Comparative Literature Studies* 26.3 (1989): 252–70. Print.

———. *The Story of Stone: Intertextuality, Ancient Chinese Stone Lore, and the Stone Symbolism in* Dream of the Red Chamber. Durham: Duke UP, 1992. Print.

Wang Lanzhi 王蘭止. *Qilou chongmeng* 綺樓重夢 [Revisiting the Silken Chambers]. Beijing: Beijing Daxue, 1990. Print.

Wang Liqi 王利器, ed. *Yuan Ming Qing san dai jinhui xiaoshuo xiqu shi liao* 元明清 三代禁毀小說戲曲史料 [Historical Sources on the Prohibition and Destruction of Novels and Plays during the Yuan, Ming, and Qing Dynasties]. Shanghai: Shanghai Guji, 1981. Print.

Wang Mengruan 王夢阮 and Shen Ping'an 沈瓶庵. *Honglou meng suoyin* 紅樓夢索引 [The Key to Dream of the Red Chamber]. Shanghai: Zhonghua, 1916. Print.

———. *The Story of the Western Wing* [*Xixiang Ji* 西廂記]. Trans. Stephen West and Wilt Idema. Berkeley: U of California P, 1995. Print.

———. *Xinkan dazi kuiben quanxiang canzeng qimiao Xixiang ji* 新刊大字魁本全相 參增奇妙註釋西廂記 [Newly Cut, Large-Character, Folio-Size, Completely Illustrated, Expanded, Deluxe, Annotated Story of the Western Wing]. *Quan Yuan zaju* 全元雜劇 [The Northern Plays of the Yuan Dynasty]. Vol. 4. Ed. Yang Jialuo 楊家駱. Taipei: Shijie shuju, 1962. Print.

Wang Shucun 王樹村, ed. *Minjian zhenpin tushuo Hongloumeng* 民間珍品圖說紅樓 夢 [Precious Paintings from the Popular Tradition: The Illustrated *Dream of the Red Chamber*]. Taipei: Dongda Tushu, 1996. Print.

Wang Wenjuan 王文娟. "Wo yan Lin Dai-yu de tihui" 我演林黛玉的體會 [My Experience of Playing Lin Dai-yu]. *Xiju bao* 戲劇報 20 (1960): 67–71. Print.

Wang Xiaochuan 王曉傳, ed. *Yuan Ming Qing sandai jinhui xiaoshuo xiqu shiliao* 元明清三代禁毀小說戲曲史料 [The Prohibited and Destroyed Works of Fiction and Dramas in the Periods of the Yuan, Ming, and Qing]. Beijing: Zuojia, 1958. Print.

Wang Xilian 王希廉. "Hongloumeng zongping" 紅樓夢總評 [General Comments on *Dream of the Red Chamber*]. *Zengping butu Shitouji* 增評補圖石頭記 [*Story of the Stone* with Added Commentaries and Supplemented Illustrations]. Facsim. of 1834 ed. Beijing: Zhongguo, 1988. 1–21. Print.

Wang Zhao 王釗. *Honglou meng xie zhen* 紅樓夢寫真 [Portrait of *Dream of the Red Chamber*]. *Hongloumeng guhua lu* 紅樓夢古畫錄 [A Catalog of the Paintings of *Dream of the Red Chamber*]. Ed. Hong Zhenkuai 洪振快. Beijing: Renmin Wenxue, 2007. 285. Print.

Wang Zhongjie 王仲傑. "Changchungong bihua de zuozhe" 長春宮壁畫的作者 [The Author of the Murals in the Palace of Eternal Spring]. *Zijincheng* 紫禁城 [The Forbidden City] 1 (1994): 7. Print.

Watson, Burton. *Chinese Rhyme-Prose: Poems in the Fu Form from the Han and Six Dynasties Periods.* New York: Columbia UP, 1971. Print.

———. *Chuang-tzu* [Zhuangzi]: *Basic Writings.* New York: Columbia UP, 1964. Print.

———. "Discussion on Making All Things Equal." *The Complete Works of Chuang Tzu.* New York: Columbia UP, 1968. 36–49. Print.

Watt, Ian. *The Rise of the Novel: Studies in Defoe, Richardson and Fielding.* London: Chatto, 1957. Print.

Wei Hong 衛宏. Preface. *The Book of Songs* [*Shi Jing* 詩經]. Trans. Pauline Yu. Damrosch et al., A: 1045.

Wei Qingyuan 韋慶遠, Wu Qiyan 吳奇衍, and Li Su 魯素. *Qingdai nüpu zhidu* 清代奴婢制度 [The Qing Slave System]. Beijing: Zhongguo Renmin Daxue, 1982. Print.

Weissbort, Daniel, and Astradur Eysteinsson, eds. *Translation, Theory and Practice: A Historical Reader.* New York: Oxford UP, 2006. Print.

Widmer, Ellen. *The Beauty and the Book: Women and Fiction in Nineteenth-Century China.* Cambridge: Harvard UP, 2006. Print.

———. "Xiaoqing's Literary Legacy and the Place of the Woman Writer in Late Imperial China." *Late Imperial China* 13.1 (1992): 111–55. Print.

Widmer, Ellen, and Kang-i Sun Chang, eds. *Writing Women in Late Imperial China.* Standford: Stanford UP, 1997. Print.

Wilhelm, Richard. *The I Ching; or, Book of Changes.* Trans. Cary F. Baynes. Princeton: Princeton UP, 1967. Print.

Wolf, Werner. *The Musicalization of Fiction: A Study in the Theory and History of Intermediality.* Amsterdam: Rodopi, 1999. Print

Wong Ain-ling 愛玲. "Honglou meng wei xing" 紅樓夢未醒 [The Dream of the Red Chamber Lingers On]. *Meng yu shuo meng* 夢餘夢 [Dream Discourse in the Wake of Dreams]. Vol. 2. Hong Kong: Oxford UP, 2012. 139–42. Print.

———. ed. *Li Han-hsiang, Storyteller.* Hong Kong: Hong Kong Film Archive, 2007. Print.

Wong, Laurence. *A Study of the Literary Translations of the* Hong Lou Meng: *With Special Reference to David Hawkes's English Version.* Diss. U of Toronto, 1992. Print.

Wong, Young-tsu. *A Paradise Lost: The Imperial Garden Yuanming Yuan.* Honolulu: U of Hawai'i P, 2001. Print.

Wu Cheng-en 吳承恩. *The Journey to the West* [*Xi you ji* 西遊記]. Trans. Anthony C. Yu. 4 vols. Chicago: U of Chicago P, 1980–84. Print.

Wu Ch'eng-en. *Monkey* [*Xi you ji* 西遊記]. Trans. and abr. Arthur Waley. New York: Grove, 1943. Print.

Wu Cuncun. *Homoerotic Sensibilities in Late Imperial China*. London: Routledge, 2004. Print.

Wu Hung. "Beyond Stereotypes: The Twelve Beauties in Qing Court Art and the *Dream of the Red Chamber*." Widmer and Chang 306–65. Print.

———. *The Double Screen: Medium and Representation in Chinese Painting*. Cambridge: Harvard UP, 1996. Print.

———. "Emperor's Masquerade: 'Costume Portraits' of Yongzheng and Qianlong." *Orientations* 26.7 (1995): 25–41. Print.

Wu, I-Hsien. "Portraits of a Lady: Lin Daiyu's Makeover in *Honglou meng* Pictures." *The Story of the Stone* and *The Tale of Genji* in Modern China and Japan: Issues in Media, Gender, and Cultural Identity. Columbia U. 20 Nov. 2010. Address.

Wu Jianren 吳趼人. *Xin Shitouji* 新石頭記 [New Story of the Stone]. Zhengzhou: Zhongzhou guji, 1986. Print.

Wu Shicheng 吳世澄. "Yu Xiaohui xiansheng nianpu" 余孝惠先生年譜 [Chronicle of Yu Zhi's (Yu Xiaohui's) Life]. *Zun xiaoxue zhai ji* 尊小學齋集 [The Collection of Honoring Primary Learning Studio]. By Yu Zhi 余治. Vol. 4. Dejian Zhai, 1883. 1–17. Print.

Wu Shih-Chang. *On* The Red Chamber Dream. Oxford: Clarendon, 1961. Print.

Wu Shijian 吳士鑒, ed. *Qing gongci* 清宮詞 [Qing Court Poetry]. Beijing: Beijing Guji, 1986. Print.

Wu, Silas H. L. *Communication and Imperial Control in China: Evolution of the Palace Memorial System, 1693–1735*. Cambridge: Harvard UP, 1970. Print.

———. *Passage to Power: K'ang-hsi and His Heir Apparent, 1661–1722*. Cambridge: Harvard UP, 1979. Print.

Wumu Shanseng 烏目山僧. *Haishang daguanyuan* 海上大觀園 [The Grand Prospect Garden in Shanghai]. Shanghai: Dongya, 1924. Print.

Xiao Chi. *The Chinese Garden as Lyric Enclave: A Generic Study of* The Story of the Stone. Ann Arbor: Center for Chinese Studies, U of Michigan, 2001. Print.

Xiaoyao zi 逍遙子 [Carefree Wanderer]. *Hou Hongloumeng* 後紅樓夢 [*Later Dream of the Red Chamber*]. Shanghai: Shanghai Guji, 1990. Print.

Xu Jin 徐進. Afterword. Xu Jin, *Yueju* 156–66.

———. *Yueju Honglou meng* 越劇紅樓夢 [*Dream of the Red Chamber*: A Yue Opera]. Shanghai: Shanghai Wenyi, 1959. Print.

Xu Ke 徐珂. *Qingbai leichao* 清稗類鈔 [An Unofficial History of the Qing Dynasty, Arranged by Categories]. Vol. 8. Beijing: Zhonghua, 1984. Print.

Yampolsky, Philip B. *The Platform Sutra of the Sixth Patriarch: The Text of the Tunhuang Manuscript with Translation, Introduction, and Notes*. New York: Columbia UP, 1967. Print.

Yang, Gladys. Rev. of *The Story of the Stone*, by Cao Xueqin, trans. David Hawkes, vols. 1 and 2. *Bulletin of the School of Oriental and African Studies, U of London* 43.3 (1980): 621–22. Print.

Yang Pengyu. "Qing Gongci" 清宮詞 [Qing Court Poetry]. Wu Shijian 163–70.

Yao Xie 姚燮. *Du Hongloumeng gangling* 讀紅樓夢綱領 [Guidelines for Reading *Dream of the Red Chamber*]. Shanghai: Zhulin, 1940. Print.

Yau Ching. "A Sensuous Misunderstanding: Women and Sexualities in Li Han-hsiang's *Fengyue* Film." Trans. Agnes Lam. Wong Ain-ling, *Li* 100–13.

Yau, Ka-fai. "Realist Paradoxes: The Story of the *Story of the Stone.*" *Comparative Literature* 57.2 (2005): 117–34. Print.

Ye Jiaying 葉嘉瑩. *Wang Guowei jiqi wenxue piping* 王國維及其文學批評 [Wang Guowei and His Literary Criticism]. Taipei: Yuanliu, 1982. Print.

Yee, Angelina C. "Counterpoise in *Honglou meng.*" *Harvard Journal of Asiatic Studies* 51.2 (1990): 613–50. Print.

———. "Self, Sexuality, and Writing in *Honglou meng.*" *Harvard Journal of Asiatic Studies* 55.2 (1995): 373–407. Print.

Yeh, Catherine Vance. "Reinventing Ritual: Late Qing Handbooks for Proper Customer Behavior in Shanghai Courtesan Houses." *Late Imperial China* 19.2 (1998): 1–63. Print.

———. *Shanghai Love: Courtesans, Intellectuals, and Entertainment Culture, 1850–1910.* Seattle: U of Washington P, 2006. Print.

Yeh, Emilie Yueh-yu. "From Shaw Brothers to Grand Motion Picture: Localisation of Huangmei Diao Films." Trans. Barbara Yang. Wong Ain-ling, *Li* 116–25.

Yim, Chi-hung. "The 'Deficiency of Yin in the Liver': Dai-yu's Malady and *Fubi* in *Dream of the Red Chamber.*" *Chinese Literature: Essays, Articles and Reviews* 22 (2000): 85–111. Print.

Yisu 一粟, ed. *Hongloumeng juan* 紅樓夢卷 [Compendium on *Dream of the Red Chamber*]. 2 vols. Beijing: Zhonghua, 1963. Print.

———, ed., *Hongloumeng shulu* 紅樓夢書錄 [A Bibliography of *Dream of the Red Chamber*]. Shanghai: Shanghai Guji, 1981. Print.

Yu, Anthony C. *Rereading the Stone: Desire and the Making of Fiction in* Dream of the Red Chamber. Princeton: Princeton UP, 1997. Print.

Yu Da 俞達. *Qinglou meng* 青樓夢 [Dream of the Green Chamber]. Shanghai: Shenbaoguan, 1878. Print.

Yu, Hsiao-Jung. "The Interrogatives Employed in *Honglou meng* and Their Bearing on the Problem of Authorship." *Journal of the American Oriental Society* 116.4 (1996): 730–35. Print.

Yu Mingzhen 俞明震. "Gu'an manbi" 觚庵漫筆 [Casual Notes by Gu'an]. *Xiaoshuo lin* 小説林 [The Forest of Fiction] 5, 7, 10, and 11, 1907–08.

Yu, Pauline. "Cao Xueqin." Damrosch et. al. 77–80.

Yu Pingbo 俞平伯. *Hongloumeng bian* 紅樓夢辨 [Explicating *The Dream of the Red Chamber*]. Shanghai: Yadong tushuguan, 1923. Print.

———. *Hongloumeng yanjiu* 紅樓夢研究 [Studies on *The Dream of the Red Chamber*]. Shanghai: Tangdi, 1953. Print.

Yu Xuelun 喻血輪. *Lin Daiyu Biji* 林黛玉筆記 [Lin Dai-yu's Notes]. Shanghai: Shanghai Guangwen, 1918. Print.

———. *Lin Daiyu Riji* 林黛玉日記 [Lin Dai-yu's Diary]. Shanghai: Shijie, 1936. Print.

Yu Zhi 余治. "Ge shufang gongjin yinshu yidan tiaoyue" 各書坊公禁淫書議單條約 [Compact to Prohibit the Obscene Books by Bookstores]. *Deyi lu* 得一錄 [A Record of Keeping All the Virtues]. Ed. Yu (Liancun 蓮村). Taipei: Wenhai, 2001. 10–11. Print.

Yuan Mei 袁枚. "Suiyuan shi hua" [Notes on Suiyuan Poems]. Yisu, *Hongloumeng juan* 12–13.

Yuan Zhen. "The Story of Ying-ying." *Ways with Words: Writing about Reading Texts from Early China.* Ed. Pauline Yu et al. Berkeley: U of California P, 2000. 173–82. Print.

Yung Sai-shing 容世成. *Yueyun liusheng: Changpian gongye yu Guangdong quyi (1903–1953)* 粵韻留聲: 唱片工業與廣東曲藝 (1903–1953) [Phonographs of Cantonese Arias: Music Record Industry and Cantonese Opera, 1903–53]. Hong Kong: Tiandi Tushu Youxian, 2006. Print.

Zaehner, R. C. *Our Savage God.* London: Collins, 1974. Print.

Zeitlin, Judith T. *Historian of the Strange: Pu Songling and the Chinese Classical Tale.* Stanford: Stanford UP, 1993. Print.

———. *The Phantom Heroine: Ghosts and Gender in Seventeenth-Century Chinese Literature.* Honolulu: U of Hawai'i P, 2007. Print.

———. "Shared Dreams: The Story of the Three Wives' Commentary on *The Peony Pavilion.*" *Harvard Journal of Asiatic Studies* 54.1 (1994): 127–79. Print.

———. "Xiaoshuo." Moretti 249–61.

Zhang Ailing. *See* Chang, Eileen

Zhang Henshui 張恨水. *Jinfen shijia* 金粉世家 [Old Grand Family]. Hefei: Anhui Wenyi, 1985. Print

Zhang Hui 張惠. "Chengjiaben banhua goutu yuyi yu qita *Hongloumeng* banhua bijiao" 程甲本版畫構圖寓意與其他紅樓夢版畫比較 [The Composition of the 1791 Woodblock Illustrations of the *Dream of the Red Chamber* and Their Implications: A Study from a Comparative Perspective]. *Hongloumeng xuekan* 紅樓夢學刊 [Journal on *Dream of the Red Chamber*] 3 (2009): 319–32. Print.

Zhang Jinghao 張經浩 and Chen Kepei 陳可培. *Mingjia Minglun Mingyi* 名家名論名翻 [Renowned Translators: Their Theory and Practice]. Shanghai: Fudan, 2005. Print.

Zhang, Xudong. *Chinese Modernism in the Era of Reforms: Cultural Fever, Avant-Garde Fiction, and the New Chinese Cinema.* Durham: Duke UP, 1997. Print.

Zhang Yanfeng 張燕風. *Lao yuefenpai guanggao ji* 老月份牌廣告畫 [A Collection of the Old Posters and Advertisements Published in Shanghai]. 2 vols. Taipei: Yingwen Hansheng Chuban Youxian, 1994. Print.

Zhang, Yingjin, ed. *Cinema and Urban Culture in Shanghai: 1922–1943.* Stanford: Stanford UP, 1999. Print.

———. *The City in Modern Chinese Literature and Film: Configurations of Space, Time, and Gender.* Stanford: Stanford UP, 1996. Print.

Zhang Zhen. *An Amorous History of the Silver Screen: Shanghai Cinema, 1896–1937*. Chicago: U of Chicago P, 2005. Print.

Zhao Liewen 趙烈文. "Nengjingju biji" 能靜居筆記 [Notes Made in the Studio of Tranquility]. Yisu, *Hongloumeng juan* 378.

Zheng Bixian 鄭碧賢. *Honglou meng zai Falanxi de mingyun* 紅樓夢在法蘭西的命運 [The Fate of *Honglou meng* in France]. Beijing: Xinxing, 2005. Print.

*Zhiyan zhai chongping Shitou ji* 脂硯齋重評石頭記 [Repeated Commentary on the *Story of the Stone* by Red Inkstone Studio]. *Gengchen* 庚辰 (1760) MS. Beijing: Renmin, 1975. Print. Photographic rpt.

Zhong, Xueping. *Masculinity Besieged? Issues of Modernity and Male Subjectivity in Chinese Literature of the Late Twentieth Century*. Durham: Duke UP, 2000. Print.

Zhou Fengling 周芬伶. "Zhang Ailing mengyi: Ta de liufeng jiashu" 張愛玲夢魘: 她的六封家書 [Zhang Ailing's Nightmare: Her Six Letters Home]. *INK Literary Monthly* 11 (2002): 59–68. Print.

Zhou Ruchang 周汝昌. *Between Noble and Humble: Cao Xueqin and the* Dream of the Red Chamber. Ed. Mark S. Ferrara and Ronald R. Gray. New York: Lang, 2009. Print.

———. *Hongloumeng de zhengushi* 紅樓夢的真故事 [The True Story of *Story of the Stone*]. Beijing: Huayi, 1995. Print.

———. "*Honglou* sibi zhu Changchun" 紅樓四壁駐長春 [Retaining the Scenes from the *Dream of the Red Chamber* on the Four Walls in the Palace of Eternal Spring]. *Zijincheng* 紫禁城 [The Forbidden City] 6 (1981): 14–16. Print.

———. "Zi bi badou da 2" 字比笆斗大 2 [A Word Is Larger than a Basket 2]. *Dingshi Honglou meng li ren: Zhang Ailing yu Honglou meng* 定是紅樓夢里人: 張愛玲與紅樓夢 [She Must Have Been a Character in *The Dream of the Red Chamber*: Eileen Chang and *The Dream of the Red Chamber*]. Beijing: Tuanjie, 2005. 221–22. Print.

Zhou Ruchang and Zhou Yueling 周月苓. *Gongwangfu yu Hongloumeng: Tongwang Daguanyuan zhilu* 恭王府與紅樓夢: 通向大觀園之路 [Prince Gong's Palace and *Dream of the Red Chamber*: The Path toward the Grand Prospect Garden]. Beijing: Yanshan, 1992. Print.

Zhou Shu 周澍. "Honglou xinyong" 紅樓新詠 [New Poems on *Dream of the Red Chamber*]. Yisu, *Hongloumeng juan* 490–94.

Zhou, Zuyan. *Androgyny in Late Ming and Early Qing Literature*. Honolulu: U of Hawai'i P, 2003. Print.

Zhu Min 朱敏. "Honglou qingyou ru hua lai: 'Daguanyuan' tu kao" 紅樓清幽入畫來: 大觀園圖攷 [The *Dream of the Red Chamber* Found Its Way into a Painting: A Study of "The Grand Prospect Garden"]. *Zhongguo guojia bowuguan guancang wenwu yanjiu congshu*, huihua juan (lishi hua) 中國國家博物館館藏文物研究叢書, 歷史畫 [Series of the Studies on the Collections of the National Museum, Beijing, the Volume on Historical Paintings]. Ed. Zhongguo guojia bowuguan. Shanghai: Shanghai Guji, 2006. 312–15. Print.

Zhu Yixuan 朱一玄, ed. *Hongloumeng ziliao huibian* 紅樓夢資料匯編 [A Collection of Documents on *Dream of the Red Chamber*]. Tianjin: Nankai Daxue, 1985. Print.

Žižek, Slavoj. "'I Hear You with My Eyes'; or, The Invisible Master." *Gaze and Voice as Love Objects*. Ed. Renata Salecl and Žižek. Durham: Duke UP, 1996. 90–126. Print.

Zou Tao 鄒弢. *Haishang chentian ying* 海上塵天影 [The Shadows of Earth and Heaven in Shanghai]. Shanghai: Shanghai Guji, 1990. Print.

# INDEX OF CHINESE CLASSIC TEXTS

An asterisk indicates that the work is not available in English translation; two indicate an abridged translation.

## Philosophical, Religious, and Historical Texts

## Fictional, Dramatic, and Poetic Texts

# INDEX OF NAMES